BLOOD LIES

The Evidence that Every Accusation against Joseph Stalin and the Soviet Union in Timothy Snyder's *Bloodlands* Is False

Plus: *What Really Happened*: The Famine of 1932-33; the "Polish Operation"; the "Great Terror"; the Molotov-Ribbentrop Pact; the "Soviet invasion of Poland"; the"Katyn Massacre"; the Warsaw Uprising; "Stalin's Anti-Semitism"

By Grover Furr

Red Star Publishers
August 2014

BLOOD LIES: The Evidence that Every Accusation against Joseph Stalin and the Soviet Union in Timothy Snyder's Bloodlands Is False

Plus: What Really Happened: The Famine of 1932-33; the "Polish Operation"; the "Great Terror"; the Molotov-Ribbentrop Pact; the "Soviet invasion of Poland"; the"Katyn Massacre"; the Warsaw Uprising; "Stalin's Anti-Semitism"

First Corrected Edition July 2014

Published by Red Star Publishers

PO Box 1641, Manhattanville Station

365 125th Street

New York NY 10027

webmaster@redstarpublishers.org

Locally Assigned LC-type Call Number DJK49 .F87 2014

Furr, Grover C. (Grover Carr)

BLOOD LIES: The Evidence that Every Accusation against Joseph Stalin and the Soviet Union in Timothy Snyder's Bloodlands Is False / Grover C. Furr; translations by Grover C. Furr

ISBN: 978-0-692-20099-5

565 pp. Includes index.

1. Snyder, Timothy. Bloodlands. 2. Europe, Eastern--History--1918-1945. 3. Poland--History--1918-1945. 4. Ukraine--History--1921-1944 . 5. Stalin, Joseph, 1879-1953. 6. Soviet Union--History--1917-1956. 7. World War, 1939-1945--Atrocities. 8. Massacres--Europe, Eastern--History--20th century. 9. Antisemitism--Poland--History--20th century. 10. Fascism--Ukraine.

Table of Contents

Acknowledgements and Dedication

I would like to express my continuing thanks to the staff of Harry A. Sprague Library, Montclair State University, and especially to Kevin Prendergast and Arthur Hudson, the indefatigable and extremely helpful Inter-Library Loan librarians.

Without their help I simply could not obtain the many hard-to-find books and articles, in many languages, that make my research possible.

* * * * *

I dedicate this book to Vladimir L'vovich Bobrov, of Moscow, Russia.

A fine historian, superb translator, a tactful yet sharp critic, he contacted me first in March 1999 to suggest that we begin collaboration on a thorny mystery concerning Soviet history of the Stalin period. When I was hesitant to do so, his patient, persuasive voice convinced me. From there our collaboration has continued for more than fifteen years.

We have coauthored a number of articles and, at this point, one book. But everything I have written under my own name owes a great deal to him.

Without his collaboration, encouragement, and limitless help I would not have written this book or any of my previous books and articles. Words cannot fully express my debt to him, and my gratitude.

List of Abbreviations

Lubianka 1922-1936: *Lubianka. Stalin i VChK-GPU-OGPU-NKVD. IAnvar' 1922 - dekabr' 1936.* Moscow: IDF, 2003.

Lubianka 1937-1938: *Lubianka. Stalin i Glavnoe Upravlenie Gosbezopasnosti NKVD.* 1937-1938. Moscow: "Materik", 2004.

Lubianka 1939-1946: Lubianka. Stalin i NKVD-NKGB-GUKR "Smersh". 1939 – mart 1946. Moscow: MDF, 2006.

Lubianka Golgofa: *Lubianka. Sovetskaia elita na stalinskoi golgofe. 1937-1938.* Ed. V.N. Khaustov (Moscow: MDF, 2011.

RKEB 1: *Reabilitatsiia: Kak Eto Bylo. Mart 1953 - Fevral' 1956 gg. Dokumenty Prezidiuma TsK KPSS i Drugie Materialy.* Moscow: Mezhdunarodniy Fond "Demokratiia", 2000.

RKEB 2: *Reabilitatsiia. Kak Eto Bylo. Febral' 1956 - nachalo 80-kh godov. T. 2.* Moscow: "Materik", 2003.

RKEB 3: *Reabilitatsiia. Kak Eto Bylo. Seredina 80-kh godov - 1991. Dokumenty. T. 3.* Moscow: "Materik", 2004.

R-PP: *Reabilitatsia: Politicheskie Protsessy 30-x - 50-x gg.* Moscow: Izdatel'stvo politicheskoi literatury, 1991.

Introduction:

What is *Bloodlands* and Why

Do We Need to Expose It?

In 2010 a book was published that rewrites the history of the Soviet Union, Poland, and Ukraine between the years 1932 and 1945.
Its title is *Bloodlands. Europe Between Hitler and Stalin.*[1] Its author
is Timothy Snyder, a professor of Eastern European history at Yale
University in New Haven, Connecticut, USA. In *Bloodlands* Snyder
equates the Soviet Union with Nazi Germany and Stalin with Hitler.[2]

Bloodlands is a worldwide success. It has been lavished with praise
in dozens of book reviews worldwide, "praised as a work of near-
perfect history by many critics."[3] A selection of the awards and
praise can be seen at the special web page created for this book.[4]

> Editor's Pick, *New York Times Book Review*; *Die
> Welt*, Book of the Week; *NRC Handelsblad*, Book of
> the Week, *El País*, Book of the Week; *NDR* Sachbuch
> des Monats; *New York Times* non-fiction bestseller,
> *Der Spiegel* non-fiction bestseller (Germany);
> *Gazeta Wyborcza* non-fiction bestseller (Poland);
> *Dziennik Polski* bestseller (Poland), *Wall Street
> Journal* #1 hardback history bestseller.

---

[1] New York: Basic Books, 2010

[2] Although Snyder concludes that the Nazis did kill somewhat more people than did the
Soviets, he still equates them in a moral sense.

[33] Oliver Bullough. "Poking with the human rights stick." January 20, 2012. At
http://www.opendemocracy.net/od-russia/oliver-bullough/poking-with-human-rights-
stick

[4] Translations are listed at http://timothysnyder.org/books-2/bloodlands/ Awards and
selection are at pages listed at http://timothysnyder.org/

It has received high praise not only from predictable right-wing sources but from liberal outlets like *The Nation* (New York City). It has been translated into at least 25 languages, including Ukrainian, Polish, Hungarian, Romanian, and all three Baltic languages, plus German, French, Spanish, and all three Scandinavian languages.

And yet it is a complete fraud, false from beginning to end. It is no exaggeration to say that Snyder's *Bloodlands* is a litany of falsehoods. That fact is exemplified by the following story.

"Petro Veldii"

During 2011 and 2012 Snyder had a standard book talk on *Bloodlands* that he delivered many times. Here are some passages transcribed from the Youtube video of that standard talk as delivered in Chicago in 2011:[5]

> This is a difficult book to introduce, and I'd like to introduce it by way of what's most important to me — namely, the individuals who are its subject

> In early 1933, in what was then the Soviet Ukraine, a young man dug his grave. The reason he dug his grave was that he was sure he was going to die of starvation — and he was right. The other reason he dug his own grave was that he knew that once he died his body would lie in a field beside the road until it was picked up, thrown in the back of a cart, and then dumped with a number of other corpses in a mass grave where there would be no marker. So he knew that he was going to die but he wished to preserve some element of dignity. So he dug his own grave. Then when the day came he went there.

Snyder returns to this story at the end of the talk:

> So 14 million is not just 14 million but it is 14 million times one, where that one is not just an interchangeable unit but that one is an individual who is different than the individual that came before and

---

[5] http://www.youtube.com/watch?v=qcXMV-4HfXs accessed 02.15.2014.

> the individual who came after . In other words, the
> book is ultimately about people and it succeeds in-
> sofar as it turns numbers back into people. I can't
> succeed with a lecture like this but what I would
> like to leave you with is the names of the three peo-
> ple that I mentioned at the beginning. The young
> man in Ukraine who dug his own grave is Petro
> Veldii...

This incident is described in *Bloodlands* on page 47, where it reads
as follows:

> To die of starvation with some sort of dignity was
> beyond the reach of almost everyone. Petro Veldii
> showed rare strength when he dragged himself
> through his village on the day he expected to die.
> The other villagers asked him where he was going:
> to the cemetery to lay himself down. He did not
> want strangers coming and dragging his body away
> to a pit. So he had dug his own grave, but by the
> time he reached the cemetery another body had
> filled it. He dug himself another one, lay down, and
> waited.[69]

Snyder's source for this story (n. 69, p. 466) is as follows: "On
Vel'dii, see Kovalenko, *Holod,* 132." Snyder spells the man's name
"Veldii" in the text but "Vel'dii" in the footnote (the apostrophe is
the transcription of a Ukrainian letter.) As we shall see, neither is
correct.

Kovalenko's book[6] is rare in the United States, so few if any readers will check this story.

Here is the original, at page 132:

> Бачу як сьогодні: йде селом Бельдій Петро, несе
> в руках якийсь клуночок. Люди стоять біля
> сільради, на майдані. Йде Петро у святковій

---

[66] *33-у Holod: Narodna Knyha-memorial.* Uporiadnyky L.B. Kovalenko, V.A. Maniak. Kyiv:
Radians'kyy pis'mennyk, 1991. (33-й: Голод: Народна Книга-меморіал / Упорядники
Л.Б.Коваленко, В.А. Маняк. - Київ : Радянський письменник, 1991). Worldcat gives the
title's transcription as "*33 Holod...*"

> полотняній сорочці, штанах полотняних , з
> ціпком у руках. «Куди?» — питають люди. «На
> цвинтарь.» — «Чого?» — «Умирати. Таки не
> хочу, щоб мене на гарбі вивозили, йду сам».
> Пішов, але яма, яку сам для себе ще раніш був
> викопав, була уже зайнята. Петро ще викопав
> собі ямку і таки помер на цвинтарі.

Translated:

> I can see like [it happened] today: Petro Bel'diy is
> going to the village and is carrying in his hands
> some kind of little bundle. People stand by the vil-
> lage Soviet, in the square. Petro is walking in a fes-
> tive linen shirt, linen trousers, with a *tsipok*[7] in his
> hands. "Where are you going?" — the people ask.
> "To the cemetery." "Why?" "To die. Since I do not
> want to be carried in a cart, I will go myself." He
> went, but the pit that he had dug earlier for himself
> was already occupied. Petro dug himself another
> grave and so died at the cemetery.

Snyder has seriously distorted this story.

* The man's name was not "Veldii" or "Vel'dii" but "Bel'diy."

* There is nothing at all about starvation or famine in the story. There is no indication that Bel'diy is even hungry.

* The original has nothing about Bel'diy "dragging himself
through his village." It simply says that he walked to the village.

Snyder's phrase "dragging himself" suggests weakness, and is
no doubt also intended to suggest starvation and the famine.
It permits Snyder to claim that "Veldii" "showed rare
strength." But the original suggests nothing of the kind. In it

---

[7] "Tsipok' (Ціпок) can mean a stick or cane. Bel'diy is dressed in his best! The cane would
suggest he was elderly or infirm. I have been informed that *tsipok* can also mean one of
several different kinds of digging implements depending on the specific area in the Ukraine
where the word is used. Since Bel'diy thinks his grave has already been dug, he would probably not bring a digging implement. But then how does he dig himself another grave?

the villagers standing around the village Soviet (local gov-ernment headquarters) just wonder what he is doing.

* In the original Bel'diy is carrying a "little bundle." This ac-count does not say what was in it. One likely possibility would be food. Snyder omits the bundle altogether.

* In the original Bel'diy is dressed in his holiday clothes. Clearly he wants to be buried looking his best. Snyder omits this detail.

* Snyder claims that Bel'diy "did not want strangers coming and dragging his body away to a pit." But there is nothing like this in the original. Kovalenko quotes Bel'diy as telling some of his fellow villagers that he did not want to be carried away in a cart. Since this is what normally happens when a person dies — the body is taken away in a cart — it means that Bel'diy has some private reason for not wanting this.

* In the original Bel'diy dies in the cemetery after digging himself a second grave. In Snyder's version he "lay down and waited."

* In his book talk Snyder calls "Veldii" a "young man." But in Snyder's source there is no indication at all of his age.

Snyder has falsified this story. He has appropriated it to the famine by adding some details that are not in the original story while omitting other details that are in it.

Even in Kovalenko's book the story says nothing at all about the cause of the 1932-33 famine, or anything about any famine at all. But more than that — Snyder's version simply can't be true. This man who, in Snyder's version, was starving to death — starving so badly that he thought he would die on that very day — dug not just one grave, but two!

It's no good to dig a shallow grave — the body would probably be dug up by dogs. Digging a deep grave is hard work. It shows exact-ly the opposite of the lassitude that accompanies slow starvation. But according to Snyder "Veldii" was not just starving — he was so far gone that he expected to die *that very day!*

This is impossible. A starving person would not have had the ener-gy to dig these two graves — one some days before, when he must have been starving as well (or why dig the grave?) and another on the very day he expected to actually die of starvation (in the original story, he does die). Sure enough, the original story has nothing about starvation, famine, "dragging himself," "strangers dragging his body to a pit," or even anything that suggests hunger.

This story has the form of a legend or folklore: "The man who dug his own grave and then waited for death to come." Here is a similar story about a legendary French Canadian *voyageur*, preserved in a ballad or folk-song:

> ... Pursued by the Indians through the forest, Cailleux gradually weakened; he dug his own grave, erected a cross above it and composed a ballad about his misfortune, which he wrote in blood on birchbark; it was found by those who came to look for him.[8]

In any case, no conclusion can be drawn from this rumor, or from any rumor. It does not even mention famine or starvation. Even if the original version in Kovalenko's book could somehow be verified it would not prove anything relevant to Snyder's book.

Kovalenko"s Book

This book was the first collection in Ukraine of testimonies about the famine. Under the prodding of the anticommunist "Memorial" association Stanislav Kul'chyts'kyy, a Ukrainian scholar, published an advertisement in the widely-circulated newspaper *Sil's'ki Visti* ("Rural News") in which solicited letters from those who had experienced the famine. He obtained 6000 replies. According to Ukrainian scholar Heorhiy Kas'ianov:

> Paradoxically, these questions and the memories they stimulated, regardless of the motives that led to their appearance, could have become one important element in a more adequate reconstruction in the picture of the events of 1932-33. However, the final product, that is the book created on the ba-

---

[8] "Cailleux, Jean." *The Canadian Encyclopedia* (Edmonton, AB: 1985), Vol. 1 p. 254.

sis of the materials thus gathered, testified to the
fact that at the turn of the 1990s the concept of the
project had changed fundamentally. For the book
they selected only information from eyewitnesses
who painted terrible pictures of people dying in
their own homes and related excesses.[9]

Though Kovalenko's book, from which Snyder took this story before falsifying it, is hard to find in the USA it is famous and widely available in Ukraine.

In fact it is famous as the first collection in Ukraine, still at that time a Soviet Republic, of stories by those who lived through the famine of 1932-33. The book is so well known that we might expect that the Ukrainian translation of Snyder's book would reprint the original story from Kovalenko's volume. But instead, it translates Snyder's distorted version, even to the point of getting Bel'diy's name wrong as Snyder did!

Петро Вельдій виказав рідкісну силу волі й з
останніх сил пішов у село в день, коли чекав, що
по нього прийде смерть. Односельчани питали
його, куди він іде: на цвинтар — лягати в
могилу. Він не хотів, щоб чужі люди тягнули
його тіло у яму. Тож він викопав собі могилу,
але коли дошкандибав до цвинтаря, там уже
лежало інше тіло. Він викопав собі ще одну, ліг і
почав чекати (69).[10]

Translated:

Petro Vel'diy showed rare strength of will and with
his last strength went into the village on the day
that he was waiting for death to come for him. His
fellow villagers asked him where he was going: to

---

[9] Georgii Kas'ianov, "Разрытая могила: голод 1932-1933 годов в украинской историографии, политике и массовом сознании*. Ab Imperio 3 (2004) 248-9. The editors Lidia Kovalenko and Volodymyr Maniak were husband and wife. This article is in Russian; "Georgii" is the Russian transliteration of the Ukrainian "Heorhiy."

[10] "Про Петра Вельдія див.: Коваленко, Голод, 132."("About Petrov Vel'diy see Kovalenko, Holod, 132"). In the Ukrainian translation of Snyder, Krivavy Zemli. Vydavnytsvo Grani-T, at http://www.istpravda.com.ua/ukr/research/2011/11/25/62973/ at note 69.

> the cemetery, to climb into a grave. He did not want
> strangers to drag his body to a pit. So he dug him-
> self a grave, but when he reached the cemetery, an-
> other body was already lying in it. He dug himself
> another grave, lay in it, and began to wait.

Anyone who checks the original version of this story against Snyder's version would see immediately that Snyder has seriously falsified it. It is hard to believe that no one — the translator, the Ukrainian publisher, the Ukrainian historians who work with Snyder, those who arranged for his many talks to Ukrainian audiences in Ukraine, the US, Canada — has ever done this. But they chose to remain silent about it.

The "Petro Veldii" story is an example of something we will see a great many times in this book: Snyder cannot be trusted to use his sources honestly. When Snyder makes an assertion of fact, or fact-claim, about something involving communists, the Soviet Union, or Stalin, the sources for this fact-claim must be double-checked.

Upon checking Snyder's source we normally find either (1) that his source does not support what Snyder's text says or implies that it does; or (2) that the source does reflect what Snyder says in his text but that source itself is dishonest, in that (a) does not reflect what its own evidence states or (b) its source is yet another secondary source which, when examined, does not support the fact-claims given; or (c) it cites no evidence at all.

In his standard book talk Snyder names three people who were, supposedly, victims of Hitler and Stalin. He claims that two of these were in fact victims of Stalin. One is "Petro Veldii." That story is a fabrication. In fact the falsification goes far beyond the story of this one man. We shall show that there was no "Holodomor" at all — no "deliberate" or "man-made" famine in 1932-33.

Snyder's "Petro Veldii" falsification ought to make us curious about the second "victim of Stalin" whom Snyder features at the start of his book talk. He is Adam Solski, one of the Polish officers whose corpse was disinterred by the Nazis at Katyn in April-June 1943. Unlike "Veldii / Vel'dii / Bel'diy" there is no doubt about Solski's identity: he was a real person whose corpse was indeed unearthed by the Germans at the Katyn forest. However, the evidence available today points to German rather than Soviet guilt in the murders of Solski and the other Polish prisoners. We will discuss the "Katyn massacre" later in this book.

*   *

*

The present book presents a detailed, heavily documented critique of *Bloodlands*. It concludes that virtually all of Snyder's charges and statements about Stalin and the Soviet Union are false. I prove this by checking the evidence Snyder cites; by including when appropriate the evidence Snyder's sources cite; and by citing other evidence he omits.

Snyder's book has become a Bible for East European neo-Nazis and right-wingers generally. Here is a collection of articles from the Holocaust research site "Defending History" (collected February 2014):

> Foreign Minister of Lithuania invokes Timothy Snyder in launch of newest European Union campaign for Double Genocide.

> Vytautas Magnus University professor tells Lithuanian daily that Timothy Snyder is the one great hope...

> Kaunas Professor tells the leading Lithuanian daily that reburial of the wartime Nazi puppet prime minister reconfirms the "drama of Lithuanian history" while attacking "the Jews" who allegedly threatened university and national officials with "getting hit over the head with a club" over the reburial. He also refers to Timothy Snyder as his one great ray of hope.

> Book Event for Lithuanian Edition of Bloodlands at Lithuanian Foreign Ministry; Historians Use the Occasion to Besmirch Holocaust Survivors who Joined the Anti-Nazi Partisans and to Cement Red-Equals-Brown Equation

> Professor tells Lithuanian radio audience that 'It's not all hopeless' thanks to — Timothy Snyder's *Bloodlands.*

> At a symposium of historians speaking for a wider Lithuanian audience, one accomplished professor put on the record, when discussing the difficulties in selling the revisionist history to the West: 'But it's not all hopeless. Timothy Snyder has written an important book called *Bloodlands'*.[11]

Some Holocaust researchers have appealed to Snyder to dissociate himself from the political uses of his book:

> List of Experts Cited during Preparation of Lithuanian Parliament Sponsored Film Glorifying the Local Holocaust Killers

> For the record, I do sincerely regret the inclusion of Professor Snyder's name in the planning stages of a 2011 ultranationalist film, supported by the Lithuanian parliament, which glorifies the Holocaust-perpetrating LAF (Lithuanian Activist Front) as 'freedom fighters'. Its Vilnius premiere on 22 June 2011 included swastika stamped souvenir tickets (report on the event here; review of the film by the longtime editor of the last Jewish newspaper in Lithuania here; image of the souvenir ticket here).

> I respectfully call on Professor Snyder to publicly disavow and/or sever any links to the planning for the film (which would have simply been naive), and to now condemn the final product as the product of ultranationalist, anti-Semitic East European Holocaust revisionism designed to glorify the perpetrators and deflect attention from local participation in the Holocaust in the making of state-sponsored revisionist history.

---

[11] At http://defendinghistory.com/east-european-nationalist-abuse-of-timothy-snyders-bloodlands

Good luck with that! There is no way that Snyder is not completely aware of the political tendency of *Bloodlands* and whom the falsehoods and distortions in his book benefit.

The page in question is titled "East European Nationalist (Ab)use of Timothy Snyder's 'Bloodlands'."[12] But it is not an "abuse" at all. This is in fact the political tenor of *Bloodlands*. The East European "nationalists" and neo-Nazis have understood it all too well.

I have specialized in researching the history of the Soviet Union during the Stalin years, particularly the crucial decade between 1930 and the Nazi invasion of June 22, 1941. I first became acquainted with Snyder's research some years ago when studying the Volhynian massacres, the mass murders by Ukrainian Nationalist forces of 50,000 to 100,000 or more Polish civilians in the Western part of the Ukrainian SSR then under German-occupation. In the 1990s Snyder published the only scholarly studies in the English language of these horrifying slaughters, although his anti-communism and tendency to minimize the crimes of anticommunist nationalists are already evident in these articles.

Several years ago a friend and colleague asked me what I thought about one of Snyder's essays in the influential American journal *The New York Review of Books*. There Snyder asserted, without evidence of any kind, that the famine of 1932-33 was "man-made" and deliberately directed by Stalin to kill and terrorize Ukrainians.

Serious students of Soviet history have long known that there is, in fact, no evidence of any "Holodomor", any deliberate famine. This has been described as a fiction by mainstream Western anticommunist scholars since at least Robert Conquest's book *Harvest of Despair* was published in 1987.[13] Conquest himself has withdrawn his accusation that the famine was deliberate. We discuss this matter thoroughly in Chapters One through Three of the present book.

It is clear to any objective student of Soviet history that Snyder is wrong about the famine. But non-specialists like my friend and

---

[12] Ibid.

[13] See Jeff Coplon, "In Search of A Soviet Holocaust: A 55-Year-Old Famine Feeds the Right." *Village Voice* (New York) January 12, 1988. At http://msuweb.montclair.edu/~furrg/vv.html

colleague do not know it. So I began collecting Snyder's essays. He publishes widely in intellectual and semi-popular journals, where he is assumed to be an expert on Eastern European history. It soon became clear to me that Snyder's book gives a false account not only the famine of 1932-33 but virtually every point of Soviet history with which I was familiar.

It is the professional responsibility of historians to acknowledge disputes and disagreements in the fields they research. But Snyder never informs his readers about the scholarly disputes that exist over many of these issues, whether it be the famine, the *Ezhovshchina* or "Great Terror," the "Katyn massacre," the Molotov-Ribbentrop Pact, the partisan war, the Warsaw Ghetto revolt, the Warsaw Uprising, or others. Without exception Snyder repeats an anti-Soviet, anticommunist position without any qualification.

It is not only that many statements in Snyder's book are factually false. There are so many such false statement that they could not be the result of carelessness. Moreover, there is a systematic quality to all of them: every one is tendentiously anticommunist. I realized that I would have to systematically check every factual statement about the Soviet leadership or Soviet actions that had a negative tendency, every allegation of a crime or an atrocity.

In April 2012 Snyder was invited to speak at a Holocaust commemoration event at Kean University of New Jersey, not far from my own university. I wrote a two-sided flyer detailing a small number of Snyder's most brazen falsehoods and distributed 100 copies of it at the talk. The flyer was well received by the audience of students (who had been required to attend) and others interested in the Holocaust.[14] I am pleased that the present book, in which Snyder's falsehoods about Soviet history are exposed and refuted in a more detailed and complete manner, is now available to readers.

Like any work of history *Bloodlands* contains a great many assertions of fact — statements that affirm that something occurred. The present book examines and checks all of the assertions of fact

---

[14] "I Protest the Appearance of Professor Timothy Snyder!" (April 17, 2012). At http://msuweb.montclair.edu/~furrg/research/timothy_snyder_protest_0412.html

that have a clearly anti-Soviet or anticommunist tenor. It does not verify other of Snyder's fact-claims, in particular, Snyder's statements about Nazi Germany. There are a great many experts on the history of Nazi Germany. If Snyder has made any factual errors in his discussion of Nazi crimes it is unlikely that this will escape notice.

My working hypothesis was as follows: I would find that many of Snyder's anti-Soviet assertions or "fact-claims" were false, not supported by the evidence Snyder cites or indeed by any other evidence. My further hypothesis was that the secondary sources Snyder cites in support of these statement would either not support Snyder's fact-claims, or would themselves be fallacious, unsupported by the evidence (if any) that they cited.

My research has fully corroborated both of these hypotheses. In fact, I discovered that my initial hypothesis was too cautious. I have found not that many, but that virtually *all* of Snyder's fact-claims of an anti-Soviet and/or anticommunist tendency are false. In this book I present the results of that research.

Organization of This Book

The chapters in this book adhere to the following method of presentation. After an introductory section I quote every passage in which Snyder makes a fact-claim that accuses the Soviet Union or one of its leaders (e.g. Stalin) or communists generally of some crime or that tends to reflect negatively upon Stalin or Soviet actions. Then the evidence Snyder cites to support his statement(s), normally found in a footnote, is identified and, where possible, reproduced. Then each of the sources in that footnote, whether primary or, usually, secondary, is checked and verified in order to assess whether that source provides support for Snyder's fact-claim.

In the case of secondary sources I have checked further for the primary sources that these secondary sources use. This is essential because the fact that one historian agrees with another does not constitute evidence. Only primary sources are evidence. Accordingly, in each instance where Snyder cites another secondary source in his footnote I have obtained and studied the primary source evidence upon which that secondary source relies. This procedure continues until we reach the primary sources upon which all the other secondary sources are based, or until we discover that, in reality, there is no primary source evidence supporting the series of fact-claims, which are thereby revealed to be falsifications. This method is essential in order to verify Snyder's fact-claims concerning Soviet "crimes" — or, as it turns out, in order to demonstrate that they are false virtually without exception.

Whenever possible a summary title, or subheading, has been given to each of the passages from Snyder's book. The purpose of this subheading is to aid the reader in deciding whether he or she wants to examine these fact-claims, or wishes to pick and choose, examining some and passing over others.

In the case of the most famous alleged Soviet or "Stalinist" crimes: the 1932-33 famine, the "Ezhovshchina" or "Great Terror," the Molotov-Ribbentrop Pact, the "Katyn massacre," the Warsaw Uprising of 1944, and Stalin's alleged antisemitism — I have preceded my investigation of Snyder's account with a section titled "What Really Happened."

No one else has taken the trouble to do this. This would not be a bad thing if Snyder's book were generally ignored. Historians of the USSR, like historians generally, should spend their time in discovering the truth rather than in double-checking every fact-claim and allegation made by other historians. But Snyder's book is very influential, as are his published articles in semi-popular journals. Snyder's fact-claims are normally *assumed* to be true while the reality is that they are virtually always false. Through books such as *Bloodlands* falsehoods become accepted as truths, the current of historical understanding polluted.

The Anti-Stalin Paradigm

In the present book I demonstrate, using Snyder's own sources and other evidence, that the fact-claims in *Bloodlands* are false; that *not a single one of the accusations Snyder levels against Stalin, the Soviet leadership, or pro-communist forces such as partisans, is true.* Such a conclusion demands explanation, and I outline my own views in the Conclusion. One important element of that explanation is what I call the "anti-Stalin paradigm", about which a little should be said here at the outset.

Since the Bolshevik Revolution itself the academic field of Soviet history has been dominated by anticommunist bias. In February 1956, at the 20th Congress of the Communist Party of the Soviet Union, Nikita Khrushchev, First Secretary of the Party and leader of the Soviet state, gave a "secret speech" in which he accused Stalin (and Lavrentii Beria) of great crimes. Khrushchev and other Party leaders under him went even further in their attacks on Stalin at the 22nd Party Congress in 1961. After that and until Khrushchev's ouster in October 1964 a flood of pseudo-scholarly Soviet works were published in which accusations about Stalin's "crimes" multiplied wildly.

Khrushchev's 1956 "Secret Speech", the anti-Stalin speeches at the 22nd Party Congress and the ensuing torrent of Khrushchev-orchestrated fabrications became the basis for the avalanche of anti-Stalin books that followed. Notable among them was, for example, Robert Conquest's tome *The Great Terror*, which drew heavily upon these Khrushchev-era materials (although Conquest also used, indiscriminately, any and all anti-Stalin works he could find, including many that preceded Khrushchev's speech). In an earlier article Vladimir L. Bobrov and I examined the last chapter of Stephen F. Cohen's book *Bukharin and the Bolshevik Revolution* (1973), another of the anti-Stalin books based on Khrushchev-era materials. There we showed (a) that Cohen relied entirely upon Khrushchev-era "revelations" in this chapter of Bukharin's fate between 1930 and 1938; and (b) that every single "revelation" Cohen makes in that long chapter is demonstrably false, thanks to evidence from Soviet archives now available to researchers.[15]

The Khrushchev-era Soviet works were not simply the result of bias. Rather, they were deliberate lies. Khrushchev and his men had all the evidence of the Soviet archives — everything we have today plus much, much more. The same is true of Gorbachev's

---

[15] Grover Furr and Vladimir L. Bobrov. "Stephen Cohen's Biography of Bukharin: A Study in the Falsehood of Khrushchev-Era 'Revelations'." *Cultural Logic* 2010. At http://clogic.eserver.org/2010/Furr.pdf

people, who churned out another and even larger avalanche of anti-Stalin falsehoods after 1987, an avalanche that continues to the present day.

The academic field of Soviet history of the Stalin period has been constructed around the more or less uncritical acceptance of, first, Khrushchev-era, and second, of Gorbachev-era and post-Soviet-era lies. These lies cannot be sustained in the face of the evidence now available from former Soviet archives. However, to admit this would entail exposing the fact that the work of dozens of historians of the USSR are poisoned at the root.

Therefore the "anti-Stalin paradigm," as I call this model of Stalin-era Soviet history, goes unchallenged. As long as it continues to serve anticommunist ideological purposes, and as long as the truth can be ignored, buried, hidden, or otherwise disregarded, the demonization of Stalin, the Soviet leadership of his day, and the communist movement continues to perform its useful function in the economy of anticommunist propaganda, propped up by the prestige of academic experts in many countries. This is the tradition that has produced works like Snyder's *Bloodlands*.

Books like Snyder's do not have to fear that their falsehoods will be exposed by their peers in the field of Soviet history because anti-Stalin lies are very seldom exposed as such. In such an atmosphere, where the historian can accuse Stalin and the USSR of almost any crime, can say virtually anything as long as it has an anti-Stalin bias, a kind of "Gresham's Law" comes into play. Bad research drives out the good or — at the very least — makes the good research very cautious, very careful not to challenge the prevailing paradigm. This is the academic and political environment that makes completely fraudulent works like *Bloodlands* possible.

Concerning the portrayal of Stalin by anticommunist historians like Snyder Professor Domenico Losurdo of the University of Urbino, Italy, writes:

> Les philosophes aiment à s'interroger en évoquant
> non seulement les événements historiques mais
> aussi les catégories avec lesquelles nous interprétons ces événements. Aujourd'hui, quelle est donc la
> catégorie avec laquelle on interprète Staline ? Celle

de folie sanguinaire. Cette catégorie a été déjà utili-
sée contre Robespierre, contre la révolution de
1848, contre la Commune, mais jamais contre la
guerre, ni contre Louis XVI, ni contre les Girondins
ou Napoléon. Pour ce qui concerne le XXème siècle,
nous avons des études psychopathologiques sur
Lénine, Staline, Trotski, Mao, mais pas, par exemple
contre Churchill. Or, tout le groupe dirigeant bolchevik se prononçait contre l'expansionnisme colonial, tandis que Churchill écrivait « la guerre est un
jeu auquel il faut sourire . » Il y eut ensuite le carnage de la Première Guerre mondiale, le groupe
dirigeant bolchevik, Staline compris, est contre ce
carnage, mais Churchill déclare encore : « la guerre
est le plus grand jeu de l'histoire universelle, nous
jouons ici la mise la plus élevée, la guerre constitue
l'unique sens aigu de notre vie ». Alors, pourquoi
l'approche psychopathologique dans un cas et pas
dans l'autre?[16]

Translated:

In their discussions philosophers like to evoke not
only historical events but also the categories with
which we interpret these events. Today, what is the
category with which Stalin is interpreted? That of
bloodthirsty madness. This category has already
been used against Robespierre, against the Revolution of 1848, against the Paris Commune, but never
against war, or against Louis XVI, or against the Girondins or Napoleon. Regarding the twentieth century, we have psychopathological studies of Lenin,
Stalin, Trotsky, Mao, but not, for example, of

---

[16] Losurdo, ""Staline et le stalinisme dans l'histoire (2)" (Debate with Nicolas Werth), April
12, 2012. At http://www.lafauteadiderot.net/Staline-et-le-stalinisme-dans-l,855 Losurdo's
quotations from Churchill may be found in his book *Stalin. Storia e critica di una leggenda
nera.* Rome: Carocci, 2008, p. 243. Their ultimate source is A. P. Schmidt, (1974), *Churchills
privater Krieg. Intervention und Konterrevolution im russischen Burgerkrieg, November 1918-
März 1920*, Atlantis, Ziirich, 1974, pp. 48-49.

Churchill. However, all of the Bolshevik leaders spoke up against colonial expansionism, while Churchill wrote: "War is a game at which one should smile." Then there was the carnage of the First World War. The Bolshevik leadership group, including Stalin, was against this carnage, but Churchill said again: "War is the greatest game in world history, here I play with the highest stakes, war is the sole acute sensation of our lives." So why the psychopathological approach in the one case and not in the other?

Fabrications, Falsifications, and Lies

It will surprise, even shock, many to learn that a major work by a prominent historian can be, at base, nothing but a chain of untruths, its scholarly trappings a demonstrable fraud, a trap intended to lure the unwary or the hopelessly biased into believing falsehoods. Yet *Bloodlands* is precisely such a book. That is the inevitable conclusion of my study.

It will appear to readers that many of Snyder's fact-claims are almost certainly "lies" in the strict sense. That is, they must have been made by conscious decision rather than as the expression of bias coupled with ignorance. At the same time many readers will assume that the word "lie" should only be used when *deliberate* dishonesty by a writer can be clearly demonstrated.

For this reason I am reluctant to have recourse to the word "lie." In all cases where deliberate intent to deceive cannot be clearly demonstrated by the evidence I use another term such as "fabrication" or "falsification" that connotes something made up, not contained in any of the evidence cited. As I have written elsewhere,

> [I]t is easy to underestimate the power of a well-established, privileged preconceived framework of analysis on the minds of any researcher who is himself seriously biased. The pressures, both psychological and academic, to reach a conclusion acceptable to leading figures in the field of Soviet history, as well as to officials in Russia who control ac-

cess to archives, are considerable indeed. Consequently, the disadvantages, professionally and otherwise, of reaching a conclusion that, no matter
how well demonstrated, will be displeasing to powerful forces in the archival, political, and academic
communities, are clear to anyone who is familiar
with the highly politicized nature of the field of Soviet and indeed of all of communist history.[17]

Accordingly I consider the word "lie" to be appropriate only when
the evidence clearly shows that Snyder has made a statement in
flagrant disregard for the truth, such as a statement that is not
supported in the source Snyder cites in support of it or is even
contradicted by that source. Yet even in such cases we should not
rule out the power of a preconceived framework plus a strong bias
to "blind" a non-objective historian like Snyder to inconvenient
evidence and conclusions.

Objectivity and the Truth

It is a commonplace today that Stalin committed mass murders
and gross atrocities. This belief is like the notions almost universal
before the 20th century (and by no means dead today) that women
and non-whites were "intellectually inferior." Those notions were
"common sense", taken for granted by almost every "white" male
of European ancestry, including scientists. They were questioned
by few, firmly rejected by fewer still. Yet they were never true.
They were (and are) avidly promoted because they served (and, in
some circles, still serve) definite political and economic interests.

An objective study of the evidence now available shows that, contrary to "what everybody knows" — what I call "the anti-Stalin
paradigm" — none of the mass murders and atrocities alleged
against Stalin and the Soviet leadership of his day can be verified
by the evidence.

Because this conclusion will strike many readers as outrageous,
the evidence supporting it must be more fully expounded than is

---

[17] Grover Furr, *The Murder of Sergei Kirov: History, Scholarship, and the Anti-Stalin Paradigm*. Kettering, OH: Erythrós Press & Media, LLC, 2013, p. 7.

normally the case in historical studies. After all, a major conclusion of this book is that, on any important matter, the fact-claims of historians should not be simply "believed" — accepted as true — but must be verified. Why, then, should any reader believe the fact-claims in this book — namely, that some statement in *Bloodlands* is false — when the same book cautions them not to believe Snyder?

Accordingly, the footnotes, references, and — where necessary — the primary documents essential for any reader to check my conclusion, are reproduced here. This adds to the length of this study. But there is no other way to document such a travesty of historical scholarship as *Bloodlands* presents us with. In some cases I have put longer passages from primary or secondary sources on the Internet as web pages and provided URLs to them.

The aim of the present study is to examine the allegations by Snyder against Stalin, the Soviet leadership, and pro-communist forces. Although *Bloodlands* reads something like a "prosecutor's brief" against Stalin and the USSR the present study is fundamentally different. It is not a "defense attorney's brief." It is not an attempt to prove either guilt or innocence. Rather, it is an attempt to find the truth.

I have tried hard to do what an investigator does in the case of a crime in which he has no *parti pris* but only wishes to solve the crime. This is what all historians are supposed to do, and what most historians who investigate the more distant past do all the time. I wish to persuade the fair-minded, objective reader that I have carried out a competent, honest investigation. Namely, that I have done the following:

* collected all the evidence that Snyder has cited to prove his allegations against Stalin et al., and also any "negative" evidence that contests those allegations;

* studied all this evidence carefully and honestly;

* drawn my conclusions on the basis of that evidence.

Political prejudice predominates in the study of communism and in particular of Soviet history. Conclusions that contradict the dominant anti-Stalin paradigm are routinely ignored or dismissed.

Conclusions that cast doubt upon accusations against Stalin or whose implications tend to make him look either "good" or even less "evil" than the predominant paradigm holds him to have been, are called "Stalinist." Any objective study of the evidence now available is bound to be called "Stalinist" simply because it must reach conclusions that are politically unacceptable to those who have a strong anticommunist bias, those who are in thrall to the false "anti-Stalin paradigm."

I wish to persuade the objective reader that I have reached my conclusions on the basis of evidence and its analysis and not on any other basis such as political bias. My aim is neither to arraign or "convict" Snyder nor to "defend" Stalin, the Soviet leadership, or pro-communist forces. Specifically, I assure the reader that I remain ready to be convinced that Stalin et al. did commit the atrocities alleged by Snyder if and when evidence is disclosed that supports that conclusion and that evidence can withstand the scholarly scrutiny to which all evidence should be subject.

Evidence

Before proceeding to study the relevant evidence we must briefly consider the question of evidence itself. Whereas "documents" are material objects — in our case, writing on paper — "evidence" is a relational concept. In the present study we are concerned with investigating Snyder's allegations in *Bloodlands* of criminal, atrocious activity by Stalin, the Soviet leadership, and pro-communist forces.

There is no such thing as "absolute" evidence. All evidence can be faked. Any statement — a confession of guilt, a denial of guilt, a claim one has been tortured, a claim one has not been coerced in any way — may be true or false, an attempt to state the truth as the speaker (or writer) remembers it or a deliberate lie. Documents can be forged and, in the case of Soviet history, often have been. False documents have on occasion been inserted into archives in order to be "discovered." Or it may be alleged that a given document was found in an archive when it was not. Photographs can be faked. Eyewitnesses can lie, and in any case eyewitnesses are so often in error that such evidence is among the least reliable kind. In principle there can be no such thing as a "smoking gun" — evidence that is so clearly genuine and powerful that it cannot be denied.

Identifying, locating, gathering, studying, and interpreting evidence are skills that can be taught to anyone. The most difficult and rarest skill in historical research is the discipline of objectivity. In order to reach true conclusions — statements that are more truthful than other possible statements about a given historical event — a researcher must first question and subject to doubt any preconceived ideas she may hold about the event under investigation. It is one's own preconceived ideas and prejudices that are most likely to sway one into a subjective, inaccurate interpretation of the evidence. Therefore, the researcher must take special steps to make certain this does not happen.

This can be done. The techniques are known and widely practiced in the physical and social sciences. They can and must be adapted to historical research as well. If such techniques are not practiced the historian will inevitably be seriously swayed from an objective understanding of the evidence by her own pre-existing preferences and biases. That will all but guarantee that her conclusions are false even if she is in possession of the best evidence and all the skills necessary to analyze it.

Nowhere is a devotion to objectivity more essential or less in evidence than in the field of Soviet history of the Stalin period. As it is impossible to discover the truth absent a dedication to objectivity, the present study strives to be objective at all costs. Its conclusions will displease, even outrage, a good many persons who are dedicated not to objectivity and the truth but to promoting some nationalist anticommunist narratives or to defending the Cold War — anticommunist paradigm of Soviet and European history.

The Role of Appropriate Skepticism

Throughout this essay I have tried to anticipate the objections of a skeptical critic. This is no more than any careful, objective researcher should do. In the body of the essay I follow each presentation of evidence with a critical examination.

Scholarship is the attempt to ascertain the truth. Arguments that proceed not from an objective search for truth but from some other motive, such as an attempt to attack or defend some specific allegation or historical paradigm, may fairly be labeled "propaganda." When accompanied by the trappings of scholarship — references, bibliography, assurances of objectivity devoid of its essence — such writing in reality constitutes not scholarship but "propaganda with footnotes." It is the conclusion of the present study that *Bloodlands* is precisely such a work.

I am aware that there is a subset of readers for whom evidence is irrelevant, for whom — to put it politely — this is not a matter of evidence but one of belief or loyalty. In any historical inquiry as in any criminal case "belief" and "loyalty" are irrelevant to the truth or falsehood of the hypothesis. By definition, a belief that is not rationally founded on evidence cannot be dispelled by a sound argument and evidence.

However, those who cannot bring themselves to question their preconceived ideas may nevertheless be provoked by those same prejudices to look especially critically at the evidence and to find weaknesses in its interpretation that might escape other readers for whom there is less at stake. This sometimes makes objections from such quarters worthy of attention. I have tried hard both to anticipate and to deal with such objections in an objective and satisfactory manner.

True Fact-Claims Are Acknowledged

The results of my study of *Bloodlands* are so overwhelmingly negative that some readers may suspect that this study lacks objectivity. I wish to assure the reader that I have done my best to point out those very few cases in which Snyder makes a fact-claim about the Soviet Union that both is of a negative tendency and is true.

Polish and Ukrainian "Nationalism"[18]

Snyder's falsehoods about Soviet history are not original to him. Snyder is a captive, albeit a willing one, of right-wing Polish and Ukrainian nationalists who have ruled these countries since the end of the Soviet Union and Soviet bloc. The lies and other falsehoods Snyder repeats come mainly from those sources.

This fact can be most easily seen from the books Snyder cites. When writing about Soviet history Snyder almost never cites Russian-language sources. His main sources are in Polish, secondarily in Ukrainian. But Snyder also frequently cites Ukrainian and Belarusian works in Polish translation. Polish nationalist, anticommunist writers, then, are the main fount from which Snyder draws.

I ask the reader to imagine how competent research on, say, the history of the United States could be done without citing a great many sources in the English language, or the history of France written without a preponderance of French sources. Yet Snyder seldom uses a Russian-language source. The blatant fraudulence of such an approach should be obvious — though many reviewers, sympathetic to Snyder's anti-Stalin and anticommunist bias, seem not to have remarked it at all!

Snyder repeats and thus conveys to an unsuspecting audience the mythology of Polish and, secondarily, of Ukrainian nationalists. This is the distortion of history that is taught as truth in today's Poland and Ukraine, but also in Eastern Europe generally and increasingly, thanks to books like *Bloodlands*, in the rest of the world as well.

Here are some of the chief elements, the principal falsehoods, of Polish and Ukrainian historical mythology that compose the framework around which *Bloodlands* is constructed. We will examine all of them in the course of the present study.

---

[18] In this chapter and in the Conclusion I have put scare quotes around the words "nationalism" and "nationalist." I do so because the right-wing "nationalists" claim that *only* anticommunists can be really "nationalist." Communist Poles, Ukrainians, Russians, and others claim "nationalism" too — "national in form, socialist in content" is one formulation. There is no reason that the right-wing, conservative, fascist, etc. definition of "nationalist" should be conceded to be the only "legitimate" nationalism. In fact the very concept of nationalism has long since been deconstructed, though we cannot go into that here.

Poland:

* The USSR was an "ally of Hitler's."

* The "Treaty of Non-Aggression between Germany and the Union of Soviet Socialist Republics," popularly known as the "Molotov-Ribbentrop Pact" and called "The Hitler-Stalin Pact" by anticommunists, was an agreement to "attack" and "divide up" Poland and the Baltics;

* Western Ukraine and Western Belorussia were integral "parts of Poland", the "kresy wschodnie" or Eastern territories.

* The Soviets aimed to "eliminate the Polish elites" — a kind of "genocide" not unlike that of the Nazis.

* The Soviets shot about 22,000 Polish prisoners of war in the massacres called the "Katyn Massacre."

* The Polish "Home Army" (Armia Krajowa, AK,), loyal to the Polish exile government in London, fought the Nazis but was duplicitously betrayed by their supposed ally the USSR.

* The Red Army stood by and allowed the German Army to suppress the Warsaw Uprising.

* Polish Home Army soldiers who remained armed and underground after June 1945 were fighting for "independence" and were unjustly hunted down and "repressed" by communist security forces.

* The Polish government and civilians were no more anti-Semitic than many other Europeans.

Ukraine:

* Stalin and his henchmen created the famine of 1932-33 by their criminal plan to collectivize agriculture.

* Then they deliberately starved Ukrainian peasants in order to "punish" Ukraine and/or to sell its grain abroad.

* The Volhynian Massacre during the war of 50,000-100,000 or more Polish civilians by armed forces of the Organization of Ukrainian Nationalists (OUN), who were armed by, allied with, and loyal to Nazi Germany, was a minor episode unworthy of more than the briefest attention.

* The Ukrainian nationalists in the OUN were "freedom fighters", "against both Stalin and Hitler." They were not significantly implicated in the Jewish Holocaust or other mass murders.

> * The armed Ukrainian nationalist forces who re-
> mained after the war in the underground, killing
> Soviet civilians, soldiers, and policemen, were not
> terrorists but "heroic freedom fighters."

It is hard to exaggerate the vehemence with which these false historical mythologies are officially propagated in Poland and
Ukraine, as well as in the rest of Eastern Europe. Snyder feeds
them to a largely Western public that is unaware of the history of
Eastern Europe and has been indoctrinated over many years to
accept as true any accusations of crimes against Stalin and the Soviet Union.

Both nationalist mythologies are based on historical falsehoods.
Both mythologies are aimed to cover up the crimes of the Polish
and Ukrainian nationalists of the 1930s and wartime period. These
crimes include:

Poland:

> * Poland's imperialist invasion of Soviet Russia in 1919.

> * Poland's seizure by conquest of Western Ukraine and Belo-
> russia, ignoring the Curzon Line drawn by the Allies to show
> where Poles were in the minority.

> * Poland's killing of between 18,000 and 60,000 Russian
> prisoners of war in Polish POW camps.

> * Poland's imperialist seizure by force of Lithuania's capital
> Vilnius in 1922, restored to Lithuania by the USSR in October
> 1939.

> * The sending of Polish veterans as "settlers" (Polish "osadni-
> cy") to "Polonize" the conquered territories.

> * Polish racist oppression against Ukrainians, Belorussians,
> and Jews, and suppression of their languages and cultures.

> * The pervasive nature of anti-Semitism in Polish society dur-
> ing the Second Republic (1919-1939), an anti-Semitism offi-

cially promoted by the Polish government and Polish Roman Catholic Church[19], which made Poland perhaps the most anti-Semitic country in the world at that time.

* The Polish government's deliberate sabotage of the Soviet attempts to build collective security against Hitler's Germany.

* Poland's participation with Germany in the partitioning of Czechoslovakia.

* The Polish government's abandonment of the country by fleeing to internment in Rumania on September 17, 1939, thus destroying the Polish state and condemning the Polish people to Nazi occupation and mass murder.

* The Polish Home Army's collaboration with the German Army against Soviet partisans and the Red Army.

* The Polish Home Army's murderous anti-Semitism and anticommunism.

* The Polish Home Army's failure to help the Warsaw Ghetto uprising of 1943.

* The crime of the Warsaw Uprising of 1944.

* The Polish Home Army's clandestine terrorism,[20] murder and sabotage in socialist Poland after 1945.

Ukrainian "Nationalism"

Since the Second World War the two pillars of Ukrainian nationalism have been (a) the "Holodomor", or deliberate starvation of several million Ukrainians by Stalin in the so-called "man-made famine" 1932-33; and (b) the supposed "heroism" of the armed forces of the OUN as "freedom fighters" against both Germany and the Soviet Union, for independence.

Both are myths. No "Holodomor" occurred. The terrible famine of 1932-33 was caused by natural phenomena. The OUN forces were Nazis and Nazi-like mass murderers. We discuss the 1932-33 famine, and Snyder's lies about it, in a separate chapter. The principal

---

[19] Not the much smaller Polish Catholic Church, a different Catholic sect.

[20] The term "terrorism" here is used in its objective sense of organized violence by forces not representing any state.

characteristics of Ukrainian nationalism, all of which Snyder either omits or mentions only in passing, include the following:

* The fascist nature of Ukrainian Nationalism.

* The collaboration of the Organization of Ukrainian Nationalists (OUN) with the Nazis during the invasion of the USSR in 1941 and during the war.

* The OUN's participation in the mass murder of Soviet Jews (the Holocaust) and of a great many other Soviet citizens.

* The mass murder by Ukrainian Nationalist forces of 50,000 to 100,000 Polish civilians.

* The OUN's underground terrorism against Soviet citizens after the war, including collaboration with the American OSS/CIA.

Why Now?

During the period of the Cold War Polish and Ukrainian nationalists pushed this mythology hard. It is easy to understand why they did so. Their aim was to try to help the Western capitalist powers to weaken and perhaps overthrow socialism in the USSR and Eastern Europe. Following the principles of the "Big Lie" outlined by Hitler they considered any means — in this case, any degree of lying and falsehood — to be legitimate towards this goal.

After 1990 (Poland) and 1992 (Ukraine) the nationalists found themselves in power in capitalist states. The goal of capitalists is to enrich themselves by extracting value from the working class. This meant lowering the standard of living of the working class of Poland and Ukraine. Nationalism — the myths of the "heroic past" and of the "two Holocausts", one by the Nazis, the other by the Soviets — has been the main way the economic and intellectual elites of Poland and Ukraine have attempted to "create a history" useful to the new anticommunist ruling elites. By constructing nationalist lies they also cover up the shameful truth about the past. Such national mythology also serves the important function of distracting the population away from the fact that its own rulers, through their government, are exploiting them more, lowering their standard of living. Most other "post-Soviet" countries, from the Baltics to

Hungary have witnessed the imposition of similar false nationalist and anticommunist historical constructions by their new capitalist rulers.

Until recently this nationalist mythology was virtually unknown outside Eastern Europe. Why is it now being popularized in the rest of the world? There appear to be several reasons.

Anticommunism

The anticommunist motive is simplest to understand. Polish and Ukrainian nationalist mythologies, like those of the other former Soviet and Soviet bloc countries, rely on pushing anticommunist lies, the more the better. They do this in order to disguise or minimize the fascist, racist, and pro-Nazi crimes of their nationalist predecessors, most of whom are praised as "heroes" today.

For capitalists anywhere it is always logical to promote anticommunism in order to disarm protests against the injustices of exploitation. By demonizing communism, and then by describing protests against socio-economic inequality as "communist", capitalists attempt to delegitimize any protest against their exploitative policies. Militant trade unionists, students fighting for lower tuition or free education, struggles against imperialist wars and military expenditures — all can be, and are, condemned as "communist." If communism can be equated with Nazism, then anticommunism — and, thereby, exploitation — can be portrayed as praiseworthy, even virtuous. Meanwhile the essential similarity between Nazi-type anticommunism and ordinary capitalist anticommunism can be obscured, as can the fact that fascism was and is another form of capitalism.

Twenty years after the end of the Soviet bloc many citizens of Eastern Europe look back upon it with some, often much, nostalgia. Like the USSR these were social welfare states that provided basic benefits and jobs to all, or almost all, citizens: free or low-cost medical care, education, job training, retirement pensions, and many benefits for the youth. This basic economic security is entirely lacking in capitalist states, leaving most citizens vulnerable and fearful. Cultural activities were popular, free or low-cost, and encouraged by the government. Racism — the ethnic hatreds and rivalries that have been the curse of Eastern Europe in the 20th century and are now coming back — was at a minimum. The sense of internationalism within the socialist bloc, taken for granted at the time, is often remembered now with fondness.

Geopolitics

The United States encouraged and aided the breakup of the Soviet Union and the socialist bloc in an effort to weaken its main political and economic rival. An important ideological weapon in this effort was the demonization of the Soviet Union generally and especially of the Stalin era. Since then the United States and NATO have engaged in wars and killed civilians on a scale that no one could blame the Soviet Union for — a million civilians, mostly children, by the war and then boycott on Iraq from 1991 — 2003, and another several hundred thousand at least since then. This boycott and these invasions would have been impossible if the USSR and Soviet bloc had still been in existence.

Stimulated once again by the US and NATO ethnic hatreds have flared up again throughout Europe — hatred against immigrants, gypsies, and anybody of the "wrong" national background. These have led to terrible wars and anti-civilian atrocities in the former Yugoslavia, and to racist violence and murders and the rise of fascist parties throughout Europe.

When the USSR sent an army into Afghanistan in December 1979 the USA and Western capitalist governments howled with protest, cancelled the 1980 Olympic Games, armed and trained the future Al-Qaida terrorists. In 2001 the United States invaded Afghanistan, in 2003 it invaded Iraq. Now the USA has gone far beyond what the Soviet Union ever did in the Middle East. The US is more heavily involved in military imperialist ventures in Africa as well. American influence has been challenged in Latin America by mildly reformist governments in Venezuela (Hugo Chavez), Ecuador (Rafael Correa), Bolivia (Evo Morales), and throughout the region.

In the Eurasian area one of the United States' main obstacles to expansion is Russia, still a major regional military and economic power now that the period of collapse and shrinkage of the post-Soviet period has ceased. China is now another major economic and military rival to American power — a fact which threatens to drive Russia and China into closer alliance against the United States.

US Competition With Russia

This is the geopolitical context for the escalation of hostility in American scholarship and elite discourse concerning Soviet history, especially history of the Stalin period. The United States did not split up the Soviet Union. Top figures in the Soviet Communist Party did that. But the United States ruling elite has benefitted tremendously from the way the USSR broke up. Most of the countries that had previously been in the Soviet bloc, plus most of the new countries that had been part of the USSR itself, instantly became anti-Russian, more closely allied to the United States and Western Europe (NATO) than to Russia. This was a great geopolitical victory for the US ruling elite. It is presumably helpful to their interests to accept large parts of the nationalist mythology promoted by Polish and Ukrainian elites.

Russia is blamed as the successor state to the Soviet Union. The more crimes that can be attributed to the USSR, the more negative, even criminal Russia can be made to appear. The campaign to associate the Soviet Union with Nazi Germany serves to obscure the far more accurate parallels between the prewar capitalist states and Nazi Germany, and the fascist mass murders by capitalist states before and after World War 2. It is similar to the French and American "rewriting" of their wars to preserve colonialism in Vietnam by calling them "wars of liberation against communist aggression", since the anti-colonial movement in Vietnam was indeed led by the communist party.

One could argue that there has indeed been a "second Holocaust" — not by the Soviet Union during 1930-1945 but by the Western imperialist nations in their colonial empires during their final century of roughly 1880-1975, with tens of millions of victims. This "second Holocaust" has only escalated since the demise of the Soviet bloc.

Method of Presentation

The present book takes upon itself the task of examining and checking every single statement in *Bloodlands* that has an anti-Soviet or anticommunist tendency, and reporting the results of this research of verification. It presents for the reader's consideration the proof that virtually every fact-claim of an anti-Soviet tendency in Snyder's book is false.

Most people rely upon the statements by supposedly "authoritative" figures such as Snyder. They trust that scholars from respected institutions of learning with renowned academic reputations do not fabricate evidence and consciously lie about important historical events. It is this trust that enables false scholarship to shape opinion on important historical questions.

Most of the chapters in Snyder's book focus on a single event or chain of events: the famine of 1932-33 (Chapter 1);[21] the *Ezhovshchina* (the anticommunist term is "Great Terror") (Chapter 2); the so-called "national operations", part of the *Ezhovshchina* (Chapter 3); the Molotov-Ribbentrop Pact (Chapter 4); the Resistance (Chapter 9); the post-war deportations intended to separate people of different nationalities (Chapter 10); Soviet suppression of Zionism within the USSR during the period up to 1953 (Chapter 11). Chapters 5 through 7 are not organized about a single main event but deal with a number of events related to the war. Only Chapter 8, "The Nazi Death Factories", which is devoted solely to Nazi crimes, contains no fact-claims of an anti-Soviet tendency.

It is no exaggeration to state that, as concerns Soviet history, Snyder's *Bloodlands* is a work of falsification from beginning to end. I have established that this is so through an exhaustive process of checking every footnote, every reference that Snyder cites in support of any fact-claim or statement of an anti-Soviet tendency.

---

[21] The first chapter of *Bloodlands* contains a great many more falsifications than those concerning the famine. Not only the first chapter, but most of the chapters of Snyder's book consist of a veritable litany of fact-claims whose purpose is to show the Soviet Union, its leadership, and its policies in a very negative light.

The "Big Lie" Technique

A normal practice for those who intend to deceive others is to mainly tell the truth, and smuggle in the falsehoods intermingled among the true statements. Snyder did not choose to follow this technique of deception. Rather, Snyder employs method of "The Big Lie." Though it is ostensibly not a work of propaganda Snyder's book follows the technique of propaganda recommended by Adolf Hitler in *Mein Kampf*, such as the following:

> The function of propaganda is, for example, not to weigh and ponder the rights of different people, but exclusively to emphasize the one right which it has set out to argue for. Its task is not to make an objective study of the truth, in so far as it favors the enemy, and then set it before the masses with academic fairness; its task is to serve our own right, always and unflinchingly.

> It was absolutely wrong to discuss war-guilt from the standpoint that Germany alone could not be held responsible for the outbreak of the catastrophe; it would have been correct to load every bit of the blame on the shoulders of the enemy, even if this had not really corresponded to the true facts, as it actually did.[22]

The "Big Lie" was not original with Hitler. He learned of it by studying the anti-German propaganda put out by the Western Allies during the First World War. After the war a number of books were written, often by shocked and deceived journalists, exposing these Allied falsifications.[23] Thus there was no need for Snyder to learn the "Big Lie" technique from Hitler. That Snyder does utilize this technique is beyond question. The present book establishes this

---

[22] Adolf Hitler. *Mein Kampf.* Part 1, Chapter 6: War Propaganda. At
http://www.hitler.org/writings/Mein_Kampf/mkv1ch06.html

[23] There is a large literature about these Allied lies. A famous example is Arthur Ponsonby, *Falsehood in war-time, containing an assortment of lies circulated throughout the nations during the great war.* London: G. Allen & Unwin Ltd., 1928. In the USA the so-called "Creel Committee" co-ordinated false propaganda for the American home front.

fact by carefully checking every one of the references Snyder uses to support his anti-Soviet fact-claims.

Snyder makes no attempt at objectivity. Indeed, his anti-Soviet hostility often boils over in passages of heated rhetoric, fervent moralizing, and moral condemnation that serve no analytical purpose. Yet objectivity is first among the requirements of any historian worthy of the name. If one does not strive for objectivity from the outset of one's study one will never discover the truth. The truth was never Snyder's goal in the first place.

Hitler also succinctly explained why the "Big Lie" technique is so effective:

> In this they proceeded on the sound principle that the magnitude of a lie always contains a certain factor of credibility, since the great masses of the people in the very bottom of their hearts tend to be corrupted rather than consciously and purposely evil, and that, therefore, in view of the primitive simplicity of their minds they more easily fall a victim to a big lie than to a little one, since they themselves lie in little things, but would be ashamed of lies that were too big. Such a falsehood will never enter their heads and they will not be able to believe in the possibility of such monstrous effrontery and infamous misrepresentation in others; yes, even when enlightened on the subject, they will long doubt and waver, and continue to accept at least one of these causes as true. Therefore, something of even the most insolent lie will always remain and stick — a fact which all the great lie-virtuosi and lying-clubs in this world know only too well and also make the most treacherous use of.[24]

Some readers may think that it is inappropriate to compare Snyder's method to Hitler's regardless of the apparent accuracy of that comparison. As understandable as such reluctance may be,

---

[24] *Mein Kampf* Part 1 Chapter 10. At
http://www.hitler.org/writings/Mein_Kampf/mkv1ch10.html

the reader should note that Snyder often compares Joseph Stalin to Adolf Hitler but utterly fails to demonstrate that similarity because the "evidence" he cites in support of this "Stalin — Hitler" comparison is not evidence at all but is based on falsification.

Consciously or not, Snyder uses the "Big Lie" technique to compare Stalin to Hitler, the communists to the Nazis, communism to Nazism. This comparison falls apart if one sticks to the truth — the truth dismantles it entirely. Hence the lies and falsehoods, "deliberate" or not.

A full professor of history at Yale University, publishing with a major American commercial publisher, can rely on "credibility" — the only coin in the propagandist's purse. The present study shows this coin to be counterfeit.

Chapter 1.

The "Man-Made" Famine and "Deliberate Famine" Arguments in *Bloodlands*, Chapter 1.

More pages of *Bloodlands* are devoted to the subject of the famine of 1932-33 than to any other single event. Though he has never done research on the famine Snyder promotes a view that contradicts all the evidence as well as the view of the best scholars of this subject: that the famine was "man-made" and "deliberate." We present the conclusions of these scholars here.

In the course of studying Snyder's account of the famine and proving it wrong we also consider, and disprove, the works of scholars who are motivated not by objectivity and a desire to discover the truth but by ideological partisanship: anticommunism and Ukrainian nationalism.

Snyder devotes the whole first chapter of *Bloodlands* to insistence that the famine was deliberate. This is all wrong. Moreover, Snyder ought to be aware that it is wrong because the unanimous conclusion of the best experts who have studied this question is that the famine was a secular one caused by weather conditions and plant diseases. Snyder cites the works of these scholars. But he never informs his readers that they reject entirely the "deliberate starvation" notion that is central to Snyder's book.

There are two distinct though related parts to the "man-made famine" allegation. First, it is asserted that the Soviet government — "Stalin" — deliberately "murdered" the several million people, mainly Ukrainian peasants, who died from the famine. The reasons alleged for the decision to "murder" vary. Sometimes it is claimed that starvation was used to crush Ukrainian nationalism. Sometimes it is suggested that the Soviet government decided to export grain to fuel the program of crash industrialization in full knowledge that this meant death of millions by starvation. These two explanations are not mutually exclusive and are raised in an inconsistent manner, an inconsistency attributable to the fact that there is not the slightest evidence to support either one of them.

As a preface to our detailed critique of Snyder's account in Chapter One of *Bloodlands* we note the following passages from Snyder's articles in influential American and British intellectual journals. These passages attest to the fact that Snyder promotes this false position with great energy and persistence. We have emphasized some phrases for the readers' convenience.

A. The Famine Itself Was Deliberate Murder

Jewish communist partisans in Belarus or Ukraine obviously seem heroic as enemies of the Nazis and avengers of their families. Their legacy is muddled by the fact that they bore arms to defend **a system that had killed 3.5 million Ukrainians and a similar number of Kazakhs by famine** 10 years before, and a million other Soviet citizens by execution in 1937-1938. (2004-2)

The Soviets hid their mass shootings in dark woods and falsified the records of regions in which they had **starved people to death**... (2009-2)

...the Soviet policies that killed people directly and purposefully, by starvation... (2009-2)

Of the Stalinist killing policies, two were the most significant: the collectivization famines of 1930—1933 and the Great Terror of 1937—1938. It remains unclear whether the Kazakh famine of 1930—1932 was intentional, although it is clear that over a million Kazakhs died of starvation. **It is established beyond reasonable doubt that Stalin intentionally starved to death Soviet Ukrainians in the winter of 1932—1933.** Soviet documents reveal a series of orders of October—December

> 1932 with evident malice and intention to kill. By
> the end, more than three million inhabitants of So-
> viet Ukraine had died. (2009-2)

Here Snyder says "over a million Kazakhs" died. In the previous
quotation, from the same article, he says "3.5 million Ukrainians
and a similar number of Kazakhs."

> ...millions of Ukrainians were **deliberately starved**
> by Stalin. (2009-2)

> The preoccupation with Ukraine as a source of food
> was shared by Hitler and Stalin. Both wished to
> control and exploit the Ukrainian breadbasket, and
> both caused **political famines**: Stalin in the country
> as a whole, Hitler in the cities and the prisoner-of-
> war camps. (2009-2)

> The **famine** certainly did happen, and it was **delib-
> erate**. (2010-1)

> He threatened local officials with the Gulag, **forcing
> them to collect grain from the starving;** and he
> sealed the internal borders of the republic so that
> they could not beg in other parts of the Soviet Un-
> ion. (2010-1)

> ...the **deliberate starvation** of the three million in-
> habitants of Soviet Ukraine by the Stalinist regime...
> (2010-2)

> While it is true that Stalin's policy of collectivization
> — the state seizure of farmland and the coercive
> employment of peasants — brought enormous suf-
> fering throughout the USSR in the early 1930s, it is
> also true that Stalin made **deliberate decisions**
> about grain requisitions and livestock seizures that
> **brought death to three million people in
> Ukraine who did not have to die**. Some of the very
> worst of the **killing** took place in southeastern
> Ukraine, where Stalin is now being celebrated and
> where Yanukovych has his political base. The fam-
> ine destroyed that region's rural society by killing

many, cowing more, and permitting the immigra-
tion of people from beyond Ukraine — chiefly Russians, some of whom inherited the homes of the
starved. The cult of Stalin is thus no empty symbol
in Ukraine; it is a mark of active identification with
a person who owed his mastery of Ukraine to a
campaign of death. (2010-2)

We now know, after 20 years of discussion of Soviet
documents, that in 1932 Stalin knowingly transformed the collectivization famine in Ukraine into **a
deliberate campaign of politically motivated
starvation**. (2010-5)

Of those who starved, the 3.3 million or so inhabitants of Soviet Ukraine who died in 1932 and 1933
were victims of **a deliberate killing policy related
to nationality**. (2011-1)

Stalin requisitioned grain in Soviet Ukraine **knowing that such a policy would kill millions**. (2011-
1)

(All emphases added.)

In these semi-popular articles Snyder is at liberty to make the
charge of "deliberate famine" and "mass murder" without citing
evidence of any kind. In *Bloodlands* Snyder finally has to present
his "evidence" to the scrutiny of his readers. We shall examine his
argument in detail and expose it for the fraud that it is.

The "Ukrainian Famine" and post-Soviet nationalism

Since the 1950s Ukrainian Nationalist organizations have been
claiming that Stalin and Bolshevik leaders deliberately starved the
Ukraine in order to punish Ukrainian nationalist spirit. The same
Ukrainian nationalist groups entered the USSR with the Nazis and
collaborated in massacring at least hundreds of thousands of Soviet citizens — mainly other Ukrainians, as they were largely confined to the Ukraine, as well as Jews. They also committed the
"Volhynian massacres" of 50,000 - 100,000 Polish peasants in their

attempt at "ethnic cleansing" — a little-known holocaust that has received attention only since the end of the USSR and Eastern bloc. Their version of the famine, which they call "Holodomor," or "deliberate death by starvation," is best known in the West from the 1986 book by Robert Conquest, *Harvest of Sorrow: Soviet Collectivization and the Terror-Famine.* Conquest has retracted his claim, as we shall see below.

The thesis of Conquest's book, that the famine was deliberate and aimed at Ukrainians, is today's "Holodomor" thesis, though this term was not yet used in the 1980s. Anticommunist Soviet-studies experts rejected it at the time the book was published.

> "There is no evidence it was intentionally directed against Ukrainians," said Alexander Dallin of Stanford, the father of modern Sovietology. "That would be totally out of keeping with what we know — it makes no sense."

> "This is crap, rubbish," said Moshe Lewin of the University of Pennsylvania, whose Russian Peasants and Soviet Power broke new ground in social history. "I am an anti-Stalinist, but I don't see how this [genocide] campaign adds to our knowledge. It's adding horrors, adding horrors, until it becomes a pathology."

> "I absolutely reject it," said Lynne Viola of SUNY-Binghamton, the first US historian to examine Moscow's Central State Archive on collectivization. "Why in god's name would this paranoid government consciously produce a famine when they were terrified of war [with Germany]?"

> These premier Sovietologists dismiss Conquest for what he is — an ideologue whose serious work is long behind him. But Dallin stands as a liberal exception to the hard-liners of his generation, while Lewin and Viola remain Young Turks who happen to be doing the freshest work on this period. In Soviet studies, where rigor and objectivity count for less than the party line, where fierce anti-

> Communists still control the prestigious institutes
> and first-rank departments, a Conquest can survive
> and prosper while barely cracking a book.
>
> "He's terrible at doing research," said veteran Sovi-
> etologist Roberta Manning of Boston College." He
> misuses sources, he twists everything."[1]

In a polite but firmly negative review of Conquest's book in the
London Review of Books in 1987 American Soviet scholar J. Arch
Getty wrote:

> Conquest's hypothesis, sources and evidence are
> not new. Indeed, he himself first put forward his
> view two years ago in a work sponsored by the
> American Enterprise Institute. The intentional fam-
> ine story, however, has been an article of faith for
> Ukrainian émigrés in the West since the Cold War.
> Much of Conquest's most graphic description is tak-
> en from such period-pieces as *The Golgoltha of the
> Ukraine* (1953), *The Black Deeds of the Kremlin*
> (1953) and *Communism the Enemy of Mankind*
> (1955). Conquest's book will thus give a certain ac-
> ademic credibility to a theory which has not been
> generally accepted by non-partisan scholars out-
> side the circles of exiled nationalities. In today's
> conservative political climate, with its 'evil empire'
> discourse, I am sure that the book will be very pop-
> ular.[2]

Despite their best efforts Ukrainian researchers have been unable
to find *any* documentary support for their claim of deliberate starvation. A huge number of archival documents, a few of them reproduced in a Library of Congress volume *Revelations from the*

---

[1] Quoted in Jeff Coplon. "In Search of a Soviet Holocaust. A 55-Year-Old Famine Feeds the Right." *Village Voice* (New York City) January 12, 1988.

[2] "Starving the Ukraine." Review of Conquest, *The Harvest of Sorrow the terror-famine*. *London Review of Books* January 22, 1987 pp. 8-9. Conquest's reply, Getty's response to it, and the ensuing back-and-forth, bitter on Conquest's part and skillful on Getty's, was online on October 24, 2013 when I accessed it. Now only ¼ of it is available for free.

Russian Archives,[3] documents in English translation, make it clear that no such deliberate starvation occurred.

Nevertheless the myth of the "Holodomor" is now constitutive of the nationalist identity promoted by the independent state of Ukraine and is taught compulsorily in Ukrainian schools as fact. A few articles by the world's leading scholar on the 1932-33 famine, Mark Tauger of West Virginia University, whose work contradicts the Ukrainian nationalist account have just begun to appear in Russian-, though not in Ukrainian-language publications.

Even Robert Conquest has backed off his initial claim that the famine was deliberate, as Davies and Wheatcroft have revealed.

> Our view of Stalin and the famine is close to that of Robert Conquest, who would earlier have been considered the champion of the argument that Stalin had intentionally caused the famine and had acted in a genocidal manner. In 2003, Dr Conquest wrote to us explaining **that he does not hold the view that 'Stalin purposely inflicted the 1933 famine. No.** What I argue is that with resulting famine imminent, he could have prevented it, but put "Soviet interest" other than feeding the starving first — thus consciously abetting it'.[4] (Emphasis added)

Yet the "man-made famine" claim continues to be presented either as settled fact, as Snyder does, or as one plausible theory among others.

In 1995 Davies, Tauger, and Wheatcroft outlined their conclusions about the famine in this way:

> We therefore conclude:
>
> 1. All planners' stocks — the two secret grain reserves, Nepfond and Mobfond or Gosfond, together

---

[3] I have put these documents from this collection online at
http://msuweb.montclair.edu/~furrg/research/ukfaminedocs97.pdf

[4] R. W. Davies & Stephen G. Wheatcroft. "Debate. Stalin and the Soviet Famine of 1932 — 33: A Reply to Ellman." *Europe-Asia Studies* 58 (4) June 2006, 629; Also in Davies & Wheatcroft, *The Years of Hunger: Soviet Agriculture, 1931 — 1933* (Basingstoke, Palgrave Macmillan, 2004), 441 n.145.

with "transitional stocks" held by grain organizations — amounted on 1 July 1933 to less than 2 million tons (1.997 million tons, according to the highest official figure). Persistent efforts of Stalin and
the Politburo to establish firm and inviolable grain
reserves (in addition to "transitional stocks")
amounting to 2 or 3 million tons or more were almost completely unsuccessful. ...

2. We do not know the amount of grain which was
held by grain-consuming organizations, notably the
Red Army, but we suspect that these "consumers'
stocks" would not change the picture substantially.

3. These findings do not, of course, free Stalin from
responsibility for the famine. It is difficult, perhaps
impossible, to assess the extent to which it would
have been possible for Stalin to use part of the grain
stocks available in spring 1933 to feed starving
peasants. The state was a monopoly supplier of
grain to urban areas and the army; if the reserves of
this monopoly supply system — which amounted to
four-six weeks' supply — were to have been
drained, mass starvation, epidemics and unrest in
the towns could have resulted. Nevertheless, it
seems certain that, if Stalin had risked lower levels
of these reserves in spring and summer 1933, hundreds of thousands — perhaps millions — of lives
could have been saved. In the slightly longer term, if
he had been open about the famine, some international help would certainly have alleviated the disaster. And if he had been more far-sighted, the agricultural crisis of 1932-1933 could have been mitigated and perhaps even avoided altogether. But
Stalin was not hoarding immense grain reserves in
these years. On the contrary, he had failed to reach

the levels which he had been imperatively demanding since 1929.[5]

In their major work on the subject published in 2004 Davies and
Wheatcroft outline their conclusions as follows:

> Our study of the Famine has led us to very different
> conclusions from Dr. Conquest's. He holds that Sta-
> lin "wanted a famine," that "the Soviets did not
> want the famine to be coped with successfully," and
> that the Ukrainian famine was "deliberately inflict-
> ed for its own sake." This leads him to the sweeping
> conclusion: "The main lesson seems to be that the
> Communist ideology provided the motivation for an
> unprecedented massacre of men, women and chil-
> dren."
>
> We do not at all absolve Stalin from responsibility
> for the famine. His policies towards the peasants
> were ruthless and brutal. But the story which has
> emerged in this book is of a Soviet leadership which
> was struggling with a famine crisis which had been
> caused partly by their wrongheaded policies, but
> was unexpected and undesirable. The background
> to the famine is not simply that Soviet agricultural
> policies were derived from Bolshevik ideology,
> though ideology played its part. They were also
> shaped by the Russian revolutionary past, the expe-
> riences of the civil war, the international situation,
> the intransigent circumstances of geography and
> the weather, and the *modus operandi* of the Soviet
> system as it was established under Stalin. They
> were formulated by men with little formal educa-
> tion and limited knowledge of agriculture. Above
> all, they were a consequence of the decision to in-

---

[5] R.W. Davies, M.B. Tauger and S.G. Wheatcroft. "Stalin, Grain Stocks and the Famine of
1932-1933." *Slavic Review* Volume 54, Issue 3 (Autumn, 1995), 642-657, at 656-7.

dustrialize this peasant country at breakneck
speed.[6]

Mark Tauger did not coauthor this book. Of these three authors
only Tauger has devoted his professional life to the study of the
1932-33 famine, Russian famines, and famines generally. In his
review of Davies' and Wheatcroft's book Tauger both sums up
their conclusions and expresses some criticisms of them.

> Popular media and most historians for decades
> have described the great famine that struck most of
> the USSR in the early 1930s as "man-made," very of-
> ten even a "genocide" that Stalin perpetrated inten-
> tionally against Ukrainians and sometimes other
> national groups to destroy them as nations. The
> most famous exposition of this view is the book
> *Harvest of Sorrow*, now almost two decades old, by
> the prolific (and problematic) historian Robert
> Conquest, but this perspective can be found in His-
> tory Channel documentaries on Stalin, many text-
> books of Soviet history, Western and even World
> Civilization, and many writings on Stalinism, on the
> history of famines, and on genocide.
>
> This perspective, however, is wrong. The famine
> that took place was not limited to Ukraine or even
> to rural areas of the USSR, it was not fundamentally
> or exclusively man-made, and it was far from the in-
> tention of Stalin and others in the Soviet leadership
> to create such as disaster. A small but growing lit-
> erature relying on new archival documents and a
> critical approach to other sources has shown the
> flaws in the "genocide" or "intentionalist" interpre-
> tation of the famine and has developed an alterna-
> tive interpretation. The book under review, *The
> Years of Hunger*, by Robert Davies and Stephen
> Wheatcroft, is the latest and largest of these revi-

---

[6] R. W. Davies and Stephen G. Wheatcroft, *The Years of Hunger: Soviet Agriculture, 1931-1933*. New York: Palgrave Macmillan, 2004, p. 441.

sionist interpretations. It presents more evidence than any previous study documenting the intentions of Soviet leaders and the character of the agrarian and agricultural crises of these years.

Tauger also expresses some serious criticisms of Davies' and Wheatcroft's work:

> Second, the book still does not satisfactorily explain why the famine took place when it did and especially why it ended. The authors' chapters on agriculture and procurements in 1933, which was of course the crucial agricultural year because this was when the famine basically ended, are substantially shorter than those on 1931 and 1932 and have a certain "rushed" quality. Davies and Wheatcroft identify several objective factors to which they attribute the declines in food production in 1931-1933 that in great part caused the famine. Most of those factors that they identify for 1932, however, still prevailed or were even worse in 1933. The decline in livestock numbers and draft forces, for example, continued into 1933 and possibly 1934 (depending on how one calculates the value of a tractor); the disorder in crop rotation was not overcome even by the reduced sowing plans of 1933, or for some years thereafter. Most important, famine conditions were much worse. The authors cite a few sources claiming that peasants somehow knew in 1933 that they had to work hard (p. 238), but they also acknowledge in another context that at least some peasants worked hard in 1932 as well (p. 418). In any case, all evidence about peasants' resistance is anecdotal and can be shown not to be representative of their views and actions generally (see my article "Soviet Peasants and Collectivization: Resistance and Adaptation"). Without any doubt, however, working conditions for peasants in

1933, because of the more severe famine conditions, were much worse in 1933 than in 1932.

Given these inconsistencies, there remains one factor in explaining the cause of the small harvest of 1932 that can account for the improved harvest in 1933, and that is the complex of environmental factors in 1932. As I documented in a recent publication, the USSR experienced an unusual environmental disaster in 1932: extremely wet and humid weather that gave rise to severe plant disease infestations, especially rust. Ukraine had double or triple the normal rainfall in 1932. Both the weather conditions and the rust spread from Eastern Europe, as plant pathologists at the time documented. Soviet plant pathologists in particular estimated that rust and other fungal diseases reduced the potential harvest in 1932 by almost nine million tons, which is the largest documented harvest loss from any single cause in Soviet history (*Natural Disaster and Human Action*, p. 19). One Soviet source did estimate higher rust losses in 1933 than 1932 for two provinces in the Central Blackearth Region, which is a small region of the country (approximately 5 percent of the total sown area). Davies and Wheatcroft cite this and imply that it applied to the rest of the country (p. 131-132 fn. 137), but that source does not document larger losses from rust in 1933 anywhere else. Further, the exceptional weather and agricultural conditions of 1932 did not generally recur in 1933.

Consequently I would still argue, against Davies and Wheatcroft, that the weather and infestations of 1932 were the most important causes of the small harvest in 1932 and the larger one in 1933. I would also like to point out for the record here that the criticism they make (p. 444-445) of my harvest data is invalid and represents an unjustified statistical manipulation of what are in fact the only genuine harvest data for 1932 (see "The 1932 Harvest").[7]

Tauger attributes more importance to climatic conditions, and less to communist party ideology, policies, incompetence, and/or brutality, than do Davies and Wheatcroft.

B. Collectivization caused the famine

Snyder also links the famine to collectivization. He writes:

> ...both regimes [i.e. the Nazi and Soviet] integrated mass murder with economic planning. (2009-2)

> Eighty years ago, in the autumn of 1930, Joseph Stalin enforced a policy that changed the course of history, and led to tens of millions of deaths across the decades and around the world. In a violent and massive campaign of "collectivization," he brought Soviet agriculture under state control. (2010-5)

> Once the agricultural sector of the USSR was collectivized, the hunger began. (2010-5)

> ...the shooting and deportation of the best farmers..." (2010-5)

> After Mao made his revolution in 1948, Chinese communists followed the Stalinist model of development. This meant that some 30 million Chinese starved to death in 1958-1961, in a famine very similar to that in the Soviet Union. Maoist collectivization, too, was followed by mass shooting campaigns. (2010-5)

As we have seen above, Tauger believes that climatic conditions played a greater role in the famine than policy factors such as collectivization.

There have been hundreds of famines in Russian history, about one every 2nd or 3rd year. There were serious famines in 1920-

---

[7] Mark Tauger. Review of R. W. Davies and Stephen G. Wheatcroft, *The Years of Hunger: Soviet Agriculture, 1931-1933*. New York: Palgrave Macmillan, 2004. At http://eh.net/book_reviews/years-hunger-soviet-agriculture-1931-1933

1921, 1924, 1927, and 1928. The "Volga famine" of 1920-1921 is well known, in part because of the Nansen relief commission which took many horrifying photographs of the suffering. There was another weather-induced famine in 1924.

In 2001 Tauger published an article about the 1924 and 1928 famines titled "Grain Crisis or Famine?"[8] Official Soviet Ukrainian primary sources prove that the 1928-29 famine was a serious famine, including in the Ukraine, which received more aid than it sent to other parts of the USSR. This disproves the "exploitation" theory of some Ukrainian nationalists. The 1928-1929 famine was caused by natural disaster, mainly drought. It was not induced by Soviet taxation or procurement policies. Moreover, government relief efforts and agencies organized the shortage to distribute very significant amounts of food to the poorest persons, undoubtedly saving many lives.

But the famines of 1924 and 1927-1928 are largely ignored. When they don't ignore them anticommunist researchers deny that these were "famines," calling them instead "regional and local problems." Evidently they do this in order to hide the fact that famines of greater or lesser intensity occurred in Russia very frequently. Anticommunist writers would like others to believe that such famines were rare until collectivization.

But in reality famines were common. Collectivization was in large part an attempt to solve this perennial problem. In a famous passage in his memoir of World War 2 *Hinge of Fate* Churchill quoted Stalin as saying:

> "Ten millions," he said, holding up his hands. "It was fearful. Four years it lasted. It was absolutely necessary for Russia, if we were to avoid periodic famines, to plough the land with tractors. We must mechanise our agriculture. When we gave tractors to the peasants they were all spoiled in a few

[8] Mark Tauger, "Grain Crisis or Famine? The Ukrainian State Commission for Aid to Crop-Failure Victims and the Ukrainian Famine of 1928-29." In Donald J. Raleigh, ed. *Provincial Landscapes. Local Dimensions of Soviet Power* 1917-1953. Pittsburgh: University of Pittsburgh Press, 2001, 146-170.

> months. Only Collective Farms with workshops
> could handle tractors.[9]

Churchill wrote these volumes years later and his memory was probably far from precise. But no one has suggested that Churchill invented this passage about "avoiding periodic famines."

Therefore, collectivization was necessary not simply to fund industrialization, although it was indeed essential for that purpose. It was essential to put an end to periodic famines, during which a great many people died. Indeed, 1932-33 was the last famine, except for the postwar famine of 1946-1947, the basic cause of which was the worst drought in many decades combined with the immense destruction caused by the war. Stephen Wheatcroft's recent article convincingly demolishes the ideological anticommunists who tried to make this famine too a "man-made" famine to "punish peasants."[10]

This fact — that collectivization saved the Soviet people from further famines — is virtually always erased in discussions of the famine of 1932-33. Collectivization certainly caused deaths. *However, not to collectivize would also have caused deaths*. The status quo caused deaths — from famines. Continuing the NEP (New Economic Policy) would have caused deaths from famines. Poor peasants died from starvation even in non-famine years because they could not afford to buy enough grain.

The only alternatives to collectivization of agriculture were:

1. To permit famines to continue every 2-3 years indefinitely, as the Tsars had done;

2. To forego industrialization for decades, if not forever (if the Nazis had had their way all Slavs would have been killed or reduced to uneducated serfs).

In terms of the good that it did and the evils that it avoided, collectivization, with all of its problems and deaths, was one of the great triumphs of public policy of the 20th century. Had it been accom-

---

[9] Winston Churchill. *The Hinge of Fate*. RosettaBooks LLC 2002 (orig. ed. 1950), 447-8.

[10] Wheatcroft, Stephen G. "The Soviet Famine of 1946—1947, the Weather and Human Agency in Historical Perspective." *Europe-Asia Studies*, 64:6, 987-1005.

plished by a capitalist country it would probably have long since been generally acknowledged as such.

The Chinese Communists and Vietnamese Communists learned much from studying the Bolsheviks' experience with collectiviza- tion and industrialization. They resolved not to slavishly imitate the Soviet example, and they did not do so. But Stalin and the Bol- sheviks were the first. They did not have the benefit of hindsight. It is to be expected that they would make many decisions that later turned out to have been mistakes. That is always the case with pi- oneers. During collectivization the Bolsheviks made many, many errors. But it would have been an immeasurably greater mistake not to try in the first place.

And here is the problem. It is unfashionable, "politically incorrect," to point these things out. The prevailing anticommunist, and spe- cifically anti-Stalinist, orthodoxy among elites, East and West, make it literally unprintable. It's a fact, it's the truth — but "you can't say it."

Collectivization and the Famine of 1932-33: What Really Happened

This is a brief account of the 1932-1933 Soviet famine as support- ed by the primary source evidence now available. It is based upon the research of Professor Mark Tauger of West Virginia University. Tauger has spent his professional life of more than 20 years study- ing famines and is a world expert on Russian famines. He has writ- ten several special studies of the 1932-33 famine.[11]

---

[11] For this brief introductory account I have drawn the following works by Mark Tauger:

"The Harvest of 1932 and the Famine of 1933," *Slavic Review*, Vol. 50, No. I (1991), 70-89. (Tauger 1991)

"Grain Crisis or Famine? The Ukrainian State Commission for Aid to Crop Failure Victims and the Ukrainian Famine of 1928-1929" in *Provincial Landscapes. Local Dimensions of Sovi- et Power*, ed. by D.J. Raleigh (Pittsburgh, 2001), 146-170, 360-365. (Tauger 2001a)

Natural Disaster and Human Action in the Soviet Famine of 1931-1933, Carl Beck Papers No. 1506 (Pittsburgh, Penn., 2001). (Tauger 2001b)

"Soviet Peasants and Collectivization, 1930-1939. Resistance and Adaptation." *Journal of Peasant Studies* (4) 2004, 427-256. Reprinted in *Rural Adaptation in Russia*, ed. Stephen K. Wegren. London and New York: Routledge, 2005, 65-94. (Tauger 2004)

Famines in Russian History

Famine has struck Russia hundreds of times during the past millennium. A 1988 account by Russian scholars traces these famines through historical records from the year 736 A.D. to 1914. Many of these famines struck Ukraine as well.

The year of the two Russian revolutions, 1917, saw a serious crop failure leading to an urban famine in 1917-18. In the 1920s the USSR had a series of famines: in 1920-1923 in the Volga and Ukraine plus one in western Siberia in 1923; in the Volga and Ukraine again in 1924-25, and a serious and little-studied famine in Ukraine in 1928-1929.

In 1920-1923 Russia experienced a devastating famine, often called the Volga famine — a misnomer since it affected at least the Volga region, Ukraine, and the North Caucasus — with accompanying typhus epidemic. The Soviet government requested and received considerable help from abroad, including from the famous commission headed by Norwegian explorer and humanitarian Fridtjof Nansen and Herbert Hoover's American Relief Administration.[12]

Another famine struck in 1924-1925. Again in 1927-1928 a terrible crop failure struck the Ukraine, the result of a combination of natural disasters.

"Stalin, Soviet Agriculture, and Collectivisation." In *Food and Conflict in Europe in the Age of the Two World Wars*. Edited by Frank Trentmann and Flemming Just. New York and Houndsmills: Palgrave Macmillan, 2006. 109-142. (Tauger 2006)

"Famine in Russian History." *The Supplement to the Modern Encyclopedia of Russian and Soviet History*. Edited by George N. Rhyne. Volume 10 (Gulf Breeze, FL, 2011) 79-92. (Tauger 2011)

I have also drawn upon two unpublished communications by Tauger of April 12. 2012 (Tauger 2012a) and April 13, 2012 (Tauger 2012b). I cite other works of Tauger's in the discussion of Snyder's version.

[12] The Nansen commission took many photographs of the dead, dying, and starving. Some of these have been used repeatedly by Ukrainian Nationalists to illustrate their works on the 1932-33 famine.

> The Soviet Ukrainian government established a
> famine relief commission, the Uriadkom,[13] the cen-
> tral government in Moscow transported food from
> the Russian Republic to Ukraine, and the Uriadkom
> distributed food to nearly 400,000 peasants, as well
> as livestock feed, farm equipment, and credits.
> (Tauger 2012a; Tauger 2001a)

This history of a thousand years of frequent famine and of a dozen
years that witnessed three significant crop failures and subsequent famines is the essential context for understanding the famine of 1932-1933 and the response of the Soviet government to it.

> The Ukrainian famine of 1928-29 was the third
> famine in the Soviet Union in seven years due to a
> natural disaster and was the most extreme part of a
> broader food-supply crisis that affected most of the
> country. This crisis did not result exclusively or
> even mainly from price policies. The Soviet Union
> clearly had an extreme vulnerability to natural dis-
> asters, and Soviet leaders interpreted this vulnera-
> bility in comparison to the West as. a sign of agri-
> cultural backwardness.
>
> For Soviet leaders, the Ukrainian famine was an
> important part of the argument that Soviet agricul-
> ture had to be changed. (Tauger 2001a 169-70)

Collectivization

The collectivization of agriculture was designed to end the cycle of
famines that had tormented Russia and Ukraine for centuries. It
was a reform — a significant improvement in the security and
lives of the peasant population and therefore of the entire population. It was not undertaken to "tax" or "exploit" the peasants or to
extract value from the countryside. On the contrary: during the

---

[13] Abbreviation for the Ukrainian name "Uriadova komisia po dopomohi poterpilim vid
nevrozhaiu selianam" - "State Commission for Aid to Peasants Suffering from the Crop Failure" (Tauger 2001a, 147)

decade 1929-1939 the Soviet government spent tens of billions of rubles on agriculture.

> [T]heir primary goal was increasing food produc-
> tion by using what seemed to be the most modern
> and reliable methods available at the time. (Tauger
> 2004, 70)

Stalin and the Bolsheviks viewed collectivization as the only way to swiftly modernize agriculture, to put an end to the wasteful and labor-consuming cultivation of individual land holdings, often in tiny widely-scattered strips and put it on a large-scale basis. They used the large-scale, highly mechanized agriculture of certain American farms in the West as models for the *sovkhozy* (Soviet farms). They did not see collectivization as a means of exploitation or as "re-creating serfdom" and certainly not as deliberate killing or genocide. Nor was it.

Peasant Protests against Collectivization

Peasant protests did occur. According to an OGPU (police) report of March 1931, right in the midst of collectivization, about five per cent of the peasant population was involved in protests. This also means that the vast majority of peasants was not involved in such protests. Most of these protests were settled peacefully; the OGPU reported that they had recourse to force in fewer than 2% of them. Many peasants actively supported collectivization. This number increased when local activists were experienced or sensitive enough to patiently explain the purpose of collectivization to the peasants. Some peasants "spontantously form[ed] *kolkhozy* and consolidated their fields." (Tauger 2004, 75)

Tauger concludes that:

> ...the regime implemented collectivization coercive-
> ly, violently and without adequate appreciation of
> or concern for its disruptive consequences. (Tauger
> 2004, 88)

Nevertheless, he concludes:

> [C]ollectivization was a programme to achieve a
> clearly necessary goal - to increase food production

in a country plagued by famines - and that it was
implemented after the apparently successful exper-
iment of the sovkhoz project and with substantial
governmental investments. (Tauger 2004, 88)

Many historians claim that peasant opposition to and even rebellion against collectivization was widespread, and thus that collectivization produced "famine and failure." Tauger believes the facts
show otherwise:

[T]hese studies minimize or ignore the actual harvest data, the environmental factors that caused
low harvests, the repeated recovery from the famine and crop failures, the large harvests of the
1930s, the mechanization of Soviet farms in these
years, Soviet population growth, and the long-term
increases in food production and consumption over
the Soviet period. (Tauger 2004, 87)

In short, collectivization was a success for the Soviet and Ukrainian peasantry and for all of Soviet society which, of course, relied
on the peasants' agricultural labor to feed it.

... collectivisation brought substantial modernisa-
tion to traditional agriculture in the Soviet Union,
and laid the basis for relatively high food production and consumption by the 1970s and 1980s.
(Tauger 2006, 109)

Many accounts of "dekulakization" and forcible grain procurements emphasize the violence that was often necessary to force
determined opponents of collectivization off the land into exile,
and the fact that peasants who were forced to give up grain during
the famine experienced this force as cruelty. There must have been
many incidents that could be described by anyone as "cruel". In
Tauger's view "the cruel forced movement of population — dekulakization" or what Stalin called "the destruction of the class of kulaks", was "not necessarily the best means to achieve the regime's
objective" of collectivizing agriculture.

I am not convinced by those who claim that the Soviets rejected
"better" or "less cruel" methods of collectivization. The truth is

that collectivization was a massive enterprise that was unprecedented in history. Stalin and the Soviet leadership undertook it because they saw no other way to avoid devastating famines in the future. They made a plan and carried it out, and that meant disempowering any people who were determined to stop it.

The Soviet leadership was flexible. The plan was changed several times in response to feedback from local activists who worked directly with peasants. The most famous change in plan is that associated with Stalin's article "Dizzy with Success," published on March 2, 1930. This article re-emphasized the need to persuade rather than to force peasants to join collective farms.

When the famine occurred — not caused by collectivization but by environmental factors, as we discuss below — the Soviet leadership had to deal with that too. There was no choice but to take grain from peasants in the countryside in order to redistribute it in a more egalitarian manner, as well as to feed the cities and the army, which produced little food. Whatever excesses or cruelty took place were the inevitable result of errors in the plan for carrying out collectivization. Inevitable too was the unevenness in the abilities and characteristics of the tens of thousands of activists and of the peasants themselves. All were faced with a terrible situation under emergency conditions, where many people would inevitably die of starvation or its effects, simply because there was not enough food to feed the whole population.

No "perfect" plan is ever possible at any time. None was possible in 1932. A great many mistakes were made. It could not have been otherwise. But the biggest mistake would have been not to collectivize at all.

> This evidence shows, in particular, that collectivisation allowed the mobilisation and distribution of resources, like tractors, seed aid, and food relief, to enable farmers to produce a large harvest during a serious famine, which was unprecedented in Russian history and almost so in Soviet history. By implication, therefore, this research shows that collectivisation, whatever its disruptive effects on agri-

culture, did in fact function as a means to modernise and aid Soviet agriculture. (Tauger 2006, 112)

The Famine of 1932-33[14]

Two incorrect explanations of this famine are widely accepted. The Ukrainian nationalist explanation claims that Stalin and the Bolshevik leadership withheld grain from Ukrainian peasants in order to export it; deliberately starved Ukrainian peasants to suppress Ukrainian strivings for independence; or both. The alleged motives vary because there is no evidence to support any of them.

This is the myth of the "Holodomor". Consciously modeled on the Jewish Holocaust it originated in the Ukrainian diaspora, among and under the influence of the Organization of Ukrainian Nationalists and veterans of the 14th Waffen SS "Galizien" division and Ukrainian Insurgent Army (OUN-UPA). These forces had fought on the side of the Nazis and had fled to the west with German troops as the Red Army advanced. In true Nazi fashion early proponents of this "deliberate famine" myth blamed Jews for it.

> Two Ukrainian quislings of Moscow, D. Shumsky and M. Khvylovyj, who believed that Moscow as working for a better communist Ukraine but eventually realised that she was only expanding her empire, committed suicide. They were replaced by L. Kahanovych as Secretary of the Communist Party of Ukraine and 1. Shelehess, A. Shlihter, Y. Rahkis, among others, as assistant secretaries. All of them were Jews. The following Jews held positions in the Ministry of Police - V. Balicky, Karlsom, M. Latsis, F. Koch, C. Fuchs. ...

> L. Kahanovych realised he would have a monumental task in bringing the Ukrainian villagers to heel. They were hard-working farmers, fiercely proud of their livelihood and land and would defend these to the death. Moscow's plan was to take all the land

---

[14] This section is largely taken from Tauger 2001b.

> and reduce the villagers to virtual serfdom under the guise of collectivisation.
>
> To achieve this, Kahanovych and the politburo organized a man-made famine in which 7 million Ukrainians died. [15]

When Ukraine became independent in 1991 these forces flooded into the country and exercised a determining influence in historical-ideological questions. They promoted the status of the OUN-UPA forces, guilty of immense mass murders of Jews, Poles, and Soviet citizens generally, as "heroes" who were "fighting for independence". (The assumption here is that "patriotism" and "nationalism" somehow excuse mass murder.)

Thus the myth of the "Holodomor" was never based upon any evidence. Rather, it was politically motivated from the beginning. It has been officially adopted by the Ukrainian state and is now compulsorily taught in Ukrainian schools and promoted by Ukrainian academics. Since there is no evidence at all to support it, it is simply "taken for granted". It is unofficially "taboo", forbidden to dissent from this view in the public sphere in Ukraine (and in the Ukrainian diaspora as well). A law threatening anyone who publicly dissented from this view with criminal penalties was briefly considered under the presidency of Viktor Yushchenko (2005-2010), a leader of the "Orange revolution."

A more "mainstream" but still politicized interpretation states that the famine was due to the collectivization of agriculture, and excessive state grain requisitions, which led to disruptions, mismanagement, and peasant rebellion, and ultimately to famine and starvation. This is the official position of the Russian government. Neither of these explanations is borne out by primary source evidence.

---

[15] See Jurij Chumatskij, *Why Is One Holocaust Worth More Than Others?* Baulkam Hills, NSW, Australia: Busnessl Press Printing Pty, 1986, 31. The title page informs us that it is "Published by Veterans of the Ukrainian Insurgent Army." In today's Ukraine, dominated by pro-Nazi "nationalist" ideology, this group (often called by its Ukrainian initials UPA, for *Ukrains'ka Povstans'ka Armiia*) is praised as "fighters for independence."

Environmental Factors Caused The Famine

The main causes of the 1932-33 famine were environmental factors that led to a poor harvest. These factors were: drought in some areas; unusually heavy rainfall in others; serious infestations of the crop diseases rust and smut; plagues of pests, including Asian locusts, beet weevils, meadow moths, and caterpillars; and a huge infestation of mice. The harvest was so small that the amount of food available in the USSR was apparently less than was necessary to feed the whole population.

Contributing factors were due to the interaction of human agency with these environmental causes. There was a widespread and serious problem of weeds, caused by a shortage of labor to weed the fields due to population flight and the weakness of many remaining peasants. Much land remained unplanted or unharvested due to labor shortages caused by population losses both from peasants moving to towns and cities and from peasants weakened by or dying of starvation.

Horses were the chief draught animals used for plowing and other agricultural tasks. Many horses had been lost or were already severely weakened by a famine in 1931-32 and by desperate peasants eating oats, the horses' fodder. The Soviet state imported some tractors and manufactured others. This did have some effect but not enough to overcome the loss of draft power from horses. (Tauger 2001b)

Much of the land had been planted in grain for years in a row. This resulted in soil exhaustion that severely reduced fertility. Farms and agricultural officials were finding it hard to find additional land in the established agricultural regions. The increased area put the peasants under considerable strain. Nevertheless there was sufficient labor to bring in a good harvest in 1933 and so put an end to the famine. That means there had been enough labor in 1931 and 1932 as well. That the harvest in those years was fatally small was mainly due to the environmental factors listed above.

The Soviet leadership did not fully understand these environmental causes. Nor did their informants, the OGPU and local Party leaders. Therefore, they tended to blame human factors like mismanagement, faulty leadership, and, to some extent, peasant resistance and kulak sabotage. Not understanding, at least for many months, the primary importance of environmental causes, and believing reports that the harvest should have been a good one, the only logical alternative was that the famine was caused by various kinds of sabotage: direct sabotage by Ukrainian nationalists; peasants withholding grain; peasants and others hoarding grain for sale; peasants unwilling to work the fields; Party, kolkhoz, and other officials collaborating in these efforts, and so on.

Nevertheless the Soviet government did greatly reduce exports of grain. It also began to ship aid in food and seed to Ukraine and other hard-hit areas. Tauger (2004, 82-3) writes:

> By early 1933 the USSR was in the throes of a catastrophic famine, varying in severity between regions but pervasive. After efforts in January to procure more grain, the regime began desperate efforts in February to aid peasants to produce a crop. The political departments *(politotdely)*, which the regime introduced into the state farms (*sovkhozy*) and the machine tractor stations (MTS) in early 1933, played a crucial role in these efforts. These agencies, composed of a small group of workers and OGPU personnel in each MTS or *sovkhoz*, removed officials who had violated government directives on farm work and procurements, replacing them with *kolkhozniki* or *sovkhoz* workers who they thought would be more reliable, and organized and otherwise helped farms to produce a good harvest in 1933. They were supported by draconian and coercive laws enforcing labour discipline in the farms in certain regions, but also by the largest allocations of seed and food aid in Soviet history, 5.76 million tons, and by special sowing commissions set up in crucial regions like Ukraine, the Urals, the Volga and elsewhere to manage regional-level aspects of organization and supplies to the farms.

Historians seldom discuss the role of these *politotdely*. Tauger believes they made a significant contribution to the efforts to organize production and overcome the famine. He summarizes at some
length a report of December 1933 from the Central Blackearth Oblast' (south of Moscow and directly north of Ukraine) about the
important role these bodies played in helping the peasants bring
in bringing in the good harvest of 1933:

> The report first describes the crisis conditions of
> early 1933: peasants starving and dying, horses ex-
> hausted, dying and neglected, tractors repaired
> poorly or not at all, labour discipline weak among
> *kolkhozniki*, tractor drivers and individual peasants,
> with frequent cases of refusals to work and avoid-
> ance of responsibility. The *politotdely* began by talk-
> ing with and organizing the *kolkhozniki*, and by
> purging *kolkhozy*, MTS, and other local agencies of
> what it termed kulak and counter-revolutionary el-
> ements. According to the report *kolkhozniki* partici-
> pated in these actions and developed enthusiasm
> for work from them. With *politotdel* help, MTS and
> *kolkhozy* finished sowing 15 days earlier than they
> had in 1932, and sowed 3.4 million hectares instead
> of the 2.85 million hectares they had in 1932. They
> used fertilizer for the first time and sorted seed,
> they treated more seed against plant diseases, they
> weeded crops sometimes two and three times, and
> they took measures against insects. They completed
> harvesting grain crops in 65 days, versus 70 in
> 1932, and threshing in December 1933, a process
> that in 1932 had lasted in the region into March
> 1933. They completed grain procurements in No-
> vember 1933 (those of 1932 had lasted like thresh-
> ing into spring 1933), paid off all of their seed loans,
> formed the necessary internal funds in *kolkhozy*
> and still managed to distribute to *kolkhozniki* much
> more in labour-day payments than the previous
> year, thereby ending the famine in the region. The
> *kolkhozniki* also provided all their livestock with

basic fodder, and built granaries, livestock shelters, clubs and other buildings....

As a result of these efforts, the CBO harvested some 24 per cent more grain in 1933 than in 1932 [Tauger, 1991b: 81]. While weather conditions played a role in these successful results, clearly peasants worked harder and differently in 1933, during the peak of the famine, than they had earlier, and management by the *politotdely* contributed to this. (Tauger 2004, 84)

Tauger cites evidence that many peasants who hated or did not like the *kolkhozy* nevertheless worked hard in them, while many other peasants "worked willingly during the whole period ... siding with the system." (Tauger 2004, 85)

As a result, on the whole peasants accepted collectivization:

All of this is not to deny that some peasants in the 1930s, especially in famine years, used the 'weapons of the weak' against the kolkhoz system and the Soviet government. The issue is how representative evidence is of peasants generally, which is another way of asking how important such incidents were. Certainly resistance was greater and more important in 1930 and possibly 1932. But any analysis of this must also take into account natural disaster, the diversity of peasants' responses, and overall results of their work. Studies conducted in the mid-1930s found that kolkhozniki actually worked harder than non-collectivized peasants had worked in the 1920s, clear evidence of significant adaptation to the new system. (Tauger 2004, 87)

The Question of Grain Exports

Like the Tsarist governments the Soviet government exported grain. Contracts were signed in advance, which created the dilemma Tauger describes as follows:

The low 1931 harvest and reallocations of grain to
famine areas forced the regime to curtail grain exports from 5.2 million tons in 1931 to 1.73 million
in 1932; they declined to 1.68 million in 1933. Grain
exported in 1932 and 1933 could have fed many
people and reduced the famine: The 354,000 tons
exported during the first half of 1933, for example,
could have provided nearly 2 million people with
daily rations of 1 kilogram for six months. Yet these
exports were less than half of the 750,000 tons exported in the first half of 1932. How Soviet leaders
calculated the relative costs of lower exports and
lower domestic food supplies remains uncertain,
but available evidence indicates that further reduc-
tions or cessation of Soviet exports could have had
serious consequences. Grain prices fell in world
markets and turned the terms of trade against the
Soviet Union in the early 1930s, its indebtedness
rose and its potential ability to pay declined, causing western bankers and officials to consider seizure of Soviet property abroad and denial of future
credits in case of Soviet default. Failure to export
thus would have threatened the fulfillment of its industrialization plans and, according to some observers, the stability of the regime.

At the same time that the USSR was exporting it was also allocat-
ing much more grain to seed and famine relief. Tauger documents
the fact that the Central Committee allocated more than half a million tons to Ukraine and North Caucasus in February, and more
than half a million tons to Ukraine alone by April 1933. The government also accumulated some 3 million tons in reserves during
this period and then allocated 2 million tons from that to famine
relief. Soviet archival sources indicate that the regime returned
five million tons of grain from procurements back to villages
throughout the USSR in the first half of 1933 (Tauger 1991, 72; 88-
89). All of these amounts greatly exceed the amount exported in
this period.

The Soviet government was faced with a situation where there was simply not enough food to feed the whole population even if all exports had been stopped instead of just drastically curtailed, as they were.

> The severity and geographical extent of the famine, the sharp decline in exports in 1932-1933, seed requirements, and the chaos in the Soviet Union in these years, all lead to the conclusion that even a complete cessation of exports would not have been enough to prevent famine. This situation makes it difficult to accept the interpretation of the famine as the result of the 1932 grain procurements and as a conscious act of genocide. **The harvest of 1932 essentially made a famine inevitable.** (Tauger 1991 88; 89. Emphasis added)

Grain delivery targets (procurement quotas) were drastically cut back multiple times for both collective and individual farmers in order to share the scarcity. Some of what was procured was returned to the villages. (Tauger 1991, 72-3) It is these collection efforts, often carried out in a very harsh way, that are highlighted by promoters of the "intentionalist" interpretation as evidence of callousness and indifference to peasants' lives or even of intent to punish or kill.

Meanwhile the regime used these procurements to feed 40 million people in the cities and industrial sites who were also starving, further evidence that the harvest was small. In May 1932 the Soviet government legalized the private trade in grain. But very little grain was sold this way in 1932-1933. This too is a further indication of a small 1932 harvest. (Tauger 1991, 72-74)

About 10 per cent of the population of Ukraine died from the famine or associated diseases. But 90 per cent survived, the vast majority of whom were peasants, army men of peasant background, or workers of peasant origin. The surviving peasants had to work very hard, under conditions of insufficient food, to sow and bring in the 1933 harvest. They did so with significant aid from the Soviet government. A smaller population, reduced in size by deaths, weakened by hunger, with fewer draught animals, was nevertheless able to produce a successful harvest in 1933 and put an end to the famine. This is yet more evidence that the 1932 harvest had been a catastrophically poor one. (Tauger 2004)

Government aid included five million tons of food distributed as relief, including to Ukraine, beginning as early as February 7, 1933; [16] the provision of tractors and other equipment distributed especially to Ukraine; "a network of several thousand political departments in the machine-tractor stations which contributed greatly to the successful harvest in 1933" (Tauger 2012b); other measures, including special commissions on sowing and harvesting to manage work and distribute seed and food aid.

> This interpretation of the 1932-1933 famine as the result of the largest in a series of natural disasters suggests an alternative approach to the intentionalist view of the famine. Some advocates of the peasant resistance view argue that the regime took advantage of the famine to retaliate against the peasants and force them to work harder. Famine and deaths from starvation, however, began in 1928 in towns and some rural areas because of low harvests and of some peasants' unwillingness to sell their surpluses. The food supply generally deteriorated over the next few years, due not only to exports in 1930-1931 but also to the crop failures of 1931-1932. The harsh procurements of 1931 and 1932 have to be understood in the context of famine that prevailed in towns as well as villages throughout the Soviet Union by late 1931; by 1932-1933, as noted above, workers as well as peasants were dying of hunger. If we are to believe that the regime starved the peasants to induce labor discipline in the farms, are we to interpret starvation in the towns as the regime's tool to discipline blue and white collar workers and their wives and children?

---

[16] See the document here:
http://msuweb.montclair.edu/~furrg/research/aidtoukraine020733.pdf

While Soviet food distribution policies are beyond the scope of this article, it is clear that the small harvests of 1931-1932 created shortages that affected virtually everyone in the country and that the Soviet regime did not have the internal resources to alleviate the crisis.

Finally, this essay shows that while the USSR experienced chronic drought and other natural disasters earlier, those which occurred in 1932 were an unusual and severe combination of calamities in a country with heightened vulnerability to such incidents. ... The evidence and analysis I have presented here show that the Soviet famine was more serious and more important an event than most previous studies claim, including those adhering to the Ukrainian nationalist interpretation, and that it resulted from a highly abnormal combination of environmental and agricultural circumstances. By drawing attention to these circumstances, this study also demonstrates the importance of questioning accepted political interpretations and of considering the environmental aspects of famines and other historical events that involve human interaction with the natural world. That the Soviet regime, through its rationing systems, fed more than 50 million people, including many peasants, during the famine, however poorly, and that at least some peasants faced with famine undertook to work with greater intensity despite their hostility to the regime in 1933, and to some extent in previous years as well, indicate that all those involved in some way recognized the uniqueness of this tragic event. (Tauger 2001b, 46, 47)

Snyder has adopted the Ukrainian nationalists' "intentional" interpretation — the "Holodomor" myth, though Snyder chooses not to use this term. He strives to give the impression that the Soviet government cut the Ukraine off completely, making no effort to relieve the famine. Snyder ignores environmental causes — which were in fact the primary causes — and fails to mention the Soviet government's large-scale relief campaign which, together with their own hard work under the most difficult conditions, enabled the peasants to produce a large harvest in 1933. In Tauger's judgment:

> [T]he general point [is that] the famine was caused by natural factors and that the government helped the peasants produce a larger harvest the next year and end the famine. (Tauger 2012b, 3)

This is the polar opposite from what Snyder and the Ukrainian nationalists contend. The so-called "Holodomor" or "deliberate" and "man-made" famine interpretation is not simply mistaken on some important points. Its proponents misrepresent history by omitting evidence that would undermine their interpretation. It is not history but political propaganda disguised as history, what I have called elsewhere "propaganda with footnotes."

Tauger's view is also significantly different from that of R. W. Davies and Stephen G. Wheatcroft, who attribute the famine to several causes, including collectivization.[17] In their opinion environmental factors played only a secondary role. Davies and Wheatcroft believe the Soviet government could have saved many, perhaps millions, of lives if collectivization had not been undertaken and mitigated if the Soviet government had not handled the famine in a "brutal" manner. The official position of the Russian government and academic establishment is similar: that the famine was caused by excessive grain requisitioning and by collectivization.

This hypothesis is mistaken. The reality is that collectivization put an end to famines in the Soviet Union, except for a serious famine in 1946-47. Wheatcroft, author of the most recent study of this famine, has concluded that this famine too was due to environmental causes.[18]

---

[17] *The Years of Hunger. Soviet Agriculture, 1931-1933.* Palgrave Macmillan 2009 (2004).

[18] Wheatcroft, Stephen G. "The Soviet Famine of 1946—1947, the Weather and Human Agency in Historical Perspective." *Europe-Asia Studies*, 64:6, 987-1005.

Chapter 2.

The Famine of 1932-33 "Deliberate"?

Snyder's "Seven Points" of Proof

The central section of Snyder's first chapter is his attempt to prove that he has "evidence of clearly premeditated murder on the scale of millions" in the Ukraine. As evidence he outlines "seven crucial policies" that "were applied only, or mainly, in Soviet Ukraine in late 1932 or early 1933," each of which "had to kill" (42)

Snyder must have been aware that no one else — none of the bevy of Ukrainian nationalist or Russia anticommunist scholars who claim that Stalin intended to kill Ukrainian peasants by intentionally starving them to death — has proven this claim. Snyder also knows that the Western experts on this question, Tauger and Davies-Wheatcroft, as well as many other historians of the Soviet Union including bitterly anticommunist writers like Nicolas Werth, reject the notion of a "deliberate famine."

Yet Snyder must claim the deaths were the result of "premeditated murder" because, without the five million famine deaths, the whole thesis of his book, that "the Nazi and Soviet regimes murdered some fourteen million people," falls to the ground, and with it goes the "Stalin — Hitler" comparison so treasured by ideological anticommunists.

Our analysis of Snyder's first chapter begins with a detailed study of each of what Snyder calls the "seven crucial policies." Snyder does not outline these seven points until the last third of his chapter. But the whole chapter, and indeed Snyder's whole book, depends upon these seven points. They are Snyder's "proof" that the several million Soviet citizens who died as a result of the famine of 1932-33 were "murdered" by Stalin and the Soviet leadership. It will be shown that in every case Snyder falsifies his claims and his evidence.

Because of the importance of these "seven points" to Snyder's whole project, somewhat more detail is devoted to them in the main text of the present study than to most of Snyder's other fact-claims. The reader may always consult the full documentation in the Appendix to this first chapter.

Point One (pp. 42-3): Were Ukrainian Peasants Required to Return Grain Advances?

Snyder states that on November 18, 1932 "peasants in Ukraine were required to return grain advances" and that the leadership of the CP(b)U unsuccessfully protested this policy. His note to this passage cites the following sources (n. 57 p. 466):

* Graziosi, "New interpretation," 8;

* Kuśnierz, *Ukraina*, 143;

* Maksudov, "Victory," 188, 190;

* Davies, Years, 175 and, on seed grain, 151.

Graziosi — clearly Snyder's chief "source" here — indeed makes these charges. But Graziosi cites no evidence at all, not a single reference of any kind for these statements or for the entire paragraph of which they are a part. Snyder had to know this, of course, just as anyone who reads Graziosi's article would know it. But Snyder cites these statements anyway. Of course Snyder's readers will *not* know that Graziosi has no evidence for these very serious charges.

Kuśnierz has nothing about any decision of November 18, 1932 on p. 143. He has nothing about returning grain advances, taking away seed grain, the Ukrainian Party leadership trying to "protect" it, etc., as stated by Snyder. Nothing about "shooting" "hundreds of officials" or "arresting thousands" of them.

Maksudov's article, in *Harvard Ukrainian Studies* (2001), contains no evidence itself. Instead it refers the reader to a volume in Ukrainian, *Голод 1932-1933 років*. There are no relevant documents on the pages Maksudov cites from this book. Elsewhere in this volume there is a document dated November 18, 1932 regulating grain collections.[1] This is the document discussed below.[2]

---

[1] № 293 cc. 388-395.

Davies, *Years* 175 has nothing about either returning grain advances or anything at all about seed grain. On pages 151-2 Davies does record the struggle between Moscow — Stalin and Lazar Kaganovich — and the Ukraine, mainly Kosior. Both the decrees of November 18 and November 29, which in part concerned seed grain, were cancelled. In any case these decrees permitted confiscation of seed grain only in exceptional circumstances.

> On November 18 [1932], under strong pressure
> from Moscow to collect more grain, it [the Politburo
> of the Ukrainian Communist Party] granted permission to district soviet executive committees to respond to the 'completely unsatisfactory' grain collection by confiscating the Seed Fund of the kolkhoz concerned, and its other Funds held in grain...
>
> The USSR Politburo [Stalin et al., in Moscow] did
> not catch up with these Ukrainian moves until Kaganovich and Chernov descended on Ukraine towards the end of December. Following telegrams to Stalin from Kaganovich, on December 23 the USSR Politburo brusquely cancelled the Ukrainian Politburo decision of November 18. The Ukrainian Politburo itself cancelled its decision of November 29, and Kosior sent an apology to members and candidate members for this document, of which 'I was the main author.' (151-2)

On December 25, 1932 Kosior self-critically discussed his responsibility for these two documents and made it clear that it was a case of confiscating seed grain only from kolkhozes that did not fulfill their plan for delivering grain to the state:

> Остановившись перед вывозом семенных
> фондов из колхозов, которые не выполняют
> план хлебозаготовок,...[3]

---

[2] This document is online at
http://msuweb.montclair.edu/~furrg/research/pyrigno293.pdf It is also at this site:
http://www.archives.gov.ua/Sections/Famine/Publicat/Fam-Pyrig-1932.php#nom-105

[3] At http://www.archives.gov.ua/Sections/Famine/Publicat/Fam-Pyrig-1932.php#nom-126

Translated:

> Referring to the export of seed funds from the collective farms that do not fulfill the grain procurement plan,...

Conclusion to Snyder's Point One: Not only is Snyder wrong here — in fact, he has it exactly backwards. Not the Soviet, but the *Ukrainian* Politburo did approve a document allowing for confiscation of seed grain, though only under extreme circumstances. It was *Stalin and the Moscow* Politburo that cancelled this decision! As a result Ukrainian First Secretary Kosior apologized for drafting the document in question. This is the opposite of what Snyder claims!

Point Two (p. 43): Did the "Meat Tax" Cause Starvation?

Snyder claims that on November 20, 1932 a "meat penalty" was imposed upon peasants "who were unable to make grain quotas" and that "they [the peasants] starved" as a result. His references (n. 58 p. 466) are:

> * concerning the meat penalty, Shapoval, "Proloh trahedii holodu," 162; and Maksudov, "Victory," 188;
>
> * for the "quotation," Dzwonkowski, *Głód*, 71. "For the example described," Dzwonkowski, *Głód*, 160 and 219.

Here is what **Shapoval**, Snyder's first citation, has to say about the meat penalty (p. 162):

> 20 листопада 1932 року Раднарком УСРР ухвалив рішення про запровад- ження натуральних штрафів: «До колгоспів, що допустили розкрадання кол- госпного хліба і злісно зривають план хлібозаготівель, застосувати натуральні штрафи порядком додаткового завдання з м'ясозаготівель в обсязі 15-місячної норми здавання даним колгоспом м'яса як усуспільненої худоби, так і худоби колгоспників». 6 грудня ухвалено постанову ЦК КП(б)У і Раднаркому УСРР «Про занесення на

"чорну дошку" сіл, які злісно саботують хлібозаготівлі."Це рішення спричинило збільшення жертв голодомору.

Translated:

On November 20, 1932 the People's Commissar of the Ukrainian SSR approved a decision to introduce fines in kind: "to the collective farms, which allowed the theft of kolkhoz grain and maliciously sabotaged the grain procurement plan, to apply fines in kind of an additional task of meat requisitions in the amount of a 15-month norm in contribution by the kolkhoz in question of meat as socialized livestock and of the livestock of kolkhoz members." On December 6 was approved the decree of the Central Committee of the Ukrainian CP and of the People's Commissars of Ukrainian SSR "On entering on the 'black board' [= a "blacklist"] villages that willfully sabotage grain procurements." This decision caused an increase in the victims of the Holodomor.

We should note a few interesting things about this quotation from Shapoval's article — an article which is also available in Russian, in the volume cited by Snyder in his bibliography, and is also available in Ukrainian on the Internet. [4]

* There is no source, either printed or archival, for the quotation.

* Nothing is said about how many kolkhozes this meat penalty was applied to, or indeed whether it was ever applied at all.

* Nothing is said in the source about it contributing to the famine. This sentence is present in Shapoval's article and in all the other Internet sites, but there is no evidence to support it.

---

[4] At http://memorial.kiev.ua/statti/75-iii-konferencija-kpb-prolog-tragediji-golodu.html
For some reason Shapoval is not cited here as author of this article.

Maksudov is Snyder's second and last citation about the "meat penalty." He does discuss the meat tax, but not on page 188. On page 191 Maksudov writes as follows:

> Among the punishments for those who did not ful-
> fill required grain deliveries was the penalty of hav-
> ing to surrender a fifteen months' supply of meat in
> advance. [12] 1n other words, the state officials knew
> there was no grain to be seized in payment. The
> peasants, of course, considered their livestock as
> insurance against a famine, either slaughtering the
> animals for food or selling them in order to buy
> grain. State confiscation of this livestock was a par-
> ticularly malicious act. If a peasant sold his live-
> stock on the open market, he could easily have paid
> his tax, but the authorities did not want it, prefer-
> ring instead to take the livestock on a low fixed
> price as a form of punishment for the peasant's
> non-payment of taxes. Such penalties in meat did
> not exempt the peasant from fulfilling his original
> grain procurement quota, which remained in effect.

Maksudov's conclusion in the second sentence does not follow from the first. It is likely — neither Snyder nor Maksudov gives sufficient context — that the "meat penalty" was intended to force peasants to give up grain that they claimed they did not have but in fact had hidden. Also, Maksudov says nothing about the meat tax causing starvation.

The question naturally arises: Why don't Snyder or any of his foot-noted sources actually identify and quote the relevant passages from this meat penalty decree? As previously noted Shapoval quotes from it but does not give a reference to the original text. The document is called a "decree of the Council of People's Commissars of the Ukrainian SSR" but without any indication as to where such documents can be consulted.

As it turns out, this is the same document Maksudov refers to (see note 2, above). It may also be found in the multi-volume collection of documents on collectivization entitled *Tragediia sovetskoi derevni.* The relevant part of the lengthy decree of the Bolshevik Central Committee, dated November 18, 1932, reads as follows:

> 5. В колхозах, допустивших разворовывание колхозного хлеба и злостно срывающих хлебозаготовки, применять натуральные штрафы в виде установления дополнительного задания по мясозаготовкам в размере 15-месячной нормы сдачи для данного колхоза мяса, как по обобществленному, так и индивидуальному скоту колхозника.
>
> Применение этого штрафа проводится райисполкомом с предварительного разрешения в каждом отдельном случае облисполкома. Причем райисполкомы устанавливают сроки взыскания и размеры штрафа для каждого колхоза (в пределах 15-месячной нормы мясосдачи) применительно к состоянию отдельных колхозов.
>
> Наложение штрафа не освобождает колхоз от полного выполнения установленного плана хлебозаготовок. В случае, если колхоз принял действительные меры к полному выполнению плана хлебозаготовок в установленный срок, штраф может быть отменен с предварительного разрешения облисполкома.[5]

Translated:

> 5. In collective farms that have permitted the theft of kolkhoz grain and are willfully frustrating grain procurement, to apply penalties in kind in the form of fixing additional targets for giving in meat procurements on the order of a 15-month delivery of meat for the collective farm in question, for both socialized livestock and that of the individual farmer.

---

[5] *Tragediia sovetskoi derevni. T. 3. Konets 1930 — 1932.* M.: ROSSPEN, 2001, p. 543.

The application of this penalty is to be carried out
by the regional (raion) executive committee with
prior approval in each case of the provincial (oblast') executive committee. Moreover, regional executive committees are to set deadlines for the recovery and the size of the fine for each farm (within
the limits of the 15-month norm of meat delivery)
according to the situation of the individual collective farms.

The imposition of this penalty does not relieve the
collective farm of the requirement of full compli-
ance with the established grain procurement plan.
If the collective farm has made real efforts for the
full implementation of the grain procurement plan
within the prescribed period, the penalty can be
waived with the prior approval of the provincial executive committee.

This Russian text corresponds exactly to the text published in
Ukrainian by Shapoval. But Shapoval gave only the first paragraph.
With the full text in hand, including the part that describes the
"meat penalty" it is clear that Shapoval and Snyder have withheld a
few important details from their readers:

* The local officials — those most closely in touch
with each farm — were to impose this meat fine.

* They had to receive prior permission from the
provincial government each time before imposing
this fine.

* The 15-month meat delivery was the limit of the
fine, its maximum size. A lesser fine could be levied
"according to the situation of the individual kolkhoz."

* The third paragraph makes it clear that the purpose is to push recalcitrant kolkhozes to make "real
efforts" to fulfill its grain collection plan. If they did
so the fine could be cancelled even if already levied.

This means the purpose was to get each kolkhoz to make "real efforts" rather than to withhold — hide — grain and then claim that they had none. Clearly, the government felt that it had to have some way of forcing recalcitrant peasants and collective farms to cough up hidden stores of grain. If they did not, what was to prevent every kolkhoz and peasant from claiming that they had no more grain while hiding whatever amount they could? The result would be starvation in those areas that genuinely had no grain, including the cities and towns.

Conclusion on Snyder's Point Two: If Snyder did find and read this text, he falsified its contents to his readers. But most likely Snyder never troubled himself to find this text. Yet it constitutes the evidence for his fact-claims in his "Point Two." It is his responsibility to verify that the fact-claims he makes are backed up by evidence.

Point Three (p. 43): Did the "Black List" Cause "Zones of Death"?

Snyder claims that the "black list," introduced in late November, 1932, required kolkhozes (= collective farms) that had not met their grain collection targets to give up fifteen times a one-month's tax in grain. As a result, says Snyder, such kolkhozes "became zones of death." His evidence (n. 59 p. 466):

> Shapoval, "Proloh trahedii holodu," 162;
>
> Maksudov, "Victory,"188;
>
> Marochko, *Holodomor*, 172;
>
> Werth, *Terreur*, 123.

None of these sources even mentions Snyder's central accusation here: the supposed "requirement to immediately surrender fifteen times the amount of grain."

Here, once again, is what **Shapoval** states:

> 6 грудня ухвалено постанову ЦК КП(б)У і
> Раднаркому УСРР «Про занесення на "чорну
> дошку" сіл, які злісно саботують хлібозаготівлі."
> Це рішення спричинило збільшення жертв
> голодомору. (162)

Translated:

> On December 6 was approved the decree of the
> Central Committee of the Ukrainian CP and of the
> People's Commissars of Ukrainian SSR "On entering
> on the 'black board' [= a "blacklist"] villages that
> willfully sabotage grain procurements." This deci-
> sion resulted in an increase in the number of vic-
> tims of the Holodomor.

Shapoval cites no evidence that anyone died as a result of the
"blacklisting" of some villages.

Maksudov has nothing like this on page 188 or on any page of
"Victory." He merely refers to the "meat procurement" of 15
months in advance (see discussion above). Marochko, *Holodomor*
does not refer to such a policy on page 172 or on any page of this
book, which in any case is merely a brief chronology of events. November 28, 1932 is dealt with on page 162; no such "black list"
document is mentioned here. The December 6 1932 document,
identified above, is mentioned on page 166. It says nothing about
any fine of "fifteen times the amount of grain."

It is not clear that this "new regulation" was introduced on November 28, 1932. The collection by Georgii Papakin "Archival documents on the 'blacklist' as a weapon of Soviet genocide in the
Ukraine in 1932-1933" mentions many documents, but none of
them fit this description.[6]

Perhaps the following resolution mentioned by Shapoval and dated December 6, 1932, is the one meant (the complete text of this
document may be found in the Appendix at the end of this chapter):

> № 219
>
> Постановление СНК УССР и ЦК КП(б)У «О
> занесении на черную доску сел, злостно
> саботирующих хлебозаготовки»1*

---

[6] Georgiy Papakin. "Arkhivni dokumenty pro 'chorni doshky' jak znariaddia radians'kogo
genotsidu v Ukraini v 1932-1933 rokakh." In *Golodomor 1932-1933 rokiv — Genotsid
ukrains'kogo narodu.* (2008), 14-28.

...

СНК и ЦК постановляют:

За явный срыв плана хлебозаготовок и злостный саботаж, организованный кулацкими и контрреволюционными элементами, занести на черную доску следующие села:

1. с. Вербка Павлоградского района Днепропетровской обл.

2. с. Гавриловка Межевского района Днепропетровской обл.

3. с. Лютеньки Гадячского района Харьковской обл.

4. с. Каменные Потоки Кременчугского района Харьковской обл.

5. с. Святотроицкое Троицкого района Одесской обл.

6. с. Пески Баштанского района Одесской обл.

В отношении этих сел провести следующие мероприятия:...[7]

Translated:

No. 219

Decree of the SNK of the Ukrainian SSR and CC of the CPU(b) "On inscribing on the black board of villages that maliciously sabotage grain collection."

...

The SNK and CC decree:

For flagrant disruption of the grain collections plan and malicious sabotage organized by kulak and counterrevolutionary elements, the following villages are inscribed on the black board:

1. v[illage]. Verbka, Pavlogradsk raion, Dnepropetrovsk obl[ast'].

---

[7] ТСД Т. 3, cc. 562-3. The same decree in Ukrainian is widely available on the Internet.

2. v. Gavrilovka, Mezhevsk raion, Dnepropetrovsk obl.

3. v. Liuten'ki, Gadiachsk raion, Khar'kov obl.

4. v. Kamennye Potoki, Kremenchug raion, Khar'kov obl.

5. v. Sviatotroitskoe, Troitsk raion, Odessa obl.

6. v. Peski, Bashtansk raion, Odessa obl.

In relation to these villages the following measures to be carried out...

This decree is restricted to *six villages*. No evidence is given about any "zones of death," much less as a result of this regulation.

The "black board"— "chorna doshka" (Ukrainian) or "chiornaia doska" (Russian) had been used in the Russian empire since the 1840s and in the USSR since the 1920s.[8]

Werth, *Terreur*, 123 and surrounding pages consist mainly of quotations from Kaganovich's letters to Stalin and a mention of the "black list." There is no mention of anything concerning "fifteen times the amount of grain..." Werth, by the way, asserts that collectivization caused the famine — a claim that Tauger and Davies-Wheatcroft both disprove.

But Werth strongly rejects the notion that the famine was deliberate:

> On a beaucoup de documents durs et forts sur les terribles famines qui se sont abattues à la suite de la collectivisation forcée, **qu'il serait absurde de qualifier de famines organisées**, mais qui sont des conséquences directes de cet énorme chaos, de cette désorganisation de tout le système de production traditionnel, au moment de la collectivisation forcée,...[9]

Translated:

---

[8] For example see http://uk.wikipedia.org/wiki/Чорні_дошки / http://ru.wikipedia.org/wiki/Чёрные_доски

[9] Nicolas Werth, "Staline et le stalinisme dans l'histoire." April 12, 2012. At http://lafauteadiderot.net/Staline-et-le-stalinisme-dans-l,854

> ... the terrible famines that took place following
> forced collectivization, **which it would be absurd
> to call organized famines**... (Emphasis added, GF)

Conclusion on Point Three: None of Snyder's sources show any
knowledge of the text of the resolution to which he refers — one
"requiring" the "immediate" "surrender of fifteen times the
amount of grain that was normally due in a whole month" (43).
Snyder certainly never saw it himself.

Point Four (pp. 43-44): Did Vsevolod Balitskii Terrorize Ukrainian Party Officials?

According to Snyder, Vsevolod Balitskii, NKVD chief of the Ukrainian SSR[10] "handpicked" by Stalin, "terrorized" Ukrainian party officials by treating anyone who "failed to do [their] part" in the grain
collection as a "traitor to the state."

His sole source (n. 60, p. 466) is "Shapoval, "Holodomor" (no page
number). This article has been "forthcoming" for several years
now in the journal *Harvard Ukrainian Studies*.[11] Evidently it was
delivered at a conference at the Harvard Ukrainian Institute on
November 17-18, 2008.[12] It has finally been published (2013) in
English translation in a collection devoted to this 2008 conference.[13] There is nothing in this article about "terrorizing" the
Ukrainian Party officials or treating anyone as a "traitor to the

---

[10] This was Balitskii's office from July 15, 1934 to May 11, 1937, according to Petrov and
Skorkin, *Kto rukovodil NKVD 1934-1941. Spravochnik.* (Moscow, 1999). At
http://www.memo.ru/history/NKVD/kto/biogr/gb31.htm

[11] This journal is subsidized by Ukrainian nationalists. As of December, 2012 the last issue
of this journal published is that of 2007. Snyder's book was published in 2010 and, presumably, written a year or more before that time. Shapoval's article has now been "forthcoming"
for six years. The article is probably the same one that has now been published in a 2013
collection; see below.

[12] Cf. *Свобода*, № 46 п'ятниця, 14 листопада 2008 року, с. 14: «Конференція про
Голодомор.»

[13] Yuri Shapoval, "The Holodomor. A Prolog to Repressions and Terror in the Soviet
Ukraine." In *After the Holodomor. The Enduring Impact of the Great Famine in Ukraine*. Ed.
Andrea Graziosi et al. (Cambridge, MA: Ukrainian Research Institute, 2013) 99-122.

state", as Snyder claims. As will be shown later in the present chapter, Shapoval has a history of making false claims.

According to Snyder Balitskii claimed he had uncovered a Ukrainian Military Organization and underground Polish groups:

> He would report, in January 1933, the discovery of more than a thousand illegal organizations and, in February, the plans of Polish and Ukrainian nationalists to overthrow Soviet rule in Ukraine.[61] (44)

Snyder's sources: (n. 61 p. 466) are Davies, *Years* 190; Marochko, *Holodomor*, 171.

Davies, *Years* 190 simply quotes a part of a Politburo resolution of December 14, 1932, stating in part:

> [C]ounter-revolutionary elements — kulaks, former officers, Petlyurians, supporters of the Kuban' Rada and others — were able to penetrate into the kolkhozes [and the village soviets, land agencies and cooperatives]. They attempt to direct the work of these organizations against the interests of the proletarian state and the policy of the party; they try to organize a counter-revolutionary movement, the sabotage of the grain collections, and the sabotage of the village.

Marochko, *Holodomor* 171 does mention Balitskii's report of December 20, 1932 on Polish and Ukrainian nationalists as follows:

> В. Балицького про арешт 27 тис. осіб за хлібозаготівельними справами, про засудження до розстрілу 108, про виявлення 7 тис. ям та «чорних комор» і вилучення з них 700 тис. пудів хліба, про викриття великих повстанських груп польського походження, організованих урядом УНР.

Translated:

> V. Balitskii [reported] the arrest of 27 thousand persons for grain procurement cases of condemnation to death 108, the discovery of seven thousand holes and "black barns" and removing them from

> 700 thousand poods of grain, the exposure of major
> insurgent groups of Polish descent, organized by
> the leadership of the UNR [Ukrainian National Rada,
> = anticommunist nationalist Ukrainian Party from
> the time of the Civil War].

In other documents Balitskii refers to the arrests of 38,000 village residents on various charges, and the fight against Ukrainian Nationalist rebels. But Snyder does not refer to these documents at all.[14]

Conclusion to Snyder's Point Four: There is nothing in the passages cited by Snyder about January or February 1933 reports by Balitskii. Snyder gives no reference to such reports, so he has not seen them himself.

There is no documentation of Snyder's claim that "anyone who failed to do his part in requisitions was a traitor to the state." Snyder claims that it is documented in Shapoval's article but, as we have seen, nothing like it is there. But even if Balitskii did say this, that is not evidence of 'deliberate starvation" — only of the efforts of the State to obtain and share the little existing grain among as many people as possible.

Point Five (pp. 44-45): Did Kaganovich Condemn Millions To Die of Starvation?

In his fifth point Snyder makes the following claims:

> * On December 21, 1932 Stalin and Kaganovich confirmed the grain collection quota for the Ukrainian SSR;

> * Kaganovich arrived on December 20 and forced the Ukrainian Politburo to meet and reaffirm the quota.

> * This was "a death sentence for about three million people."

Snyder concludes:

> A simple respite from requisitions for three months
> would not have / harmed the Soviet economy, and
> would have saved most of those three million lives.

---

[14] Pyrig, R. ed., *Holodomor 1932-1933 rokiv v Ukraini: dokumenty i materialy* (Kyiv, 2007), No. 458, pp. 631-634; № 476, cc. 672-3.

Yet Stalin and Kaganovich insisted on exactly the contrary. The state would fight "ferociously," as Kaganovich put it, to fulfill the plan.[63]

Snyder's sources for this paragraph (n. 63 p. 466) are:

* Quotation: Davies, *Years*, 187.

* For the December 20 meeting, Vasiliev, "Tsina," 55;

* Graziosi, "New Interpretation," 9;

* Kuśnierz, *Ukraina*, 135.

None of the statements in this paragraph of Snyder's are supported by the sources in Snyder's footnote 63 to this passage.

* **Davies**, Years, 187: The only "quotation" in this paragraph is the single word "ferociously." Davies, 187, does not mention Kaganovich and does not contain the word "ferociously."

* **Vasiliev**, "Tsina," 55 — the December 20th meeting is actually discussed on page 54. Vasil'ev is honest enough to note that:

> Виступаючі були переконані в тому, що збіжжя сховано селянами в «чорних» коморах або закопано в ямах.

Translated:

> The speakers were convinced that grain was hidden by peasants in "black" closets or buried in pits.

As we show below, there is clear evidence that peasants did indeed hide grain in pits and other places.

Graziosi, "New Interpretation," has no page 9. Snyder may have in mind this passage on the ninth page of the article, page 105:

> On the night of 20 December, at the urging of Kaganovich, the Ukrainian Politburo committed itself to new targets for grain requisitions. Nine days later it declared that the precondition to fulfilling the plan was the seizure of seed stock reserves. [28]

Note 28 on p. 114 of Graziosi reads:

> "28. Danilov, Manning, and Viola. *Tragediia so-*
> *vetskoi derevni*, 3: 603, 611"

Now to check Graziosi's sources:

> * Vol. 3 p. 603 is Kaganovich's letter to Stalin of December 22,
> 1932, concerning the meeting of the Politburo of the Ukraini-
> an CP on measures for strengthening the collection of grain.[15]

> * Vol. 3 p. 611 is the same document briefly considered above
> from the volume *Golod 1932-1933 rokiv na Ukraini*. There it is
> document number 129.[16] The text is as follows:

> До сих пор еще районные работники не
> поняли, что первоочередность
> хлебозаготовок в колхозах, не
> выполняющих своих обязательств перед
> государством, означает, что все имеющееся
> наличное зерно в этих колхозах, в том числе
> и так называемые семенные фонды, должно
> быть в первую очередь сдано в план
> хлебозаготовок.

> Именно поэтому ЦК ВКП(б) отменил
> решение ЦК КП(б)У от 18 ноября о невывозе
> семенных фондов как решение,
> ослабляющее наши позиции в борьбе за
> хлеб.

> ЦК КП(б)У предлагает в отношении
> колхозов, не выполнивших план
> хлебозаготовок, немедленно, на протяжении
> 5-6 дней, вывезти все наличные фонды, в
> том числе так называемые семенные, на
> выполнение плана хлебозаготовок.

> ЦК обязывает немедленно мобилизовать
> для этого все перевозочные средства, живую
> тягловую силу, автотранспорт и трактора. В

---

[15] See http://tragedia-sovetskoy-derevni-3.blogspot.com/2008/09/17-3.html № 236; also
http://archive.is/cFaS № 236.

[16] At http://www.archives.gov.ua/Sections/Famine/Publicat/Fam-Pyrig-1932.php#nom-
129

однодневный срок дать твердый
ежедневный наряд на поставку
необходимого количества лошадей, в том
числе и единоличниками.

Всякую задержку в вывозе этих фондов ЦК
будет рассматривать как саботаж
хлебозаготовок со стороны районного
руководства и примет соответствующие
меры.

Translated:

Even at this point the regional (*raionnye*) workers have not understood that the priority of
grain collections **in those collective farms that
have not fulfilled their obligations** to the
state means that all the grain on hand in these
collective farms, including the so-called seed reserves, must be included as a priority in the
plan of grain collection.

That is the reason that the CC of the VKP(b) set
aside the decision of the CC of the CP(b)U of
November 18 on not exporting the seed re-
searves as a decision that weakens out position
in the struggle for grain.

The CC of the CP(b)U proposes **in relation to
those collective farms that have not fulfilled
the plan for grain collection** to immediately,
within the next 5-6 days, bring forth all the reserves they have, including the so-called seed
reserves, for the fulfillment of the grain collection plan.

The CC demands immediate mobilization for
this purposes of all means of transportation,
live animal power, automobile and tractor
transportation. Within one day give a firm daily
accounting to supply the required number of
horses, including by individual farmers.

> The CC will regard any and all delay in the transportation of these reserves as sabotage of the grain collections on the part of the regional (*raion*) leadership and will take appropriate measures.

Here it is Graziosi who has falsified the meaning of the document. Recall that Graziosi wrote:

> Nine days later it declared that the precondition to fulfilling the plan was the seizure of seed stock reserves.

But the document says nothing about any "precondition" and strictly limits seed stock seizures, as the bold-faced passages above indicate.

The issue seems to be as follows. Some kolkhozes had stated that they had no more grain except for seed grain. The Party did not believe them. If the Party accepted the statement of every such kolkhoz, then more kolkhozes would make the same claim, in order to avoid grain collections, and the grain collection would fail. That would mean starvation in the cities and towns, where the residents could not grow their own grain. Therefore, the excuse that "we only have our seed grain left" was not to be accepted.

Note that Graziosi lied when he stated that all seed grain had to be given in. The document Graziosi himself identifies as his source clearly states that seed grain was to be collected only from those kolkhozes that had failed to fulfill their quota in the grain collections.

Kuśnierz, *Ukraina* 135 simply outlines a few of the events and decisions of late November to late December 1934.

Snyder (45) stays that Kaganovich toured the Ukrainian SSR, demanding "100% fulfillment" of the grain collection quota while "sentencing local officials and ordering deportation of families as he went." Moreover, Snyder claims, on December 29, 1932 Kaganovich told Ukrainian party leaders that they also had to collect the seed grain. His evidence (n. 64 p. 466): "Davies, Years, 190-192."

Davies does discuss Kaganovich's trip, though only on page 192. But Davies' outline of what Kaganovich's message was is quite different from Snyder's characterization of it.

> When the Plenipotentiary of the USSR party central committee in Chernigov declared that the region would complete 85 per cent of its plan by January 1, Kaganovich interrupted: "For us the figure 85% does not exist. We need 100%. Workers are fed on grain and not on percentages."

> He addressed a conference of district secretaries in Odessa region in even more uncompromising terms:

>> There is no need to punch people in the jaw. But carefully organized searches of collective farmers, communists and workers as well as individual peasants are not going too far. The village must be given a shove, so that the peasants themselves reveal the grain pits... When our spirit is not as hard as metal the grain collections don't succeed.

According to Davies Kaganovich specifically opposed the demand that collective farmers return the grain they had been issued as advance payment for their labor days.

> ...the compulsory return of part of their grain advances by collective farmers risked 'creating a united front against us, insulting the shock worker, and undermining the basis of the labor days.' Instead he [Kaganovich] advocated an intensive search for stolen grain... (194).

As for the seed grain,

> Kaganovich defended the seizure of seed on the grounds that it could be assembled again after the grain collection was complete. (194)

In other words *Kaganovich never planned to keep the seed grain* but, evidently, to hold it hostage to guarantee grain deliveries and then to return it. Davies concludes:

> The decision was perverse, and was ultimately inef-
> fective. Its consequence was that the central au-
> thorities had to issue substantial seed loans to
> Ukraine during the spring sowing. (195, emphasis
> added)

So some seed grain was to be collected from recalcitrant peasants but it was returned for sowing in the spring.

Conclusion to Snyder's Point Five: There is no evidence for Snyder's claim that the demand that "requisition targets were to be met" meant "a death sentence for about three million people." Nor does Snyder cite any evidence at all for his claim that "A simple respite from requisitions for three months would not have harmed the Soviet economy, and would have saved most of those three million lives." These are pure assertions by Snyder. They are good examples of the logical fallacy of "begging the question" — of "asserting that which should be proven."

According to Davies and Wheatcroft, where seed grain was collected it was returned for spring sowing. Since seed was not intended to be eaten in the first place, no one starved as a result of all the confiscating and returning.

Point Six (p. 45): Did Stalin Doom Peasants to Starve by Forbidding Train Travel?

That the borders of the Ukrainian SSR and certain other areas were sealed is not disputed. But did this cause starvation? Snyder claims it did, concluding (45-6):

> By the end of February 1933 some 190,000 peas-
> ants had been caught and sent back to their home
> villages to starve.

His evidence (n.65 p. 466):

> * "On the interpretation of starving people as spies, see Shapoval, "Holodomor.""

> * "On the 190,000 peasants caught and sent back, see Graziosi, "New Interpretation," 7.

> * "On the events of 22 January, see Marochko, *Holodomor*, 189; and Graziosi, "New Interpretation," 9.""

As noted above **Shapoval**'s Ukrainian language article "Holodo-mor" has not appeared but the English version has been published (2013). There is nothing about "interpreting starving people as spies" in it. Moreover, it is hard to believe that primary documents with contents as dramatic as Stalin describing starving people as "spies" have not been published somewhere else. But Shapoval may simply mean the document reproduced below.

Graziosi, "New Interpretation," p. 105 (not, as Snyder has it, page 7 or page 9) refers (note 29, p. 114) to the well-known order of January 22, 1933, to stop peasants generally, not just Ukrainian peasants, from moving to other areas. Here is the text:[17]

> 22 января 1933 г.
>
> Ростов-Дон, Харьков, Воронеж, Смоленск,
>
> Минск, Сталинград, Самара
>
> N. 65/ш
>
> До ЦКВКП(б) и СНК дошли сведения, что на Кубани и Украине начался массовый выезд крестьян «за хлебом» в ЦЧО, на Волгу, Московскую обл., Западную обл., Белоруссию. ЦК ВКП и Совнарком СССР не сомневаются, что этот выезд крестьян, как и выезд из Украины в прошлом году, организован врагами Советской власти, эсерами и агентами Польши с целью агитации «через крестьян» в северных районах СССР против колхозов и вообще против Советской власти. В прошлом году партийные, советские и чекистские органы Украины прозевали эту контрреволюционную затею врагов Советской власти. В этом году не может быть допущено повторение прошлогодней ошибки.
>
> Первое. ЦК ВКП и Совнарком СССР предписывают крайкому, крайисполкому и ПП

---

[17] *Tragediia sovetskoi derevni t.3*, 634-5; Document No. 258. Also at http://ru.wikisource.org/wiki/Директива_ЦК_ВКП(б)_и_СНК_СССР_от_22.01.1933_№_65 /ш

ОГПУ Северного Кавказа не допускать массовый выезд крестьян из Северного Кавказа в другие края и въезд в пределы края из Украины.

Второе. ЦК ВКП и Совнарком предписывают ЦК КП(б)У, Балицкому и Редену не допускать массовый выезд крестьян из Украины в другие края и въезд на Украину из Северного Кавказа.

Третье. ЦК ВКП и Совнарком предписывают ПП ОГПУ Московской обл., ЦЧО, Западной обл., Белоруссии, Нижней Волги и Средней Волги арестовывать пробравшихся на север «крестьян» Украины и Северного Кавказа и после того, как будут отобраны контрреволюционные элементы, водворять остальных в места их жительства.

Четвертое. ЦК ВКП и Совнарком предписывают ТО ГПУ Прохорову дать соответствующее распоряжение по системе ТО ГПУ.

Предсовнарком СССР

В. М. Молотов

Секретарь ЦК ВКП(б)

И. Сталин

(РГАСПИ. Ф. 558.Оп. 11. Д. 45. Л. 109-109об.)

Translated:

It has come to the attention of the CC of the VCP(b) and the SNK that there has begun a massive exodus of peasants "in search of bread" into the Central Black Earth District, the Volga, Moscow oblast', the Western oblast', and Belorussia. The CC VCP(b) has no doubt that this exodus of peasants, like the exodus from the Ukraine last year, is being organized by enemies of the Soviet Government, Socialist Revolutionaries, and agents of Poland with the goal of agitating, "through the peasants," in the northern regions of the USSR against the collective farms and against Soviet power in general. Last year party, Soviet and Chekist organs of the Ukraine neglected this counterrevolutionary plot by enemies of Soviet power. This year a repetition of last year's mistake cannot be permitted.

First. The CC VCP(b) and the Council of People's Commissars [in Russian, "Sovnarkom," abbreviated SNK] of the USSR instructs the area committees, the area executive committee, and the PP [plenipotentiary representatives] of the OGPU of the Northern Caucasus not to permit a massive exodus of peasants from the Northern Caucasus into other areas or entry into the regions of the area from the Ukraine.

Second: the CC of the VCP(b) and the Sovnarkom instructs the CC of the CP(b)U, Balitskii, and Redens, not to permit any massive exodus of peasants from the Ukraine into other regions or entry into the Ukraine from the Northern Caucasus.

Third: the CC VCP and the Sovnarkom require the PP of the OGPU of the Moscow oblast', Central Black Earth District, Western oblast', Belorussia, the Lower Volga, and the Middle Volga to arrest "peasants" making their way north from the Ukraine and Central Caucasus and, after detaining counterrevolutionary elements, to return the rest to their places of residence.

Fourth. The CC of the VCP and the Snovarkom require the director of the GPU service division Prokhorov to give appropriate directives throughout the system of the service division of the GPU.

Representative of the Sovnarkom V.M. Molotov

Secretary of the CC of the VCP(b) J. Stalin

(RGASPI f. 558. Op. 11. D. 45. L. 109-109ob.)

Graziosi continues:

> In the following month, the decree led to the arrest
> of 220,000 people, predominantly hungry peasants
> in search of food; 190,000 of them were sent back
> to their villages to starve. (105)

This conclusion and these figures, which Snyder simply repeats verbatim, are not supported by any primary sources Graziosi cites.

Graziosi has no way of knowing how many of the persons stopped were "hungry peasants." In reality, very few of them, if any, could have been. Starving people do not travel long distances by train to seek food — they do not have the energy for long trips, much of which would have to be on foot. Nor do starving people spend their money on train tickets. They would remain at home and use their money to buy food.

As in previous famines, most of these travelers would have been speculators trying to purchase grain and foodstuffs in areas not as hard-hit by the famine in order to return to famine areas to resell them at a high profit. This "market" process benefitted the well-to-do and guaranteed that only the poor would starve. In fact, poor peasants starved even when harvests were good, since speculators could drive up the price by buying it for resale elsewhere.

Note too that the document in question makes it clear that peasants were moving from the North Caucasus and Kuban *into* the Ukraine as well as the other way around. This is consistent with the movements of people buying and selling grain, but not of people who were starving.

Why would Snyder mention only the Ukraine? Probably to please Ukrainian nationalists, who have indeed celebrated Snyder's book, invited him to give talks in Ukraine, and published a Ukrainian translation of *Bloodlands*.

Marochko, 188-189, summarizes Stalin's and Balitskii's outline of peasant movements in and out of the Ukraine and why they should not be permitted. Graziosi, "New Interpretation," 9 (really, p. 105, as already noted) briefly summarizes the document of January 22, 1933, reproduced in full above.

Conclusion to Snyder's Point Six: Snyder's claims are not supported by his documentation. There is no evidence that those who were travelling by train were "begging" or "starving," and of course few if any of them could have been.

Point Seven (pp. 45-6): Did Stalin Seize the Seed Grain in December 1932?

As his seventh point Snyder claims that in December 1932 Stalin decided that seed grain should be seized to meet the grain collection quota, while the USSR still had a reserve of three million tons of grain and continued to export grain. He further claims that "many" of the the 37,392 people recorded as having been arrested that month were "presumably trying to save their families from starvation." His evidence (n. 66, page 466):

> * "On the 37,392 people arrested, see Marochko, *Holodomor*, 192."

> * Davies, *Years*, 161-163.

Marochko, *Holodomor*, 192, gives the number of 37,797, not 37,392.

> Протягом січня скоєно 150 «терористичних актів», з них «фізичний терор» становив 80,9 % випадків, а в селах арештовано 37 797 осіб. Серед арештованих із «політминулим» —8145 осіб, 1471 голова колгоспу, 388 голів сільських рад, 1335 голів правлінь колгоспів, 1820 завгоспів та комірників,7906 колгоспників. Розглянуто 12 076 справ звинувачених, із них до розстрілу засуджено 719, до концтаборів — 8003, до виселення — 2533, до примусових робіт — 281 / *Holodomor 1932—1933 років в Україні: Документи і матеріали.* — К.,2007. — С. 633—634.

Translated:

> During January, 150 "terrorist acts" were committed, of which "physical terror" amounted to 80.9% of the cases, and in villages 37,797 persons were arrested. Among those arrested were "fugitives" - 8145 people, 1,471 heads of kolkhozes, 388 heads

of village councils, 1335 chairmen of boards of collective farms, 1820 steward and storekeepers, 7,906 kolkhozniks. 12,076 cases of those indicted were reviewed, including 719 sentenced to death, to labor camps - 8003, to exile - 2533, to forced labor - 281 /

This is a simple list of arrests and dispositions of cases during January, 1933. There is no indication whatsoever that even a single one of these cases have to do with "trying to save their families from starvation," as Snyder claims. Even Snyder has to add the word "presumably" — an admission that he has invented the business about "saving their families from starvation."

Davies, *Years,* 161-163, is entirely concerned with the illegal trade in grain and Soviet attempts to suppress it — with good, though far from complete, success.

The grain trade harmed everything the Soviets were trying to do: collect grain as tax from the collective farms to feed workers in the cities; ration grain so as to spread out what was available as equitably as possible given the crop failures and famine. Collective farmers who sold grain sometimes stole it from the kolkhoz, which meant it was not available either for grain collection by the State or for the use of the other kolkhozniks. Only those with money — that is, not the village poor — could buy grain, so the grain trade threatened to destroy any attempt to ration grain in the famine conditions. That would mean that, as in all previous famines, those better off would eat while the poor would starve.

One last point here: Snyder claims that the Soviet Union had three million tons [of grain] in reserve. Davies and Wheatcroft do not directly state how much "reserve" (they use the term "stocks") were on hand in December 1932, but they say "the June [1933] plan" was for 3.608 million tons, and conclude:

> This hopeful estimate must have been regarded with great skepticism by the few officials who knew the fate of previous attempts to stockpile grain. (186-7)

Later they state that in fact "on July 1, 1933 total stocks amounted to 1.392 million tons," some of which was seed grain. (229) Snyder does not tell us where has found the figure of 3 million tons of re-serves in December 1932.

Conclusion to Snyder's Point Seven: All of the significant claims in Snyder's paragraph are entirely undocumented by either of the sources he cites.

The following statement of Snyder's reveals his dishonesty with special clarity:

> At the end of December 1932, Stalin had approved
> Kaganovich's proposal that the seed grain for the
> spring be seized to make the annual target. This left
> the collective farms with nothing to plant for the
> coming fall. (46)

Of course nothing of the kind happened. Stalin and Kaganovich would have indeed been stupid to take away seed grain and leave nothing to sow. This is probably a reference to the Politburo directive of December 29, 1932, and the other decisions discussed above under Snyder's point 5.

The government refused to accept less than the grain delivery quota, assuming that kolkhozes and individual peasants who did not fulfill their grain collection quota were hiding grain. Why hide grain? To eat, of course — but also, to sell. Large profits could be made by selling grain illegally, on the black market, during a famine, when its price would be much higher than normal.

The Fraud of Snyder"s "Seven Points"

Snyder requires the "deliberate starvation" thesis in order to compare the Soviets with the Nazis, Stalin with Hitler, in respect to "mass murder." The "seven points" are supposed to represent Snyder's evidence that the Soviet leadership was deliberately starving the Ukraine. Readers should satisfy themselves that every reference Snyder cites to document his claims in the "seven points" has been carefully checked. Not a single one of them provides any evidence for Snyder's claim of deliberate starvation.

Types of Dishonest Citations

Snyder employs several kinds of phony citations. In one type, the citation Snyder gives simply does not contain evidence to support Snyder's statement. Such citations are "bluffs." The reader is evidently supposed to assume that a full professor of history at Yale University, as Snyder is, would cite his sources honestly, and therefore assume that Snyder does in fact have evidence to support the claims he makes in his text.

Phony citations of a second type do contain statements like those in Snyder's own text. But these citations either have no evidence to support these claims or they give further citations to yet other works — which do not support their statements either. An example of this type is Kuśnierz's book, which is Snyder's single most frequent secondary source on the famine. It is mainly a summary of Ukrainian nationalist studies rather than a work of independent scholarship. Moreover, Kuśnierz falsifies his summary of the scholarship on the famine. For example, Kuśnierz says the following:

> Istnieją także inne, nie poparte w zasadzie żadnymi poważnymi dowodami, poglądy nt. powodów pojawienia się głodu na Ukrainie. Np. według Amerykanina Marka Taugera głód był rezultatem nieurodzaju, a Stalin musiał podjąć trudną decyzję o ratowaniu ludności miejskiej kosztem wsi. (197)

Translated:

> There are also other views, not supported, in principle, by any serious evidence, about the reasons for the emergence of famine in the Ukraine. For example, according to the American Mark Tauger the famine was the result of crop failures, and Stalin had to make a difficult decision to save the urban population at the expense of the village.

This is a lie. All of Mark Tauger's research on the famine of 1932-33 is heavily documented. But few of Kuśnierz's Polish readers will check Tauger's works and realize that Kuśnierz is lying here.

Kuśnierz is guilty of the same kind of scholarly malpractice as is Snyder: of pretending to do objective research while in reality supporting a preconceived idea. Kuśnierz's book, like that of Snyder, has no evidence at all either that the famine of 1932-33 was "caused by collectivization" or constituted "deliberate starvation" whether of Ukrainians or of anyone else.

A third type of phony citation is a form of "bias by omission." Snyder does not inform his readers about crucial information concerning the works to which he refers. For example, the long and detailed study by Davies and Wheatcroft, one of Snyder's major sources, concludes that the Soviet regime was not guilty of deliberate starvation — but Snyder fails to inform his readers of their conclusion.

None of the many Ukrainian nationalist or anticommunist researchers who proclaim that "Stalin" deliberately starved the Ukraine has ever produced any evidence to support this claim. Of course Snyder, who is not a specialist in this field and who simply relies upon the work of other anticommunists, has not produced any such evidence either.

The anticommunists and Ukrainian nationalists have been searching assiduously for evidence to support their preconceived notion of "deliberate starvation" since at least the 1980s. The fact that they have never found any such evidence is perhaps the best possible evidence that there was no such deliberate starvation.

In fact there was no "Holodomor" — no deliberate or "man-made" starvation. There was just "holod" — a famine, as there had been every few years for centuries. Thanks to collectivization and mechanization of agriculture, the famine of 1932-33 was to be the last famine in Russian history (except for the post-war famine of 1946-47, which was also not "man-made").[18]

---

[18] This postwar famine is briefly discussed in a later chapter. For the present, see Stephen G. Wheatcroft, "The Soviet Famine of 1946—1947, the Weather and Human Agency in Historical Perspective." *Europe-Asia Studies* 64 no. 6 (2012), 988-1005.

False Statements in Shapoval"s article "Lügen und Schweigen."

Snyder cites Yurii Shapoval's work very frequently. Shapoval is a leading Ukrainian nationalist, and highly anticommunist, scholar. But Shapoval cannot be trusted to quote his sources accurately. Here is one example from the very beginning of the article, "Lügen und Schweigen," that Snyder cites here:

> Čuev hat diese Begegnungen in einem Büchlein aufgearbeitet: "Einhundertvierzig Gespräche mit Vjaceslav Molotov," in dem folgendes zu lesen ist:
>
>> - Unter Schriftstellern wird darüher gesprochen, daß die Hungersnot 1933 ahsichtlich von Stalin und Ihrer gesamten Fuhrung organisiert worden ist.
>>
>> - Das sagen die Feinde des Kommunismus!
>>
>> - Aber es hat den Anschein, daß beinahe 12 Millionen Menchen bei der Hungersnot 1933 zugrunde gegangen sind.
>>
>> Ich halte diese Fakten für nicht bewiesen, behauptete Molotov.
>>
>> - Nicht bewiesen?
>>
>> - Nein, keinesfälls. Ich bin in jenen Jahren bei der Getreidebeschaffung herumgereist. Ich komme an solchen Dingen nicht vorbeigehen. Ich bin damals zweimal in der Ukraine wegen der Getreidebeschaffung gewesen, in Sichevo, im Ural war ich, in Sibirien — have ich etwa nichts gesehen? Das ist ja absurd! Nein, das is völlig absurd!
>
> Das ist tatsächlich absurd, denn auf der Sitzung des Politbüros des ZK der VKP(B) am 3. August 1932 sagte niemand anderes als Molotov: "Wir stehen tatsächlich vor dem Gespenst einer Hungersnot, und zwar in den reichen Getreiderayons."'

Translated:

Felix Chuev wrote an account of this meeting in a little book, *One Hundred Forty Talks with Viacheslav Molotov,"* where we read the following:

> - Some writers have said to one another that the famine of 1933 was organized on purpose by Stalin and your whole leadership.
>
> - The enemies of communism say that.
>
> - But it appears that almost 12 million persons died because of the famine of 1933.
>
> - I consider that these facts are unproven, asserted Molotov.
>
> - Unproven?
>
> - No, not at all. During those years I travelled around to the grain collections. I never encountered such things. At that time I was in the Ukraine twice because of the grain collection, I was in Sichevo, in the Urals, in Siberia — and was there something I did not see? That is absurd. No, that is completely absurd.

That is certainly absurd, because at the session of the CC of the VCP(b) on August 3, 1932 Molotov, and no one else, said: "We are really facing the spector of a famine, and particularly in the rich grain regions."

Here is what the text of this book, *Molotov. Poluderzhavnyi Valstelin* (Moscow, 1999), p. 453, actually says:

> — В писательской среде говорят о том, что голод 1933 года был специально организован Сталиным и всем вашим руководством.
>
> — Это говорят враги коммунизма! Это враги коммунизма. Не вполне сознательные люди. Не вполне сознательные...
>
> Нет, тут уж руки не должны, поджилки не должны дрожать, а у кого задрожат — берегись! Зашибем! Вот дело в чем. Вот в этом дело. А у

вас все — давай готовенькое! Вы как дети. Подавляющее большинство теперешних коммунистов пришли на готовое, и только давай все, чтоб у нас хорошо было все, вот это главное. А это не главное.

Найдутся люди, которые займутся этим. Найдутся такие люди. Борьба с мещанским наследием должна быть беспощадной. Не улучшается жизнь — это не социализм, но даже если жизнь народа улучшается из года в год в течение определенного периода, но не укрепляются основы социализма, неизбежно придем к краху.

— Но ведь чуть ли не 12 миллионов погибло от голода в 1933-м...

— Я считаю, эти факты не доказаны, — утверждает Молотов.

— Не доказаны?..

— Нет, нет, ни в коем случае. Мне приходилось в эти годы ездить на хлебозаготовки. Так что я не мог пройти мимо таких вещей. Не мог. Я тогда побывал на Украине два раза на хлебозаготовках, в Сычево, на Урале был, в Сибири — как же, я ничего не видел, что ли? Абсурд! Нет, это абсурд. На Волге мне не пришлось быть. Там, возможно, было хуже. Конечно, посылали меня туда, где можно хлеб заготовить.

Нет, это преувеличение, но такие факты, конечно, в некоторых местах были. Тяжкий был год.

Translated:

- Some writers have said to one another that the famine of 1933 was organized on purpose by Stalin and your whole leadership.

- The enemies of communism say that. That's the enemies of communism. Not completely conscious persons. Not completely conscious…

No, here our hands, or muscles could not tremble, and beware those whose do tremble — beware! We'll throw them out. And if you have everything — give up what you have prepared! You are like children. The vast majority of present-day communists came when everything had been prepared, and just make it so everything is good for us, that's the main thing. But that is not the point.

There are those who will be engaged in it. There are people. The fight against the bourgeois heritage must be ruthless. If you don't improve life — that is not socialism, but even if the life of the people is improving from year to year for a specified period, but the foundations of socialism are not being strengthened, we will inevitably come to ruin.

- But almost 12 million persons died of hunger in 1933….

- I consider that these facts are unproven, asserted Molotov.

- Unproven?

- No, not at all. During those years I had to travel around to the grain collections. I could not have missed such things. Impossible. At that time I was in the Ukraine twice because of the grain collection, I was in Sichevo, in the Urals, in Siberia — and was there something I did not see? That is absurd. I did not go to the Volga. Perhaps it was worse there. Naturally, they sent me to places where it was possible to get grain.

No, that is an exaggeration, but such things, of course, did exist in some places. It was a very difficult year.

Note that:

* Molotov does not deny that a famine existed. Rather, he denies that "12 million people died of hunger in 1933."

* Shapoval has omitted Molotov's last two sentences: "No, this is an exaggeration, but such things did exist in some places. It was a very difficult year."

Shapoval quotes this passage to "prove" that Molotov was "telling lies and remaining silent" ("Lügen und Schweigen") about the famine. In reality Molotov *did* know and *did* speak about it in 1932. In addition, Molotov did *not* remain silent about the famine. Shapoval simply omitted Molotov's reference to it!

* Molotov did not "lie." What he said was correct: (a) the estimate of 12 million dead of starvation in 1933 was an exaggeration — in fact, a gross, "absurd" exaggeration; and (b) this story was indeed spread by "the enemies of communism" — specifically, the Ukrainian Nationalists who collaborated with the Nazis. They originated the false story about the "Holodomor" after the war.[19]

Shapoval's statement should not be accepted as accurate any more than Snyder's should. Every fact-claim has to be checked. In practice this ruins his usefulness as a historian — as it does Snyder's.

For Snyder's story about "Petro Veldii / Vel'dii" , which occurs at this point in Bloodlands, see the Introduction.

Snyder Falsifies Gareth Jones's Story

Snyder praises Gareth Jones as one of "a very few outsiders" who "were able to record" something of the famine. He states that Jones boarded a train from Moscow to Khar'kiv, "disembarked at random at a small station and tramped through the countryside with a backpack full of food." He found "famine on a colossal scale." Snyder concludes his account of Jones' account as follows:

---

[19] Heorhiy Kar'ianov. *Danse macabre. Holod 1932-1933 rokiv u polititsi, masoviy svidomosti ta istoriiografii (1980-ti — pochatok 2000-kh)*. Kiev, 2000, gives the history of the concept of the "Holodomor."

> Once, after he had shared his food, a little girl ex-
> claimed: "Now that I have eaten such wonderful
> things I can die happy."[70] (47)

Snyder (n. 70 p. 466) gives his source as "New York Evening Post,
30 March 1933." According to the Gareth Jones website the only
article in the *New York Evening Post* by Jones is the one of March
29, 1933. It does not contain this story. However, in an article published in the London (UK) *Daily Express* of April 6, 1933 Jones
wrote:

> When I shared my white bread and butter and
> cheese one of the peasant women said, "Now I have
> eaten such wonderful things I can die happy."[20]

Not "a little girl" but a peasant woman! Perhaps Snyder felt that
putting these words into the mouth of "a little girl" would make
the story more pathetic? Or perhaps Snyder never bothered to
read the article at all? Whatever the case, it is another of Snyder's
false statements.

Raphael Lemkin and the Accusation of "Soviet Genocide"

Snyder says:

> Rafał Lemkin, the international lawyer who later
> invented the term genocide, would call the Ukraini-
> an case "the classic example of Soviet genocide."
> (53)

Lemkin's view was never accepted by the United Nations Genocide
Convention. Lemkin's attempts to redefine the concept of genocide
to cover Soviet actions have been universally rejected.[21] So why
does Snyder mention Lemkin and his long-discredited attempt to
redefine genocide so as to cover the USSR? According to Anton

---

[20] At
http://www.garethjones.org/soviet_articles/daily%20express%20archives/DExp_1933_04
_06_011.pdf The quotation is in the third column of the story.

[21] See Anton Weiss-Wendt, "Hostage of Politics: Raphael Lemkin on "Soviet Genocide." *Journal of Genocide Research* 7 (4) 2005, 551-559.

Weiss-Wendt Lemkin's efforts received support in one corner only — that of right-wing Eastern European émigrés:

> At the time when Lemkin and his ideas found little support in government offices, East European ethnic communities became Lemkin's most trusted allies. (Weiss-Wendt 555)

Lemkin became closely involved with these right-wing anticommunist groups.

> Lemkin was actively involved with émigré organizations: he attended their meetings, participated in their lobbying campaigns, and even edited their public appeals. For example, on December 20, 1954, the Assembly of Captive European Nations adopted a resolution which had the following line: "Communist puppet governments have suppressed all freedoms and all human rights." Lemkin augmented that sentence by adding: "By resorting to genocide they are threatening our civilization and weaken the forces of the free world." For his planned three-volume History of Genocide Lemkin intended to write a chapter on Soviet repression in Hungary. The chapter was to be drawn from the "UN report" on the Soviet invasion of the country. (Weiss-Wendt 556).

Weiss-Wendt concludes that the term "genocide" became just another expression of Lemkin's strong anticommunism — in short, an insult:

> Lemkin explicitly stated that for him "Soviet genocide" was just an expedient: "genocide is a concept that carries the highest moral condemnation in our cold war against the Soviet Union."

Snyder has to be aware of this well-known critique of Lemkin but withholds it from his readers.

Snyder: "Almost No One Claimed that Stalin Meant To Starve Ukrainians To Death…"

Snyder laments that the famine "never took on the clarity of an undisputed event. Almost no one claimed that Stalin meant to starve Ukrainians to death …" (56) Indeed, "deliberate famine" was not reported at the time — but that was because the myth of the "deliberate famine" had not yet been invented! The notion of a "deliberate famine" or "Holodomor"[22] was invented by pro-Nazi, anti-communist Ukrainian nationalists after World War II. One of the earliest statements of it, if not the earliest, is in Volume 2 of *The Black Deeds of the Kremlin* published in Toronto in 1953. Some of the coauthors of this book were complicit in the mass murder of Ukrainian Jews during the Nazi occupation and had written hair-raising anti-Semitic propaganda linking Jews with communism.[23] The same book also claims that there was no starvation outside the Ukraine — completely false, of course.

Snyder"s Dishonest Attack on Walter Duranty

Snyder claims that New York Times Moscow correspondent Walter Duranty "did his best to undermine Jones's accurate reporting."

> Duranty, who won a Pulitzer Prize in 1932, called Jones's account of the famine a "big scare story." Duranty's claim that there was "no actual starvation" but only "widespread mortality from diseases due to malnutrition" echoed Soviet usages and pushed euphemism into mendacity. … Duranty knew that millions of people had starved to death. Yet he maintained in his journalism that the hunger served a higher purpose. Duranty thought that "you

---

[22] The term "Holodomor," or "famine-death" to denote that the famine was deliberate and aimed at Ukrainians did not come into official use until the 1990s. See J.-P. Himka, "Encumbered Memory. The Ukrainian Famine of 1932—33," *Kritika* 14, 2 (Spring 2013), 420.

[23] See Douglas Tottle. *Fraud, Famine, and Fascism. The Ukrainian Genocide Myth from Hitler to Harvard* (Toronto, Canada: Progress Books, 1987), Appendix: "From Third-Reich Propagandist to Famine-Genocide Author," outlining the career of Olexa Hay-Holowko. This book can be downloaded at a number of Internet sites including http://rationalrevolution.net/special/library/tottlefraud.pdf

can't make an omelette without breaking eggs."
(56)

Snyder's evidence (n. 95 p. 468): "For Duranty, see *New York Times*, 31 March 1933."

Snyder is wrong about Duranty and Duranty's article of March 31, 1933. Duranty did use the words "a big scare story" — but to refer to Jones' "conclusion that the country was 'on the verge of a terrific smash'." Duranty said of Jones' words to him, "nothing could shake his conviction of impending doom." This is where Duranty said he disagreed with Jones. Of course it was not Jones but Duranty who was right — the USSR did not suffer "a terrific smash."

Then Duranty goes on to say that he agreed with Jones! He wrote:

> But to return to Mr Jones. He told me there was vir-
> tually no bread in the villages he had visited and
> that the adults were haggard, gaunt and discour-
> aged, but that he had seen no dead or dying animals
> or human beings.

> I believed him because I knew it to be correct not
> only of some parts of the Ukraine but of sections of
> the North Caucasus and lower Volga regions and,
> for that matter, Kazakstan, ... (Emphasis added, GF)

According to Duranty Jones himself had said he had seen "no actu-al starvation" — that is, "no dead or dying animals or human be-ings." Snyder gives no evidence that "Duranty knew that millions of people had starved to death."

As for this claim of Snyder's:

> Yet he maintained in his journalism that the hunger
> served a higher purpose. Duranty thought that "you
> can't make an omelette without breaking eggs."

Here is what Duranty actually wrote:

> But — to put it brutally — you can't make an ome-
> lette without breaking eggs, and the Bolshevist
> leaders are just as indifferent to the casualties that
> may be involved in their drive toward socialization
> as any General during the World War who ordered

> a costly attack in order to show his superiors that
> he and his division possessed the proper soldierly
> spirit. In fact, the Bolsheviki are more indifferent
> because they are animated by fanatical conviction.

Snyder is deliberately deceiving his readers. There is no hint here that Duranty "maintained... that the hunger served a higher purpose." In reality Duranty explicitly stated that Bolshevik leaders were even more "indifferent to the casualties" than were commanders in WW1 who callously ordered attacks for purposes of career advancement only.

Why does Snyder go out of his way to attack this article of Duranty's when in it Duranty states plainly that he agrees with what Jones told him concerning what he, Jones, had observed; called the Bolsheviks "indifferent" to casualties; and termed them "fanatical," therefore even "more indifferent to casualties"?

The reason seems to lie in his sponsors, the Ukrainian nationalists. For some reason the Ukrainian Nationalists have tried time and again to have Duranty's Pulitzer Prize posthumously revoked on the grounds that he did not report the famine. Their latest effort of about a decade ago was unsuccessful, in large part due to the fact that Duranty's Pulitzer was for reporting done in 1931, before any famine existed, and therefore had nothing to do with anything he wrote (or did not write) about the famine later on.

Evidently, therefore, Snyder's misrepresentation of Duranty's March 31, 1933 article is simply a "tell," a signal that he is taking his cues from the Ukrainian nationalists.

Duranty was one of the *New York Times* Russian correspondents whose reporting on the Russian Revolution and ensuing Civil War was so anticommunist and biased that it completely distorted the truth, as determined in the famous study "A Test of the News" by Walter Lippmann and Charles Merz, published as a supplement to the August 4, 1920 edition of *The New Republic*. Lippmann went on to be advisor to presidents and Merz to being an editor of *The New York Times*. After this experience, it seems, Duranty determined to curb his anticommunist bias and report only what he himself had witnessed, as reporters are trained to do in the US.

Resolution of the Soviet of People's Commissars of the Ukrainian SSR and the CC of the Communist Party of the Ukraine on the "Black Board"

This is the full text, the first part of which we quoted verbatim in the main part of this chapter.

№ 219

Постановление СНК УССР и ЦК КП(б)У «О занесении на черную доску сел, злостно саботирующих хлебозаготовки»1*

6 декабря 1932 г.

Ввиду особо позорного провала хлебозаготовок в отдельных районах Украины, СНК и ЦК ставят перед облисполкомами и обкомами, райисполкомами и райпарткомами задачу сломить саботаж хлебозаготовок, организованный кулацкими и контрреволюционными элементами, уничтожить сопротивление части сельских коммунистов, ставших фактически проводниками саботажа, и ликвидировать несовместимую со званием члена партии пассивность и примиренчество к саботажникам, обеспечить быстрое нарастание темпов, полное и безусловное выполнение плана хлебозаготовок.

СНК и ЦК постановляют:

За явный срыв плана хлебозаготовок и злостный саботаж, организованный кулацкими и контрреволюционными элементами, занести на черную доску следующие села:

1. с. Вербка Павлоградского района Днепропетровской обл.

2. с. Гавриловка Межевского района Днепропетровской обл.

3. с. Лютеньки Гадячского района Харьковской обл.

4. с. Каменные Потоки Кременчугского района Харьковской обл.

5. с. Святотроицкое Троицкого района Одесской обл.

6. с. Пески Баштанского района Одесской обл.

В отношении этих сел провести следующие мероприятия:

1. Немедленное прекращение подвоза товаров, полное прекращение кооперативной и государственной торговли на месте и вывоз из соответствующих кооперативных и государственных лавок всех наличных товаров.

2. Полное запрещение колхозной торговли как для колхозов, колхозников, так и единоличников.

3. Прекращение всякого рода кредитования, проведение досрочного взыскания кредитов и других финансовых обязательств.

4. Проверку и очистку органами РКИ кооперативных и государственных аппаратов от всякого рода чуждых и враждебных элементов.

5. Проверку и очистку колхозов этих сел с изъятием контрреволюционных элементов, организаторов срыва хлебозаготовок.

СНК и ЦК обращаются с призывом ко всем честным, преданным Советской власти колхозникам и трудящимся крестьянам-единоличникам организовать все свои силы для беспощадной борьбы с кулаками и их пособниками для преодоления кулацкого саботажа хлебозаготовок в своих селах, за честное добросовестное выполнение хлебозаготовительных обязательств перед советским государством, за укрепление колхозов.

Председатель Совнаркома УССР В. Чубарь
Секретарь ЦК КП(б)У С.Косиор

РГАСПИ. Ф. 17. Оп. 26. Д. 55. Л. 71—72. Заверенная копия.[24]

Translated:

Number 219

Resolution of the Council of People's Commissars [CPC] of the USSR and the Communist Party (Bolshevik) "On the inscription on the black board of villages that maliciously sabotage grain reserves."

December 6, 1932

In view of the particularly shameful failure of grain procurements in some regions of the Ukraine , the CPC and Central Committee [CC] pose before the regional executive committees and regional committees, district executive committees and regional party committees the task of breaking the sabotage of grain procurements organized by kulak and counterrevolutionary elements, of destroying the resistance of a part of the rural communists, who have become in fact agents of sabotage and eliminate passivity and conciliation towards saboteurs, which is incompatible with the title of party member, and of ensuring a rapid increase in the rate of full and unconditional implementation of the grain procurement plan.

The CPC and CC decree:

For blatant failure of the grain procurement plan and malicious sabotage organized by kulak and

---

[24] *Tragediia sovetskoi derevni t. 3*, pp. 562-3. The same decree in Ukrainian is widely available on the Internet.

counterrevolutionary elements, to inscribe on the black board the following villages :

1. Verbka, Pavlograd district, Dnepropetrovsk oblast'.

2. Gavrylivka, Mezhevskii district, Dnepropetrovsk oblast'.

3. Liuten'ki, Gadiach district, Khar'kov oblast'.

4. Kamennye Potoki, Kremenchug district, Khar'kov oblast'.

5. Sviatotroitskoe, Trotskii district, Odessa oblast'.

6. Peski, Bashtansky district, Odessa oblast'.

With regard to these villages to conduct the following activities:

1. Immediate cessation of the transport of goods, the complete cessation of cooperative and state trade in place and removal from the relevant cooperative and state stores of all available products .

2. Complete prohibition of collective farm trade for both collective farms, kolkhoz farmers, and individual farmers.

3. Termination of any kind of lending, the holding of early loan credits, and other financial obligations.

4. Verification and purging by the organs of the Workers and Peasants

 Inspection Bureau of the cooperative and state apparatus from any kind of alien and hostile elements.

5. Verification and purging of the collective farms in these villages by removing counter-revolutionary elements and organizers disrupt grain procurements.

The CPC and CC call upon all collective farmers and individual peasants who are honest and loyal to the Soviet government to organize all their forces for a ruthless struggle with kulaks and their accomplices in order to overcome kulak sabotage of grain procurements in their villages, for procuring an honest conscientious fulfillment of grain collection obligations to the Soviet state , and for the strengthening of the collective farms.

Chairman of the Council of People's Commissars of the Ukrainian SSR V. Chubar

Secretary of the Communist Party (Bolshevik) of the Ukrainian SSR S.Kosior

RGASPI . F. 17. Op. 26. D. 55 . L. 71-72 . Certified copy

Chapter 3.
Snyder, Chapter 1 - Appendix

In order to make the main text of this book a more readable narrative we have added Appendices to several of the chapters of this analysis. In these Appendices are presented direct quotations from *Bloodlands* together with our dissection and critique of the assertions Snyder makes in them.

We have examined and critiqued every fact-claim of an anti-Stalin or anti-Soviet tendency in *Bloodlands*. Those that are not studied and critiqued in the main chapters are covered in the Appendices. In addition, the full texts of some of the longer documents that are referred to in the body of each chapter are contained in the Appendices. This too improves the readability of the main text while still making additional important documentation available to scholars or whoever wants it.

Each such section or "unit" in the Appendices is comprised of the following elements:

> * A quotation from *Bloodlands* where the Soviet Union or a pro-Soviet force is accused of some "crime," misdeed, etc. These quotations contain some assertion or "fact-claim."

> * The text of the footnotes, which constitute the evidence or "proof" of Snyder's fact-claims;

> * Our study and analysis of the evidence in the footnotes;

> * Our conclusion as to whether Snyder's fact-claims have been verified or — as almost always is the case — proven to be fraudulent.

Whenever possible we have provided each unit with a title in bold-face. These titles are intended only for shorthand reference. They do not fully reflect the contents of the paragraph of Snyder's text that is analyzed in the unit below.

Unlike the main body of the book these Appendices do not constitute a flowing narrative. Some readers will content themselves to
studying our critique of Snyder's principal allegations, which is
contained in other chapters. Others will want to go further and
study our critique of some or all of the anti-Soviet allegations
Snyder makes in the book but that are not examined in the texts of
the chapters themselves.

The Starving Children

Snyder (22-23) gives some anecdotal accounts of famine-stricken
children. A number might be true but are not recorded in any of
the sources Snyder cites.

> Starving peasants begged along the breadlines, ask-
> ing for crumbs. In one town, a fifteen-year-old girl
> begged her way to the front of the line, only to be
> beaten to death by the shopkeeper. The city house-
> wives making the queues had to watch as peasant
> women starved to death on the side-walks. A girl
> walking to and from school each day saw the dying
> in the morning and the dead in the afternoon. One
> young communist called the peasant children he
> saw "living skeletons." A party member in industrial
> Stalino was distressed by the corpses of the starved
> that he found at his back door. Couples strolling in
> parks could not miss the signs forbidding the dig-
> ging of graves. Doctors and nurses were forbidden
> from treating (or feeding) the starving who reached
> their hospitals. The city police seized famished ur-
> chins from city streets to get them out of sight. In
> Soviet Ukrainian cities policemen apprehended
> several hundred children a day; one day in early
> 1933, the Kharkiv police had a quota of two thou-
> sand to fill. About twenty thousand children await-
> ed death in the barracks of Kharkiv at any given
> time. The children pleaded with the police to be al-
> lowed, at least, to starve in the open air: "Let me die

in peace, I don't want to die in the death barracks."[4]
(22-23)

Sources (n. 4 p. 463):

* "Quotations: Falk, *Sowjetische Städte*, 299, see also 297-301";

* Kuśnierz, *Ukraina*, 157, 160.

* "On the schoolgirl and the hospitals, see Davies, *Years*, 160, 220. See also Kuromiya, *Freedom and Terror*, 171, 184."

Snyder's claim in this paragraph that "about twenty thousand children awaited death in the barracks of Kharkiv at any given time" is not documented by any of the sources Snyder cites.

Falk, *Sowjetische Städte*, 299 contains a quotation, in German translation, from the report of a Komsomol activist to the Khar'kov city Soviet on July 4, 1933, describing peasant children coming into Khar'kov: "Wenn man auf die Kinder schaut, sieht man lebendige Skelette…" (When one looks at the children one sees living skeletons…").

Kuśnierz, 157: The quotation "Let me die in peace, I don't want to die in the death barracks" is here. Snyder states that it was the "about twenty thousand children" "in the barracks of Kharkiv" who made this "plea." This is false. According to Kuśnierz, Snyder's source, it was the homeless children in the streets who said this to policemen. What's more, the source of this is the Italian consul in Kharkov — in other words, a fascist, hardly a reliable source.

Kuśnierz, 156 (not 157), citing a Ukrainian nationalist source, says that 27,454 homeless children were "rounded up" in the whole Kharkov oblast' by May 28, 1933. It does not say that all, or indeed any, of these children were in "the barracks of Kharkiv" or "awaiting death," as Snyder claims. Evidence cited below shows that children were given special priority for emergency food supplies, and that the Soviet Politburo — "Stalin" — issued some of these orders.

Kuśnierz notes (p. 156, n. 277) that "according to other data" 6378 children had been taken from the streets of Khar'kov by the end of

May, 1933. This figure is contained in Kuśnierz's source, Document 233 of Голод 1932-1933 років. [1] This document appears to reflect attempts by the Khar'kov city authorities to aid homeless children. Snyder has fabricated the claim that the purpose was "to get them [the homeless children] out of sight." It is not in his source.

Kuśnierz, 160: "The schoolgirl" story is here, not in Davies, *Years*. Kuśnierz quotes it in Polish translation from the collection published by the U.S. Congress in 1990, "*Oral History Project of the Commission on the Ukraine Famine*, p. 1588." (Page 1588 is in volume 3 of this work.) Kuśnierz errs in copying her name, calling her "Olga Lodyga." In reality she identified herself as Ol'ga Odlyga, née Antonova. In the Ukrainian-language interview Odlyga refuses to testify that she saw policemen arresting starving people, despite leading questions by the Ukrainian-speaking interviewer.

Davies, *Years*, 160, 220, despite Snyder's claim, has nothing at all about "the schoolgirl and the hospitals."

However, on pages 221 ff. Davies and Wheatcroft outline Soviet efforts to help Ukrainian children:

> Considerable efforts were made to supply grain to hungry children, irrespective of their parents' roles in society. The Vinnitsa decision of April 29, insisting that most grain should be distributed to those who were active in agriculture, also allocated grain specifically to crèches and children's institutes in the badly-hit districts. On May 20, the USSR Politburo [in Moscow, led by Stalin — GF] issued a grain loan to the Crimea specifically for children in need and aged invalids... (Emphasis added)

Snyder fails to inform his readers about these and similar efforts documented in Davies and Wheatcroft. This work is one of the most important studies of the 1932-33 famine (along with those by Mark Tauger) and firmly concludes that it was not "deliberate" in any way.

---

[1] At http://www.archives.gov.ua/Sections/Famine/Publicat/Fam-Pyrig-1933.php#nom-233

A similar resolution of February 22, 1933, by the Kiev Oblast' buro of the Ukrainian Communist Party to provide food relief to all those struck by famine, is reproduced in translation in the 1997 Library of Congress volume *Revelations from the Russian Archives*, ed. Diane P. Koenker and Ronald D. Bachman, as document 187 on pp. 417-418.[2]

These works refute Snyder's entire hypothesis of a "deliberate famine." For if the Stalin regime wanted to deliberately starve Ukrainians, why would it take special measures to feed hungry children and aged invalids?

Kuromiya, *Freedom and Terror*, 171, 184: Page 171 relates the "fifteen year-old girl beaten to death by the shopkeeper" story. Snyder distorts the story by omitting the detail that the "store-keeper" was "communist," although the original version and Kuromiya, Snyder's source, include it. Why? Could it be because this detail — making the shopkeeper a "communist" — makes the whole story seem phony, sound like anticommunists "going over-board"?

But there is a more serious problem with this story. It is taken from *The Black Deeds of the Kremlin*, Volume 1, page 284. Its source is an unidentified person using the name "Mariupilsky" — the story is set in the town of Mariupil'. This book was published in the mid-1950s by Ukrainian émigrés in Canada who had collabo-rated with the Nazis and written hair-raising antisemitic propa-ganda to recruit other Ukrainians to the pro-Nazi forces. At least one identifiable Ukrainian fascist recounts a story in it.[3]

There's no reason to accept any of them as true. Eyewitness stories are notoriously unreliable as history under any circumstances. A volume of self-serving, largely anonymous stories by Nazi collabo-rators such as this one is even more unreliable as history. Moreo-ver, the volume claims that there was plenty of food in Russian

---

[2] I have put these documents online at
http://msuweb.montclair.edu/~furrg/research/ukfaminedocs97.pdf The document in question is on pages 17 and 18 of this 22-page collection.

[3] See the note to the book by Douglas Tottle in the previous chapter.

areas outside the Ukraine, an absurd statement that even fervent anticommunists do not make today.

This collection became known beyond the circles of Nazi collaborators only because Robert Conquest cited it many times in his 1986 book *Harvest of Sorrow.* Conquest was paid by the Ukrainian Nationalists to write this book. The work is never cited except by extreme anticommunists, such as Kuromiya. Moreover, Conquest has repudiated his original accusation that the famine is deliberate, as we discuss below.

Kuromiya, *Freedom and Terror*, 184, does not document anything at all in Snyder's paragraph.

Conclusion: Many of Snyder's claims in this paragraph are not in the sources he cites:

> * the "city housewives making the queues";

> * the "party member in Stalino";

> * the allegation that doctors and nurses were forbidden to treat the starving;

> * the quota that the Khar'kiv police supposedly had;

> * the story of the "about 20,000 children" in the "death barracks";

— none are documented. But even if they were true none of these stories would be evidence for Snyder's insistence that the famine was either caused by collectivization or constituted the "deliberate starvation of Ukrainians."

Snyder "Begs the Question" of the Famine (Assumes What He Needs To Prove)

Snyder:

> The mass starvation of 1933 was the result of Stalin's first Five-Year Plan, implemented between 1928 and 1932. In those years, Stalin had taken control of the heights of the communist party, forced through a policy of industrialization and collectivization, and emerged as **the frightful father of a beaten population.** He had transformed the

market into the plan, **farmers into slaves**, and the
wastes of Siberia and Kazakhstan into a chain of
concentration camps. His policies had killed tens of
thousands by execution, **hundreds of thousands
by exhaustion, and put millions at risk of starvation**....[8] (24-25. Emphasis added)

n. 8. For a sophisticated guide to the meanings of
the Plan, see Harrison, *Soviet Planning* , 1-5.

Snyder cites *no evidence whatsoever* to support this paragraph of
invective. We have dealt, or are dealing, with the falsehoods in
boldface. In reality, like all previous famines in Russian and
Ukrainian history this famine too had environmental, not human,
causes.

Harrison, *Soviet Planning* , 1-5, is a very brief introduction to what
Harrison sees as the tensions between balance and "voluntarism"
within Soviet economic planning in the early 1930s, concluding
that "there was a sense in which they [these two tendencies] needed each other." It contains nothing — no evidence, or even reference — to Snyder's claim of "frightful father," "beaten population,"
peasants as "slaves," or "concentration camps." It does not even
support Snyder's claim that collectivization caused the famine.

The Lie of "Slave Labor"

One hallmark of anticommunist bias and falsification is to call Soviet collective farmers or labor camp prisoners "slaves." The penal
systems of the United States today, and many other countries, em-
ploy the labor of prisoners. This is never called "slave labor." The
proper term used for prisoners' labor in all capitalist countries is
"penal labor."[4] Peasants on collective farms (kolkhozes) and Soviet
farms (sovkhozes) had nothing in common with the institution of
"slavery," any more than they did with serfdom. Neither did prisoners in the Soviet GULAG.

A writer who uses that term is making no attempt to be accurate
and so is likely to be untruthful about other matters too. But the

---

[4] See http://en.wikipedia.org/wiki/Penal_labour

basic point to note here is that Snyder "assumes that which is to be proven." Instead of citing evidence that the Five-Year Plan and collectivization resulted in the famine, Snyder simply states it as a fact.

We have already shown that Mark Tauger, and Davies and Wheatcroft have established that the famine was not caused by collectivization but by environmental factors, like virtually all the numerous famines that preceded it. Quotations from these authors are in the main body of Chapter One of this book.

Was the Threat of Mass Starvation "Clear" to Stalin by June 1932?

Snyder:

> The threat of mass starvation was utterly clear to Soviet Ukrainian authorities, and it became so to Stalin. ... That same day, 18 June 1932, Stalin himself admitted, privately, that there was "famine" in Soviet Ukraine. The previous day the Ukrainian party leadership had requested food aid. He did not grant it. His response was that all grain in Soviet Ukraine must be collected as planned. He and Kaganovich agreed that "it is imperative to export without fail immediately.[34] (34-5)

> n. 34 - On the reports of death by starvation, see Kuśnierz, 104-105. On Stalin, see Davies, *Kaganovich Correspondence*, 138. On the request for food aid, see Lih, *Letters to Molotov*, 230. On Kaganovich (23 June 1932), see Hunczak, *Famine*, 121.

Nothing in any of the sources cited by Snyder here gives any evidence that "the threat of mass starvation" "became clear to Stalin." On the contrary: these sources show that in mid-1932 the Soviet leadership was far from recognizing that a devastating famine was to come.

* **Kuśnierz**, 104-105 contains several reports about starvation. These reports contain nothing abojut and are therefore irrelevant to charges of "man-made famine" and "deliberate starvation."

* **Davies**, *Kaganovich Correspondence*, 138: In this letter of Stalin's of June 18 1932 (p. 179 of the Russian edition) Stalin explains to Kaganovich his conclusion that the starvation that does exist in places in the Ukraine is the result of improper accounting by the grain-collection teams, who instead of accounting for differences have been taking the same from everyone:

> В результате этого механически-
> уравниловского отношения к делу
> получилась вопиющая несообразность, в
> силу которой на Украине, несмотря на
> неплохой урожай, ряд урожайных районов
> оказался в состоянии разорения и голода, а
> на Урале обком лишил себя возможности
> оказать помощь неурожайным районам за
> счет урожайных районов области.[5]

Translated:

> The mechanical equalizing approach to the matter
> has resulted in glaring absurdities, so that a number
> of fertile districts in the Ukraine, despite a fairly
> good harvest, have found themselves in a state of
> impoverishment and famine, while the regional
> party committee in the Urals has deprived itself of
> the capacity to use the districts with good crops in
> the region to assist regions with bad harvests.

Five days later, on June 23, 1932, Kaganovich wrote to Stalin that, in his opinion, the quantity of grain for the 3rd quarter of 1932 must be "somewhat" reduced. Snyder does not mention this.

> 10 июля 1932 г. ПБ решило сократить
> намеченную цифру экспорта хлеба в III
> квартале и окончательно установить ее 16
> июля (Там же. Оп. 162. Д. 13. Л. 11). На заседании
> ПБ 16 июля экспорт хлеба в III квартале был
> установлен в размере 31,5 млн пудов (включая
> бобовые), 20 млн пудов для варранта и 10 млн

---

[5] *Stalin i Kaganovich. Perepiska 1931-1936 gg.* Moscow: ROSSPEN, 2001, p. 179. Online at http://grachev62.narod.ru/stalin/t17/t17_320.htm

> пудов переходящих остатков, всего — 61,5 млн
> пудов (Там же. Л. 30). 20 октября 1932 г. ПБ
> приняло решение сократить экспорт из урожая
> 1932 г. с 165 до 150 млн пудов (Там же. Л. 133).[6]

Translated:

> On July 10 1932 the PB [Politburo] decided to lower
> the indicated amount of grain for export in the 3rd
> quarter and to establish it firmly on July 16….At the
> PB session of July 16 the export of grain for the 3rd
> quarter was set at 31.5 million poods (excluding
> legumes), 20 million poods as a guarantee [i.e. in
> reserve] and 10 million poods carried over, in total:
> 61.5 million poods. On October 20 1932 the PB
> adopted a decision to reduce the export from the
> 1932 harvest from 165 to 150 million tons.

Lih, "Letters to Molotov," is a translation from the Russian original, which we reproduce and discuss below.

> 3. Forced collectivization resulted in widespread
> famine.

Before proceeding we should note that this sentence, "Forced collectivization resulted in widespread famine," is an addition by the editors, who assume this rather than trying to prove it. As we have shown, neither Davies and Wheatcroft nor Tauger think this is true.

Lih's text continues:

> On 17 June 1932, the Ukrainian Politburo sent Ka-
> ganovich and Molotov the following telegram:
>
>> On the instructions of our Central Committee,
>> Chubar' has initiated a request to grant food as-
>> sistance to Ukraine for districts experiencing a
>> state of emergency. We urgently request addi-
>> tional means for processing sugar beets, and al-
>> so supplemental aid: in addition to the 220,000,
>> and other 600,000 pounds of bread.

---

[6] *Stalin i Kaganovich*, 198 note 3. Emphasis mine (GF).

In Stalin's view, Ukrainian crop failures were caused by enemy resistance and by the poor leadership of Ukrainian officials. On 21 June 1932, the Central Committee sent a telegram, signed by Stalin and Molotov, to the Ukrainian Central Committee and Council of Commissars, proposing to ensure the collection of grain "at all costs." The telegram stated:

> No manner of deviation — regarding either amounts or deadlines set for grain deliveries — can be permitted from the plan established for your region for collecting grain from collective and private farms or for delivering grain to state farms.

On 23 June 1932, in response to S.V. Kosior's telegram requesting aid, the Politburo passed the following resolution: "To restrict ourselves to the decisions already adopted by the Central Committee and not to approve the shipment of additional grain into Ukraine." (All quotations are from *The 1932-1933 Ukrainian Famine in the Eyes of Historians and in the Language of Documents* [in Ukrainian. Kiev, 1990], 183, 186, 187,190.)

The original document reads as follows:

> В результате насильственной коллективизации в ряде районов страны, в том числе на Украине, начался голод. Руководители Украины обращались в Москву за продовольственной помощью. Так, 17 июня 1932 г. Политбюро ЦК КП(б)У приняло решение послать в ЦК ВКП(б) Кагановичу и Молотову следующую телеграмму:

>> «Чубарь по поручению ЦК КП(б)У возбудил ходатайство [об] отпуске Украине продовольственной помощи находящимся [в] тяжелом положении районам. Настоятельно просим сверх отпущенных

> для обработки свеклы, а также
> дополнительной продовольственной
> помощи 220 тысяч еще 600 тысяч пудов
> [хлеба]." (Emphasis added, GF)

По мнению Сталина провалы в сельском
хозяйстве на j Украине объяснялись
сопротивлением врагов и плохим '
руководством правительства/республики. 21
июня 1932 г. в ЦК КП(б)У и Совнарком Украины
была направлена телеграмма ЦК ВКП(б) и СНК
СССР за подписью Молото-ва и Сталина. В ней
предлагалось обеспечить зернопоставки «во
что бы то ни стало» . В телеграмме говорилось:

> «Никакие уклонения от выполнения
> установленного для вашего края ... плана по
> зернопоставке колхозами и единоличными
> хозяйствами и по сдаче зерна совхозам не
> должны быть допущены ни под каким
> видом как в отношении количеств, так и
> сроков сдачи зерна» .

23 июня 1932 г. ПБ в ответ на телеграмму
С.В.Косиора о помощи приняло следующее
постановление:

> «Ограничиться уже принятыми решениями
> ЦК и дополнительного завоза хлеба на
> Украину не производить» («Голод 1932—
> 1933 годов на Украине: глазами историков,
> языком документов» (на украинском языке)
> Киев 1990 С. 183, 186, 187, 190)[7]

The primary documents cited here are all in various editions of the
book Snyder cites.

---

[7] *Pis'ma I.V. Stalina V.M. Molotovu. 1925-1936 gg. Sbornik dokumentov.* Moscow: "Molodaia
Gvardiia" 1995, p. 242.

The June 23, 1932 telegram refusing "to approve the shipment of additional grain to Ukraine" is genuine. But note the word "additional." It implies that grain was already promised to the Ukraine.

This is indeed the case. The Ukrainian Politburo telegram of June 17, 1932 quoted in the Stalin-Molotov volume was preceded *the previous day* by the following decree of the Politburo of the All-Union Party — that is, by Stalin, Molotov, Kaganovich, et al.:

№144 Постанова Політбюро ЦК ВКП(б) про продовольчу допомогу УСРР

16 червня 1932 р.

а) Отпустить Украине 2000 тонн овса на продовольственные нужды из неиспользованной семссуды;

б) отпустить Украине 100 тыс. пудов кукурузы на продовольственные нужды из отпущенной на посев для Одесской области, но неиспользованной по назначению;

в) отпустить 70 тыс. пудов хлеба для свекловичных совхозов УССР на продовольственные нужды;

г) отпустить 230 тыс. пудов хлеба для колхозов свекловичных районов УССР на продовольственные нужды;

д) обязать т. Чубаря лично проследить за использованием отпущенного хлеба для свекловичных совхозов и колхозов строго по назначению;

е) отпустить 25 тыс. пудов хлеба для свекловичных совхозов ЦЧО на продовольственные нужды в связи с уборкой урожая, обязав т. Варейкиса лично проследить за использованием отпущенного хлеба строго по назначению;

ж) настоящим решением считать
продовольственную помощь свекловичным
совхозам и колхозам исчерпанной.[8]

Translated:

No. 144. Decree of Politburo of the CC VCP(b) [=
Central Committee of the All-Russian Communist
Party (Bolsheviks), the formal name for the Party
until October 1952] concerning foodstuff aid to the
Ukrainian SSR of June 16, 1932 [the title is in
Ukrainian; the text in Russian]:

a) To release to the Ukraine 2000 tons of oats for
food needs from the unused seed reserves;

b) to release to the Ukraine 100,000 poods of corn
for food of that released for sowing for the Odessa
oblast' but not used for that purpose;

c) to release 70,000 poods of grain for sugar-beet
Soviet farms of the Ukrainian SSR for food needs;

d) to release 230,000 poods of grain for collective
farms in the sugar-beet regions of the Ukrainian
SSR for food needs;

e) to require com. Chubar' to personally verify the
fulfillment of the released grain for the sugar-beet
Soviet and collective farms, that it be used strictly
for thisi purpose;

f) to release 25,000 poods of grain for thesugar-
beet Soviet farms of the Central Black Earth Region
for food needs in connection with the gathering of
the harvest, first requiring com. Vareikis to personally verify that the grain released is used for the assigned purpose;

g) by the present decision to consider the question
of food aid to sugar-beet producing Soviet and collective farms closed.

---

[8] *Holod v SSSR 1929-1934. Tom pervyi. 1929-iiul' 1932. Dokumenty. Kniga 2* ((Moscow: MFD, 2011), pp. 261-2. Note that Davies and Wheatcroft transliterate the first word as „Golod".

So it is true that Stalin rejected the June 17 request of the Ukrainian Party's Politburo for more food aid. But what Snyder, as well as
the editors of the Stalin-Molotov correspondence, did not disclose
to their readers is that *one day earlier, on June 16, Stalin et al. had
ordered a very large quantity of food grains to the Ukraine.*

It is crucial to Snyder's thesis to claim or imply that the Soviet government did not send food aid to the Ukraine. "Deliberation starvation of Ukraine", the "Holodomor", is incompatible with serious
attempts by the Soviet state to alleviate the famine. But that is
what happened.

Here is a passage from a 1991 article by Mark Tauger:

> The harvest decline also decreased the regime's re-
> serves of grain for export. This drop in reserves be-
> gan with the drought-reduced 1931 harvest and
> subsequent procurements, which brought famine to
> the Volga region, Siberia, and other areas. Soviet
> leaders were forced to return procured grain to
> those areas in 1932. The low 1931 harvest and real-
> locations of grain to famine areas forced the regime
> to curtail grain exports from 5.2 million tons in
> 1931 to 1.73 million in 1932; they declined to 1.68
> million in 1933. Grain exported in 1932 and 1933
> could have fed many people and reduced the fam-
> ine: The 354,000 tons exported during the first half
> of 1933, for example, could have provided nearly 2
> million people with daily rations of l kilogram for
> six months. Yet these exports were less than half of
> the 750,000 tons exported in the first half of 1932.[51]
> How Soviet leaders calculated the relative costs of
> lower exports and lower domestic food supplies
> remains uncertain, but available evidence indicates
> that further reductions or cessation of Soviet ex-
> ports could have had serious consequences. Grain
> prices fell in world markets and turned the terms of
> trade against the Soviet Union in the early 1930s,
> its indebtedness rose and its potential ability to pay
> declined, causing western bankers and officials to

consider seizure of Soviet property abroad and denial of future credits in case of Soviet default. Failure to export thus would have threatened the fulfillment of its industrialization plans and, according
to some observers, the stability of the regime.[52]

While the leadership did not stop exports, they did
try to alleviate the famine. A 25 February 1933 Central Committee decree allotted seed loans of
320,000 tons to Ukraine and 240,000 tons to the
northern Caucasus. Seed loans were also made to
the Lower Volga and may have been made to other
regions as well. Kul'chyts'kyy cites Ukrainian party
archives showing that total aid to Ukraine by April
1933 actually exceeded 560,000 tons, including
more than 80,000 tons of food. Aid to Ukraine alone
was 60 percent greater than the amount exported
during the same period. Total aid to famine regions
was more than double exports for the first half of
1933. It appears to have been another consequence
of the low 1932 harvest that more aid was not provided: After the low 1931, 1934, and 1936 harvests
procured grain was transferred back to peasants at
the expense of exports.[53]

The low 1932 harvest meant that the regime did
not have sufficient grain for urban and rural food
supplies, seed, and exports. The authorities curtailed all of these, but ultimately rural food supplies
had last priority. The harsh 1932-1933 procurements only displaced the famine from urban areas
which would have suffered a similar scale of mortality without the grain the procurements provided
(though, as noted above, urban mortality rates also
rose in 1933). The severity and geographical extent
of the famine, the sharp decline in exports in 1932-
1933, seed requirements, and the chaos in the Soviet Union in these years, all lead to the conclusion
that even a complete cessation of exports would not

have been enough to prevent famine.[54] **This situation makes it difficult to accept the interpretation of the famine as the result of the 1932 grain
procurements and as a conscious act of genocide. The harvest of 1932 essentially made a
famine inevitable.**[9] (Emphasis added.)

For our present purposes Tauger's heavily-documented account shows that:

1. The Soviet Politburo did provide a great deal of aid, both in seed grain and in food, to the Ukraine.

2. Stopping all exports would have seriously harmed, perhaps destroyed, Soviet foreign credit and either seriously delayed industrialization or caused it to fail altogether. In a footnote Tauger provides evidence from British archives that Soviet failure to meet its export obligations would have brought disaster: a refusal of future credits, seizure of Soviet assets abroad, and so, probably, the failure of the industrialization program.

But it was industrialization that, together with collectivization, broke the thousand-year cycle of famines in Russia. Industrialization was essential to preventing further famines, as well as to industrialization of other areas of the economy and the modernization of the military.

3. Tauger concludes that "even a complete cessation of exports would not have been enough to prevent famine." Davies and Wheatcroft outline the deepening crisis after the Spring of 1932, along with the extensive aid in both seed grain and food granted by the authorities to the affected areas, including to the Ukraine. They document how hunger weakened the farmers and led to late sowing and poor weeding, which further lessened the harvest. Armed with more accurate weather information they "conclude that the weather in 1932 was much more unfavourable than we had previously realized." (119) The state made advances to collective farmers in order to bring in the harvest (124-5). As we noted

---

[9] Mark Tauger, "The 1932 Harvest and the Famine of 1933." *Slavic Review* 50, 1 (Spring 1991), 88-89. Emphasis added.

in the last chapter, the best research on the environmental causes of the famine is by Tauger.

The Soviet authorities greatly overestimated the crop that would be harvested in late 1932. But so did foreign experts, as Davies and Wheatcroft show (127). Hunger limited the strength of harvest workers (128). Plant diseases were a serious problem. According to Davies and Wheatcroft:

> During the harvest of 1932, the poor weather, the lack of autumn and spring ploughing, the shortage and poor quality of the seed, the poor cultivation of the crop and the delay in harvesting all combined to increase the incidence of fungal disease. Reports in the Narkomzem [= People's Commissariat for Agriculture] archives complain that traditional campaigns to disinfect the fields, the storehouses and the sacks for the harvested grain, were all carried out extremely badly in Ukraine. Cairns [the British expert whose overestimation of the 1932 harvest they cited earlier] found that in the North Caucasus 'the winter wheat was extremely weedy and looked as though it was badly rusted', and 'all the spring wheat I saw was simply rotten with rust'. (131)

Conclusion: In June 1932 the authorities were still looking forward to a good harvest. A few pages earlier, Davies and Wheatcroft quote the opinion of one of the foreign experts:

> Andrew Cairns, the Scottish grain specialist, travelled extensively in the major grain regions in May and July [1932], reporting very bad conditions, and dismissed the official estimate that the yield would be 7.8 tsentners as 'absurdly too high'. He nevertheless concluded in a cable: 'do not like to generalise about comparative size this and last years harvest tentatively of opinion this years appreciably larger stop. (127)

Snyder conceals these facts from his readers. The result of his doing so is to suggest that the famine could have been averted through different policies but that Stalin and the Politburo refused to do so. This is false.

Snyder conceals the fact that Stalin et al. shipped large quantities of food grains to the Ukraine in June 1932. This fact alone is fatal to his "deliberate starvation" thesis: one does not ship food to those whom one wishes to starve.

"Stalin"s First Commandment": Another Snyder Fabrication

Snyder:

> Understanding this religiosity, party activists prop-
> agated what they called Stalin's First Command-
> ment: the collective farm supplies first the state,
> and only then the people. As the peasants would
> have known, the First Commandment in its biblical
> form reads: "Thou shalt have no other God before
> me.[20] (29)

Sources (n. 20, p. 464):

> * "For the Stalinist "First Commandment," see Kulczycki, *Hołodomor*, 170.
>
> * "See also Kuśnierz, *Ukraina*, 70."

Here Snyder seems to be trying to deliberately deceive his readers. For why was "the state" collecting produce from collective farms? Naturally, for the non-agricultural areas and for export. The work-ers in the cities and towns could not grow their own food. Con-tracts for export had been made a year earlier. In mid-1932 the fact that there was going to be a widespread famine was of course not known to anyone.

Kulczycki, *Hołodomor*, 170:

> "Pierwsze przykazanie"
>
> Były kleryk Józef Stalin używał niekiedy wyrażeń
> zapożyczonych z Biblii. Dzięki aparatowi
> propagandowemu największy rozgłos zdobyło
> wyrażenie "pierwsze przykazanie." Było ono
> adresowane do chłopów i chodziło w nim o to, że

> kołchoz powinien najpierw rozliczyć się z
> państwem, a dopiero potem pozostałe plony
> podzielić na podstawie roboczodni między
> pracowników. Deficyt chleba na wsi został
> spowodowany, jak już wiemy, przez dostawy
> obowiązkowe dla państwa.

Translated:

> "The First Commandment"
>
> The former seminarian Joseph Stalin sometimes use
> phrases borrowed from the Bible. Thanks to the
> propaganda apparatus the expression "the First
> Commandment" gained great circulation. It was ad-
> dressed to the peasants, and it meant that the col-
> lective farm should first settle with the state, and
> then divide the remaining crop on the basis of man-
> days among employees. The deficit of bread in the
> country was caused, as we have seen, by the supply
> required for the state.

Kuśnierz, *Ukraina*, 70: This is a phony citation. There is nothing in Kuśnierz's book about the "First Commandment" or the OGPU us-ing religious language. On the contrary, Kuśnierz records the recol-lection that *some kulaks* dressed up as devils and informed super-stitious peasants that entering the collective farm was a "pact with the devil" and that the OGPU arrested three of them and sentenced them to prison.

Conclusion: Snyder is untruthful here. Judging from the very source he cites, the term "The First Commandment" was invented by Kul'chyts'kyy as a section heading. Kul'chyts'kyy does claim that somebody — either the Party propagandists or the peasants — called the grain collection plan by this name, but he cites no ev-idence that anybody used this term, much less that it was well known.

Snyder claims "that Stalin's own policy of collectivization could cause mass starvation was also clear." (35) His evidence (n. 35 p. 465):

> * Cameron, "Hungry Steppe," chap. 2;

* Pianciola, "Collectivization Famine," 103-112;

* Mark, "Hungersnot," 119.

Chapter 2 of **Cameron**, "Hungry Steppe," a 2010 Yale Ph.D. dissertation, contains nothing that supports Snyder's claim that collectivization "could cause mass starvation," much less that this was "clear"

Pianciola, "The Collectivization Famine in Kazakhstan," was published in Harvard Ukrainian Studies, 25 (2001). It contains no evidence that collectivization "could cause mass starvation," much less of deliberate starvation.

Mark, "Hungersnot" does not appear in Snyder's bibliography. The following article is almost certainly the one meant: Rudolf A. Mark, Gerhard Simon, "Die Hungersnot in der Ukraine und anderen Regionen der UdSSR 1932 und 1933", *Osteuropa* 54 (2004), S. 5-12. This article is a long series of undocumented assertions reflecting the Ukrainian Nationalist viewpoint that Snyder also echoes. It contains no evidence to support its assertion, which is also Snyder's, that the famine was caused by collectivization, much less that this was predictable from the outset, as Snyder claims.

Davies & Wheatcroft discuss the Kazakhstan famine (322-326 and 408-9). This basic work is also cited by Cameron and Pianciola. They conclude that there was a "population deficit" by 1939 of "some 1.2 million." This is an estimate based on a projection of what they Kazakh population of Kazakhstan *would* have been if (1) its natural increase of 1926 had continued through to January 1939 — that is, if there had been no famines in 1928 and 1932-33; and (b) all Kazakhs had remained in Kazakhstan during this entire period. Davies and Wheatcroft cite evidence that large numbers of Kazakhs migrated to other regions in Kazakhstan, and to other regions and republics in search of a livelihood or simply seeking food, while others emigrated to China. (409) For these reasons we cannot know precisely how many Kazakhs died of famine — i.e. the surplus of deaths during the famine years.

None of these sources establish that collectivization was the "cause" of "mass starvation." Snyder is guilty of the logical fallacy of "begging the question" — asserting that which ought to be proven.

More False Citations; Stalin"s "Personal Politics"; "Starving Peasants on Tour"

> Stalin, a master of personal politics, presented the Ukrainian famine in personal terms. His first impulse, and his lasting tendency, was to see the starvation of Ukrainian peasants as a betrayal by members of the Ukrainian communist party. He could not allow the possibility that his own policy of collectivization was to blame; the problem must be in the implementation, in the local leaders, anywhere but in the concept itself. As he pushed forward with his transformation in the first half of 1932 ...(35)

This paragraph is really Snyder's own imagination. Snyder declares that he has determined what Stalin "intended"; what Stalin's "first impulse" was; what Stalin "could not allow"; what "problems" he "saw." How can he possibly know these things? Therefore it is both nonsense, and a deception.

This passage concerns "the first half of 1932." As the discussion above has pointed out, the famine had net yet made itself clear in early 1932. At that time Stalin wrote that he believed the incipient hunger were the result of mismanagement.

> Starving Ukrainian peasants, he complained, were leaving their home republic and demoralizing other Soviet citizens by their "whining."[36] (35)

Sources (n. 36 p. 465):

> * "Quotation: Davies, *Kaganovich Correspondence*, 138."
>
> * ("On Stalin's predisposition to personalized politics"), Kulczycki, *Hołodomor*, 180; Kuśnierz, *Ukraina*, 152.

Travelling Peasants Were "Whining" — Just Not Starving

There are a few factual statements that we can check, such as the statement about "whining." **Davies**, *Kaganovich Correspondence*,

138: The relevant part of Stalin's letter to Kaganovich of June 18, 1932 reads thus:

> Результаты этих ошибок сказываются теперь на посевном деле, особенно на Украине, причем несколько десятков тысяч украинских колхозников все еще разъезжают по всей европейской части СССР и разлагают нам колхозы своими жалобами и нытьем. (179)

Translated:

> The results of these mistakes can now be seen in the matter of sowing, especially in the Ukraine, in that several tens of thousands of Ukrainian collective farmers are still travelling all around the European part of the USSR and are degrading the collective farms for us by their complaints and whining.

So Snyder is correct that Stalin accused the kolkhozniks of "whining." But these peasants could not possibly have been starving, as Snyder claims, and he cites no evidence that they were. Train travel costs money, which starving people would spend on food, not travel. Likewise, moneyless starving people would not have the strength to travel "all over the European part of the USSR." They would need food to have the energy to travel anywhere.

If these farmers were not starving what were they doing? Most likely they were traveling to trade: either taking grain from the Ukraine to trade for other things — the harvest was bad in European Russia too — or taking money, or other goods, to trade for grain.

In normal times this activity was not immoral or illegal. But during a famine the price of food increases greatly. The Soviet government's efforts to distribute food according to need, rather than according to who had the money to buy it at inflated prices, stood in complete contradiction to permitting speculators to travel around buying and selling grain.

A capitalist approach to the famine would mean that, as usual, the well-off would eat and the poor would starve. The Bolsheviks needed to stop any trade in grain because that would destroy all attempts to ration grain, reserving grain only for those who could pay for it with money or goods.

Kulczycki, *Hołodomor*, 180 — This is a phony citation. There is nothing on this page about any "predisposition to personal politics," whatever that might mean, on Stalin's part. Stalin is not even mentioned on this page, or on the pages before and after it, 179 or 181.

Incidentally, this is a Polish translation of a Ukrainian-language book. What is the point of using it as a secondary source? It is very hard to find. Snyder cites Ukrainian-language works elsewhere, so why not here? Moreover, how could it contain any information about Stalin's "predispositions" that isn't available elsewhere? It is absurd to do what Snyder does — to write about Soviet history from Polish, Ukrainian, German, and English books and articles while failing to use Russian works.

From this and other indications in *Bloodlands* it appears that Snyder can read Polish well enough. Perhaps he reads Ukrainian too. Perhaps Snyder cannot read Russian, at least not well — or why wouldn't he use Russian primary and secondary sources for Soviet history, instead of Polish and even Ukrainian translations? Or perhaps Snyder has nationalist Polish and Ukrainian historians helping him, but not Russian scholars?

Kuśnierz, *Ukraina*, 152, is another phony citation. There is nothing about Stalin's supposed "predisposition to personalized politics" here. In fact Stalin's name does not occur on p. 152 of Kuśnierz's book. Stalin is briefly mentioned on page 148 (a report was sent to Stalin), and not again until page 174.

Did Molotov and Kaganovich Explain Starvation as "Laziness"?

Snyder claims that in July 1932 Molotov and Kaganovich

> told Ukrainian comrades that talk of starvation was just an excuse for laziness on the part of peasants who did not wish to work and activists who did not wish to discipline them and requisition grain.[40] (37)

His evidence (n. 40 p. 465): "… On talk of starvation as an excuse for laziness, see Šapoval, "Lügen," 136."

This is another phony citation. **Šapoval**, "Lügen" says nothing of the kind anywhere in this article, let alone on this specific page. The only statement even close is this:

> Im Kreml war man davon überzeugt, daß der Getreidebeschaffungsplan realistisch sei und daß die Führer der Ukraine sich mit ihren Bitten lediglich das Leben erleichtern wollen.

Translated:

> In the Kremlin they were convinced that the plan for grain collection was realistic and the leaders of the Ukraine just wanted to make their lives easier by their requests.

Shapoval's note to *this* passage is not a reference to any evidence. Rather it is to yet another secondary source: an entire article by Shapoval himself: "III Konferentsia KP(b)U: Prolog tragedii goloda," in a hard-to-find collection of articles coedited by Shapoval and Vasil'ev in Kiev in 2001. I obtained the book (written partly in Russian and partly in Ukrainian) and have studied the article. Evidently Snyder did not. Had he done so he would have — or, at any rate, should have — footnoted it instead of "Lügen…"

In any case, nothing in this article either corresponds to Snyder's claim of "talk of starvation as an excuse for laziness." As he has done many times in this book Snyder has falsely "documented" this fact-claim too with citations which do not, in fact, document it.

Were "Women Routinely Raped, Robbed of Food"?

Snyder asserts:

> Women who lived alone were routinely raped at night under the pretext of grain confiscations—and their food was indeed taken from them after their bodies had been violated. This was the triumph of Stalin's law and Stalin's state.[48] (39-40)

Source: (n. 48 p. 465): " ... On the party activists' abuses, see Kuśnierz, *Ukraina*, 144-145, 118-119; and Kuromiya, *Freedom and Terror*, 170-171."

Kuśnierz, 144-145: the relevant sentences are as follows:

> Dochodziło też do gwałtów na kobietach.
> Członkowie komisji ds. Chlebozagotowok we wsi
> Wesianyki (rejon koziatyński) po libacji
> alkoholowej w domu chłopa zgwałcili po kolei jego
> córkę, a później jeden z nich przez pół godziny
> trzymał nagą dziewczynę na mrozie.

Translated:

> There were also examples of rapes of women.
> Members of the Committee on grain collection in
> Wesianyki village (koziatyński *rayon*) after alcohol-
> ic libations in a peasant's house in turn raped his
> daughter, and later one of them for about half an
> hour held the naked girl in the cold.

Kuśnierz mentions this example at page 145. This was a crime, and Kusierz cites an archival document. It would be useful to know what kind of document this is. It might be a record of a Party report or even of a prosecution of the offender.

Rape — which is undoubtedly among the most deplorable forms of victimization — occurs in a variety of settings and conditions and is not unique to those discussed in the present narrative. No doubt that the alleged intoxication of male authorities might exacerbate these conditions as well. As such, the question of whether this crime was punished is an important one. Source criticism is a fundamental part of the historical method, but Kuśnierz makes no attempt to describe, much less to analyze, this archival source.

On page 117-118 (not 118-119) Kuśnierz writes:

> Podczas chlebozagotowok w 1932 r. we wsi Surśko-
> Mychajliwka w obwodzie niepropietrowskim
> sekretarz ośrodka komsomolskiego Kotenko
> gwałcił kobiety oraz brał udział w biciu chłopów.

Translated:

> During grain collection in 1932 in the village of
> Surśko- Mychajliwka, Dnepropetrovsk district, the
> Komsomol secretary Kotenko raped women and
> took part in the beating of peasants.

Kuśnierz's source is an article in Ukrainian by V.I. Prilutskii, "Molod' u suspil'no-politychnomu zhitti USRR (1928-1933 rr)" — "Youth' in the socio-political life of the USSR (1928-1933) — in the "Ukrainian Historical Journal" (*Український Историчний Журнал*) for 2002. The source cited by Prilutskii is a report by the Odessa district committee of the Komsomol to Andreev, head of the Ukrainian Komsomol.

The citation is as follows:

> Так, в с. Сурсько-Михайлівському
> Солонянського р-ну Дніпропетровської обл.
> секретар комсомольського осередку Котенко
> брав участь у гвалтуванні дівчат, побитті селян,
> за що був засуджений "аж" на 3 роки. (p. 73)

Translated:

> Thus, in the village of Surskaya-Mikhailovskoye,
> Solonyans'kyy raion, Dniproretrovsk oblast', secre-
> tary of the Komsomol cell Kotenko participated in
> raping women, and beating peasants, for which he
> was sentenced to "up to" 3 years.

The Odessa district party committee was reporting *a crime committed by a Komsomol member for which the guilty man was tried, convicted, and sentenced to "up to" three years.* Neither Kuśnierz nor Snyder mentions this fact. (It would be important to have the document from which Prilutskii is quoting, evidently a trial transcript or sentence, but he does not provide it.)

Conclusion: There is no evidence that rape was "routine," as Snyder claims. Moreover, neither of these examples — the only two examples given in the works he cites — concern "women living alone," the "pretext of grain confiscations," or "food taken from them after" the rape, etc.

"Stalin"s New Malice"

Snyder:

> The next day Stalin approached the problem of the
> famine with a new degree of malice. ... Two politbu-
> ro telegrams sent out on 8 November 1932 reflect-
> ed the mood: individual and collective farmers in
> Soviet Ukraine who failed to meet requisition tar-
> gets were to be denied access to products from the
> rest of the economy. A special troika was created in
> Ukraine to hasten the sentencing and execution of
> party activists and peasants who, supposedly, were
> responsible for sabotage. Some 1,623 kolkhoz offi-
> cials were arrested that month. Deportations within
> Ukraine were resumed: 30,400 more people were
> gone by the end of the year. The activists told the
> peasants: "Open up, or we'll knock down the door.
> We'll take what you have, and you'll die in a
> camp."[51] (40)

Sources (n. 51 p. 465):

> * Quotation: Kovalenko, *Holod*, 44.
>
> * The two politburo telegrams: Marochko, *Holodomor*, 152;
> and Davies, *Years*, 174.
>
> * The 1,623 arrested kolkhoz officials: Davies, *Years*, 174.
>
> * For 30,400 resumed deportations, Kuśnierz, *Ukraina*, 59.

Kovalenko, *Holod*, 44: The quotation is actually on p. 45. It is the
recollection of a child of a kulak family; a 1927 photo of the family
is also on p. 45. The original:

> Через певний час бригада появлалась біля
> нашої хати. Рвали двері, тарабанили в шибки
> так, що ось-ось повилітають. Я й досі не забуду
> погроз: «Відчини, бо виб'ємо двері. Заберемо — і
> зогинєш в тюрмі.»

Translated:

> After a certain time the team appeared near our
> house. They tore down the door, and drummed on

the windowpanes so that they were about to shat-
ter. I still have not forgotten their threat: "Open up
or we'll knock down the door. We will take away
[what we want] — and you will die in jail. "

Snyder claims that "the activists told the peasants" in a general
sense. But this is false: the account in question is a single incident.

Moreover, "the activists" had good reason to threaten this peasant.
In another part of this same account not quoted by Snyder the author describes how his family did in fact hide wheat, potatoes, and
other beets in two holes, in case one was found. The authorities
had the obligation to collect any food over and above a minimal
amount for the peasant family's own survival, in order to distribute it to others who were starving to death. In fact the peasants
were obliged to do this, hence the threat of prison.

Petro Danilovich Gumeniuk, the person whose account this is, born
in 1923, would have been 8 or 9 at this time (no year is given). He
went on to become a doctor of economics and professor at the
Ternopil' Institute of Finance and Economics. His membership in a
prosperous peasant family did not prevent him from having a fine
career in the USSR. And his family did not starve.

Davies, *Years* 174 states:

> On November 8, Stalin and Molotov insisted in a
> telegram to Kosior that 'from today the dispatch of
> goods for the villages of all regions of Ukraine shall
> cease until kolkhozy and individual peasants begin
> honestly and conscientiously to fulfill their duty to
> the working class and the Red Army for the delivery
> of grain.'

Davies indeed does report on the special commission of three, or
"troika," "to simplify further the procedure for confirming death
sentences in Ukraine." This is another of the few accurate claims
Snyder makes in this book (another is Stalin's remark about
"whining" kolkhozniks, above).

The 1,623 kolkhoz officials, plus others arrested for "counterrevolutionary offenses," are also mentioned in a document of December 9. Davies, but not Snyder, informs us that "over 2,000 of

those arrested were allegedly former supporters of Petlyura or Makhno" — that is, former anti-Soviet rebels.

It appears that none of these documents have been published in any of the great collections of documents concerning the famine. Snyder has certainly not seen them.

Marochko, *Holodomor,* 152: First telegram. Marochko says that this is from Stalin to Khataevich:

> Відповідаючи на його "шифровку про завезення товарів на Україну," Сталін підкреслив, що ЦК ВКП(б) обговорює питання про "заборону" завезення товарів для українського села на термін, поки Україна не розпочне чесно та акуратно виконувати зменшений план хлібозаготівель"

Translated:

> Responding to his "coded message about the delivery of goods to Ukraine," Stalin said that the CPSU (b) was discussing the issue of "banning" delivery of goods to the Ukrainian village until the Ukraine frankly and accurately fulfills the reduced grain procurement plan."

It would be good to have the text of the telegram, but Marochko does not give it. Even his "quotations" from it are in Ukrainian, not Russian.

Second telegram. Marochko says this is from Molotov and Stalin to the Central Committee of the Communist Party of the Ukraine:

> Повідомлено, що з 8 листопада "призупиняється відвантаження товарів для сіл всіх областей України," допоки колгоспи та "індивідуальні селяни" не розпочнуть "чесно і добросовісно виконувати свій обов'язок перед робітничим класом і Червоною Армією" в справі хлібозаготівель.

Translated:

> It is reported that on November 8 "shipment is sus-
> pended of goods to villages in all regions of
> Ukraine" as long as kolkhozes and "individual farm-
> ers" do not start to "honestly and faithfully perform
> their duty towards the working class and the Red
> Army" in the case of grain procurement.

Marochko does not identify the actual text of this telegram either.
Both these telegrams would certainly have been in Russian.

"On the 30,400 resumed deportations, see **Kuśnierz,** *Ukraina*, 59."
Here is the relevant text in Kuśnierz's book:

> Rozkułaczanie i deportacje miały również miejsce
> w okresie późniejszym. 29 marca 1932 r. Biuro
> Polityczne Komitetu Centralnego KP(b)U w tajnym
> postanowieniu uchwaliło wywózkę 5 tysięcy rodzin
> kułackich z Polesia na lewy brzeg Dniepru, w celu
> wykorzystania ich do pracy w kamieniołomach. Dla
> zesłanych utworzono tam stałe osiedla kulackie. [153]
> W okresie pomiędzy 28 listopada a 25 grudnia
> 1932 r.wysłano na północ ZSRR ponad 30 400 osób.
> [154]

Translated:

> Dekulakization and deportation also took place at a
> later date. On 29 March 1932 the Political Bureau of
> the Central Committee of the KP(b)U by secret de-
> portation order approved the deportation of 5,000
> kulak families from Polesie to the left bank of the
> Dnieper, in order to use them to work in the quar-
> ries. For the exiles there have been established
> permanent kulak settlements there. In the period
> between 28 November and 25 December 1932 r.
> more than 30,400 persons were exiled to the north
> of the USSR.[154]

> Kuśnierz's footnotes are to archival documents
> which we cannot obtain and check. However, the
> authoritative 2005 volume *Stalinskie deportatsii*

1928-1953. Dokumenty[10] records no such deportations during any period of 1932, much less the last
6 months. (790)

Conclusion: Marochko does not quote the original texts of Stalin's two telegrams as Snyder's reference suggests. Therefore Snyder has not seen the texts either.

According to what Marochko does cite, it appears that if collective farms and individual farmers were to "begin honestly and conscientiously to fulfill their duty," they would not be denied "products from the rest of the economy." The telegram quoted by Davies and by Marochko does not state that a farm or peasant had to completely fulfill their grain delivery quota, only that they had to make an "honest and conscientious" attempt.

It is difficult to find any fault with this regulation, much less to discern in it any "degree of malice" at all. If farms and peasants had money to buy, or agricultural produce to exchange for, manufactured products then they were obligated to do their best to "pay their taxes" — for that's what grain deliveries were.

Nothing in the paragraph supports Snyder's hypothesis of a "deliberate famine."

Did Stalin Call the Famine a "Fairy Tale"?

Snyder says that at the end of 1932 Stalin came to believe that the famine was "a "fairy tale", "a slanderous rumor spread by enemies." (41)

His source (n. 52 p. 465): Šapoval, "Lügen," 159; and Davies, *Years*, 199.

Šapoval, "Lügen," 159: This page does not exist. Evidently Snyder means p. 139, where the same quotation is given as is given in **Davies**, *Years*, 199. The quotation is from *Pravda*, May 26, 1964.

Davies, but not Shapoval or Snyder, states:

It is not clear whether this statement comes from
the archives, from memoirs, or from hearsay.

---

[10] Moscow: MDF, Izd. "Materik," 2005.

Either Terekhov, the man who supposedly made this statement, claimed Stalin said this to him or Stalin really did say this to him. Or the whole matter is a fabrication. This is quite possible, as Khrushchev and his men were fabricating — deliberately falsifying and lying — a great deal about Stalin and the Stalin years. We already know, and Snyder has acknowledged, that Stalin knew there was a famine in the Ukraine and elsewhere. Therefore it seems unlikely that Stalin would have used the term "fairy-tale about hunger" ("takuiu skazku o golode").

According to the *Pravda* article R.Ia. Terekhov, the Khar'kov First Secretary, told this story orally, evidently in 1964. Russian famine scholar Viktor Kondrashin states that Stalin said or wrote these words to Terekhov on *February 22, 1933*.[11] However, according to a newpaper source "Terekhov R.A." was removed from the post of First Secretary of the Khar'kov Oblast' and city committees on January 29, 1933.[12] Viktor Danilov states that this exchange with Stalin took place "*at the end of 1932*" (в конце 1932 г.) and Terekhov was removed from office "by decree of the Central Committee of the VKP(b) of January 24, 1933" ("Postanovleniem TsK K VKP(b) ot 24 ianvaria 1933 g.") [13]

None of this tells us whether Stalin actually said these words to Terekhov or why. But it seems clear that either the story is untrue, a rumor — which would account for the disagreement about when it happened — or it was a minor flare-up on Stalin's part. Terekhov was moved from Party to government and production work, where he remained until his retirement in 1956.[14] Roman Ia.

---

[11] "Историк Виктор Кондрашин: 'Не Россия убивала Украину. Вождь - свой народ.'" *Известия* 22 октября 2008, http://izvestia.ru/news/341984

[12] Сайт Новостей. «Критика на тормозах." http://novostei.com/news/past/1/2461/3

[13] The January 24 document is referred to in a published source, so we may assume it is correct. See *Golod 1932-1933 rokiv na Ukraini: ochyma istorykiv, movoiu dokumentiv.* Ed. Ia. Pyrih Kyiv: Politvydav Ukrainy, 1990, No. 157 (*Голод 1932-1933 років на Україні: очима істориків, мовою документів.* Кер. кол. упоряд. р. Я. Пиріг. - К.: Політвидав України, 1990. № 157). At http://www.archives.gov.ua/Sections/Famine/Publicat/Fam-Pyrig-1933.php#nom-157

[14] In late January and early February 1933 he was removed from his posts as secretary and member of both the Orgburo and the Politburo, and First Secretary of the Khar'kov Oblast' Committee, of the CP(b)U. However, he moved to the position of Chairman of the Central Committee of the Union of Metal Workers, and 2nd Secretary of the Donetsk Oblast' Com-

Terekov attended the 22nd Party Congress in October 1961 during which Khrushchev his most ferocious — and utterly mendacious — attack on Stalin but apparently did not speak at the Congress.[15]

Perhaps Shapoval took this story from the 1974 Russian language edition (New York: Knopf) of Roi Medvedev's book *Let History Judge* (In Russian: *K sudu istorii)*, where it occurs on page 213. Medvedev's book is the source of many rumors about Soviet history that have been passed on as "fact."

As to the rest of the quotation, Snyder again "begs the question" by "assuming that which should be proven": namely, that collectivization caused the famine. Amazingly enough, though Snyder's whole thesis of "Soviet mass murder" is largely predicated upon this statement, he never tries to prove it or provides any evidence at all that it is so. As we have already shown, it cannot be proven, because it is false. Famines had occurred every 2-4 years in Russia and Ukraine for at least a millennium.

Nor does Snyder give any evidence at all for his claim that:

> Stalin had developed an interesting new theory:
> that resistance to socialism increases as its successes mount, because its foes resist with greater desperation as they contemplate their final defeat.
> Thus any problem in the Soviet Union could be defined as an example of enemy action, and enemy action could be defined as evidence of progress. (40-41)

---

mittee of the CP(b)U. Terekhov remained a candidate member of the CC VKP(b) until the 17th Party Congress in January 1934. He was not re-elected to this position, but was transferred to government work in the Commission of Soviet control attached to the SNK of the USSR. From 1939 to 1956 Terekhov was the Assistant Chief of Light Metal Working industry, and retired in 1956.

[15] R.Ia. Terekhov appears in a photograph taken at the XXII Party Congress in *Ogoniok* 29.X. 1961, p. 17. "Tertkhov Roman Iakovlevich" is listed as a voting delete to the Congress in the transcript of the Congress. See *XXII S"ezd Kommunisticheskoi Partii Sovetskogo Soiuza. 17-31 oktiabria 1961 goda. Stenograficheskii Otchiot.* Moscow: Gos. izd. politicheskoi literatury, 1962. T. 3, p. 533. (*XXII Съезд Коммунистической Партии Советского Союза. 17-31 октября 1961 года. Стенографический Отчёт.* М.: Гос. Изд. Политической Литературы, 1962. III, с. 533.

But even in this *Pravda* version Stalin does not refer to "enemies," as Snyder claims. Therefore this is pure fabrication on Snyder's part, unless it is an oblique reference to one of the accusations Khrushchev made against Stalin in his famous "Secret Speech" to the 20th Party Congress in February 1956. The present author has fully exposed Khrushchev's falsehoods in this speech in an earlier book.[16]

Did Stalin Believe that "Starvation Was Resistence"?

Snyder makes the following claim:

> Resistance to his policies in Soviet Ukraine, Stalin argued, was of a special sort, perhaps not visible to the imperceptive observer. Opposition was no longer open, for the enemies of socialism were now "quiet" and even "holy." The "kulaks of today," he said, were "gentle people, kind, almost saintly."

His sources (n. 53 p. 465):

> * Quotations: *Ukraina*, 124.

> * "See also" Vasiliev, "Tsina," 60; Kuromiya, *Stalin*, 110.

Here we have three citations — to Kuśnierz, Vasiliev, and Kuromiya. But in reality they all refer to the very same document! Moreover, it is a document that has been available in English for 60 years and can be easily found on the Internet today.

Kuśnierz, *Ukraina*, 124 quotes from the well-known speech of Stalin's of January 1, 1933. This speech was published in 1950 in volume 13 of Stalin's *Collected Works* and has been available in English, to say nothing of Russian, for more than 60 years. It is on the internet in Russian[17] and English.[18] The fact that Snyder quotes this document from a Polish-language book once again suggests either that Snyder does not read even the most basic texts in Rus-

---

[16] Furr, Khrushchev Lied.

[17] E.g. at http://grachev62.narod.ru/stalin/t13/t13_36.htm

[18] E.g. at http://www.marx2mao.com/Stalin/WC33.html

sian, or that he is not interested in helping his readers find the sources.

In this speech Stalin was ironic in calling the "kulaks of today" "gentle, kind, almost saintly." The context shows this:

> People look for the class enemy outside the collective farms; they look for persons with ferocious visages, with enormous teeth and thick necks, and with sawn-off shotguns in their hands. They look for kulaks like those depicted on our posters. But such kulaks have long ceased to exist on the surface. The present-day kulaks and kulak agents, the present-day anti-Soviet elements in the countryside are in the main "quiet," "smooth-spoken," almost "saintly" people. There is no need to look for them far from the collective farms; they are inside the collective farms, occupying posts as store-keepers, managers, accountants, secretaries, etc. They will never say, "Down with the collective farms!" They are "in favour" of collective farms. But inside the collective farms they carry on sabotage and wrecking work that certainly does the collective farms no good. They will never say, "Down with grain procurements!" They are "in favour" of grain procurements. They "only" resort to demagogy and demand that the collective farm should reserve a fund for the needs of livestock-raising three times as large as that actually required; that the collective farm should set aside an insurance fund three times as large as that actually required; that the collective farm should provide from six to ten pounds of bread per working member per day for public catering, etc. Of course, after such "funds" have been formed and such grants for public catering made, after such rascally demagogy, the economic strength of the collective farms is bound to be undermined, and there is little left for grain procurements.

Vasiliev, "Tsina," 60: Vasiliev summarizes this same speech on pp. 59 — 61 — but in Ukrainian! It adds nothing by way of commentary.

Kuromiya, *Stalin*, 110: This is simply two quotations from Stalin's January 1933 report to the joint Plenum of the Central Committee and the Central Control Committee. This speech is the fuller version of the talk "Work in the Countryside" quoted above. It is identical to the first citation in this note.

Snyder's citation of a document in a Polish and a Ukrainian source of a document readily available in English as well as in the original Russian can have no purpose except to "impress" his readers with this show of "scholarship." Readers of *Bloodlands* will have no idea that he is doing this. They will think that Kuśnierz and Vasiliev actually have something to add. Nor is there any need here for the Kuromiya citation, when the primary source itself is available on the Internet.

"Starvation Was Resistance": Another Snyder Fabrication

There is no evidence whatever for the following statements made by Snyder here, who merely relies on the same footnote 53 as discussed above:

> People who appeared to be innocent were to be seen as guilty. A peasant slowly dying of hunger was, despite appearances, a saboteur working for the capitalist powers in their campaign to discredit the Soviet Union. Starvation was resistance, and resistance was a sign that the victory of socialism was just around the corner. These were not merely Stalin's musings in Moscow; this was the ideological line enforced by Molotov and Kaganovich as they traveled through regions of mass death in late 1932.[53] (41)

Snyder has simply invented all this. Few readers of *Bloodlands* will realize that it is a pure fabrication of Snyder's own — and that, no doubt, is why Snyder inserted it.

Snyder:

> Forced to interpret distended bellies as political
> opposition, they [Stalin's "comrades in the Soviet
> Ukraine"] produced the utterly tortured conclusion
> that the saboteurs hated socialism so much that
> they intentionally let their families die. Thus the
> wracked bodies of sons and daughters and fathers
> and mothers were nothing more than a façade be-
> hind which foes plotted the destruction of social-
> ism. (41)

Sources: (n. 54, p. 466): "On the family interpretation (Stanislaw
Kosior), see Davies, *Years*, 206."

Snyder's statement is false — a fabrication. Kosior said nothing
about "hatred of socialism" or any "tortured conclusions."

Davies, quoted below at the reference Snyder gives, accurately
summarizes Kosior's statement. We would add that Kosior gave
only two examples, and only the first was of a farmer who let his
children go hungry while keeping grain. Kosior does not give the
age of the farmer's children, whom he cast out. For all we know,
they could have been adults.

Davies, *Years*, 206:

> "And on February 9, Kosior circulated a report to
> the Ukrainian Politburo listing cases where, he
> claimed, 'malicious withholders of grain have
> brought their families to real hunger (the children
> swell up)', even though they possessed several
> tsentners of grain.[281]
>
> n. 281 — "TsDAGOU, 1/101/1282,2, published in
> *Golod 1932-1933* (1990) 375-6.

In Davies, *Years,* Bibliography, p. 526, the full title of this book is
given thus: "*Golod 1932-1933 rokiv na Ukraini: ochima istorikiv,
movoyu dokumentiv* (Kiev, 1990). The text in the original Ukrainian, from this source, is as follows:[19]

---

[19] Source: Pyrih ed., *Holod 1932-1933 rokiv*, 605. At
http://www.archives.gov.ua/Sections/Famine/Publicat/Fam-Pyrig.php

№ 161

ДОВІДКА ІНФОРМАЦІЙНОГО СЕКТОРА
ОРГІНСТРУКТОРСЬКОГО ВІДДІЛУ ЦК КП(б)У
ПРО ВИПАДКИ УДАВАНОГО ГОЛОДУВАННЯ З
МЕТОЮ НЕЗДАЧІ ХЛІБА
У ХАРКІВСЬКІЙ ОБЛАСТІ*

9 лютого 1933 р.

Некоторые РПК сообщают, что в борьбе против
хлебозаготовок злостные несдатчики хлеба
доводят свою семью до действительного голода
(дети пухнут).

Бригадировский РПК (Харьковская область)
пишет 1 февраля: в Васильевском сельсовете,
контрактант III группы Яковец Влас, имея 4,45
га посева, контрактации 27,8 ц не сдал ни
одного килограмма хлеба, но покинул детей,
которые сейчас нищенствуют.

Бригада по хлебозаготовкам обнаружила у него
закопанный хлеб в ямах: 5 ц, 2,35 ц, 5,23 ц и 6,42
ц.

Подобное же сообщает и Якимовский РПК.
Колхозник Клименко из артели им. Молотова
кричал: "Я голодный и мои дети пухнут." После
проверки у него выявлено 2,5 ц хлеба, хотя на
трудодни он получил только 90 кг.

Заведующий информационным сектором
Оргинструкторского отдела ЦК КП(б)У

Стасюк

ПА ІІП при ЦК Компартії України. Ф. 1. Оп. 101.
Спр. 1282. Арк. 2.

> * Ця довідка за дорученням С. В. Косіора була направлена для ознайомлення всім членам та кандидатам у члени Політбюро ЦК КП(б)У.[20]
>
> (РПК = Районные общества потребительской кооперации, или РайПотребКооперация.)

Translated:

> Some of the RPK reported that in the fight against grain procurements malicious withholders of grain bring their families to real hunger (the children swell up).
>
> Brigadirovsky RPK (Khar'kov region) writes on February 1: in the Vasil'evskii village hall, the contractor of group III Yakovets Vlas, with 4.45 hectares of crops, contracting 27.8 tsentners, did not give a single pound of bread, but cast his children out, and they now live by begging.
>
> The team for grain procurement found at his place, buried in pits: 5 ts[entners], 2.35 ts[entners], 5.23 ts[entners] and 6.42 ts[entners].
>
> The Iakimovski RPK gives a similar report. Collective farmer Klimenko of the Molotov artel' shouted: "I'm hungry and my children are swelling up. After verification 2.5 tsentners of grain were found at his place, although he had received only 90 kg. in workday pay.
>
> (RPK = Regional Society of Consumer Cooperatives)

Conclusion: Snyder's fabrications here are as follows:

* There is no evidence that Stalin was "forced to interpret distended bellies as political opposition."

* There is nothing here about "intentionally let[ting] their families die."

---

[20] At http://www.archives.gov.ua/Sections/Famine/Publicat/Fam-Pyrig-1933.php#nom-161

* There is nothing about "the wracked bodies of sons and daughters and fathers and mothers were nothing more than a façade behind which foes plotted the destruction of socialism."

Yet these are the statements for which Snyder cites the Davies passage as evidence. Davies cites Kosior, whose actual statement we have reproduced above. It could hardly be clearer that Snyder has invented all this.

Should Stalin Have Predicted The Future?

Snyder:

> Yet Stalin might have saved millions of lives without drawing any outside attention to the Soviet Union. He could have suspended food exports for a few months, released grain reserves (three million tons), or just given peasants access to local grain storage areas. Such simple measure, pursued **as late as November 1932**, could have kept the death toll to the hundreds of thousands rather than the millions. Stalin pursued none of them.[55] (41-2; emphasis added)

His sources (n. 55 p. 466): "For similar judgments, see, for example"

> * Jahn, *Holodomor*, 25;
> * Davies, Tauger, and Wheatcroft, "Grain Stocks," 657;
> * Kulczycki, *Hołodomor*, 237;
> * Graziosi, "New Interpretation," 12.

Jahn, *Holodomor*, 25 cites no evidence for any of the claims on this page. One might object that Snyder simply claims he makes "similar judgments." But "judgments" are of no validity without evidence. Like Snyder himself, Jahn has none. Jahn's article is in the ideologically anticommunist journal *Osteuropa*; it is a statement of his anticommunist beliefs, not a scholarly study of the famine or of anything else.

Jahn also claims that there was no natural famine caused by environmental reasons, or even from insufficient food production, but solely from deliberate "Nahrungsentzugs" — "withdrawal of foodstuffs." Jahn even doubts whether the government was aware of the starvation! None of the specialists on the famine like Davies and Wheatcroft or Tauger conclude anything like this.

Davies, Tauger, and Wheatcroft, "Grain Stocks," 657: In Snyder's list of references the only specialists on the famine with any claim to objectivity are Davies, Tauger, and Wheatcroft.[21] Here is what they have to say:

> We therefore conclude:
>
> 1. All planners' stocks — the two secret grain reserves, Nepfond and Mobfond or Gosfond, together with "transitional stocks" held by grain organizations — amounted on 1 July 1933 to less than 2 million tons (1.997 million tons, according to the highest official figure). Persistent efforts of Stalin and the Politburo to establish firm and inviolable grain reserves (in addition to "transitional stocks") amounting to 2 or 3 million tons or more were almost completely unsuccessful. In both January - June 1932 and January - June 1933 the Politburo had to allow "untouchable" grain stocks set aside at the beginning of each year to be used to meet food and fodder crises. **On 1 July 1933 the total amount of grain set aside in reserve grain stocks (fondy) amounted not to 4.53 million tons as Conquest claimed but to only 1.141 million.** It is not surprising that after several years during which the Politburo had failed to establish inviolable grain stocks, Kuibyshev in early 1933 recommended a "flexible approach" to Nepfond and Mobfond, denied that they were separate reserves and even claimed that the flexible use of the two fondy had enabled uninterrupted grain supply in spring and summer 1932. (Emphasis added)

---

[21] Kul'chyts'kiy, also a famine specialist, is so politically biased that he tailors his results to "fit" the myth of the "Holodmor." This makes his research worthless See, for example, his four-part essay in English "What Is The Crux of the Ukraine-Russia Dispute?" at http://www.day.kiev/ua/263850 (accessed 02.24.2014)

In the quotation above Snyder claims, without any reference, that the USSR held three million tons of grain in reserve "as late as November 1932."

But here Davies and Wheatcroft claim that (a) the grain reserves were likely less than two million tons; (b) that in the first half of 1932 and again in the first half of 1933 "the Politburo had to allow 'untouchable' grain stocks set aside at the beginning of each year to be used to meet food and fodder crises." That is, *the Politburo did, in fact, release grain reserves to alleviate the famine.*

Davies and Wheatcroft continue:

> 2. We do not know the amount of grain which was held by grain-consuming organizations, notably the Red Army, but we suspect that these "consumers' stocks" would not change the picture substantially.
>
> 3. These findings do not, of course, free Stalin from responsibility for the famine. It is difficult, perhaps impossible, to assess the extent to which it would have been possible for Stalin to use part of the grain stocks available in spring 1933 to feed starving peasants. The state was a monopoly supplier of grain to urban areas and the army; if the reserves of this monopoly supply system — which amounted to four-six weeks' supply — were to have been drained, mass starvation, epidemics and unrest in the towns could have resulted. Nevertheless, it seems certain that, if Stalin had risked lower levels of these reserves in spring and summer 1933, hundreds of thousands — perhaps millions — of lives could have been saved. In the slightly longer term, if he had been open about the famine, some international help would certainly have alleviated the disaster. And if he had been more far-sighted, the agricultural crisis of 1932-1933 could have been mitigated and perhaps even avoided altogether. **But Stalin was not hoarding immense grain reserves in these years. On the contrary, he had failed to**

reach the levels which he had been imperatively demanding since 1929. (Emphasis added.)

Snyder claimed that Stalin "could have kept the death toll to the hundreds of thousands rather than the millions." Davies, Tauger, and Wheatcroft surmise that "hundreds of thousands, — perhaps millions — of lives could have been saved" — but only by risking "mass starvation, epidemics and unrest in the towns."

Mark Tauger, as we have seen, goes further:

> The severity and geographical extent of the famine, the sharp decline in exports in 1932-1933, seed requirements, and the chaos in the Soviet Union in these years, all lead to the conclusion that **even a complete cessation of exports would not have been enough to prevent famine.** (Emphasis added, GF)

However, both Snyder and Davies et al. tacitly assume that the Soviet leadership — "Stalin" — could have known in advance that the famine would end in 1933 with a good harvest. Of course neither the Soviet leadership nor anyone could possibly know this. For all they or anyone knew, the famine would continue unabated during 1933. Since they could not know when the famine would end the Soviet state retained grain stocks.

Moreover, no government in the world would have deprived its army of foodstuffs. That was especially the case with the USSR, which was surrounded by hostile states. Nor would any government have deprived the cities of food reserves and risked "mass starvation, epidemics and unrest." A central aspect of the plan to end the cycle of starvation, collectivization, depended upon production of labor-saving farm machinery such as tractors and harvesters. These were produced in the cities.

The USSR had received large-scale international aid during the Volga famine of 1921-22 that followed the incredible destructiveness of the First World War and Civil War, the typhus epidemic, and very poor weather conditions. But there is no reason to think that significant international aid would have been forthcoming in the same way in 1933, the depths of the Great Depression. Davies, Tauger and Wheatcroft do not give any evidence for this assertion.

Kulczycki, *Hołodomor,* 237:

> W 1932 roku na rynki zagraniczne wysłano 107,9 miliona pudów zboża. W bilansie ziarna spożywczego i paszowego, sporządzonym przez Ukrzernocentr, na wyżywienie jednej osoby na wsi przewidziano 16 pudów rocznie. Oznacza to, że dzięki zbożu wywiezionemu w 1932 roku mozna było uratować od śmierci wszystkich zmarłych z głodu w Związku Radzieckim w 1933 roku.

Translated:

> In 1932 there were sent to foreign markets 107.9 million poods of grain. According to the balance of food and feed grains, prepared by Ukrzernocentr [Ukraine Grain Center], to feed one person in the village were required 16 poods per year. This means that the grain exported in 1932 could have saved from death all who died of starvation in the Soviet Union in 1933.

Here Kul'chyts'kyy too absurdly suggests that if only Stalin had known a year in advance that there would be a great famine in 1933, he ought not to have exported any grain in 1932!

Graziosi, "New Interpretation" has no "page 12" On p. 108, the twelfth page in the article, we do read "similar judgments," in that Graziosi asserts that the famine was deliberate. But, like Snyder, Graziosi fails to cite any evidence that this was the case. The simple assertion of Graziosi, or of anyone, is not evidence.

We discuss Snyder's "Seven Points of Proof," pages 42-46, in Chapter One of this book.

"Begging the Question" Again: Assertions Without Evidence

Snyder:

> This final collection was murder, even if those who executed it very often believed that they were doing the right thing. As one activist remembered, that spring he "saw people dying from hunger. I saw women and children with distended bellies, turning blue, still breathing but with vacant, lifeless eyes." Yet he "saw all this and did not go out of my mind or commit suicide." He had faith: "As before, I believed because I wanted to believe." Other activists, no doubt, were less faithful and more fearful. Every level of the Ukrainian party had been purged in the previous year; in January 1933, Stalin sent in his own men to control its heights. Those communists who no longer expressed their faith formed a "wall of silence" that doomed those it surrounded. They had learned that to resist was to be purged, and to be purged was to share the fate of those whose deaths they were now bringing about.[67] (46)

Sources (n. 67 page 466):

> * "For the recollections of the activist," Conquest, *Harvest*, 233.
>
> * "For quotation and details on the importance of purges," Šapoval, "Lügen," 133.
>
> * "On purges of the heights," Davies, *Years*, 138.

Snyder cites no evidence at all that "this final collection was murder." Rather, this is yet another example of "begging the question": he is supposed to *prove* "murder," not merely assert it.

The "activist" quoted by **Conquest** is Lev Kopelev, from his memoir published in 1980. The quotation only documents that people starved, a fact that no one denies. Snyder quotes this passage later in the book as well. In his old age Kopelev came to believe that the famine was "man-made" but he had no such doubts at the time.

In Chapter One of the present book we have quoted Robert Conquest's repudiation of his former position, expressed in his book *The Harvest of Sorrow* (1986) that the famine was "man-made." Snyder is aware of this too because he cites, and therefore has read, Davies and Wheatcroft, where Conquest's repudiation is published. Therefore, Snyder is simply concealing this information from his readers.

Shapoval, "Lügen," has no such quotation on p. 133. He does mention arrests of heads of kolkhozes for sabotaging grain collections, but only up to January 1, 1932 — well before the famine. He states that 80% of raion secretaries were removed in the first half of 1932, but says nothing about any relation to the famine.

But even these statements do not refer to any primary source evidence. Instead Shapoval refers us to a book of his own that is hard to find in the US. Shapoval refers to "page 160" of this book. This is a page of an article of his own, Shapoval's, in Ukrainian. The very same text — the entire article — is also published in Russian, immediately following the Ukrainian text. Ukrainian p. 160 corresponds to Russian pp. 173-174.

And this page does contain interesting information. For instance, *it reveals that the 1932 plan for grain collection from the Ukraine was officially reduced three times*. Even then it had been less than half-fulfilled by November 1, 1932.

> Делегаты конференции приняли резолюцию, которую 9 июля 1932 года утвердил пленум ЦК КП(б)У и которой «к безусловному исполнению» прини мался установленный для Украины план хлебозаготовок—356 млн.пудов по крестьянскому сектору. **Этот план впоследствии трижды сокращался**, а к 1 ноября 1932 года от крестьянского сектора Украины поступило лишь 136 млн.пудов хлеба.[22]

[22] IUrii Shapoval, "'Povelitel'naia neobkhodimost': god 1932-y." *Den'* November 23, 2002. At http://www.day.kiev.ua/ru/article/panorama-dnya/povelitelnaya-neobhodimost-god-1932-y This is a Ukrainian newspaper of nationalist tendency.

Translated:

> Delegates to the conference passed a resolution
> which was confirmed by the Plenum of the CC of the
> CP(b)U on July 9 1932 and by which "for uncondi-
> tional fulfillment" the established grain collection
> plan for the Ukraine was accepted — 356 million
> poods from the peasant sector. **This plan was
> thereafter reduced in size three times**, and by
> November 1 1932 only 136 million poods of grain
> had been obtained from the peasant sector of the
> Ukraine. (Emphasis added)

Shapoval's source for this statement is a 48-page pamphlet published in 1989 by Kul'chyts'kyy .[23] But it isn't likely that Shapoval
invented it, since it does not tend to support his anticommunist
and "Holodomor" bias. Why would Stalin et al. reduce the plan for
grain collection from the Ukraine if their aim was to starve Ukrainians?

In a later work Kul'chyts'kyy explains that *in 1989 he did not understand that the famine was a "Holodomor"!*[24] In 1990 the fabrica-
tion-myth of the "Holodomor" had not yet become obligatory, the
"Ukrainian Nationalist party line."

"To Be Purged = Death"?

Shapoval has nothing about the "purged," i.e. demoted officials
"sharing the fate of those whose deaths they were now bringing
about" — i.e., suffering execution. Snyder apparently invented this,
as he invented the "five million murdered." Even Shapoval does
not claim that these sources have any bearing at all on Snyder's
point: the question of whether the famine was "deliberate."

---

[23] Kul'chyts'kyy S.V. *1933. Tragedia holodu*. Kyiv: T-vo "Znania" URSR, 1989. (Кульчицький
С. В. *1933: трагедія голоду*. — К. Т-во «Знання» УРСР, 1989). Cited at
http://www.history.org.ua/?litera&id=1023

[24] "And I did not yet understand the special nature of the Ukrainian famine." ("Та
специфіки українського голоду я ще не розумів.") Кульчицький С. " Голодомор 1932
— 1933 рр. в україні як геноцид." (Kul'chyts'kyy S. "Holodomor 1932-1933 rr. v Ukraini
iak henotsyd.") In *Проблеми історії України: факти, судження, пошуки*. - Київ: Інститут
історії України НАН України, 2005. - №14. - с. 225-300. Quotation at p.252.

Davies, *Years*, 138 has nothing about any "purges of the heights" or of anything else in Snyder's paragraph. Davies discusses January 1933 in the pages beginning at p. 197 ff. There is nothing about "the heights" here either.

"Collective Farming Did Not Work"

Snyder makes the following claim, which can only be called bizarre:

> Ukrainians who chose not to resist the collective farms believed that they had at least escaped deportation. But now they could be deported because **collective farming did not work**. Some fifteen thousand peasants were deported from Soviet Ukraine between February and April 1933. Just east and south of Soviet Ukraine, in parts of the Russian republic of the Soviet Union inhabited by Ukrainians, some sixty thousand people were deported for failing to make grain quotas. In 1933 some 142,000 more Soviet citizens were sent to the Gulag, most of them either hungry or sick with typhus, many of them from Soviet Ukraine.[72] (47-8; emphasis added GF)

Sources: (n. 72 p. 466):

> * "On the fifteen thousand people deported," Davies, *Years*, 210.

> * "On the sixty thousand people deported from Kuban," Martin, "Ethnic Cleansing," 846.

Snyder's claim that "collective farming did not work" is ideologically-motivated nonsense. There had been famines for a thousand years in Russia and in the Ukraine, long before collective farming. Like it or not — and Snyder obviously doesn't — collective farming put an end to the age-old cycle of famines. The collective farms "worked" until the end of the USSR when they were forcibly dissolved.

Evidently Snyder is trying to please today's Ukrainian nationalists, who favor the kulaks and despise the poor peasants, many of whom helped the collectivization movement. For a great many poor peasants did help collectivization and also helped grain procurement. The late James E. Mace, a hero to Ukrainian Nationalists and a staunch anticommunist, reluctantly acknowledged the important role of the Committees of Poor Peasants, or "Komitety nezamozhnykh selian" in the collectivization movement in the Ukraine.[25]

Davies, *Years*, 211, relates that 15,000 *households*, not "peasants," were exiled "for refusing to collect in the seed, and to sow, and for much vaguer reasons." Davies refers briefly to archival materials. These persons were clearly not starving, since they had grain, including seed grain.

Deportations and Martin's Error

Martin, "Ethnic Cleansing," 846 states:

> ... ultimately, a total of approximately 60,000 Kuban Cossacks were deported for failing to meet their grain requisitions.[199]

The 2005 volume *Stalinskie Deportatsii* gives the number as 45,000 (790). However Martin's whole article is of questionable reliability since it contains at least one serious error. On this same page 846 Martin states:

> The December 14 Politburo decree ordered the deportation of the entire Kuban Cossack town of Poltava for "the sabotage of grain delivery."

Martin is in error. Poltava is a city in the Ukraine. Its inhabitants were *not* deported. Martin has confused this town with *stanitsa Poltavskaia*, or just plain Poltavskaia, a Kuban Cossack village in the Krasnodar region of Russia. All of its 9,000 inhabitants were deported in December, 1932 for sabotage of grain collection, and the town was resettled by demobilized Red Army men and renamed "Krasnoarmeiskaia" (= "Red Army village").

---

[25] James E. Mace. "The *Komitety Nezamozhnykh Selian* and the Structure of Soviet Rule in the Ukrainian Countryside, 1920-1933." *Soviet Studies* 35 (4) October 1983, 487-503.

The Bolsheviks published a booklet explaining why its inhabitants had been deported.[26] This pamphlet is cited in Roi Medvedev's book *Let History Judge*. Today the whole text of that pamphlet is available to anyone on the Internet.[27] There's no excuse for this elementary error by Martin.

The deportations in question were from the Kuban. Moreover, Martin explicitly states these were Kuban Cossacks, not Ukrainians. Cossacks do not consider themselves either Ukrainians or Russians, though Kuban Cossacks usually speak Ukrainian.

Snyder evidently wants us to believe that this was somehow an anti-Ukrainian action, and so does not say "the Kuban," but instead uses the clumsy circumlocution "parts of the Russian Republic of the Soviet Union inhabited by Ukrainians." This is another passage suggesting that Snyder is trying to conform to the historical falsehoods of Ukrainian nationalists.

According to the authoritative book *Stalinskie deportatsii 1928-1953* (2005) published by the strongly anticommunist and anti-Stalin "Memorial Society," during 1932 313,000 kulaks and others were deported "from various areas" to Western Siberia, Kazakhstan, the Urals, "and elsewhere."

Snyder gives no evidence for the following statement:

> In 1933 some 142,000 more Soviet citizens were
> sent to the Gulag, most of them either hungry or
> sick with typhus, many of them from Soviet
> Ukraine.

Neither Davies nor Martin say anything about any 1933 sending of "Soviet citizens to the Gulag," as Snyder claims in the passage under discussion, much less that they were "hungry, or sick with typhus" or that "many" were "from Soviet Ukraine."

Snyder:

---

[26] Radin, Shaumian. *Za chto zhiteli stanitsy Poltavskoi vysyliaiutsia s Kubani v severnye kraia.* Rostov-na-Donu, 1932.

[27] At http://elan-kazak.ru/sites/default/files/IMAGES/ARHIV/Krasnoe/radin-shaumyan-stanica_poltavskaya.pdf   In the 1970s I requested this book from the Lenin Library in Moscow through the Inter-Library Loan office at my university (then a college). The Lenin Library refused my request though I was able to obtain other books from Soviet libraries.

In the camps they tried to find enough to eat. Since the Gulag had a policy of feeding the strong and depriving the weak, and these deportees were already weak from hunger, this was desperately difficult. When hungry prisoners poisoned themselves by eating wild plants and garbage, camp officials punished them for shirking. At least 67,297 people died of hunger and related illnesses in the camps and 241,355 perished in the special settlements in 1933, many of them natives of Soviet Ukraine. Untold thousands more died on the long journey from Ukraine to Kazakhstan or the far north. Their corpses were removed from the trains and buried on the spot, their names and their numbers unrecorded.[73] (48)

Sources (n. 73 p. 467):

* "On the 67,297 people who died in the camps," Khlevniuk, *Gulag*, 62, 77.

* "On the 241,355 people who died in the special settlements," Viola, *Unknown Gulag*, 241.

Oleg V. **Khlevniuk**, *The History of the GULAG from Collectivization to the Great Terror* (Yale University Press, 2004), 77, does indeed cite this figure. Khlevniuk usefully gives the death rate for 1932 (4.8%) and for 1933 (15.2%). Assuming the difference is due to the famine, if 4.8% of the 440,008 prisoners in 1933 had died, that would be 21,121 people instead of 67,297, meaning that about 46,176 deaths in 1933 were above the rate of 1932 and thus largely or wholly attributable to the famine.

But this doesn't really tell us anything. Nobody denies that there was a terrible famine in 1932-33. The question is: Was the famine "man-made" by collectivization, and "deliberate," in that "Stalin" took grain away from starving people for purposes of political punishment? These figures tell us nothing about this.

Lynne **Viola**, *The Unknown GULAG. The Lost World of Stalin's Special Settlements* (Oxford University Press, 2007) cites the figure of 241,355 deaths on page 141, not page 241. Viola herself cites V.N.

Zemskov, *Spetsposelentsy v SSSR 1930-1960* (Moscow: Nauka, 2003).

Zemskov's figures are 89,754 deaths in 1932 and 151,601 in 1933 for the total of 241,355. These figures tell us nothing about the famine. The special settlements, as their name implies, were villages, not prisons, and included families — old persons, parents, children. There is no indication how many of these people died above the number that would be expected to die in non-famine years.

Conclusion: Snyder gives no evidence for the following statements:

> * that "the Gulag had a policy of feeding the strong and depriving the weak";
>
> * that "hungry prisoners" were "punished for shirking" for "eating wild plants and garbage;
>
> * that "untold thousands" died on the journey or that no records were kept of such deaths.

Evidently he has invented these "facts."

Snyder relates more horror stories of starving people. Whether these specific stories are true or not is not important. Terrible things happen during famines, so these stories could be true and, if they are not, others similar to them undoubtedly were.

But they have nothing whatsoever to do with the issue of whether the famine was "man-made," "deliberate" or not. They do not even help us understand whether the Soviet authorities should have handled it differently than they did.

Snyder: "Half a Million Youngsters in Watchtowers"

> In a broader sense, though, it was politics as well as starvation that destroyed families, turning a younger generation against an older. Members of the Young Communists served in the brigades that requisitioned food. Still, younger children, in the Pioneers, were supposed to be "the eyes and ears of the party inside the family." The healthier ones were assigned to watch over the fields to prevent theft.

Half a million preadolescent and young teenage boys and girls stood in the watchtowers observing adults in Soviet Ukraine in summer 1933. All children were expected to report on their parents.[79] (50)

Sources (n. 79 p. 467):

* "On the half a million boys and girls in the watchtowers," Maksudov, "Victory," 213.

* "Quotation," Kuśnierz, *Ukraina*, 119.

Kuśnierz does have this quotation on page 119 ("the eye and the ear of the Party in the family") — it is the familiar story of Pavlik Morozov.

Maksudov"s Falsification

Maksudov, "Victory," 213, states:

Surveillance towers appeared across the countryside; mounted patrols hid in ambush; adults and even small children were employed to spy on their friends and relatives. Kosior estimated that 500,000 Pioneers guarded the fields from their own parents during the summer of 1933.[58] The law of August 7 that threatened execution or imprisonment for anyone caught stealing grain came to be called the "ears of wheat" law.

Maksudov's note 58 (p. 234) says: "Ivan Trifonov, *Ocherki istorii klassovoi bor'by v SSSR, 1921-1937*. (Moscow, 1960), 258."

The actual title of this book is *Ocherki istorii klassovoi bor'by v SSSR v gody NEPa (1921-1937)*.[28] Here is what Trifonov actually wrote:

Лучшими помощниками политотделов являлись комсомольцы. Во всех колхозах Северного Кавказа она создали отряды «легкой кавалерии». Отряды бдительно охраняли общественное имущество, боролись с потравами, задерживали воров и расхитителей.

---

[28] Трифонов И. *Очерки истории классовой борьбы в СССР в годы НЭПа* (1921 — 1937). М.: Изд-во политической литературы, 1960.

> На Украине в 1933 г. в сборе колосков и охране урожая участвовало 540 тыс. детей. В колхозах республики работали 240 тыс. комсомольцев и 160 ударных комсомольских бригад по ремонту тракторов.

Translated:

> The best assistants of the political departments were the Komsomol members. In all the collective farms of the North Caucasus the Komsomol established "light cavalry" squads. Detachments vigilantly guarded public property and struggled against damage by animals, detained thieves and plunderers. In Ukraine in 1933 540 thousand children took part in the collection of ears and crop protection. In the collective farms of the republic worked 240 thousand Komsomol members and 160 Komsomol shock brigades in repairing tractors. (258)

Maksudov has seriously falsified this passage. Trifonov says nothing about "surveillance towers"; about any statement at all by Kosior; about Pioneers "guarding the fields from their own parents"; or about children "spying on their friends and relatives;" or — as Snyder adds — about "reporting on their parents." The "half million children" Trifonov mentions were not "standing in the watchtowers," as Snyder claims, but helping to glean the fields and protect the crops.

The "Law of Three Ears" — this is in fact the sobriquet of this law — punished theft of government property, including the property of collective farms and cooperatives.[29] Michael Ellman, a very anti-communist researcher, claims that 11,000 persons were executed under this law but gives no evidence whatsoever for this statement. (Ellman, 2007, p. 686) The relevant document, available to Ellman in 2007 but evidently not used by him, states that 2,052

---

[29] The text of the law, in Russian, is online at
http://ru.wikisource.org/wiki/Об_охране_имущества_государственных_предприятий,_колхозов_и_кооперации_и_укреплении_общественной_(социалистической)_собственности

persons had been sentenced to death under the law. A number of cases of very large-scale theft are noted in this report to Stalin of March 20, 1933 (Lubianka 1922-1936 No. 349, p. 417). It does not note how many of these death sentences were commuted, though such commutations were generally frequent.

This law was supported by many peasants, as Tauger argues:

> Without question, however, many other peasants had worked willingly during the whole period, earning many labour-days and siding with the system. As an example of this, we can consider peasants' views of the notorious 7 August 1932 law on socialist property, which authorized arrests of people for thefts and imposed capital punishment in some cases, and under which more than 100,000 people (mostly peasants) were arrested. **An OGPU study of peasant attitudes towards this law in Ivanovo oblast found that most peasants supported it and even considered it overdue, because of numerous outrages and scandals involving theft that they had witnessed and could not prevent.** (Tauger 2004 85-6. Emphasis added.)

Snyder cites a document in the multivolume *Tragediia sovetskoi derevni* ("Tragedy of the Soviet Countryside"), edited by staunch opponents of collectivization but still a very useful collection of primary source materials. The document in question, a report on the reaction of peasants in a certain region to the August 7, 1932 law, contains a section on "negative reactions" but a longer one on "positive reactions", with examples given.[30]

On February 1 1933 the Politburo decreed that the following persons should *not* be prosecuted under this law:

> лиц, виновных в мелких единичных кражах общественной собственности, или трудящихся, совершивших кражи из нужды, по

---

[30] V. Danilov et al., eds., *Tragediia sovetskoi derevni* t. 3 (Moscow: ROSSPEN, 2001), Dok. No. 170, 479-481.

> несознательности и при наличии других
> смягчающих обстоятельств.

Translated:

> those guilty of individual acts of petty theft of public
> property, or workers who have committed theft be-
> cause of need (poverty), or from lack of conscious-
> ness and in the presence of other mitigating cir-
> cumstances.

This was confirmed by an order of the Presidium (the executive body of the Soviet government) of March 27 1933. A joint instruction of the Central Committee and the Central Executive Committee — that is, the main bodies of the Party and the Government, of May 8 1933 greatly restricted the punishments under this law. Several other decrees limited punishment under this law and released persons convicted under it.[31]

In any case it is evident that the 500,000 Pioneers and their parents were not starving.

Snyder relates more horrifying stories, none of which have any bearing on the issue at hand: whether the starvation was "deliberate."

Why Were Those In Charge of the 1937 Census Arrested?

Snyder:

> The Soviet census of 1937 found eight million fewer
> people than projected: most of these were famine
> victims in Soviet Ukraine, Soviet Kazakhstan, and
> Soviet Russia, and the children that they did not
> then have. Stalin suppressed its findings and had
> the responsible demographers executed. In 1933,
> Soviet officials in private conversations most often
> provided the estimate of 5.5 million dead from
> hunger. This seems roughly correct, if perhaps
> somewhat low, for the Soviet Union in the early

---

[31] See http://ru.wikipedia.org/wiki/Закон_о_трёх_колосках

1930s, including Soviet Ukraine, Soviet Kazakhstan, and Soviet Russia.[87] (58)

n.87, p. 467:" On the Soviet census, see Schlögel, *Terror*. For discussion of 5.5 million as a typical estimate, see Dalrymple, "Soviet Famine," 259."

Karl **Schlögel**, *Terror und Traum: Moskau 1937* (Munich, 2007) isn't an easy book for most readers to find, so why pick it? Possibly because it is another work of the "USSR, land of terror" school, relentlessly anticommunist. It is devoid of any effort at historical objectivity, and is full of outright falsifications.

Dalrymple's article is from the 1960s, merely an attempt to establish that there had indeed been a famine. Far more recent estimates have been made by recent scholarly studies.

Mark Tauger estimates roughly five million deaths as a result of the famine. But others estimate a much lower figure. The careful Ukrainian-Canadian scholar John-Paul Himka writes:

> These could not be specialists in demography, however, since all recent studies based on a careful analysis of census data come up with numbers in the range of 2.6 to 3.9 million.... Jacques Vallin, France Meslé, Serguei Adamets, and Serhii Pirozhkov, "A New Estimate of Ukrainian Population Losses during the Crises of the 1930s and 1940s," *Population Studies* 56, 3 (2002): 249—64; this study arrives at the figure of 2.6 million.[32] (Emphasis added)

The 1937 census was not cancelled because the population count was "too low," as hinted by Snyder and stated by Schlögel. It was declared defective and rescheduled for 1939, when the questions about nationality were simplified, the questions about literacy were changed, and the question about religious belief was omitted altogether, so respondents did not have to say whether they were religious or not.

---

[32] "Encumbered Memory. The Ukrainian Famine of 1932—33." *Kritika* 14 (2) Spring 2013, p. 426 and note.

Several of those in charge of the census were indeed arrested, tried, and in at least one case, executed. But this had nothing to do with the census. Ivan Adamovich Kraval', the main official in charge of the census, was named by one of the defendants in the March 1938 Moscow Trial (the "Bukharin-Rykov" trial) as a member of the Right-Trotskyite conspiracy against the Soviet government and Party leadership. The census was cancelled in January 1937 but Kraval' was not even arrested until May.

In fact as early as January 11, 1937 Kraval' had been named as a clandestine Bukharinite from as far back as 1919-1921 and again in 1924 by Valentin Astrov, also a Bukharin supporter and member of his "school." This is significant because Astrov lived until 1993, long enough to write that the NKVD had not mistreated him in any way and that his testimony to them against Bukharin and his supporters was truthful, not the result of any compulsion.[33]

Lazar' S. Brandgendler, another leading census official, was also arrested, tried, and convicted of involvement in a Right-Trotskyite conspiracy. He was not executed but sentenced to 10 years in a camp.

Fortunately there are a number of Russian studies of the Soviet census of 1937 where all these matters are explained. Snyder failed to consult any of them.

---

[33] Astrov, "Kak Eto Proizoshlo.." *Literaturnaia Gazeta* March 29, 1989 ; Astrov, "...S menia sledovateli trebovali pokazaniia." *Izvestiia* February 27, 1993, p. 3. Vladimir Bobrov and I have discussed Astrov's confessions in detail in "Verdikt: Vinoven!" Chapter 1 of *Pravosudie Stalina* (Moscow: EKSMO, 2010), 13-63. I discuss it more briefly in English in Chapter 16 of *The Murder of Sergei Kirov* pp. 318-319.

Chapter 4. *Bloodlands* Chapter 2: Snyder's Claim of the Soviets' "Class Terror" Examined

In this chapter Snyder does not focus on any one central event. Instead, he touches on a number of different issues: collectivization, Hitler's coming to power, the Spanish Civil War, the Moscow Trials and the so-called "Military Purges" (also known as "the Tukhachevsky Affair") and the *Ezhovshchina* or "Great Terror," which Snyder has already dealt with in Chapter One, and to which he will return in Chapter Four. Every fact-claim that has an anti-Soviet tendency is examined here, and all of the evidence that Snyder or his sources cite, is checked.

Collectivization

> His policy of collectivization had required the
> shooting of tens of thousands of citizens and the
> deportations of hundreds of thousands, and had
> brought millions more to the brink of death by star-
> vation—as Jones would see and report. (59-60)

Snyder states that collectivization was accompanied by "tens of thousands of executions." The two most crucial years for collectivization were 1930 and 1931. In 1930 there were 20,201 executions for all crimes, and 9876 executions in 1931, for a total of 30,077. Executions in the adjacent non-collectivization years were much lower: 1383 for the year 1929; 3912 (or, alternatively, 3194) in 1932; 2154 in 1933. [1]

---

[1] Oleg Mozokhin is the expert on this question. His book, *Pravo na repressii* (Moscow, 2006), contains serious misprints: numbers are put in the wrong columns. Mozokhin's web pages give the corrected figures for executions, which are reported here. For 1931, see http://mozohin.ru/article/a-41.html ; for 1932, http://mozohin.ru/article/a-42.html

It is logical to assume that these most of the additional executions above the level of the preceding year (1929) and following year (1932) would have been related to collectivization. These would have been due to the struggle against organized armed groups rebelling against collectivization, and against other kinds of sabotage of the collectivization movement. This would make the approximate number of executions due to collectivization around 20,000 to 25,000. Snyder is correct in this instance.

It was inevitable that kulaks — rich peasants who lived by exploiting the labor of others — and other rural opponents of Soviet power would oppose collectivization, often violently. Tauger has shown that collectivization was also supported by many peasants, and by poor and landless peasants above all. Indeed, this has been admitted even by such staunch anticommunists and opponents of collectivization as James Mace.

Documents from former Soviet archives do indeed confirm hundreds of thousands of deportations of peasants who resisted collectivization, as Snyder states. But Snyder's main fact-claims here are false. Collectivization did not cause the famine. Snyder has no evidence that it did and, in fact, does not even bother to try to prove it but simply "asserts" it. We have discussed this question thoroughly in connection with our analysis of Chapter 1 of *Bloodlands*. The famine was a secular event caused by poor weather conditions. There had been famines every 2-3 years in Russian history for at least a millennium.

Snyder is also prevaricating when he tries to associate Jones' genuine account of the famine itself with his, Snyder's, falsehood that the famine had been caused by collectivization. Jones could not have "seen" the cause of the famine that he witnessed because causes cannot be "seen." Jones witnessed famine conditions. But Snyder says Jones "saw and reported" that "collectivization... had brought millions to the brink of death by starvation." This is false.

Nor did Stalin "order the shooting of hundreds of thousands more Soviet citizens" "later in the 1930s." (59) No one has ever found such an "order," so Snyder has not seen it either. Therefore,

Snyder's claim is deliberately false. We will discuss this in our analysis of Chapter 3.

Did "Soviet Cruelty" Lead to Support for Nazism?

Snyder states:

> For some of the Germans and other Europeans who favored Hitler and his enterprise, the cruelty of Soviet policy seemed to be an argument for National Socialism. (60)

Snyder's claim that that some chose choose Nazism because it was "less cruel" than communism is bizarre. As though even Nazism's supporters thought it was "not cruel!" Some kind of humanitarian alternative to communism, perhaps? But collectivization was certainly "cruel" to kulaks, as the Revolution of 1917 had been "cruel" to capitalists — and as capitalism had been "cruel" to working people the world over, for centuries. Many capitalists supported Nazism because it seemed to be the best bulwark against communism, which threatened to dispossess them of their wealth.

As we have shown, *not* to have collectivized would have been the "cruel" policy with respect to the vast majority of the Soviet population, whether peasants or workers. Collectivization stopped the centuries-old cycle of famines in Russia which mainly killed the poorest.

Did Communist Hostility to Social-Democrats Facilitate Hitler"s Rise to Power?

> Communists were to maintain their ideological purity, and avoid alliances with social democrats. Only communists had a legitimate role to play in human progress, and others who claimed to speak for the oppressed were frauds and "social fascists." They were to be grouped together with every party to their right, including the Nazis. In Germany, communists were to regard the social democrats, not the Nazis, as the main enemy.
>
> In the second half of 1932 and the first months of 1933, during the long moment of Stalin's provoca-

tion of catastrophe, it would have been difficult for
him to abandon the international line of "class
against class." The class struggle against the kulak,
after all, was the official explanation of the horrible
suffering and mass death within the Soviet Union.
(61-2)

Snyder cites no evidence at all for his contention that communist
suspicion of, and failure to work with, the Social-Democrats (SPD)
helped the rise of Nazism. We cannot go deeply into this historical
question here. But it is important to note that the Social Democrats
were intensely hostile to communism as well. Each party saw the
other as its main rival for the allegiance of the German working
class. The well-known book by noted Indian-born communist R.
Palme Dutt, *Fascism and Social Revolution* (1934) sets forth the
Comintern's view of the social democratic parties at this time and
details their numerous betrayals both of the communists and of
their own working classes.[2]

Once again Snyder tries to sneak in his unproven, and unprovable,
assertion that it was collectivization that caused the famine. The
"horrible suffering and mass death" was caused by the famine, not
by "the struggle against the kulak," which was part of the struggle
to collectivize agriculture. Nor did Stalin "provoke catastrophe."
The truth is quite the opposite: collectivization ended the cycle of
famines and enabled rapid industrialization, without which the
USSR would certainly have been defeated by Hitler's armies — a
true catastrophe.

Was Collectivization Like Hitler"s Anti-Jewish Scapegoating?

In this respect Hitler's policies resembled Stalin's.
The Soviet leader presented the disarray in the Soviet countryside, and then dekulakization, as the result of an authentic class war. The political conclusion was the same in Berlin and Moscow: the state

---

[2] It is now available online at http://www.plp.org/books/dutt.pdf (accessed February
2014)

would have to step in to make sure that the necessary redistribution was relatively peaceful. (62)

Snyder's main goal in *Bloodlands* is to argue that the USSR was similar to Nazi Germany, Stalin similar to Hitler. Here Snyder tries to smuggle past his readers the suggestion that collectivization was somehow similar to Nazi racism against Jews. But Snyder cannot find any real similarities. Therefore, he claims that collectivization was somehow "spontaneous," with the State just "stepping in." This is more than simply false — it a statement made in flagrant disregard of the facts. There is no evidence to support it.

In essence Snyder is arguing that socializing private property (collectivization in the USSR) is somehow similar to violently dispossessing German Jews while strengthening the position of large-scale industrialists, and private business generally (Hitler's policy in Germany). This absurdity is a good example of the lengths to which Snyder will go in order to force some comparison between the USSR and Nazi Germany. Nazi Germany was a form of capitalism. Collectivization was its polar opposite.

Snyder is wrong as well when he states as fact, with no evidence at all that "Stalin" — i.e. the USSR — had "policies" of "shooting," "deportation," or "starvation," As we showed in our discussion of Chapter One of *Bloodlands* Soviet policy was to collectivize agriculture. Collectivization was the only policy that could end the constant cycle of killer famines and allow the USSR to industrialize. No other policy that would accomplish either of these goals, much less both of them, has ever been dreamed up by anyone else, including anticommunist researchers.

Executions were for rebellions against the government or serious violations of laws controlling the food supply. Deportations were for less violent opposition to collectivization. They were not "policies."

Had the USSR and Germany Planned to Dismantle Poland since 1922?

Snyder writes:

> Since 1922, the two states [Germany and the USSR]
> had engaged in military and economic cooperation,
> on the tacit understanding that both had an interest
> in the remaking of eastern Europe at the expense of
> Poland. (64)

This is false. The 1922 Rapallo Treaty between Weimar Germany and Soviet Russia did not concern the "remaking of Eastern Europe" and had nothing to do with Poland at all. Moreover, if the "understanding" was "tacit," how does Snyder know about it? He cites no evidence of any such "tacit understanding" because there is none.

In reality the opposite is true. In 1939 the USSR tried many times to get Poland to sign a mutual defense treaty aimed at Germany. In a later chapter we show that the Polish government wanted no treaties at all with the USSR even if it meant facing Hitler's Wehrmacht alone.

Snyder fails to examine the legitimacy of Poland's claim to Western Ukraine and Western Belorussia. Both lie east of the Curzon Line in an area in which Poles were a distinct minority of the population. Regardless of the ethnicity or the desires of the population Pilsudski and other Polish nationalists wanted these lands because they had been within the boundaries of the Polish-Lithuanian state of 1772,. This state occupied almost all of Western Ukraine, all of Belorussia, much of Latvia and Lithuania, and had a large part of the Black Sea coast. Polish imperialist ambitions aimed to reestablish a greater Poland along these lines.[3]

Therefore, *when Poland "lost" Western Ukraine and Western Belorussia in September 1939 it lost nothing that it had any right to possess in the first place.* Even today's Polish state, both capitalist and highly nationalistic, no longer claims Western Ukraine and Western Belorussia.

---

[3] See the map at http://commons.wikimedia.org/wiki/File:Polish-Lithuanian_Commonwealth_in_1764.PNG

The *Ezhovshchina*

Aside from the famine of 1932-33 the *Ezhovshchina* or "bad time of Ezhov," called by anticommunists the "Great Terror," is the only source for mass murder that Snyder can find to blame "Stalin" (the Soviet government) for. A campaign of mass murder did indeed take place during the period July or August 1937 through September 1938. Anticommunist historians sometimes claim that these mass murders took place because Stalin either ordered them — Snyder simply states this as a "fact" — or at least authorized them.

> During the period of the Popular Front, from June
> 1934 through August 1939, about three quarters of
> a million Soviet citizens would be shot to death by
> order of Stalin... (67; emphasis added)

This is false. There is no evidence of any such "order of Stalin," so of course Snyder has never seen any and gives no reference to one. The reader of *Bloodlands* is left to assume that Snyder has such evidence when Snyder knows he does not. Snyder is deliberately misleading his readers. On the contrary, it is clear now that Stalin and the Politburo did not know that Ezhov was engaging in these massive executions of innocent people. We discuss this important matter in much more detail in Chapter Six of the present book.

The Spanish Civil War

The Spanish Civil War of 1936-1939 was a very important event, the only war on the European continent and a "prequel" to World War II. Six months after the end of the Spanish Civil War Hitler invaded Poland. Hitler and Mussolini sent thousands of troops, tanks, and aircraft to attack the bourgeois Spanish Republic. Without them the fascist army, led by General Francisco Franco, could not have won.

In a brief paragraph Snyder claims that Soviet NKVD men were "sent to Spain to shoot" Trotskyists for "treason." But none of the works in Snyder's footnote to this passage demonstrate that. The reason is that, aside from the case of Andres Nin which we discuss below, there is no firm evidence that even a single Trotskyist (or anyone else) was shot in Spain by the Soviet NKVD.[4]

Snyder is correct when he states that the communists presented Trotskyists — more accurately, Trotskyism — as "fascist." Based on the evidence we now have, it appears to be true that some Trotskyists were involved in sabotaging the Spanish Republic. We simply have far too much primary source evidence directly about this, including from Nazi sources, for all of it to be fabrication.[5] In addition, Karl Radek testified at the January 1937 Moscow Trial that Trotskyists were active in Spain and appealed to them to stop.

A few pages later Snyder briefly picks up the Spanish Civil War again:

> Orwell watched as the communists provoked clash-
> es in Barcelona in May 1937, and then as the Span-
> ish government, beholden to Moscow, banned the
> Trotskyite party [the POUM]. (75)

This is false. The Barcelona "May Days" revolt was precipitated by an Anarchist seizure of the Barcelona telephone station, which the Republican government of Barcelona took back. The phrase "beholden to Moscow," is likewise false. Neither the government of Largo Caballero (September 4 1936 to May 17, 1937) nor that of his successor Juan Negrín were under communist control. Both Caballero and Negrin were suspicious of the communists.

The "Partido Obrero de Unificación Marxista" or POUM had participated in the Barcelona revolt. The Soviets had evidence then, and we have evidence today, that both Franco's and German agents were involved in the revolt.[6] It was logical to think that the POUM leaders were conspiring with them. POUM was not an "official"

---

[4] Trotsky activists Mark Rein, Kurt Landau, and Erwin Wolf vanished. Paul Preston, the foremost historian of this period, believes they were abducted and killed either by "Soviet agents" or by the "Grup d'Informació", the secret intelligence unit for the Catalonian government, the *Generalitat.* It is logical to think so, though not proven. See Paul Preston, Paul Preston, *The Spanish holocaust: inquisition and extermination in twentieth-century Spain.* (New York: W.W. Norton, 2012) 407, 418-419.

[5] Grover Furr, "Communist Anti-Trotskyism, and the Barcelona "May Days" of 1937," in press.

[6] Furr, "Communist Anti-Trotskyism."

Trotskyist party, but it was friendly to Trotsky and unfriendly to the USSR. The head of POUM, Andres Nin, had been one of Trotsky's leading aides. The Soviets knew that Trotsky and some of his supporters — Karl Radek and IUrii Piatakov at least — had publicly denounced each other in the harshest terms as a cover for their continued secret collaboration. It was logical to assume that Nin had done likewise — as, in fact, he may well have done. Nin strongly supported the armed revolt against the Republican government, which benefitted only Franco and his Axis allies.

Meanwhile the high-ranking Soviet commanders executed on June 12, 1937 in the "Tukhachevsky Affair" confessed at trial that they had been in collaboration with both Nazi Germany and Trotsky. One of them stated that Trotsky had given him the honor of opening the Leningrad front to the rebels in the event of a successful revolt against the Soviet leadership. Nin and the POUM leadership were arrested a few days later, on June 16, 1937, by Orlov, head of the Soviet NKVD in Spain. He was not tortured but refused to confess and was murdered a few days later.[7]

Snyder Claims The Soviets Made No Progress Towards Socialism

Snyder makes the bizarre claim that Soviet "progress toward socialism" was "largely a matter of propaganda." (71) The Soviet Union built an industrial, socialist society during the decade of the 1930s. A great many visitors to the USSR reported on the phenomenal changes that had taken place in Soviet society since the late 1920s. Any number of scholars have remarked upon the same thing.[8] Snyder gives no evidence at all to support this statement,

---

[7] Details about Nin's activities, arrest, and murder are in Preston, *Spanish holocaust,* 402, 411-412. The trial of the "Tukhachevsky Affair" generals is reported and a key document examined in Vladimir L. Bobrov and Grover Furr, "Marshal S.M. Budiennyi on the Tukhachevsky Trial. Impressions of an Eye-Witness", *Klio* (St Petersburg) 2012 (2), 8-24 (in Russian). At http://msuweb.montclair.edu/~furrg/research/budennyi_klio12.pdf Reprinted in *M.N. Tukhachevskii: Kak My Predali Stalina* ("M.N. Tukachevsky. How We Betrayed Stalin"), Moscow: Algoritm, September 2012, pages 174-230.

[8] A good discussion by a noted economic historian is Robert C. Allen, *From Farm to Factory. A Reinterpretation of the Soviet Industrial Revolution.* Princeton University Press, 2003. It has a good bibliography too.

nor does he define what he means by "progress toward socialism." By social-democratic definitions of socialism — wide-ranging social welfare benefits for all workers in an industrialized or industrializing society — the Soviet Union had indeed achieved socialism by the mid-1930s.

No Foreign Subversion?

Snyder makes the following claim:

> ...the explanation of famine and misery at home depended upon the idea of foreign subversion... (72)

Snyder then claims that this idea "was essentially without merit" — that there was in fact no "foreign subversion."

Snyder does not deign to cite any evidence for either of these claims. It's no wonder that Snyder does not try to prove that there was no "foreign subversion," for Snyder himself documents considerable Polish espionage in his book *Sketches from a Secret War.*[9] There is a great deal of evidence of espionage by other countries too, especially Germany and Japan. If Snyder believes it to be false or fabricated, he should say so and state the reason for his suspicions. We examine this issue in more detail later in the present book.

Did Stalin Have No Political Opposition?

Snyder claims:

> By 1937 Stalin faced no meaningful political opposition within the Soviet communist party, but this only seemed to convince him that his enemies had learned political invisibility. Just as he had during the height of the famine, he argued again that year that the most dangerous enemies of the state appeared to be harmless and loyal. (72)

---

[9] Timothy Snyder. *Sketches from a secret war : a Polish artist's mission to liberate Soviet Ukraine.* Yale University Press, 2005. The subject of this book, Henryk Józewski, supported greater autonomy for Ukrainians in Volhynia but was a staunch anticommunist. We will return to this book in a future chapter.

Today there are available to researchers a great many primary documents giving evidence of multiple conspiracies against the Soviet government that involved high-ranking Party members along with many others. Some of these conspiracies resulted in the various trials of 1934-1938, plus the military conspiracy (Tukhachevsky Affair), Ezhov's conspiracy, and much else. This includes important evidence from outside the USSR, from sources that could not possibly have fabricated it. Much of this evidence is from 1937, the year Snyder names here. We have discussed some of this in a recent book (see the following foonote).

Since there is so much documentary evidence of these conspiracies — "political opposition" — it is incumbent on Snyder to give evidence that these documents have been forged, faked, or in some way are not what they appear to be. He does not do this because he cannot. No one has ever proven these documents fakes. Moreover, there are far too many of them, from too many different sources, for them to all have been forged or falsified.

The Murder of Sergei Kirov — Did Stalin Have No Evidence For His "Theory"?

Since 2000 a great deal of scholarly attention has been devoted to investigating the assassination of Leningrad Party First Secretary Sergei M. Kirov in the Party Headquarters in the Smolny Institute in Leningrad on December 1, 1934. Four major studies, one of them by the present writer, have been devoted to it.

Snyder writes:

> Stalin's interpretation of the Leningrad murder was
> a direct challenge to the Soviet state police. His was
> not a theory that the NKVD was inclined to accept,
> not least because there was no evidence. (73)

Snyder does not know what he is talking about. Stalin had no "interpretation." He instructed the NKVD to seek for the assassins among Zinovievites in Leningrad only after evidence of the assassin's, Leonid Nikolaev's, ties to these underground Zinovievites had been uncovered during the course of the investigation, both in

Nikolaev's own notebooks and from the assassin's own statements to the investigators.

A very large body of evidence in the Kirov murder case has now been available to researchers. Much of it has been public for over a decade. All of it supports the official position of the Soviet prosecution at the time that Kirov was murdered by a conspiracy of underground Zinovievites; that Zinoviev and Kamenev were in overall charge of the murder; and that Trotsky and his followers were at least aware of it. Few of Snyder's readers will know this.

The present writer's book on the Kirov murder has now been published in both English and Russian editions. The evidence now available — not only from former Soviet archives but from non-Soviet sources — clearly proves that the conspiracies that constituted the main accusations against the defendants at the Kirov murder trial of December 1934, the First, Second, and Third Moscow "Show" Trials of August 1936, January 1937, and March 1938, and the Military or "Tukhachevsky Affair" trial of June 1937, really did exist.[10]

Snyder on the Moscow Trials

According to Snyder,

> Beginning in August 1936, Yezhov charged Stalin's former political opponents with fantastic offenses in public show trials. (73)

Snyder is "bluffing" again. He uses the word "fantastic" in an attempt to confuse his readers, and so permit him to avoid the normal scholarly obligation to study the evidence that exists.

In reality there is a great deal of evidence that the charges against the defendants in the August 1936 Moscow Trial and the other two in January 1937 and March 1938 were true. Like other anticommunist writers Snyder prefers to pretend that it does not exist. Perhaps he is deliberately concealing it; perhaps he is unaware of

---

[10] Grover Furr, *The Murder of Sergei Kirov: History, Scholarship and the Anti-Stalin Paradigm.* Kettering, OH: Erythros Press and Media LLC, 2013. For evidence from beyond the USSR see Chapter 17. Russian translation: Grover Ferr (Furr). *Ubiystvo Kirova. Novoe issledovanie.* Moscow: Russkaia panorama, 2013.

it, and therefore incompetent to write about this subject. Again, few of his readers will know about it.

There was nothing "fantastic" in the charges brought in the Moscow trials. Leon Trotsky declared some of them to be "fantastic" — but Trotsky was secretly in league with at least some of the defendants, as we have known for more than 30 years now thanks to Trotsky's own admissions preserved in the Trotsky Archives in Harvard and the Hoover Institution.

Words like "fantastic" say nothing about the matter at hand — in this case, the charges against the Moscow Trial defendants. "The charges were fantastic" means, in fact, "*I consider* the charges to be fantastic," just as the statement "pistachio ice cream is delicious" simply means "*I think that* pistachio ice cream is delicious." In each case the statement tells us about the person who makes the statement. It says nothing about the reality.

Snyder claims that "these old Bolsheviks had been intimidated and beaten, and were doing little more than uttering lines from a script." (73) But once again, intentionally or not, Snyder is deceiving to his readers. He cannot possibly have any evidence that the defendants were "beaten" since there never has been any. In 2003 Stephen F. Cohen, the world's greatest authority of Bukharin, wrote that Bukharin was definitely not tortured. Nor has there ever been any evidence that any of the other defendants were tortured. Likewise, there has never been any evidence of any "script."

Once again Snyder's falsehood is also a "bluff." Perhaps many of Snyder's readers will think: "A full professor of history like Snyder *must* have evidence that the defendants had been 'intimidated' and 'beaten' and so gave false testimony." But neither Snyder nor anybody else has any such evidence. On the contrary, we have a lot of evidence that the defendants in the Moscow Trials testified as they wanted to. That does not mean that they always told the truth, but that if and when they lied, they did so because they chose to lie to the prosecution.

Snyder writes:

> The party newspaper, Pravda, made the connection
> clear in a headline of 22 August 1936: "Trotsky-

> Zinoviev-Kamenev-Gestapo." Could the three Bol-
> sheviks in question, men who had built the Soviet
> Union, truly be paid agents of capitalist powers?
> Were these three communists of Jewish origin like-
> ly agents of the secret state police of Nazi Germany?
> They were not, but the charge was taken seriously,
> even outside the Soviet Union. (74)

This is a falsehood — specifically, a "straw man." *None* of the testimony in the August 1936 Moscow Trial portrays Zinoviev and
Kamenev as either "paid agents of capitalist powers" or "agents of
the secret state police of Nazi Germany," as Snyder alleged. Any
reading of the trial transcript, which is widely available on the Internet, will show this.

The testimony at the August 1936 Moscow trial simply confirms
that Zinoviev and Kamenev and their followers were in touch with
Trotskyites, who were also in touch with Trotsky, and that some of
the Trotskyites had conspired with agents of the German Secret
Police. It is a shibboleth of respectability, *de rigueur* in certain cor-
ners of anticommunist scholarship, to assert that the Moscow Trials were all "faked." But there is no evidence at all that they were,
and much evidence that corroborates the confessions of the most
important defendants.

It is striking that Snyder seems to believe that he can tell whether
the charges against and confessions of the defendants in the August 1936 Moscow Trial were true or not simply by ratiocination.
This is the fallacy of disbelief, a version of the logical fallacy of
'begging the question": "I cannot believe it, therefore it is not true."
It is a statement about the speaker, not a statement about the matter at hand, as competent historians are aware.

Snyder falsely claims that:

> He [Stalin] believed that the Spanish government
> was weak because it was unable to find and kill
> enough spies and traitors....[35] (74)

Sources (n. 35 p. 470):

   * Werth, *Terreur*, 282.

   * "See also" Kuromiya, *Stalin*, 121.

This is a false statement. Here follows an examination of these sources.

Werth, *Terreur*, 282: This reference contains no evidence to support Snyder's statement. Werth merely refers to a conference presentation by Oleg Khlevniuk, claiming that Khlevniuk has "shown" (*montré*) that that the defeats of the Spanish Republic were caused by their inability to uproot spies from their midst. These conference papers have proven impossible to obtain. At any rate Snyder never read this essay, or he would have referred directly to it. Therefore, Snyder does not know what Khlevniuk actually said, only what Werth claims he said.

Kuromiya, *Stalin*, 121, quotes from essays published by Khlevniuk in 1995 and 1998. It is likely that Khlevniuk said the same thing here as in the unpublished essay cited by Werth. Here is the relevant quotation from Kuromiya:

> As Oleg Khlevniuk has convincingly shown, the Spanish Civil War (which Stalin closely followed) demonstrated to him that 'the situation in Spain itself, the acute contradictions between the different political forces, including those between the Communists and Trotsky's adherents, provided Stalin with the best possible confirmation of the need for a policy of repression as a means of strengthening the USSR's capacity for defense'.

The part in quotation marks above is evidently from Khlevniuk. However, even Kuromiya gives no evidence to support this statement of Khlevniuk's.

Kuromiya continues (121):

> As Soviet military dispatches from Spain in 1936 and 1937 made clear, the war was characterised by 'anarchy, partisan and subversive and divisionist [*sic*, diversionist] movements, relative erosion of the frontiers between front and rear, betrayals.' The events in Spain were for Stalin direct proof that there existed, and very obviously, just such a threat from within.

This represents either Khlevniuk's views, with which Kuromiya agrees, or Kuromiya's views alone. In either case, they deliberately omit some crucial facts:

> * At the January 1937 Moscow Trial former Trotskyist Karl Radek called upon Trotskyists in Spain to stop their subversive activities there.

> * In May 1937 anarchist and Trotskyists forces rebelled against the Republican government of Barcelona in an event known as the "May Days" revolt. This rebellion during wartime was regarded as a stab in the back by the Republican government and by the Soviets as well.

> * We have documentary evidence of Nazi German and Francoist involvement in the May Days revolt. Trotskyists like Andres Nin and the POUM, friendly to Trotsky, were also involved.

> * The Tukhachevsky Affair defendants testified that Trotsky was in collaboration with them and the German general staff in planning a revolt within the USSR.

> * On June 4, 1937, in the midst of the Tukhachevsky Affair, Stalin told an expanded meeting of the Military Soviet that the accused Soviet generals had wanted to make of the Soviet Union "another Spain."

Kuromiya (121-2) claims that from the disorder within the Spanish Republic Stalin drew the conclusion that subversion was rife and a "quiet rear" was essential.

 None of Snyder's sources — or anybody else — claims that Stalin believed the Spanish Republic should "find and kill enough spies and traitors." Evidently Snyder has invented this.

The Tukhachevsky Affair

Snyder:

> Eight high commanders of the armed forces were show-tried that same month; about half of the generals of the Red Army would be executed in the months to come....[37] (75)

This is an unusually incompetent falsehood even for Snyder. The definition of "show trial" in the Oxford English Dictionary conforms to common usage — a highly publicized, public trial. But the trial of the eight "Tukhachevsky Affair" defendants on June 11, 1937, was top-secret.

Although the transcript exists no one, even anticommunist Russian scholars trusted by the Russian government, has been allowed to see it since Col. Viktor Alksnis in 1991. After reading the transcript Alksnis, who until that time thought the generals had been framed, changed his mind and concluded that they were guilty. This information has been available since 2001 when Alksnis revealed these facts in an interview in Russia. He has recently repeated this in print).[11]

In addition, Marshal Semion Budiennyi's letter to Marshal Voroshilov, and NKVD General Genrikh Liushkov's statements to his Japanese handlers, leave no room for doubt that Tukhachevsky and the military leaders convicted with him, plus many others, were guilty. Either Snyder does not know about all this evidence or he has withheld this information from his readers.

Snyder"s "Fundamental" Source — A Hitler Supporter

Snyder's footnote to this statement about the Military Purges reads as follows:

> n. 37 ... On the Red Army generals, see
> Wieczorkiewicz, *Łańcuch*, 296. **This is a funda-**
> **mental work on the military purges.** (Emphasis
> added, GF)

The book by Pawel Wieczorkiewicz that Snyder recommends here, *Łańcuch śmierci* (= "Chain of Death"), it is not only not a "fundamental work" — it is worthless. Wieczorkiewicz's book reflects

---

[11] Alksnis's recent statement of February 2013 is at
http://www.echo.msk.ru/programs/graniweek/1012648-echo/#element-text For Alksnis'
earlier statements see «Последний полковник империи». Интервью «Элементов» с
народным депутатом СССР Виктором Алкснисом // Элементы, 1993. No 3; also
Алкснис В.И. Я не согласен! // Русский обозреватель. 2009, 31 окт. см.:
http://www.rus-obr.ru/opinions/4577

pre-1991 "scholarship" — essentially, Khrushchev- and Gorba-chev-era falsehoods. It does not use any of the large quantity of evidence that has been published since the end of the USSR in 1991, especially during the past decade. It is never cited by any of the highly anticommunist Russian scholars who write on the Tu-khachevsky Affair.[12] This is another of the many references that suggest that Snyder does not study Russian-language materials and is not familiar with the scholarship, yet insists on writing about Soviet history.

But Snyder is concealing from his readers something that is widely known in Poland. The late Pawel Wieczorkiewicz (he died in 2009) was a far right-wing crackpot whose views were extreme even among far-right Polish nationalists.

Wieczorkiewicz's admiration for Hitler's Germany led him to wish that Poland had united with Hitler to invade the USSR. He had great trust in Hitler and wished Polish leaders could have stood beside Hitler in Red Square, taking a victorious salute after the de-feat of the USSR.

> Nie chcieliśmy znaleźć się w sojuszu z Trzecią Rzeszą, a wylądowaliśmy w sojuszu z tak samo zbrodniczym Związkiem Sowieckim. A co gorsza, pod jego absolutną dominacją. Hitler zaś nigdy nie traktował swoich sojuszników tak jak Stalin kraje podbite po II wojnie światowej. Szanował ich suwerenność i podmiotowość, nakładając jedynie pewne ograniczenia w polityce zagranicznej. Nasze uzależnienie od Niemiec byłoby więc znacznie mniejsze niż to, w jakie wpadliśmy po wojnie wobec Związku Sowieckiego. Moglismy znaleźć miejsce u boku Rzeszy prawie takie jak Włochy, a na pewno lepsze niż Węgry czy Rumunia. W efekcie stanęlibyśmy w Moskwie i tam Adolf Hitler wraz z Rydzem-Śmigłym odbieraliby defiladę zwycięskich wojsk polsko-niemieckich. Ponurą asocjacją jest

---

[12] The present author bought and studied a copy of Wieczorkiewicz's book 10 years ago while researching the Tukhachevskii Affair.

> oczywiście Holokaust. Jeżeli jednak dobrze się nad
> tym zastanowić, można dojść do wniosku, że
> szybkie zwycięstwo Niemiec mogłoby oznaczać, że
> w ogóle by do niego nie doszło. Holokaust był
> bowiem w znacznej mierze funkcją niemieckich
> porażek wojennych.

Translated:

> We did not want to be in an alliance with the Third
> Reich and ended up in alliance with the also crimi-
> nal Soviet Union. And what is worse, under its abso-
> lute domination. Hitler never treated its allies as
> Stalin did the conquered countries after World War
> II. He respected their sovereignty and subjectivity,
> requiring only some limitations in foreign policy.
> Our dependence on Germany would have been
> much less than the one in which we ended up with
> after the war against the Soviet Union. We could
> have found a place at the side of the Reich almost
> like Italy, and definitely better than Hungary or
> Romania. As a result, we would have been in Mos-
> cow and there Adolf Hitler together with Rydz-
> Smigly would have reviewed the parade of the vic-
> torious Polish-German armies. A grim association
> is, of course, the Holocaust. If, however, you consid-
> er it well, one can conclude that a rapid German vic-
> tory would have meant it would not have come to
> that. The Holocaust was in fact largely a function of
> the German military defeats.

Wieczorkiewicz's favorite historian was British pro-Nazi, forger, and Holocaust denier David Irving, about whom Wieczorkiewicz said:

> To najlepszy i najwybitniejszy znawca historii II
> wojny światowej. Badacz, dla którego miarodajne
> są źródła, a nie poglądy historiografii, opinie
> kolegów, czy wrzask mediów. Człowiek, któremu z
> racji ogromnych zasług - zebrania lub odtajnienia i
> udostępnienia kluczowych dokumentów III Rzeszy,

czapką buty czyścić by trzeba. Historyk tej miary, że
ma prawo napisać i powiedzieć wszystko.

Translated:

> He is the best and most prominent expert on the
> history of World War II. A researcher for whom
> sources, not the viewpoints of historiography, the
> opinions of colleagues, or the media uproar, are
> what is meaningful. A man, who by virtue of his
> enormous merits — of collecting or declassifying
> and sharing key documents of the Third Reich —
> we should shine his boots with our hat. A historian
> of such caliber that he has the right to write and tell
> everything.[13]

Wieczorkiewicz openly wished that Poland had sided with Nazi
Germany in World War II! In an interview published in the Polish
journal *Wiadomosci* on January 2, 2006, Wieczorkiewicz said the
following:

> Talaga: Wybuch wojny poprzedziło zawarcie paktu
> Ribbentrop-Mołotow. Co by się stało, gdyby Polska
> zgodziła się wówczas na żądania Niemiec?
> Początkowo Hitler wcale nie chciał atakować Polski,
> uderzenie było raczej efektem okoliczności niż
> przemyślanego, tworzonego wiele lat planu. Czy
> Polska swoim twardym stanowiskiem
> sprowokowała poniekąd układ sowiecko-
> niemiecki?
>
> Wieczorkiewicz: Beck zrobił, moim zdaniem,
> kardynalny błąd: nie dostrzegł czynnika
> sowieckiego. Rozgrywał grę polityczną
> perfekcyjnie, ale przy założeniu, że nie ma Związku
> Sowieckiego. Co by było, gdybyśmy poszli z
> Hitlerem na Związek Sowiecki? Polska byłaby

---

[13] "Polityczna poprawność, a prawda historyczna, rozmowa z profesorem Pawłem Piotrem
Wieczorkiewiczem z Uniwersytetu Warszawskiego." ("Political correctness and historical
truth - conversation with Professor Pawel Piotr Wieczorkiewicz of Warsaw University").
Templum Novum, March 2006.

jednym z głównych twórców — obok Niemiec i
Włoch — zjednoczonej Europy ze stolicą w Berlinie
i z niemieckim językiem urzędowym.

Translated:

Talaga: The outbreak of war was preceded by the
conclusion of the Molotov-Ribbentrop Pact. What
would have happened if Poland agreed to the re-
quests of Germany? Initially, Hitler did not want to
attack Poland, the strike was the result of circumstances rather than a deliberate plan that was years
in creation. Did Poland provoke somewhat by its
hard position the Soviet-German agreement?

Wieczorkiewicz: Beck committed, in my opinion, a
cardinal error: he overlooked the Soviet factor. He
played the political game perfectly, but without taking the Soviet Union into account. What would have
happened if we had gone with Hitler against the Soviet Union? Poland would have been one of the
main creators, along with Germany and Italy, of a
united Europe with its capital in Berlin and with
German as the official language.[14]

Snyder continues:

The Germans, however, were not counting on help
from the Soviet population in that coming war. In
this respect, Stalin's scenario of threat, the union of
foreign enemies with domestic opponents, was
quite wrong. Thus the still greater terror that Stalin
would unleash upon his own population in 1937
and 1938 was entirely fruitless, and indeed coun-
terproductive. (78)

This is all wrong. From non-Soviet sources interested scholars
have known since the late 1980s that Hitler was indeed expecting
a military coup in the USSR and the establishment of a pro-German

---

[14] At http://wiadomosci.onet.pl/kiosk/historia/zabraklo-
wodza,3,3331024,wiadomosc.html

military regime.[15] It has been clear since the late 1990s that the military conspiracies really did exist and were coordinated with the conspiracy of the "Rights and Trotskyites," and much more evidence has come to light since the late Alvin D. Coox's work.[16] And there is even more evidence of these conspiracies today.

All this evidence accords very well with the great deal of evidence that we have from former Soviet archival documents now declassified.[17] This is as good confirmation of Tukhachevsky's collaboration with the Germans as we are likely to ever have. Snyder is either ignorant of this fact (incompetent) or knows about it but fails to tell his readers (dishonest).

Collaboration with the Germans was the substance of many of the confessions of defendants in the Moscow Trials and in the Tukhachevsky Affair. In 1939 Nikolai Ezhov, head of the NKVD during the so-called "Great Terror", admitted that by means of mass murder the conspirators under his command were trying to make enough people dissatisfied with the Soviet government that they would either revolt in the case of invasion, or would not oppose it. There is no evidence that these confessions were coerced or fabricated. Certainly Snyder has never seen any such evidence. If he

---

[15] We refer to the Mastny-Benes note of February 9, 1937, concerning Mastny's private talk with German emissary von Trouttmannsdorff. See, for example, Ivan Pfaff, *Die Sowjetunion und die Verteidigung der Tschechoslowakei 1934-1938: Versuch der Revision einer Legende.* Koeln — Weimar — Wien: Bohlau Verlag, 1996, "Prag unde die Affaere Tuchacevski," 191-216. First published in Pfaff, "Prag und der Fall Tuchatschewski." *Vierteljahresheft fuer Zeitgeschichte* 35 (1987), 95-134. Pfaff's own interpretation of this important document is very faulty. We have obtained a copy of the document and plan to publish a study in the future.

[16] See, Coox, "The Lesser of Two Hells: NKVD General G.S. Lyushkov's Defection to Japan, 1938-1945." *Journal of Slavic Military Studies* 11, 3 (1998) 145-186 (Part One) (Coox 1); 11, 4 (1998) 72-110 (Part Two).

[17] These documents are published, mostly in excerpt, in Kantor, Iulia. *Voina i mir Mikhaila Tukhachevskogo.* Moscow: Izdatel'skii Dom Ogoniok "Vremia," 2005, and Kantor, Iulia. *Zakliataia druzhba. Sekretnoe sotrudnichestvo SSSR I Germania v 1920-1930-e gody.* M-Spb: "Piter," 2009. Kantor tries to contend that Tukhachevsky was innocent nonetheless. The documents alone are in a series of articles by Kantor in *Istoriia Gosudarstva i Prava* (2006). I have put them on line at
http://msuweb.montclair.edu/~furrg/research/kantor_4articles_igp06.pdf

had, he would have cited it.[18] Once again, Snyder's statement is a "bluff."

Snyder Says There Were No Such People as "Kulaks"

Snyder claims that there were in reality no such people as "kulaks" and that the Soviets had invented the term:

> As a social class, the kulak (prosperous peasant) never really existed; the term was rather a Soviet classification that took on a political life of its own. (78-9)

This is either incompetence or deliberate deception. The term "kulak" had existed long before the Russian Revolution or Russian Marxism. Kulaks were defined as those peasants who employed other workers on their farms.

Here are quotations from three pre-revolutionary non-Russian writers who commented on the "koolaks" and their role in the peasant society. English author Emile Joseph Dillon wrote:

> ...this type of man was commonly termed a Koolak, or fist, to symbolize his utter callousness to pity or truth. And of all the human monsters I have ever met in my travels, I cannot recall any so malignant and odious as the Russian Koolak.
>
> - Emile J. Dillon. *The Eclipse of Russia*. New York: George H. Doran, 1918, p. 67.

Other prerevolutionary references to the kulak are the following:

> The great advavntage the *koulaks* possess over their numerous competitors in the plundering of the peasants, lies in the fact that they are members, generally very influential members, of the village commune. This often enables them to use for their

---

[18] For the complete texts in Russian and in English translation of all of Ezhov's confessions that had been published by 2010 see Grover Furr, ""The Moscow Trials and the "Great Terror" of 1937-1938: What the Evidence Shows.." At http://msuweb.montclair.edu/~furrg/research/trials_ezhovshchina_update0710.html See also Bobrov and Furr, "Marshal S.M. Budiennyi."

private ends the great political power which the self-governing *mir* exercises over each individual member. The distinctive characteristics of this class are very unpleasant. It is the hard, unflinching cruelty of a thoroughly uneducated man who has made his way from poverty to wealth, and has come to consider money-making, by whatever means, as the only pursuit to which a rational being should devote himself.

- "Stepniak" (a pseudonym), *The Russian Peasantry*. London: George Routledge; New York: E.P. Putnam & Co., 1905, p. 55.

On the other side arise the *kulak* (literally, the "fist"), a name coined to designate those ex-serfs and simple peasants who, utilising the unpropitious condition of their fellow members of the commune. made one after another their debtors, next their hired labourers, and appropriated for their own individual use the land shares of those economical weaklings.

The *kulak* is a very interesting figure in rural Russia ... There is no doubt that the methods used by this usurer and oppressor in the peasant's blouse have not been of the cleanest.... The conspicuous position he now occupies came about during the last twenty or thirty years. In Russian literature he has been dubbed he "village eater," and has been clothed with all sorts of diabolical qualities. ... He is the natural product of a vicious system. ...

- Wolf von Schierband, *Russia, her Strength and her Weakness*. New York and London: G.P. Putnam's, 1904, p. 120.

Conclusion: The category of "kulak" is well documented from pre-Soviet times. Snyder's false claim that it was a "Soviet classification" is ignorant.

The *Ezhovshchina*, Again

> In a telegram entitled "On Anti-Soviet Elements,"
> Stalin and the politburo issued general instructions
> on 2 July 1937 for mass repressions in every region
> of the Soviet Union. The Soviet leadership held ku-
> laks responsible for recent waves of sabotage and
> criminality, which meant in effect anything that had
> gone wrong within the Soviet Union. The politburo
> ordered the provincial offices of the NKVD to regis-
> ter all kulaks who resided in their regions, and to
> recommend quotas for execution and deportation.
> Most regional NKVD officers asked to be allowed to
> add various "anti-Soviet elements" to the lists... (80-
> 1)
>
> ... The killing and imprisonment quotas were offi-
> cially called "limits," though everyone involved
> knew that they were meant to be exceeded. Local
> NKVD officers had to explain why they could not
> meet a "limit," and were encouraged to exceed
> them. No NKVD officer wished to be seen as lacking
> élan when confronting "counter-revolution," espe-
> cially when Yezhov's line was "better too far than
> not far enough." (81)

This outline of the *Ezhovshchina* — called the "Great Terror" by anticommunists — is all wrong. The text of the Politburo Decree "On Anti-Soviet Elements" is online in Russian as is a facsimile of the original telegram.[19] It is published in a well-known documentary collection.

---

[19] Text of decree at http://www.alexanderyakovlev.org/fond/issues-doc/61096 Facsimile of the original at http://upload.wikimedia.org/wikipedia/commons/6/6f/Решение_Политбюро_ЦК_ВКП(б)_№_П5194.jpg?uselang=ru This translation is from Getty and Naumov, 470-1. They capi-

Extract from Protocol #51 ofthe Politburo ofthe CC resolution of 2 July 1937

STRICTLY SECRET Central Committee All-Union Communist Party (Bolshevik)

No. P51/94 3 July 1937

To: Comrade Yezhov, secretaries of regional and territorial committees, CCs of the national Communist parties.

#94. On anti-Soviet elements.

The following telegram is to be sent to secretaries of regional and territorial committees and to the CCs of national Communist parties:

"It has been observed that a large number of former kulaks and criminals deported at a certain time from various regions to the north and to Siberian districts and then having returned to their regions at the expiration of their period of exile are the chief instigators of all sorts of anti-Soviet crimes, including sabotage, both in the kolkhozy and sovkhozy as well as in the field of transport and in certain branches of industry. The CC of the VKP(b) recommends to all secretaries of regional and territorial organizations and to all regional, territorial, and republic representatives of the NKVD that they register all kulaks and criminals who have returned home in order that the most hostile among them be forthwith administratively arrested and executed by means of a 3-man commission [troika] and that the remaining, less active but nevertheless hostile elements be listed and exiled to districts [raiony] as indicated by the NKVD. The CC of the VKP (b) recommends that the names of those comprising the 3-man commissions be presented to the C within five

talize the text. The Russian language edition above does not, so we have restored the text to normal sentence format.

days, as well as the number of those subject to execution and the number of those subject to exile."

Secretary of the CC I. Stalin[20]

It is not a "general instruction" for "mass repressions" but instructions for opposing rebellions against the government. This volume
and other documentary collections make it clear that the Soviet
leadership was correct in believing that a serious crisis existed.

The disclosure of a widespread conspiracy by the top leaders of
the Red Army, and the continuing uncovering of high- and medi-
um-ranking Party leaders and officials in several secret conspiratorial organizations, proved that plans — probably several plans
— for a coup against the government and Party leadership in favor
of Germany and Japan had been far advanced.

In his recent study *Practicing Stalinism* Soviet historian J. Arch Getty has written:

> Stalin and his associates seem to have believed that
> a large-scale conspiracy was about to overthrow
> them.[21]

Getty points out that both Molotov and Kaganovich continued to
believe this decades later. (263-4). We have excellent evidence today that such conspiracies did in fact exist. The Tukhachevsky Affair defendants gave details about some of them. Existence that
these military conspiracies not only existed but were connected to
the Rightist conspiracy involving Nikolai Bukharin and Aleksei Rykov, defendants at the third Moscow Trial of March 1938, come
from NKVD escapee Genrikh Liushkov, who informed the Japanese
of them after he fled the USSR in 1938.[22]

What Stalin and the Party leadership did not know was that Nikolai Ezhov, head of the NKVD, was also a conspirator. Ezhov conspired with other Party leaders and with his own subordinates to

---

[20] *Lubianka. Stalin I Glavnoe Upravlenia Gosbezopasnosti NKVD 1937-1938 Dokumenty.* Moscow: MFD, 2004, No. 114, pp. 234-5. (Лубянка. Сталин и Главное Управление
Госбезопасности НКВД. 1937-1938. Документы). Hereafter Lubianka 1937-1938.

[21] J. Arch Getty. *Practicing Stalinism: Bolsheviks, Boyars, and the Persistence of Tradition.* Yale
University Press, 2013, 263.

[22] For a summary and further bibliography see Furr, *Murder of Sergei Kirov,* Chapter 17.

kill as many Soviet citizens as he could, in order to spread discontent with the Soviet system and aid any invasion by Germany or Japan.

Snyder claims that there were "quotas" for executions — and then admits that there were none. In fact all the documents we have today show that the center — Stalin and the top leadership — insisted that the **limits** on executions and imprisonments be restricted. Snyder's claim that "everybody knew" that "limits" really meant "quotas" is false. Like other anticommunist writers Snyder would like to have evidence that Stalin set "quotas" for executions. But Snyder goes too far when he implies that he does have such evidence. And he does imply this, for otherwise how would he know that "everybody knew"?

Arch Getty makes this clear:

> Order No. 447 established limits (*limity*) rather
> than quotas; maximums, not minimums. (*Practicing*
> 201)

He goes on to insist that Stalin could not possibly have intended these numbers to be exceeded (232). Getty also pointed adds the following about the "limits — quotas" issue:

> One of the mysteries of the field [of Soviet history
> — GF] is how *limity* is routinely translated as "quo-
> tas." (*Practicing* 340 n. 109)

Getty's specific example is Oleg Khlevniuk, another researcher whose anticommunist bias and lack of objectivity ruin his scholarship. But it applies to Snyder as well. Maximums are different from minimums. Ideological anticommunists like Khlevniuk and, as here, Snyder, would like their readers to believe that Stalin demanded "maximums," so that's what they write.

Snyder is fabricating again when he states the following:

> Under time pressure to make quotas, officers often
> simply beat prisoners until they confessed. Stalin
> authorized this on 21 July 1937. (82)

It is certainly true that Ezhov and his men beat prisoners until they made false confessions. Some of Ezhov's men confessed to doing this and/or observing other NKVD men doing it. We know this because it is documented, and these documents exist because Ezhov and his men were prosecuted, tried, and punished for these crimes after Ezhov had been removed as Commissar of the NKVD and replaced by Lavrentii Beria.

But the claim that Stalin "authorized this" is false. Neither he nor anyone else has seen any such authorization by Stalin of July 21, 1937, or any other date, because none has been found. If it existed, it would have been well publicized — it is just the kind of evidence that anticommunist writers have been eagerly looking for. It is needless to add that Snyder provides no source for his claim. But few of his readers will know this.

Snyder fills pages 82-84 with accounts of mass shootings. Not all are reliable — many of the secondary sources Snyder uses are by scholars just as lacking in objectivity and prone to making undocumentable statements as Snyder is. Ezhov and his men did shoot hundreds of thousands of Soviet citizens. The point is that Ezhov's mass murders were part of his anti-government conspiracy.

Snyder makes a number of false statements in these pages too. For example:

> Yet even as Stalin presented his own policies as inevitable... (85)

This is false. Snyder cites no such statement by Stalin, nor — to our knowledge — has anyone else.

Phony NKVD "Shorthand"

Snyder claims that NKVD men justified "victimizing" Poles in the following manner:

> In a kind of operational shorthand, NKVD officers said: "Once a Pole, always a kulak.[62] (86)

Snyder's note to this statement reads as follows: "n. 62 - Gurianov, "Obzor," 202." This is a reference to the following work:

> A. Ie. Gurianov, "Obzor sovetskikh repressivnykh kampanii protiv poliakov i pols's'kikh grazhdan," in A. V. Lipatov and I. O. Shaitanov, eds., *Poliaki i russkie: Vzaimoponimanie i vzaimoneponimanie*, Moscow: Indrik, 2000, 199-207.

This is a phony reference. This is no such passage in the article by Gur'ianov (note correct spelling of his name). The expression "Raz poliak — znachit, kulak" was in use in the USSR at the time, perhaps mainly in Ukraine and Belorussia.[23] Crude as it was, such an expression made some sense. Poles in Western Ukraine and Western Belorussia were likely to be "osadnicy," imperialist "settlers," and therefore landlords.

Conclusion to *Bloodlands*, Chapter Two: Every fact-claim Snyder makes in this chapter that alleges some kind of criminal or immoral action by Stalin and/or the Soviet leadership is false.

---

[23] Per Anders Rudling suggests that this term was used in Belorussia during 1937-1938. "Vialikaia Aichynnaia vaina u sviadomastsi belaruau (The Great Patriotic War in the minds of Belorussians)"*Arkhe* (Minsk) 5 (2008), p. 44.

Chapter 5. Examining Snyder's Claim of "National Terror" in *Bloodlands*, Chapter 3

In Chapter 3 of *Bloodlands* Snyder turns to the *Ezhovshchina* of 1937-1938 and specifically the "Polish Operation", Nikolai Ezhov's mass murders of Soviet citizens of Polish descent. Snyder also discusses the NKVD campaign against Polish espionage and the "Polish Military Organization."

Snyder's account is completely false. This is partly due to Snyder's deliberate falsifications and withholding of evidence from his readers. Without doubt, it is also due in part to Snyder's ignorance of Soviet history. It seems clear that Snyder has never devoted any serious study to the extremely important issue of the illegal mass murders called the *Ezhovshchina*.

A full history of the *Ezhovshchina* is beyond the scope of this book. We can state that all the evidence available to researchers today confirms that the mass murders, and especially the "national operations" against persons of various nationalities, were part of the conspiracy by Nikolai Ezhov to maximize discontent with the Soviet system and so facilitate uprisings in the wake of any invasion of the USSR by hostile powers such as Germany or Japan.[1]

This chapter of *Bloodlands* is of sufficient interest that we will deal with most of it in the body of this book. In the following chapter we'll discuss a few aspects of the *Ezhovshchina* in more depth, and also point out some falsifications in a few of Snyder's published articles.

---

[1] See Furr, "The Moscow Trials and the "Great Terror" of 1937-1938: What the Evidence Shows," cited in the last chapter.

Another Falsification by Snyder…

> People belonging to national minorities "should be
> forced to their knees and shot like mad dogs." It
> was not an SS officer speaking but a communist
> party leader, **in the spirit of the national opera-**
> **tions of Stalin's Great Terror**….[1] (89) (Emphasis
> added, GF)

Snyder's note to this passage (n.1 p. 471):

> * Martin, "Origins," which, Snyder claims "brings analytical
> rigor to the national operations."[2]
> * "Quotation": Jansen, *Executioner*, 96;
> * "See also" Baberowski, *Terror*, 198.

The quotation is actually in **Jansen and Petrov**, page 98 at note
96. It reads as follows:

> In the words of the Krasnoiarsk province Party sec-
> retary, Sobolev: "Stop playing internationalism, all
> these Poles, Koreans, Latvians, Germans, etc. should
> be beaten, these are all mercenary nations, subject
> to termination… all nationals should be caught,
> forced to their knees, and exterminated like mad
> dogs." This may have been an exaggeration, but (af-
> ter Ezhov's fall) he was accused of this by the Kras-
> noiarsk state security organs' Party organization:
> "By giving such instructions, Sobolev **slandered**
> the VKP(b) and comrade Stalin, in saying that he
> had such instructions from the Central Committee
> and comrade Stalin personally."[60] (Emphasis added,
> GF)

The revised and updated Russian version of 2007 reads similarly.[3]
The words of the original edition, "this may have been an exagger-

---

[2] Martin, "Origins" is in fact an overview of Soviet ethnic policy. But it is composed from the materials available in the mid-1990s, when a great many important primary sources on the Ezhovshchina had not yet been published, and so is of limited usefulness today.

[3] "Так, первый секретарь Красноярского крайкома С. М. Соболев, выступая на оперативных совещаниях УНКВД, заявлял: «Довольно играть в интернационализм, надо бить всех этих поляков, корейцев, латышей, немцев и т.д., все это продажные

ation," are omitted in the later Russian edition. No doubt this omission is intended to lend a more anticommunist flavor to the passage. Petrov is a leading figure in the "Memorial Society", a fervently anticommunist organization, and Petrov's publications on Soviet history, tendentious and full of vituperation, cannot be trusted.

Once again, Snyder is misleading his readers here. He claims that this statement was "in the spirit of the national operations of Stalin's Great Terror." *But the very quotation he cites says precisely the opposite of this — that this statement was "slander"* (see above).

Jansen and Petrov (henceforth J&P) inform us that this statement is an accusation made against Sobolev during the investigations, arrests, and prosecutions against Ezhov and his men (their footnote is to an archival document in Ezhov's files). In fact we only know about the statement at all because of this investigation — it is attributed to Sobolev by his accusers, Beria's men, who were working to investigate and prosecute Ezhov's massive crimes. They and Beria were of course doing so at the behest of Stalin and the Soviet leadership.

Jansen and Petrov, both extremely anticommunist and anti-Stalin writers, admit that the NKVD claim that Sobolev made this statement "may have been an exaggeration." But Snyder does not inform his readers of this fact. Nor was it, in Snyder's words, "Stalin's Great Terror." On the contrary: it was Ezhov's. Ezhov and hundreds of his men were investigated, prosecuted, and many of them executed, because the massacres they committed were *not* authorized by Stalin or the Soviet Party or government. Later in this chapter we cite some of the relevant evidence.

Another Lie by Jörg Baberowski

The second reference Snyder cites here — **Baberowski**, *Terror*, 198, — falsifies just as flagrantly as does Snyder. Baberowski

---

нации, подлежащие истреблению... Всех националов надо ловить, ставить на колени и истреблять как бешеных собак». После падения Ежова, парторганизация УНКВД осудила Соболева, посчитав, что «давая такие указания, Соболев клеветал на ЦК ВКП(б) и тов. Сталина, говоря, что он такие указания имеет от ЦК ВКП(б) и *лично от тов. Сталина*.»" (114)

claims that Ezhov said "The Poles must be completely annihilated" (*Die Polen müssen vollständig vernichtet werden*). Baberowski's own footnote to this paragraph gives two references:

> [92] Zitiert in Suvenirov, *Tragedija*, S. 208; Jansen/Petrov, *Stalin's Loyal Executioner*, S. 98.

Anyone who checks these sources will discover that the supposed "quote" from Ezhov is Baberowski's own creation — a fabrication. Neither Suvenirov nor J&P documents it. It would not be surprising if Ezhov did say it, or something like it, since it is consistent with his conspiracy. But Baberowski does not say that "it would be logical" for Ezhov to have said it — he says that Ezhov *did* say it. Therefore, he is lying.

Baberowski frequently falsifies as he does here. Several years ago I wrote an article about another example of his dishonesty: "Baberowski's Falsification."[4] But Snyder is responsible for this lie as well. It is a historian's duty to verify the fact-claims he cites, as we are doing in the case of Snyder's book. This is a "circular citation" — a reference that simply refers again to materials Snyder has already cited. The Jansen/Petrov reference is to the same passage Snyder has also cited dishonestly.

Suvenirov, *Tragediia RKKA 1937-1938*, p. 208, quotes from interrogations of Ezhov's men by Beria's men — in other words, the investigation of Ezhov's unauthorized mass murders, undertaken by Beria at the instigation of the Politburo and, of course, of Stalin.

Neither Snyder, nor any of the "sources" he cites here tell their readers that *such evidence as they have comes from prosecutions of Ezhov's men, and Ezhov himself, for massive illegal repressions.* All these authors — Snyder, Jansen/Petrov, Baberowski, and Suvenirov — deliberately give the impression that this was official Soviet policy, sanctioned by Stalin and the Politburo when, in reality, the opposite was the case.

---

[4] Grover Furr, "Baberowski's Falsification." At http://www.tinyurl.com/baberowski

The Case of "The Polish Military Organization"

The "Polish operation" was a part of Ezhov's mass murder campaign. Snyder seriously falsifies it. He writes:

> Stalin was a pioneer of national mass murder, and the Poles were the preeminent victim among the Soviet nationalities. (89)

This is false; the national mass murder was Ezhov's. Snyder continues:

> The Polish national minority, like the kulaks, had to take the blame for the failures of collectivization. The rationale was invented during the famine itself in 1933, and then applied during the Great Terror in 1937 and 1938. In 1933, the NKVD chief for Ukraine, Vsevolod Balytskyi, had explained the mass starvation as a provocation of an espionage cabal that he called the "Polish Military Organization." According to Balytskyi, this "Polish Military Organization" had infiltrated the Ukrainian branch of the communist party, and backed Ukrainian and Polish nationalists who sabotaged the harvest and then used the starving bodies of Ukrainian peasants as anti-Soviet propaganda. It had supposedly inspired a nationalist "Ukrainian Military Organization," a doppelganger performing the same fell work and sharing responsibility for the famine.[2] (89-90)

Source: (n. 2 p. 471): "For greater detail on the Polish line, see Snyder, *Sketches*, 115-132."

Snyder is wrong. We showed in the first chapter that Balitskii[5] did not "explain the mass starvation as a provocation" of Polish military intelligence or of any other organization — and, of course, Snyder does not cite any evidence that he did.

---

[5] Snyder uses "Balytskyi", a Ukrainian spelling (another, more accurate, transliteration of the Ukrainian would be "Balyts'kyy") though almost all the sources we have concerning him are in Russian. I will use the Russian spelling.

Snyder cites Chapter Six of his own book *Sketches from a Secret War: A Polish Artist's Mission to Liberate Soviet Ukraine*, 115-132. In this work Snyder documents the fact that Polish espionage really did exist in the USSR during the 1930s![6] In *Sketches*, but not in *Bloodlands*, Snyder admits that Polish spies were active in the USSR in the 1930s — the hero of his book, Henryk Józefski, ran some of them — and that some of these spies were indeed active within the Polish Communist Party. For example, he writes:

> These, and similar sources, such as the records of the counterintelligence sections of the Polish Army's field commands, can now be read in a different light. They suggest the degree of Polish penetration of the Soviet Union in the late 1920s and the early 1930s, and the political design that lay behind the border crossings, the sabotage, and the support of local nationalists. (Sketches, xviii)

> Jozewski's Volhynia Experiment united these two goals, supporting Ukrainian culture in Poland while serving as a base for espionage operations within the Soviet Union. (xxi)

> By 1932 the work of the Lwow command brought measurable results. In March it could boast sixty-one active agents, and missions in the GPU in Proskuriv, Iampol, Shepetivka, and Kam'iants' Podil's'kyi, in the Dniester fleet, and in the Kyiv and Kharkiv garrisons of the Red Army. (89; emphasis added.)

Many more such quotations from Snyder's *Sketches* could be cited.

In the one confession statement by Witold Wandurski now available to scholars and cited by Snyder in *Sketches* (but not in *Bloodlands*), Wandurski says concerning his Polish communist contacts working in the USSR:

---

[6] It is possible that the Polish military intelligence no longer referred to itself as the POW, the Polish acronym for the "Polska Organizacja Wojskowa" or Polish Military Organization, although some of those arrested as Polish spies had been in the POW and referred to the Polish underground intelligence organization as the POW.

> W okresie moich kontaktów z wymienionymi osobami przekonałem się, że mam do czynienia z ludźmi, grającymi podwójną rolę: z jednej strony zajmowali wysokie stanowiska w partii, a z drugiej byli zagorzałymi piłsudczykami. (504)

Translated:

> In the course of my contacts with these people I realized that I was dealing with people who were playing a double role: on the one hand they held high positions in the party, on the other, they were staunch Pilsudski supporters.

Wandurski outlines the way he himself was torn between his desire for social reform, which drew him towards the communist party and resulted in his being arrested several times in Poland, and his Polish nationalism. Due to his close relations with Polish nationalists he was finally drawn into subversive work in the USSR:

> Jeśli chodzi o Granta, to po rozmowach i kontaktach z nim nie miałem nawet cienia wątpliwości, że zachował on przekonania peowiaka i wciąga mnie w szeregi POW, abym później pracował w ZSRR.
>
> Tak więc, gdy w 1929 r. przyjechałem do ZSRR, byłem już w gruncie rzeczy, choć nie formalnie, członkiem POW. (504)

Translated:

> As for Grant, after my conversations and dealings with him I did not have even the shadow of a doubt that he retained the beliefs of a "Peowiak" (POW member) and he drew me into the ranks of the POW for later work in the USSR.
>
> So when in 1929 I came to the USSR, I was already fundamentally, though not formally, a member of the POW.

As these passages prove, Snyder is perfectly aware that Polish espionage was a real threat in the USSR at this time. But he withholds this information from his readers and pretends that there was no such threat (see below).

Snyder gives no evidence at all that Balitskii "explained the mass starvation" as the result of espionage. This section of Snyder's paragraph appears to be a falsification of his own invention.

The Polish Military Organization (PMO)

(Note: The PMO is often referred to the "POW" and "PVO", Polish and Russian abbreviations respectively for "Polish Military Organization")

Snyder's chief falsification in this section is his statement that the PMO no longer existed, and therefore was an invention by the Soviet NKVD. He states:

> This was a historically inspired invention. There was no Polish Military Organization during the 1930s, in Soviet Ukraine or anywhere else. It had once existed, back during the Polish-Bolshevik War of 1919-1920, as a reconnaissance group for the Polish Army. The Polish Military Organization had been overmastered by the Cheka, and was dissolved in 1921. Balytskyi knew the history, since he had taken part in the deconspiracy and the destruction of the Polish Military Organization back then. (90)

This is a particularly bizarre falsehood by Snyder since many sources, including some Snyder himself cites in his book *Sketches*, document the continued existence of the PMO. We shall demonstrate this below.

Snyder then claims that during the 1930s Polish espionage in the USSR "played no political role" — i.e. was impotent.

> In the 1930s Polish spies played no political role in Soviet Ukraine. They lacked the capacity to do so even in 1930 and 1931 when the USSR was most vulnerable, and they could still run agents across the border. They lacked the intention to intervene after the Soviet-Polish nonaggression pact was initialed in January 1932. After the famine, they gen-

erally lost any remaining confidence about their ability to understand the Soviet system, much less change it. Polish spies were shocked by the mass starvation when it came, and unable to formulate a response. Precisely because there was no real Polish threat in 1933, Balytskyi had been able to manipulate the symbols of Polish espionage as he wished. This was typical Stalinism: it was always easier to exploit the supposed actions of an "organization" that did not exist.[3]

Sources (n. 3 p. 471):

* Snyder, *Sketches*, 115-116.

* "The 'Polish Military Organization' idea seems to have originated in 1929, when a Soviet agent was placed in charge of the security commission of the Communist Party of Poland." (Snyder refers to Stroński, *Represje*, 210.)

Snyder's claims that "this was a historically inspired invention" and that "there was no Polish Military Organization" are false. Not only did the PMO exist during the 1930s; *it continued to exist in the 1940s, under German occupation.* In 1942 German intelligence considered the PMO to be the largest continuing Polish threat in Nazi-occupied Lithuania:

Из отчёта оперативной группы А полиции безопасности о положении в Прибалтике, Белоруссии, Ленинградской области, за период с 16 октября 1941 г. по 31 января 1942 г....

3. Литва...

Из польских тайных организаций, действовавших еще в советское время, сегодня доказано существование следующих:

1. ПОВ — Польска организация войскова

2. Млода польска — Молодая Польша

3. ЦВП — Связь вольных поляков

4. Блок сражающейся Польши

Эти организации в большинстве своем возглавляются бывшими офицерами. Однако и польские священнослужители широко представлены в их руководстве. Главной организацией является ПОВ. Она обучает свои подразделения военному делу и готовит их к партизанской войне....

Source: РГВА. Ф. 500к «Главное управление имперской безопасности (РСХА)» (г.Берлин). Оп. 4 Д.92 Л. 120-147[7]

Translated:

From the report of operative group A of the security police concerning the situation in the Baltics, Belorussia, and the Leningrad oblast' for the period from October 16, 1941 to January 31, 1942...

3. Lithuania...

Of the Polish secret organizations still active during Soviet times today we have evidence of the existence of the following:

1. PMO — Polish Military Organization ("Polska Organizacja Wojskowa")

2. Młoda Polska — Young Poland.

3. TsVP — Union of Free Poles.

4. The Bloc of Fighting Poland.

These organizations, for the most part, are led by former officers. However, Polish priests are widely represented in their leadership as well. The main organization is the PMO. It gives its units military training and prepares them for partisan warfare...

Source: RGVA, F. 500k "Reichssicherheitshauptamt (RSHA)" (Berlin) Op. 4 D. 92. ll.120-147. (Emphasis added)

---

[7] At http://9may.ru/unsecret/m10009059

Snyder's bizarre claim that no PMO existed after the early 1920s can, I think, only be explained if we assume that Snyder believed (a) his readers will be too ignorant of the history of this period to realize how incompetent (or dishonest) his statement really is; and (b) those researchers who might know it will be too anticommunist to expose such a useful anticommunist falsehood.

Snyder cites his own book *Sketches*, pp. 115-116, where he describes the beginning of the "POV" (= PMO) case, evidently as outlined by his secondary sources. But Snyder presents no evidence that the PMO had ceased to exist in 1921, "was a historically inspired invention", no longer existed, etc., nor that "there was no real Polish threat."

In reality, there can be no such evidence in principle. Any country with a secret military espionage service in an enemy country would surely deny its existence. Therefore, such a denial would not constitute evidence worthy of attention that the group did not in fact exist. But Snyder does not even cite any official Polish denial of the PMO's existence!

The reference Snyder cites here — "**Stroński**, *Represje*, 210" — states that the Polish Communist Party was riven by fights and splits. In 1929 Viktor Zytlowski, a Polish immigrant to the USSR and "an employee of the GPU" was appointed head of a "security commission" for the Party by its Politburo. In 1934 Zytlowski announced the discovery of a PMO cell in the Polish Party's leadership. Stroński cites no evidence that this charge was false.

In fact the evidence now available strongly suggests the contrary, as we shall see. We have a great deal of testimony concerning the existence and activities of the PMO.

> The "Polish Military Organization," Balytskyi had argued back in summer 1933, had smuggled into the Soviet Union countless agents who pretended to be communists fleeing persecution in their Polish homeland. ...The arrests of Polish political émigrés in the Soviet Union began in July 1933. The Polish communist playwright Witold Wandurski was jailed in August 1933, and forced to confess to participation in the Polish Military Organization. With

this link between Polish communism and Polish espionage documented in interrogation protocols,
more Polish communists were arrested in the USSR.
The Polish communist Jerzy Sochacki left a message
in his own blood before jumping to his death from a
Moscow prison in 1933: "I am faithful to the party
to the end."[4] (90)

Sources (n. 4 p. 472):

* Stroński, *Represje*, 211-213.

* "On Sochacki, see Kieszczyński, "Represje," 202."

* For further details on Wandurski, see Shore, *Caviar and Ashes*."

* "At least one important Polish communist did return from the Soviet Union and work for the Poles: his book is Reguła, *Historia*."

Stroński, *Represje*, 211-213 simply summarizes the PMO conspiracy, especially in the Ukraine, that the NKVD had allegedly uncovered, including alleged contacts with Ukrainian nationalists.
Stroński does *not* claim that the conspiracy was fabricated by the
GPU, did not exist, etc.

Kieszczyński, "Represje," 202: This essay was published in 1989.
It is basically a list of information that was known — or merely
suspected, since little documentation is given — about the fates of
the members of the Central Committee of the Polish Communist
Party. At that time, in 1989, virtually none of the Soviet archival
materials now available had been made public. Therefore, aside
from a few bits of biographical information, therefore, the
Kieszczyński article is outdated and useless. Snyder must have
known this. But it is unlikely that his readers will know it.

Much more information about Sochacki is now available. We discuss it more fully below. As for Marci Shore, in *Caviar and Ashes*
she simply assumes, without evidence, that Wandurski was innocent. This is an invalid assumption in principle: a scholar should
always require evidence. Moreover, there is a lot of other evidence
concerning Wandurski too. One confession of Wandurski's has

been published.[8] Wandurski is also named by others who were arrested and confessed to espionage for Poland.[9]

In his earlier book *Sketches* Snyder cites the one published confession of Witold Wandurski, in which Wandurski states that he was indeed recruited to the POW:

> Tak więc w 1929 r. wyjechałem do ZSRR będąc już przygotowany do praktycznej działalności w POW, chociaż ani Bratkowski, ani Wróblewski czy Wojewódzki nie używali tego terminu w rozmowach ze mną.

Translated:

> So, already in 1929 I left for the USSR, being prepared for practical work with the POW, although Bratkowski, Worblewski and Wojewodski did not use that term in their talks with me. ("Zezanania Wandurskiego," 493)

Snyder deceives his readers concerning "the Polish communist Jerzy Sochacki" by omitting the evidence that Sochacki really was a Polish spy. In *Sketches* Snyder writes:

> In November 1933, a Polish officer in Kyiv implied in a report to his superior that the communist Jerzy Czeszejko-Sochacki, arrested that summer, was working for Polish intelligence. (123)

Snyder then adds the following remark:

> It is perhaps worthy of note that the Second Department's information about Jan Bielewski, the representative of the Polish Party in the Communist International, was much more precise. (123)

---

[8] Maria Wosiek. "Zeznania Witolda Wandurskiego we wienzeniu GPU." *Pamietnik Teatralny*, Nos 3-4, 1996, pp. 487-510.

[9] *Sprava 'Pol's'koi Orhanizatsii Viys'kovoi' v Ukraini 1920-1938 rr. (Справа «Польської Організації Військової» в Україні. 1920—1938 рр.)* Kyiv, 2011, pp. 197, 198, 220, 299. See following footnote.

Snyder knows, but hides from his readers, that Sochacki was named as a leader of PMO work within the USSR in detailed confession statements by Wandurski. For example:

> Przez cały okres naszych kontaktów Grant
> ostrożnie i stopniowo przygotowywał mnie do
> pracy na rzecz POW, co zakończyło się
> wciągnięciem mnie do działalności tej organizacji.
> Grant był jedną z osób najbliższych Bratkowskiemu
> i poinformował go o wciągnięciu mnie do POW.
> Stało się to dla mnie jasne po kilku spotkaniach z
> Bratkowskim, podczas których wieloznacznie
> podkreślał, że jest zadowolony z układu, jaki
> powstał między mną a Grantem. (508)

Translated:

> Throughout the period of our contacts Grant was
> cautiously and gradually preparing me to work for
> the POW, which ended up by my being drawn into
> the activities of this organization. Grant was one of
> the people closest to Bratkowski (= Sochacki) and
> told him about my being drawn into the POW. This
> became clear to me after several meetings with
> Bratkowski, during which ambiguously emphasized
> that he was satisfied with the arrangement between
> me and Grant.

In the recent document collection *Sprava POV v Ukraini 1920-1938 rr.*[10] (The Case of the PMO in the Ukraine, 1920-1938) Sochacki is named by one of those arrested as a leader of the Moscow branch of the POW, along with Wandurskii and others.

> Руководящий центр «Польской Военной
> Организации» на территории СССР находился в
> Москве (ранее он находился в Киеве, затем в
> Минске). В его состав входили:

---

[10] *СПРАВА «Польської Організації Військової» в Україні. 1920 — 1938 рр. Збірник документів та матеріалів.* Київ 2011.

СОХАЦКИЙ-БРАТКОВСКИЙ — б[ывший] секретарь ППС, агент 2-го отдела Польглавштаба, непосредственно был связан с начальником 2-го отделения военной контрразведки ВОЕВУДСКИМ, зав[едующим] пол[ьским] сектором в Институте Маркса-Энгельса-Ленина.

...

ВАНДУРСКИЙ — б[ывший] член КПП, писатель, б[ывший] директор поль[ского] театра в Киеве, и др. (197)

Translated:

The leadership center of the "Polish Military Organization" on Soviet territory is situated in Moscow (formerly it was in Kiev, then in Minsk). Among its members:

Sochacki-Bratkowski — former secretary of the PPS [=Polish Socialist Party], agent of the 2nd section of the Polish General Staff, was directly connected to the chief of the 2nd division of military counterintelligence WOJEWÓDSKI, head of the Polish sector in the Marx-Engels-Lenin Institute.

...

WANDURSKI — former member of the PKK [=Polish Communist Party], writer, former director of the Polish theater in Kiev, and others (197)

Sochacki is named many times in the various interrogations.[11] In his published interrogation Wandurski names Sochacki as well (503). Both Sochacki and Wandurski, along with many others, are named in interrogations of others accused of PMO activities in 1933 published in 2010.[12]

---

[11] See pages 198, 200, 201, 202, 203, 204, 209, 210, 216, 217, 218, 225, 241, 249, 268, 270, 271, 272, 286, 287, 288, 289, 290, 293, 296, 298, 308, 312, 316, 354, 408.

[12] Томазова Наталія. Олександр Скібневський: *До Історії Польського Театру в Києві. Пам'ятки*. 2010, сс. 215-245. (Natalia Tomazova. Oleksandr Skibnevs'kyy. *Do istorii*

The unavoidable implication of all this evidence is this: Sochacki was indeed a leader of Polish espionage for military intelligence. The name "PVO", the Russian abbreviation for PMO, is the one uniformly used in all these documents. Whether the "official" name for this service, if it had one at all, was still PMO or not would appear to make no difference.

As for Snyder's claim that the Polish Military Organization had been shut down in 1921, here is what Wandurski had to say in his confession (cited above):

> Jednak również po drugim aresztowaniu
> Skarżyński nie został zdemaskowany i wyjechał do
> Polski, gdzie w 1922 r. przypadkowo spotkałem go
> w Warszawie w jednej z kawiarni. Ucieszył się z
> naszego spotkania i z pasją opowiadał mi o pracy w
> szeregach POW na Radzieckiej Ukrainie.

Translated:

> But even after his second arrest Skarzynski was not
> exposed and went to Poland, where in 1922, I acci-
> dentally met him in Warsaw in one of the cafés. He
> was pleased with our meeting and passionately told
> me about working in the ranks of the POW in the
> Soviet Ukraine.

The continued existence of the PMO is cited many times in the published interrogations and in NKVD reports now available. How likely is it that all of them could have been "forged" or otherwise faked? At any rate, as with any historical statement such a forgery cannot be simply *assumed*, as Snyder does — it would have to be supported with evidence. But it is very likely that a clandestine military intelligence — espionage organization would keep its existence secret and "deniable." Therefore there is no reason to assert, as Snyder does, that the PMO no longer existed.

---

pol's'koi teatru v Kyevi. Pam'iatki, 2010.) At
http://archive.nbuv.gov.ua/portal/Soc_Gum/Pam/2010_11/14.pdf

In his study of the Comintern[13] during the 1930s William Chase records Bielewski's report to the Executive Committee of the Communist International (ECCI) about the dangers of infiltration by Polish intelligence of the Polish Communist Party.

> On 4 September, Bielewski wrote a "top secret" document entitled "On the Issue of the Crisis of the Leadership of the CPP" that focused on the dangers posed by fascists, reactionaries, and their agents, especially the Trotskyists. In light of the alleged dangers, he asserted that the destruction of these counterrevolutionary elements by the "NKVD under the direction of comrade Yezhov is a necessary act of self-defense." According to Bielewski, the arrested leaders of the CPP pursued an emigration policy designed to penetrate agents of the Polish Military Organization into the USSR. After listing and decrying the party leadership's errors, which dated back to 1919, and its repeated failure to promote workers' causes, he recommended that the "healthy elements" carry out a complete reorganization of the party and its leadership and enhance its ties to the masses.

Chase expresses skepticism about the charges in Bielewski's report, and suggests that Bielewski's arrest a week later was unfounded.

> As fantastic as this conspiratorial explanation seems, it was the assumption upon which Yezhov's NKVD built its case against present and former leaders of the CPP, including Bielewski, who was arrested a week after writing his report. The NKVD's assumption became the ECCI's conclusion. (264)

Evidently the NKVD's suspicions of Bielewski were correct. And Bielewski was on the ECCI (Executive Committee of the Com-

---

[13] William Chase. *Enemies Within the Gates? The Comintern and the Stalinist Repression, 1934—1939*. New Haven, CT: Yale University Press, 2001.

munist International), the highest Comintern body. This is evidence of Polish espionage at the highest levels. Chase prints the notes ordered by Georgy Dimitrov, head of the Comintern, of the confession of Julian Lenski, another high-ranking Polish CP member, concerning the investigation of the Polish Communist Party. (266-273). Along with many others, Bielewski is named as a Polish spy:

> [We] also agreed on using Cichowski, Bielewski, Redens [Mieczyslaw Bernstein], and Maksymowski. We used the first three and planted [them] in the Comintern. (271)

> I suggested appointing the following individuals, who were the POW members, to the verification commission: Próchniak, Skulski, Bielewski, Bortnowski, Krajewski. (272)

Snyder cites no evidence disproving the existence of the PMO. Soviet NKVD reports do document clandestine Polish spies, some of whom confessed to being members of the PMO.

Thus there is no evidence that Wandurski, Bielewski, or any of the others was forced to *falsely* confess, as implied by Snyder's phrase "forced to confess." (*Bloodlands* 90) Stroński too claims that Sochacki was "forced to confess" (*Wymuszone na nim zeznania*, p. 210). But Stroński also fails to cite any evidence that this was so. Shore, whose book Snyder cites here, also affirms that Wandurski was forced to make a false confession, and also without any evidence. Use of such language as "forced to confess" implies that the confession was a fabrication. In fact *none* of these authors has any evidence that it Wandurski's confession was false.

According to William Chase, Sochacki was denounced as a police provocateur by the Politburo of the Polish Communist Party:

> On 10 October, [Osip] Pyatnitsky sent to Lazar Kaganovich, a VKP Politburo member and one of Stalin's staunchest allies, a draft declaration by the Central Committee of the Polish CP asserting that Sochacki was a provocateur. Jan Bielewski (aka Jan

> Paszyn), a member of the Politburo of the Polish CP,
> composed the declaration…(119)

Chase gives the political context for these suspicions on pages 118 ff. It was not a case of being suspicious of Poles, but of the heterogeneous origins and history of the Polish CP.

Snyder does mention the "Soviet agent" in the Polish CP. Chase has more to say about this man, Mitskevich-Kapsukas:

> An early May 1929 report from Mitskevich-
> Kapsukas provided material to support that suspi-
> cion. Entitled "The Work of Polish Wreckers," the
> report expressed concern over the growth of fac-
> tionalism and the increasing influence of former
> Mensheviks within the Polish CP. It asserted that a
> wide network of provocateurs had weakened the
> party's ability to function and that Polish police had
> hamstrung many organs of the CPWU and CPWB.[14]
> (118)

Even Snyder suggests that "at least one" Polish communist was, or became, a Polish spy. The Comintern suspected many more than this. At least some of them confessed. Chase's study provides much more evidence about these suspicions. As we have seen, those allegations that we can now check against published primary documents appear to be true.

It is clear from the documents Chase quotes that the initiative for such suspicions came from the Comintern leadership. Stalin was reacting to them, not initiating them.

More Falsehoods by Snyder About Polish Espionage

> Yezhov followed Balytskyi's anti-Polish campaign in
> Soviet Ukraine, and then reconceptualized it. As the
> show trials began in Moscow in 1936, Yezhov drew
> his subordinate Balytskyi into a trap. While promi-
> nent communists confessed in Moscow, Balytskyi

---

[14] Communist Party of Western Ukraine and Communist Party of Western Belorussia.

was reporting from Kiev that the "Polish Military Organization" had been re-created in Soviet Ukraine. No doubt he simply wished to claim attention and resources for himself and his local apparatus at a time of security panic. Yet now, in a turn of events that must have surprised Balytskyi, Yezhov declared that the "Polish Military Organization" was an even greater danger than Balytskyi claimed. It was a matter not for the regional NKVD in Kiev but for the central NKVD in Moscow. Balytskyi, who had invented the plot of the "Polish Military Organization," now lost control of the story. Soon a confession was extracted from the Polish communist Tomasz Dąbal, who claimed to have directed the "Polish Military Organization" in the entire Soviet Union.[7] (91-2)

Sources: (n. 7 p. 427):

* Stroński, *Represje*, 227;

* Snyder, *Sketches*, 119-120.

Neither of these sources provides any evidence for the statements in this paragraph. **Stroński**, *Represje*, 227 concerns events in 1938. None of the matters in this paragraph are discussed there. **Snyder**, *Sketches* 119-120 outlines the investigation and suppression of the PMO espionage within the USSR during the mid-1930s.

Snyder has no evidence whatsoever to sustain his repeated claim that there was no such espionage and that those who were arrested, named by others, confessed, etc., as Polish spies were not guilty. But instead of acknowledging this fact Snyder uses "argument by quotation mark", putting "scare quotes" around everything he would like his readers to believe is false. This is a form of the logical fallacy of "begging the question" — assuming that which ought to be proven.

Snyder's claim that the PMO did not exist and was a falsification by the NKVD is itself a falsification, an attempt to mislead his readers. As we have shown above, Snyder himself, in his earlier book *Sketches*, acknowledges the seriousness of Polish espionage inside the USSR in the 1930s. Moreover, Snyder cites materials in that book that document Polish spies confessing to participation in the PMO. We have also cited the recent Ukrainian book about the PMO in the USSR and a German intelligence document of 1942 that states that the PMO was the most active Polish underground organization in Nazi-occupied Lithuania at the time.

Snyder, like Stroński, assumes that Dombal (Russian spelling of Dąbal) was innocent, forced to confess. This is "begging the question" again — assuming that which should be proven. There is no evidence that Dombal was forced to falsely confess. We do have one confession of Dombal's, dated January 16, 1937 (Lubianka 1937-1938, No. 5). Dombal was arrested on December 29, 1936.

We also have two very detailed reports by Ezhov concerning the "Polish Operation" (Lubianka 1937-1938 Nos. 167, 200). Balitskii is not mentioned in any of them.

Snyder continues:

> Thanks to Yezhov's initiative, the "Polish Military Organization" lost any residue of its historical and regional origins, and became simply a threat to the Soviet Union as such. On 16 January 1937 Yezhov presented his theory of a grand Polish conspiracy to Stalin, and then with Stalin's approval to a plenum of the central committee. In March Yezhov purged the NKVD of Polish officers. Although Balytskyi was not Polish but Ukrainian by nationality, he now found himself in a very awkward position. If the "Polish Military Organization" had been so important, asked Yezhov, why had Balytskyi not been more vigilant? Thus Balytskyi, who had summoned up the specter of the "Polish Military Organization" in the first place, became a victim of his own creation. He yielded his Ukrainian position in May to his former deputy, Izrail Leplevskii—the NKVD officer who carried out the kulak operation in Soviet Ukraine with such vigor. On 7 July Balytskyi was arrested on charges of espionage for Poland; a week later his name was removed from the stadium

> where Dynamo Kiev played its soccer matches—to be replaced by Yezhov's. Balytskyi was executed that November.[8] (92)

Snyder's sources (n. 8 p. 471):

> * Nikol's'kyi, *Represyvna*, 337;
>
> * Stroński, *Represje*, 227.
>
> * "For details on Balyts'kyi, see Shapoval, "Balyts'kyi," 69-74."

Snyder is inventing stories again. There's nothing in any of his sources about Ezhov asking Balitskii why he had not been more vigilant or Balitskii "becoming a victim of his own creation."

Nikol's'kyi, *Represyvna*, 337 simply describes the beginning of the *Ezhovshchina* of July 1937 onwards, with quotations from a few of the central NKVD texts. There's nothing about the POW/PMO, Ezhov report, Balitskii, Leplevskii, or any of the matters specifically mentioned in this paragraph.

Stroński, *Represje*, 227 does discussion Ezhov and the PMO case. But it does not deal with any of the matters in this paragraph: Ezhov's January 1937 report, or Balitskii, or Leplevskii. Stroński does not mention Balitskii after 1936.

According to the Bibliography in *Bloodlands* **Shapoval**, "Balyts'kyi", is an article in a Ukrainian language collection.[15] The text of the article ends on p. 73, so the reference cannot be "69-74." Only pages 69 — 70 give relevant information about Balitskii, but that is interesting.

> Балицького заарештували 7 липня 1937 р. у службовому вагоні за ордером № 15 без дати за підписом М.Єжова. Провели обшук, відібрали урядові нагороди: три ордени Червоного прапора, ордени Червоної Зірки та Трудового Червоного Прапора УРСР, два знаки почесного чекіста. Він протримався недовго, і в заяві від 17 липня зізнався, що був втягнутий И Якіром наприкінці 1935 р. у "військово-фашистський

---

[15] Юрій Шаповал, Володимир Пристайко, Вадим Золотарьов. *ЧК-ГПУ-НКВД в Украіні: особи, факти, документи*. К.: Абрис. 1997.

заколот." А на допиті 26 липня, який провели
заступник наркома внутрішніх справ СРСР
Л.Бельський, начальник 5-го відділу ГУДБ НКВД
СРСР М.Ніколаєв-Журід та помічник останнього
Р.Лістенгурт, Балицький засвідчив, що особисто
завербував своїх заступників М.Бачинського та
В.Іванова, начальника 6-го відділу УДБ НКВД
УРСР Я.Письменного та начальників УНКВД по
Харківській області С.Мазо та по Воронезькій
області О.Розанова.

Translated:

Balitskii was arrested July 7, 1937 in his official car
on the undated warrant number 15 signed by N.
Ezhov. They searched him and took away his government awards: three Orders of the Red Banner,
the Order of Red Star and the Red Banner of Labor
of the USSR, two awards "Honorable Chekist." He
did not hold out long, and his statement of July 17
admitted that he was recruited by I. Yakir at the end
of 1935 into the "military-fascist rebellion." And on
July 26 interrogation, conducted by deputy People's
Commissar of Internal Affairs of the USSR L. Belsky,
head of the 5th Division HUDB NKVD of the USSR N.
Nikolayev-Zhurid and his assistant R. Listengurt,
Balitskii testified that he personally recruited his
deputies M. Bachinskii and B. Ivanov, chief of the
6th Division UDB NKVD USSR Ia. Pismennyi and
heads UNKVD in the Kharkov region S. Mazo and in
Voronezh region O. Rozanov. (69)

The dates of these interrogations may or may not be correct —
Shapoval gives only an archival identifier that of course cannot be
verified.

(Parenthetically, it would appear inexcusable in this day of the Internet for honest researchers to cite archival documents as evidence without either publishing them, perhaps online, or else stating plainly that archival authorities will not allow their publication.)

A statement summarizing Balitskii's confessions and including all the information Shapoval gives above is printed in Lubianka 1937-1938 No. 144, dated July 21, 1937. Snyder shows no familiarity with this vital and widely-known collection of Soviet primary documents that bear directly upon his subject. Shapoval does not refer to it either.

Balitskii's other confessions have not been declassified. But his statements are corroborated in a very long and detailed confession of D.M. Dmitriev, another NKVD head (Sverdlovsk) of October 16, 1938, after Beria had effectively taken over the NKVD from Ezhov. (Lubianka 1937-1938 No. 356, pp. 577 ff.) Some of Dmitriev's confession can be verified by comparing it with other evidence we now have.

None of Snyder's sources document his statement that "Balytskyi was arrested on charges of espionage for Poland." It appears that Snyder has invented this, or copied it from someone else who invented it first.

We now have overwhelming evidence, including evidence from beyond the borders of the USSR, that the conspiracy of Soviet military leaders against the Stalin regime, often called the "Tukhachevsky Affair", really did take place.[16] There has never been any evidence — as opposed to assertions by Soviet and Russian authorities — that this was a frameup of innocent men. In view of the evidence we now have, it could not have been.

Therefore there is no basis — no evidence — to sustain any doubt that Balitskii really was involved with the Tukhachevsky military conspiracy. Snyder could and should have used these primary sources instead of the older secondary source by Shapoval. As for Shapoval himself, we cannot accept his unsupported word. As we showed in Chapter One by examining one of his articles Shapoval cannot be trusted to quote his sources honestly.

---

[16] For example, see Grover Furr, *The Murder of Sergei Kirov* Chapter 17; Furr and Vladimir L. Bobrov, "Marshal S.M. Budiennyi on the Tukhachevsky Trial. Impressions of an Eye-Witness" (in Russian). *Klio* No. 2 (2012), pp. 8-24, available at http://msuweb.montclair.edu/~furrg/research/budennyi_klio12.pdf

There is some very interesting and important material about Balitskii in Shapoval's article, and in other documents not cited by Snyder but which he should have used. But Snyder ignores all these matters, perhaps because he doesn't know about them, perhaps because they do not support his conspiracy theories.

> Even if the idea of a deep Polish penetration of Soviet institutions persuaded Yezhov and Stalin, it could not serve as the evidentiary basis for individual arrests. There simply was nothing resembling a vast Polish plot in the Soviet Union. ... Yezhov told Stalin that Polish political émigrés were major "suppliers of spies and provocateur elements in the USSR." Leading Polish communists were often already in the Soviet Union, and sometimes already dead. Some sixty-nine of the hundred members of the central committee of the Polish party were executed in the USSR. Most of the rest were behind bars in Poland, and so were unavailable for execution. And in any case, these numbers were far too small.[13] (94)

Sources (n. 13 p. 472):

* "On the "suppliers," see Kuromiya, *Stalin*, 118."

* "On the Polish diplomats, see Snyder, *Sketches*, 121-127."

* For the data on the central committee, see Kieszczyński, "Represje," 198.

* "On the experiences of Polish communists in the USSR, Budzyńska's *Strzępy* is invaluable."[17]

In contrast to Snyder **Kuromiya**, *Stalin* 118 admits that "there may well have been assassination plans against Soviet leaders." Snyder chooses not to inform his readers that Kuromiya, who is extremely hostile to Stalin, considers the idea of conspiracies plausible. In fact we have a great deal of evidence concerning such plots.

---

[17] Budzyńska, "Strzępy" is a book of personal memoirs, not relevant to any of the specific assertions Snyder makes here.

As for Jansen and Petrov, on the pages cited by Kuromiya (J&P 40-1) they also assert that the the "Polish Military Organization" (POW/POV/PMO) no longer existed. But this is a bluff. As we have explained above, they cannot possibly know whether a secret organization did or did not exist. All they, or Snyder, can in fact know is that it had been *publicly* disbanded — but they do not cite any evidence of that either. We have already shown that there is plenty of evidence that the "Polish Military Organization" continued to exist as late as 1942.

Jansen and Petrov also add:

> In September 1935 a new wave of arrests started, with a view to end an alleged POV network. [86] During the same month, the representative of the Polish Communist Party in the Comintern Executive Committee, B. Bronkowski (Bortnowski), sent Ezhov a memorandum on deficiencies in the NKVD work concerning the exposure of the agent provocateur and espionage role of Polish agents.[87]

In the more recent Russian edition of 2007 this passage is the same (page 54).

As head of the NKVD whose duties included state security Ezhov would have been a fool not to heed such a warning from one of the leaders of the Polish Communist Party. In note 87 Jansen and Petrov inform their readers that they "were not allowed to see the document." They repeated this note in the recent Russian language edition of this book (p. 54). But they believe it exists, or they would not have included this information in their book.

Snyder, *Sketches*, 121-127 documents the considerable network of spies that the Polish government did in fact have in the USSR. On pp. 125-6 Snyder quotes documents indicating that by November 1937 Polish intelligence had very little remaining of its network. Of course that means that Polish intelligence did have such a network prior to that date. By the evidence Snyder himself cites, that network was active earlier in the decade.

No "central committee" is mentioned by **Kieszczyński,** "Represje," 198.[18]

Snyder Falsifies A Quotation

In the following paragraph Snyder makes a dramatic charge:

> One Moscow NKVD chief understood the gist of the order: his organization should "destroy the Poles entirely." His officers looked for Polish names in the telephone book.[14] (94-95)

Snyder's sources are the following (n. 14 p. 472):

> * "Quotation: Petrov, "Pol'skaia operatsiia," 23."

> * "The phone book anecdote is in Brown, *No Place*, 158."

This is the passage in Petrov (really, Petrov and Roginskii, two leading researchers of the Moscow-based "Memorial" Society):

> По признанию А.О.Постеля, сотрудника УНКВД по Московской области, «когда нам, начальникам отделений, был зачитан приказ Ежова об аресте абсолютно всех поляков (о всех поляках в приказе не говорилось, но характерно, что было услышано именно это. — Авт.), польских политэмигрантов, бывших военнопленных, членов польской коммунистической партии и др., это вызвало не только удивление, но и целый ряд кулуарных разговоров, которые были прекращены тем, что нам заявили, что этот приказ согласован со Сталиным и Политбюро ЦК ВКП(б) и что нужно поляков громить вовсю»[3].

Translated:

> As A.O. Postel', UNKVD officer in Moscow oblast', admitted: "When we, heads of departments, heard Ezhov's order to arrest absolutely all Poles (the order did not say "all Poles", but it was characteristic

---

[18] If there were, why go to a Polish book published in the 1980s to find out about it? There has to be a great deal of detailed information in former communist archives.

that it was heard that way — Authors), Polish political emigres, former POWs, members of the Polish Communist Party, et al., this caused not just amazement but a number of unofficial conversations that only ceased when we were told that this order had been approved by Stalin and the Politburo of the CC VKP(b) and that it was necessary to smash the Poles completely.

Snyder does not inform us, as Petrov and Roginskii do, of the source of this statement:

n.3 - Архив УФСБ по Москве и Московской области. Следственное дело А.О.Постеля № 52668. Допрос от 11 декабря 1939 г.

Translated:

"Archive of the UFSB for Moscow and Moscow oblast'. Investigative file of A.O. Postel' No. 52668. Interrogation of December 11, 1939.

Postel' was being interrogated in 1939 in the case of the mass murders carried out by Ezhov and his men. We have further evidence of this fact in Suvenirov's work:

Бывший начальник 3-го отделения 3-го отдела по УНКВД Московской области лейтенант госбезопасности А. О. Постель за грубые нарушения законности (необоснованные аресты, применение физических методов и т. n.) был в апреле 1940 г. осужден к 15 годам лишения свободы. (207)

Translated:

Former chief of the 3rd division of the 3rd department of the UNKVD of Moscow oblast', Lieutenant of State Security A.O. Postel', was sentenced in April 1940 to 15 years deprivation of freedom for serious violation of the law (arrests without foundation, application of physical force, etc.).

Postel', that is, was arrested on January 9, 1939[19], shortly after Beria had replaced Ezhov, and investigated for the crimes he had committed as an NKVD man. He was punished with a long sentence. This is further evidence of Beria's — and, therefore, of Stalin's — prosecution of Ezhov's men for participating in Ezhov's conspiracy against the Soviet government.

Brown, *No Place*, 158 (actually 158-159) writes:

> [NKVD agent Stanislav] Redens confessed that
> agents hunted down Polish spies by looking
> through the Moscow phone book for Polish last
> names.[20]

Brown's source for this is a 1993 article in a rare Ukrainian journal by Ukrainian nationalist historian Serhii Bilokin'.[21] This interrogation of Redens is also reprinted in a book by Leonid Naumov that Snyder cites three times in his footnotes, including on the very next page of his book![22] Why didn't he tell his readers that they can find it there? Evidently he did not know this because he had not taken the trouble to check the original source.

Here is the passage Snyder and Brown refer to:

> После моего отъезда в Казахстан Заковский
> провел явно преступную деятельность по этим
> делам, он за 2 месяца арестовал 12500 человек,
> причем аресты проводились по телефонной
> книжке, лишь бы фамилия была похожа на
> польскую, латышскую, болгарскую и т.д. (Bi-
> lokin', 41; Naumov, 526)

---

[19] "Документ № 22. Из материалов расследования прокуратуры Московского военного округа методов проведения «латышской операции» НКВД СССР в 1938 г. 26.04.1955. In «...Рано или поздно Сталина все равно убьют»: Оппозиционеры под ударом Кремля и Лубянки. 1926—1936 гг. Архив Александра Н. Яковлева. At http://www.alexanderyakovlev.org/almanah/inside/almanah-doc/1012583 , Title page at http://www.alexanderyakovlev.org/almanah/inside/almanah-intro/1012214

[20] Kate Brown. *A Biography of No Place. From Ethnic Borderland to Soviet Heartland*. Cambridge, MA: Harvard University Press, 2004 (2003).

[21] «Документи з історії НКВД УРСР» *Наше Минуле* 1 (6) 1993, 39-41. ("Dokumenty z istorii NIVD URSR". *Nashe Minule* 1 (b) 1993, 39-41)

[22] Леонид Наумов. *Сталин и НКВД* (М.: Новый Хронограф, 2010). (Leonid Naumov. *Stalin I NKVD*. Moscow: Novyi Khronograf, 2010).

Translated:

> After my departure to Kazakhstan Zakovskii carried
> out obviously criminal activity in these cases. In
> two months he arrested 12,500 persons and arrests
> were made by consulting a telephone book, as long
> as the name seemed Polish, Latvian, Bulgarian, etc.

Both Snyder and Brown have interpreted this passage incorrectly.

Redens testified that *he had heard* that Zakovskii's men used the telephone book to look for Polish last names. This happened after he had left for Kazakhstan, so Redens did not know this at first hand. Rather, Redens accused Zakovskii and his men of doing so after he, Redens, left to become Commissar of the Kazakhstan NKVD. This was in January 1938, when Zakovskii had just been appointed head of the UNKVD in Moscow oblast' (the Commissar was, of course, Ezhov).

Snyder compounds this error by misreading what Brown wrote. Snyder claims that the officers who used the telephone book were under the command of the "NKVD chief" who thought Ezhov said to "destroy the Poles entirely." The NKVD man who understood Ezhov's order in this way — Petrov and Roginskii add that Ezhov did not actually say this — was Postel', not Zakovskii. Zakovskii was the "NKVD chief", not Postel'.

Redens made this statement under arrest, while he was being investigated for helping Ezhov in mass murder. Redens was arrested on November 22, 1938, virtually as soon as Beria took Ezhov's place as the head of the NKVD. According to Bilokin' (40) Redens made this specific statement in a confession of April 14, 1939. He was tried, convicted, and executed in January 1940, at the same time as many other top Ezhov NKVD leaders.

Snyder omits all the facts above and the entire context in which these statements were made. The result is that Snyder gives the impression that these tactics were Soviet, and therefore Stalin's, policies. In fact the *opposite* was the case: these men were arrested, and being investigated, for flagrant violations of Soviet law by Ezhov and his cronies. The context, which Snyder completely omits, is crucial, as it is part of the vast amount of evidence we now have that Ezhov carried out these "national operations" independently, without the knowledge of the Stalin government and in an attempt to further its overthrow.

Snyder Claims That Stalin Hated All Poles

Snyder claims that Stalin made a racist anti-Polish statement:

> Yezhov reported to Stalin that 23,216 arrests had already been made in the Polish operation. Stalin expressed his delight: "Very good! Keep on digging up and cleaning out this Polish filth. Eliminate it in the interests of the Soviet Union."[17] (96)

Sources (n. 17 p. 472):

> * "Quotation and number: Naumov, *NKVD*, 299-300."

> * "For examples, see Stroński, *Represje*, 223, 246."

Snyder's statement is false. According to Naumov, Snyder's own source, Stalin wrote "pol'sko-shpionskuiu griaz'" — "Polish spy filth" or "the filth of Polish spies" (this sounds wrong in English but is correct in Russian.) That is, the "filth" were spies who happened in this case to be Polish. The Stalin quotation is indeed in Naumov.[23] The original source — a note by Stalin on a report sent to him by Ezhov dated September 14, 1937, is at the foot of page 359 of the important document collection we have noted before (Lubianka 1937-1938).[24]

Here is Stalin remark on Ezhov's report:

> «*Т. Ежову*. Очень хорошо! Копайте и вычищайте и впредь эту польско-шпионскую грязь. Крушите ее в *интересах СССР*. И. Сталин. 14/IX—37 г.

Translated:

---

[23] In my edition of Naumov's book this quotation is on page 209 and 210.

[24] It is also online at the very bottom of the page at http://www.alexanderyakovlev.org/fond/issues-doc/61182

> "Com. Ezhov. Very good! Dig up and clean out in the
> future too this Polish spy filth. Smash it in the inter-
> ests of the USSR. I. Stalin 14/IX/-37"

To be able to discern Snyder's falsehood you have to read Russian
and to know where to look. Snyder's readers will believe — falsely
— that "Stalin called Poles 'filth'!" — as Snyder intends they
should.

Snyder tries to make it seem as though Stalin hated all Poles. Later
on the same page (96) Snyder says:

> People such as the Juriewiczes, who had nothing to
> do with Polish espionage of any kind, were the
> "filth" to which Stalin was referring.

He also repeated this same falsehood in one of his essays

> ...Stalin spoke of "Polish filth." (2010-4)

Evidently Snyder thinks that none of his readers will bother to
check the dramatic allegation that Stalin made such a racist statement. Snyder uses this phony quotation in his standard "talk" on
his book as well.[25] Later in this same chapter Snyder repeats the
accusation that Stalin hated Poles and deliberately set out to murder them:

> Although Stalin, Yezhov, Balytskyi, Leplevskii, Ber-
> man, and others linked Polish ethnicity to Soviet se-
> curity... (104)

This is yet another falsehood. Snyder has no evidence that Stalin
ever did anything of the kind; no such evidence exists.

> But perhaps, Stalin reasoned, killing Poles could do
> no harm. (105)

The breathtaking dishonesty of such a statement hardly needs to
be pointed out. Stalin never supported "killing Poles", and of
course Snyder has no evidence that he did. Those responsible for

---

[25] Stroński, *Represje*, 223, 246: the former page recounts some sentences of terms in a camp
or to death; the latter, of some persons whose bodies were found by the Germans in Vinnitsa in 1943, where they organized another mass exhumation for propaganda purposes and
wrote a report along lines identical to their Katyn report. Stroński's point here is simply
that some of these victims had Polish-sounding names.

the mass murders of the Ezhov period, including of Poles, were arrested, tried, convicted, and in many cases executed for these immense crimes.

Snyder Falsifies Yet Another Citation

On the next page — this whole chapter concerns the period 1937-1938 — Snyder writes the following:

> Leningraders and Poles had little idea of these pro-portions at the time. There was only the fear of the knock on the door in the early morning, and the sight of the prison truck: called the black maria, or the soul destroyer, or by Poles the black raven (nevermore). As one Pole remembered, people went to bed each night not knowing whether they would be awakened by the sun or by the black ra-ven...[21] (97-8)

His source (n. 21 p. 472) is:

> * "Awakened: Dzwonkowski, *Głód*, 236. Black raven appears in Polish and Russian, black maria in Russian...."

Snyder cites no evidence at all to support his claim about the "fear" of Leningraders. He has only one anecdotal story about the "fear" of Poles — and this is about a period a few years earlier (the Dzwonkowski passage[26]). Without evidence to support his claim about the "fear" of "Leningraders and Poles" it is misleading and dishonest for Snyder to insert these claims into his book.

Was The "Belorussian Intelligentsia" the Special Target of the NKVD?

Snyder makes the following dramatic accusation:

> The mass killing in Soviet Belarus included the de-liberate destruction of the educated representatives of Belarusian national culture.

---

[26] In Dzwonkowski, *Głód*, 236 the passage about the "czarny kruk", or "black raven" con-cerns 1933 and 1934, during the famine, while Snyder's text concerns the "Polish Opera-tion" of 1937-1938.

Snyder gives the following details:

> As one of Berman's colleagues later put it, he "destroyed the flower of the Belarusian intelligentsia." No fewer than 218 of the country's leading writers were killed. Berman told his subordinates that their careers depended upon their rapid fulfillment of Order 00485: "the speed and quality of the work in discovering and arresting Polish spies will be the main consideration taken into account in the evaluation of each leader."[23] (98)

Source (n. 23 p. 472):

> * "On the national purge, see Naumov, *NKVD*, 262-266; flower quotation at 266."

> * Berman quotation: Michniuk, "Przeciwko Polakow," 115." [This should be "Polakom" – GF]

> * "On the 218 writers, see Mironowicz, *Białoruś*, 88-89."

> * "See also Junge, *Vertikal'*, 624.

As is almost always the case, a check of Snyder's sources reveals quite a different story.

Junge, *Vertikal'*, 624 is a only very short list of the NKVD "troikas" in Belorussia of 1937-1938. It adds nothing to any understanding of what happened. It appears that Snyder added it to "pad" his footnote, make it look more thoroughly researched. Meanwhile, as we demonstrate, Snyder omitted crucial information that his sources do supply.

Mironowicz, *Białoruś,* 88-89: I had access to the 2004 Belarusian[27] and 2007 Polish editions. The figure of 218 writers killed is in both of them (Polish 2007 edition on p. 94): "Of 238 Belorussian literary figures of the Stalin period only some 20 survived." ("Spośród 238 literatów białoruskich epokę Stalina przeżylo jedynie dwudziestu"; (Belarusian edition: "З ліку 238 беларускіх

---

[27] As a republic of the Soviet Union the country, now called Belarus after its name in its official language (Belarusian), was usually called "Belorussia" or "the Belorussian SSR." Between 1921 and 1939 Belorussia was divided between the USSR and Poland.

літаратараў эпоху Сталіна пражыло толькі 20 тварцоў."). But no evidence or source for this information is cited.

Nor is "the Stalin period" defined. But Mironowicz certainly means the period of the *Ezhovshchina*, 1937-1938, when Ezhov was killing as many Soviet citizens as he could in order to sow discontent with the USSR among the population and facilitate an uprising to coincide with an invasion by one or more imperialist countries.[28]

As we shall see, Belarussian historian Shybeka (Polish spelling Szybieka), whom Snyder cites elsewhere, claimed that the anticommunist Polish AK (Armia Krajowa, Home Army) killed thousands of Belorussian teachers and intellectuals — a fact Snyder omits.

In my 2010 edition of **Naumov**, NKVD, the national operation is covered not on pp. 262-266 but on pp. 207 and following. The "flower of the Belarusian intelligentsia" quotation is indeed in Naumov. Its origin is a quotation from the book by famed Soviet spy D.A. Bystrioletov (sometimes spelled Bystroliotov), *Pir Bessmertnykh*. (The Feast of the Immortals). This is a quotation at third hand. Bystroliotov claimed that these were the words of A.A. Nasedkin, Boris Berman's successor as NKVD chief of Belorussia.

> — Слушайте: Борис расстрелял в Минске за
> неполный год работы больше восьмидесяти
> тысяч человек. Слышите?
>
> — Слышу.
>
> — Он убил всех лучших коммунистов
> республики. Обезглавил советский аппарат.
> Истребил цвет национальной белорусской
> интеллигенции. Тщательно выискивал,
> находил, выдёргивал и уничтожал всех мало-
> мальски выделявшихся умом или
> преданностью людей из трудового народа —
> стахановцев на заводах, председателей в
> колхозах, лучших бригадиров, писателей,
> учёных, художников. Воспитанные партией

---

[28] See Furr, "The Moscow Trials and the Great Terror...", for the evidence for this statement.

национальные кадры советских работников. Восемьдесят тысяч невинных жертв... Гора залитых кровью трупов до небес...

- http://jz7k.narod.ru/archive/a/005.html

Translated:

- Listen: in Minsk during less than one year of work Boris shot more than eighty thousand people. Do you understand me?

- I understand you.
- He killed all the best communists in the [Belorussian] republic. He decapitated the Soviet apparatus. He destroyed the flower of the national Belorussian intelligentsia. He carefully sought out, found, pulled up and destroyed every one of the working people who stood out in terms of intelligence or dedication — Stakhanovite workers in factories, chairmen of collective farms, the best team leaders, writers, scholars, and artists. The national cadres of Soviet workers who had been trained by the Party. Eighty thousand innocent victims ... A sky-high mountain of blood-soaked corpses...

Third-hand quotations — Nasedkin to Bystroliotov to us, over a period of many years — are notoriously subject to distortion or even invention. However, we should note what Snyder does *not* mention in this quotation. Nasedkin allegedly told Bystroliotov that Berman had killed:

* the best communists in Belorussia;

* government officials ("the Soviet apparatus");

* "the flower of the national Belorussian intelligentsia";

* Stakhanovite workers;

* chairmen of collective farms;

* team leaders;

* writers, scholars, artists.

But Snyder mentions only the "Belorussian intelligentsia." This implies that they were Berman's special target. But Bystroliotov mentions them third of seven or eight groups of people that he says were targeted by Berman.

Moreover, by omitting the essential context of this statement, Snyder leaves the impression that this mass murder was not just Berman's and Ezhov's aim, but also that of Stalin and the Soviet government. In reality, it was just the opposite: Ezhov, Berman, Nasedkin, and others were being prosecuted, and were to be executed, for their mass murders.

Berman was arrested in September, 1938. At this time Ezhov was still the head (People's Commissar) of the NKVD. But Lavrentii Beria had been appointed as his deputy in August 1938, unquestionably to oversee Ezhov's activities, which had finally aroused the suspicions of Stalin and the Soviet leadership. Berman's arrest must reflect Beria's involvement.

Of equal interest is this: a study of the pages from Naumov's book that Snyder cites, 262-266, reveals some important information that Snyder withheld from his readers.

For example:

> Интересно, что в январе 1939 г. был арестован
> С. Н. Миронов-Король и почти сразу он дал
> показания, что еще в июле 1937 г. Фриновский в
> частной беседе сказал ему о намерении Ежова
> придти к власти, опираясь на своих соратников
> в НКВД. Конечно, это можно было бы списать на
> фантазии бериевских следователей. Но вот
> интересная деталь. Жена Миронова — **Агнесса
> Миронова в своих мемуарах говорит
> практически то же самое: «Нам казалось, что
> Ежов поднялся даже выше Сталина»** 365.
> Мысли эти, судя по тексту мемуаров, относятся
> где-то к середине 1938 г. **А вот кто это «мы», у
> которых такие мысли? Судя по тексту
> мемуаров Мироновой, общалась она тогда
> только с членами своей семьи, с братом С.
> Миронова — разведчиком Давидом Король и
> его семьей, и с семьей Фриновских...** (209)

Translated:

> Interestingly, in January 1939, S. Mironov-Korol'
> was arrested, and almost immediately testified that
> in July 1937 in a private conversation Frinovsky
> told him of Ezhov's intention to come to power on
> the basis of their group in the NKVD . Of course, one
> might attribute this to the imagination of Beria's in-
> vestigators. But here's an interesting detail.
> **Mironov's wife Agnes Mironov in her memoirs
> says almost the same thing: "We thought that
> Ezhov had risen even higher than Stalin."** These
> thoughts, according to the text of memoirs, are from
> some time in mid-1938. **But who is this "we" who
> were thinking such thoughts? Judging by the
> text of Mironova's memoirs, she was then talk-
> ing only with the members of her family, with
> Mironov's brother, the intelligence official Da-
> vid Korol' and his family, and with the Fri-
> novsky family.** (Emphasis added)

We have a great deal of other documentary evidence that Ezhov
led a conspiracy of his own that was linked to other Right conspiracies, including that of Bukharin and Rykov and that of Tukhachevsky. For example, we have confessions by Frinovsky, Ezhov
himself, and others which I have made available online in Russian
and in English translation.[29]

Once again Snyder has deliberately deceived his readers. This passage from Naumov's book, which Snyder cites several times, is the
proof that he knows about it. Jansen and Petrov also discuss
Ezhov's conspiracy. The more recent Russian-language edition of
their book, Petrov and Jansen (the author's names are reversed for
the Russian edition) discusses it in even more detail. But Snyder
fails to tell his readers about it. No doubt this is because *it reveals*

---

[29] Grover Furr. "The Moscow Trials and the "Great Terror" of 1937-1938: What the Evidence Shows." (Written July 2010). At
http://msuweb.montclair.edu/~furrg/research/trials_ezhovshchina_update0710.html

that Stalin and the Soviet state had not ordered the Ezhov mass murders.

Michniuk, "Przeciwko Polakom," 115 does record the statement quoted by Snyder:

> Po raz drugi uprzedzam, ze tempo i jakość pracy
> dotyczącej wykrywania i aresztowania polskich
> szpiegów będą przede wszystkim brane pod uwagę
> przy ocenianiu pracy każdego naczelnika. —
> Berman 22 pażdziernika 1937 r.[30]

Translated:

> Once again I warn you that the pace and quality of
> work on the detection and arrest of Polish spies will
> first of all be taken into account when evaluating
> the work of each director. — Berman, 22 October
> 1937

In order to evaluate this statement we need to know more about Berman. Snyder has failed to inform us that Berman was part of Ezhov's conspiracy against Stalin and the Soviet government.

On August 4, 1939 Ezhov gave a lengthy and very important confession about his anti-Soviet conspiracy, during which he mentioned Berman's role in the "National Campaign." This confession is printed for the first time in Petrov and Jansen. In it Ezhov describes his plan, which included massive illegal repressions so as to sow dissent among the Soviet population and facilitate an anti-Soviet uprising.

> Question: Are you aware of the facts concerning
> how the dissatisfaction of the population was con-
> cretely expressed?
>
> Answer: ... From what Uspensky said I know that
> flights through the border posts into Poland in-
> creased as a result of the provocational conduct of
> the mass operations, especially in the border re-
> gions of the Ukraine. The families of those re-
> pressed began to be expelled from kolkhozes, and

---

[30] If this document dated October 22, 1937 has been published, I can't find it.

in connection with that, robberies, arson, and thefts began. There were even a few examples of terrorist acts against workers of the village soviets and kolkhozes. Not only families of the repressed, but rank-and-file kolkhoz members and even Party members began to write complaints.

Dissatisfaction with the punitive policy was so great that local party organizations began to insist that all the family members of persons who had been repressed be resettled from the Ukraine to other regions.

Such in general terms were the results of the provocational conduct of the mass operations in the Ukraine.

We were successful in achieving about the same results in Belorussia too.

At the time the mass operations were taking place B. Berman was in charge of the NKVD of Belorussia.

Question: Was Berman a member of the conspiratorial organization in the NKVD?

Answer: Berman was not a member of our conspiratorial organization. However, Frinovsky, Bel'sky, and I knew by the beginning of 1938 that he was an active member of Yagoda's anti-Soviet conspiratorial group.

We did not plan to draw Berman into our conspiratorial organization. Already at that time he was sufficiently compromised and was subject to arrest. However, we delayed his arrest. In turn Berman, who feared arrest, worked very hard. I only had to give him general directives that Belorussia was badly infested and that it was necessary to purge it in a thoroughgoing way, and he carried out the mass operations with the same result as Uspensky.

Question: With what result specifically?

Answer: He incessantly demanded an increase of "limits" and, following Uspensky's example, put "nationalists" into the category of persons subject to repression, carried out completely unfounded arrests, created exactly the same kind of dissatisfaction in the border regions of Belorussia, and left the families of those repressed where they were.

There were even more warnings sent to the NKVD and the Procuracy concerning dissatisfaction among the population of the border regions of Belorussia than in the Ukraine. We left all these too without investigating them and hid them from the Central Committee of the Party and the government.[31]

Two days earlier, on August 2, 1939, Ezhov had testified as follows concerning Berman:

In Belorussia you sent **Boris Berman? Did you know that he was an old German agent?**

Yes. Artnau told me that Berman was working for German intelligence as soon as I became Commissar of Internal Affairs. He had been recruited at the beginning of the 'thirties, when irhe was [Soviet] resident in Germany. I immediately established espionage contact with him, then he was the assistant chief of the INO [Foreign Department]. In 1937 I specially sent him from our organization to Belorussia and made him Commissar of Internal Affairs. There he met with German agents and received assignments and instructions.

That means your widespread espionage organization in the case of an attack on the USSR by Japan and Germany could seize power not only in Moscow

[31] Nikita Petrov, Marc Jansen. "Stalinskii pitomets" — Nikolai Ezhov. Moscow: ROSSPEN, 2008, pp. 367-379. At http://msuweb.montclair.edu/~furrg/research/ezhov080439eng.html Russian original at http://msuweb.montclair.edu/~furrg/research/ezhov080439ru.html

but in border areas, opening the road to the invaders. Do I understand this correctly from your
confessions?

Yes. That was exactly what we had planned. It's useless to deny such things.[32] (Emphasis added, GF)

Berman was tried, convicted, and executed in February, 1939, after Beria had replaced Ezhov. According to Ezhov Berman was really a "Iagoda" man. A.A. Nasedkin, on the other hand, was one of
Ezhov's men, tried and sentenced to death in January 1940 with
many other of Ezhov's closest NKVD collaborators (Ezhov himself
was tried and executed in early February, 1940). As one of Ezhov's
chief henchmen it is hard to imagine Nasedkin claiming somebody
else was "bloody." It would be "the pot calling the kettle black."

Snyder has omitted all the evidence long available that Berman,
along with Ezhov, were conspiring against Stalin and the Soviet
government. The effect is to create the false impression that Berman and Ezhov were carrying out the orders of the Soviet government. This is in fact what Snyder states. Once again Snyder has
deceived his readers.

There is no hint of all these important details in Snyder's account,
and that account is false to boot. Either Snyder knows virtually
nothing about the *Ezhovshchina* — i.e. he has not studied the
scholarship on it — or he does know something but has concealed
it from his readers in order to give his book a suitably "anti-Stalin"
and anti-Soviet bias.

According to Jansen and Petrov:

Aleksei Nasedkin, the former Smolensk NKVD chief
and from May 1938 on Interior People's Commissar[33] of Belorussia, described the situation at the
conference this way: Ezhov approved of the activity
of those NKVD chiefs, who cited "astronomic" num-

---

[32] Ezhov interrogation 08.02.39 by Rodos, In Aleksei Polianskii,. *Ezhov. Istoriia «zheleznogo»*
stalinskogo narkoma. Moscow: «Veche», «Aria-AiF», 2001. 275-280. At
http://msuweb.montclair.edu/~furrg/research/ezhovinterrogs.html Russia original at
http://msuweb.montclair.edu/~furrg/research/ezhovpokazaniia.html

[33] Jansen and Petrov mean "People's Commissar of Internal Affairs."

> bers of persons repressed, such as, for instance, the NKVD chief of Western Siberia, citing a number of 55,000 people arrested, Dmitriev of Sverdlovsk province— 40,000, Berman of Belorussia—60,000, Uspenskii of Orenburg— 40,000, Liushkov of the Far East—70,000, Redens of Moscow province—50,000. The Ukrainian NKVD chiefs each cited numbers of people arrested from 30,000 to 40,000. Having listened to the numbers, Ezhov in his concluding remarks praised those who had "excelled" and announced that, undoubtedly, excesses had taken place here and there, such as, for instance, in Kuibyshev, where on Postyshev's instruction Zhuravlev had transplanted all active Party members of the province. But he immediately added that "in such a large-scale operation mistakes are inevitable."
>
> (J&P 131; same quotation in Russian, P&J 146).

Nasedkin made this statement on July 16, 1939, under arrest and during the investigation of his case by Beria's men. *Having regained control of the NKVD from Ezhov Stalin and his forces were investigating the enormous atrocities committed by Ezhov and his men and punishing the guilty parties.* It is this that the ideological anticommunists like Snyder wish to conceal from their readers.

Snyder Claims That Japan Did Not Move Against the USSR After Mid-1937

> The Japanese leadership had decided upon a southern strategy, toward China and then the Pacific. Japan intervened in China in July 1937, right when the Great Terror began, and would move further southward only thereafter. (105)

It is hard to imagine how anyone could make such an ignorant statement and think it would not be noticed. In reality Japan attacked the USSR *twice* after 1937. In the "Lake Khasan" or "Changkufeng" incident of July — August 1938 the Red Army lost about 236 killed, the Japanese Army perhaps twice that number.

But from May to mid-September 1939 a real war was fought between the USSR and Japan. This was the "Battles of Khalkhin Gol"
or "Nomonhan Incident." The Soviet Union and Japan each lost
about 8,000 soldiers. It played an important part in Soviet negotiations with the UK and France, since the USSR was determined not
to fight two wars at the same time, one in Europe against Germany,
and the second in Asia against Japan. The Soviet victory at Khalkhin Gol convinced the Japanese not to attack the USSR.

Snyder has to know about this. Evidently he thinks his readers are
so ignorant that they would accept his statement here at face value.

Snyder Invents "Stalin"s Theory of Interrogation"

> Stalin had brought to life his theory that the enemy
> could be unmasked only by interrogation. (107)

Where did this "theory" come from? Snyder has no documentation
for this statement, not even false "documentation." There is no evidence that Stalin had any such "theory." This is yet another falsehood.

Snyder Reads Stalin"s Mood

It is evidently important to Snyder's project that Stalin be personally responsible for the mass murders of the *Ezhovshchina*. The
problem is that all the evidence now available points in the opposite direction. Presumably this is why Snyder, like other ideologically-motivated writers, repeatedly invents his "facts."

For example, Snyder claims that Stalin was made happier, or
something like that, by all the mass murders:

> Yet the conversion of columns of peasants and
> workers into columns of figures seemed to lift Sta-
> lin's mood... (107)

Snyder has fabricated this weird factoid. How can Snyder know
"Stalin's mood" anyway? Its purpose, evidently, is to portray Stalin
as some kind of bloodthirsty monster. Once again, there is no evidence to support it. Historians have no business engaging in this
cheap psychologizing, propaganda disguised as history.

The *Ezhovshchina* as "Stalin"s policy"

At this point in Chapter 4 Snyder inserts the quotation with which we open our discussion of the *Ezhovshchina* (see the following chapter).

> ...and the course of the Great Terror certainly con-
> firmed Stalin's position of power. Having called a
> halt to the mass operations in November 1938, Sta-
> lin once again replaced his NKVD chief. Lavrenty
> Beria succeeded Yezhov, who was later executed.
> The same fate awaited many of the highest officers
> of the NKVD, blamed for the supposed excesses,
> which were in fact the substance of Stalin's policy.
> (107-8)

For ideologically anticommunist researchers it is important that these mass murders be Stalin's plan and intention. But this is false. When Stalin acted he did so on the basis of reports sent to him through Ezhov. According to V.N. Khaustov, a very anti-Stalin researcher and one of the compilers of several of these invaluable document collections, these reports were falsified..

> И самым страшным было то, что Сталин
> принимал решения, основываясь на показаниях,
> которые являлись результатом вымыслов
> конкретных сотрудников органов
> госбезопасности. Реакция Сталина
> свидетельствовала о том, что он воспринимал
> эти показания в полной мере серьезно.[34]

Translated:

> And the most frightening thing was that Stalin
> made his decisions on the basis of confessions that
> were the result of the inventions of certain employ-
> ees of the organs of state security. Stalin's reactions

---

[34] Lubianka Golgofa p. 6. Now online at
http://www.k2x2.info/politika/lubjanka_sovetskaja_yelita_na_stalinskoi_golgofe_1937_193
8/p4.php

attest to the fact that he took these confessions completely seriously.

Snyder: Stalin Didn"t Lose, Therefore He Was Always In Control

Snyder then says:

> Because Stalin had been able to replace Yagoda with Yezhov, and then Yezhov with Beria, he showed himself to be at the top of the security apparatus. Because he was able to use the NKVD against the party, but also the party against the NKVD, he showed himself to be the unchallengeable leader of the Soviet Union. Soviet socialism had become a tyranny where the tyrant's power was demonstrated by the mastery of the politics of his own court.[43] (107-8)

Source (n. 43 p. 474):

> * "Khlevniuk, "Party and NKVD," 23, 28;"
>
> * Binner, "Massenmord," 591-593.

The false logic in this paragraph of Snyder's is worth examining also because it is used by other anticommunist researchers as well. Snyder commits the logical fallacy of "post hoc ergo propter hoc." Because Iagoda and then Ezhov both conspired to overthrow Stalin but both failed, Snyder concludes that Stalin was always in control.

Imagine applying this to football games: the team that won was always going to win, and the fact that they won proved that they were in control of the outcome the whole time! "Logic" like this is evidently intended to "absolve" anticommunist researchers of the normal scholarly trouble of having to find evidence to support their assumptions.

These are puzzling statements that require examination. Of course it has to be true that Stalin ended up "at the top of the security apparatus" after Ezhov's removal. But this does not address the main question here, which is: did Ezhov violate the Politburo's — "Stalin's" — orders in pursuring these mass executions of innocent persons, or not? And when did Stalin "use the party against the NKVD"?

Evidently Snyder is trying to imply that Stalin planned everything that Ezhov did because Stalin had succeeded in removing Ezhov. Of course the latter does not imply the former at all. If Stalin did not know about Ezhov's criminal mass murders and then found about about them, he would have wanted to remove him. From the evidence we have this appears to be what happened.

Once again Snyder appears to be trying to insinuate something that he cannot prove. Naturally Stalin did not have any "court." Nor was he a "tyrant" — whatever that means — or a dictator, one "whose word is law." Stalin had been openly challenged at the June 1937 Central Committee Plenum, and was to be decisively defeated in October 1937 in his desire to have competitive elections to the Soviets as stipulated by the new constitution.[35]

Turning for clarification to the sources Snyder cites here, we find that **Khlevniuk**, "Party and NKVD, " 23, 28 contains no evidence to support any of the claims in this paragraph. It merely summarizes in very general terms the situation after Ezhov's resignation in late 1938.

Binner, "Massenmord" — actually Binner and Junge, and titled "Wie der Terror 'Gross' Wurde: Massenmord under Lagerhaft nach Befehl 00447" — also summarizes the events of September to November, 1938. While insinuating their conviction that Stalin was in control of what Ezhov was doing — this assumption is common to all anticommunist researchers — neither Binner and Junge nor any of the other anticommunist researchers have any evidence to support their conviction.

This is pure ideology, common to most if not all anticommunist writers. They "want" evidence that Stalin was "in charge" of Ezhov's mass murders. Unfortunately, all the evidence points in the opposite direction so they just *assert* that Stalin was "really" in charge.

---

[35] See Grover Furr, "Stalin and the Struggle for Democratic Reform. Part One." *Cultural Logic* 2005, paragraphs 112 ff. , and the sources cited there. At http://clogic.eserver.org/2005/furr.html

Binner and Junge do note that as early as 1993 Boris Starkov claimed that Ezhov "had not informed Stalin of his actions." Although Binner and Junge disagree with this statement of Starkov's they have no evidence to support their disagreement. It should not surprise us that Snyder fails to mention this. But we know now that Starkov was correct. In fact he did not go nearly far enough. We now have the evidence that Ezhov's mass murders were not authorized at all, and were part of Ezhov's conspiracy to overthrow the government and Party leadership.[36]

Snyder: Noting A Person"s Nationality Is "Not So Very Different From" Nazism

> Germany's Nuremberg laws of 1935 excluded Jews from political participation in the German state and defined Jewishness according to descent. German officials were indeed using the records of synagogues to establish whose grandparents were Jews. Yet in the Soviet Union the situation was not so very different. The Soviet internal passports had a national category, so that every Soviet Jew, every Soviet Pole, and indeed every Soviet citizen had an officially recorded nationality. In principle Soviet citizens were allowed to choose their own nationality, but in practice this was not always so. In April 1938 the NKVD required that in certain cases information about the nationality of parents be entered. By the same order, Poles and other members of diaspora nationalities were expressly forbidden from changing their nationality..." [47] (110)
>
> n. 47 - Hirsch, *Empire*, 293-294.

This is another dishonest attempt by Snyder to bracket Soviet policy with Nazi racism.

Snyder has certainly not read the NKVD "requirement" he refers to. He does not even give a date for it. His source, Francine

---

[36] Starkov's statement is in his essay "Narkom Ezhov", in J. Arch Getty and Roberta T. Manning, eds., *Stalinist Terror. New Perspectives* (Cambridge University Press, 1993), p. 38.

Hirsch[37], discusses the fact that both the cancelled 1937 census and the subsequent 1938 census permitted all citizens to "declare their national identities 'according to their conscience and not their birth.'" Hirsch then cites, though without quoting it, an archival document according to which in April 1938 the NKVD began to require *new* passports to record the nationality of the holder's *parents*.

In later pages Hirsch goes on to discuss the struggle between census officials, who wanted to retain self-designation of nationality, and the NKVD, which was concerned about the possible loyalty conflicts of persons with foreign roots. Hirsch explicitly disagrees with two other anticommunist researchers (Tony Martin and Eric Weitz) who she believes greatly exaggerate the significance of this NKVD directive.

Hirsch completely rejects any comparison of Soviet and German Nazi policies on nationality because, in fact, they were very different. In a very multinational state such as the USSR nationality was an important component of individual identity. It had nothing to do with Nazi notions of genetic superiority and inferiority.

However, there are some problems with Hirsch's analysis. For one thing, Hirsch interprets the new NKVD policy as indicative of Soviet policy, as she does "terror." She appears ignorant of the fact that in 1937-1938 the NKVD, under Nikolai Ezhov, was out of control.

We have taken the trouble to obtain the text of this document. It has never been reprinted since its first appearance in an obscure Memorial Society newsletter. Now that we have the text of the NKVD directive of April 1938 we can discern a more serious problem with Hirsch's discussion: she misrepresents what the NKVD directive actually says. She states:

> The explicit aim [of the " NKVD passport decree of April 1938"] was to ferret out members of "suspect" nations who, the NKVD claimed, were "concealing" their true identities. (275)

---

[37] *Empire of Nations. Ethnographic Knowledge and the Making of the Soviet Union* (Cornell U.P. 2005), 293-4.

> The NKVD introduced this decree in April 1938, directing registrars to write the nationality of a passport recipient's parents — and *not* the self-defined nationality of the passport recipient — in newly-issued passports....If a person's parents belonged to two different nationalities and one "belonged to a foreign state," the registrar was to write the nationality of both parents in the passport. ... Even Poles and Germans who had lived in Russia for generations were designated as people who "belonged to" a foreign state... (294)

Hirsch cites archival documents, so we cannot be certain that she is referring to the April 1938 NKVD passport decree we quote below. But this document is the only one now available. It contains nothing about "suspect" nations and does not mention "foreign states" at all.

Hirsch spreads false information about this NKVD regulation, making it appear much more sinister than its text actually warrants. This is possible only because the document is so hard to locate. Petrov and Roginskii, both of the "Memorial Society", refer to it and certainly read it since it is published in a "Memorial Society" publication. Hirsch must have read it too. But her description of it varies widely from the text we have.

Snyder fails to inform his readers that the NKVD order is discussed, and quoted in part, in Petrov and Roginskii, "'Pol'skaia operatsiia' NKVD 1937-1938 gg." Snyder is certainly aware of this fact, as he repeatedly cites this work.

Petrov and Roginskii mention two different NKVD documents of two different dates: "Circular No. 65 of April 2, 1938" and "Explanatory directive of the Department of Citizenship of the NKVD of the USSR No. 1486178 of April 29, 1938." Footnote 18 in Petrov/Roginskii states that the second of these documents was published in the very rare journal *Memorial-Aspekt* in 1994. They give no source at all for the first document.

> 18 Разъясняющее указание Отдела актов гражданского состояния НКВД СССР № 1486178

от 29 апреля 1938 г. см.: Мемориал-аспект. 1994.
№ 10.[38]

Here is the text of this document from the rare *Memorial-Aspekt*
journal (no longer published)[39]:

ОТДЕЛ АКТОВ

Гражданского Состояния

29 апреля 1938 г.

№ 1486178

Всем Начальникам ОАГС НКВД и УНКВД

Циркуляром НКВД СССР №65 от 2 апреля 1938 г.
(разосланный нач. УРКМ) установлен новый
порядок указания национальности при выдаче
или обмене паспортов, обязывающий при
записи национальности владельца паспорта
исходить исключительно из национальности по
рождению (по родителям).

В связи с этим, существовавшее до настоящего
времени положение, когда национальность
граждан при регистрации актов гражданского
состояния записывалась та, к которой
причислял себя регистрирующийся —
изменяется.

Во всех случаях актовых записей
национальность должна указываться на

---

[38] This is confirmed in Ален Блюм, Мартина Меспуле. *Бюрократическая анархия Статистика и власть при Сталине*. Москва: РОССИЯН 2008, p. 223. At http://burokraticheskaya-anarhiya.blogspot.com/2011/10/67.html ; note 52 to Chapter 10 at http://burokraticheskaya-anarhiya.blogspot.com/2011/10/77.html : (Title page at http://burokraticheskaya-anarhiya.blogspot.com/search/label/Бюрократическая анархия Статистика и власть при Сталине) This is a translation of Alain Blum et Martine Mespoulet. *L'anarchie bureaucratique. Statistique et pouvoir sous Staline*. Paris, Éditions la Découverte 2003.

[39] The journal *Memorial-Aspekt* is apparently not held by any American library. I would like to thank my valued colleague Vladimir L. Bobrov of Moscow for obtaining this document for me.

основании предъявленных при регистрации паспортов.

Там. где паспортизация отсутствует, уточнение вопроса о национальности регистрирующегося проводится в процессе записи, путем опроса заявителей. При этом надо иметь в виду, что запись национальности должна быть произведена в соответствии с фактическим национальным происхождением родителей регистрирующегося. Если родители немцы, поляки и т.д .. вне зависимости от их места рождения, давности проживания в СССР или перемены подданства и друг., нельзя записывать регистрирующегося русским, белоруссом и т.д.

В случаях несоответствия указанной национальности родному языку или фамилии, как например: фамилия регистрирующегося Попандопуло, Мюллер, а называет себя русским. белоруссом и т.д. и если во время записи не удастся установить действительную национальность регистрирующихся, — графа о национальности не заполняется до представления заявителями документальных доказательств о принадлежности регистрирующегося к той или иной национальности.

Разъяснить сотрудникам загс, что непредставление документов о национальности может повлиять только на запись о национальности, но ни в коем случае не задерживать регистрацию вообще, руководствуясь в этих случаях указаниями главы 3 22 инструкции о записях актов.

Национальность ребенка при рождении, если родители разных национальностей, записывать по желанию родителей, о чем в графе «особые отметки» указывать, что национальность ребенку записана на основании соглашения родителей, т.е. по национальности отца или матери. При отсутствии соглашения — вопрос разрешается органами опеки (согласно ст. 39 Кодекса законов РСФСР и соответствующих ст.ст. кодексов союзных республик). До вынесения решения пункт о национальности не заполняется

Нач. Отдела актов граждан. состояния

майор государственной бе'зопасности

Алиевский.

Translated:

BUREAU OF REGULATIONS

CIVIL STATUS

April 29, 1938

No 1486178

To All chiefs of the OAGS[40] of the NKVD and UNKVD

Circular NKVD number 65 of April 2, 1938 ... has established a new procedure for indicating nationality at the time of the issuance or exchange of passports, requiring that the nationality of the passport holder be based solely on birth nationality by birth (of the parents).

In this regard, the situation which has existed up to now when nationality of citizens in registering civil documents is recorded as that reported by the registrant — is changing.

In all cases of documentation that nationality should be indicated on the basis of the passports presented at registration.

---

[40] "Otdel aktov grazhdanskogo sostoiania" — Division of documents of civil status.

Where no passport is present, the determination of
the nationality of the registrant is to be done by
questioning the individual present. Bear in mind
that the notation of nationality must be carried out
in conformity with actual national origin of the registrant's parent. If the parents were German, Poles,
etc., regardless of their place of birth,, length of time
they have resided in the USSR, or change of citizenship,etc., the registrant must not be recorded as a
Russian, a Belorussian, etc.

When the indicated nationality does not correspond
to [the registrant's] native language or surname —
for example: a registrant's surname is Popandopu-
lo, Mueller, but [the registrant] calls himself Russian, Belorussian, etc., and if at the time of recording it is not possible to establish the actual nationality of the registrant — do not fill out the section on
nationality until the individual has presented documentary proof that the registrant belongs to one
or another nationality.

Explain to the employees of the ZAGS that failure to
present documents about nationality can influence
only the recording of nationality, but may not delay
the registration in general, which is guided in such
cases by directives of chapter 3 22 of the instruction on recording documents.

Record the nationality of a baby at birth, if the parents are of different nationalities, according to the
parents' wishes. In such cases indicate in the section "special remarks" that the baby's nationality
has been recorded on the basis of the agreement of
the parents, i.e. according to the nationality of the
father or the mother. If they do not agree, the matter should be decided by the organs of guardianship
(according to article 39 of the Code of Laws of the
RSFSR and corresponding articles of the Codes of

the union republics). Do not fill in the nationality
until a decision has been reached.

Chief of the Bureau of regulations of civil status

Major of state security

Alievskii

A study of this document yields some important results.

* Although they do not admit as much, evidently even Petrov
and Roginskii have not seen "NKVD USSR circular No. 65 of
April 2, 1938." It is simply referred to at the beginning of the
document above.

* The examples cited in the document make it clear that the
aim of the new requirement — to determine a citizen's nationality on the basis of his parents' nationality or statement
— is to avoid absurdities. The examples given are of persons
surnamed "Popandopoulo" and "Müller" who claim that they
are Russian by nationality.

* In such cases the directive requires officials to request documentary proof of nationality. It does not give officials the
right to determine this themselves.

In the USSR nationality was an important marker of citizenship.
Persons of certain nationalities had certain privileges in certain
areas of the USSR where that nationality comprised a substantial
part of the population. In Soviet institutions an attempt was made
to have "affirmative action" — a proportion of citizens of minority
nationalities that approximated their percentage of the Soviet
population. Failure to do this would run the danger of the domina-
tion of all important posts by Russians, Ukrainians, or Jews, who
usually did predominate unless affirmative steps were taken to
promote persons of minority nationalities.

It is outrageous for Snyder to suggest that official registration of a
citizen's nationality was "not so very different" from the Nazi practice of racial stigmatization, removal of civil and legal rights, repression, persecution, imprisonment and murder. Snyder's doing

so demonstrates how desperately he strives to bracket Soviet actions with Nazism whatever the cost to the truth.

Snyder sums up his treatment of the *Ezhovshchina* as follows:

> The Soviet Union benefited from the public violence
> in Nazi Germany. In this atmosphere, supporters of
> the Popular Front counted on the Soviet Union to
> protect Europe from the descent into ethnic vio-
> lence. Yet the Soviet Union had just engaged in a
> campaign of ethnic murder on a far larger scale. It is
> probably fair to say that no one beyond the Soviet
> Union had any notion of this. A week after Kris-
> tallnacht, the Great Terror was brought to an end,
> after some 247,157 Soviet citizens had been shot in
> the national operations. As of the end of 1938, the
> USSR had killed about a thousand times more peo-
> ple on ethnic grounds than had Nazi Germany. The
> Soviets had, for that matter, killed far more Jews to
> that point than had the Nazis. The Jews were tar-
> geted in no national action, but they still died in the
> thousands in the Great Terror—and for that matter
> during the famine in Soviet Ukraine. They died not
> because they were Jews, but simply because they
> were citizens of the most murderous regime of the
> day. (111)

This is an important paragraph, in that it combines one truthful
fact — the number of people killed in the *Ezhovshchina* — with a
fallacious interpretation of that fact. The phrases "the Soviet Union
had just engaged", "the USSR had killed", "the Soviet had…killed",
and "the most murderous regime" are falsifications, in that they
express the assumption that these killings were the policy of the
Soviet government and the Politburo headed by Stalin.

It is a substitute for understanding what was going on. The 1932-
1933 famine was not deliberate, so the USSR didn't "kill" anybody
in it. Nor did "the regime" kill people on a national basis. It was
Ezhov who did this, in pursuit of his own conspiracy to overthrow
the Soviet government.

In the official sense the Soviet government, the Politburo, Stalin, all bore responsibility for Ezhov's mass murders in that they were, formally, in overall charge of the country, and therefore were obliged to take steps to stop criminal activity and to punish those responsible. This is true of all governments and heads of state anywhere at any time.

However, no one holds a government morally responsible for *illegal* crimes and atrocities committed by government officials unless the government discovers those crimes and yet refuses to punish the perpetrators. The Stalin government did vigorously pursue, investigate, prosecute, and punish Ezhov and the NKVD men under him who were responsible for these atrocities.

Therefore it is not true that the Soviet government or "regime" was guilty of these mass murders or that Ezhov was some kind of "scapegoat." Ezhov's mass murders were a rebellion against the Soviet government, Party, and Stalin.

Snyder Admits That Poland Was Anti-Semitic, Like Nazi Germany

Grand deportation schemes made a kind of sense in 1938, when leading Nazis could still delude themselves that Poland might become a German satellite and join in an invasion of the Soviet Union. More than three million Jews lived in Poland, and Polish authorities had also investigated Madagascar as a site for their resettlement. Although Polish leaders envisioned no policies toward their large national minorities (five million Ukrainians, three million Jews, one million Belarusians) that were remotely comparable to Soviet realities or Nazi plans, they did wish to reduce the size of the Jewish population by voluntary emigration. After the death of the Polish dictator Józef Piłsudski in 1935, his successors had taken on the position of the Polish nationalist right on this particular question, and had established a ruling party that was open only to ethnic Poles... (112)

Here Snyder finally admits the truth: *it was prewar Poland that was racist like Nazi Germany.* The USSR was not in the least.

Snyder Denies Poland Wanted to Invade the USSR Alongside Germany

> Piłsudski's heirs in this respect followed Piłsudski's line: a policy of equal distance between Berlin and Moscow, with nonaggression pacts with both Nazi Germany and the Soviet Union, but no alliance with either. On 26 January 1939 in Warsaw, the Poles turned down the German foreign minister, Joachim von Ribbentrop, one last time. (113)

In one of his articles Snyder makes the same false claim:

> Ribbentrop's master Adolf Hitler wanted a deal so that he could begin a war. For the Nazis, the Soviet Union was the main enemy, and its agriculture and oil the prize. But between Germany and the USSR lay Poland, and the Poles expressed no interest in being the junior partner in the adventure. (2009-4; emphasis added)

This is all false. Up till the beginning of 1939, when Hitler decided to turn against Poland before making war on the USSR, the Polish government was maneuvering to join Nazi Germany in a war on the USSR in order to seize more territory.

Here is what really happened on January 26, 1939, the date Snyder mentions. Polish Foreign Minister Josef Beck was in negotiations with Nazi Foreign Minister Joachim von Ribbentrop in Warsaw. Ribbentrop wrote:

> ... 2. I then spoke to M. Beck once more about the policy to be pursued by Poland and Germany towards the Soviet Union and in this connection also spoke about the question of the Greater Ukraine and again proposed Polish-German collaboration in this field.
>
> M. Beck made no secret of the fact **that Poland had aspirations directed toward the Soviet Ukraine**

and a connection with the Black Sea...[41] (Emphasis added.)

Beck told Ribbentrop that Poland would like to seize much of the Ukraine from the USSR, for that was the only way Poland could have had "a connection with the Black Sea." Such aspirations could not have been fulfilled without an invasion of the Ukraine. Poland could never have undertaken such an invasion by itself. Therefore Beck was stating his openness to a joint Polish-German invasion of the Ukraine, if the conditions became favorable.

This means that, far from "expressing no interest in being the junior partner" with the Nazis in carving up the USSR, Beck expressed considerable interest — but, given the current political situation, begged off. Snyder withholds this information from his readers.

Snyder Terms Stalin"s Anti-Hitler Move a „Pro"-Hitler Move

> In spring 1939, Stalin made a striking gesture toward Hitler, the great ideological foe. Hitler had pledged not to make peace with Jewish communists; Nazi propaganda referred to the Soviet commissar for foreign affairs, Maxim Litvinov, as Finkelstein. Litvinov was indeed Jewish—his brother was a rabbi. Stalin obliged Hitler by firing Litvinov on 3 May 1939. Litvinov was replaced by Stalin's closest ally, Molotov, who was Russian. The indulgence of Hitler ...[56] (115)

Source (n. 56 p. 474):

> * Haslam, *Collective Security*, 90, 153.

> * "On Litvinov, see Herf, *Jewish Enemy*, 104; and Orwell, *Orwell and Politics*, 78."

This is completely wrong. Let's look at Snyder's sources.

---

[41] Original in *Akten zur deutschen auswärtigen Politik... Serie D. Bd. V.* S. 139-140. English translation in *Documents on German Foreign Policy. 1918-1945. Series D. Vol. V.* The document in question is No. 126, pp. 167-168; this quotation on p. 168. Also in Russian in *God Krizisa T. 1*, Doc. No. 120.

Haslam, *Collective Security*, page 90 concerns Litvinov's gloomy conclusions in late 1935 that France was drifting in an anti-Soviet direction. Jakob Surits was sent to "activate contacts in Berlin", since the last thing the USSR wanted was any kind of Franco-German alliance against the Soviet Union. Surits, by the way, was Jewish. At page 163 Haslam outlines similar remarks by Litvinov to the effect that if France would not ally, or "have anything to do with" the USSR, then the Soviets would have to turn towards Germany.

Snyder's reference "On Litvinov, see **Herf**, *Jewish Enemy*, 104" is pure bluff. Page 104 of Herf's book discusses *how satisfied Goebbels was to see Litvinov back in a prominent position after the Nazi invasion*. This says the opposite of what Snyder states, so Snyder probably meant "Herf, 93." There Herf writes:

> The replacement of the Jewish foreign Minister
> Maxim Litvinov by Vycheslav [sic] Molotov had sig-
> naled the end of Soviet support for popular-front
> antifascism. As the historians of the Soviet Union
> Mikhail Heller and Alexander Nekrich put it, "for
> the first time since the founding of the Soviet state
> anti-Semitism was becoming official policy.[2]"

Soviet policy was becoming "officially" anti-Semitic? What is Herf's evidence for such a serious accusation? Herf's footnote 2 is to Heller and Nekrich, *Utopia in Power* (NY, 1986), p. 364. But there the search for evidence ends, for Heller and Nekrich, visceral haters of Stalin, have *no evidence at all* to support this statement.

Here is what Geoffrey Roberts, one of the best academic historians of the Stalin period in the West, says:

> Why did Stalin choose to replace Litvinov at such a
> critical moment? A common interpretation is that it
> was a prelude to the pact with Nazi Germany signed
> in August 1939. The problem with this explanation
> is that far from abandoning the triple alliance nego-
> tiations with Britain and France, Molotov pursued
> them with even more vigor than Litvinov. The most
> likely explanation is that Molotov's appointment
> was connected to Litvinov's failure to make any

headway in the negotiations. (Roberts, *Molotov*, p. 21. Emphasis added, GF)

As Roberts concludes, Snyder, Herf, and Heller and Nekrich, are all wrong. In fact *the opposite* was the case. Molotov was the closest person to Stalin in the Soviet leadership. His appointment signaled redoubled Soviet efforts to get "collective security" — guarantees from Britain and France that they would fight Germany if the USSR did. These talks only failed in the end because the British envoy, Admiral Drax, arrived in the USSR by slow boat and without any authority to sign any agreement. There is no evidence that any desire to "indulge Hitler" had anything to do with Litvinov's replacement.

Snyder appears to recognize this, in a vague way, in the following paragraph:

> The alternative to a German orientation, an alliance with Great Britain and France, seemed to offer little. London and Paris had granted security guarantees to Poland in March 1939 to try to deter a German attack, and tried thereafter to bring the Soviet Union into some kind of defensive coalition. **But Stalin was quite aware that London and Paris were unlikely to intervene in eastern Europe if Germany attacked Poland or the Soviet Union.** (Emphasis added.)

Once again Snyder is completely wrong in claiming that London and Paris "had 'tried...to bring the Soviet Union into some kind of defensive coalition." In reality, *just the opposite* was the case. The USSR had tried to negotiate a mutual defense pact with the UK and France. This attempt foundered because the British did not want it, and the French went along with the UK. The transcript of the negotiations between the British, French, and Soviet representatives was published in the Soviet Union in 1959 in two successive issues of the Soviet journal *Mezhdunarodnaia Zhizn'* [= "International Life"].[42] The texts are available online (in Russian), including:

---

[42] "Peregovory voennykh missii SSSR, Anglii I Frantsii v Moskve v Avguste 1939 g." *Mezhdunarodnaia Zhizn'* 2 (1959), 144-158; 3 (1959), 139-158.

* the August 12, 1939 session, during which British Admiral Drax admits that he has no powers to conclude any agreement;[43]

* the August 16 telegram from French Foreign Minister Bonnet to the French Ambassador to Poland Noel, insisting that he make clear to the Poles that their agreeing to allow Soviet troops to cross Polish territory to engage German forces is absolutely essential for any collective security agreement;[44]

* Polish Foreign Minister Josef Beck's August 20 telegram to Juliusz Łukasiewicz, Polish Ambassador to France, declaring that Poland refuses any military agreements with the Soviet Union. This is the document that definitively sabotaged any collective security agreement, thus guaranteeing both the Molotov-Ribbentrop Pact and Poland's defeat in September 1939.[45]

> Французский и английский послы обратились ко мне в результате переговоров франко-англо-советских штабов, во время которых Советы потребовали предоставления возможности вступления в контакт с германской армией в Поморье, на Сувалщизне и в восточной Малой Польше. Эта позиция поддержана английским и французским демаршем.
>
> Я ответил, что недопустимо, чтобы эти государства обсуждали вопрос о военном использовании территории другого суверенного государства. Польшу с Советами не связывают никакие военные договоры, и польское правительство такой договор заключать не намеревается.
>
> Французский посол сказал, что в таком случае они ответят Советам, что польское правительство отказалось от обсуждения или что французское правительство не взялось

---

[43] At http://www.hrono.info/dokum/193_dok/19390812cccp.html

[44] At http://www.hrono.info/dokum/193_dok/19390816bonne.html

[45] At http://www.hrono.info/dokum/193_dok/19390820bek.html

сделать формальный демарш, будучи уверено в отрицательном ответе.

Оставляю вопрос об ответе Советам на усмотрение Франции и Англии, оговаривая, чтобы ответ не давал повода для недоразумений.

Бек

A Polish source states that this document was sent to Polish Ambassador to London Edward Raczynski rather than to Łukasiewicz and gives the Polish original as follows, of which the Russian text above is a faithful translation:[46]

> Telegram ministra Józefa Becka do ambasadora RP w Londynie Edwarda Raczyńskiego
>
> w związku z propozycjami wkroczenia wojsk sowieckich na terytorium Polski w wypadku wojny

Ambasadorowie francuski i angielski zwrócili się do mnie w wyniku negocjacji sztabowej francusko-angielsko-sowieckiej, w której Sowiety zażądały możności wejścia w kontakt z armią niemiecką na Pomorzu, Suwalszczyźnie i w Małopolsce Wschodniej. Démarche angielskie i francuskie popierały to stanowisko.

Odpowiedziałem, że jest rzeczą niedopuszczalną, aby te państwa dyskutowały o wyzyskaniu wojskowym terytorium innego państwa suwerennego. **Polskę z Sowietami żadne układy wojskowe nie łączą i nie jest intencją Rządu Polskiego taki układ zawrzeć.**

Ambasador francuski zaproponował, że odpowiedzą Sowietom, iż Rząd Polski odmówił dyskusji lub że Rząd Francuski nie podjął się formalnej démarche, będąc pewny odpowiedzi odmownej.

---

[46] At http://www.ibidem.com.pl/zrodla/1918-1939/polityka/miedzynarodowa/1939-08-20-telegram-beck-londyn.html

> Pozostawiam sprawę odpowiedzi Sowietom
> uznaniu Francji i Anglii, zastrzegając się, aby
> odpowiedź nie dała powodu do nieporozumień.
>
> /-/ Beck
>
> Otrzymuje: Londyn, Paryż, Moskwa.
>
> Źródło:
>
> "Bellona", Londyn 1955, z. I, s. 74.

English translation:

> The French and English ambassadors have ap-
> proached me as a result of negotiations of the Fran-
> co-Anglo-Soviet staffs, during which the Soviets
> demanded the possibility of entering into contact
> with the German army in the Pomorze, Suwal-
> szczyna, and in eastern Little Poland [i.e. Western
> Belorussia and the Western Ukraine — GF]. This
> position is supported by an English and French de-
> marche.
>
> I responded that it is impermissible that these
> states discussed the question of the military use of
> the territory of another sovereign state. **No mili-
> tary treaties bind Poland with the Soviets, and
> the Polish government does not intend to con-
> clude a treaty of this kind.**
>
> The French ambassador said that in that case they
> will reply to the Soviets that the Polish government
> has refused any discussion or that the French gov-
> ernment has not undertaken a formal demarche
> since it is certain of a negative reply.
>
> I leave the question of a response to the Soviets to
> France and England, with the stipulation that the
> answer not give any reason for misunderstanding.
>
> Beck
>
> (Emphasis added.)

This was the direct cause of the failure of collective security against German aggression. It was thereby also the direct cause of the German invasion of Poland. Hitler feared a two-front war; his general staff even more so. He would not have invaded had collective security been established. And it would have been established — except for England and Poland.

In his interview in *Izvestiia* of August 27 1939 Marshal Voroshilov put it this way:

> Советская военная миссия считала, что СССР, не имеющий общей границы с агрессором, может оказать помощь Франции, Англии, Польше лишь при условии пропуска его войск через польскую территорию, ибо не существует других путей для того, чтобы советским войскам войти в соприкосновение с войсками агрессора. Подобно тому как английские и американские войска в прошлой мировой войне не могли бы принять участия в военном сотрудничестве с вооруженными силами Франции, если бы не имели возможности оперировать на территории Франции, так и Советские Вооруженные Силы не могли бы принять участия в военном сотрудничестве с вооруженными силами Франции и Англии, если они не будут пропущены на территорию Польши.
>
> Несмотря на всю очевидность правильности такой позиции, французская и английская военные миссии не согласились с такой позицией советской миссии, а **польское правительство открыто заявило, что оно не нуждается и не примет военной помощи от СССР.**
>
> Это обстоятельство сделало невозможным военное сотрудничество СССР и этих стран.

В этом основа разногласий. На этом и
прервались переговоры.[47]

Translated:

The Soviet military mission considered that the
USSR, having no common frontier with an aggressor, can render assistance to France, Great Britain,
and Poland only if its troops will be allowed to pass
through Polish territory, because there is no other
way for Soviet troops to establish contact with the
aggressor's troops.

Just as the British and American troops in the past
World War would have been unable to participate
in military collaboration with the French armed
forces if they had no possibility of operating in
French territory, the Soviet armed forces could not
participate in military collaboration with armed
forces of France and Great Britain if they are not allowed access to Polish territory.

Despite the fact that this position is obviously correct, the French and English military missions did
not agree with this position of the Soviet mission,
**and the Polish government openly declared that
they did not need and would not accept military
help from the USSR.**

This circumstance made military collaboration between the USSR and these countries impossible.

This is the basis of the disagreements. Over this the
negotiations have been broken off.[48] (Emphasis
added)

---

[47] "Интервью главы советской военной миссии К. Е. Ворошилова о переговорах с
военными миссиями Великобритании и Франции." At
http://www.hrono.ru/dokum/193_dok/19390827vorosh.html

[48] Translation of the first two paragraphs of Voroshilov's statement is taken from "Soviet
'Explains' Break with Allies", *New York Times* August 27 1939, p. 28

There is also good evidence that Beck had been well paid by the Germans to act in their interest — that he was, in fact, a German agent.[49]

Snyder Falsifies the "Molotov-Ribbentrop" Nonaggression Pact

Snyder states "[t]he two regimes immediately found common ground in their mutual aspiration to destroy Poland." (116)

In fact, the very opposite is the truth. Far from "destroying Poland", the Molotov-Ribbentrop Pact was intended to guarantee the continued existence of Poland in case the German Army overran it. Here is the test of the secret protocol to the Molotov-Ribbentrop Pact[50]:

> Article II. In the event of a territorial and political rearrangement of the areas belonging to the Polish state, the spheres of influence of Germany and the U.S.S.R. shall be bounded approximately by the line of the rivers Narev, Vistula and San.

> The question of whether the interests of both parties make desirable the maintenance of an independent Polish State and how such a state should be bounded can only be definitely determined in the course of further political developments.

By this secret protocol, as long as "an independent Polish State" continued to exist, it would be east of the Narev-Vistula-San line and Germany could not occupy it.[51] That would be desirable for the USSR. Such a rump Polish state would (a) provide a buffer between German troops and the Soviet border; and (b) be hostile to Germany and more likely to agree to a mutual defense treaty with the

---

[49] See the document cited at http://tinyurl.com/beck-german-agent-1 from a large collection of documents from Soviet archives. A discussion of this important document took place in 2011 on the H-RUSSIA mailing list. See the posts beginning June 29, 2011 at http://tinyurl.com/beck-german-agent-1 and ending November 21, 2011 at http://tinyurl.com/beck-german-agent-11 .

[50] From Paul Halsall's "Modern History Sourcebook", Fordham University. At http://www.fordham.edu/halsall/mod/1939pact.html

[51] See here for a map http://msuweb.montclair.edu/~furrg/research/mlg09/m-rpact.html

USSR, something that, as we have seen, Poland rejected as late as August 1939, less than a month before the Polish-German war.

But no one had foreseen that the Polish government would abandon its country without appointing a successor government, thus leaving Poland without any government at all. Without any command for the military and without any entity with which to negotiate a surrender Hitler had the pretext — and, in fact, a good case in international law — to take the position that Poland as a state no longer existed.

German declaration that Poland as a state no longer existed amounted to a threat to repudiate the Molotov-Ribbentrop Pact, which concerned "the Polish state." If Germany insisted there was no "Polish state" any longer it was free to send its troops hundreds of miles further to the East, to the borders of Western Ukraine and Western Belorussia. And this is exactly what happened. Hitler's government stopped referring to "Poland" and began referring to "in the area lying to the east of the German zone of influence."

The USSR could not stand by while Hitler's army rolled up to its pre-1939 borders. No state in the world would have acted this way. Nor did international law demand it. This compelled the USSR to enter "the former Polish state" in order to prevent the German army from marching up to the 1939 Soviet border.

Chapter Seven of the present book is devoted to a more detailed examination of the issue of the German-Soviet Nonaggression Pact and questions related to it.

Snyder Fabricates a "Justification for Mass Murder" by Stalin

> The irony was that Stalin had very recently justified the murder of more than one hundred thousand of his own citizens by the false claim that Poland had signed just such a secret codicil with Germany under the cover of a nonaggression pact. (116)

This statement is just another outright falsification by Snyder. Stalin never made any such statement, and — naturally — Snyder does not cite a shred of evidence that he did.

Snyder Begins His False Account of the "Molotov-Ribbentrop Pact"

> Officially, the agreement signed in Moscow on 23
> August 1939 was nothing more than a nonaggres-
> sion pact. In fact, Ribbentrop and Molotov also
> agreed to a secret protocol, designating areas of in-
> fluence for Nazi Germany and the Soviet Union
> within eastern Europe: in what were still the inde-
> pendent states of Finland, Estonia, Latvia, Lithuania,
> Poland, and Romania.... **now the Soviet Union had
> agreed to attack Poland along with Germany**.
> (116) (Emphasis added, GF)

This is a lie. We have quoted the Secret Protocol above. It contains
no agreement whatever to "attack Poland" at all, ever, much less
"along with Germany." Of course Snyder cannot cite any evidence
in support of his statement here.

Throughout the rest of his book, and in many of his articles, Snyder
writes about the "alliance" between Nazi Germany and the Soviet
Union: For example:

> ... the Nazi-Soviet alliance... ...the union between
> Moscow and Berlin... (116-7)

> Two days after the Soviet military victory over Ja-
> pan, on 17 September 1939, the Red Army invaded
> Poland from the east. The Red Army and the
> Wehrmacht met in the middle of the country and
> organized a joint victory parade. (117)

All these statements are false, and of course Snyder has no evidence to support any of them.

1. There was no "Nazi-Soviet alliance." Snyder repeats this over
and over again. But it never existed, so of course he has no evidence that it did. Nor was there any "union between Moscow and
Berlin."

2. The Red Army did not "invade Poland." It sent troops into "the
former Polish state" only after the Germans had informed the
USSR that there was no longer any "Poland." This meant that the

Molotov-Ribbentrop Pact was no longer in effect, because it was a pact concerning Poland — and Germany considered that Poland no longer existed. Germany told the Soviets that if they did not send in troops, "new states" would be formed in Western Belorussia and Western Ukraine. That meant a pro-Nazi Ukrainian Nationalist state, as the Soviets no doubt knew. [52]

Given this situation the Soviets had no choice but to send in the Red Army. No state in the world would have permitted the German Wehrmacht to march right up to its borders without taking some kind of action to prevent it.

3. There was no "joint victory parade." In the next chapter we will expose, in detail, Snyder's lies about the Molotov-Ribbentrop Pact and related issues.

> By opening half of Poland to the Soviet Union, Hitler would allow Stalin's Terror, so murderous in the Polish operation, to recommence within Poland itself. Thanks to Stalin, Hitler was able, in occupied Poland, to undertake his first policies of mass killing. In the twenty-one months that followed the joint German-Soviet invasion of Poland, the Germans and the Soviets would kill Polish civilians in comparable numbers for similar reasons, as each ally mastered its half of occupied Poland. (117-118)

Every one of these statements is false. Naturally Snyder has no evidence for any of them.

* The "Polish operation" was not "Stalin's Terror." The many murders in the "Polish operation" were carried out by Ezhov in pursuit of his conspiracy against the Soviet government and Party. Stalin had nothing to do with them. This is well demonstrated by the evidence we have. At least one expert though highly anticommunist historian, Khaustov, has admitted that this is what happened.

---

[52] Some primary source documentation of these statements may be found in an appendix to my article on the M-R Pact at
http://msuweb.montclair.edu/~furrg/research/mlg09/no_partition.html See also Chapter Seven of the present work.

* The USSR did not carry out any "terror" in Poland at all. As we shall see, Snyder is unable to find any evidence of such a "terror."

* To say that Hitler's "mass killing" was "thanks to Stalin" is the reverse of the truth. As though Hitler would not have killed Poles if he had occupied all of Poland instead of just the Western half! On the contrary: he would have killed many more Poles if he had had the whole country under his control.

* Hitler's conquest of Poland and the subsequent mass killings of Polish citizens were the direct result of the Polish government's rejection of collective security, and then of their abandonment of their own country, leaving it without any government. *The Polish government must share with Hitler the responsibility for the immense death and destruction visited upon Poland by Hitler.*

The Polish regime's refusal either to agree to collective security with the USSR or to avoid war with Germany by yielding to Hitler's demands (more German rights in Danzig and a "corridor" to it and to East Prussia) was suicidal. No one believed that the Polish army could stand up to the German army unaided. Yet the Polish regime flatly refused any alliance with the Red Army, the only military force that could have intervened in a timely manner if Germany should attack Poland, as in fact it did.

* The Polish government made the situation qualitatively worse by committing an unprecedented act of cowardice. The government, along with the military leaders, abandoned the country and crossed the border to internment in Rumania. Since Rumania was neutral in the war it had to "intern" the Polish government, rather than permit it to operate safely on Rumanian soil, or be guilty of a hostile act against Germany.

Moreover, the Polish government failed to appoint a successor government, either within Poland or in exile, before fleeing into Rumania and being interned. Once interned, the former Polish government figures could not perform any governmental functions. That meant that there was no Polish government and no one with whom Hitler could negotiate. It also meant that the Polish Army, parts of which were still fighting — Warsaw had not yet fallen to the Germans, for example — no longer had a legitimate commander. Therefore, as a state Poland had ceased to exist. No other government in World War 2 acted in this manner.

Naturally, one could also blame the governments of Great Britain and France, who failed to honor their obligation to attack Germany if Germany attacked Poland. Their actions proved that Soviet suspicions were correct. The Western Allies were not inclined to hinder Hitler as long as he kept "moving East", towards the hated Soviet Union.

Even Winston Churchill acknowledged that the Soviet Union was correct to enter Poland rather than allow the German army to march right up to the pre-1939 Soviet border. In his radio speech of October 1, 1939, printed in the *New York Times* on October 2, 1939, p. 6, Winston Churchill, First Lord of the Admiralty, said:

> Russia has pursued a cold policy of self-interest. We could have wished that the Russian Armies should be standing on their present line as the friends and allies of Poland. **But that the Russian Armies should stand on this line was clearly necessary for the safety of Russia against the Nazi menace.**

Churchill also agreed that it was in the interest of the Allies to have the Red Army occupying these territories:

> **... here these interests of Russia fall into the same channel as the interests of Britain and France.** (Emphasis added, GF)

The Soviets declared their neutrality in the German-Polish war. Their neutrality was accepted by every state as well as by the League of Nations.

* The Soviets killed *no* "Polish civilians" in the following 21 months, let alone for "comparable reasons" to Hitler's. Hitler's reason was the extermination of Slavs!

* The part of Poland "occupied" by the Soviet Union had been seized by Poland in an imperialist war in 1919-1920. Poles were a minority among the population. The Western Allies immediately

recognized that Poland had no claim to these territories and they would not be returned to Poland after the war ended.

Since 1939 these same lands have been part of Belarus and Ukraine and remain so today. The Polish government no longer claims that these lands are a part of Poland or should be returned to Poland.

Chapter 6. The *Ezhovshchina*, or "Great Terror", and the "Polish Operation": What Really Happened

Snyder's fourth chapter relies upon a completely falsified account of this important topic.

> ...and the course of the Great Terror certainly confirmed Stalin's position of power. Having called a halt to the mass operations in November 1938, Stalin once again replaced his NKVD chief. Lavrenty Beria succeeded Yezhov, who was later executed. The same fate awaited many of the highest officers of the NKVD, blamed for the supposed excesses, which were in fact the substance of Stalin's policy. (107-8)

Snyder is wrong. We know now, from primary source evidence, that Ezhov acted directly against "Stalin's" — the Soviet leadership's — "policy", i.e. intentions. This information was available when Snyder was writing his book. Either he was ignorant of this research and evidence or he knew about it but suppressed any discussion of it from his book. If the former, Snyder is incompetent and had no business writing about the subject at all. If the latter, he has deliberately deceived his readers.

We now have the telegram sent on June 17, 1937, just prior to the June Central Committee plenum, in which Ezhov transmits the request of S.M. Mironov, NKVD chief in Western Siberia, reporting the threat of revolts by subversives in concert with Japanese intelligence. In it Mironov reports that Robert I. Eikhe, Party First Secretary of Western Siberia, will request the ability to form a "troika" to deal with this threat.[1] We also have at least one of the reports Mironov sent to Ezhov to justify this request.[2]

Apparently Eikhe, and then a number of other First Secretaries, approached Stalin and the Politburo after the Plenum and asked for these special powers to deal with conspiracies, rebellions, and revolts in their areas. This led to the Politburo Decree "On Anti-Soviet elements" of July 2, 1937, which authorized all First Secretaries to arrest "kulaks and criminals" who had returned to their areas, shoot the "most dangerous" of them, and exile the rest to other areas.[3]

This vision of organized internal revolts in conjunction with foreign powers (Japan, in the case of Western Siberia) occurred in the context of the Tukhachevsky Affair of less than a month earlier. In that case the top commanders of the Red Army were convicted of collaboration with foreign powers and a plot to overthrow the Soviet government. The loyalty of the military commanders was in grave doubt — rightly so, as we now know. The NKVD appeared to be the only force that Soviet power could rely upon. It did not become clear until much later that Ezhov himself was conspiring with foreign powers to overthrow the government and Party leadership, and was using massive executions of innocent people to stir up resentment.

The document authorizing the NKVD to proceed on a virtual war footing against rebels is Order No. 00447 of July 30, 1937. It is available in Russian in many places, and (in excerpt) also in English.[4]

This document authorizes actions only against those involved in rebellions and criminal activities:

I. GROUPS SUBJECT TO PUNITIVE MEASURES.

---

[1] Vl. Khaustov, Lennart Samuelson. *Stalin, NKVD, I repressii 1937-1938 gg.* Mocow: ROSSPEN, 2009, 332-333. Вл. Хаустов, Леннарт Самуэльсон. *Сталин, НКВД, и репрессии 1937-1938 гг.* М.: РОССПЭН, 2009). Online at http://istmat.info/node/24544

[2] Danilov, et al., eds. *Tragediia sovetskoi derevni t. 5,1*, pp. 256-7.

[3] At http://istmat.info/node/14917 ; widely reprinted in Russian. Available in English in Getty & Naumov Doc. 169 pp. 470-471.

[4] English translation in Getty & Naumov, Doc. 170 pp. 473-478 (in excerpt). Hereafter G&N.

1. Former kulaks who have returned home after having served their sentences and who continue to carry out active, anti-Soviet sabotage.

2. Former kulaks who have escaped from camps or from labor settlements, as well as kulaks who have been in hiding from dekulakization, who carry out anti-Soviet activities.

3. Former kulaks and socially dangerous elements who were members of insurrectionary, fascist, ter-roristic, and bandit formations, who have served their sentences, who have been in hiding from pun-ishment, or who have escaped from places of con-finement and renewed their anti-Soviet, criminal activities.

4. Members of anti-Soviet parties (SRs, Georgian Mensheviks, Dashnaks, Mussavatists, Ittihadists, etc.), former Whites, gendarmes, bureaucrats, members of punitive expeditions, bandits, gang abettors, transferees, re-emigres, who are in hiding from punishment, who have escaped from places of confinement, and who continue to carry out active anti-Soviet activities.

5. Persons unmasked by investigators and whose evidence is verified by materials obtained by inves-tigative agencies and who are the most hostile and active members of Cossack-White Guard insurrec-tionary organizations slated for liquidation and fas-cist, terroristic, and espionage-saboteur coun-terrevolutionary formations. In addition, punitive measures are to be taken against elements of this category who are kept at the present under guard, whose cases have been fully investigated but not yet considered by the judicial organs. 6. The most active anti-Soviet elements from former kulaks, members of punitive expeditions, bandits, Whites, sectarian activists, church officials, and others, who are presently held in prisons, camps, labor settle-

ments, and colonies and who continue to carry out in those places their active anti-Soviet sabotage.

7. Criminals (bandits, robbers, recidivist thieves, professional contraband but not yet considered by the judicial organs.

8. Criminal elements in camps and labor settlements who are carrying out criminal activities in them.

9. All of the groups enumerated above, to be found at present in the countryside- i.e., in kolkhozy, sovkhozy, on agricultural enterprises-as well as in the city-i.e., at industrial and trade enterprises, in transport, in Soviet institutions, and in construction-are subject to punitive measures. (G&N 474-5)

For the next year or more Stalin was flooded with reports of conspiracies and revolts from all over the USSR. A large number of these have been published (in Russian). Undoubtedly a great many more remain unpublished in former Soviet archives throughout the former Soviet Union. According to Khaustov, a very anti-Stalin researcher and one of the compilers of several of these invaluable document collections, Stalin believed these reports.

> И самым страшным было то, что Сталин принимал решения, основываясь на показаниях, которые являлись результатом вымыслов конкретных сотрудников органов госбезопасности. Реакция Сталина свидетельствовала о том, что он воспринимал эти показания в полной мере серьезно.[5]

Translated:

> And the most frightening thing was that Stalin made his decisions on the basis of confessions that were the result of the inventions of certain employees of the organs of state security. Stalin's reactions

---

[5] Lubianka golgofa, p. 6.

attest to the fact that he took these confessions
completely seriously.

It is important to ideologically anticommunist researchers that
these mass murders be seen as Stalin's plan and intention.
Khaustov is honest enough to admit that the evidence does not
bear this out. Some, and no doubt many, of the confessional and
investigative documents Ezhov sent on to Stalin and the Soviet
leadership must have been falsifications. But in reality Khaustov
has no idea which were fabrications and which were not.

What is important here is that *Khaustov admits the existence of a
major conspiracy by Ezhov and concedes that Stalin was deceived by
him.* Ezhov admits as much in the confessions of his that we now
have. *Khaustov admits that Stalin acted in good faith on the basis of
evidence presented to him by Ezhov,* much of which must have been
false.

Russian historian Iurii Zhukov suggests that after Eikhe got these
special powers for Western Siberia the other First Secretaries
asked Stalin for the same powers, and received them. Evidently
there was a connection between this campaign of repressions, carried out as a virtual war against rebellious anti-Soviet forces
throughout the country, and the cancellation of the competitive
elections that had been stipulated under the new 1936 Soviet Constitution. Stalin and his supporters in the central Soviet government and Party fought for such elections but failed to win the Central Committee to approve them. Zhukov has traced the final decision not to hold such elections to October 11, 1937. He also located
a draft or sample ballot for contested elections — a ballot never
used but preserved in a Soviet archive.[6]

Ezhov"s Conspiracy Gradually Uncovered

Beginning perhaps at the January 1938 Central Committee Plenum
Stalin and the Politburo began to uncover evidence of massive illegal repressions, first of all against Party members. Politburo mem-

---

[6] See Grover Furr, "Stalin and the Struggle for Democratic Reform, Part One", in *Cultural
Logic* 2005, paragraphs 60 — end. At http://clogic.eserver.org/2005/furr.html Much of
this material is summarized from IUrii N. Zhukov, *Inoi Stalin. Politicheskie Reformy v SSSR v
1933-1937 gg.*,Moscow: Vagrius, 2003.

ber Pavel Postyshev was dismissed from his post on the grounds that he was killing off the Party infrastructure.[7] From what we can tell from the documents now published the suspicions continued to grow in the Politburo that massive, unauthorized repressions were going on. In August 1938 Ezhov's second-in-command, Mikhail Frinovskii, was replaced by Lavrentii Beria. Evidently Beria was chosen as a reliable person to keep watch over Ezhov, as Ezhov himself later stated.

In November 1938 Ezhov was convinced to resign his position as Commissar of the NKVD. We are not sure exactly how everything happened. There is some evidence that Ezhov and his men planned one final desperate effort at seizure of power by assassinating Stalin and others at the November 1938 celebration of the Bolshevik Revolution but that timely arrests forestalled this.[8] Zhukov claims to have seen Ezhov's actual resignation and claims that it was done in a rushed way, on any scrap of paper available. Zhukov concludes from this that Ezhov was only persuaded to resign with difficulty.[9]

As soon as Ezhov resigned, to be replaced by Beria, orders were given to immediately stop all the repressions, to repeal all the NKVD Operational Orders that enabled them, to stop the work of the *troikas*, and to re-emphasize the need for oversight by the Prosecutor's Office of all cases of arrest. This document is available in English.[10]

After this there began a flood of reports to Beria and the central Party leadership concerning massive illegitimate repressions and shootings on the part of local NKVD groups. We have many of these documents now, and no doubt there are many more of them. The central Party leadership began to investigate.

---

[7] On Postyshev see Furr, Khrushchev Lied, 45ff; 282-288.

[8] See "transcript of the interrogation of the arrested person Ezhov Nikolai Ivanovich of April 26 1939," Lubianka 1939-1946 at pp. 68 ff. English translation at http://msuweb.montclair.edu/~furrg/research/ezhov042639eng.html

[9] IU.N. Zhukov, "Zhupel Stalina", *Komsomolskaia Pravda* 20 November 2002.

[10] Getty & Naumov Doc. 190 pp. 532-537.

On January 29, 1939 Beria, Andreev, and Malenkov signed a report about the massive abuses during Ezhov's tenure.[11] It begins as follows:

> We consider it essential to report to you the following conclusions about the situation of cases in the NKVD USSR:
>
> 1. During the period of time that com. Ezhov headed the Narkomvnudel [People's Commissariat of Internal Affairs, the NKVD] of the USSR right up until the moment he left the duties of People's Commissar a majority of the leading positions in the NKVD USSR and in the organs under its supervision (the NKVDs of union and autonomous republics, the UNKVDs of the krais and oblasts) have been occupied by enemies of the people, conspirators, and spies.
>
> 2. Enemies of the people who penetrated the organs of the NKVD have consciously distorted the punitive policy of Soviet power, have carried out massive, unfounded arrests of completely innocent persons, while at the same time covering up real enemies of the people.
>
> 3. The methods of conducting investigations have been perverted in the most brutal manner. They had recourse to beatings of prisoners on a massive level in order to force them into false confessions and "admissions." The quantity of admissions that each investigator was supposed to obtain from prisoners in the course of 24 hours has been decided upon in advance. In addition, the quotas have often reached several dozen "admissions."
>
> Investigators have widely made use of the practice of fully informing one another concerning the con-

---

[11] Nikita Petrov, Marc Jansen. *"Stalinskii pitomets" - Nikolai Ezhov*. Moscow: ROSSPEN, 2008, pp. 359-363.Russian text online at http://istmat.info/node/24582 English translation at http://msuweb.montclair.edu/~furrg/research/beria_andreev_malenkov012939eng.html

tent of the confessions they obtained. This gave the investigators the ability, during interrogators of "their" prisoners, to suggest to them by one means or another facts, circumstances, and names of persons about whom confessions had earlier been given by other prisoners. As a result this kind of investigation very often led to organized false slanders against persons who were completely innocent.

In order to obtain a greater number of admissions a number of organs of the NKVD had recourse to direct provocation: they convinced prisoners to give confessions about supposed espionage work for foreign intelligence services by explaining that these kinds of fabricated confessions were needed by the party and government in order to discredit foreign states. They also promised the prisoners that they would be liberated after they gave such "admissions."

The leadership of the NKVD in the person of com. Ezhov not only did not put a stop to this kind of arbitrariness and extremism in arrests and in the conduct of investigations, but sometimes itself abetted it.

The slightest attempts by Chekist party members to oppose this arbitrariness were stifled.

. . . . .

Com. Ezhov concealed in every way from the Central Committee of the ACP(b) the situation of the work in the NKVD organs. Besides that he hid from the CC ACP(b) materials that compromised leading NKVD workers.

. . . . .

In addition we believe it essential to note that all the above disgraceful actions, distortions and excesses <in the matter of arrests and the conduct of investigation> were carried out with the sanction

and knowledge of the organs of the Procuracy of the
USSR (coms. Vyshinsky and Roginsky). Assistant
Procuror of the USSR Roginsky has been especially
zealous in this matter. Roginsky's practice of work
raises serious doubts about this political honesty
<and reliability>.

The report continues in this vein. Reports and investigations of
NKVD abuses continued rapidly.

In April Mikhail Frinovskii, Ezhov's "zam", or deputy commissar,
and Ezhov himself were arrested. They immediately began to confess. All the confessions published so far are now available online
in both the Russian original and in English translation.[12] These
confessions revealed the broad outlines of Ezhov's conspiracy
against and deception of the Soviet leadership and of Stalin. During
the next few years, up to the beginning of the war, further investigations and prosecutions of guilty NKVD men proceeded. Over
100,000 persons were released from camps and prisons after reviews of their cases.[13]

The "Polish Operation"

The "Polish Operation" of the NKVD was enabled by NKVD Order
No. 00485 of August 11, 1937. It has been published many times in
Russian and is also online.[14] We have now made it available in Eng-
lish translation for the first time.[15]

The following are the major scholarly works on the Polish Operation. The second and fourth are cited by Snyder.

> * James Morris. "The Polish Terror: Spy Mania and Ethnic
> Cleansing in the Great Terror." *Europe-Asia Studies* 56, 5 (July
> 2004), 751-766.

---

[12] See "Additional Bibliography — Documents" at the bottom of the following page:
http://msuweb.montclair.edu/~furrg/research/trials_Ezhovshchina_update0710.html

[13] Okhotin and Roginskii of the "Memorial Society", both highly antcommunist and anti-
Stalin researchers, estimate "about 110,000 persons formerly accused of counterrevolutionary crimes" were freed during 1939 as a result of Beria's investigation of NKVD crimes
under Ezhov. *Tragedia sovetskoi derevni* t. 5, 2 (Moscow: ROSSPEN, 2006), p. 571.

[14] One site is http://ru.wikisource.org/wiki/Приказ_НКВД_от_11.08.1937_№_00485

[15] At http://msuweb.montclair.edu/~furrg/research/no00485.html

* A. Ie. Gur'ianov, "Obzor sovetskikh repressivnykh kampanii protiv poliakov i pol'skikh grazhdan," in A. V. Lipatov and I. O. Shaitanov, eds., *Poliaki i russkie: Vzaimoponimanie i vzaimoneponimanie,* Moscow: Indrik, 2000, 199-207.

* A. Ie. Gur'ianov, "Obzor sovetskikh repressivnykh kampanii protiv poliakov i pol'skikh grazhdan," in *Massovye repressii protiv poliakov.* Memorial Society. At http://www.memo.ru/history/polacy/vved/index.htm [This is a brief summary of Gur'ianov's longer article above.]

* N. V. Petrov and A. B. Roginskii, "'Pol'skaia operatsiia' NKVD 1937-1938 gg.," in A. Ie. Gur'ianov, ed., *Repressii protiv poliakov i pol'skikh grazhdan,* Moscow: Zven'ia, 1997, 22-43.

All these studies agree in the following conclusions:

* The "Polish Operation" was aimed at Polish spies only, not at Poles as such. This can of course be seen from the text of Operational Order No. 00485 itself.

> The intention of the regime was not to terrorize or murder minority populations... (Morris 759)

> ... it [NKVD Order No. 00485, the "Polish Operation" order] did not concern Poles as such, but Polish spies... (Petrov & Roginskii)

Least of all was the massive nature of the repression "along Polish lines" the result of some kind of special personal hatred by Stalin of Poles. It was not a matter of Poles as such, but of Poland.

> ... their nationality was not a criterion of "criminal guilt" (*prestupnosti*) ...

> ...to equate the concept of "Poles" and "Polish operation" would be a mistake.

> (Petrov & Roginskii)

* Many of those arrested and either executed or imprisoned were not Poles or of Polish background at all.

> These numbers show that many of the victims were not ethnic Poles. (Morris 762)

* Petrov and Roginskii stress repeatedly that nationality itself was not a criterion for arrest or execution. The central NKVD did not keep records of the nationality of those arrested.

* Ezhov confessed that he and his men had arrested people who were not Poles on the pretext that they were Poles:

> As a result of this pressure the practice of repressions without any incriminating evidence whatsoever on the sole basis of one criterion alone, that the person repressed belonged to such-and-such a nationality (Pole, German, Latvian, Greek, etc.), was broadly expanded.

> However, that was not enough. The practice of including Russians, Ukrainians, Byelorussians, et al. in the category of Poles, Finns, Germans, et al., became a rather mass phenomenon, especially in certain oblasts.

> Of those who especially distinguished themselves in this manner were the People's Commissars of Internal Affairs of such republics as: the Ukraine, Belorussia, Turkmenia, and the heads of the UNKVDs of such oblasts as the Sverdlovsk, Leningrad, and Moscow.

> So for example Dmitriev, former head of the NKVD of the Sverdlovsk oblast included a great many Ukrainians, Byelorussians, and even Russians under the category of repressed Polish refugees. In any case for every arrested Pole there were no fewer than ten Russians, Ukrainians, and Byelorussians.

> There were many cases in which Russians, Ukrainians, and Byelorussians generally were made into Poles with falsified documents.

> The practice in Leningrad was the same. Instead of Finns Zakovsky arrested many native inhab-

itants of the USSR — Karelians, and "transformed" them into Finns.

**Uspensky, under the pretence of their being
Poles, arrested many Ukrainian Uniates**, that
is, selected them not on the basis of national
origin but according to their religion. I could
multiply many times examples of this kind.
They are characteristic for the majority of oblasts.

(Ezhov interrogation of August 4, 193. Emphasis added [16])

* There were few guidelines from Stalin and the Politburo — if,
indeed, there were any at all. The whole operation was run by
Ezhov and his men, who themselves gave little specific guidance to
the local NKVD men. (Petrov & Roginskii)

Through neglect of his responsibilities Soviet Prosecutor (*Prokurator*) Vyshinskii was partly responsible for the fact that Ezhov
and his men were able to get away with these immense crimes. In
his 1939 confessions Ezhov claimed that the Prosecutor's Office
failed to conduct the oversight it was supposed to, and Ezhov and
his men could shoot and imprison people with virtually no hin-
drance from Vyshinskii's office. This passage from Ezhov's interrogation of August 4, 1939 illustrates this negligence of Vyshinskii's
office:

Question: Confess in what manner you managed to
deceive the organs of prosecutorial oversight in implementing this clear, obvious, and criminal practice of repression?

Answer: I can't say that we had any special
thought-out plan to consciously deceive the organs
of the Procuracy.

---

[16] This was published for the first time in Nikita Petrov, Marc Jansen. *"Stalinskii pitomets"* —
Nikolai Ezhov. Moscow: ROSSPEN, 2008, pp. 367-379. Russian original online at
http://msuweb.montclair.edu/~furrg/research/ezhov080439ru.html ; English translation
at http://msuweb.montclair.edu/~furrg/research/ezhov080439eng.html

The prosecutors of the oblasts, krais, and republics, and also the Procuracy of the USSR could not have been unaware of such a blatant criminal practice of mass provocational arrests and falsification of investigative facts, since they bore responsibility, together with the NKVD, for the review of such cases.

This inactivity of prosecutorial supervision can only be explained by the fact that in charge of the Procuracy in many oblasts, krais, and republics were members of various anti-Soviet organizations who often practiced even more widespread provocational repressions among the population.

Another group of the prosecutors, those who were not involved in participation in anti-Soviet groupings, simply feared to argue with the heads of the UNKVDs on these questions, all the more so since they did not have any directives on these matters from the center, where all the falsified investigative reports that had been mechanically signed by themselves, i.e. the prosecutors, went through without any kind of restraint or remarks.

Question: You are talking about the local organs of the Procuracy. But didn't they see these criminal machinations in the Procuracy of the USSR?

Answer: The Procuracy of the USSR could not, of course, have failed to notice all these perversions.

I explain the behavior of the Procuracy of the USSR and, in particular, of Prosecutor of the USSR Vyshinsky by that same fear of quarreling with the NKVD and by [the desire] to prove themselves no less "revolutionary" in the sense of conducting mass repressions.

I have come to this conclusion also because Vyshinsky often spoke to me personally about the tens of thousands of complaints coming in to the Procuracy and to which he was paying no attention. Likewise, during the whole period of the conduct of the operations I do not recall a single instance of a protest by Vyshinsky concerning the mass operations, while there were instances when he insisted on more severe sentences in relation to some persons or other.

This is the only way I can explain the virtual absence of any prosecutorial supervision at all during the mass operations and the absence of any protests from them to the government against the acts of the NKVD. I repeat, we the conspirators and specifically, I myself did not have any kind of thought-out plans.

The first document issued after Ezhov had been induced to resign from office stressed the lack of Prosecutorial oversight. In 1939 Vyshinskii was replaced as Prosecutor. It seems likely that this was because he had failed to do his duty during the *Ezhovshchina*.

* The notion that the *Ezhovshchina* and the "Polish Operation" of which it was a part were undertaken to forestall a potential "fifth column" is false. This theory was evidently first stated by Oleg Khlevniuk in 1996[17] and has been uncritically repeated ever since, including by Snyder.

Bukharin, Not Stalin, Was To Blame for the Massive Repressions

One interesting fact that emerges from the primary sources now available — and, we note, available during the time Snyder was writing *Bloodlands* — is that Nikolai Bukharin, leading name among the Rightists and one of its leaders, knew about the *Ezhovshchina* as it was happening, and praised it in a letter to Stalin that he wrote from prison.

---

[17] Note 14 in Petrov & Roginskii states this as a fact. Khlevniuk's only evidence is an off-the-cuff statement by an aged Molotov to his biographer Felix Chuev.

Bukharin knew that Ezhov was a member of the Rightist conspiracy, as he himself was. No doubt that is why he welcomed Ezhov's appointment as head of the NKVD — a view recorded by his widow in her memoirs.[18]

In his first confession, in his now-famous letter to Stalin of December 10, 1937, and at his trial in March 1938 Bukharin claimed he had completely "disarmed" and had told everything he knew. But now we can prove that this was a lie. Bukharin knew that Ezhov was a leading member of the Rightist conspiracy — but did not inform on him. According to Mikhail Frinovsky, Ezhov's right-hand man, Ezhov probably promised to see that he would not be executed if he did not mention his own, Ezhov's, participation. This is documented in Mikhail Frinovskii's confession of April 11, 1939. Frinovskii was Ezhov's second-in-command.

> An active participant in investigations generally, Ezhov kept himself aloof from the preparation of this trial. Before the trial the face-to-face confrontations of the suspects, interrogations, and refining, in which Ezhov did not participate. He spoke for a long time with Yagoda, and that talk concerned, in the main, of assuring Yagoda that he would not be shot.
>
> Ezhov had conversations several times with Bukharin and Rykov and also in order to calm them assured them that under no circumstances would they be shot.[19]

If Bukharin had told the truth — if he had, in fact, informed on Ezhov — Ezhov's mass murders could have been stopped in their tracks. The lives of hundreds of thousands of innocent people could have been saved.

But Bukharin remained true to his fellow conspirators. He went to execution — an execution that Bukharin himself swore in his ap-

---

[18] Anna Larina (Bukharina), *Nezabyvaemoe.* Moscow: Izdatel'stvo APN, 1989, 269-70.

[19] See the English translation at
http://msuweb.montclair.edu/~furrg/research/frinovskyeng.html#The%20preparation%20of%20the%20trial%20of%20Rykov,%20Bukharin,%20Krestinsky,%20Yagoda%20and%20others

peal for clemency that he deserved "ten times over" — without revealing Ezhov's participation in the conspiracy.

This point cannot be stressed too much: the blood of the hundreds of thousands of innocent persons slaughtered by Ezhov and his men during 1937-1938, is on Bukharin's hands.

Bukharin's two appeals for clemency, both dated March 13, 1938, were reprinted in *Izvestiia* on September 2, 1992. They were rejected, and Bukharin was executed on March 15, 1938. I have translated them and put them online in English.[20]

Ezhov"s Confessions

All ideologically anticommunist accounts suppress the evidence of Ezhov's conspiracy against the Soviet government. None of them refer to the confessions of Ezhov and his men, though these confessions were all available to them.

The apparent reason for the failure to discuss Ezhov's conspiracy is the desire on the part of ideologically anticommunist researchers to falsely accuse the Soviet leadership, Stalin most of all, of having ordered all the huge number of executions carried out by Ezhov. However, Ezhov explicitly states many times that his repressions and executions were carried out in pursuit of his own private conspiratorial goals and that he had deceived the Soviet government. Thus Ezhov's own confessions are evidence that Stalin and the central Soviet leadership were not responsible for his massive executions.

Ezhov's confessions that he deceived the government for his conspiratorial purposes are not contradicted by any other evidence. In addition, we now have the judgment of Khaustov, an anticommunist researcher himself, who concludes on the basis of massive evidence at his disposal that Stalin believed the false reports Ezhov was sending to him.

Thus, the only conclusion supported by the evidence contradicts the "anti-Stalin" ideological aims of these anticommunist researchers. It is important to them that Stalin and the Soviet leader-

---

[20] At http://msuweb.montclair.edu/~furrg/research/bukharinappeals.html

ship be "guilty" of "mass murders." By omitting evidence that tends to disprove this conclusion — Ezhov's confessions — their assertions may be accepted by their readers.

All of the confessions of Ezhov that the Russian government has seen fit to make public to date, plus one of Ezhov's "zam" or Deputy Commissar Mikhail Frinovskii, are available online in both Russian and English.[21]

In his confession of August 4, 1939 Ezhov specifically states that he deceived the Soviet government about the extent and nature of espionage:

> **Question**: Did you succeed in obtaining a government decision to prolong the mass operations?
>
> **Answer:** Yes. We did obtain the decision of the government to prolong the mass operation and to increase the number of those to be repressed.
>
> **Question:** What did you do, deceive the government?
>
> **Answer:** It was unquestionably essential for us to prolong the mass operation and increase the number of persons repressed.
>
> However, it was necessary to extend the time period for these measures and to set up a real and accurate account so that once we had prepared ourselves, we could strike our blow directly on the most dangerous part, the organizational leadership of the counterrevolutionary elements.
>
> The government, understandably, had no conception of our conspiratorial plans and in the present case proceeded solely on the basis of the necessity to prolong the operation without going into the essence of how it was carried out.

---

[21] See the following web page, under "Additional Bibliography" "Documents" - http://msuweb.montclair.edu/~furrg/research/trials_Ezhovshchina_update0710.html

In this sense, of course, we were deceiving the government in the most blatant manner. (Emphasis added.)

Was Ezhov a Polish Spy?

Of the sources on the Polish Operation only Morris mentions this fact:

> Ironically, Ezhov was accused of being a Polish spy when he was arrested a short time later. (763)

Morris cites no evidence or source at all here. He may well have taken it from Jansen & Petrov (2000, p. 187), where it is briefly stated as one of the charges against Ezhov at trial on February 1, 1940. But we now know somewhat more about this. Pavliukov had access to some of Ezhov's confessions including those of April 18-20, 1939, shortly after his arrest. After a brief verbatim quote Pavliukov (520-521) summarizes thus:

> Ezhov related that he was drawn into espionage work by his friend F.M. Konar, who had long been a Polish agent. Konar learned political news from Ezhov and gave them to his bosses in Poland and on one occasion told Ezhov about this and proposed that he volunteer to begin working for the Poles. Since Ezhov had in fact already become an informant of Polish intelligence, since he had transmitted to them via Konar many significant party and state secrets, he supposedly had no other choice than to agree with this proposal.

> The Poles supposedly shared a part of the intelligence received from Ezhov with their allies the Germans, and so after a time an offer of collaboration from the latter was also made.

> According to Ezhov Marshal A.I. Egorov, first assistant Commissar for Defense, acted as the middleman [between Ezhov and the Germans]. He met with Ezhov in the summer of 1937 and told him that he knew about the latter's ties with the Poles,

> that he himself was a German spy who on orders
> from the German authorities had organized a group
> of conspirators in the Red Army, and that he had
> been given a directive to establish close working
> contact between his group and Ezhov.
>
> Ezhov agreed with this proposal and promised to
> protect Egorov's men from arrest.

This corresponds generally to other evidence we have about the
military conspiracies and the charges against Egorov.

Objectivity and Evidence

I agree with historian Geoffrey Roberts when he says:

> In the last 15 years or so an enormous amount of
> new material on Stalin ... has become available from
> Russian archives. I should make clear that as a his-
> torian I have a strong orientation to telling the truth
> about the past, no matter how uncomfortable or
> unpalatable the conclusions may be. ... I don't think
> there is a dilemma: you just tell the truth as you see
> it.[22]

The conclusions about the *Ezhovshchina* outlined here will be unacceptable to persons motivated not by the pursuit of the objective
truth bsions out of any desire to "apologize" for the policies of Stalin or the Soviet government but because they are the only objective conclusions possible based on the available evidence.

---

[22] "Stalin's Wars", February 12, 2007. At http://hnn.us/roundup/entries/35305.html

Chapter 7. The Molotov-Ribbentrop Pact: What Really Happened [1]

Introduction

Did the Soviet Union Invade Poland on September 17, 1939? Why ask? "We all know" this invasion occurred. "You can look it up!" Almost all contemporary authoritative accounts agree that this historical event happened.

Here is how Snyder puts the matter in an article in *The New York Review of Books* (April 30, 2009, p. 17) .

> Because the film (although not the book)* begins
> with the German invasion of the Soviet Union in
> 1941 rather than the joint German-Soviet invasion
> and division of Poland in 1939... the Soviet state had
> just months earlier been an ally of Nazi Germany...
> (* "Defiance")

The Public Broadcasting System's documentary "Behind Closed Doors" (2009) describes the invasion as an unproblematic fact:

> After invading Poland in September 1939, the Nazis
> and the Soviets divided the country as they had
> agreed to do in the Molotov-Ribbentrop pact...[2]

The Wikipedia article: "Soviet invasion of Poland", undoubtedly composed by Polish nationalists like virtually all Wikipedia material on Poland and the USSR:

---

[1] The formal name for this agreement is the Nonaggression Pact between the USSR and Germany. It is often called the "Molotov-Ribbentrop Pact" or "Treaty" after the two foreign ministers who signed it. Ideological anticommunists call it the "Hitler-Stalin Pact", in furtherance of the goal of associating the USSR to Nazi Germany and Stalin to Hitler. An earlier version of this essay is at http://www.tinyurl.com/furr-mlg09

[2] At http://www.pbs.org/behindcloseddoors/in-depth/struggle-poland.html

...on 17 September, the Red Army invaded Poland from the east...[3]

The Soviet Union Did Not Invade Poland in September, 1939

The truth is that the USSR did not invade Poland in September, 1939. However, so completely has this non-event passed into historiography as "true" that I have yet to find a recent history book from the West that actually gets this correct.

And, of course, the USSR had never been an "ally" of Nazi Germany. The Molotov-Ribbentrop Pact (henceforth "M-R Pact") was a non-aggression pact, not an alliance of any kind. The claim that the USSR and Hitler's Germany were "allies" is simply stated over and over again but is never backed up with any evidence.

The present chapter and the one preceding it present a great deal of evidence in support of this statement. There is a great deal more evidence to support what I say — much more than I can present here, and no doubt much more that I have not yet identified or located. Furthermore, at the time it was widely acknowledged that no such invasion occurred.

The Soviet Union and Hitler"s Germany Were Never "Allies"

Strictly speaking, it is impossible to prove a negative — in this case, that no "alliance" existed. The burden of proof is on those who use the terms "alliance", "allies", and "ally" with respect to the USSR, Germany, and the M-R Pact. The complete text of the Pact is online at the Modern History Sourcebook.[4] It is short. Anyone who reads it can see that there is no "alliance" of any kind.

The truth about these matters is another victim of the post-WWII Cold War, when a great many falsehoods about Soviet history were invented and popularized. The truth about this and many other

---

[3] At http://en.wikipedia.org/wiki/Soviet_invasion_of_Poland
[4] At http://www.fordham.edu/halsall/mod/1939pact.html

questions concerning the history of the first socialist state has simply become "politically incorrect." In "respectable academia" it is "taboo."[5]

Demonizing — I use the word advisedly; it is not too strong — the history of the communist movement and anything to do with Stalin has become *de rigeur,* a shibboleth of respectability. And not only among avowed champions of capitalism but also among those on the left and opponents of capitalism generally, including many Marxists, the natural constituency of a movement for communism.

The Nonaggression Treaty between Germany and the USSR of August 1939[6]

Before examining the question of the invasion that did not take place, the reader needs to become familiar with some misconceptions about the Nonaggression Treaty and why they are false. These too are based on anticommunist propaganda that is widely, if naively, "believed."

The most common, and most false, of these is stated above in the PBS series "Behind Closed Doors:"

> ...the Nazis and the Soviets divided the country as they had agreed to do in the Molotov-Ribbentrop pact...

This is completely false, as any reading of the text of the M-R Pact itself will reveal.

---

[5] Some time ago a colleague on an academic mailing list tweaked me for supposedly "defending Stalin." He wrote:

> "I could make a crack about what defenses of Stalin have to do with a 'sensible materialism,' but that would be beneath me."

My colleague thinks he knows something about Stalin and the USSR during Stalin's time. He doesn't! But you can't blame him too much, since almost none of us do. More precisely: We "know" a lot of things about the Soviet Union and Stalin, and almost all of those things are just not true. We've been swallowing lies for the truth our whole lives.

[6] For a discussion of the events that led up to the Molotov-Ribbentrop Pact of 1939 an excellent account is still Bill Bland, "The German-Soviet Non-Aggression Pact of 1939" (1990) at http://marxism.halkcephesi.net/Bill%20Bland/german%20soviet%20pact.htm I have checked every citation in this article; most are available online now. It's very accurate, but far more detailed than the present account requires.

The Secret Protocols to the M-R Pact Did NOT Plan Any Partition of Poland

Up to at least September 7 Hitler was considering making peace with Poland if Poland sued for peace. General Franz Halder, Chief of the General Staff of the Army (*Chef des Generalstabs des Heeres*), wrote in his "War Diary" — Halder F. *Kriegstagebuch. Tägliche Aufzeichnungen des Chefs des Generalstabes des Heeres 1939-1942.* Stuttgart: W. Kohlhammer Verlag, 1962-1964. I have used *Band I. Vom Polenfeldzug bis zum Ende der Westoffensive (14.8.1939 - 30.6.1940).*

> OB beim Führer (7.9. nachmittag): 3 Möglichkeiten:
>
> 1. Polen kommen zu Verhandlungen: er bereit zur Verhandlung: Trennung von Frankreich und England, Restpolen wird anerkannt. Narew — Warschau = Polen. Industriegebiet wir. Krakau, Polen. Nordrand Beskiden wir. Ukraine selbständig. (I, S. 65)
>
> 7 September 1939
>
> The High Command with the Fuehrer (second half of the day 7 September): Three different ways the situation may develop.
>
> 1. The Poles offer to begin negotiations. He [Hitler - GF] is ready for negotiations [on the following conditions]: [Poland must] break with England and France. A part of Poland will be [preserved and] recognized. [The regions from the] Narev to Warsaw - to Poland. The industrial region—to us. Krakow—to Poland. The northern region of the Beskidow mountains—to us. [The provinces of the Western] Ukraine—independent.

So on September 7 Hitler was considering independence for Western Ukraine even though, according to the "Secret Protocol" of the

Molotov-Ribbentrop Pact the Western Ukraine lay within the Soviet sphere of influence. This shows that:

* The Secret Protocol about spheres of influence was not about the "partition of Poland."

* Hitler was prepared to negotiate over the Western Ukraine with the Poles, not with the Soviets. The Western Ukraine lay entirely within the Soviet "sphere of influence" as defined by the Secret Protocol of the M-R Pact.

* As late as September 7 Hitler was planning to preserve a shrunken Polish state.

In his entries for September 9 and September 10 Halder repeats that the Germans are discussing the formation of an independent state in the Western Ukraine. This is further evidence that the Secret Protocols of the M-R Pact did not concern any "partition of Poland."

> September 9:
>
> *OB vormerken:* ... b) Selbstständigkeit der West-Ukraine. (I, S. 67)
>
> *Bring to the attention of the Supreme Command:* ... b) The independence of the Western Ukraine.
>
> September 10:
>
> *Warlimont:* a) Aufruf Westukraine kommt. (I, S. 68)
>
> *Warlimont:* a) A call to the Western Ukraine is imminent.

Col. Walter Warlimont was deputy head of operations at the German High Command. A note in the annotated text of Halder's diary reads:

> Nämlich für die Errichtung eines selbständiges Staates aus der polnischen Ukraine. (I, S. 68 Anm. 6)

Translated:

That is, for the setting up of an independent state out of Polish Ukraine.

Under September 11 Halder noted that:

> Grenzübertritt polnischer *aktiver Soldaten* nach Rumänien hat begonnen. (I, S. 71)

Translated:

> The flight of *active* Polish *soldiers* [= combat troops] into Rumania has begun.

On September 12 Halder noted: "Talks between the High Command and the Fuehrer" and said:

> *ObdH-Führer:* Russe will wahrscheinlich nicht antreten…. [Russe] halt Friedenswunsch Polens für möglich. (I, S. 72)

Translated:

> The Russian apparently does not want to come in…. [The Russian] believes it possible that Poland wants [to conclude a] peace [with Germany].

This is further proof that the Germans had no agreement with the USSR to partition Poland. It is also evidence that the USSR expected that a negotiated settlement would leave a rump Polish state in existence between Germany and the Soviet border.

Halder also noted:

> Rumänien will polnische Regierung nich aufnehmen; [Grenzen] zumachen. (I, S. 72)

Translated:

> Rumania does not wish to accept [the entry of] the Polish government; will close [its borders].

Halder:

> [Hitler] denkt an sich bescheiden mit Ost-
> Oberschlesien und Korridor, wenn Westen
> wegbleibt. (I, S. 72)

Translated:

> He [Hitler] is prepared to be content with the East-
> ern part of Upper Silesia and the Polish Corridor, if
> the West doesn't interfere.

This would have meant that most of Western Poland would have remained part of a shrunken Poland. This is additional evidence that Hitler did not plan on liquidating the Polish state.

By September 12 the issue of whether the Polish government might try to flee to Rumania had obviously been raised, but it had not yet happened. This means that on September 12 Hitler still believed the Polish government would stay in Poland - because he assumed he would have someone to negotiate peace with.

The same date General Wilhelm Keitel, Head of the Supreme Command of the Armed Forces (*Chef des Oberkommandos der Wehrmacht*) ordered Admiral Canaris to activate units of the Organization of Ukrainian Nationalists (OUN) on Polish territory with the aim of forming an independent Polish and Galician Ukraine. This was to be accompanied by a general massacre of, Poles and Jews. During post-war interrogation by Soviet authorities General-major Erwin von Lahousen of the *Abwehr* (German Military Intelligence) confirmed this:

> **Oberst Amen**: Was, wenn überhaupt etwas, wurde
> über eine mögliche Zusammenarbeit mit einer
> Ukrainischen Gruppe gesagt?
>
> **Lahousen**: Ja, es wurde — und zwar vom da-
> maligen Chef OKW als Weitergabe einer Rechtlinie,
> die er offenbar von Ribbentrop empfangen hatte,
> weil er sich in Zusammenhang mit dem politischen
> Vorhaben des Reichsaußenministers Ribbentrop
> bekanntgegeben hat — es wurde Canaris aufgetra-
> gen, in der Galizischen Ukraine eine

Aufstandsbewegung hervorzurufen, die die
Ausrottung der Juden und Polen zum Ziele haben
sollte...

Nach den Eintragungen im Tagebuch von Canaris
fand sie am 12. September 1939 statt. Der Sinn die-
ses Befehls oder der Anweisung, die von Ribbentrop ausging, von Keitel und Canaris weitergegeben
war und dann in kurzer Unterredung nochmals von
Ribbentrop Canaris gegenüber aufgezeigt wurde,
war folgende: Die Organizationen nationaler
Ukrainer, mit denen das Amt Ausland / Abwehr im
militärischen Sinne, also im Sinne militärischer Op-
erationen zusammenarbeitete, sollten in Polen eine
Aufstandsbewegung hervorrufen — in Polen mit
den Ukrainern. Die Aufstandsbewegung sollte den
Zweck haben, Polen und Juden, also vor allem Ele-
mente oder Kreise, umdie es sich ja bei diesen Be-
sprechungen immer wieder drehte, auszurotten.[7]

Translated:

Colonel Amen [interrogator]: What, if anyting, was
said about possible collaboration with a Ukrainian
group?

Lahousen: Yes, and it was given by the then Chief
of Staff of the Supreme Command of the Wehrmacht
[General-Fieldmarshal Keitel] as the transmission
of a straight line, which he had evidently received
from Ribbentrop, because he had announced it in
connection with the political project of Reichs Foreign Minister Ribbentrop — Canaris was assigned
to bring about an insurgency in the Galician
Ukraine, which should have as its goal the extermination of Jews and Poles....

According to the entries in Canaris' diary this meeting took place on September 12, 1939. The purpose

---

[7] Julius Mader, *Hitlers Spionagegenerale sagen aus*. Berlin: Vlg. der Nation. 1971, 122; 124.

of this command or the statement that came from Ribbentrop, was passed by Keitel and Canaris and was in a short conversation again assigned by Ribbentrop to Canaris, was as follows: The organizations of national Ukrainians [i.e. the Organization of Ukrainian Nationalists] with which the Office Ausland / Abwehr was collaborating in a military sense , that is in the sense of military operations, should produce an insurgency in Poland - in Poland, with the Ukrainians. The insurgency should have the purpose of exterminating Poles and Jews, that is, in particular the elements or circles that were repeatedly the subjects of these meetings.

The Soviets Wanted to Protect the USSR — and Therefore to Preserve Independent Poland

It is conventionally stated as fact that the M-R Pact was an agreement to "partition Poland", divide it up. This is completely false. I've prepared a page with much fuller evidence.[8]

No doubt a big reason for this falsehood is the inconvenient fact that *Britain and France did sign a Nonaggression Pact with Hitler that "partitioned" another state — Czechoslovakia*. That was the Munich Agreement of September 30, 1938.[9]

Poland also took part in the "partition" of Czechoslovakia. Poland seized a part of the Teschen (Polish: Cieszyn) area of Czechoslovakia, even though only a minority of the population was Polish. This invasion and occupation was not part of the Munich Agreement. But neither France nor Britain did anything about it. Therefore, they consented to it. Later, in March 1939 Hitler seized the remaining part of Czechoslovakia. This had not been foreseen in the Munich Agreement either. Once again Britain, France, and Poland did nothing about it.

---

[8] See'"The Secret Protocols to the M-R Pact Did NOT Plan Any Partition of Poland" at
http://msuweb.montclair.edu/~furrg/research/mlg09/no_partition.html

[9] For a brief overview see "Munich Agreement" at
http://en.wikipedia.org/wiki/Munich_Agreement

So the anticommunist "Allies" Britain, France, and Poland really did participate in the partitioning of a powerless state! Perhaps this may explain, at least in part, why the anticommunist position today is that the USSR did likewise. But whatever the reason, it is a lie.

The Soviet Union signed the Nonaggression Pact with Germany not to "partition Poland" like the Allies had partitioned Czechoslovakia, but in order to defend the USSR. The Treaty included a line of Soviet interest within Poland beyond which German troops could not remain in the event that Germany routed the Polish army in a war.

The point here was that, if the Polish army were beaten, it and the Polish government could retreat beyond the line of Soviet interest and so find shelter, since Hitler had agreed not to remain further into Poland than that line. From there they could make peace with Germany. The Polish state would still exist.

The Soviets — "Stalin", to use a crude synecdoche (= "a part that stands for the whole") — did not do this out of any love for a ferociously anticommunist and anti-Soviet Poland that was rapidly becoming fascist. The Soviets wanted a Polish government — *any* Polish government — as a buffer between the USSR and the Nazi armies. The betrayal by the Polish Government of its own people frustrated this plan.

In the event that, as all military experts expected, its army was smashed by the German army the Polish government had two alternatives:

> * It could stay inside the country, moving its capital to the East, away from the advancing German army into the Soviet sphere of influence. From there it could have sued for peace.

> * Or the Polish government could have fled to either France or England, Allied countries that were at war with Germany.

But the Polish government did neither. Instead, the Polish government and General Staff fled into neighboring Rumania. Rumania was neutral in the war. By crossing into neutral Rumania the

Polish government became "interned." Under internment it could not function as a government from Rumania, or pass through Rumania to a country at war with Germany like France. To permit the Polish government to do either would be a violation of Rumania's own neutrality and a hostile act against Germany.[10]

The USSR did not invade Poland - and everybody knew it at the time

When Poland had no government, Poland was no longer a state. That meant that Hitler had nobody with whom to negotiate a cease-fire, or treaty. Furthermore, the M-R Treaty's Secret Protocols were void, since they were an agreement about the state of Poland. But *no state of Poland existed any longer.*

Unless the Red Army came in to prevent it, there was nothing to prevent the Nazis from coming right up to the Soviet border. Or — as we now know they were in fact preparing to do — Hitler could have formed one or more pro-Nazi states in what had until recently been Eastern Poland. That way Hitler could have had it both ways. He could claim to the Soviets that he was still adhering to the "spheres of influence" agreement of the M-R Pact while in fact setting up a pro-Nazi, highly militarized fascist Ukrainian nationalist state on the Soviet border.

Once the Germans had told the Soviets that they, the German leadership, had decided that the Polish state no longer existed, then it did not make any difference whether the Soviets, or some hypothetical body of international jurists, agreed with them or not. In effect the Nazis were telling the Soviets that they felt free to come right up to the Soviet border. Neither the USSR nor any state would have permitted such a thing. Nor did international law demand it.

At the end of September a new secret agreement was concluded. In it the Soviet line of interest was to the East of the "sphere of influence" line decided upon a month earlier in the Secret Protocol and published in *Izvestiia* and in the *New York Times* during September

---

[10] I discuss "internment" and the international law on this question extensively below.

1939.[11] In this territory Poles were a minority, even after the "polonization" campaign of settling Poles in the area during the '20s and '30s.[12]

How do we know this interpretation of events is true?

How do we know the USSR did not commit aggression against, or "invade", Poland when it occupied Eastern Poland beginning on September 17, 1939 after the Polish Government had interned itself in Rumania? Here are nine pieces of evidence:

1. The Polish government did *not* declare war on USSR.

The Polish government declared war on Germany when Germany invaded on September 1, 1939. It did not declare war on the USSR.

2. The Polish Supreme Commander Rydz-Smigly ordered Polish soldiers not to fight the Soviets, though he ordered Polish forces to continue to fight the Germans.[13]

3. The Polish President Ignaz Moscicki, interned in Rumania since Sept. 17, tacitly admitted that Poland no longer had a government.

4. The Rumanian government tacitly admitted that Poland no longer had a government.[14]

The Rumanian position recognized the fact that Moscicki was lying when he claimed he had legally resigned on September 30. So the Rumanian government fabricated a story according to which Moscicki had already resigned back on September 15, just before entering Rumania and being interned (NYT 10.04.39, p.12). But even Moscicki himself did not make this claim!

Rumania needed this legal fiction to try to sidestep the following issue: once Moscicki had been interned in Rumania — that is, from

---

[11] See the map here:
http://msuweb.montclair.edu/~furrg/research/mlg09/new_spheres_0939.html

[12] A map that shows'ethnic and linguistic population is here:
http://msuweb.montclair.edu/~furrg/research/mlg09/curzonline.html

[13] See the documents at this page:
http://msuweb.montclair.edu/~furrg/research/mlg09/rydz_dont_fight.html

[14] See the evidence at
http://msuweb.montclair.edu/~furrg/research/mlg09/moscicki_resignation.html

September 17 1939 on — he could not function as President of Poland. Since resignation is an official act, Moscicki could not resign once he was in Rumania.

For our present purposes here's the significant point: Both the Polish leaders and the Rumanian government recognized that Poland was bereft of a government once the Polish government crossed the border into Rumania and were interned there. Both Moscicki and Rumania wanted a legal basis — a fig-leaf — for such a government. *But they disagreed completely about this fig-leaf, which exposes it as what it was — a fiction.*

5. Rumania had a military treaty with Poland aimed against the USSR. Yet Rumania did not declare war on the USSR.

The Polish government later claimed that it had "released" Rumania from its obligations under this military treaty in return for safe haven in Rumania. But there is no evidence for this statement. It is highly unlikely that Rumania would have ever promised "safe haven" for Poland, since that would have been an act of hostility against Nazi Germany. Rumania was neutral in the war and, as discussed below, insisted upon interning the Polish goverment and disarming the Polish forced once they had crossed the border into Rumania.

The real reason for Rumania's failure to declare war on the USSR is probably the one given in a *New York Times* article of September 19, 1939:

> The Rumanian viewpoint concerning the Rumanian-Polish anti-Soviet agreement is that it would be operative only if a Russian attack came as an isolated event and not as a consequence of other wars.
>
> - "Rumania Anxious; Watches Frontier." *NYT* 09.19.1939, p.8.

That means Rumania recognized that the Red Army was *not* allied with Germany in its war with Poland.

6. France did not declare war on the USSR, though it had a mutual defense treaty with Poland. See this page[15] for the reconstructed

---

[15] http://msuweb.montclair.edu/~furrg/research/mlg09/m-rpact.html

text of the "secret military protocol" of this treaty, which has been "lost" — which probably means that the French government still keeps its text secret.

7. England never demanded that the USSR withdraw its troops from Western Belorussia and Western Ukraine, the parts of the former Polish state occupied by the Red Army after September 17, 1939. On the contrary, the British government concluded that these territories should not be a part of a future Polish state. Even the Polish government-in-exile agreed![16]

8. The League of Nations did not determine the USSR had invaded a member state.

Article 16 of the League of Nations Covenant required members to take trade and economic sanctions against any member who "resorted to war."[17] But no country took any sanctions against the USSR. No country broke diplomatic relations with the USSR over this action.

However, when the USSR attacked Finland in 1939 the League did vote to expel the USSR, and several countries broke diplomatic relations with it. This very different response tells us that the League viewed the Soviet action in the case of Poland as qualitatively different, as not a "resort to war."[18]

9. All countries accepted the USSR's declaration of neutrality.

All, including the belligerent Polish allies France and England, agreed that the USSR was *not* a belligerent power, was *not* participating in the war. In effect they accepted the USSR's claim that it was neutral in the conflict. Here is President Franklin Roosevelt's "Proclamation 2374 on Neutrality", November 4, 1939:

> ...a state of war unhappily exists between Germany
> and France; Poland; and the United Kingdom, India,

---

[16] See the texts reproduced here:
http://msuweb.montclair.edu/~furrg/research/mlg09/maisky_101739_102739.html

[17] See http://avalon.law.yale.edu/20th_century/leagcov.asp#art16

[18] The League of Nations Resolution is reproduced here:
http://www.ibiblio.org/pha/policy/1939/391214a.html

> Australia, Canada, New Zealand and the Union of
> South Africa,...[19]

FDR's "Statement on Combat Areas" of November 4, 1939, defines

> belligerent ports, British, French, and German, in
> Europe or Africa...[20]

The Soviet Union is not listed among the belligerent states. That means the United States government did not consider the USSR to be at war with Poland.

For more detail on the Soviet Union's claim of neutrality see the texts reproduced here.[21]

Naturally, a country cannot "invade" another country and yet credibly claim that it is "neutral" with respect to the war involving that country. But no country — not the United States, or Britain, or France, or any country in the world — declared the USSR a belligerent. Even the Polish government-in-exile, at first in Paris, did not declare war on the Soviet Union.

In 1958 UCLA professor George Ginsburgs published an article examining the Soviet Union's claim of neutrality in the German-Polish war. With reference to international law and the statements of the parties at the time Ginsburgs concluded that the USSR was indeed neutral and that this neutrality was internationally recognized.

> In spite of the doubtful legality of its action, the Soviet Government succeeded in not losing its status as a neutral. Even after the invasion of Eastern Poland by the Red Army the USSR continued to be treated as a neutral both by the belligerents and by third parties. No municipal neutrality laws were applied to the Soviet-Polish hostilities. The major reason for the Narkomindel's success lies, of course, in the political decision of France and Great Britain

---

[19] At http://www.presidency.ucsb.edu/ws/index.php?pid=15831&st=&st1=

[20] At http://www.presidency.ucsb.edu/ws/index.php?pid=15833&st=&st1=

[21] For the Soviet Union's claim of neutrality see
http://msuweb.montclair.edu/~furrg/research/mlg09/soviet_neutrality.html

who found it politically inexpedient to challenge the Soviet action. Questions of law apart, Soviet neutrality was confirmed simply because the belligerents thought it impractical to question it.

It emerges quite clearly that the main preoccupation of the Soviets was to act so as not to jeopardize Soviet neutrality, or, in Molotov's words, to act so as not to 'injure our cause and promote unity among our opponents.' Thus the march of the Red Army was held up until Warsaw had fallen, until the military disintegration of Poland was far advanced and its total collapse was clearly imminent. In these circumstances the action of the USSR, buttressed by not unreasonable legal arguments, took upon itself less and less of the appearance of a full-:fledged military intervention on the side of Germany. To many Poland's doom already appeared sealed by 17 September 1939, and, by and large, it was thought that in the East the war had already come to an end with Poland's defeat. For all these various reasons, the Soviet move did not assume the proportions of a flagrant violation of its duties as a neutral and the USSR succeeded in maintaining the legal status quo.

From 1939 to 1941 it seems to have been in the interests of the USSR to pursue a more or less scrupulous policy of neutrality and to have this policy recognized by the world at large *de jure* and *de facto*. [22]

The Collapse of the Polish State

By September 17, 1939, when Soviet troops crossed the border, the Polish government had ceased to function. The fact that Poland no longer had a government meant that Poland was no longer a state. On September 17 when Molotov met with Polish Ambassador to the USSR Grzybowski the latter told Molotov that he did not

---

[22] "The Soviet Union as a Neutral, 1939-1941." *Soviet Studies* 10 (1) (July 1958), pp. 12-35. At pp. 25, 25-6; 33.

know where his government was, but had been informed that he should contact it through Bucharest.[23] The last elements of the Polish government crossed the border into Rumania and so into internment during the day of September 17, according to a United Press dispatch published on page four of the *New York Times* on September 18 with a dateline of Cernauti, Rumania.[24]

Without a government Poland as a state had ceased to exist under international law. This fact is denied — more often, simply ignored — by Polish nationalists, for whom it is highly inconvenient, and by anticommunists generally.

We take a closer look at this issue in the next section below. But a moment's reflection will reveal the logic of this position. With no government — the Polish government was interned in Rumania and had not appointed a successor before interning itself — there was no Polish body to claim sovereignty over those parts of Poland not yet occupied by Germany; no one to negotiate with; no body to which the police, local governments, and the military were responsible. Polish ambassadors to foreign countries no longer represented their government, because there was no government. See the page "Polish State Collapsed" cited in a previous footnote, and especially the NYT article of October 2, 1939 quoted there.[25]

Germany No Longer Recognized the Existence of the State of Poland

By September 15 German Foreign Minister Joachim von Ribbentrop was writing to Friedrich Werner von der Schulenburg, German ambassador to Moscow, that if the USSR did not enter Eastern Poland militarily there would be a political vacuum in which "new states" might form:

---

[23] See the documents reproduced at this page:
http://msuweb.montclair.edu/~furrg/research/mlg09/polish_state_collapsed.html

[24] See the articles at
http://msuweb.montclair.edu/~furrg/research/mlg09/polish_leaders_flee.html

[25] At
http://msuweb.montclair.edu/~furrg/research/mlg09/polish_state_collapsed.html#Polish%20Government%20Blamed

Also the question is disposed of in case a Russian intervention did not take place, of **whether in the area lying to the east of the German zone of influence** a political vacuum might not occur. Since we on our part have no intention of undertaking any political or administrative activities in these areas, apart from what is made necessary by military operations, without such an intervention on the part of the Soviet Government there might be the possibility of the construction of new states there.[26] (Emphasis added)

Ribbentrop no longer referred to "Poland", only to"...the area lying to the east of the German zone of influence..." This shows that he considered that the Polish government was no longer functioning and so no longer had sovereignty even in the East where there were no German forces and where the Soviets had not yet entered.

Schulenburg reported this to Molotov and summarized Molotov's reply (to Ribbentrop) the next day, September 16:

Molotov added that he would present my communication to his Government but he believed that a joint communiqué was no longer needed; the Soviet Government intended to motivate its procedure as follows: the Polish State had collapsed and no longer existed; therefore all agreements concluded with Poland were void; third powers [i.e. Germany] might try to profit by the chaos which had arisen...[27]

So even if the USSR had disagreed with the Germans and had held to the position that a Polish state still existed, the Soviets would have to deal with the fact that Germany no longer did. Germany considered that a Polish state no longer existed. Therefore the Secret Protocol about spheres of influence, agreed upon in the Secret Protocol to the M-R Pact a few weeks earlier, was no longer in effect.

---

[26] At http://avalon.law.yale.edu/20th_century/ns072.asp.

[27] At http://avalon.law.yale.edu/20th_century/ns073.asp

Germany felt it was now free either to occupy what had been Eastern Poland right up to the Soviet border or — as we now know Hitler was planning — to form one or more pro-Nazi, anti-Soviet puppet states there. The USSR simply could not permit either of these outcomes.

German General Kurt von Tippelskirch, in his *Geschichte des Zweiten Weltkrieges* (Bonn, 1954) wrote:

> When the Polish government realized that the end was near on September it fled from Warsaw to Lublin. From there it left on September 9 for Kremenetz, and on September 13 for Zaleshchniki, a town right on the Rumanian border. **The people and the army, which at that time was still involved in furious fighting, were cast to the whim of fate.**[28] (Emphasis added)

The Question of the State in International Law[29]

Every definition of the state recognizes the necessity of a government or "organized political authority." Once the Polish government crossed the border into Rumania, it was no longer a "government." Even the Polish officials of the day recognized this by trying to create the impression that the government had never been interned since it had been handed over to somebody else before crossing into Rumania. See the discussion concerning Moscicki and his "desire to resign" on September 29, 1939, also cited above.[30]

Everybody, Poles included, recognized that by interning itself in Rumania the Polish government had created a situation whereby Poland was no longer a "state." This is not just "a reasonable interpretation" — not just one logical deduction among several possible deductions. It was virtually everybody's interpretation at the time.

---

[28] I have used the Russian edition of Tippelskirch's book. The passage in question is online at http://militera.lib.ru/h/tippelskirch/02.html

[29] See this page for more detail:
http://msuweb.montclair.edu/~furrg/research/mlg09/state_international_law.html

[30] At http://msuweb.montclair.edu/~furrg/research/mlg09/moscicki_resignation.html

Every major power, plus the former Polish Prime Minister himself, shared it.

Once this problem is squarely faced, everything else flows from it:

* The Secret Protocol to the M-R Pact was no longer valid, in that it was about spheres of influence in the state of Poland. By September 15 at the latest Germany had taken the position that Poland no longer existed as a state We have discussed this further at this page.[31]

Once Poland ceased to exist as a state this Secret Protocol did not apply any longer. If they wanted to the Germans could march right up to the Soviet frontier. Or — and this is what Hitler was in fact going to do if the Soviet Union did not send in troops — they could facilitate the creation of puppet states, like a pro-Nazi Ukrainian Nationalist state.

In any case, once Hitler had taken the position that Poland no longer existed as a state and therefore that the Molotov-Ribbentrop Pact's agreement on spheres of influence in the state of Poland was no longer valid, the Soviet Union had only two choices. It could send the Red Army into Western Ukraine and Western Belorussia to establish sovereignty there. Or it could stand passively by and watch Hitler send the Nazi army right up to the Soviet border.

* Since the Polish state had ceased to exist, the Soviet-Polish non-aggression pact was no longer in effect. The Red Army could cross the border without "invading" or "committing aggression against" Poland.

By sending its troops across the border the USSR was claiming sovereignty, so no one else could do so — e.g. a pro-Nazi Ukrainian Nationalist state, or Nazi Germany itself.

* Legitimacy flows from the state, and there was no longer any Polish state. Therefore the Polish Army was no longer a legitimate army, but a gang of armed men acting without any legitimacy. Having no legitimacy, the Polish Army should have immediately laid

---

[31] At
http://msuweb.montclair.edu/~furrg/research/mlg09/no_partition.html#Germany%20N o%20Longer%20Recognized%20the%20Existence%20of%20Poland

down its arms and surrendered. Of course it could keep fighting —
but then it would no longer be fighting as a legitimate army but as
partisans. Partisans have no rights at all except under the laws of
the government that does claim sovereignty.

Some Polish nationalists claim that the Soviets showed their "per-
fidy" by refusing, once they had sent troops across the Soviet frontier, to allow the Polish army cross the border into Rumania. But
this is all wrong. The USSR had diplomatic relations with Rumania.
The USSR could not permit thousands of armed men to cross the
border from areas where it held sovereignty into Rumania, a
neighboring state. Imagine if, say, Mexico or Canada tried to permit
thousands of armed men to cross the border into the USA!

The Soviet Position Was Valid Under International Law

In a 1958 article in *The American Journal of International Law*
UCLA professor Ginsburgs determined that the Soviet claim that
the State of Poland no longer existed was basically a sound one:

> For all these various reasons, it may safely be con-
> cluded that on this particular point the Soviet ar-
> gument was successful, and that the "above consid-
> erations do not allow for any doubt that there did
> not exist a state of war between Poland and the
> U.S.S.R. in September, 1939."

> In spite of scattered protests to the contrary, the
> consensus heavily sides with the Soviet view that
> by September 17, 1939, the Polish Government was
> in panic and full flight, that it did not exercise any
> appreciable control over its armed forces or its re-
> maining territory, and that the days of Poland were
> indeed numbered.

> De facto, then, one may well accept the view that
> the Polish Government no longer functioned as an
> effective state power. **In such a case the Soviet
> claim that Eastern Galicia was in fact a *terra nul-***

lius **may not be unjustified and could be sustained.**[32] (Emphasis added)

Re-negotiation of "Spheres of Influence" September 28 1939[33]

All this is referred to directly in Telegram No. 360 of September 15-16 1939 from German Foreign Minister Joachim von Ribbentrop to Graf Werner von Schulenburg, German ambassador to Moscow, with its reference to "the possibility of the formation in this area of new states."[34]

Note that Ribbentrop was very displeased with the idea that the Soviets would "tak[e] the threat to the Ukrainian and White Russian populations by Germany as a ground for Soviet action" and wants Schulenberg to get Molotov to give some other motive. He was unsuccessful; this was exactly the motive the Soviets gave:

> Nor can it be demanded of the Soviet Government that it remain indifferent to the fate of its blood brothers, the Ukrainians and Byelo-Russians inhabiting Poland, who even formerly were without rights and who now have been abandoned entirely to their fate.

> The Soviet Government deems it its sacred duty to extend the hand of assistance to its brother Ukrainians and brother Byelo-Russians inhabiting Poland.[35]

---

[32] "A Case Study in the Soviet Use of International Law: Eastern Poland in 1939." *The American Journal of International Law* 52 (1) 69-84, at pp. 72 and 73. The term "terra nullius" is described on Wikipedia as follows: "*Terra nullius* (/ˈtɛrə nʌˈlaɪ.əs/, plural terrae nullius) is a Latin expression deriving from Roman law meaning "land belonging to no one",[1] which is used in international law to describe territory which has never been subject to the sovereignty of any state, or over which any prior sovereign has expressly or implicitly relinquished sovereignty."

[33] For more documentation and a map see
http://msuweb.montclair.edu/~furrg/research/mlg09/new_spheres_0939.html

[34] Text of the telegram at http://avalon.law.yale.edu/20th_century/ns072.asp

[35] TASS, September 17, 1939; quoted in *New York Times* September 18, 1939, p. 5; also Jane Degras (Ed.), *Soviet Documents on Foreign Policy 1933-1941*, vol. III (London/New York: Oxford University Press, 1953), pp. 374-375.

Polish Imperialism

We should try to understand the Soviet explanation regarding the reference to "the fate of its blood brothers, the Ukrainians and Byelo-Russians inhabiting Poland."

At the Treaty of Riga signed in March 1921 the Russian Republic (the Soviet Union was not officially formed until 1924), exhausted by the Civil War and foreign intervention, agreed to give half of Belorussia and Ukraine to the Polish imperialists in return for a desperately-needed peace.

We use the words "Polish imperialists" advisedly, because Poles — native speakers of the Polish language — were in the minority in Western Belorussia and Western Ukraine, the areas that passed to Poland in this treaty. The Polish regime then encouraged ethnic Poles to populate these areas to "polonize" them (make them more "Polish"). The Polish government put all kinds of restrictions on the use of the Belorussian and Ukrainian languages.

Up till the beginning of 1939, when Hitler decided to turn against Poland before making war on the USSR, the Polish government was maneuvering to join Nazi Germany in a war on the USSR in order to seize more territory. As late as January 26, 1939, Polish Foreign Minister Beck was discussing this with Nazi Foreign Minister Joachim von Ribbentrop in Warsaw. Ribbentrop wrote:

> ... 2. I then spoke to M. Beck once more about the policy to be pursued by Poland and Germany towards the Soviet Union and in this connection also spoke about the question of the Greater Ukraine and again proposed Polish-German collaboration in this field.
>
> M. Beck made no secret of the fact that **Poland had aspirations directed toward the Soviet Ukraine and a connection with the Black Sea...**[36]

---

[36] Original in Original in *Akten zur deutschen auswärtigen Politik... Serie D. Bd. V. S.* 139-140. English translation in *Documents on German Foreign Policy. 1918-1945. Series D. Vol. V.* The document in question is No. 126, pp. 167-168; this quotation on p. 168. Also in Russian in *God Krizisa T. 1*, Dok. No. 120.

Polish Foreign Minister Beck was telling Ribbentrop that Poland would like to seize ALL of the Ukraine from the USSR, for that was the only way Poland could have had "a connection with the Black Sea."

In occupying Western Belorussia and Western Ukraine the USSR was reuniting Belorussians and Ukrainians, East and West. This is what the Soviets meant by the claim that they were "liberating" these areas. The word "liberation" is conventionally used when an occupying imperialist power withdraws. That is what happened here.

Ginsburgs wrote:

> ...theoretically the U.S.S.R. still retains a better claim than Poland to the incorporated territories on the basis of the principle of national self-determination, if the ethnic composition of the area's population is taken into account. For, though the Soviet title rests on a plebiscite of doubtful validity, the Polish one derives from a direct act of force and military conquest, not even remotely claiming parentage with the concept of national self-determination.[37]

The Polish Government-In-Exile

At the beginning of October 1939 the British and French governments recognized a Polish government-in-exile in France (later it moved to England). This was an act of hostility against Germany, of course. But the UK and France were already at war with Germany. The US government wasn't sure what to do. After a time it took the position of refusing to recognize the conquest of Poland, but treated the Polish government-in-exile in Paris in an equivocal manner.

The USSR could not recognize it for a number of reasons:

> * Recognizing it would be incompatible with the neutrality of the USSR in the war. It would be an act of hostility against Germany, with which the USSR had a non-aggression pact

---

[37] Ginsburgs, Case Study, 80.

and a desire to avoid war. (The USSR did recognize it in July 1941, after the Nazi invasion).

* The Polish government-in-exile could not exercise sovereignty anywhere.

* Most important: if the USSR were to recognize the Polish government-in-exile, the USSR would have had to retreat back to its pre-September 1939 borders — because the Polish government-in-exile would never recognize the Soviet occupation of Western Belorussia and Western Ukraine. Then Germany would have simply marched up to the Soviet frontier. To permit that would have been a crime against the Soviet people as well as against all residents of these areas, including Poles, because they would have been abandoned to Hitler. And, as the British and French soon agreed, a blow against them, and a big boost to Hitler as well.[38]

The Polish Government Was Uniquely Irresponsible

No other government during WW2 acted as the Polish government did. Many governments of countries conquered by the Axis formed governments in exile to continue the war. But only the Polish government interned itself in a neutral country, thereby stripping itself of the ability to function as a government and stripping their own people of their existence as a state.

What should the Polish government leader have done, once they realized they were completely beaten militarily?

* The Polish government should have remained somewhere in Poland — if not in the capital, Warsaw, then in Eastern Poland. If its leaders had set up an alternative capital in the East — something the Soviets had prepared to do East of Moscow, in case the Nazis captured Moscow — then they could have preserved a "rump" Poland. There it should have capitulated — as, for example, the French Government did in July 1940.

---

[38] See the further discussion at
http://msuweb.montclair.edu/~furrg/research/mlg09/should_the_ussr_have_permitted.html

Or, it could have sued for peace, as the Finnish government did in March 1940. Then Poland, like Finland, would have remained as a state. It would certainly have lost a great deal of territory, but not *all* of it.

* Or, the Polish government could have fled to Great Britain or France, countries already at war with Germany. Polish government leaders could have fled by air any time. Or they could have gotten to the Polish port of Gdynia, which held out until September 14, and fled by boat

Why didn't they do either of these things?

* Did Polish government leaders think they might be killed? Well, so what? Tens of thousands of their fellow citizens and soldiers were being killed!

*Did they perhaps really believe that Rumania would violate its neutrality with Germany and let them pass through to France? If they did believe this, they were remarkably stupid. There is no evidence that the Rumanian government encouraged them to believe this.

* Did they believe Britain and France were going to "save" them? If so, that too was remarkably stupid. Even if the British and French really intended to field a large army to attack German forces in the West, the Polish army would have had to hold against the Wehrmacht for at least a month, perhaps longer. But the Polish Army was in rapid retreat after the first day or two of the war.

Perhaps they fled simply out of sheer cowardice. That is what their flight out of Warsaw, the Polish capital, suggests. Warsaw held out until early October, 1939. The Polish government could have simply remained there until the city capitulated.

Everything that happened afterwards was a result of the Polish government being interned in Rumania. Here's how the world might have been different if a "rump" Poland had remained after surrender to Hitler:

* A "rump" Poland might finally have agreed to make a mutual defense pact that included the USSR. That would have restarted "collective security", the anti-Nazi alliance between

the Western Allies and the USSR that the Soviets sought but UK and French leaders rejected.

That would have:

* greatly weakened Hitler;

* probably prevented much of the Jewish Holocaust;

* certainly prevented the conquest of France, Belgium, and the rest of Europe;

* certainly prevented the deaths of many millions of Soviet citizens.

Poland could have emerged from WW2 as an independent state, perhaps a neutral one, like Finland, Sweden, or Austria. All this, and more — if only the Polish government had remained in their country at least long enough to surrender, as every other government did.

Chapter 8. Snyder's Fraudulent Claims About the Molotov-Ribbentrop Pact in *Bloodlands* Ch. 4

Snyder"s Fraudulent Claims About the Molotov-Ribbentrop Pact in *Bloodlands* Ch. 4

Snyder writes more often about the Molotov-Ribbentrop Pact than about any other single subject except the Soviet famine of 1932-33. These events — or, to be accurate, a fraudulent version of them — are foundational to contemporary right-wing anticommunist Polish and Ukrainian nationalism respectively. This cannot be mere coincidence. Snyder's articles and *Bloodlands* present this nationalist mythology to English readers with something the nationalists are not able to provide for themselves: the prestige of a Yale professor.

Snyder does not cite any of the primary source evidence concerning the Molotov-Ribbentrop Pact and Soviet actions in September 1939. In fact he shows no knowledge of it at all. Nor does he cite, much less refute, the accounts of Western, Soviet, or Russian historians. Perhaps this is because all except a few of the most right-wing of these scholars disagree with him completely.

"Joint Invasion" of Poland by "Allies": The "Big Lie" At Work

The notion that the Soviet Union and Hitler's Germany were "allies" from 1939 to 1941 is one of the central falsehoods in Snyder's book. This allegation is false and there is no evidence whatever to support it. But by the principle of the "Big Lie" a falsehood repeated over and over again as if it were simply the obvious truth may eventually be *assumed* to be true by those who hear or read it enough times. This is especially so if the Big Lie emanates from a source thought to be "authoritative" such as a full professor at Yale University.

Therefore Snyder simply assumes — takes for granted — his contention that the USSR and Nazi Germany had an alliance. Snyder refers to the Molotov-Ribbentrop Pact as an "alliance" fifteen times in this book. He calls Germany and the USSR "allies" eight times. He uses the term "ally" with reference to Germany and the USSR eight times. He asserts three times that they were "allied." Snyder uses the word "joint" or "jointly" fifteen times to refer to the "invasion" and occupation of Poland. This is The Big Lie at work with a vengeance![1]

The USSR did not invade Poland. As a practical matter Poland as a state had ceased to exist when its government abandoned its governmental functions. It ceased to exist in a legal sense when its government interned itself in Rumania without appointing a successor government, even one in exile.[2]

As a legal as well as a practical matter Poland ceased to exist as a state when Germany could no longer locate the Polish government to try to open negotiations with it. On September 15, 1939, German Foreign Minister Joachim von Ribbentrop informed the Soviet Union that Poland no longer existed.[3] This implied that Germany no longer recognized the Molotov-Ribbentrop Pact[4] since that was an agreement about "the Polish state."

Despite German insistence that the USSR invade Poland the Soviet leadership was slow to send any troops into Eastern Poland. When the Red Army did cross the border it was only to prevent German troops from coming right up to the Soviet frontier. No government would have permitted that to happen. Winston Churchill recog-

---

[1] Chapter Six of Adolf Hitler's *Mein Kampf* is the classic source for the doctrine of the "Big Lie."

[2] See http://msuweb.montclair.edu/~furrg/research/mlg09/moscicki_resignation.html

[3] See
http://msuweb.montclair.edu/~furrg/research/mlg09/no_partition.html#Germany_No_Lo
nger_Recognized_the_Existence_of_Poland

[4] See
http://msuweb.montclair.edu/~furrg/research/mlg09/did_ussr_invade_poland.html#The
%20Question%20of%20the%20State%20in%20International%20Law

nized this in a speech of October 1, 1939; we quoted his remarks in the previous chapter.[5]

The USSR was not an "ally" of Nazi Germany, as Snyder repeatedly claims. There was no "alliance." The USSR declared its neutrality in the German-Polish war. This claim was accepted by all the powers at the time and by the League of Nations.[6]

That the Soviet Union was not in any way "allied" militarily with Hitler's Germany can be shown by the facts. A good source of these facts is the book by Russian historian Oleg Vishliov, *On The Eve of June 22 1941*.[7] Vishliov demonstrates in great detail that there is no evidence for any "military collaboration," which is a fiction constructed by anticommunists:

> Publications that pursue the aim of exposing the "Polish policy" of the USSR in 1939 are distinguished by one remarkable trait: they fail to set forth any concrete examples of how the Russians and Germans fought against the Poles "shoulder to shoulder." The difficulties of authors who write about the "military cooperation" of the USSR and Hitlerite Germany but who fail to cite any concrete evidence of such collaboration, may be easily accounted for. There is no such evidence, and there is no place to obtain any, since the Soviet Union never intended to take part in, and never did take part in Germany's war against Poland, and the Red Army command did not work out with the Wehrmacht command any operational plans aimed at Poland, did not plan any military operations against the Polish army together with the German armed forces, and did not carry out any such. Germany had its

---

[5] See
http://msuweb.montclair.edu/~furrg/research/mlg09/should_the_ussr_have_permitted.ht ml

[6] See http://msuweb.montclair.edu/~furrg/research/mlg09/soviet_neutrality.html

[7] Олег Викторович Вишлёв, Накануне 22 июня 1941 года. М.: 2001. (Oleg Viktorovich Vishliov. *Nakanune 22 iiulia 1941 goda.* Moscow 2001). At http://militera.lib.ru/research/vishlev/index.html

war of conquest, the USSR its campaign of liberation. Their actions were not synchronized, different
in character, and were directed towards the at-
tainment of different aims.[8]

Who Destroyed the Polish State?

There was no "joint invasion" of "Poland." There was no Polish
government, legitimate or otherwise, after sometime in the middle
of September of 1939. Neither the Soviets nor even the Germans
"destroyed the Polish state." The Polish government did that by
interning itself in Rumania and leaving no government behind.

The Polish government was uniquely cowardly and unprincipled.
Hitler himself was ready to negotiate with the Polish government
and leave a shrunken Poland in existence. But there was no government with which to negotiate — it had fled the country and de-
serted its people. No other government on any side of the war did
this.[9]

There Was No "Joint Victory Parade"

Snyder twice refers to a supposed "joint victory parade" by German and Soviet troops. This is a falsehood. There was no such
"joint victory parade." Brest, on the border between the German
and Soviet spheres of influence, was handed over to the Soviet
commander General Semion M. Krivoshein by the German commander, Heinz Guderian.

Both men wrote about this event in their memoirs. Krivoshein
wrote that a parade had been stipulated in the agreement between
the Soviet and German commands and therefore he was forced to
agree to one, though unwillingly. But Krivoshein refused to have a
joint parade since the German troops had been rested for a week
while his own had just made a night march of 120 Km and would
not have the spit-and-polish appearance necessary for a parade.

---

[8] Vishliov, Ch. 4. - Вишлёв, гл. 4: «"Дружба, скрепленная кровью"? (К вопросу о
характере советско-германских отношений. 1939-1940)." At
http://militera.lib.ru/research/vishlev/04.html

[9] See http://msuweb.montclair.edu/~furrg/research/mlg09/no_partition.html and in the
preceding chapter.

The two commanders agreed that the German troops would march by while the Soviet troops, upon entering Brest, would stand on the side of the road and salute the German troops while the two orchestras played military marches.[10]

Guderian called this a "farewell parade" and "ceremony of changing of flags", after which the German troops withdrew from Brest:

> Eine Abschiedsparade und ein Flaggenwechsel in Gegenwart des Generals Kriwoschein beendete unsern Aufenthalt in Brest-Litowsk.[11]

Krivoshein described the great joy with which the Belorussian inhabitants of Brest greeted the Soviet forces as they approached the city:

> Подъезжаем к окраине, все улицы забиты народом, поздравления, радость, слезы. Танки остановились, пройти невозможно. Люди лезут прямо на танки, целуют, обнимают ребят, угощают яблоками, арбузами, молоком — ну, словом, всем, что есть. Народ с красными транспарантами и лозунгами: «долой панскую Польшу!», «да здравствует Советский Союз — освободитель белорусского народа от ига польских панов!» Из окон и с балконов многих домов свисают целые красные полотнища. На мой танк поднялся старый крестьянин, в лаптях и рваной свитке. Долго, по-крестьянски обстоятельно, рассказывал он о горькой доле белорусов в панской Польше.
>
> Другой оратор — старый рабочий — говорил о том, что в панской Польше для получения работы недостаточно было иметь квалификацию отличного слесаря. Требавались еще свидетельство о благонадежности от полиции, справки о прохождении исповеди от

---

[10] Krivoshein, *Mezhdubur'e.* Voronezh-Belgorod, 1964, p. 258.

[11] Heinz Guderian, *Erinnerungen eines Soldaten* (1951) p. 74.

ксендза и рекомендация от фашистской организации «Стрелец». Затем на танк взобрался ученик старшего класса и со слезами на глазах кричал, что они больше не позволят, чтобы их секли розгами и били линейками.

— Такая встреча — доказательство того, что нам здесь рады, что нас считают большими друзьями, — сказал я. — Это очень хорошо. Теперь займемся подготовкой людей к проводам немецких частей из города. Разыщи, пожалуйста, нашего капельмейстера и передай ему мое приказание, чтобы шумел не меньше немцев.

(Krivoshein 263-4)

Translated:

We drive to the outskirts, the streets clogged with people, congratulations, joy, tears. The tanks have stopped, it is impossible to pass. People are climbing right on the tanks, kissing, hugging children, giving us apples, watermelons, milk - well, in a word, everything. People with red banners and slogans: "Down with bourgeois Poland", "Long live the Soviet Union - the liberator of the Belorussian people from the yoke of the Polish *pans* [gentry]!" From the windows balconies of many homes hang the whole lengths of red cloth. An old peasant in bast shoes and tattered peasant's overcoat climbed upon my tank. At length, in peasant fashion and in detail, he told me about the bitter lot of Belorussians in Poland of the *pans*.

Another speaker, an old worker, said that in the Poland of the *pans,* to get a job it was not enough to have the qualifications of an expert mechanic. They also demanded a certificate of loyalty from the police, a priest's certification that you had taken confession, and a recommendation of the fascist organization "Sagittarius" (*Strzelec*). Then a student from

the senior class climbed up on the tank and with
tears in his eyes shouted that they would no longer
allow hemselves to be whipped with rods and beat-
en with rulers.

— A meeting like this is proof that people are glad
to see us, that they consider us to be great friends, I
said. It is very good. Now let us prepare the people
for the transit of German units out of the city.
Please locate the conductor of our orchestra and
tell him that I command him to make no less noise
than the Germans.

Krivoshein and — surprisingly — Guderian agree that the Soviet
forces prevented the Germans from driving off with trucks of booty looted from Brest. There is an article online, in Russian, that
gives yet more evidence.[12] Vishliov's well-documented refutation
of the "joint parade" fiction is strongly recommended.[13]

The Soviets Did Not "Occupy" or "Annex" "Poland" or "Polish Territory"

The areas of the former Polish state that the Red Army entered
had been taken by Poland by conquest from the Russian Republic
at the Treaty of Riga in 1921. They were east of the Curzon Line —
the line marking the area west of which speakers of Polish were in
the majority — and had only a minority of Polish inhabitants. Most
of the inhabitants were Belorussians and Ukrainians, as well as a
great many Jews, who were counted as a separate nationality.[14]

Western Belorussia and Western Ukraine were in Poland solely
due to the Polish imperialist conquest during the Russo-Polish
War of 1920. The Polish leadership wanted Ukraine and Belorussia, or as much of both as they could conquer, because at its height

---

[12] "Myth: The Joint Soviet-German Parade in Brest" - «Миф: Совместный советско-
германский парад в Бресте» -http://wiki.istmat.info./миф:совместный_парад_в_бресте
[13] Vishliov 108-110.

[14] The Curzon Line and the boundaries since 1919 may be seen here
http://msuweb.montclair.edu/~furrg/research/mlg09/curzonline.html . A slightly different view, with the post-1945 borders clearly marked along with the Curzon Line, is here
http://en.wikipedia.org/wiki/File:Curzon_line_en.svg

in the 18th century the Polish-Lithuanian Commonwealth had possessed Belorussia and most of Ukraine.15 The map shows that it reached to the Black Sea. Readers should recall that in January 1939 Polish Foreign Minister Jósef Beck told German Foreign Minister Joachim von Ribbentropp that Poland still had aspirations to the Black Sea.

Within a month representatives of the populations of Western Belorussia and Western Ukraine had voted to join the USSR. Whatever one thinks about this vote, we note that Poland had never permitted the inhabitants of these areas to hold any plebiscite about whether they preferred to be part of Poland.

What "Legitimate Polish Government"?

Snyder claims the Polish government in exile, first in Paris, then in London, was the "legitimate" government. This is the logical fallacy of *petitio principii*, "assuming that which must be proved"; in plain English, of "begging the question." Who says the "legitimate" government of Poland was in London?

The Polish government ceased to be a government when it interned itself in Rumania without appointing a successor government. Great Britain and France recognized the Polish government in exile in Paris because they were at war with Germany and that government was anti-German. But by international law the former Polish government now in internment in Rumania could not perform any political function, including appointing a successor government in Poland or in exile. And without a government Poland was no longer a state.

The USSR only recognized the Polish government-in-exile, which had by that time having moved to London, once Germany had invaded and the USSR was at war with Germany. The USSR withdrew its recognition of the London Polish government when that government took Hitler's side on the "Katyn massacre" issue despite its formal alliance with the USSR. The USSR severed relations with the London Polish government on April 25, 1943 and then recognized another, pro-Soviet Polish entity, the Union of Polish

---

15 See the map of 1764 here: http://en.wikipedia.org/wiki/File:Poland1764physical.jpg

Patriots. After the war the UPP became the basis of the pro-Soviet socialist government of Poland.

Why doesn't Snyder explain this issue for his readers? That is the responsibility of an historian. Instead, he simply "assumes what is to be proven" — that the London-based Polish government was the "legitimate" one.

Great Britain and the United States withdrew recognition of the London Polish government on July 6, 1945, and recognized the pro-Soviet Polish government in Warsaw. Thereafter the self-proclaimed London-based "Polish government" remained in the U.K., recognized by no major country.

Specific Falsehoods in *Bloodlands*, Chapter 4

On page 120 Snyder states, without explanation:

> Poland fought alone.

Poland did indeed fight Germany alone — because of the anti-communism and brinksmanship of its government. The Polish government refused any military alliance with the Soviet Union, the one force that could have had troops in Poland in time to fight the German army. The British had tried in vain to point out to the Poles the obvious: that only the Red Army could give them any real help in the event of a German invasion. The Poles were firm in re-jecting any treaties with the USSR. This sealed their fate.

On pages 120-121 Snyder outlines some German atrocities against the Poles. Snyder ignores alleged Polish atrocities against German civilians in Poland. For example, Polish nationalists have long de-nied the Nazi charges that Poles massacred German civilians in Bromberg / Bydgoszcz when the war began. Włodzimierz Ja-strzębski, a professor at the Bydgoszcz University who had spe-cialized in studying this event, concluded in 2003 that there was no "German provocation" and that the German civilians were in-deed massacred by Poles.[16]

---

[16] See http://ru.wikipedia.org/wiki/Кровавое_воскресенье_(1939) : "Włodzimierz Jastrzębski: To co się zdarzyło w Bydgoszczy miało podłoże emocjonalne." *RMF* September 1, 2003. At http://www.rmf24.pl/tylko-w-rmf24/wywiady/news-wlodzimierz-jastrzebski-to-co-sie-zdarzylo-w-bydgoszczy-mial,nId,138894

On page 122, Snyder states:

> Poland never surrendered, but hostilities came to
> an end on 6 October 1939.

Once again Snyder fails to explain something important: Why did Poland never surrender? The answer is simple: *The Polish govern-ment could not surrender because there was no Polish government.* Having interned itself in Rumania it could not exercise any governmental functions, including that of surrender, cease-fire, negotiation. Because the Polish government had failed to appoint a successor government outside the country, no one else could exercise those functions either. No doubt the reason Snyder does not state why "Poland never surrendered but hostilies came to an end" is that the true explanation would expose the bankruptcy of the Polish regime.

The Lie the USSR Entered the German-Polish War on Germany"s Side

Snyder states:

> Germany had all but won the war by the time the
> Soviets entered it on 17 September. (123)

This statement is false. The USSR never entered the German-Polish war at all. The USSR declared its neutrality from the very outset. This neutrality was accepted by all parties, including the U.K. and France, who were, in a formal sense, at war with Germany.[17]

Snyder begins to pay at least some lip-service to the political reality of statelessness that the Polish government created.

> The Soviets claimed that their intervention was
> necessary because the Polish state had ceased to
> exist. Since Poland could no longer protect its own
> citizens, went the argument, the Red Army had to
> enter the country on a peacekeeping mission. Po-
> land's large Ukrainian and Belarusian minorities,

---

[17] For the evidence see the preceding chapter and Furr, "Did The Soviet Union..." generally, and specifically the section "Soviet Neutrality" at
http://msuweb.montclair.edu/~furrg/research/mlg09/soviet_neutrality.html

went the Soviet propaganda, were in particular
need of rescue.

True enough — but Snyder does not tell his readers the evidence
for and against this position. Nor has he given his readers any of
the explanation or context for these statements. He never explains
why the Soviets claimed "the Polish state had ceased to exist" —
i.e. what realities this claim was based on. He never outlines Polish
oppression of the Belorussian and Ukrainian majorities. He fails to
inform his readers about the anti-Polish uprisings that accompanied the outset of the Polish-German war.

Snyder continues:

> Yet despite the rhetoric the Soviet officers and sol-
> diers were prepared for war, and fought one. The
> Red Army disarmed Polish units, and engaged them
> wherever necessary.

Snyder fails to explain to his readers why the Polish army had to
be disarmed. It was no longer the army of the Polish state, which
had disappeared when its government interned itself in Rumania
without appointing a successor. But some Polish units did not
know their government had abandoned them — the Polish government had not informed them. So some Polish military units did
oppose the Red Army and had to be fought.

Whereupon Snyder writes:

> Half a million men had crossed a frontier that was
> no longer defended, to fight an enemy that was all
> but defeated.

This is false. The Red Army did not cross the border to fight with
the Poles but to keep German troops away from its borders and to
keep a fascist pro-German state, probably a Ukrainiian Nationalist
state, from being formed there. Quotations from the relevant documents can be found in the preceding chapter and my online article.[18]

---

[18] At http://msuweb.montclair.edu/~furrg/research/mlg09/no_partition.html

The Lie that Stalin Spoke of an "Alliance" with Hitler

Snyder concludes:

> Soviet soldiers would meet German soldiers, demarcate the border, and, in one instance, stage a joint victory march. Stalin spoke of an alliance with Germany "cemented in blood." It was mainly the blood of Polish soldiers, more than sixty thousand of whom died in combat.[12] (123)

This paragraph is replete with evasions and falsehoods. The Soviet Union entered Poland because not to do so would have been to allow the German Army to stand on the Russian border. Since there was no government any longer that claimed sovereignty in Western Ukraine and Western Belorussia, the Soviet Union claimed sovereignty. Germany had already informed the USSR that "new states" — most likely, a Ukrainian fascist state closely tied to Nazi Germany — would arise if the Soviets did not claim sovereignty.

An essential aspect of sovereignty is the monopoly of force. The Red Army became the only legitimate military force. Since there was no Polish government anywhere, the Polish Army has no legal status and was obliged to disarm. Some commanders did not know about this, and the Red Army had to engage them.

Snyder writes that "Stalin spoke of an alliance with Germany '"cemented in blood.'" He gives his source for it as follows:

> n. 12 - Quotation: Weinberg, *World at Arms*, 57.

Snyder's statement is false. Weinberg notes that Stalin did not mention the term "alliance" at all. Instead, in response to von Ribbentrop's congratulations to him on his 60th birthday in December 1939, Stalin used the word "friendship."

Here is the full text of Stalin's reply telegram to Ribbentrop.

> Министру иностранных дел Германии
> господину Иоахиму фон Риббентропу
> Берлин

> Благодарю Вас, господин министр, за поздравления. Дружба народов Германии и Советского Союза, скрепленная кровью, имеет все основания быть длительной и прочной.
>
> И. Сталин[19]

Translated:

> To the German Foreign Minister Mr. Joachim von Ribbentrop, Berlin:
>
> Thank you, Mr. Minister, for your congratulations. Friendship between the peoples of Germany and the Soviet Union, cemented by blood, has every reason to be long and strong.
>
> J. Stalin

Weinberg uses the word "friendship", as did Stalin. This means that Snyder deliberately deceived his readers when he used the word "alliance." The USSR vigorously declared its neutrality in the Polish-German war.

The term "cemented in blood" cannot refer to fighting the Polish Army. As Vishliov points out, Stalin did not speak of friendship between the German and Soviet *governments*, but between the German and Soviet *people*.

> Не о "дружбе" большевизма и нацизма говорил Сталин, как это нам сегодня преподносят, а о дружбе народов двух стран. Эту дружбу он с полным основанием мог назвать скрепленной кровью. Напомним, что немцев и русских связывали прочные революционные традиции, что народы обеих стран принесли немалые жертвы на алтарь общей борьбы за социальный прогресс, что немецкие и советские интернационалисты плечом к плечу сражались против фашизма на земле Испании.[20]

---

[19] Text at http://old.novayagazeta.ru/data/2009/092/22.html

[20] Vishliov, 502. - Вишлёв, «О какой дружбе говорил Сталин?». http://militera.lib.ru/research/vishlev/04.html c. 502.

Translated:

> Stalin spoke not of "friendship" between Bolshe-
> vism and Nazism, as we are falsely told today, but of
> the friendship of the peoples of the two countries.
> This friendship he could describe as "cemented by
> blood." Let us remember that strong revolutionary
> traditions bound Germans and Russians, that the
> peoples of both countries had made great sacrifices
> on the altar of the common struggle for social pro-
> gress, that German and Soviet internationalists
> fought shoulder to shoulder against fascism on the
> earth of Spain.

Concerning Polish POWs taken by the Red Army Snyder writes:

> The removal of these men—and all but one of them
> were men—was a kind of decapitation of Polish so-
> ciety. The Soviets took more than one hundred
> thousand prisoners of war, but released the men
> and kept only the officers. More than two thirds of
> these officers came from the reserves. Like Czapski
> and his botanist companion, these reserve officers
> were educated professionals and intellectuals, not
> military men. Thousands of doctors, lawyers, scien-
> tists, professors, and politicians were thus removed
> from Poland.[15] (125)

Sources: (n. 15 p. 475):

* "Hrycak[21] estimates 125,000 prisoners of war ("Victims,"
179)";

* Cienciala, 230,000-240,000 (*Crime*, 26).

* "The Soviets also kept about fifteen thousand people for
hard labor in the mines and in road-building, of whom some
two thousand died in 1941 during evacuations; see Hryciuk,
"Victims," 180."

Hryciuk does cite the figure of 125,000 POWs (on page 180, not
page 179). The problem with all of Hryciuk's other estimates is

---

[21] This is a misprint; Snyder obviously means Polish nationalist scholar Grzegorz Hryciuk.

that they come from the Polish Katyn volumes, which are based upon tendentious interpretations of Soviet archival materials. On the same page he gives the figure of approximately 2,000 killed during the 1941 evacuations.

Here as elsewhere Hryciuk's numbers do not add up. On page 180 he states that "nearly 39,000 [Polish] prisoners" remained in the USSR in December 1939, while on the next page he states that in July 1941, after the alleged Katyn killings and the 2000 supposedly killed during evacuations there still remained 25,184 Polish prisoners "in Soviet captivity." That would mean a difference of about 12,000, far fewer than the number of victims usually attributed to the Katyn massacres.

Cienciala ("Crime", page 26) states that Polish historians figure about 10,000 Polish officers ended up in Soviet captivity. This figure too does not tally with the total number of officers supposedly killed in the Katyn massacre plus those remaining to join the "Anders army" in 1941. Numerical problems like those of Hrycak's and Ciencala's contribute to the mystery of the Katyn massacres. We discuss this controversy further in Chapter 10 of the present work.

Meanwhile, Snyder "wants it both ways." If the officers were the "head of Polish society", then *the Polish Army itself "decapitated" Poland by surrendering to the German forces and by fleeing to internment* in Hungary (35,000), Rumania (32,000), and the Baltic states (12,000). Meanwhile the Polish government and military high command "decapitated Poland" by interning themselves in Rumania, thus leaving their country with no leadership.

How Many Poles Did the NKVD Arrest, and Why?

> In the background, the NKVD entered the country, in force. In the twenty-one months to come it made more arrests in occupied eastern Poland than in the entire Soviet Union, seizing some 109,400 Polish citizens. The typical sentence was eight years in the Gulag; about 8,513 people were sentenced to death.[17] (126)

Sources (n. 17 p. 476):

> * "On the typical sentence, see Jasiewicz, *Zagłada*, 172."

* "On the 109,400 people arrested and the 8,513 people sentenced to death, see Hryciuk, 182.

* "On the disproportion between arrest and imprisonment numbers, see Khlevniuk, *Gulag*, 236; and Głowacki, *Sowieci*, 292."

Jasiewicz, *Zagłada*, 172 states correctly that the *maximum* sentence was eight years. The *Osoboe Soveshchanie* (Special Commission) of the NKVD, essentially "troikas" operating like military courts and without appeal, was not empowered to impose sentences longer than eight years.

According to Jasiewicz, 74% of the sentences *of Polish residents of Western Belorussia* who were put on trial were for the maximum eight years. This was the Polish imperialist infrastructure: police, government officials, and the "settlers" (*osadnicy*) sent to "polonize" the conquered territories.[22]

Hryciuk, 182 does give the number 109,400 for "Polish citizens" arrested — that is, including Belorussians and Ukrainians from Western Belorussia and Western Ukraine (on the following page Hryciuk says "roughly 110,000"). In reality, of course, all these people were *former* Polish citizens since the state of Poland no longer existed and Western Ukraine and Western Belorussia were now part of the USSR. These arrests were for all reasons.

Hryciuk notes that:

> Among those imprisoned, an increasingly large
> group came from Polish conspiratorial organiza-
> tions, which had begun to take shape in 1939 after
> the September defeat. They made up a considerable
> part of all Poles arrested in 1940 and 1941. (182)

In a good example of "bias by omission" Snyder fails to mention this important fact. Naturally the USSR was justified in arresting such people, as any government would do. No state would permit hostile conspiratorial groups to carry on their activities with impunity.

---

[22] All Polish citizens in the USSR were freed after the fascist invasion of the USSR in June 1941and the treaty of alliance between the Soviet government and the Polish government in exile.

Snyder also fails to note that on page 183 Hryciuk includes "7,305 persons murdered" in the Katyn massacres. That is, once again Hryciuk rejects the numbers normally given for the Katyn killings of 14,000, 22,000 etc. Hryciuk doesn't explain this. We discuss "Katyn" in a later chapter.

Khlevniuk (*Gulag*, 236) says nothing at all about "the disproportion between arrest and imprisonment numbers." In any case Khlevniuk's book is biased by many assertions that are not supported either by the documents Khlevniuk cites or by any footnotes.

Głowacki (*Sowieci*, 292) says nothing about any "disproportion between arrest and imprisonment numbers" either. The top half of the page is a list of political crimes and the sentences for them. This passage does occur:

> Ustalenie bezpośredniej zależności między wysokością kary a narodowością ofiary jest trudne. **Związek taki chyba nie istniał**. Niewątpliwa surowość wymiaru „sprawiedliwości„ miała w założeniu działać odstraszająco wobec wszystkich obywateli.

> Establishing a direct relationship between the amount of the punishment [i.e. sentence] and the nationality of the victims is difficult. **I do not think such a link existed.** The undoubted severity of the dimension of "justice" was designed to act as a deterrent to all citizens. (Emphasis added, GF)

If this is the passage that Snyder had in mind when he referred to a "disproportion between arrest and imprisonment numbers", then he has misunderstood the passage. The remainder of the page is a summary of the statistics of persons imprisoned and in exile in 1939-1941 published by the well-known article by the Russian scholar Viktor N. Zemskov in 1991.

Snyder writes:

> After the conquest of Poland was complete, the Germans and their Soviet allies met once again to reassess their relations. On 28 September 1939, the

> day Warsaw fell to the Germans, the allies signed
> their treaty on borders and friendship,... Poland
> had ceased to exist. (127)

This is all wrong.

* Germany and the USSR were never "allies." No agreement between Germany and the USSR mentions any "alliance." Like some other anticommunist writers Snyder simply asserts that the Soviet Union and Hitler's Germany were "allies." They do this repeatedly. Perhaps their aim is to create the impression in the readers' minds that this is "common knowledge" for which no evidence needs to be cited.

* Poland ceased to exist not on September 28, 1939 but from the time the Polish government ceased to exercise control over it. This was, at the latest, on September 17 when the Polish government crossed into Rumanian internment. As a practical matter it was some days before that, when the government was in flight towards the Rumanian border and out of touch with its military command and its ambassadors.

Snyder writes:

> On 4 December 1939 the Soviet politburo ordered
> the NKVD to arrange the expulsion of certain
> groups of Polish citizens deemed to pose a danger
> to the new order: military veterans, foresters, civil
> servants, policemen, and their families. Then, on
> one evening in February 1940, in temperatures of
> about forty below zero, the NKVD gathered them
> all: 139,794 people taken from their homes at night
> at gunpoint to unequipped freight trains bound for
> special settlements in distant Soviet Kazakhstan or
> Siberia. ... The special settlements, part of the Gulag
> system, were the forced-labor zones to which the
> kulaks had been sent ten years before.[24] (129)

Sources: (n. 24 p. 476):

> * "On the 139,794 people taken from their homes, see
> Hryciuk, "Victims," 184."

* "Głowacki records temperatures of minus 42 Celsius, which is minus 43 Fahrenheit; see *Sowieci*, 328."

* Jolluck, *Exile*, 16.

Hryciuk does cite the number 139,794 (on page 186, not 184) while admitting that this count is approximate. The recent Russian account, *Sovetskie deportatsii,* states "approximately 140,000."

Głowacki (*Sowieci*, 328) states the following:

> Akcję wysiedleńczą rozpoczęto o świcie 10 II 1940 r. Mróz dochodził wtedy nawet do minus 42°C....

Translated:

> The resettlement began at dawn on February 10, 1940. The frost reached as low as minus 42° Celsius (=Centigrade)...

What is the evidence that the temperature at the time of deportation was minus 42° Celsius (= -44° Fahrenheit)? Głowacki admits that he has no definite reference, much less any evidence, for this assertion.

Jolluck, (*Exile*, 17), whom Snyder cites here, quotes an account from one of the deportees that mentions "that freezing and gloomy day 10 February 1940." "Freezing" suggests at or below 0° C or 32° F, whereas minus 40° C equals minus 40° F, literally a killing temperature. It is unlikely that anyone would refer to a temperature of -40° C as "freezing." To establish such facts is the job of historians; Snyder ignores this responsibility.

It is interesting to note that Głowacki does not claim anyone died from the cold. Some surely would have, if they had really been shipped off in -42° C temperatures. He states that he has taken his accounts of deportation from personal accounts:

> Jej przebieg szczegółowo dokumentuje bardzo liczna już dziś literatura wspomnieniowa, relacje i wydawnictwa żródlowe (patrz bibliografia). W tym miejscu ograniczę się jedynie do wskazania przykładowych pozycji: „W czterdziestym nas Matko na Sibir zesłali„. *Polska a Rosja 1939-42.* Wybór i opracowanie J.T. Gross, I. Grudzińska-

> Gross. Wstęp J.T. Gross [Warszawa 1990];
> *Wspomnienia Sybiraków*,[t.] 1-9, Warszawa 1989-
> 1997.

Translated:

> A very large body of literature — memoires, reports
> and primary source publications available today —
> documents in detail the course of the deportations
> (see references). At this point I will confine myself
> only to indicate the sample items: "On the fortieth
> day Mother sent us to Siberia." *Poland and Russia
> 1939 to 1942*. Selection and development by J.T.
> Gross, I. Grudzinska-Gross. Introduction J.T. Gross
> [Warsaw 1990], *Memories of Siberians*, [t] 1-9, War-
> saw, 1989-1997.

Though it's not our purpose here to delve deeply into this memoir
literature we note in passing that this very paragraph of
Głowacki's — evidently a direct quotation from the memoir in his
footnote — contains some important contextual information. For
example:

> Do otoczonych domów (mieszkań) osób
> przewidzianych do zsyłki załomotali uzbrojeni
> funkcjonariusze NKWD. Nierzadko asystowali im
> cywile - przedstawiciele lokalnych władz.

Translated:

> Armed NKVD officers were called to the surround-
> ed homes or apartments of the persons proposed
> for exile. They were often assisted by civilians —
> representatives of the local authorities.

And:

> Czasami wręczali gospodarzom spis
> pozostawionego przez nich dobytku, który miał być
> później sprzedany, a uzyskany przychód - przesłany
> na zesłanie (w zasadzie cały majątek zesłańców
> powinien zostać opisany przez rejestratorów i
> oddany pod kontrolę komitetów chłopskich).

Translated:

> Sometimes a list was handed to the owners of their
> property, which was to be later sold and the result-
> ing money sent to them in exile (in fact all the prop-
> erty of the exiles was supposed to be described by a
> recorder and put under the control of the peasant
> committees).

The "local authorities" and "peasant committees" were made up of the local peasants — Ukrainians or Belorussians — who had been exploited by the Polish landowners imposed upon them after the conquest of Western Ukraine and Western Belorussia by Poland in 1920.

This account confirms what is well known: those exiled were the "osadniki" (in Polish, *osadnicy*), settlers or colonists sent to "polo-nize" these non-Polish areas. When Poland had conquered West-ern Ukraine and Western Belorussia in 1920 the Polish authorities had repressed Ukrainian and Belorussian communists, and then all the non-Polish ethnics. The Soviets could hardly have tolerated the presence of the Polish imperialist administration in what was now the Ukrainian and Belorussian Republics of the USSR.

The term "forced labor" implies imprisonment. This is false: they were not imprisoned but sent to settlements where, of course, they had to work to support themselves.

Did Soviet Journalists and Teachers Keep Saying "Poland Will Never Rise Again?

Snyder writes:

> As Soviet journalists kept writing and teachers kept
> saying, Poland had fallen and would never rise
> again. (130)

If this statement were true — "Soviet journalists kept writing and teachers kept saying" — there must be considerable written rec-ord of it. But Snyder does not give a single citation for this state-ment! Surely he would cite at least one if he could do so. In fact this sounds like a quotation from one of Hitler's speeches after the conquest of Poland, when he said: "Poland of the Versailles Treaty will never rise again."[23]

In the following statement Snyder tells a part of the truth:

> When the Soviets said that they were entering eastern Poland to defend Ukrainians and Belarusians, this had at least a demographic plausibility: there were about six million such people in Poland. (131)

But Snyder fails to inform his readers that in Western Belorussia and Western Ukraine there were more Belorussians and Ukrainians than there were Poles. Nor does Snyder mention the Curzon Line, Polish imperialism, the Polish government's "polonization" policy, or the official racism against non-Polish nationalities.

Snyder describes the prisoner-of-war camps where the Polish officers were kept as follows:

> The three camps were a sort of laboratory for observing the behavior of the Polish educated classes. Kozelsk, Ostashkov, and Starobilsk became Polish in appearance. (134)

Snyder has invented the "laboratory" fantasy. It has no basis in reality. It sounds sinister; as though the Soviets were planning to do something to "the Polish educated classes" and wanted a "laboratory" to see how they behaved. No doubt this is the effect Snyder is trying to achieve. But what evidence is there that the Soviets used the camps "for observing the behavior of the Polish educated classes?" None.

Moreover, Snyder does not bother to argue that these prisoners were representative of "the Polish educated classes" — as, of course, they were not. Snyder does not mention the fact that, even if the Katyn "smoking gun" documents were genuine — there has long been serious doubt about that — they mention only 9631 Polish officers. All the rest mentioned in these documents are:

---

[23] "Das Polen des Versailler Vertrags wird niemals wieder erstehen!" — Speech before the Reichstag, October 6, 1939. In *Der Grossdeutsche Freiheitskampf. Reden Adolf Hitlers vom 1. September 1939 bis 10 März 1940*. Munich: Franz Eher Vgl, 1940, p. 93. English at http://www.humanitas-international.org/showcase/chronography/speeches/1939-10-06.html

> civil servants, landlords, policemen, intelligence
> agents, military policemen (gendarmes), immigrant
> settlers, and prison guards; ... 11,000 members of
> various counter-revolutionary organizations en-
> gaged in spying and sabotage, former landlords,
> manufacturers, former Polish officers, clerks and
> refugees:...

This is not a sample of the "Polish educated classes." Yet Snyder
has to claim that they were because he wishes us to believe that
the Soviets were "decapitating" Polish society, "killing off its elite",
etc.

The Nazis were indeed killing off the Polish elite in a special murder program called "AB-Aktion." Therefore, since Snyder wants to
compare or equate the Soviets with the Nazis whenever he can, he
has invented this fiction. Here as throughout *Bloodlands* Snyder is
simply parroting the rightwing Polish nationalist historical "line."

We will discuss the "Katyn massacre" story, and Snyder's treatment of it, in Chapter 10.

Snyder claims:

> At the same time, in March 1940, NKVD chief Beria
> had ordered a deportation of people who had de-
> clined to accept a Soviet passport. This meant a re-
> jection of the Soviet system, and also a practical
> problem for Soviet bureaucrats. Polish citizens who
> refused to allow their identities to enter Soviet rec-
> ords could not be observed and punished with de-
> sirable efficiency.

This is just anticommunist nonsense. The Soviets did not need a
person's permission to "enter their identities in Soviet records."
Snyder wishes his readers to believe that the Soviets wanted to
"observe and punish" everybody. Of course he has no evidence to
support this statement; he has invented it. Historians are not supposed to "make things up."

> As it happened, the vast majority of people who had
> rejected the Soviet passport were Jewish refugees
> from western Poland. These people had fled the

> Germans, but had no wish to become Soviet citizens. They feared that, if they accepted Soviet documents, they would not be allowed to return to Poland — once it was restored. So, in this way, Jews proved to be loyal citizens of Poland, and became victims of both of the regimes that had conquered their homeland.

Snyder has no evidence concerning what they "wished" or whether some of them wanted to "return to Poland." Then we have this interesting factoid:

> They had fled the depredations of the SS, only to be deported by the NKVD to Kazakhstan and Siberia. Of the 78,339 people deported in the June 1940 action that targeted refugees, about eighty-four percent were Jewish.[54] (141)

Source: (n. 54 p. 478):

> "Of the 78,339 people deported, about eighty-four percent were Jewish; see Hryciuk, "Victims," 189."

This statement is false. There are problems with Hryciuk's figures. Hryciuk cites the "84% Jewish" figure (though on page 191, not page 189) from a 1989 article by Parsadanova. On page 175 of his article Hryciuk notes a very serious error of exaggeration in Parsadanova's article. Gur'ianov, whose work on the repression of Poles Snyder cites, also notes Parsadanova's "curious error in interpretation."[24] Since Snyder cites both Hryciuk and Gur'ianov, he knows this but fails to inform his readers.

In addition to whatever errors she made Parsadanova's article was published in 1989, long before the release of many documents from former Soviet archives. There seems to be no evidence that "the vast majority of people who had rejected the Soviet passport were Jewish refugees from western Poland", as Snyder claims.

---

[24] A. Ie. Gur'ianov, "Obzor sovetskikh repressivnykh kampanii protiv poliakov i pols's'kikh grazhdan," in A. V. Lipatov and I. O. Shaitanov, eds., *Poliaki i russkie: Vzaimoponimanie i vzaimoneponimanie*, Moscow: Indrik, 2000, 199-207, at 205.

The recent Russian collection of documents on Soviet deportations includes nothing about the ethnic breakdown of the deportees.[25] However, it does discuss the intention of the Soviet state to find them all employment fit for their qualifications.[26]

Snyder has this to say concerning the city of Vilnius:

> Throughout the interwar period Lithuania had claimed the city of Vilnius and its environs, which lay in northeastern Poland. (142)

Snyder fails to inform his readers how Vilnius came to "lie in northeastern Poland" and how it was that "Lithuania had claimed this city." The reason for Snyder's silence is not hard to understand. The seizure of Vilnius from Lithuania by Poland in 1920 was another egregious example of Polish aggression and imperialism. The Red Army had given Vilnius to the new Lithuanian state on July 7, 1920. Poland recognized Vilnius as belonging to Lithuania. Nevertheless, two days later a Polish army occupied Vilnius and part of Lithuania. Lithuania never recognized this annexation and continued to refer to its capital as "occupied Vilnius."

Thus Vilnius "lay in northeastern Poland" because Poland had seized it by force. Just as Poland had seized Western Ukraine and Western Belorussia by force in 1919-1921. On October 10, 1939 the USSR returned Vilnius and the part of Lithuania formerly annexed by Poland to Lithuania.

Did Stalin Refuse Hitler"s Offer to Accept Two Million Jews? (No, He Didn"t)

Snyder claims:

> "The Germans proposed a transfer of European Jews in January 1940. Stalin was not interested. ... The Soviets had rejected a deportation of Jews to the Soviet Union,..." (144-145)

---

[25] *Stalinskie deportatsii 1928-1953. Dokumenty.* Moscow: MDF / Izd. "Materik", 2005, 156-168. - Сталинские депортации, сс. 156-158.

[26] Ibid. № 2-37 cc. 159-160.

Snyder has made this claim elsewhere as well:

> In early 1940, the German leadership tried to persuade its Soviet ally to take two million Jews from Polish territory; Stalin refused. (2011-2)

Snyder's evidence is as follows (n. 60 p. 478):

> "On Eichmann and the January 1940 proposal, See Polian, "Schriftwechsel," 3, 7, 19."

It is instructive to check this reference. The bibliography in *Bloodlands* informs us that this is a reference to the following article:

> Pavel Polian, "Hätte der Holocaust beinahe nicht stattgefunden? Überlegungen zu einem Schriftwechsel im Wert von zwei Millionen Menschenleben," in Johannes Hurter and Jürgen Zarusky, eds., *Besatzung, Kollaboration, Holocaust*. Munich: R. Oldenbourg Verlag, 2008, 1-20.

But this is a secondary source; what we need is evidence. Continued searching reveals that the source is in Gennady Kostyrchenko's very anticommunist book *Tainaia politika Stalina. Vlast' i Antisemitizm* (Moscow: Mezhdunarodnye otnosheniia, 2001). Here we read:

> Между тем нацистами предпринимается новая попытка давления на Москву. На сей раз инициатива исходила из структур Центральной имперской службы по делам еврейской эмиграции, которой также руководил Гейдрих. Но, как и следовало ожидать, советские власти ответили категорическим отказом, / 189 / обоснованным начальником Переселенческого управления Е.М. Чекменевым в записке к Молотову от 9 февраля 1940 г.:
>
> «Переселенческим управлением при СНК СССР получены два письма от Берлинского и Венского переселенческих бюро по вопросу организации **переселения еврейского населения из Германии в СССР** — конкретно в Биробиджан и Западную Украину. По

соглашению Правительства СССР с Германией об эвакуации населения на территорию СССР эвакуируются лишь украинцы, белорусы, русины и русские. Считаем, что предложения указанных переселенческих бюро не могут быть приняты».

Translated:

Meanwhile, a new attempt was made by the Nazis to put pressure on Moscow. This time the initiative came from the structure of the Reich Central Service for Jewish Emigration, which was also headed by Heydrich. But, as expected, the Soviet authorities responded with a categorical refusal, / 189 / which was explained by the head of the Resettlement Department E.M. Chekmenev in a note to Molotov on February 9, 1940:

"The Resettlement Department at the CPC [Council of People's Commissars, the executive part of the Soviet government] has received two letters from the Berlin and Vienna Offices of Resettlement on the question of **the resettlement of the Jewish population from Germany** to the Soviet Union — particularly to Birobidzhan and the Western Ukraine. According to the agreement between the Government of the USSR and Germany concerning the evacuation of the population into the territory of the USSR only Ukrainians, Belorussians, Ruthenians, and Russians are to be evacuated. We consider that the proposals of the Offices of Resettlement cannot be accepted." (Emphasis added)

Now we have the text from a primary source — something Snyder should have given is readers but did not, possibly because he never bothered to locate it himself. From it we can draw certain conclusions.

* The German letters have not been published or even directly referred to. Apparently they have not been located.

* Judging from the Soviet reaction reproduced above Heydrich offered to resettle not "European" but **German** Jews to the USSR. The wording is unequivocal: "the resettlement of the Jewish population from Germany."

Hitler did not allow non-German Jews into Germany. Therefore the Jews in question were German Jews — no more than 214,000 persons (see below).

* These people were not volunteering to be deported to the rugged pioneer agricultural life of of Birobidzhan, the Soviet Jewish Autonomous Region in Eastern Siberia. Nor were they volunteering for Western Ukraine, where there were already millions of inhabitants. They were not volunteering to be sent to the USSR at all!

German Jews had applied in large numbers to be allowed to move to Western Europe and the United States. As is well known, in 1939 the United States and Canada rejected the Jewish refugees on the MS St Louis, a trip often called "Voyage of the Damned" after a book about this event. They were eventually accepted by Great Britain, France, Belgium and the Netherlands. None of these countries was willing to accept more than 288 of them, the number accepted by Great Britain.

* Neither the figure two million nor "Polish territory" are mentioned in the Russian original. In fact no number of Jews is mentioned in the Russian document. By the beginning of the war there were only about 214,000 Jews remaining in Germany.[27]

* In his 2011 article Snyder falsely states that the Germans wanted the Soviets "to take two million Jews from Polish territory." In *Bloodlands*, published the previous year (2010), Snyder appears confused. In the passage quoted above he mentions neither the two-million figure nor anything about "Polish territory", only "a transfer of European Jews." Later, on pp. 160-161, he again cites the "two million" figure.

Snyder may have copied the error from Polian's article. Polian writes:

---

[27] United States Holocaust Memorial Museum. Holocaust Encyclopedia. "German Jews During the Holocaust. 1939-1945." At
http://www.ushmm.org/wlc/en/article.php?ModuleId=10005469

> Jedoch hat Čekmenev den wesentlichen Inhalt der
> fehlenden deutschen Briefe ebenso knapp wie deut-
> lich übermittelt: Hitler schlägt Stalin vor, **alle Juden
> zu übernehmen, die sich zu diesem Zeitpunkt
> unter dem deutschen Stiefel befinden**. (3)

Translated:

> However Chekmenev did briefly and clearly trans-
> mit the essential content of the missing German let-
> ter: Hitler proposes that Stalin accept **all the Jews
> who were under the German boot at that point
> in time**. (Emphasis added)

Now it is obvious that Polian was in error. The Russian document
says nothing about "all the Jews who were under the German boot
at that point in time." Nor is it a question of mistranslation, for the
German translation quoted by Polian clearly says "Umsiedlung der
jüdischen Bevölkerung aus Deutschland" — the resettlement of
the Jewish population **from Germany**, not "under German control"
or "from German-occupied territory." In other words, at most
about 214,000 unwilling persons.

Once again, Snyder's claim is false.

> The Wnuk brothers, who hailed from a region that
> had once been in east-central Poland but was now
> quite close to the German-Soviet border, met the
> same fate. Bolesław, the older brother, was a popu-
> list politician who had been elected to the Polish
> parliament. Jakub, the younger brother, studied
> pharmacology and designed gas masks. Both mar-
> ried in 1932 and had children. Jakub, along with the
> other experts from his institute, was arrested by the
> Soviets and killed at Katyn in April 1940. Bolesław
> was arrested by the Germans in October 1939, tak-
> en to Lublin castle in January, and executed in the
> AB-Aktion on 29 June 1940. He left a farewell note
> on a handkerchief: "I die for the fatherland with a
> smile on my lips, but I die innocent."[75] (149)
>
> n. 75 *Zagłada polskich elit*, 77.

This book is a catalog of an exhibition. It does not document the quotations, and only makes the claim without evidence.

Jakub Wnuk is number 4121 in the German list, p. 272 in the official German report *Amtliches Material zum Massenmord von Katyn*. We explore the Katyn issue in Chapter 10.

Deportations Just Prior to June 22, 1941

According to Snyder:

> The Organization of Ukrainian Nationalists now began to take action against the institutions of Soviet power. Some leading Ukrainian nationalists had interwar connections with German military intelligence and with Reinhard Heydrich's SS intelligence service, the Sicherheitsdienst. As Stalin knew, several of them were still gathering intelligence for Berlin. Thus a fourth Soviet deportation from the annexed territories of eastern Poland chiefly targeted Ukrainians. The first two operations had targeted mainly Poles, and the third mainly Jews. An action of May 1941 moved 11,328 Polish citizens, most of them Ukrainians, from western Soviet Ukraine to the special settlements. The very last deportation, on 19 June, touched 22,353 Polish citizens, most of them Poles.[78] (151)

As we have seen above, Snyder has no evidence of a deportation that "targeted...mainly Jews," nor is this recorded by the most authoritative Soviet volume.

Snyder's evidence is as follows (n. 78 p. 479):

> * "On the Ukrainians targeted, see HI 210/14/7912. These operations were part of a series of June 1941 deportation actions that were then organized throughout the newly annexed regions of the Soviet Union, from the Baltics to Romania."

> * "On the 11,328 and 22,353 Polish citizens, see Hryciuk, "Victims," 191, 193."

> * "See also Olaru-Cemirtan, 'Züge.'"

"HI 210/14/7912" is an archival identifier of the Hoover Institution in Palo Alto, CA. The Hoover Institution Library has informed me that this number is insufficient to identify the document in question.

Moreover, no citation of this nature is of any use unless it is accompanied by source criticism. The mere fact that a piece of paper is in an archive somewhere does not make it "evidence." Much less can we assume it is truthful. We need to know what the document is — when written, by whom, its relationship to the events recorded in it, etc. Snyder knows this — or ought to know it, since he is a historian. But he tells his readers nothing about any of this.

The Ukrainian Nationalists were fascists like the German Nazis. They were more active in the Western Ukraine than in the Eastern Ukraine in the USSR. Naturally the Soviets had to deal with them.

Snyder's second source, **Hryciuk**, ("Victims," 191, 193) does not mention any "11,328 Poles." He does mention 22,353 Poles from Western Belorussia. These are described as family members of the Polish imperialist infrastructure: persons arrested, sentenced to death, persons "in hiding", i.e. fleeing arrest, persons who had fled the country, "leaders and active members of counterrevolutionary insurgent organizations," imprisoned landowners, arrested gendarmes and policemen, merchants, traders, repressed Polish military officers and former high-ranking Polish officials.

Hryciuk takes his figures from a Polish article published in 1994 and therefore written well before that year. But we cannot consider the information in this article to be accurate, as most Soviet archives now available had not been opened by 1994, and no other sources would have recorded accurate data about deportations. Snyder has to know this — or should know it, since he is a historian working in this area. But if he does, he ignores it.

Olaru-Cemirtan, "Züge" is a Rumanian article translated into German that outlines the deportation of Rumanian governmental and other figures from Bessarabia, which was being transferred to the USSR from Rumania and renamed Moldavia. It has nothing to do with Poland at all.

The recent Russian document collection to which I have referred previously records 21,000 "counterrevolutionaries and nationalists" deported from Western Belorussia (p. 792, l. 3 col. 5), without accompanying documents.

Snyder then states:

> Germany invaded the Soviet Union in a surprise attack on 22 June, and its bombers caught up with the Soviet prison trains. About two thousand deportees died in the freight cars, **victims of both regimes**.
> (Emphasis added, GF)

This is a good example of Snyder's bias. Members of the Polish imperialist infrastructure were hardly "victims" of the Soviets by any normal meaning of the word. When the Germans killed them, they were "victims" only of Germany, not of the Soviets. Moreover, *the Soviets were, in fact, moving them out of the way of the Nazi invasion — that is, attempting to fulfill internationally-recognized obligations to care for prisoners.*

> In the previous two years, the Soviets had repressed about half a million Polish citizens: about 315,000 deported, about 110,000 more arrested, and 30,000 executed, and about 25,000 more who died in custody....[80] (151)

Sources: (n.80 p. 479):

* "Some 292,513 Polish citizens were deported in four waves, along with thousands more individually or in smaller actions. See *Deportacje obywateli*, 29"

* "... and Hryciuk, "Victims," 175."

* "Of the deportees, some 57.5 percent were counted by the Soviets as Poles, 21.9 percent as Jews, 10.4 percent as Ukrainians, and 7.6 percent as Belarusians; see Hryciuk, "Victims," 195.

* "For overall counts I rely on Hryciuk, "Victims," 175;

* "...and Autuchiewicz, "Stan," 23."

* "See also Gurianov, "Obzor," 205."

A highly anticommunist historian of the Russian "Memorial Socie-ty" has stated that Polish historians have exaggerated the figure of roughly 300,000 Poles deported by five to eight times — that is, that the real figure should be in the order of 40,000.

> Таким образом, **оценки традиционной польской историографии (от 200 тысяч до свыше 300 тысяч человек)**[11,12] **оказываются завышенными в пять-восемь раз**. Возможно, что не все высланные с указанных территорий сами считали себя польскими гражданами, даже если они формально и были таковыми до 17 сентября 1939 г. — например, члены семей участников Организации украинских националистов, составлявшие, согласно донесениям УНКВД/НКВД регионов расселения, большинство среди ссыльнопоселенцев из западных областей УССР.

Translated:

> Therefore **the evaluation of traditional Polish historiography (from 200,000 to over 300,000 people) is too high by from five to eight times**. It is possible that not all those expelled from these territories regarded themselves as Polish citizens, even if they were formally until September 17, 1939 — for example, the family members of the Or-ganization of Ukrainian Nationalists [OUN], which constituted, according to the reports of the UNKVD / NKVD regional settlement, the majority of exiles from the western regions of the USSR[28].(Emphasis added)

The OUN members were pro-Nazi nationalists on whom Hitler counted heavily and who later participated in the Holocaust of

---

[28] A.E. Gur'ianov, "Masshtaby deportatsii naselenia v glub' SSSR v mae-iiune 1941 g." *Repressii protiv poliakov I pol'skikh grazhdan.* Moscow: Zven'ia, 1997. At http://www.memo.ru/history/polacy/G_2.htm (TOC at http://www.memo.ru/history/polacy/)

Jews and immense mass murders of Poles known as the "Volhynian massacres."

Who was deported? The best evidence we have is the order signed by NKVD Commissar Lavrentii Beria. It specifies deportation of the following groups:

> 1. Members of counterrevolutionary parties and anti-Soviet nationalist organizations;
>
> 2. Former policemen, security guards, leaders of the police and prisons, and rank and file police.
>
> 3. Officers and jailers if there is evidence to incriminate them;
>
> 4. Landowners, large-scale merchants, factory owners and officials of the bourgeois state apparatus;
>
> 5. Former officers and White Guards [= those who had fought against the Soviets during the Civil War], including officers of the Tsarist army and the officers who had served in the territorial corps of the Red Army (formed from the units and the national armies of the former independent states of Lithuania, Latvia and Estonia after their incorporation into the Soviet Union);
>
> 6. Criminals;
>
> 7. Prostitutes registered with the police and continuing to work as prostitutes;
>
> 8. Family members of persons enumerated in points 1-4;
>
> 9. Family members of participants in the counterrevolutionary nationalist organizations, whose heads were sentenced to capital punishment or who went into hiding;
>
> 10. Anyone who had escaped from Poland and refused to accept Soviet citizenship;

> 11. Persons repatriated from Germany as well as
> Germans, who were registered to emigrate and re-
> fuse to go to Germany.[29]

Here we will discuss only Snyder's allegations about those who were killed or died.

1. Snyder gives no source at all for his claim that "25,000 more who died in custody." This factoid is another of Snyder's fabrications.

2. By "30,000 executed" Snyder appears to be just "rounding up" the figure of 22,000 allegedly shot by the Soviets at Katyn, Ostashkov, and Starobelsk, the "Katyn massacre." We will return to the Katyn issue in much more detail in Chapter 10. But where do the other 8,000 "executed" come from? All the footnotes above concern deportations. Snyder appears to have invented this figure.

> Together, between September 1939 and June 1941,
> in their time as allies, the Soviet and German states
> had killed perhaps two hundred thousand Polish
> citizens, and deported about a million more. Poles
> had been sent to the Gulag and to Auschwitz, where
> tens of thousands more would die in the months
> and years to come. Polish Jews under German occu-
> pation were enclosed in ghettos, awaiting an uncer-
> tain fate. Tens of thousands of Polish Jews had al-
> ready died of hunger or disease. (153; emphasis
> added, GF)

"Allies" again! There was no alliance between the USSR and Germany. Snyder evidently thinks that if he repeats it often enough his readers — or some of them, at least — will believe it. This is the technique of "the Big Lie."

But the main falsehood is this: To write "the Soviet and German states had killed perhaps two hundred thousand Polish citizens" is to suggest some kind of equivalence between the numbers killed by each. But Snyder claims the Soviets "killed" 30,000 Poles. Even

---

[29] Gur'ianov, "Masshtaby deportatsii naseleniia v glub' SSSR v mae- iiune 1941 g." At http://www.memo.ru/history/polacy/g_2.htm This information is not in the 2000 version of Gur'ianov's article that Snyder cites.

if that were true that would still be only 15% of 200,000, which would mean that the Germans killed 170,000, or 85%. And Snyder ignores the whole scholarly dispute over Katyn while blithely attributing 22,000 of those 30,000 dead Poles to the Soviets.

So even with his fraudulent arithmetic Snyder cannot really demonstrate any equivalence at all between the number of Poles killed by Germany and those killed by the Soviets. All he can do is *assert* that there was such an equivalence. Moreover, Snyder assumes that all of the Poles "executed" by the Soviets were "innocent", since those killed by the Nazis certainly were — they were killed on a racial basis because the Nazis wanted to eradicate any Polish elite through mass murder. No one has ever claimed that the Soviets had any such aim.

Did the Soviets Aim to "Decapitate Polish Society?" (No, they didn't)

Snyder declares that the Nazis and the Soviets had similar, basically genocidal, intentions:

> A particular wound was caused by the intention, in both Moscow and Berlin, to decapitate Polish society, **to leave Poles as a malleable mass that could be ruled rather than governed**. (153, emphasis added, GF)

Snyder does cite some evidence that this was the Nazis' intention:

> Hans Frank, citing Hitler, defined his job as the elimination of Poland's "leadership elements."

But what is his evidence that the Soviets intended anything of the kind?

> NKVD officers took their assignment to a logical extreme by consulting a Polish "Who's Who" in order to define their targets.

A "Who's Who? So what?" you may ask. Here is Snyder's exegesis:

> **This was an attack on the very concept of modernity, or indeed the social embodiment of Enlightenment** in this part of the world. In eastern Europe the pride of societies was the "intelligent-

sia," the educated classes who saw themselves as
leading the nation, especially during periods of
statelessness and hardship, and preserving national
culture in their writing, speech, and behavior. The
German language has the same word, with the same
meaning; Hitler ordered quite precisely the "extermination of the Polish intelligentsia." The chief in-
terrogator at Kozelsk had spoken of a "divergent
philosophy"; one of the German interrogators in the
AB-Aktion had ordered an old man to be killed for
exhibiting a "Polish way of thinking." It was the intelligentsia who was thought to embody this civilization, and to manifest this special way of thinking.[85] (153-4) (Emphasis added, GF)

So by consulting a "Who's Who" the Soviets were "attacking the
social embodiment of Enlightenment", "the very concept of modernity" — or so Snyder claims. How terrible! Just as though the
Soviets were promoting the geocentric theory of the universe or
the burning of witches!

But what is Snyder's evidence? He cites the following: (n. 85 p.
479):

> * "On Frank, see Longerich, *Unwritten Order*, 47."

> * "On the NKVD, see Kołakowski, *NKWD*, 74."

> * "On Hitler, see Mańkowski, "Ausserordentliche," 7. Compare
> Aly, *Architects* , 151."

Of these works only Kołakowski, *NKWD*, is about the Soviets' the
other books are about the Germans. Checking Kołakowski, we see
that, once again, Snyder has fabricated this "fact" — invented it.

Kolakowski, NKVD, 74:

> Dane te potwierdzają pogląd o skierowaniu
> pierwszej fali represji na ziemiach północno-
> wschodnich II Rzeczypospolitej głównie przeciwko
> przedstawicielom społeczeństwa polskiego. Objęły
> one rzeczywistych i domniemanych przeciwników
> systemu komunistycznego spośród wszystkich
> warstw społecznych. Listy osób przewidzianych do

zatrzymania sporządzono posługując się miejscowymi informatorami oraz wykorzystując dokumenty przejęte z polskich archiwów, urzędów i przedsiębiorstw, a także zarekwirowane podczas rewizji w mieszkaniach. Do celów tych wykorzystywano **książki i opracowania, które wymieniały nazwiska osób walczących o granice II Rzeczypospolitej w latach 1918-1921.** Takimi wydawnictwami były m.in.: Książka Bolesława Waligóry "Bój pod Radzyminem" lub opracowanie pod red. Stanisława Łozy "Czy wiesz, kto to jest", wydane w Warszawie w 1938 r. jako polskie "Who is who."

Translated:

These data support the view of directing the first wave of repression in the north-east of the Second Republic mainly against representatives of the Polish society. These include real and suspected opponents of the communist system **from all social strata.** Lists of people prepared for detainment were prepared using local informants and documents seized from Polish archives, offices and businesses and confiscated his review of residences. For these purposes they **used books and studies containing the names of those who fought for the boundaries of the Second Republic in 1918-1921.** Such releases included the book of Boleslaw Waligora "The Battle of Radzymin" [a battle in the Polish-Soviet War, August 12-15, 1920] or the work, edited by Stanislaw Łoza "Do you know who this is", published in Warsaw in 1938 as a Polish "Who's Who." (Emphasis added.)

Kołakowski makes it clear that the two books he cites were used by the Soviets to identify "the names of those who fought for the boundaries of the Second Republic in 1918-1921." Snyder's own source contradicts Snyder's statement that the Soviets aimed repression at "the leadership elements" of Polish society. The Soviets had no aim to "decapitate Polish society" or to target the intelligentsia. They aimed to remove the structures of Polish imperialism that had been responsible for the racist oppression of Belorussians, Ukrainians, and Jews in Western Belorussia and Western Ukraine.

Moreover, Kołakowski says that "real and suspected opponents of the communist system *from all social strata*" were targeted. Kolakowski does not even mention "the intelligentsia." Much less does he claim that the Soviets targeted it.

So this is yet another attempt by Snyder to associate the Soviets with the Nazis, and again Snyder has to flagrantly abuse his sources in order to do it.

Chapter 9. Snyder's Fact-Claims in *Bloodlands* Chapters 5 and 6 Examined

Snyder's fifth chapter deals with the period immediately before the German invasion of the Soviet Union. There is little new here. Many of the fact-claims he makes about the Soviet Union, Stalin, etc., in this chapter are repeated from other chapters.

Bloodlands Chapter 5:

The Oft-Repeated Lie: "German-Soviet Alliance"

Snyder frequently repeats the falsehood that there was an "alliance" between the Soviet Union and Nazi Germany.

> ...in the second, during the German-Soviet alliance (1939-1941), the killing was balanced. (155)

> How could the Soviets make an alliance with the Nazis? (155)

> What was it about the Nazi and Soviet systems that permitted mutually advantageous cooperation, between 1939 and 1941, but also the most destructive war in human history between 1941 and 1945? (156)

> After this ideological compromise ("socialism in one country"), Stalin's alliance with Hitler was a detail. (157)

Here Snyder *assumes* that Leon Trotsky was correct in claiming that "socialism in one country" was in opposition to Lenin's ideas. He does not even allude to the well-known debate over this question. Evidently Snyder is eager to seize upon any argument that is "anti-Stalin."

> The allied Soviet Union had rejected Germany's proposal to import two million Jews. (160-161)

We have discussed this falsehood in the preceding chapter. In addition, we should note that all the Western capitalist countries had "mutually advantageous cooperation" with Nazi Germany. What else was the Munich Accord, or the trade agreements between the U.K. and Germany?

The Lie that the USSR Wanted to "Destroy the Polish Upper Classes"

> Thus it was legitimate to destroy the Polish upper classes (Stalinism)... (156)

Snyder cites no evidence whatsoever that the Soviets wanted to "destroy the Polish upper classes" — because, of course, they did not. Nothing of the kind occurred. Polish "settlers" (*osadnicy*) and the Polish imperialist officials were not "destroyed" — they were deported from the lands they had occupied, Western Belorussia and Western Ukraine.

Snyder Equates Nazi Imperialism with Soviet Anti-Imperialism

> Hitler wanted the Germans to become an imperial people; Stalin wanted the Soviets to endure the imperial stage of history, however long it lasted. The contradiction here was less of principle than of territory. (157)

If this convoluted statement means anything at all it suggests that genocidal and imperialist Nazism and Soviet anti-imperialism are basically the same. If you want to "endure the imperial stage of history" — that is, to survive it — you are somehow similar to those who want to impose it! True nonsense.

In reality, Nazi imperialism was fundamentally similar to the imperialism of Great Britain, France, Italy, Spain, Belgium, Portugal, and Japan. The difference was that Hitler wanted an empire in Europe — specifically, Eastern Europe and the USSR — while the Western imperialists had imposed their imperial rule on other continents. The worldwide communist movement was the single most significant force opposing all of these imperialisms.

> Hitler's Garden of Eden, the pure past to be found in
> the near future, was Stalin's Promised Land, a terri-
> tory mastered at great cost, about which a canonical
> history had already been written (Stalin's *Short
> Course* of 1938). (157)

If *this* means anything, it is that the racist and genocidal Nazi Ary-
an empire, in which all except ethnic Germans would be killed off
or reduced to slavery, was the same as the Soviet ideal of a multi-
racial state free of exploitation — a breathtakingly cynical statement.

Snyder is also wrong on elementary facts. Stalin's *Short Course* was
a history of the Bolshevik Party, not a history of the USSR. Its title
is *History of the Communist Part of the Soviet Union (Bolsheviks).
Short Course.* Either Snyder is deliberately misleading his readers,
or he has never read the book and does not know what he is talking about.

Was Collectivization of Agriculture a Form of Colonialism?

> The secret of collectivization (as Stalin had noted
> long before) was that it was an alternative to ex-
> pansive colonization, which is to say a form of in-
> ternal colonization. (159)

This is not only nonsense — it is yet another dishonest attempt to
equate the USSR with Nazi Germany. There is no such thing as "internal colonization." And where did Stalin "note" that collectivization was "an alternative to colonization"? Snyder does not even
attempt to document this claim, which is no more than name-
calling. Basically, Snyder assumes, without evidence, that the purpose and function of collectivization was exploitation. This is false,
as Tauger has argued. (Tauger 2006)

> Collectivization had brought starvation to Soviet
> Ukraine, first as an unintended result of inefficien-
> cies and unrealistic grain targets, and then as an in-
> tended consequence of the vengeful extractions of
> late 1932 and early 1933. (162)

Snyder is relating two distinct falsehoods here. First, collectivization did not cause the famine. Snyder does not even attempt to
prove that it did; he simply asserts it. In reality, as we have seen,
collectivization put an end to the age-old cycle of famines caused
by Russia's and Ukraine's extreme vulnerability to natural disasters and the primitive — actually, medieval — methods of traditional Russian and Ukrainian peasant agriculture. Second, there
was no "intended" famine or "vengeful extraction." We have examined this question in Chapter One.

> Stalin himself received more than a hundred such
> indications [that Hitler would invade the USSR in
> 1941], but chose to ignore them. (165)

This is false. Everybody makes mistakes of judgment; Stalin unquestionably made them as well. As, of course, did the British and
French, who were caught totally unprepared when Hitler sent his
army against them in May 1940, even though they had officially
been at war for more than eight months.

But Stalin did not make this specific error. We now have a great
deal of evidence that Stalin and the Soviet leadership were expecting a German attack around June 21, 1941. I have collected many
of them in *Khrushchev Lied*.[1] We also have American sources, such
as the following:

> In Moscow on June 20, Steinhardt received a cable
> from Washington that advised him to evacuate all
> American citizens from Russia. On June 21 a United
> States diplomatic official traveling east to Vladivos-
> tok observed between 200 and 220 westbound
> trains, of twenty-five cars each, partially loaded
> with troops and army supplies. The same day, Ni-
> kita S. Khrushchev, Ukrainian Communist Party
> leader, lifted the phone in his Kiev office to hear

---

[1] Grover Furr. *Khrushchev Lied: The Evidence That Every "Revelation" of Stalin's (and Beria's)
Crimes in Nikita Khrushchev's Infamous "Secret Speech" to the 20th Party Congress of the
Communist Party of the Soviet Union on February 25, 1956, is Provably False.* Kettering, OH:
Erythrós Press & Media LLC, 2011 See the two sections titled "30. Stalin Did Not Heed
Warnings About War", 84-86 and 334-340.

> Stalin alert him that the Nazis might begin military
> operations against Russia the next day, June 22.[2]

We now know that the Red Army commanders were instructed to go to battle stations on June 18, 1941, though some failed to do so. This question was the source of an interesting and acrimonious debate in a leading Soviet / Russian military journal 20 years ago. General Dmitrii Pavlov, commander of the Belorussian front, was tried and executed for failing to bring his army to battle readiness. The very partial evidence in his case that has been released suggested that there is some evidence that he was deliberately aiding Hitler.

The Red Army did indeed suffer serious defeat during the early months of the German invasion. This was certainly a mistake — it was not supposed to happen. However, the same is true of the other armies that Hitler's forces had attacked. At the war's outset none of the Allied armies were prepared to deal with the German *Blitzkrieg*.The entire French army was smashed in less than six weeks and Paris occupied. The British expeditionary force on the continent was routed, barely saving some of its remnants at Dunkirk thanks to bad weather for the Luftwaffe and indecisiveness on the part of the German commander. American forces were badly defeated in their first battle with German forces by German Field Marshal Rommel's *Afrika Korps* in February 1943 at the Kasserine Pass in Tunisia.

> Eight years before, it had taken a strong Soviet state
> to starve Soviet Ukraine…. Under his rule, people in
> Soviet Ukraine (and elsewhere) stooped over their
> own bulging bellies to harvest a few sheaves of
> wheat that they were not allowed to eat. (172)

This is a grotesque idea, false in every detail, as we have shown in Chapter One. The image of starving peasants harvesting grain that they could not eat is absurd. Needless to say, Snyder did not document any examples of this. All of the available documentation shows that those who were working in the fields had a priority

---

[2] Robert H Jones. *The Roads To Russia: United States Lend Lease To The Soviet Union*, Norman, University of Oklahoma, 1969, 31- 32.

claim on whatever limited food was available during 1932 and 1933.

> It was near Kharkiv that starving peasant children
> in 1933 had eaten each other alive in a makeshift
> orphanage. (172)

There was a serious famine, so of course terrible things occurred. But Snyder gave no evidence for this statement in his chapter on the famine and cites none here.

> During the Great Terror, Stalin had made sure that
> Finns were targeted for one of the deadliest of the
> national actions, believing that Finland might one
> day lay claim to Leningrad. (172)

Not only does Snyder state as a fact that Stalin "targeted" Soviet Finns but also claims that he knows the reason Stalin supposedly did so. Yet he gives not a single citation to any evidence, or any document of any kind, to substantiate his claims. There is no evidence that Stalin even knew at the time about Ezhov's murder of thousands of ethnic Finns.

During interrogations in 1939 Ezhov admitted that he deceived the Soviet government concerning these national actions:

> The government, understandably, had no concep-
> tion of our conspiratorial plans and in the present
> case proceeded solely on the basis of the necessity
> to prolong the operation without going into the es-
> sence of how it was carried out.

> In this sense, of course, we were deceiving the gov-
> ernment in the most blatant manner.[3]

---

[3] Nikita Petrov, Marc Jansen. *Stalinskii pitomets — Nikolai Ezhov.* Moscow: ROSSPEN, 2008, p. 368. "No. 21. From the transcript of the interrogation of the accused Ezhov Nikolai Iva-novich. August 4, 1939." Online at
http://msuweb.montclair.edu/~furrg/research/ezhov080439eng.html

Was Stalin"s "No Retreat" Order Similar to Nazi-type Racism?

> By treating Soviet soldiers horribly, he [Hitler] wished to ensure that German soldiers would fear the same from the Soviets, and so fight desperately to prevent themselves from falling into the hands of the enemy. It seems that he could not bear the idea of soldiers of the master race surrendering to the subhumans of the Red Army. **Stalin took much the same view:** that Red Army soldiers should not allow themselves to be taken alive. He could not counsel the possibility that Soviet soldiers would retreat and surrender. They were supposed to advance and kill and die. .... This tyranny of the offensive in Soviet planning caused Soviet soldiers to be captured. Soviet commanders were fearful of ordering withdrawals, lest they be personally blamed (purged, and executed). Thus their soldiers held positions for too long, and were encircled and taken prisoner. **The policies of Hitler and Stalin** conspired to turn Soviet soldiers into prisoners of war and then prisoners of war into non-people.[41] (175. Emphasis added.)

This is false, yet another attempt by Snyder to yoke the Soviet Union with Nazi Germany. Specifically, Snyder is trying to blame Stalin for Hitler's mass murder of Soviet POWs.

In one of his published articles Snyder writes:

> Germans took so many Soviet prisoners of war in part because Stalin ordered his generals not to retreat. (2011-1)

Stalin"s "No Retreat" Order and Those of the Allies in 1918 Compared

There are more similarities between the policies of Hitler and Great Britain than between those of Hitler and the USSR. Stalin's orders not to retreat recall that given by Field Marshal Sir Douglas

Haig, Commander-in-Chief of the British Army, on April 11, 1918, which reads in part:

> There is no other course open to us but to fight it out. Every position must be held to the last man: there must be no retirement [= retreat]. With our backs to the wall and believing in the justice of our cause each one of us must fight on to the end.[4]

At the same time Sir Arthur Currie, Commander of the Canadian Corps, issued a similar order:

> ...I place my trust in the Canadian Corps, knowing that where Canadians are engaged there can be no giving way.
>
> Under the orders of your devoted officers in the coming battle you will advance or fall where you stand facing the enemy.[5]

Stalin's orders were the same as these of the Allied commanders in 1918 — no retreat, fight till death. Both Haig and Currie ordered "fight on to the end", "fall where you stand," no retreat.

But there is a big difference between Stalin's orders and those of Haig and Currie. British and Canadian troops were being told to fight to the end, without retreat, simply to hold a given position at a given time. The British and Canadians were fighting on the soil of France. Their homes and families were not at all threatened in the case of a German victory. Even French homes and families were not threatened, any more than were German homes and families when the Allies won the war.

But for Red Army soldiers the situation was far different. They really were fighting for their homes and families. The Germans were bent on mass extermination. Hitler had already murdered millions of Soviet civilians. Even Snyder admits that Hitler planned to murder tens of millions more Soviet people if Germany were victorious. Snyder fails to make this distinction or to even inform his readers about the World War I precedents for Stalin's order.

---

[4] At http://www.firstworldwar.com/source/backstothewall.htm

[5] At http://www.firstworldwar.com/source/lys_currie.htm

> For hundreds of thousands of prisoners of war, this
> was the second political famine in Ukraine in the
> space of eight years. (181)

And:

> As during the Soviet starvation campaign of 1933...

Snyder is just repeating his falsehoods. As we demonstrated in our
examination of Chapter One, there was no "political famine in
Ukraine" or "Soviet starvation campaign of 1933." Snyder falsifies
his "evidence" at every turn. In fact, he has no real evidence to
support his contention of "political famine."

> At Buchenwald in November 1941, the SS arranged
> a method of mass murder of Soviet prisoners that
> strikingly resembled Soviet methods in the Great
> Terror, though exhibiting greater duplicity and so-
> phistication. Prisoners were led into a room in the
> middle of a stable, where the surroundings were ra-
> ther loud. They found themselves in what seemed
> to be a clinical examination room, surrounded by
> men in white coats—SS-men, pretending to be doc-
> tors. They would have the prisoner stand against
> the wall at a certain place, supposedly to measure
> his height. Running through the wall was a vertical
> slit, which the prisoner's neck would cover. In an
> adjoining room was another SS-man with a pistol.
> When he saw the neck through the slit, he would
> fire. The corpse would then be thrown into a third
> room, the "examination room," be quickly cleaned,
> and the next prisoner invited inside. Batches of thir-
> ty-five to forty corpses would be taken by truck to a
> crematorium: a technical advance over Soviet prac-
> tices.[58] (182-3)

Snyder's sole source (n. 58 p. 483): Streim, *Behandlung*, 102-106.

The only reference Snyder cites here refers to German murders.
Snyder has no evidence whatever to support his statement that
"Soviet methods in the Great Terror" resembled those of the Nazis.

Evidently this is another cheap attempt to associate the USSR with Nazi Germany.

Moreover, there were no "*Soviet* methods in the Great Terror" because these was Ezhov's unauthorized mass murders, not those of the Soviet government, for which he and many of his men were tried and executed. But Snyder has no evidence, not even phony evidence, for this spurious claim.

Again the Lie that Stalin Rejected Jews from Germany

> By late 1941 the Nazi leadership had already considered, and been forced to abandon, four distinct versions of the Final Solution. The Lublin plan for a reservation in eastern Poland failed by November 1939 because the General Government was too close and too complicated; the consensual Soviet plan by February 1940 **because Stalin was not interested in Jewish emigration;**... (185. Emphasis added).

There was no such plan for Jewish emigration to the USSR. We have examined this falsehood of Snyder's in a previous chapter.

*   *
*

Bloodlands Chapter 6

This chapter is mainly about the Germans. It makes very limited reference to the Soviets. However, Snyder continues his attempt to put the Nazis and the Soviets side by side.

> ...in June 1940, eastern Poland had been annexed by the Soviets nine months before that, in September 1939. Here the Germans found evidence of a social transformation. Industry had been nationalized, some farms had been collectivized, and **a native elite had been all but destroyed**... (194, Emphasis added, GF)

This statement exposes Snyder's own elitist assumptions. The So-viets did not "destroy" any "native elite." The Poles deported from Western Belorussia and Western Ukraine were not "native" to those lands at all. They were mainly *osadnicy*, the Polish imperial-ist "settlers."

The Soviets also had what may be termed a "class-conscious un-derstanding" of what an "elite" was — and it wasn't the same as Snyder's. For the Soviets, the "elite" consisted of leading Party members and advanced workers such as Stakhanovites, as well as intellectuals.

For the pre-war Polish ruling class, and for Snyder, the "elite" was the rich — the landowners, government officials, retired military men, and police commanders, together with the upper level of the intelligentsia. These people were not "destroyed" — killed — at all. They were "demoted" — their property confiscated, and they and their families subject to deportation so that the common people and the Soviets could be rid of them.

> The Soviets had deported more than three hundred thousand Polish citizens and shot tens of thousands more. The German invasion prompted the NKVD to shoot some 9,817 imprisoned Polish citizens rather than allow them to fall into German hands. The Germans arrived in the western Soviet Union in summer 1941 to find NKVD prisons full of fresh corpses. These had to be cleared out before the Germans could use them for their own purposes.[16]
>
> Soviet mass murder provided the Germans with an occasion for propaganda.
>
> (194; emphasis added)

Sources (n. 16 p. 485):

> * "The 9,817 count in *Verbrechen* is at 93."
>
> * "See also Wnuk, *Za pierwszego Sowieta*, 371 (11,000-12,000);
>
> * Hryciuk, "Victims," 183 (9,400).

We have already pointed out that the figure of 300,000 Polish citizens deported is exaggerated by a factor of five to eight.

Böhler, **Verbrechen,** is not a work of scholarship but a catalog of an exhibition about German army crimes in Poland in September-October 1939. Böhler himself is a specialist on the German war and German crimes in Poland. He has not researched Soviet history.

Hryciuk, "Victims," does state that 9400 persons — not "Polish citizens" — were killed by the Soviets:

> * In Western Ukraine, "Of 20,094 prisoners in custody on 10 June 1941 ... more than 8700 were murdered...";

> * In Western Belorussia, "Of the 6,375 prisoners in custody as of 10 June 1941... over 700 were murdered (mainly those in prison in Głębokie)..."

However, Hryciuk provides no evidence for these figures.

Nazi propaganda claimed that the Soviet NKVD shot many prisoners in L'vov and elsewhere before retreating from the city. Other sources claim that Ukrainian Nationalists killed many communists and Jews when the German army occupied L'vov. There is a controversy about just what happened, with little agreement.[6]

Soviet documentary evidence exists, as does at least one article by the anticommunist "Memorial" association that examines that evidence: "The Evacuation of the Prisons 1941," by Aleksandr Gur'ianov and Aleksandr Kokurin.[7] Both of these authors, like the "Memorial Society" itself, are extremely anti-Soviet and anticommunist. It is impossible that they would *under*estimate, let alone ignore, Soviet murders or crimes of any type.

According to the evidence cited and examined by Gur'ianov and Kokurin the only prisoners executed were those convicted of or, in

---

[6] See "The Lviv prgroms controversy at
http://en.wikipedia.org/wiki/The_Lviv_pogroms_controversy_(1941 and Alfred De Zayas' account, "The Lviv Massacre", at
http://www.alfreddezayas.com/Chapbooks/Lembergmassacre.shtml De Zayas is well known as an apologist for the Nazis. Naturally, he is also a strong anticommunist, so other anticommunists continue to rely on his work.

[7] «Evakuatsiia tiurem 1941." At http://www.hro.org/node/6729

some cases, under investigation for, capital crimes. Many or most of those were probably members of the Organization of Ukrainian Nationalists (OUN), active Nazi collaborators. This article is well documented from Soviet-era records and seems credible, though of course it cannot claim any precision in numbers of persons killed.

Other prisoners were shot while attempting to escape either from prisons under bombardment or from evacuation columns. A great many prisoners were either left in the prisons or set free by their NKVD guards. It is doubtful, therefore, whether Hryciuk's use of the term "murdered" here is legitimate.

We note in passing that Snyder fails to mention the murders of Ukrainian nationalists in Lviv after the Soviets had retreated. A good recent account is that by anticommunist but also anti-nationalist scholar John-Paul Himka: "The Lviv Pogrom of 1941" (2011). Himka concludes:

> In sum, the Lviv pogrom was an action undertaken at German initiative, but carried out largely by the Ukrainian militia set up by the Bandera faction of the OUN [Organization of Ukrainian Nationalists, allied with the German Nazis] as the policing arm of the newly proclaimed Ukrainian State. Mob participation supplemented the violence. The pogrom took place on 1 July 1941, a day after Lviv was occupied by the Germans and the Ukrainian nationalists declared statehood. The pogrom itself probably took dozens or at most hundreds of lives, but systematic executions during the pogrom and in its aftermath took thousands. In the executions, OUN militia were also active in the round up and beating of Jews, just as they had been during the pogrom preceding them.[8]

---

[8] Himka, Paper for ASN Convention, April 2011. At
https://www.academia.edu/1314919/The_Lviv_Pogrom_of_1941_The_Germans_Ukrainian
_Nationalists_and_the_Carnival_Crowd Accessed June 2, 2014).

Snyder has done no research on these matters and evidently doesn't know anything about them. On the next page (197) he states:

> The NKVD, usually discreet, had been revealed as the murderer of prisoners. Germans broke through the levels of mystification, secrecy, and dissimulation that had covered the (far greater) Soviet crimes of 1937-1938 and 1930-1933. The Germans (along with their allies) were the only power ever to penetrate the territory of the Soviet Union in this way, and so the only people in a position to present such direct evidence of Stalinist murder. Because it was the Germans who discovered these crimes, the prison murders were politics before they were history. Fact used as propaganda is all but impossible to disentangle from the politics of its original transmission.

A page after claiming that the Soviets shot roughly 10,000 prisoners, Snyder admits that it is impossible to extract the truth from German — that is Nazi — documents! Snyder has evidently not consulted, is ignorant of, or at least does not cite, the Soviet studies and documents that reveal that the killings were not "murders", as the Germans and Ukrainian Nationalists described them. And, of course, such logic applies to the Katyn Massacres, which were "politics before they were history."

> The act of killing Jews as revenge for NKVD executions confirmed the Nazi understanding of the Soviet Union as a Jewish state. ...
>
> Yet this psychic nazification would have been much more difficult without the palpable evidence of Soviet atrocities. The pogroms took place where the Soviets had recently arrived and where Soviet power was recently installed, where for the previous months Soviet organs of coercion had organized arrests, executions, and deportations. They were a joint production, a Nazi edition of a Soviet text.[21] (196)

Here Snyder tries to make the Soviets share the blame for Nazi murders and pogroms! In reality Poles and Ukrainians had carried out antisemitic pogroms long before the Soviets came along.

Snyder's long footnote 21 (on pages 485-6 of *Bloodlands*) has to be read to be believed. It contains no sources or evidence, only a convoluted "theoretical" argument with which Snyder tries to justify blaming the Nazi pogroms and murders on the Soviets. It is too long to reproduce here.

In reality, *there is no evidence of "Soviet atrocities."* To say this is not denial, or even defensiveness. It is the simple truth: we have no such evidence. The evidence cited by the "Memorial Society" authors above is of executions of prisoners convicted or under investigation for capital crimes, and shootings of prisoners while the NKVD guards suppressed prison escapes and uprisings or escapes from evacuation convoys. These are not atrocities but acts under conditions of martial law, when normal judicial procedures do not apply.

> Soviet atrocities would help German SS-men, policemen, and soldiers justify to themselves the policies to which they were soon summoned: the murder of Jewish women and children. Yet the prison shootings, significant as they were to the local people who suffered Soviet criminality, were for Nazi leaders rather catalyst than cause. (197)

It would be interesting if Snyder had cited some accounts from memoirs, or indeed from any primary source, of German "SS-men, policemen, and soldiers" who actually "justified to themselves" the mass murder of "Jewish women and children" with reference to "Soviet atrocities." Historical honesty should prevent him from making such a statement unless he had evidence to support it. Of course such self-justification would still be Nazi thinking, not sober historical analysis. But this is what Snyder is doing here — engaging in such Nazi thinking — and he is the only one doing it! Once again Snyder is trying to connect Nazi atrocities to the Soviets without even a fig-leaf of evidence.

There was a group whose activities at this time could validly be connected to Nazi atrocities, because they were engaged not only in aiding the Nazis in committing mass murders but were carrying out mass murders of their own. That group is the Organization of Ukrainian Nationalists. But the OUN is praised as "freedom-fighters" and "heroes" in today's Ukraine. It was also the OUN that invented the "Holodomor" fabrication.

Bloodlands is popular among today's Ukrainian Nationalists. Snyder has been honored repeatedly by Ukrainian nationalist groups in Ukraine and elsewhere. It is no wonder, then, that Snyder has virtually nothing to say about their atrocities. Instead, he fabricates Soviet crimes that did not happen.

> The Reichskommissar [of the Ukraine], Erich Koch, was a man known for his brutality. Hitler's advisors called Koch a "second Stalin," and they meant it as a compliment....[70] (222)

Snyder has evidently invented this falsehood too, as he has so many others. He does not cite any evidence to support it. It is not made in any of the sources Snyder cites in his footnote 70. I have tracked it down in a biography of Erich Koch:[9]

> ... als „brauner Zar" der Ukraine soll er sich als „zweiter Stalin" geriert haben... (12)

> ... as "Brown Tsar" of the Ukraine he is said to have boast-ed of himself as "a second Stalin."

It is not at all a reference to Koch's brutality — something Hitler's advisors would not object to in any case. Nor was it a "compli-ment." Rather it was Koch's own arrogant posturing. The Ukraine was once ruled by the Tsar, then by Stalin, and now by "the brown Tsar" and "second Stalin." It means only that Koch saw himself as the successor to the other two.

---

[9] Ralph Meindl, *Ostpreußens Gauleiter: Erich Koch — eine politische Biographie*. Osnabrück: fibre Verlag, 2007. In his note Meindl cites a report of September 1941 to Alfred Rosenberg.

Chapter 10. The "Katyn Massacre"

What Really Happened?

Anticommunists claim that there is an historical consensus about the "Katyn massacre" issue. This is not true. Rather, "Katyn" has become a shibboleth, a marker of historical partisanship. Anticommunists accept without question the version that blames the Soviets for all the shootings and demand that everybody else do so as well — or the anticommunists will call them bad names. Critics of this version often call it the "Goebbels" version since taking this position means assuming that the Nazi report of 1943 tells the precise truth.

It is almost impossible to have a rational discussion about the "Katyn massacre."[1] I would appear even-handed, neutral, and therefore objective if I could honestly lay the blame for this state of affairs equally on both "sides:" those who think the Soviets shot 14,800 to 22,000 Polish POWs, and those who think the Germans did it. But that is not the case. In reality it is the "Soviets-did-it" side that has declared the matter "settled" and demonizes or ridicules anyone who dares to question this position.

This makes political sense: Why acknowledge your opponents and thus bring them to public notice when you have a monopoly on public opinion concerning this issue? But from the historiographical point of view it is irresponsible.

In normal historical discussion it is considered essential to outline the disputes and disagreements among the experts. In the case of Katyn it is just the opposite. Proponents of the "Soviets-did-it" position normally refuse to acknowledge the viewpoint they oppose. This is Snyder's practice. Or, in a few case, they insult and belittle those who think that the Soviets did *not* "do it", or call them "communists." This is not scholarship but political propaganda —

---

[1] I use scare quotes — "Katyn massacre" — to remind the reader that the "official version" is certainly incorrect.

as though communists cannot be trusted while, by contrast, anti-communists, including the German Nazis, can be. Under such conditions it is already a declaration of partisanship to acknowledge and discuss the controversy at all.

The only objective way to approach the historical dispute about the "Katyn massacre" is to begin by acknowledging that such a dispute actually exists. Anyone who studies the "Katyn massacre" dispute carefully, in detail, and over a long period of time, and tries their best to do so without predetermining their conclusions, will see that there is indeed more than one "side" to the dispute.

The Historical Dispute

There is a very important historical debate concerning the question of the "Katyn massacre." Unfortunately for those who want to know "what really happened" this debate is divided along purely political lines.

The viewpoint that the Soviets shot all the Poles and that the Nazi report of 1943, aside from its anti-Semitic statements, is entirely truthful, is accepted without question by all anticommunists everywhere, including in Russia.[2] The viewpoint that the Germans shot all the Poles and that the Soviet Burdenko report of 1944 is the accurate one is accepted by communists and pro-communists (except for Trotskyists) and by many Russian nationalists.

A few researchers tend toward a more nuanced position something like the following. First the Soviets shot some of the Polish POWs, perhaps because they were found guilty of anti-Soviet or anticommunist crimes. This is the version that Lazar' Kaganovich, a former Politburo member very close to Stalin, reportedly told

---

[2] Russian President Vladimir Putin has voiced a somewhat different version of this viewpoint. He does not question that the Soviets shot the Poles but has suggested that they may have done so "in revenge for" the tens of thousands of Russian POWs who died or were killed in Polish captivity in 1920-1921. "Putin dopuskaet, chto Katyn mogla byt' mest'iu Stalina za gibel' v Pol'she sovetskikh plennykh."(Putin concedes that Katyn could have been Stalin's revenge for the deaths in Poland of Soviet prisoners). Корреспондент.net 7 апреля 2010 г. http://korrespondent.net/world/russia/1064467/print Accessed March 23 2014.

military historian A.N. Kolesnik in November 1985.[3] Then the Germans shot the rest of the Poles, obviously for very different reasons. Then in 1943 the Germans staged a "discovery" of bodies — really a propaganda stunt — unearthing corpses of Polish officers they had shot elsewhere (and so the location of which they knew) and bringing them for reburial and "discovery" to "Katyn" (in reality the small area called Koz'i Gory).

In 1990-1992 Mikhail Gorbachev and Boris Eltsin claimed that the Stalin-era leadership of the USSR had indeed shot the Poles, confirming virtually all the details of the anticommunist Polish nationialist version. In 1992 Eltsin presented to Polish officials facsimiles of documents from "Closed Packet No. 1" which, if genuine, would put Soviet guilt beyond reasonable doubt.

But beginning in 1995 Russian researchers began to argue that these documents were forgeries. Analysis of these documents mainly by Russian researchers who reject the "official version" of Katyn has continued since, growing ever more detailed and sophisticated. These studies have shown there is at least a *prima facie* case for suspecting that the documents are forgeries. But long before this positions on both sides had hardened. Among those who believed the Soviets guilty very few changed their opinion on the basis of the new evidence. I count myself among the few since I changed my own view, shifting from thinking that "the Soviets did it" to an agnostic position.

Recent years have seen two dramatic developments in the Katyn issue. The first was in October 2010, when material evidence came to light that the documents in the famous "Closed Packet Number 1" may be forgeries. Documents were published that appear to be drafts prepared for the final forgery. This had long been suspected by some in Russia. But these revelations represent the first documentary evidence of such a forgery. Thereafter the question became, and remains: Which set of documents is genuine — those

---

[3] See Sergei Strygin, "L.M. Kaganovich o Katynskom dele" (L.M. Kaganovich on the Katyn affair), "Pravda o Katyne" site. At
http://www.katyn.ru/index.php?go=Pages&in=view&id=936

from "Closed Packet No. 1" or those disclosed in 2010 — and which set is a forgery?[4]

The Ukrainian Excavations

Since 2010 much more important evidence has come to the fore that casts the strongest doubt upon the "official version" of Katyn. In Volodymyr-Volyns'kiy, Ukraine, Polish and Ukrainian archeologists found evidence that at least two Polish policemen believed to have been shot by the Soviets in April or May 1940 in or near Kalinin (now Tver'), Russia, were in fact murdered by the Germans and their Ukrainian Nationalist allies in the second half of 1941, after the fascist invasion of the USSR. This fact alone dismantles the "official" version of the "Katyn massacre" narrative.[5] The present writer has endeavored to describe and examine this new evidence and to explain just how it proves that the "official" version has to be false.[6]

These discoveries illustrate how corrupt the history around the "Katyn massacre" has become. The discovery of the badges of the two Polish policemen previously said to have been shot and buried sixteen months or more later and seven hundred miles away is by far the most important find at the Volodymyr-Volyns'kiy excavation. It is the most important development in the Katyn issue since the disclosure of the "forgery evidence" in October 2010. So why has it not received the publicity that it merits? Undoubtedly because powerful political forces in Poland and Ukraine do not want to publicize it — because it casts doubt on Soviet guilt.

Therefore it has been hushed up. The Polish archeological report mentions only one of the Polish policemen's badges. Even that is buried in a footnote with only the most cryptic reference to Katyn

---

[4] It is also possible that *both* sets of documents — those from "Closed Packet No.1" and the "draft forgery" documents and materials disclosed in October 2010, may be forgeries. It is not possible that both sets of documkents are genuine. See the mor detailed discussion at my web page "The Katyn Forest Whodunnit" at http://www.tinyurl.com/katyn-the-truth

[5] Sergei Strygin. "'Volynskaia Katyn' okazalas' delom ruk gitlerovtsev." — Сергей Стрыгин. "Волынская Катынь" оказалась делом рук гитлеровцев. At http://katyn.ru/index.php?go=News&in=view&id=253

[6] Grover Furr. "The 'Official' Version of the Katyn Massacre Disproven? Discoveries at a Mass Murder Site in Ukraine." *Socialism and Democracy* 27 (2) July 2013. 96-129.

— literally a "coded" reference, understandable only to those who are extremely familiar with the Katyn issue. But at least the Polish report draws the obvious conclusion that the victims in this mass grave were shot by Germans and their Ukrainian nationalist collaborators in 1941. The Ukrainian archeological report does not mention the discovery of the Polish policemen's badges at all! Moreover, one of the Ukrainian archeologist explicitly said that this site could "cast doubt "on other shootings of Polish prisoners by Soviets" — that is, on the "official version" of the "Katyn massacre."[7]

The coverup began before this. The October 2010 revelations of the "draft forgery" documents were presented on the floor of the Russian Duma by Duma deputy Viktor Iliukhin. Yet this dramatic story was virtually blacked out of the mainstream Russian media. I was able to find only one article about it, and that was a snide dismissal. The mass media outside Russia has completely ignored the 2010 discovery of the "draft forgery" documents, while the mass media outside Poland Ukraine has ignored the Volodymyr-Volyns'kiy discoveries. I have been unable to find any articles about either of these discoveries in Western European or American mass media. The left-wing and Internet media did cover it, a fact that makes the absence of coverage in the mainstream news media all the more noteworthy.

Judging from early media reports on this excavation it appears that they believed the victims had been shot by the Soviet NKVD.[8] It is safe to assume that Poland and Ukraine would never have proceeded with the excavation of the mass graves at Volodymyr-

---

[7] Furr, Official version 127.

[8] See, for example, "Volyn's Own Katyn." *The Ukrainian Week*, October 3, 2011. At http://ukrainianweek.com/Investigation/32076 ; "Poland will finance the excavation of NKVD victims' graves in Volyn." Day (Den', Kyiv, Ukraine). http://www.day.kiev.ua/en/article/society/poland-will-finance-excavation-nkvd-victims-graves-volyn (both accessed 03.14.2014); "Mass Graves in Ukraine Hold Polish Victims?", Polish Radio August 4, 2009. At http://www.polskieradio.pl/thenews/international/?id=113330 (accessed 01.15.2010; no longer online here); at http://forum.axishistory.com/viewtopic.php?f=6&t=156119 (accessed 03.15.2014).

Volyns'skiy if either had thought for a moment that the results would cast doubt upon the "Katyn massacre."

There is good evidence that OUN (Ukrainian Nationalist) forces participated in the mass murders of the victims at Volodymyr-Volyns'kiy. The OUN is honored in Western Ukraine. Volodymyr-Volyns'kiy even has a street named after OUN leader and Nazi collaborator Stepan Bandera, whose men participated in the mass murders there.[9]

Soviet guilt in the "Katyn massacre" is literally constitutive of post-1990 Polish nationalism. Poland has transformed "Katyn" into an anticommunist and anti-Russian orgy of veneration for its victims. Polish governments have spent hundreds of millions of dollars on hundreds of monuments and memorials to "Katyn." Hundreds of ceremonies, some very large in scope, have been devoted to "Katyn, " as have hundreds or thousands of publications and the efforts of dozens of scholars. The "official version" of Katyn is taught in all Polish schools. In addition to the motive of anticommunism "Katyn" is kept alive as a weapon to beat Russia with, for Russia is the heir to the Soviet Union. Poland continues its years-long struggle to have "Katyn" declared "genocide" and make Russia pay reparations to the families of the victims.

Yet now we know that there was no "Katyn" — no single chain of events during which the Soviets shot all the Polish POWs. But Poland, Ukraine, and anticommunists generally do not want to acknowledge this. Much less do they want their own citizens or the world at large to doubt Soviet guilt at Katyn.

The story of "Katyn" is a fascinating historical conundrum. Any similar event in, for example, American history would have long ago attracted the attention of scores of researchers, professional and amateur. But in Poland it is "taboo" to question even for a minute the "official", "Soviets-did-it" version of "Katyn." Hence the coverup and the denial.

---

[9] It is marked as route P15 on the Googlemaps map but shown clearly on Ukrainian maps, such as the map at OpenStreetMap.org - http://www.openstreetmap.org/relation/2101524#map=19/50.84526/24.31109 (Accessed 03.14.2014)

The "Katyn Massacre": What Really Happened

We don't know what really happened, at least not in any detail. There are a number of reasons for this. First, according to one of the documents from "Closed Packet No. 1", the "Shelepin letter" dated March 3, 1959, thousands of relevant documents have been destroyed. Whether the "Shelepin letter" is genuine or a forgery those documents were certainly destroyed; the only question would be by whom and when.

Second, a great many Soviet-era documents concerning controversial historical matters are still classified in Russia today, inaccessible even to trusted historians. Russian scholar Sergei Strygin claims to have learned of many such documents that disprove the "official version" of Katyn. He enumerates some of them in his now-famous "voluntary confession" of December 6, 2012.[10] Among the most interesting of these: a report of an inter-agency commission that supposedly worked in 1952-53 as a response to the U.S. Congressional Madden Commission on Katyn that held hearings in 1952. According to Strygin the archival materials of this Soviet commission, still kept secret, confirm German guilt in the mass murders at Katyn and the findings of the 1944 Soviet Burdenko commission.

Strygin also claims that more bodies wearing Polish policemen's uniforms were discovered in the Koz'i Gory / Katyn area in March 2000 but the finding was covered up. This claim is echoed in a recent Polish book (which, naturally enough, assumes these are victims of the Soviets). If these documents alleged by Strygin do indeed exist they would definitively prove Soviet innocence.

Our ignorance about "what really happened" is also is in large part the fault of Polish historians. They continue to pretend that the "official version" of Katyn is seamless, without contradictions, and unquestionable. In short, they "do not want to know" anything that might cast doubt on this foundational myth of right-wing Polish

---

[10] "Координатор "Правды о Катыни" Сергей Стрыгин направил в ФСБ России "'Заявление о явке с повинной'." ("The Manager of 'Truth about Katyn' Sergei Strygin has sent to the Russian FSB a 'Declaration of Voluntary Confession'") At http://katyn.ru/index.php?go=News&in=view&id=224

nationalism. If archeologists at the dig in Volodymyr-Volyns'kiy should uncover evidence of more victims thought to have been shot at one of the three sites where the "official version" of the "Katyn massacre" says they were shot, we will surely never learn about it.

There is no reason to think that only two of the Polish POWs are in these mass graves just because — at least, as far as we know — only two badges have been found. Parts of Polish policemen's uniforms and other Polish military relics, along with many other Polish artifacts, have been found there. For all we know there could be hundreds of "Katyn" victims buried in these same mass graves, shot by German troops and their Ukrainian Nationalist allies collaborators in late 1941. A thorough excavation of the hundreds or thousands of mass graves in the former Soviet Union would surely turn up more evidence of Polish POWs.

Although the Volodymyr-Volyns'kiy discoveries definitively refute the "official" Polish version of Katyn they do not tell us what really happened. The hypothesis that most closely fits the evidence we have today is that the Germans and/or their Ukrainian Nationalist allies shot most of the Polish POWs. It is likely that the Soviets shot some Poles too. Even those Russian researchers who have long argued that the official version of the "Katyn massacre" is false this it is likely that some of them were executed by the Soviets for some crimes or other. But all the evidence we now have suggests that the Germans and Ukrainian Nationalists, not the Soviets, shot the Polish officers whose corpses the Germans exhumed at Katyn in April-June 1943.[11]

Therefore there was no "Katyn massacre" in the sense of the event known to history by that name. The Polish POWs, officers and others, were killed, but probably in different places where their bodies have never been recovered, as the Volodymyr-Volyns'kiy site was unexcavated until a few years ago.

---

[11] Strygin, "Volynskaia Katyn" - Сергей Стрыгин. «"Волынская Катынь" оказалась делом рук гитлеровцев». Katyn.ru 06 Январь 2013. At http://katyn.ru/index.php?go=News&in=view&id=253 (Accessed 03.14.2014); Furr, Official Version.

It is possible that we will never learn any more. Neither Poland nor Ukraine — nor, at this time, Russia — wants to find any evidence that casts doubt upon the "official version" of Katyn.

Meanwhile, where are the 14,800+, or 22,000, or whatever the number of missing Polish POWs? Those executed by the Soviets may well be buried at Mednoe (near Kalinin / Tver') and/or Piaty-khatky (near Khar'kov / Kharkiv) as the "official version" claims. But all are under the earth somewhere in the Western part of the former Soviet Union — Russia, Ukraine, Belarus. They are among the millions of victims of fascist[12] aggression, both soldiers and civilians, who were slaughtered and whose bodies were never re-covered, Indeed, the 22,000 Polish POWs are a very small per centage of all the missing victims of the war in the Soviet Union.

The Katyn Shell Casings

The Polish officers whose bodies were unearthed at Koz'i Gory, near Katyn, near Smolensk, Russia, by the Germans in April-June 1943, then again by the Russians in October — January 1943-44, were almost certainly shot by German and/or Ukrainian national-ist forces, for German shell casings were found in these mass graves. The official German report contains photographs of the shell casings. In a telling omission, these photographs are side views of these casings. There are no photographs of the "head-stamps" or ends where the percussion cap and identifying marks are located. Most German bullets of the era had date stamps, just as most of those found at Volodymyr-Volyns'kiy did. If any of those had been stamped 1940 or earlier the Germans would surely have photographed them, since they would have been excellent proof of Soviet guilt. The fact that they did not suggests that the head-stamps contained numbers or codes indicating manufacture in 1941. This is consistent with the other circumstantial evidence now available that points strongly to German, not Soviet, guilt.

---

[12] I prefer the term "fascist" rather than "German" invasion, advisedly, for it was not Germa-ny alone that invaded the USSR on or shortly after June 22, 1941. The armies of Italy, Roma-nia, Hungary, and Finland did as well. Among the fascist forces were units from almost eve-ry European country. Ukrainian Nationalist forces were involved in the Volodymyr-Volyns'kiy murders. It is more accurate to say: "Europe invaded the Soviet Union in June 1941."

Snyder"s Account of Katyn

It is the duty of an honest historian to explain this important and polarized historical dispute to his readers. Snyder cannot possibly be unaware of it. But he fails to inform his readers about it. Once again, Snyder commits the fallacy of "assuming that which is to be proven" — in this case, that the Soviets shot the Poles in question.

In *Mein Kampf* Hitler wrote that no one interested in swaying the public should ever tell the truth — only what benefits one's own cause. Those who take the position that the Soviets shot all the Poles tacitly assume that *in this one case* the Nazis' investigation told the pure truth (except for blaming the Jews). Under any other circumstances to accept a Nazi propaganda report as an honest piece of research would be considered a risky thing to do. But in the case of "Katyn" it is a leap that anticommunists insist that everyone make. World public opinion has followed them, but only because the arguments against it have been excluded from public consciousness.

In the case of the "Vinnitsa massacre", the other large-scale disinterment staged by the Nazis of what they claimed were victims of Soviet mass shootings in which they followed their "Katyn" script very closely, it appears that the Germans insisted upon "gilding the lily" by burying some of the bodies of Soviet citizens they themselves had killed, then later digging them up, putting them with buried corpses of victims of NKVD shootings during the *Ezhovshchina* of 1937-1938, and blaming the Soviets for everything. But even this is not certain — nothing about these hotly contested events is "certain."[13]

It is interesting that anticommunist Ukrainian nationalists, who once paid a great deal of attention to the Vinnitsa massacre, just as the anticommunist Poles had always done with Katyn, have not written much about it in recent years. The "Holodomor" has be-

---

[13] See "Erwin Bingel. Eyewitness to Mass Murder at Uman and Vinnitsa in the Ukraine." At http://www.holocaustresearchproject.org/einsatz/bingel.html This is an abbreviated version of the article "The Extermination of Two Ukrainian Jewish Communities. Testimony of a German Officer." *Yad Vashem Studies* 3 (1959), 303-320.

come one of the two cornerstones of right-wing Ukrainian nationalism.[14] Vinnitsa has received much less attention.

Snyder is closely aligned in sympathy with contemporary anticommunist Polish nationalism. He supports the anticommunist myths of the Ukrainian nationalists only when they do not clash with those of the Polish nationalists. This is not the only form of Polish nationalism. Pro-communist Poles had and still have a competing form of pro-socialist nationalism.[15]

But with the end of the USSR the anticommunist brand of nationalism has become hegemonic in Poland. This ideology bans any overt expression of doubt about the "Katyn massacre." Soviet guilt is literally constitutive of anticommunist Polish national identity. No discussion of Katyn as an historical controversy is tolerated. Questioning Soviet responsibility for Katyn is virtually outlawed in Poland, as well as in anticommunist circles, including academic circles, in the rest of the world. Polish nationalists and anticommunists generally make none but the most derogatory reference to the alternative versions.[16]

The Case of the Two Sets of Siblings: Snyder"s Nazi-Soviet Parallel Again

Snyder's main purposes in *Bloodlands* is to draw as many parallels between the Nazis and the Soviets as possible, in order to suggest that these regimes were more similar than different.

---

[14] The other "cornerstone" issue for today's rightwing Ukrainian Nationalists is their claim that the "Ukrainian Insurgent Army" were "freedom fighters" and opposed both the Soviets and the Germans. In reality the UPA was comprised of Ukrainians who worked under the Germans and took a personal oath to Adolf Hitler. There is a huge literature about the UPA. A good, objective article is Per Anders Rudling, "'The Honor They So Clearly Deserve': Legitimizing the Waffen-SS Galizien," *The Journal of Slavic Military Studies* 26:1 (2013): 114-137.

[15] See the essay by the late Professor Ryszard Nazarewicz, "Kontrowersje Wokół Najnowszej Historii Polski" (ca. 1998). At http://smp.republika.pl/polemiki/Nazarewicz.kontrowersje.htm A veteran of the Warsaw Uprising Nazarewicz worked for Polish communist security and then became a noted historian in socialist Poland.

[16] The present author has created an extensive web page on this controversy: "The Katyn Forest Whodunnit", at http://www.tinyurl.com/katyn-the-truth

> Some of the people going to their deaths in the AB
> Aktion were thinking of family who had been taken
> prisoner by the Soviets. Although the Soviets and
> the Germans did not coordinate their policies
> against the Polish educated classes, they targeted
> the same sorts of people. The Soviets acted to re-
> move elements that they regarded as dangerous to
> their system, on the pretext of fighting a class war.
> The Germans were also defending their territorial
> gains, though also acting on their sense that the in-
> ferior race had to be kept in its place. **In the end,
> the policies were very similar**, with more or less
> concurrent deportations and more or less concur-
> rent mass shootings. (149, Emphasis added)

This is false. The Nazis AB-Aktion[17] was explicitly aimed at murdering members of the Polish elite. Snyder would like to be able to
prove that the Soviets did the same thing, and so were in this way
like the Nazis. But there is no evidence of this, so he simply asserts
it.

It is true that the Soviets "removed elements that they regarded as
dangerous to their system" — but through arrest and deportation,
not murder. Nor does a class war have anything in common with
murderous racist violence. The Polish government too had "removed dangerous elements", mainly communists, when they took
control of Western Belorussia and Western Ukraine after the Treaty of Riga in 1921. Snyder never compares this policy to the Nazis.
Indeed, he never mentions it.

Snyder claims that "In the end, the policies [Nazi and Soviet] were
very similar." In reality there is no similarity at all between them.
If there is any similarity it is between the racism of the Polish nationalists, who refused to consider Jews, Ukrainians, or Belorus-

---

[17] There is a Wikipedia page on AB-Aktion in English and in Polish, though not in Russian.
Both these pages include the deliberate lie that the Nazis "discussed" these murders "with
Soviet officials during a series of secretive Gestapo-NKVD Conferences."
(http://en.wikipedia.org/wiki/AB-Aktion) In reality there were no such conferences, even
though there is a Polish nationalist Wikipedia page about them. See О.В. Вишлёв, «Миф об
'антипольском соглашении'», Накануне 22 июня 1941 года. М.: Наука, 2001, сс. 120-
122. On the web at http://militera.lib.ru/research/vishlev/04.html

sians as "Poles" even if they spoke Polish and were citizens of Poland, and Nazi racial doctrines that refused to consider Jews as
"Germans" even if they were culturally German and were German
citizens. In contrast, all citizens of the Soviet Union regardless of
nationality were considered equally part of "the Soviet people."

Snyder then turns to the "case of the two sets of siblings", which
we will now briefly investigate.

> In at least two cases, the Soviet terror killed one
> sibling, the German terror the other. (149)

Set #1: The Wnuk Brothers

> The Wnuk brothers, who hailed from a region that
> had once been in east-central Poland but was now
> quite close to the German-Soviet border, met the
> same fate. Bolesław, the older brother, was a popu-
> list politician who had been elected to the Polish
> parliament. Jakub, the younger brother, studied
> pharmacology and designed gas masks. Both mar-
> ried in 1932 and had children. Jakub, along with the
> other experts from his institute, was arrested by the
> Soviets and killed at Katyn in April 1940. Bolesław
> was arrested by the Germans in October 1939, tak-
> en to Lublin castle in January, and executed in the
> AB Aktion on 29 June 1940. He left a farewell note
> on a handkerchief: "I die for the fatherland with a
> smile on my lips, but I die innocent.[75]

Source:

> n. 75 *Zagłada polskich elit*, 77.

Snyder took the case of the two sets of siblings directly from this
book without informing his readers that this is merely a catalog of
an exhibition. It contains a photograph of Bolesław's farewell note.
But it offers no evidence about who killed Jakub, about the "Katyn
massacre," or about anything.

Jakub Wnuk is number 4121 in the German list, page 272 in the
official German report *Amtliches Material zum Massenmord von*

Katyn. But the question is not whether he was killed, but rather by whom — the Soviets or the Germans?

He is on the Soviet transit list of prisoners sent on April 2, 1940 from the Polish POW camp at Kozel'sk to the NKVD at Smolensk. Aside from the German — that is, Nazi — report of 1943 there is no evidence that he or any other Polish POWs were shot by the Soviets. Recent archeological discoveries have proven that the "transit" lists are not lists of Polish POWs being sent to execution, as has long been assumed. As of this writing the evidence is that the Soviet Burdenko Commission report of January 1944 was correct: the Polish POWs disinterred at Katyn were shot by the Germans.[18]

Set #2: The Dowbor Sisters: The Legend of Janina Lewandowska

Snyder writes:

> Janina Dowbor was the only female among the Polish officers taken prisoner by the Soviets. An adventurous soul, she had learned as a girl to hang glide and parachute. She was the first woman in Europe to jump from a height of five kilometers or more. She trained as a pilot in 1939, and enlisted in the Polish air force reserve. In September 1939 she was taken prisoner by the Soviets. According to one account, her plane had been shot down by the Germans. Parachuting to safety, she found herself arrested by the Soviets as a Polish second lieutenant. She was taken to Ostashkov, and then to Kozelsk. She had her own accommodations, and spent her time with air force comrades with whom she felt safe. On 21 or 22 April 1940, she was executed at Katyn, and buried there in the pits along with 4,409 men. Her younger sister Agnieszka had remained in the German zone. Along with some friends, she had joined a resistance organization in late 1939. She

---

[18] See Furr, Official version.

was arrested in April 1940, at about the time that her sister was executed. She was killed in the Palmiry Forest on 21 June 1940. Both sisters were buried in shallow graves, after sham trials and shots to the head.[74] (149)

Sources:

n. 74 - Dunin-Wąsowicz, "Akcja," 22-25; Bauer, *Dowbor*, 217, 241; *Crime of Katyń*, 33; *Zagłada polskich elit*, 73.

Snyder asserts that Janina Lewandowska was shot at Katyn by the Soviets. This allows him to further assume that her fate parallels that of of her sister Agnieszka, shot by the Nazis. For some reason Snyder says that Janina had a "sham trial." Even in the version of Katyn that blames the Soviets for all the shootings there is no talk of any "trials", "sham" or otherwise.[19] Moreover, there is no decent evidence that Janina Lewandowska was shot by the Soviets at all.

The Mystery of Janina Lewandowska, Part 1: Khar"kov

During the period 1990 to 1992 retired Soviet NKVD man Mitrofan Vasil'evich Syromiatnikov gave six interviews to Soviet (1990-1991), Polish (1991), and Ukrainian (1992) investigators, and one to Polish journalist Jerzy Morawski (1991). Syromiatnikov had been a guard at the NKVD prison in Khar'kov where, he testified, he had participated in the execution of Polish officers and policemen in the spring of 1940.

In two of these interviews Syromiatnikov testified that one female was among the prisoners. During his third interrogation, on May 15, 1991, Syromiatnikov referred briefly to the female prisoner:

Pamiętam. ze do budynku więzienia wewnętrznego UNKWD wśród polskich wojskowych była dostarczona jedna kobieta. Teraz nie przypominam

---

[19] Snyder may have been thinking of the end of the "Beria letter", which talks about a review of 14,800+ files by an NKVD "troika." This is the main "smoking gun" document from "Closed Packet No.1." Its bona fides are in serious doubt. For much more detail about this fascinating matter see the account on my "Katyn Forest Whodunnit" page at http://www.tinyurl.com/katyn-the-truth

> sobie dokladnie, kto to był, czy była wojskowym, jednakże dobrze pamiętam, że wsród dostarczonych Polaków była kobieta. Jej dalsze losy nie są mi wiadome, najwidoczniej także zostala rozstrzelana.[20]

> I remember that to the building of the internal prison of the NKWD among Polish military men one woman was [also] delivered. I do not remember now exactly who it was, whether she was military, but I remember well that among the Poles brought there was a woman. Her fate thereafter is unknown to me, apparently she was also shot.

The Polish editor of this interrogation attached a note to this passage explaining that this must have been Janina Lewandowska, as she was the only female among the Polish prisoners.

> Jedyna znana kobieta jeniec wojenny, zamordowana na podstawie decyzji z 5 marca 1940 r ., to ppor. Janina Lewandowska z obozu kozielskiego, nr 53 na liście śmierci 040/1 z [20] kwietnia 1940 r. (481)

> The only known female military prisoner, murdered according to the decision of March 5, 1940, was second lieutenant Janina Lewandowska from the Kozel'sk camp, number 53 on the death list 040/1 of [20] April 1940.[21]

This should have raised a problem for the editors of these confessions. Syromiatnikov was in Khar'kov, where Polish POWs from the Starbelsk camp were sent. Smolensk, where the Kozel'sk prisoners were sent, is about 700 Km (= 450 miles) from Khar'kov.

---

[20] *Katyń. Dokumenty zbrodni, Tom 2, Zagłada. Marzec-Czerwiec 1940* (Warsaw, 1998), 480-481.

[21] The list number refers to the Russian transit lists given to the Polish government and published in Jędrzej Tucholski, *Mord w Katzniu. Kozielsk, Ostaszków, Starobielsk. Lista ofiar.* Warsaw: Instytut Wydawniczy Pax, 1991. Lewandowska is indeed listed on p. 703, number 53, though the list in Tucholski does not specify April 20. As mentioned above, we now know that these lists were *not* "death lists" but merely transit lists, lists of what POWs were being sent where, when, and in what convoy (Furr, Official version).

Syromiatnikov gave more detail about the female prisoner in his fourth interview on July 30, 1991. Now he is certain that the woman was shot.

> Syromiatnikow: Tak. Była wśród nich kobieta. Ubrana zwyczajnie, w płaszczyku.
>
> Przywieziono ją z Polakami. Ją także rozstrzelano.
>
> ...
>
> Trietiecki: Czy jest Pan pewien, że kobieta również została rozstrzelana?
>
> Syromiatnikow: Mogę z całą pewnością powiedzieć, że była rozstrzelana, dlatego że sam ją prowadziłem. Rozumiecie. Uściślam swoje poprzednie zeznania. Wiem, że jej palto zostało rzucone pod wiatą. Podniosłem je, był tam pierścionek miedziany lub złoty. Pokazałem go komendantowi, on powiedział, abym odniósł Karmanowowi magazynierowi.

Translated:

> Syromiatnikov: Yes. Among them was a woman. Dressed casually in a coat.
>
> They brought her with the Poles. She was also shot.
>
> ...
>
> Trietiecki: Are you sure that the woman also was shot?
>
> Syromiatnikov: I can say with complete certainty that she was shot dead, because I myself accompanied her. Understand. I am refining my previous testimony. I know that her coat was thrown in the carport. I picked it up, there was a copper or gold ring. I showed it to the commander and he told me to bring it to Karmanov the quartermaster.

In his 1991 interview with Polish journalist Jerzy Morawski Syromiatnikov changed his story again. He now claimed that he did not know whether the woman had been shot or not, and said she might have been a Russian, not a Pole.

— Czy pan potwierdza, że wśród polskich jeńców znajdowała się kobieta?

— Kobieta? Tak, widziałem ją, jak przechodziłem przez podwórze. Właśnie ją prowadzili. Tak, tak.

— Co stało się z nią?

— Nie wiem, czy to była Polka czy Rosjanka. Akurat wychodziłem z komendantury, a ją prowadzili.

Translated:

- Can you confirm that among Polish prisoners was a woman?

- A woman? Yes, I saw it as I walked through the yard. They were just leading her. Yes, yes.

- What happened to her?

- I do not know if it was a Pole or Russian. Just left the headquarters, and they were leading her.

Here Syromiatnikov retracts the most important details of the previous confessions. He says "they were leading her", and he did not know whether she was a Pole or a Russian. There's nothing about execution, and he no longer claims that he himself accompanied her.

There are many such contradictions and inconsistencies in the confessions of the three aged NKVD men. However, instead of carefully studying these confessions and parsing the contradictions in and among them, the Polish and Russian researchers of the "Katyn massacre" have just neglected them entirely. We do not even have the Russian originals of their statements — only Polish translations. This neglect may be due to the Polish attempt to make the "official version" appear seamless and unproblematic.

The Mystery of Janina Lewandowska, Part 2: Katyn

Nevertheless as of 1991 it seemed that the question of Janina Lewandowska's fate was somewhat confused. Supposedly she had been brought to Khar'kov prison where she was then supposedly executed along with an undetermined number of other Polish POWs and buried in the Piatykhatky forest outside Khar'kov.

Sometime in the late 1990s, a new story is created that contradicts this story while leaving the Lewandowska story as mysterious as ever. We are told that Lewandowska was buried at Katyn and her skull identified. We are told that she was shot not at Khar'kov but at Katyn in April 1940. This explanation is confidently stated in Polish sources. But a careful study reveals that there is no evidence for it at all.

Snyder's source, the exhibition catalog-booklet *Zagłada polskich elit* states that Lewandowska's body was exhumed by the Germans:

> Zwłoki Janiny Lewandowskiej odnaleźli Niemcy podczas pierwszej ekshumacji katyńskiej. (73)

Translated:

> The Germans discovered the remains of Janina Lewandowska during the first Katyn exhumation.

But there is no evidence at all for this statement. Lewandowska's name does not appear in the German list of names of identified corpses at Katyn. At least Jacob Wnuk's name does appear in this official German propaganda report.

Some Polish accounts offer the explanation that the Germans were confused or embarrassed by finding the body of a single woman and so they never mentioned it. But there is no evidence for this explanation. Nor is it likely. The whole purpose of the German disinterments at Katyn was to embarrass the Soviets and hopefully drive a wedge between the Soviets and the rest of the Allies. Reporting the body of a woman would not have interfered with German propaganda. Ideed, it would probably have made Soviet actions seem even more heinous.

Lewandowska's presence in the Soviet camp for Polish officer POWs at Kozel'sk, near Katyn, was supposedly attested by two Polish officers, Rafał Bniński and Wacław Mucho, who themselves survived this camp.[22] Mucho is identified at the Griazowiec camp (Tucholski 528). Tucholski also mentions Mucho as a doctor at Koziel'sk (19). Rafał Bniński is named at Kozel'sk by Tucholski (77) but is not named in any of the "transit lists." How he got out of Kozel'sk is unclear. Perhaps he was never there in the first place. Evidently Tucholski includes him only because he is *said* to have been there.

These two men claimed Lewandowska had assumed a false name to hide her identity. But this is not true either. The Soviet "transit list" of prisoners shipped from Kozel'sk to Smolensk, as printed by an official Polish source, lists her by her real first and last names but with a false name for her father and an age 6 years younger than her real age:

> 53. ЛЕВАНДОВСКОЙ Янины Марьяновны 1914 г.р.[23]

Either Soviet records are in error or Lewandowska tried to conceal her father's identity and, for some reason, her own age. This is a poor means of disguising one's identity! It would only work if there were multiple people with the same first and last names, so that the only way of distinguishing among them was by age or patronymic. That was clearly not the case here. Did she give some false information in a private act of defiance? But wouldn't her military identification papers record accurately her patronymic and, at the very least, her year of birth?

Lewandowska's skull was supposedly one of six skulls from Katyn saved by the German medical chief Dr. Gerhard Buhtz that after his death passed into the hands of a Polish scientist, Dr. Jerzy Popielski. Supposedly Popielski did not reveal the existence of these skulls until 1997, "before he died." We are not told why he waited so long; pro-Soviet Poland had come to an end in 1990. We are told that the skull, or fragments of it, were identified as Lewan-

---

[22] This account was evidently first published in *Zbrodnia Katyńska w świetle dokumentów*, preface by General Władysław Anders. The first edition was in 1948; I have checked the third, enlarged edition: London: "Gryf", 1962, pp. 30-31.

[23] Jędrzej Tucholski. *Mord w Katyniu. Kozielsk, Ostaszków, Starobielsk. Lista ofiar.* Warszawa: Instytut Wydawniczy Pax, 1991, l. 703.

dowska's by "computer analysis", not by DNA analysis.[24] To our knowledge there is no process that can do this.

The Mystery of Janina Lewandowska, Part 3: The Falsification

Lewandowska could not have been shot at Khar'kov, as Syromiatnikov suggested, but buried at Katyn, near Smolensk. That means that somebody — or everybody — is in error.

There are various possible scenarios:

* Bniński is said to have told Lewandowska's family that she was flying a Polish plane when she was shot down and captured by the Red Army.[25] However, Polish-American historian Professor Anna Cienciala, a leading expert on Katyn, recently rejected this story:

> Please note that the brief information on Lewandowska in the 2007 edition of the Katyn book, is wrong. She was not shot down, but was evacuated to eastern Poland by train and taken prisoner there. This corrected information is in the revised reprint of the book isued in 2009 (see Lewandowska in Index for pages).[26]

Cienciala does not state where she has learned this new information. It may come from the booklet *Zagłada polskich elit* used by Snyder, which says more or less the same thing. However, it directly contradicts what Bniński reportedly told to Lewandowska's family in January 1941. The only way Bniński could have learned that Lewandowska had been shot down was from Lewandowska herself or from others at the Kozel'sk POW camp. If Lewandowska had not been shot down, why would she tell Bniński that she had been?

---

[24] These details come from a number of sources, mainly the article by Kamila Baranowska, "Jedyna kobieta wśród ofiar Katynia: Janina Lewandowska" *Rzeczpospolita* April 22, 2008.

[25] Zbrodnia Katyńska, 31.

[26] Cienciala, post to the H-POLAND list of August 15, 2012. At http://tinyurl.com/lewandowska-1 (original URL: http://h-net.msu.edu/cgi-bin/logbrowse.pl?trx=vx&list=H-Poland&month=1208&week=c&msg=It7PC1MnEdGRd9URRqycvQ&user=&pw=)

The Russian record reproduced in Tucholski's book is good evidence that Lewandowska was indeed at Kozel'sk and was shipped to Smolensk, near Katyn. As we have argued elsewhere, recently discovered evidence makes it next to impossible that she was shot by the Soviets.[27]

> * But if Syromiatnikov was telling the truth, then Lewandowska was shot at Khar'kov and buried outside the town at Piatykhatky. In that case the story about her being disinterred by the Germans, her skull taken by Buhtz, its rediscovery and identification in Poland, etc., is a fabrication.

> * Perhaps Syromiatnikov was mistaken. Then Lewandowska was not shot and buried at Khar'kov. Instead she was taken to Katyn, and shot and buried there — from the evidence we now have, by the Germans.

> * Perhaps Syromiatnikov was telling the truth about the "one female" among the prisoners, but the Polish records are wrong — there were at least two female Polish prisoners. The one shot and buried at Khar'kov was not Lewandowska. The problem is that the Soviet transit records of Polish P.O.W.s shipped from Starobelsk P.O.W. camp to Khar'kov do not record any other female prisoners.

We have no idea what Syromiatnikov was told informally. It is possible that he told the very brief story about the "female prisoner" in order to provide closure to the Polish story about Lewandowska and so to please his interrogators. In 1991 the "skull at Katyn" story had not yet appeared. But it is also possible that he told the truth as he remembered it. He said himself that he had a poor memory of those long-ago events and he contradicted himself on some points, including this one.

With the appearance in the late 1990s of the version that Lewandowska was shot by the Soviets at Katyn, disinterred by the Germans who never mentioned it, and finally identified through a skull that had ended up in the possession of a Polish scientist, Syromiatnikov's confession has been forgotten. None of the histo-

---

[27] See Furr, Official version.

rians and writers on the Katyn question mentions it or the problem of falsification that it raises. Snyder does not mention it either.

The significance of this is that it casts further doubt upon the confessions of the three NKVD men who, in the early 1990s, were important evidence of Soviet guilt in the Katyn massacre. Russian researchers of the Katyn story have long doubted these confessions. This would be further evidence that they are indeed corrupted, at least partly false, probably an attempt to tell the Polish and Russian interrogators what they wanted to hear.

Why spend all this space on the question of Janina Lewandowska and Katyn, which occupies few pages in *Bloodlands*? One reason is to show that what we have called the "official version" of the "Katyn massacre", the "Soviets-did-it" story, is not a simple matter. The fascinating complexity of the Janina Lewandowska story highlights the fact that Snyder is uncritically repeating the official Polish nationalist version not only of Lewandowska but of the whole Katyn question without acknowledging — informing his readers — that he is doing so.

The "Janina Lewandowska" story shows that the "official version" — really, the anticommunist and Polish nationalist version — of Katyn is very far from the seamless narrative, devoid of contradictions, that its proponents pretend it is. And it does not even help Snyder's "numbers game." Given that his goal is to make the Soviets into mass murderers on almost the Nazi scale, Katyn is scarcely relevant. Even if the Soviets had "done it" — shot all the Polish POWs — that would be 22,000, scarcely a drop in the bucket compared to the millions of mass murder victims he needs in order to make his Soviet-Nazi comparison even remotely credible.

Chapter 11. The Partisan War and Related Issues in *Bloodlands* Chapter 7

This chapter deals principally with the partisan warfare in Western Belorussia and Western Ukraine, which the Polish exile government in London and its underground army the Home Army (Armia Krajowa, AK) still considered to be part of Poland.

Snyder's obvious aim throughout is to portray pro-Soviet partisans as murderous, completely insensitive to the safety and needs of civilians, misogynistic, opponents of independence, and illegitimate. By "independent" Snyder means "capitalist", and by "legitimate" he means "obedient to the Polish government-in-exile in London" (e.g. on page 298).

Setting aside the language of propaganda, the London-based Polish government-in-exile was completely dependent upon, thus not at all "independent" of, the U.K. and the Western Allies. Nor was it any more "legitimate" than was the pro-Soviet formation that became the Polish government. In July 1945 the pro-Soviet Polish government was officially recognized by the Allies, thereby making it the only "legitimate" government of Poland.

An honest historian would explain these matters to his readers rather than foist Polish nationalist propaganda onto them through the use of value-laden terms like "legitimate" and "independent" without explanation. In fact much of Snyder's book is anticommunist Polish "nationalist"mythology and moralizing thinly disguised as historiography.

Did Stalin"s Speech of November 7, 1941 Favor Russians?

In November 1941 Stalin was thus preparing an ideological as well as a military defense of the Soviet Union. The Soviet Union was not a state of the Jews, as the Nazis claimed; it was a state of the Soviet peoples, first among whom were the Russians. On 7 November, as the Jews marched through Minsk to their deaths, Stalin reviewed a military parade in Moscow. To raise the spirits of his Soviet peoples and to communicate his confidence to the Germans, he had actually recalled Red Army divisions from their defensive positions west of Moscow, and had them march through its boulevards. In his address that day he called upon the Soviet people to follow the example of their "great ancestors," mentioning six prerevolutionary martial heroes—all of them Russians. At a time of desperation, the Soviet leader appealed to Russian nationalism.[5] (227)

Source (n. 5 p. 489): Brandenberger, *National Bolshevism*, 118-119.

Properly speaking this is not an anti-Soviet statement. Apparently Snyder included it so he could accuse Stalin of being "pro-Russian" instead of simply "pro-Soviet."

Brandenberger says: "... all of Stalin's examples were defenders of the old regime if not outright counterrevolutionaries." (118) Brandenberger is correct to note the appeals to Russian nationalism in Soviet rhetoric during the war. But this specific statement is nonsense. It is an anarchronism and thus an absurdity to call these historical figures of centuries ago "counterrevolutionaries", as though they were living in the 20th century.[1]

Stalin's speech on November 7 1941 mentions six traditional Russian military heroes.[2] One might suspect that Stalin referred to Russian heroes because he spoke in Moscow, the historic capital of

---

[1] Brandenberger does note the establishment in 1943 of the order of Bogdan Khmel'nitskii, awarded to Ukrainians in the Ukrainian language. This caused much dissatisfaction because of the anti-Jewish pogroms carried out by Khmel'nitskii's men in the mid-17th century. Along with his Ukrainian provenance Khmel'nitskii's alliance with the Tsar and organizing the struggle of Ukrainian peasants against Polish exploiters appear to have been the reason for the award.

[2] An English translation of Stalin's speech is at http://www.marxists.org/reference/archive/stalin/works/1941/11/07.htm The Russian text is at http://grachev62.narod.ru/stalin/t15/t15_14.htm

Russia that in November 1941 was again threatened with capture as it had been in earlier wars. All six leaders were relevant to the situation the USSR found itself in on November 7, 1941: defeating an invader, or fighting successful retreats (Suvorov) as the Red Army had been forced to do since June 22, 1941

* Alexander Nevsky, who defeated the Teutonic Knights (Germans) and later the Finns.

* Dmitry Donskoy, who defeated the Mongols at Kulikovo when they tried to conquer Moscow in 1380.

* Kuz'ma Minin, who raised a volunteer army (*opol'chenie*) in Nizhnii Novgorod and worked with Pozharsky (see below). During World War 2 the Soviet "home guard" of those unfit for service in the regular Red Army were also called "opol'chenie."

* Dmitry Pozharsky: Minin's army led by Pozharsky cleared the Kremlin of Polish-Lithuanian forces in 1612.

* Alexander Suvorov, who led a great strategic retreat across the Alps in 1799.

* Mikhail Kutuzov, who fought the French army at Borodino and then drove the Grand Army out of Russia in 1812. This war was also referred to as the "Patriotic War" (*Otechestvennaia*), as the war against the Nazis was already being called.

The Marxist view of history is that the Tsars were indeed imperialist exploiters, but also that the great land empire they had built laid the basis for socialism to seize one-sixth of the world. In the latter task the Tsars' expansion was progressive in both the bourgeois and Marxist senses of the word, as were all the bourgeois imperialist expansions from the 16th century on. Similarly, Ivan IV ("the Terrible") and Henry VII of England were progressive in unifying their kingdoms and suppressing the power of the feudal nobility because by doing so they laid the political basis for the development of capitalism and the capitalist class, precursor to socialism and communism.

The vast majority of Muscovites (as well as of Russians and Soviet citizens generally) were not communists. They had to fight and, in many cases, die for something — not for communism, then, but for their country. For all these reasons an appeal to traditional Russian patriotism at that critical time must have seemed logical.

Snyder continues:

> People who had distinguished themselves in the Minsk of the 1930s had been shot by the NKVD at Kuropaty. ... Left to themselves, they would have endured Hitler for fear of Stalin.[13] (231)

His source (n. 13 p. 490): Epstein, *Minsk*, 130.

This is another fraudulent reference. There is nothing about Kuropaty[3] in **Epstein**'s whole book, let alone on this page. Neither Snyder nor anyone else knows who was "shot by the NKVD at Kuropaty," much less whether the victims buried there were "people who had distinguished themselves in the Minsk of the 1930." Kuropaty has never been thoroughly studied and there is no list of identified victims. If Snyder had written: "It is a reasonable surmise that some people who had distinguished themselves....", he would have been on firmer ground.

Snyder also fabricated — invented — this "fact":

> Left to themselves, they would have endured Hitler for fear of Stalin.

On the very page Snyder cites for this statement Epstein stresses that the Minsk underground did not act out of fear. On the contrary, "they supported the Soviet concept of authority..." (130).

Did Soviet Partisans Cause Nazi Atrocities?

> Hitler, who saw partisan warfare as a chance to destroy potential opposition, reacted energetically when Stalin urged local communists to resist the Germans in July. Even before the invasion of the Soviet Union, Hitler had already relieved his soldiers

---

[3] Kuropaty (Russian) / Kurapaty (Belarusian) is an area outside Minsk, Belarus, where an unknown number of persons shot by the NKVD, probably in 1937- 1938 under Ezhov, plus an unknown number of other persons including, possibly, victims of the Nazis, may have been buried. It has never been thoroughly excavated and studied. Estimates of the total number of persons buried there vary from 7000 to 250,000. The higher numbers are promoted by anticommunist Belarusian nationalists.

of legal responsibility for actions taken against civilians. Now he wanted soldiers and police to kill anyone who "even looks at us askance."[20] (234)

Source: n. 20 p. 490): "...Quotation: Lück, "Partisanbekämpfung," 228.

Here Snyder tries to blame Soviet partisans, and therefore Stalin, for Hitler's murders of civilians. He implies that Hitler stepped up his killing of civilians because of Stalin's setting up of partisan warfare. Snyder does this repeatedly in the last part of his book.

The citation from Lück is from Martin Bormann's notes of a discussion in Hitler's HQ of July 16, 1941. Bormann quotes Hitler as saying:

> Die Russen haben jetzt einen Befehl zum Partisanen-Krieg hinter unserer Front gegeben. Dieser Partisanenkrieg hat auch wieder seinen Vorteil: er gibt uns die Möglichkeit, auszurotten, was sich gegen uns stellt.[4]

Translated:

> Now the Russians have given the order for a partisan war behind our front. This partisan war also has an advantage: it gives us the possibility to exterminate anything that opposes us.

However, Lück notes that this was nothing new for Hitler:

> ... diese "Strategie" hatte die SS ohnehin schon längst angewendet... (Lück 228 n. 17)

Translated:

> ... this "strategy" had long been used by the SS...

Snyder suggests that Hitler's words should be taken literally: that he needed an "opportunity" to take murderous action against civilians, an "excuse" that Hitler did not have before. That is to say, Snyder is suggesting that if the Soviets had not begun partisan warfare Hitler would not have exterminated so many people! But

---

[4] Martin Bormanns Abschrift einer Besprechung im Führerhauptquartier (16. Juli 1941). At http://www.ns-archiv.de/krieg/1941/nationalsozialistische-besatzungspolitik.php

Lück, Snyder's own source, makes it clear to his readers that in reality Hitler had been exterminating people long before Stalin's order for partisan warfare.

Hitler also made the second statement claimed by Snyder — to "kill anyone 'who even looks at us askance'":

> Der Riesenraum müsse natürlich so rasch wie
> möglich befriedet werden; dies geschehe am besten
> dadurch, daß man Jeden, der nur schief schaue,
> totschieße.[5]

Translated:

> Naturally the huge area had to be pacified as quick-
> ly as possible and the best way to do this is to shoot
> dead anybody who looks wrong.

It is not true, as Snyder suggests, Hitler also made this statement in relation to Soviet declaration of partisan warfare. Rather, Hitler just suggested that shooting as many people as possible on any pretext at all was the best way to "pacify this gigantic area."

By Snyder's logic all the Allies were facilitating Nazi mass murders, for French, Czech, Italian, and other partisans also fought the Nazis. Polish partisans fought the Nazis too, though the Polish underground generally considered Jews and communists just as much their enemies as the Germans and Ukrainian nationalists. But Snyder never raises this issue in connection with them. Snyder's goal to associate the Soviet Union, but not Poland or the Allies, with Nazi atrocities.

Snyder does the same thing in the following passage:

> Partisan operations, effective as they sometimes
> were, brought inevitable destruction to the Belarus-
> ian civilian population, Jewish and gentile alike.
> When the Soviet partisans prevented peasants from
> giving food to the Germans, they all but guaranteed
> that the Germans would kill the peasants. A Soviet
> gun threatened a peasant, and then a German gun
> killed him. Once the Germans believed that they had

---

[5] Ibid.

lost control of a given village to the partisans, they would simply torch houses and fields. If they could not reliably get grain, they could keep it from the Soviets by seeing that it was never harvested. When Soviet partisans sabotaged trains, they were in effect ensuring that the population near the site would be exterminated. When Soviet partisans laid mines, they knew that some would detonate under the bodies of Soviet citizens. The Germans swept mines by forcing locals, Belarusians and Jews, to walk hand in hand over minefields. In general, such loss of human life was of little concern to the Soviet leadership. The people who died had been under German occupation, and were therefore suspect and perhaps even more expendable than the average Soviet citizen. German reprisals also ensured that the ranks of the partisans swelled, as survivors often had no home, no livelihood, and no family to which to return.[34] (238-9)

Sources (n. 34 p. 491):

* Musial, *Mythos*, 189, 202;

* Lück, "Partisanbekämpfung," 238;

* Ingrao, *Chasseurs*, 131;

* Verbrechen, 495.

Lück, Ingrao, and the volume "Verbrechen der Wehrmacht" do not discuss Soviet Partisans at all, much less blame them for German atrocities. **Musial**, an intensely anticommunist Polish nationalist historian, notes that the communist partisans forced the Belorussian peasants to feed them and "often" robbed them, while the German forces murdered them. But even Musial does not claim that the German murders were due to the Soviet partisans – the claim that Snyder makes here.

Once again Snyder is trying to blame the Soviet partisans, and therefore Stalin and the Soviet leadership, in part for Nazi atrocities against civilians. Again Snyder fails to acknowledge that all the Allies, including the Polish nationalist Home Army, to whom

Snyder is sympathetic, supported partisan groups and therefore were, in Snyder's sense, all as "responsible" for Nazi atrocities as were the pro-Soviet partisans.

It must be noted that Soviet partisans could not "take control of a given village" — only pro-German Ukrainians or Polish partisans working with the Germans could do that.

> The logic of the Soviet system was always to resist
> independent initiatives and to value human life
> very cheaply...

Snyder cites no evidence to support his statement that the Soviets "valued human life very cheaply." There is evidence to the contrary, as witness this exchange between Marshal Vasilevskii and Stalin concerning a military operation to liberate Leningrad:

> On January 10 Stalin and Marshal Vasilevsky talked
> with him [Marshal Meretskov] by direct wire. They
> expressed the frank opinion that the operation
> would not be ready even by January 11 and that it
> would be better to put it off another two or three
> days. 'There's a Russian proverb,' Stalin said. 'Haste
> makes waste. It will be the same with you: hurry to
> the attack and not prepare it and you will waste
> people'.[6]

The same thing — "valuing human life very cheaply" — was said of American commanders in World War 2 — for example, in the island-hopping campaign in the Pacific, where tens of thousands of American soldiers were killed in frontal assaults on islands that could have been bypassed, leaving the Japanese garrisons to starve or surrender. And what about the "over-the-top" tactics of the commanders on all sides of the First World War, when they could think of no better way of dealing with trench warfare than to order suicidal charges against barbed wire and machine guns at the enemies' trenches, often losing thousands of men in a day? Here, as elsewhere, Snyder's judgment is ruined by his strong anticommunist bias.

---

[6] Harrison Salisbury. *The 900 Days. The Siege of Leningrad.* New York: Harper & Row, 1969, p. 559.

The Polish Home Army leadership that unleased the Warsaw Uprising without a hope of victory and led to the deaths of a quarter million Polish civilians at Nazi hands, was far more guilty of "valuing human life very cheaply" than the Soviets. We will discuss the Warsaw Uprising later.

> The previous hesitation of local Minsk communists turned out to be justified: their resistance organization was treated as a front of the Gestapo by the Central Staff of the Partisan Movement in Moscow. The people who rescued Minsk Jews and supplied Soviet partisans were labeled a tool of Hitler.[35]

Source: (n. 35 p. 491): Slepyan, *Guerillas*, 17, 42.

Slepyan, *Guerillas,* pages 17 and 42, is a phony reference; Slepyan has nothing to say about anything in this passage of Snyder's.

But Barbara Epstein's book, which Snyder recommends elsewhere, does indeed discuss the Soviet authorities' suspicion against the Minsk Ghetto partisans and the persecution of its surviving members. What Epstein writes concerning this tragic and mistaken suspicion is worth quoting:

> Why did Ponomarenko[7] and others want to discredit the Minsk underground, and why did they continue their campaign against it for so many years? **The simplest answer is that Ponomarenko honestly thought that the Minsk underground was a nest of German spies,** and was determined to protect partisan units in the Minsk region from betrayal by its members. Ponomarenko was no doubt informed of the mass arrests of underground members that took place in late September and early October 1942. He no doubt heard that all the members of the City Committee had been arrested, that Kovalyov and some others were providing the names of other underground members, and that photographs apparently of Kovalyov giving a speech to

---

[7] During most of the war Pantaleimon Kondrat'evich Ponomarenko, first secretary of the Communist Party of Belorussia,was head of the Central Staff of the Partisan Movement.

factory workers in which he urged them to drop
their resistance to the Germans appeared in the
Minsker Zeitung, that the City Committee had been
created by the Germans to lure Soviet patriots and
lead to just such a mass arrest. Certainly the second
failure of the Minsk underground could be used to
bolster such a view, as could the first failure, which
had similar features: leaders of the Military Council,
under arrest, had given the Germans names, and a
mass arrest of underground members had followed.
(244-245. Emphasis added.)

However tragically mistaken he may have been in this case
Ponomarenko had reason to suspect a Gestapo connection.[8]

Snyder writes:

Since both sides knew that their membership was
largely accidental, they would subject new recruits
to grotesque tests of loyalty, such as killing friends
or family members who had been captured fighting
on the other side. (244)

Sources (n. 45 p. 491):

    * Szybieka, *Historia*, 345, 352;

    * Mironowicz, *Białoruś*, 159.

This is a phony citation. Neither Szybieka nor Mironowicz say anything at all about "killing friends or family members" or any such
"grotesque tests of loyalty." Szybieka does state that many Belorussians fought in the ranks of Soviet partisans, seeing the USSR as
the only way to defeat the Nazis. He also describes battles between
Belorussian partisans and the Polish Home Army.

---

[8] Ponomarenko has been called an anti-Semite. However, Epstein's book, the latest and very
thorough study of the Minsk partisan movement, gives no evidence that he was one.

It Was the Polish Home Army Who Massacred the Belorussian[9] "Elite"

Both Mironowicz and Szybieka are virulently anti-Soviet. Their sympathies are with the far-right Belorussian nationalists who paid lip service to "independence for Belorussia" — that is, with the Nazi collaborators. A further problem with both of these books (Szybieka's is a translation from the Belarusian) is that they contain few footnotes or other evidentiary information.

Szybieka — this is the Polish spelling of his Belarussian surname; the proper English transliteration is "Shybeka" — is a Belarusian professor. Mironowicz is a Polish professor who specializes in Belarusian history. He too is strongly anticommunist and respectful of the Nazi collaborators who presented themselves as "nationalists."

However, according to Mironowicz it was not the Soviet partisans but the Polish Home Army that was responsible for massacring Belorussian teachers and other "elites":

> Urzędnicy białoruscy w przypadku konfliktu
> interesów z reguły wydawali decyzje niekorzystne
> dla Polaków. Chętniej także wysyłali na
> przymusowe roboty do Niemiec młodzież polską
> niż białoruską (wcześniej czynili tak urzędnicy
> polscy wobec młodzieży białoruskiej). Na
> narastającą dominację białoruską w strukturach
> władzy okupacyjnej AK odpowiedziała
> antybiałoruskim terrorem. W okręgu lidzkim
> konflikt przerodził się w wojnę na wyniszczenie
> elit. W współdziałanie AK i dominującej w tym
> okręgu polskiej policji pomocniczej doprowadziło
> do fizycznej likwidacji znacznej części
> organizatorów białoruskiego życia narodowego -
> nauczycieli, urzędników i działaczy Związku
> Młodzieży Białoruskiej. Współpraca z policją była

---

[9] As part of the Soviet Union the republic was normally spelled "Belorussia," which is a Russian spelling. Since independence the country is called Belarus, its name in the Belarusian language. Both Russian and Belarusian are official languages in Belarus today as during Soviet times.

tak widoczna, że miejscowi Białorusini postrzegali AK jako ugrupowanie militarne realizujące dyrektywy władz niemieckich. Niemiecki historyk pisze, że spółpracujący z AK policjanci polscy zastrzelili kilkuset Białorusinów, w lidzkim komisariacie rejonowym. Komendant nowogródzkiego okręgu AK pisał natomiast, że jego żołnierze w drugiej połowie 1943 r. wykonali ponad 300 wyroków śmierci na Białorusinach, a 80 zadenuncjowali na gestapo jako komunistów. Źródła białoruskie podają liczbę 1200 Białorusinów zabitych w 1943 r. przez polskie podziemie jedynie w rejonie lidzkim. **Według historyków białoruskich podczas okupacji z rąk żołnierzy AK miało zginąć około 10 tys. Białorusinów.**[10]

Translated:

Belarusian officials in the event of a conflict of interest as a rule made decisions unfavorable to the Poles. Also they were more likely to send Polish rather than Belarusian youth to forced labor in Germany (previously Polish officials had done the same to Belarusian youth). To the growing Belarusian dominance in the structures of the occupying power the AK responded with an anti-Belarusian terror. In the district of Lida the conflict escalated into a war of the annihilation of elites. In cooperation of the AK with the Polish auxiliary police who were dominant in the sub-district this led to the physical liquidation of a large part of the organizers of Belarusian national life — teachers, officials and activists of the Belarusian Youth Union. Cooperation with the police was so apparent that the Belarusian locals saw the AK as a military group implementing the directives of the German authorities. A German historian writes that the Polish police, in coopera-

---

[10] Mironowicz, *Bialorus*, 217-218.

> tion with the AK, shot and killed hundreds of Bela-
> rusians in the Lida police district. The commander
> of the AK in the Novgorod district, however, wrote
> that his troops in the second half of 1943 carried
> out more than 300 death sentences against Belarus-
> ians, and denounced 80 to the Gestapo as com-
> munists. Belarusian sources cite the number of
> 1200 Belarusians killed in 1943 by the Polish un-
> derground in the region of Lida alone. **According to
> Belarusian historians, during the occupation
> about ten thousand Belarusians perished at the
> hands of AK soldiers**. (Emphasis added.)

Snyder cites Mironowicz's book elsewhere — but not this passage,
in which Mironowicz claims to expose mass murders by the Polish
Home Army of Belorussians, including of "elites"! This fact serves
to remind us once again that Snyder's book is not historiography,
but "propaganda with footnotes."

Snyder Falsifies the Nalibocki Incident

> Polish civilians were massacred by Soviet partisans
> when Polish forces did not subordinate themselves
> to Moscow. In Naliboki on 8 May 1943, for example,
> Soviet partisans shot 127 Poles.[50] (247)

Sources (n. 50 p. 492):

> * "On the shooting of 127 Poles, see Musial, *Mythos*,
> 210."

> * "See also Jasiewicz, *Zagłada* , 264-265."

As in the case of the Katyn Massacres there is a scholarly dispute
about Nalibocki. And as in the former case Snyder conceals the
dispute from his readers and presents the anti-Soviet version as
the only version. Everyone agrees that the Soviet partisans attacked a fortified police outpost in Nalibocki. However, this armed
outpost could not have existed without German permission and
German-supplied weapons. Snyder does not mention this important fact to his readers. A Russian language source states:

> В отчете советских партизан было указано, что
> в бою в селе разбит немецкий гарнизон
> самообороны. Было также установлено, что
> силы самообороны в Налибоках в виде
> вооружённой ячейки Армии крайовой
> действовали под контролем оккупационных
> властей и сотрудничали с ними. По
> воспоминаниям узника минского гетто
> Михаила Окуня, в 1943 году «очень много
> партизан погибло от рук этих аковцев, и с ними
> началась война."[11]

Translated:

> In the report of the Soviet partisans it was stated
> that in the battle in the village German self-defense
> garrison was smashed. It was also found that the
> self-defense forces in Naliboki, an armed cell of the
> Armia Krajowa (Polish Home Army) were function-
> ing under the control of the occupying authorities
> and cooperating with them. According to the mem-
> oirs of Minsk ghetto prisoner Mikhail Okun, in
> 1943, "a lot of guerrillas were killed by these AKers
> [akovtsev] and we began a war with them."

German historian Bernhard Chiari has documented the collaboration between the Home Army and the German army against their
mutual enemy, the Red Army. We will return to Chiari's research
later in this book.

Bogdan **Musial** is a anticommunist Polish nationalist historian. But
even one of Musial's books records a different version from
Snyder's account. According to this account[12] the Nalibocki attack
was

---

[11] At http://ru.wikipedia.org/wiki/Массовое_убийство_в_Налибоках Accessed on December 1, 2012. Since then the last sentence, quoting Okun, has been removed. This page is
highly contested.

[12] Musial, ed. *Sowjetische Partisanen in Weißrussland*, 116 Doc. 2 — Soviet partisan report.

> ... einen überraschenden Angriff auf die deutsche Garnison der Selbstverteidigung in der Ortschaft Naliboki [und zerstorten sie].

Translated:

> ... a sudden attack against the German self-defense garrison in the village of Naliboki [and destroyed it].

In a note Musial claims that 128 "unbeteiligte Zivilisten" — "civilians not involved in the fight" — were killed and the village "plundered and burned." However, Musial's only source is interviews with surviving villagers. He made no effort to get the surviving Soviet partisans' accounts, as anyone would who was interested in the truth rather than simply in writing anticommunist propaganda.

The different perspectives on the Nalibocki affair can be illustrated by comparing the pages from different language versions of Wikipedia. For example, on the English Wikipedia page[13] there's no ambiguity — the Soviet partisans broke an agreement with the Polish Home Army and slaughtered the townspeople. But the Russian Wikipedia[14] says that the Soviet partisans attacked a unit of the Home Army that was armed and collaborating with the German army, and quotes Mikhail Okun, a veteran of the Minsk ghetto who states that these Home Army men ("akovtsev") killed many Soviet partisans, so the Soviet partisans fought them.[15]

The English page stresses that the Bielski Jewish partisan group was not involved in the Naliboki attack. But the Polish Wikipedia page[16] specifically accuses the Bielsky partisans of collaborating with the Soviet partisans in murdering the innocent villagers, emphasizing that they were "of Jewish ethnicity" — "osób

---

[13] At http://en.wikipedia.org/wiki/Naliboki_massacre Accessed June 2, 2014.

[14] At http://ru.wikipedia.org/wiki/Массовое_убийство_в_Налибоках Okun's claim is in the version of this page from March 23, 2013. As of June 2, 2014 it had been removed.

[15] The source of Okun's account is the excerpt from his memoirs "106-I evreiskii partizanskii..." (106th Jewish Partisan Unit) at the Mark Solonin site http://http://www.solonin.org/live_106-y-evreyskiy-partizanskiy

[16] At http://pl.wikipedia.org/wiki/Zbrodnia_w_Nalibokach

narodowości żydowskiej." The reality is that not just the Bielski partisan group, but all Jewish partisan groups, collaborated with the Soviets since Polish partisans consistently murdered Jewish partisans, as well as Jewish civilians, whenever they could do so.

So there is a serious controversy — one with more than a little anti-Semitism by the Polish nationalists — about what happened at Nalibocki and why. Snyder ignores his responsibility as an historian to objectively explore the different versions, or even to inform his readers that they exist.

Jasiewicz, *Zagłada*, 264-265 claims that the Soviet partisans attacked pro-German Polish farms and killed some Poles, families included. Perhaps some communist partisans did consider pro-German civilians — that is German collaborators — to be fair targets, as French and Italian partisans did. But these allegations are anecdotal, like Musial's account of Nalibocki. Ukrainian insurgents also disguised themselves as Soviets and committed atrocities.

Snyder Claims that Collective Farms Were Similar to Nazi Racism

> The collective farm was to be maintained to extract food; Kube proposed to dissolve it and allow Belarusians to farm as they wished. By undoing both Soviet and Nazi policies, Kube was revealing their basic similarity in the countryside. Both Soviet self-colonization and German racial colonization involved purposeful economic exploitation. (249)

The comparison is nonsense. Snyder again tries to force some similarity between Nazi and Soviet policies. If collective farms maintained by the Nazis to feed German troops and by the Soviets to feed the Soviet population had a "basic similarity", as Snyder claims, then so would individual farms, whether under Nazi or Soviet control.

Snyder hates collective farms — that's clear! So he tries to associate collective farms with Nazi genocide whenever he can. But there is no such thing as "self-colonization." Collective farmers paid a tax on what they produced so that the rest of the society could be fed, the army maintained, industry built. This has nothing in common with deliberately murderous German exploitation. Moreover, Soviet peasants benefitted immensely from collectivization, which put an end to the age-old cycle of deadly famines.

> The Jews who became partisans were serving the Soviet regime, and were taking part in a Soviet policy to bring down retributions upon civilians. The partisan war in Belarus was a perversely interactive effort of Hitler and Stalin, who each ignored the laws of war and escalated the conflict behind the front lines. (250)

This is another instance of a lie that Snyder often repeats. The Soviets had no "policy to bring down retribution upon civilians" any more than did all the other Allies, including the London Polish government. Of course Snyder has no evidence to support his contention — and no responsible historian would make such a serious charge without at least some evidence. In addition, Snyder touches here on a point which he tries to avoid throughout: the fact that Jewish partisans always sided with communist partisans because they had no choice. The Home Army, loyal to the Polish government in exile in London, did not accept Jews in its ranks and normally murdered Jews whenever it could do so.

Partisan warfare was also carried on by the Polish Home Army and Ukrainian Nationalists, to say nothing of General De Gaulle's partisan forces in France. Snyder never makes this statement about the Home Army partisans, who also (sometimes) fought the Germans. Why not?

"Ponomarenko"s Report" — Another Example of Snyder"s Bias

Snyder:

> Red Army officers invited Home Army officers to negotiate in summer 1943, and then murdered them on the way to the rendezvous points. The commander of the Soviet partisan movement believed that the way to deal with the Home Army

was to denounce its men to the Germans, who would then shoot the Poles. (247)

Sources: (n. 51 p. 492):

* Brakel, *Unter Rotem Stern*, 317;

* Gogun, *Stalinskie komandos*, 144.

Let's take a look at this interesting question.

Brakel does claim that at a session of the Central Committee on June 24, 1943 Panteleimon Ponomarenko, First Secretary of the Belorussian Party and head of the partisan movement in Belorussia, ordered that as much information as possible concerning Home Army units be collected and passed to the Germans, who would then presumably liquidate the Home Army partisans.

> Zwei Tage später konkretisierte er [Ponomarenko] auf einer Sitzung des Büros des ZK KP(b) B seine Anweisungen noch, indem er forderte, möglichst viel Informationen über die Einheiten der Heimatarmee zu sammeln und sie (wohl über Mittelmänner) bei den Deutschen zu denunzieren.
>
> - n. 437 Stenogramm der Sitzung des Büros ZK KP(b)B vom 24.6.1943, zit. nach Dokumenty o stosunki, S. 233-245, hier S. 243.

Translated:

> Two days later he [Ponomarenko] concretized his instructions at a meeting of the Bureau of the CC CP(b)B by demanding the collection of as much information about the units of the Home Army and the denunciation of these units (probably through intermediaries) to the Germans.

But Brakel has biased his account by significant omission. Here is the fuller context of Ponomarenko's remarks from the document published in the Polish journal from which Brakel took it:

> Следовательно, с точки зрения предстоящей борьбы с польскими националистическими организациями и польскими соединениями, а она будет при вступлении на территорию

Западной Белоруссии, при чем здесь разумеется очень широка борьба, здесь не исключена возможность, а нужно предвидеть, что польские подпольные боевые организации, для того, чтобы ослабить влияние партизанских отрядов и наших подпольных коммунистических организаций на массы, **они обязательно будут ставить под удар немецких оккупантов наши партизанские отряды и партийные организации.**

Это нужно предвидеть и поэтому сейчас нужно уже в своих указаниях, которые мы будем давать в части конспирации наших партийных организаций, в части контактов со стороны партизанских отрядов с различными представителями польскими, которые приходят для переговоров о совместной борьбе и т.д., а поляки очень умеют вести крепко разведывательную работу и умеют конспирировать свою деятельность, - это нужно иметь в виду. Поэтому параллельна с этой работой нам нужно ориентировать наши партизанские отряды и партийные организации на то, чтобы все эти польские организации, польские соединения, которые создаются, их выявлять и всячески ставить под удар немецких оккупантов. Немцы не постесняются расстрелять, если узнают, что это организаторы польских соединений или других боевых польских организаций.

Но тут нужна организация. Как это сделать? Методами тут не нужно стесняться. На это нужно идти широко, но обставлять нужно таким образом, чтобы это было гладко. Повидимому, прийдется поставить вопрос о разоружении **польсних националистических**

патриотов, разоблачении их, как агентов
Сикорского и предателей польского народа.[17]

Translated:

> Accordingly, from the point of view of the coming
> struggle with the Polish nationalist organizations
> and Polish units, and there will be one upon the en-
> try [of the Red Army] into the territory of Western
> Belorussia — and by this we must understand a
> very broad struggle — here not only is it not impos-
> sible but it is necessary to foresee, in order to
> weaken the influence of our partisan detachments
> and our underground communist organizations up-
> on the masses, **that the Polish underground mili-
> tary organization will expose our partisans and
> party organizations to the German occupiers.**
>
> **We need to anticipate this** and so now it is neces-
> sary in the instructions that we will give in terms of
> the conspiratorial work of our Party organizations,
> in terms of contacts by guerrilla groups with vari-
> ous Polish representatives who arrive for talks con-
> cerning fighting together, etc., and the Poles are
> very skilled in the conduct of intelligence work and
> are able to keep their activities secret — you need
> to keep this in mind. Therefore, in parallel with this
> work, we need to focus our partisan units and party
> organizations to ensure that all of these Polish or-
> ganizations and Polish units that are being created
> should be discovered and exposed in every way to
> the blows of the German occupiers. The Germans
> will not hesitate to shoot them if they find that the-
> se are the organizers of the Polish units or other
> Polish fighting organizations.

---

[17] "Stenogramma zasedaniia biuro TsK KP(b) B of 24 iiunia 1943 goda." In Michal
Gnatowski. "Dokumenty o stosunku radzieckiego kierownictwa do polskiej konspiracji
niepodległościowej na północno—wschodnich kresach rzechypospolitej w latach 1943-
1944." *Studia Podlaskie* (Białystock) V (1995), p. 243.

> But here organization is necessary. How to do it?
> We must not restrict ourselves in the way of meth-
> od. We must take this on broadly, but we must ar-
> range things so that they go smoothly. Evidently we
> will have to raise the question of disarming the
> **Polish nationalist patriots**, of exposing them as
> agents of Sikorski and traitors to the Polish people.
> (Emphasis added)

Brakel is quoting document in a Belarusian archive published by a Polish journal. Several issues with this document should excite our suspicions about it. In the notes immediately before this one Brakel cites another document by Ponomarenko dated June 22, 1943, from a *Russian* archival source. Evidently he could not locate the June 24, 1943 report in question in a Russian archive or the June 22 document in a Belarusian archive.

Another account of this same June 24 meeting records it different-ly:

> 24 июня 1943 года состоялось заседание бюро
> Центрального Комитета Компартии
> Белоруссии. Обсуждался один вопрос — «О
> разрушении железнодорожных коммуникаций».
> С небольшим докладом выступил П. К.
> Пономаренко.
>
> — Задача состоит в том, чтобы за короткий
> период подорвать как можно больше
> железнодорожных путей, — подчеркнул он. —
> Противник вынужден будет проводить
> огромные трудоемкие работы по замене
> рельсов. Потребуется колоссальное количество
> стали, проката, которых у немцев теперь не так
> уж много...
>
> В принятом постановлении отмечалось, что
> железные дороги в Белоруссии почти на всем
> протяжении находятся под контролем
> партизан, а это имеет огромное значение для

срыва оперативных и стратегических замыслов противника.[18]

Translated:

> On June 24, 1943 there took place a meeting of the Central Committee of the Communist Party of Belarus. One question was discussed: "Concerning the destruction of rail communications." P. K. Ponomarenko made a short report.
>
> — The task is to blow up as many railroad lines as possible in a short period of time, - he stressed. The enemy will be forced to carry out huge time-consuming works to replace the rails. That will require an enormous amount of steel and rolling stock, of which the Germans now do not now have very much...
>
> It was noted in the adopted resolution that the railways in Belorussia throughout most of their length are controlled by the guerrillas, and that fact is of great importance for the disruption of the operational and strategic plans of the enemy.

The assertion that there was only one topic discussed at this meeting — the question "Concerning the destruction of rail communications" — is repeated in Vladimir P. Ilin, *Partizany ne zdaiutsia!*[19]

Brakel's source is a Polish collection of supposedly Soviet documents. A more detailed account of this same meeting is widely cited with all citations coming back to the book by Bogdan Musial, *Sowjetische Partisanen in Weißrussland* (Munich, 2004), p. 223. Musial cites a Russian archive but also cites the same Polish source as Brakel.[20]

---

[18] Petr Zakhkarovich Kalinin. *Partizanskaia respublika*. M.: Voenizdat, 1964. Part 3: "Partizanskaia razvedka", p. 292. At
http://militera.lib.ru/memo/russian/kalinin_pz/10.html

[19] Ilin, *Partizany ne zdaiutsia!* (Moscow: Eksmo, 2007) Chapter 3, p. 375. At http://militera.lib.ru/memo/russian/ilin_vp/03.html

[20] An article by Musial translated into Russian from the newspaper *Frankfurter Allgemeine* includes what is supposed to be a quotation from Ponomarenko's directive to pass information about the AK on to the Germans:

Musial has been described as an anti-Semitic writer who strives in his research to blame all Polish anti-Semitism on the fact that Jews were "pro-Soviet" — essentially the Nazi "Judaeo-Bolshevism" argument.[21]

There are a number of points about this document that are relevant to our evaluation of Snyder's book:

First: Is the lengthy account from the Belorussian archive of the June 24, 1943 meeting of the Central Committee of the Communist Party of Belorussia genuine? There are reasons to question its authenticity:

* The two accounts by Kalinin and Ilin claim that there was only one topic discussed at the meeting, and that Ponomarenko's report was short. The *Studia Podlaskie* document quoted by Brakel, which Snyder then cites, is a lengthy document (pages 233-245 in the journal), and Ponomarenko's remarks are part of a discussion, not of a report.

* In this document Ponomarenko calls the Polish underground "patriots." But it is unlikely that the real Ponomarenko would have used the word "patriots" to refer to the anticommunist Polish underground. By this time the Soviets had already formed a pro-Soviet Polish organization and military. The Home Army was attacking and murdering Soviet and Jewish partisans. Ponomarenko

---

> В выборе средств можете не стесняться. Операцию нужно провести это широко и гладко.

Translated:

> We must not restrict ourselves in the way of method. We must take this on broadly, but we must arrange things so that they go smoothly.

These two sentences, but no more of Ponomarenko's directive, are widely reproduced on the Internet. They do not correspond to the text of the document we cite above. Evidently they are a re-translation back into Russian of the German-language passage quoted by Musial himself in *Sowjetische Partisanen*:

> Bei der Wahl der Mittel dürft ihr keine Skrupel haben. Dies muß breit angelegt werden und so, dag es glatt vor sich geht. (223)

Like Brakel Musial does not quote the actual document, much less the context of the quotation.

[21] Joanna B. Michlic. "Anti-Polish and Pro-Soviet? 1939-1941 and the Stereotyping of the Jew in Polish Historiography." *Shared History — Divided Memory. Jews and Others in Soviet-Occupied Poland, 1939-1941*. (Leipzig, 2007), 67-101, at 85 ff.

might well call pro-Soviet Polish partisans "patriots." But how could he also call these hostile, anticommunist forces "patriots"? This ought to awaken the suspicions of any competent historian.

Second: Even if it is genuine Brakel — and, therefore, Snyder — have omitted a number of important facts necessary to evaluate Ponomarenko's statement:

* Ponomarenko claims that the Polish underground will expose the Soviet Party organizations and pro-Soviet partisans to the Germans, and therefore the Soviet forces must plan to do the same thing to the Polish underground. Brakel, like Musial, omits this context.

* Brakel and Snyder know that the Home Army was extremely hostile to communists as well as to Jews. The Polish Government-in-exile in London regarded the Soviets as an enemy just as much as they did the Germans. By February 1943 the massive German defeat at Stalingrad had already taken place, and everyone recognized that Germany would eventually lose the war. The Soviets suspected Polish collaboration with the Germans over the Katyn affair in April, 1943, when the London Poles worked closely with the Germans in a manner that completely undermined any sense of alliance with the Soviet Union. Soviet partisans would have regarded Katyn as a Nazi-Polish government-in-exile provocation, since this was Moscow's position.

With eventual German defeat inevitable and a pro-Soviet Polish leadership and army already set up, by June 1943 it was obvious that the Home Army would begin to fight the Soviets in any way they could. This is the context for Ponomarenko's remarks — assuming they are genuine, and they may not be. By the end of 1943 at the latest some officers of the Home Army were beginning direct military collaboration with the German Army against the Soviets.

Gogun, *Stalinskie komandos*, 144: Snyder gets this all wrong. The page is 145, not 144; the time is not "summer 1943" but November 6, 1943; the Polish nationalists were allegedly shot not before but *after* the meeting took place; and they are not identified as Home Army men.

Blood Lies

Gogun claims that a commander of the guerrilla band of the famous Soviet Ukrainian partisan leader Aleksei Fedorov invited three Polish nationalist commanders to a celebration of the Bolshevik Revolution and then asked them to join the Soviet partisans. The Polish nationalist partisans refused and then left, whereupon the Soviet partisans shot them in the back and hid their bodies.

Did this event happen this way? Snyder did not check. Gogun cites two sources. One is a Polish nationalist history of an Home Army unit to which we do not have access. The other is the diary of the Soviet partisan commander — but this is unpublished, cited from an archive. Moreover, the Soviet commander's diary says only this:

> «Тов. Зубко (заместитель Балицкого. — А. Г.)
> организовал убийство польских националистов
> — заядлые были враги нашей советской
> Родины»

Translated:

> "Comrade Zybko (Balitsky's assistant — A.G.) organized the killing of Polish nationalists — they were inveterate enemies of our Soviet Motherland."

It is Gogun who identifies the event referred to in this statement as the same murder described by a Polish nationalist source, asserting that they are "obviously" the same. But he cites no evidence that this is so. Evidently, neither source describes what took place at the meeting.

Other works on Soviet partisans and on the Home Army note occasions when Home Army forces killed pro-Soviet partisans. For example, there are several such accounts in the collection of essays edited by Bernhard Chiari, *Die Polnische Heimatarmee* in which Snyder himself has an essay. Snyder does not mention them.

Chapter 12. *Bloodlands* Chapter 9: Poland and the Home Army

Snyder"s Falsehoods about the Home Army

Snyder states:

> Like the Polish government, by now in exile in London, the Home Army was to represent all political and social forces in the country. It was to fight for the restoration of Poland within its prewar boundaries, as a democratic republic with equal rights for all citizens. (281)

The reference for this statement, footnote 6, reads as follows:

> 6 On fighting for the restoration of Poland as a democratic republic, see Libionka, "ZWZ-AK," 19, 23, 34. (495)

But the passages in Dariusz Libionka's article "ZWZ-AK" contradict Snyder's statement. On page 19 Libionka quotes "several vague but significant declarations" by General Sikorski "dictated by the need to clearly distance itself from the pre-war Polish policy towards national minorities, which had terrible connotations in Western Europe."[1] But Libionka goes on to say that "[t]hese pronouncements were met with violent resistance from agents in the country" that spoke out strongly about "Jewish treason in the *Kresy*", a "deepening anti-Semitism of Polish society", "criticism of the government's position on national minorities", and so on. The rest of Libionka's paragraph details the strong anti-Semitism of forces in occupied Poland and their opposition to Sikorski's statements.

---

[1] "...kilku ogólnikowych, lecz znaczących deklaracji, podyktowanych potrzebą wyraźnego zdystansowania się od polskiej przedwojennej polityki wobec mniejszości narodowych, mającej fatalne konotacje w Europie Zachodniej."

On page 23 Libionka notes that a member of the Polish exile government issued a declaration about the government's position that
after the war the Jewish minority was to be granted equal rights.
But again it did not speak for the forces in occupied Poland which
were more concerned with "resolving the Jewish question"
through emigration.

On page 34 Libionka quotes statements by Sikorski of January 1
and February 24, 1942 concerning the government's determination to grant equal rights to national minorities, including Jews.
But Libionka shows that these general statements by London government officials were contradicted in the pro-London Polish
press. One publication ("Rzeczpospolita Polska", = "Polish Republic") interpreted the January statement as supporting

> ...[t]he settlement of the Jewish question in a man-
> ner consistent with Christian traditions of Polish
> politics, but at the same time so that it ceased to be
> a factor that makes of us us a crippled nation, se-
> verely suffering due to the fact that the disparity in
> many areas of our economic and cultural life rests
> in the hands of strangers [that is, of Jews].

Another pro-government periodical wrote:

> In Poland the current war, more strongly than any
> other period in our history, has demonstrated the
> alien nature of the Jewish masses for the political
> and historical aspirations of the Polish nation.

The Polish exile government-in-exile adhered to the racist policy
of its predecessor regimes by refusing to call all citizens of Poland
"Poles." It did issue some general statements promising equal
rights for all "inhabitants" of Poland. Perhaps it felt obliged to
make such statements in order to placate the Allies.

Polish Government-in-Exile Plan for Postwar Fas-
cism

Meanwhile the Delegatura, the Polish government inside occupied
Poland, was preparing for a very different post-war policy. The
documents below were quoted by a few scholars during the 1970s

and 1980s, while the pro-Soviet socialist government was still in power. Since then they have been ignored.

> W instrukcji bezpięczeństwa wydanej przez Departament Spraw Wewnętrznych Delegatury przewidywano, iż bezpośrednio po uchwyceniu władzy przez obóz londyński nastąpi, jak określano - "ograniczenie swobód obywatelskich", które postawi poza prawem opozycję. Przygotowany w tym celu projekt Ustawy antykomunistycznej przewidywał uznanie za zbrodnię, karaną śmiercią lub więzieniem nie niższym niż 10 lat, przynależności do organizacji komunistycznych, propagandy komunizmu itp. Za zbrodnie zostały uznane także "(...) wywoływanie strajków, propaganda przeciwko prawu własności, przeciwko .rodzinie, religii, armii, urzędom."

Translated:

> The Security Instructions issued by the Department of Internal Affairs of the Delegatura provided that immediately after the capture of power by the London-based camp will take place, as it is described - "a restriction of civil liberties," which puts the opposition outside the law. The draft of the Anticommunism Act prepared for this purpose provided for recognition as a crime punishable by death or imprisonment of not less than 10 years, membership in Communist organizations, propaganda for communism, etc. Also considered as crimes were "(...) calling strikes, propaganda against the law of property, against family, religion, the military, the authorities [urzędom]."[2]

---

[2] Ryszard Nazarwicz. *Z problematyki politycznej Powstania Warszawskiego 1944*. Warsaw: Wydawn. Ministerstwa Obrony Narodowej, 1985, p. 78. Nazarewicz, *Drogi do wyzwolenia : koncepcje walki z okupantem w Polsce i ich treści polityczne*, 1939-1945.Warsaw: Książka i Wiedza, 1979, p. 379.

432   Blood Lies

A somewhat fuller citation from the same archival document is
found in another book:

> W opracowanej przez „Antyk" „ustawe
> antykomunistycznej" zawarto art. 14, którego § 1
> brzmiał: „Kto w zamiarze obalenia Państwa i
> zburzenia ładu społecznego organizuje związek lub
> stoi na czele związku mającego za cel propaganda
> komunizmu lub anarchizmu, w szczególności przez
> wywoływanie strajków, propagandę przeciwko
> prawa własności, przeciwko rodzinie, religii, armii,
> urzędom podlega karze śmierci lub więzienia do lat
> 10, lub dozywotnio.[3]

Translated:

> In the "Anticommunist Law" developed by "Antyk"
> is article14, § 1, which stated: "Whoever with intent
> to overthrow the state and the destruction of social
> order organizes an association or is the head of an
> association having as a goal the propaganda of
> communism or anarchism, in particular by calling
> strikes, by propaganda against property rights
> against the family, religion, the military, the gov-
> ernment authorities, is punishable by death or im-
> prisonment up to 10 years, or for life.

These documents show that the London government was planning
for a polity that was essentially fascist: a conservative, anticommunist and anti-labor regime similar to the prewar Polish regimes. Homicidal anti-Semitism is not mentioned here but was
carried out during and after the war by the anticommunist Polish
underground.

Therefore, contrary to Snyder's claim, in reality the London Polish
Government in exile and its arm the Home Army never aspired to
"represent all political and social forces." It did not recruit among
Jews and firmly rejected communists. It fought against Jewish and

---

[3] Czesław Żerosławski. *Katolicka myśl o ojczyżnie. Ideowopolityczne komcepcje klerzkalnego podyiemia 1939-1944*. Warzawa: Państwo widawnicnwo naukowe, 1987, 264.

communist partisan units. Moreover, both during and after the war the Polish underground murdered Jews and communists.

The prewar Polish government had vigorously opposed "equal rights for all citizens" and discriminated against all who were not ethnic Poles. It was explicitly anti-Semitic and strongly anticommunist. There is no reason or evidence to suggest that the London Polish government would not be the same, or similar.

Further evidence of the London Poles' lack of interest in democracy: they, and their arm the Home Army, insisted on a Poland "within its prewar boundaries," including Western Belorussia and Western Ukraine. The prewar Polish government had never held plebiscites to ask the Belorussian and Ukrainian majorities whether they "chose" to be in Poland. On the contrary: the Polish governments had discriminated against them and sent "settlers" to "Polonize" these areas.

Snyder Tries to Excuse Home Army Antisemitism

None of the Allied powers supported the restoration of Western Ukraine or Western Belorussia to Poland. Poland never had any legitimate claim to these lands in the first place. Even today's Polish state, the successor to the London Polish government, no longer claims that these lands ought to be returned to Poland.

> Warsaw Home Army commanders had strategic concerns that militated against giving the Jews any weapons at all. Although the Home Army was moving in the direction of partisan action, it feared that a rebellion in the ghetto would provoke a general uprising in the city, which the Germans would crush. The Home Army was not ready for such a fight in late 1942. (284)

There are a number of falsehoods and evasions here. Snyder has just finished assuring his readers that "the Home Army was to represent all political and social forces in the country." But the Jews were Polish citizens. Therefore, Snyder is tacitly admitting that the Home Army was *refusing* to represent its own citizens. It refused because of its racist and anti-Semitic definition of national identity.

In this respect it was the prewar Polish government, the London Poles, and the Home Army who resembled the Nazis. The Soviets and Polish communists did not. The prewar Polish government and its underground partisan arm the Home Army privileged Roman Catholic Poles who were born of Polish-speaking parents above all other citizens of Poland, whether Jewish (not Roman Catholic), Ukrainian, Belorussian, Czech, German, etc.

The Polish government's racist idea of the Polish nation was similar to the Nazis' idea of the German "Volk" (people). It remains so to the present day. The President of Poland's "Instytut Pamięci Narodowej" (Institute of National Memory) swears "to serve faithfully the Polish nation." Leon Kieres, founding president of the IPN, still refers to "fellow citizens of Jewish nationality"[4] — that is, he does not consider Jews a part of the "Polish nation."

Roman Dmowski, a prewar politician and political theorist who promoted the idea that only Roman Catholics can be true Poles and who was an outspoken anti-Semite, is honored by the governments of today's capitalist Poland. Dmowski was a Polish fascist — a "Hitlerite," as the editor of the Polish edition of *Le Monde Diplomatique* has called him.[5] Dmowski was a virulent Polish imperialist who advocated harsh treatment of national minorities. Yet in January 1999 the Polish Sejm (Parliament) passed a resolution honoring Dmowski as an "outstanding Pole."[6]

Snyder:

> Home Army commanders saw a premature uprising as a communist temptation to be avoided. They knew that the Soviets, and thus the Polish communists, were urging the local population to take up arms immediately against the Germans. The So-

[4] Marci Shore, "Conversing with Ghosts: Jedwabne, Zydokomuna, and Totalitarianism." *Kritika: Explorations in Russian and Eurasian History*, 6 (2), Spring 2005 (New Series), p. 362.

[5] Stefan Zgliczyński, „Roman Dmowski — hitlerowiec." December, 2010. At http://monde-diplomatique.pl/LMD58/index.php?id=1_5

[6] "Uchwała Sejmu Rzeczypospolitej Polskiej z dnia 8 stycznia 1999 r o uczczeniu pamięci Romana Dmowskiego" (Resolution of the Polish Sejm of 8 January 1999 to commemorate Roman Dmowski). Text at http://orka.sejm.gov.pl/proc3.nsf/uchwaly/783_u.htm

> viets wanted to provoke partisan warfare in Poland
> in order to weaken the Germans — but also to hin-
> der any future Polish resistance to their own rule
> when it came. The Red Army's task would be easier
> if German troops were killed by partisan warfare, as
> would the NKVD's if Polish elites were killed for re-
> sisting Germans. (284)

This is a particularly odious lie. Snyder suggests that the Soviets encouraged resistance to the Germans because they "wanted" German troops to kill "Polish elites." But he cites no evidence to support this statement — because there isn't any.

Slurs like this are indicative. Snyder evidently wants to find any and all "dirt" he can on Stalin, Soviet policies in Poland, and Polish communists. If he could find any genuine crimes by these parties against Poles or Poland he would certainly include them. Asser-tions of "crimes" that are unsupported by evidence, or — as here — assertions that the Soviets had "bad intentions" (as though Snyder can read minds) expose his failure. Despite his best efforts, Snyder is unable to document *any* Soviet or Polish communist "crimes." But this is an unacceptable result: it is essential to claim that such crimes occurred if one is to curry favor with Polish na-tionalists. Apparently this is the motive behind Snyder's undocu-mented insults such as this one.

> The Jewish Combat Organization included the
> communists, who were following the Soviet line,
> and believed that Poland should be subordinated to
> the Soviet Union. (284)

So what? If, as Snyder claimed on page 281 (see above),

> Like the Polish government, by now in exile in Lon-
> don, the Home Army was to represent all political
> and social forces in the country.

then it should have tried to "represent" both Jews and communists too.

But Snyder does not even cite any evidence that the communists "believed that Poland should be subordinated to the Soviet Union." Moreover, the London Polish government was "subordinate to" first France, then to the U.K. and the Western Allies, without whose support at every step it simply would have ceased to exist.

Snyder's statement is also an evasion — as though "independence," not anticommunism and support for capitalism, was what kept the London Polish government and the Home Army from including communists. A communist Poland would certainly have friendly relations with the USSR. But Snyder cites no evidence that Polish communists "believed" in "subordination" to the Soviet Union.

The London Polish regime, like the Western Allies, wanted a capitalist and anticommunist Poland, which would necessarily mean an anti-Soviet Poland. As for the Soviet Union, it required friendly countries on its borders, as did all of the Western Allies. The USA would never tolerate a hostile Mexico, for example, and has invaded Mexico every time that country threatened to become hostile.

> As the Home Army command could not forget, the Second World War had begun when both the Germans and the Soviets had invaded Poland. Half of Poland had spent half of the war inside the Soviet Union. The Soviets wanted eastern Poland back, and perhaps even more. (284)

Snyder's talk about "eastern Poland," meaning Western Ukraine and Western Belorussia, is dishonest. Both territories had been seized from Soviet Russia by Poland through conquest; Polish speakers were in a minority in both. There was no reason they should not have been taken back by the USSR at the first opportunity. Snyder avoids the whole issue of the Curzon Line and Polish imperialism. He does not wish his audience to remember that *none* of Poland West of the Curzon Line, the line that divided majority Polish territory from majority Ukrainian or Belorussian lands, had been occupied by the Soviets, and none ever would be.

To say "the Soviets wanted eastern Poland back" is not objective. One could just as accurately say "Poland wanted Western Belorussia and Western Ukraine back." Then the question would be obvious: "Why should Poland have them? Why should Poland *ever* have had them?"

> From the perspective of the Home Army, rule by the
> Soviets was little better than rule by the Nazis. Its
> goal was independence. There were hardly any cir-
> cumstances that would seem to justify a Polish in-
> dependence organization arming communists in-
> side Poland. (284)

Snyder's statement here is a devastating criticism of the Home
Army — though Snyder, evidently, does not understand this. The
Nazis considered Poles to be "Untermenschen" (subhumans) and
targeted Poles for extermination — mass murder. The Soviets had
no such racist concepts or genocidal goals. The Soviets did not
commit mass murder against Poles or anybody else. Their desire
was to build a socialist state that would benefit the working people
rather than the traditional elites and that would be friendly to the
USSR, unlike the prewar Polish regime which was as hostile as can
be imagined.

The Soviets helped in rebuilding a socialist Polish state after the
war. The Polish communists organized the reconstruction and carried it out. Would the Nazis have rebuilt a Polish state? The question answers itself.

If the Home Army really did consider "rule by the Soviets" "little
better than rule by the Nazis," that means they cared nothing for
the fate of the majority of Poles as long as the status of the Polish
elite was maintained. This might well be true.

If the Home Army and London Polish government really did strive
to "represent all Poles," as Snyder has claimed, then they should
have armed communists and Jews just as they armed other Poles.
But the London Polish government in exile and the Home Army
were anticommunist and anti-Semitic — just as the Nazis were.

In reality, of course, the Home Army did *not* merely want "independence." The Home Army and the Polish government in exile
were fighting for capitalism and against communism. They were
fighting for Polish imperialism too — to regain Western Ukraine
and Western Belorussia, which they regarded as "theirs" despite
the fact that Poles had never been the majority of the population.

After World War Two "imperialism" becomes a dirty word to most of the world's peoples. Therefore the imperialist countries, Poland included, stop describing their imperialist aims as such and begin describing them as "fighting communism," "fighting for freedom," and so on.

Dariusz Libionka"s Account of Warsaw Ghetto Revolt Contradicts Snyder"s

The note to the five passages from page 284 reproduced above from reads:

> n. 13 (p. 496): Libionka, "ZWZ-AK," 60, 71.

Dariusz Libionka is widely regarded as one of the foremost experts on the subject of Jews in Poland during the war. It is not surprising that Snyder cites him as a source — except for one thing: Libionka's article does not really support what Snyder says. Libionka details the Home Army's almost total indifference to the Jewish fighting groups. Libionka's discussion on these pages documents the lack of interest of the Home Army in Jewish issues and Jewish rebels generally.

In the Appendix to this chapter we have quoted at length, with translations, some of the passages from these two pages of Libionka's so readers may judge for themselves. Some especially striking passages have been boldfaced for the reader's convenience. But all the passages are worth studying, as is the entire article for those who can read Polish.

Snyder then claims that subsequently the Home Army did give much of its own cache of weapons to the Jewish rebels:

> This worked powerfully against the anti-Semitic stereotype, present in the Home Army and in Polish society, that Jews would not fight. Now the Warsaw command of the Home Army gave the Jewish Combat Organization a substantial proportion of its own modest arms cache: guns, ammunition, explosives.[17] (286)

Sources: (n. 17 p. 496):

> * "On the arms cache, see Libionka, "ZWZ-AK," 69";

* "...and Moczarski, *Rozmowy*, 232."

* "On the anti-Semitic minority, see Engelking, *Żydzi*, 193, and passim."

Kazimierz **Moczarski**, *Rozmowy z katem*, is a book about the author's imprisonment with Jürgen Stroop, the German and fanatical Nazi who who commanded the destruction of the Warsaw Ghetto and murder of thousands of its Jewish citizens.

There is nothing on page 69 of Libionka's long article, cited here by Snyder, about the Polish government or Home Army giving any arms to the Jews. In the Appendix to this chapter we also quote much of Libionka's page 70, where discussion of the arms question is continued. These passages make clear that Libionka does not believe that the Home Army sent the Jewish forces any significant arms.

Yet this is the very source Snyder cites! Why? We suspect that very few of Snyder's readers will bother to obtain Libionka's article, written in Polish in a journal that is not easy to find and check to see whether Libionka's research does in fact support what Snyder says. Meanwhile, Snyder can appear as though he is citing one of the most respected authorities on the subject in favor of his conclusions.

Engelking, *Żydzi* 193 recounts an aborted attempt by a Home Army man to shoot unarmed Jews found hiding in a cellar simply because they were Jews. There are indeed many examples of Home Army men murdering Jews.

Snyder Claims the Home Army Aided the Warsaw Ghetto Rebels

> Among the western Allies, only Polish authorities took direct action to halt the killing of Jews. By spring 1943 Żegota[7] was assisting about four thousand Jews in hiding. The Home Army announced that it would shoot Poles who blackmailed Jews. On

---

[7] Żegota was an organization set up by the Polish Government-in-Exile in London to rescue Jews from the Germans.

4 May, as the Jews of the Warsaw ghetto fought on,
Prime Minister Władysław Sikorski issued an appeal: "I call on my countrymen to give all help and
shelter to those being murdered, and at the same
time, before all humanity, which has for too long
been silent, I condemn these crimes." As Jews and
Poles alike understood, the Warsaw command of
the Home Army could not have saved the ghetto,
even if it had devoted all of its troops and weapons
to that purpose. It had, at that point, almost no
combat experience itself. Nevertheless, seven of the
first eight armed operations carried out by the
Home Army in Warsaw were in support of the ghetto fighters. Two Poles died at the very beginning of
the Warsaw Ghetto Uprising, trying to breach the
ghetto walls. Several further attempts to breach the
walls of the ghetto failed. All in all, the Home Army
made some eleven attempts to help the Jews.[29]
(291)

Source: (n. 29 p. 496):

* "Quotation: Engelking, *Warsaw Ghetto*, 795."

* "On the eleven attempts to help Jews, see Engelking, *Getto warszawskie*, 745;

* "... and Libionka, "ZWZ-AK," 79.

None of Snyder's sources identify any Home Army announcement about "shooting Poles who blackmailed Jews." The reference in **Engelking**[8] to the "eleven attempts" is as follows:

According to Strzembosz, acts of armed assistance
to the ghetto, which included about eleven documented stories, "were usually restricted to attacking individual posts or gun emplacements." Did
[they] constitute real help for the Jewish fighters
who were defending themselves for four weeks?

---

[8] Here I quote from the English edition of Engelking, p. 792, rather than from the much harder-to-find Polish edition. Oddly, Snyder also refers to the English edition in this same footnote!

Engelking clearly believes this Home Army "support" was symbolic only.

The passages from **Libionka**'s essay quoted in the Appendix show that the Home Army was indeed "reluctant" to arm the ghetto fighters and in fact provided very few arms. More evidence of this reluctance is seen in the quotations from pages 79-80 of Libionka's work that are reproduced in the Appendix to this chapter. Libionka, Snyder's source, says that Home Army actions to help the Warsaw Ghetto revolt were very weak. Libionka also states communist groups did take part in helping the Revolt, though he does not specify precisely what they did.

Joshua D. Zimmerman, a source that Snyder cites, but not here, is equally negative about the Home Army's attitude towards helping the Warsaw Ghetto rebels.

> Rather it was "not possible," Komorowski wrote, to extend "extensive aid" to Jews for the following reasons:
>
> > 1. The population treats Jews as a foreign element and in many cases as being inimical to Poland which was documented by their actions during the Soviet occupation...
> >
> > 2. Large numbers of armed Jews are brigands or members of communist groups which plague the nation. Jews who are members of these groups have displayed extreme cruelty to Poles.
> >
> > 3. Societal opinion as well as the rank and file of the underground would not be amenable to greater assistance to Jews as they would see this as a depletion of their own resources...[9]

Following the Polish nationalist position Snyder tries to depict Home Army support for the Warsaw Ghetto rebels in a positive light. But the evidence he himself cites reinforces the view that the

---

[9] Joshua D. Zimmerman, "The Attitude of the Polish Home Army (AK) to the Jewish Question during the Holocaust: the Case of the Warsaw Ghetto Uprising." In *Varieties of Antisemitism. History, Ideology, Discourse.* Eds. Murray Baumgarten, Peter Kenez, and Bruce Thompson. Newark: University of Delaware Press, 2009, 109-126; at 121.

Polish government in exile and Home Army were rife with anti-Semitism and wished to do as little as possible to help the Uprising. And, as we have seen before, the Polish government in exile and Home Army did not consider Polish Jews to be Poles.

As for the quotation of **Engelking** — it is on pages 794-5 — it is taken from the account by Iranek-Osmecki. Sikorski may well have said it. But it was hypocrisy, as forces loyal to the Polish government in exile in London continued to murder Jews in large numbers and with complete impunity. Iranek-Osmecki is an apologetic source, a command officer of the Home Army in occupied Poland and one of those responsible for starting the disastrous Warsaw Uprising in July 1944 without coordination with the Red Army.

Snyder admits the Anti-Semitism of the Home Army:

> Some Jews did survive the ghetto uprising, but found a hard welcome beyond the ghetto. In 1943 the Home Army was even more concerned about communism than it had been in 1942. As a result of an arrest and a plane crash in summer 1943, a more sympathetic Polish commander and prime minister were replaced by less sympathetic ones. Despite its promises to do so, the Home Army never organized a Jewish unit from veterans of the Warsaw Ghetto Uprising. Over the course of 1943, units of the Home Army sometimes shot armed Jews in the countryside as bandits. In a few cases, Home Army soldiers killed Jews in order to steal their property.

Here Snyder begins, correctly, to relate the Home Army's anti-Semitism to its anticommunism. Polish nationalists, like other right-wing nationalists in the Baltics, Ukraine, Hungary, Rumania, and elsewhere, had a concept of "Jew-communism" (*żydokomuna*) virtually identical to that of the Nazis.[10]

---

[10] See the useful Polish-language Wikipedia page on this topic at http://pl.wikipedia.org/wiki/Żydokomuna The English-language page has been extensively written up in a highly apologetic and anticommunist manner. (Accessed 06.19.2013)

Snyder greatly understates the extent of Home Army anti-Semitism. He does not use the term "anti-Semitism" with respect to the Home Army. Instead he suggests that Home Army discrimination against Jews was a reflection only of their anticommunism. In anticommunist historiography it is considered illegitimate to be anti-Semitic, but essential to be anticommunist. Later in this book we will present evidence of the truly shocking extent of anti-Semitism in the Polish underground forces including the Home Army.

Then, as though to mitigate these unpleasant truths, Snyder adds:

> On the other hand, the Home Army did execute Poles who turned in Jews or tried to blackmail them.[33] (292-3)

> n.33 -See Zimmerman, "Attitude," 120; and Libionka, "ZWZ-AK," 119-123.

This is not true. The very source Snyder cites, Dariusz **Libionka**'s article, documents a number of incidents of Home Army murders of Jews and communists. But it does not document a single execution of a Pole because he murdered Jews or the punishment of any Poles because he had blackmailed Jews.

Concerning Home Army commander codenamed "Orzel" (= eagle) Libionka states that he was put on trial and shot, but Libionka states clearly that this was **not only** for his actions against the Jewish partisans:

> W czerwcu 1944 r. "Orzeł" został rozstrzelany z
> wyroku Wojskowego Sądu Specjalnego, lecz
> powodem była **nie tylko** likwidacja oddziału ŻOB.
> („ZWZ-AK", 121)

Translated:

> In June 1944, "Orzeł " was shot by sentence of a
> Special Military Court, but **not solely** for the elimi-
> nation of the Jewish Fighting Organization branch.
> (Emphasis added.)

Zimmerman, "Attitude," 120 does not support Snyder's statements in the least. Zimmerman documents Home Army commander Komorowski's relentlessly anti-Semitic attitude during the war, including towards Jewish partisans. Zimmerman points out that

Komorowski claimed the Home Army had provided only "limited supplies" to the Jews because, in his estimate, the Polish population regarded Jews as "a foreign element" (these were Polish citizens!), liable to be pro-communist, and the Home Army underground did not want to share their supplies.

Back to the Same Old Lie of Soviet "Invasion" and "Alliance with Hitler"

> Although their British and American allies could afford to have illusions about Stalin, Polish officers and politicians could not. They had not forgotten that the Soviet Union had been an ally of Nazi Germany in 1939-1941, and that its occupation of eastern Poland had been ruthless and oppressive. (297)

Snyder repeats the same lie again. The Soviet Union was never an "ally of Nazi Germany." The British and Americans knew this very well — they had accepted the USSR's claim of neutrality in the German-Polish war of September 1939. It may have been the "position" of the Polish government-in-exile that the USSR had been an "ally" of Hitler's, but the rest of the world knew better.

Snyder Ignores Oppression by the Polish Government

Poland's own occupation of Western Ukraine and Western Belorussia had been both "ruthless and oppressive" to Ukrainians, Belorussians, and Jews, who did not enjoy the same civil liberties and rights as did Poles. Poland also oppressed communists, who likewise did not have civil rights in Poland.

In a response to one of Snyder's articles Jeffrey Burds outlines something Snyder left out: Polish government terror against Ukrainians in pre-war Western Ukraine:

> Alexander Motyl has described the roots of Ukrainian violent opposition to Polish rule.[3] But the brutality of ethnic Poles towards ethnic Ukrainians is rarely discussed outside of tendentious nationalist accounts. The most widespread and intense vio-

lence took place in the anti-Ukrainian pogroms of 1934-1938. For this, alas, we do not need to rely on Polish or Ukrainian accounts alone. Monsignor Dr. Philippe Cortesi, the Papal Nuncio in Warsaw, condemned the violence in a private letter to the Polish Minister of Internal Affairs regarding just one such event of 2-3 November 1938. Polish members of the 'En-De' ('National Democracy', a militant Polish patriotic-nationalist organization) attacked Ukrainian students in their dormitories in Warsaw, unhindered by Polish police who stood by watching the brutal violence, and who waited until the end of the riots to arrest Ukrainian students for disturbing the peace. Several Ukrainian institutes were attacked, with the subsequent "destruction of everything that falls into the hands of the aggressors." A Ukrainian shop was destroyed when Polish "nationalist fanatics" set fire to the interior and then hurled a screaming young Ukrainian woman into the flames. The worst violence occurred at the Ukrainian Catholic seminary, located a mere 200 meters from the central office of the Polish state police. In the Polish crowd's iconoclastic rage, irreparable damage was done to the interior of the Ukrainian church, where icons were defiled and a priceless portrait of St. Peter destroyed. The seminary was ravaged as the angry Polish crowd systematically broke apart furniture and hurled the pieces through broken windows to the streets below. In all, at least eight Ukrainians were hospitalized with serious injuries, and two were killed. Consistent with its usual policy, the official Polish press remained mysteriously silent about such incidents. And wherever possible, the Polish police confiscated and suppressed Ukrainian underground newspapers and publications where the incidents were discussed.[11]

---

[11] Jeffrey Burds, "Comment on Timothy Snyder's article...," At

Evidently it is inconsistent with Snyder's aim — which is to portray Polish nationalists as "victims" and yoke the Soviets with the Nazis — to honestly point out the truth: *It was the Polish nationalists who had a great deal in common with the Nazis*, who were similarly racist German nationalists. The Soviet state was proudly internationalist and favored ordinary working people over "elites."

There was no "Eastern Poland" to occupy. Poland had ceased to exist. This happened entirely because of the Polish government. They had rejected collective security and then abandoned their country, leaving it without a government.

> The Soviet Union never had any intention of supporting any institution that claimed to represent an independent Poland. (299)

Here Snyder tacitly assumes that only a capitalist Poland, no matter how anticommunist, racist, anti-working class and undemocratic, could be "independent," while a communist Poland could somehow not be "independent." This linguistic deception simply reveals his anticommunist bias.

The United States has never tolerated a country anywhere near its borders that was not "closely assigned" to it. Canada and Mexico are both "closely aligned" with the United States today yet they are regarded as "independent." Therefore this is less a question of independence than of who was going to hold state power in independent Poland after the war.

> The Soviet leadership and the NKVD treated every Polish political organization (except the communists) as part of an anti-Soviet plot.[45] (299)
>
> n. 45 — *Operatsia "Seim,"* 5 and passim.

Snyder fails to tell his readers that "Operatsia 'Seim'" was aimed only against the Polish political underground *inside the USSR*. Operation "Seim" was the NKVD program to uproot underground nationalist Polish political parties — but only those in the Western Ukraine, Belorussia, and the Vil'no oblast'. These were the areas incorporated into the Soviet Union (in the case of the Vil'no oblast', into Lithuania) in 1939, and were part of the Soviet Union. The document on page 5 cited by Snyder specifies precisely this: a campaign to identify Polish nationalist organizations in these areas of the USSR and infiltrate "anti-Soviet formations" (14). The interested reader may find the document at page 5-14 of *Operatsia "Seim"* on the Internet.[12]

It would have been more accurate to say that the London Polish government and the Home Army treated every Jewish and communist-oriented political organization as part of a plot against them! In fact the Polish Socialist party and other such parties were courted by the communists during and after the war.

> Indeed, in some cases Soviet partisans were turned
> against the Polish fighters. The partisan unit of Tu-
> via Bielski, for example, took part in the disarming
> of the Home Army. (299)

Snyder is being dishonest here by implying there was something wrong in disarming the Home Army. In fact it was the London Polish government itself that ordered the Home Army to disband and give its arms to the Red Army. Moreover, the Home Army was intensely hostile to the Red Army.

The Home Army was highly anticommunist and anti-Semitic and often murdered Jews and communists. The prewar Polish government had not even considered communists and Jews to be Poles. The sources that Snyder himself uses — Chiari and Libionka — document this. In contrast to the murderous anti-Semitism of the Home Army the Soviet partisan leaders combatted anti-Semitism. Siding with them was the only sensible thing for Jewish partisans to do.

Snyder knows, but conceals from his readers, that the Home Army conspired with the German army against Soviet partisans and against the Red Army. German historian Bernhard Chiari has written about this in a volume on the "Myth of the Home Army" in which Snyder himself also has an article.[13]

---

[12] At http://msuweb.montclair.edu/~furrg/research/operatsia_seim05-14.pdf

[13] Bernhard Chiari, "Kriegslist oder Bündnis mit dem Feind? Deutsch-Polnische Kontakte 1943-44." In *Die Polnische Heimatarmee. Geschichte und Mythos der Armia Krajowa seit dem*

The Warsaw Uprising: What Really Happened

On July 31, 1944 General Komorowski, commander of the Home Army loyal to the Polish Government In Exile (GIE) in England, gave the order for an uprising in Warsaw against the German occupying forces. The Warsaw Uprising of August 1 to October 2 1944 was a disastrous defeat for the hugely outgunned and, in the end, outnumbered partisan forces in the city. At least 17,000 insurgents were killed, while the Germans and their allied forces killed about 200,000 civilian residents of Warsaw and destroyed 60% of the buildings in the city.

The uprising was directly militarily against the Germans, but politically against the Soviet Union and especially the Polish forces allied with the Red Army: the Polish Army (Wojsko Polskie) and the People's Army (Armia Ludowa). The Uprising was a part of the Polish GIE's "Operation Storm" (*Burza*). This plan was designed to try to seize power in Polish towns once the Red Army crossed into Western Belorussia and Western Ukraine. Poland had seized these regions by conquest from Soviet Russia in 1921 and they had been retaken in 1939 after Poland's defeat and merged into the Belorussian and Ukrainian Republics of the USSR. The Polish GIE continued to insist that these lands were part of Poland until the early 1990s.

Operation Storm was designed to present the Soviet government with the necessity of either recognizing the Polish GIE or of having to arrest its authorized representatives, thus admitting that it was a conqueror, not a liberator. The plan was for Home Army forces in the towns to wait until the Red Army was on the point of liberating a town from the Germans. In the interval between the German troops' withdrawal and the arrival of the Red Army the Home Army was to occupy the government buildings. When the Red Army arrived the Home Army was to greet them as the lawful government and representatives of the GIE. When the Red Army removed them from office and replaced them with their own Polish forces the Home Army was to inform the GIE which would then make a

Zweiten Weltkrieg. Munich: R. Oldenbourg Vlg, 2003, 497-527. Snyder's article is on pp. 549-561.

formal protest to the Allies. The Allies would then, supposedly, make a protest to the Soviet government.

Operation Storm did not work as planned in those cities where the Home Army did manage to time its exit from the underground precisely enough to seize the government buildings without too much fighting against superior German forces and before the Red Army arrives. In these cases the Allies showed no interest in disturbing their relations with the Red Army, which was taking huge casualties and bearing by far the brunt of the war against the fascists. In the case of Warsaw, the Normandy landing had occurred on June 6, 1944 and the Western Allies faced hard fighting.

General Komorowski, Home Army commander in Warsaw, was authorized by the GIE to declare an uprising at a time of his choice. The plan was still to wait until the Soviet forces were on the point of entering Warsaw and the German forces on the point of leaving it, and then seize power. Taking power in Warsaw would be of symbolic importance as it was the capital of Poland.

On July 31 Komorowski and his staff were mistakenly informed that Soviet tanks were on the point of crossing the Vistula and entering Warsaw. Komorowski gave the order for the uprising to begin at 5 p.m. on August 1. On the same day Col. Iranek-Osmecki, head of intelligence, told the staff that this information was false and suggested the uprising be called off. Komorowski refused. This decision ignited the chain of events that ended in the defeat of the Uprising and the destruction of Warsaw, called by many Poles at the time a "crime" and a "disaster."

No one ever thought that the Home Army and other partisan forces in Warsaw would be able to defeat the German and allied forces there. These included, at various times, part or all of five tank divisions, one of them an SS division, the German 9th Army, a company of the 29th SS grenadier division, the "Sonderkommando" Dirlewanger, infamous for its savagery against civilians, and a number of Cossack and other forces recruited from anticommunists within the USSR. These forces were supported by Stuka dive bombers and Messerschmitt fighters.

The only chance for success for the Uprising was to count on the Red Army's defeating the German forces and driving them out of the city. Then, with a minimum of fighting against retreating troops, the Home Army hoped to take control of Warsaw and present the Red Army with a *fait accompli.*

Given the hostility to the USSR on the part of the GIE and its representatives in Poland, the Soviet government could not be blamed if it did indeed stand by and let the German forces slaughter the Home Army. This is in fact what some anticommunist Polish writers and politicians have alleged ever since. But others equally anticommunist, and virtually all who are not, plus the Soviet government, Red Army commanders, and even the anticommunist Russian government today, reject this charge. More important, there is no evidence at all that the Red Army acted in this way. Like its inception, the defeat of the Warsaw Uprising was purely the responsibility of the GIE and the Home Army leadership.

The Home Army leadership started the "blame game", pointing fingers at others, during the Uprising itself. At first they tried to blame the British. Subsequently they decided it was all the Soviets' fault — despite the fact that the Uprising was supposed to be directed against the Soviets in the first place. One person Komorowski never blamed was himself. But a great many other Poles, including anticommunists and his own Home Army members, blamed him and continue to do so.

During the first two weeks of the Uprising the British sent aircraft from Italy to try to drop supplies to the Home Army forces in Warsaw. At first Stalin refused to have anything to do with the Uprising, even preventing the British airplanes from landing at Soviet airports for refueling. Stalin's position was that the Uprising was a crime because it had been undertaken without any coordination with the Red Army, which was the only way it could have been successful. Nevertheless, after pressure from the British Stalin started Soviet supply flights. British, American, and Soviet flights dropped many tons of supplies, though it appears that most either fell into German hands or were destroyed by being dropped from too high an altitude. In any case such drops were symbolic only. No amount of air drops could enable poorly-armed and largely civilian partisans to defeat heavily-armed, trained, and utterly ruthless German forces.

Post-1990 anticommunist Polish governments and scholars vacillate on the question of blaming Stalin for not coming to rescue the Uprising. This is impossible to prove for lack of evidence, though some researchers continue to make the attempt. Komorowski and the GIE leaders are honored as heroes on the grounds that the Uprising was necessary because it was a "fight for independence" that had to be attempted whatever the cost. "Independent" is a deliberate obfuscation, a code word for "anticommunist", anticommunists generally holding that being pro-Soviet means lacking independence while being pro-British — indeed, wholly dependent upon the British — and pro-capitalist is the only way to "independence."

Snyder"s Falsifications about the Warsaw Uprising

Snyder claims:

> Almost certainly, more Jews fought in the Warsaw
> Uprising of August 1944 than in the Warsaw Ghetto
> Uprising of April 1943.[50] (302)

Sources: (n. 50 p. 497):

* Engelking, *Żydzi*, 91 for Zylberberg, and passim;

* National Armed Forces[14] at 62, 86, 143.

Engelking's book at pages 91-2 does quote from Michael Zylberberg's *A Warsaw Diary, 1939- 1945.* But Zylberberg also makes it clear that these were Jews with Polish surnames. Zylberberg fought under his assumed name of Jan Zielinski (p. 92). **Libionka** records that in the communist-led "People's Army" (Armija Ludowa) Jews could fight under their Jewish names:

> Warto zwrócić też uwagę na to, że Żydzi, którzy
> walczyli w strukturach AL nie musieli się już dłużej
> ukrywać, mogli się czuć bezpiecznie, powrócić do
> własnego nazwiska.[15]

Translated:

---

[14] There is no entry in Snyder's bibliography for "National Armed Forces." Snyder cites it only twice, in notes 50 and 51, page 497. The NSZ was an especially racist and murderous group in the Polish underground. It is now officially honored in Poland; see Zgliczyński, *Jak Polaci* 10, n. 4.

[15] From the review by Kasia Przyborska in the Appendix to this chapter.

> It is also interesting to turn one's attention to the
> fact that Jews who fought in the structures of the AL
> did not have to hide anymore, could feel themselves
> safe, return to their own surnames.

Here's what Snyder wrote in a *New York Review of Books* review of
June 24, 2009:

> Indeed, it is quite possible that more people of Jew-
> ish origin took part in the Warsaw Uprising of 1944
> than in the Ghetto Uprising of 1943. (Emphasis
> added)

Evidently Snyder has no evidence that "most of these Jews joined
the Home Army" — *but those who did felt that they had to hide the
fact that they were Jews.* As Libionka points out it was the communist-led People's Army, or Armia Ludowa, not the anticommunist Home Army, or Armia Krajowa, that accepted the Jewish
fighting group into its ranks. Snyder obviously knows this but
hides it from his readers.

Snyder Blames the Soviets for the Warsaw Uprising Disaster and Exonerates Those Really Responsible

Snyder states:

> From the Soviet perspective, an uprising in Warsaw
> was desirable because it would kill Germans — and
> Poles who were willing to risk their lives for inde-
> pendence. The Germans would do the necessary
> work of destroying the remnants of the Polish intel-
> ligentsia and the soldiers of the Home Army, groups
> that overlapped. (306)

This is a shameful fabrication by Snyder. Stalin and Soviet generals
said over and over again that the uprising, uncoordinated with the
Red Army, was highly undesirable. Snyder has no evidence to the
contrary.

> As soon as the Home Army soldiers took up arms,
> Stalin called them adventurers and criminals. (306)

This too is a falsehood. Stalin did not call the "Home Army soldiers" any such thing, so of course Snyder does not cite any evidence for this assertion. Stalin did refer in similar terms to the *leaders* of the Uprising, the Polish commanders who had begun it.

Moreover, it was not only Stalin — General Wladyslaw Anders thought the Uprising was a "crime":

> Generał Władysław Anders uważał powstanie warszawskie za kardynalny błąd z politycznego i wojskowego punktu widzenia, a z moralnego za zbrodnię, za którą odpowiedzialność ponosili jego zdaniem dowódca Armii Krajowej gen. Tadeusz Bór-Komorowski i jego sztab.[16]

Translated:

> General Wladyslaw Anders considered the Warsaw uprising as a cardinal mistake from a political and military point of view, and from the moral point of view a crime, for which, in his opinion, commander of the Army General Tadeusz Bor-Komorowski and his staff bore the responsibility.

This was widely known at the time as well, as recorded in the following source from 1948:

> Znane jest powiedzenie ANDERSA o powstańcach warszawskich „Niech giną, kiedy głupi."[17]

Translated:

> Anders' statement about the Warsaw rebels is well known: "Let them die, since they are stupid."

If Snyder's readers knew that General Anders and other anticommunist Poles thought the Warsaw Uprising was "criminal," Stalin's agreeing with him would not ring the anticommunist tone that Snyder desires. So he does not tell his readers.

Snyder does admit that:

---

[16] Jan M. Ciechanowski. "Nie tylko głupota, ale zbrodnia" ("Not only stupidity, but a crime"). *Przegląd Tygodnik* 30 (2010). At http://www.przeglad-tygodnik.pl/pl/artykul/nie-tylko-glupota-ale-zbrodnia As we discuss below6 this is Ciechanowski's own view as well..

[17] *Obóz reakcji Polskiej w latach 1939-1945.* (Warszawa, Maj 1948 r.), 118.

> Given German anti-partisan tactics, an uprising
> looked like suicide to many. The Germans had been
> killing Poles in massive reprisals throughout the
> war; if an uprising failed, reasoned some com-
> manders in Warsaw, the entire civilian population
> would suffer. (300, emphasis added.)

But Snyder vastly understates the matter. The Uprising was far worse than "suicide." Suicide means killing only oneself. The Uprising entailed the killing of several hundred thousand citizens of Warsaw and the destruction of much of the city. As Snyder admits, this was predictable in advance. Yet the Home Army leadership went ahead anyway! No wonder, then, that like Stalin, General Anders called it a crime against Poland.

Anders was not alone in condemning the Warsaw Uprising as a crime. Jan M. Ciechanowski, an anticommunist and historian at both British and Polish universities and, at the age of 14 years, a fighter in the Uprising, has long condemned the Uprising. Here, at the end of an article where his views are briefly summarized, Ciechanowski's conclusion is given:

> Ciechanowski zgadza się z oceną Władysława
> Andersa, który wybuch powstania określił jako
> "nieszczęście" i "zbrodnię."[18]

Translated:

> Ciechanowski agrees with the assessment of An-
> ders, who described the uprising as a "disaster" and
> "crime."

In his own book *Powstanie Warszawskie*, which has had many editions in both English and Polish, Ciechanowski writes that this "criminal" act was undertaken *because it was directed politically against the Soviets*:

> Within a few hours of learning of it Gen Anders in-
> formed his superiors in London that he considered
> it to be 'a misfortune'. Some days later he stated

---

[18] "Prof. Jan Ciechanowski: Powstanie Warszawskie było klęską i błędem." Dzieje.pl 07.24.09 - http://dzieje.pl/aktualnosci/prof-jan-ciechanowski-powstanie-warszawskie-bylo-kleska-i-bledem

that he and his soldiers regarded the order for the rising as 'a serious crime'. In his considered opinion the capital was 'doomed to be annihilated' in spite of 'the heroism, unparalleled in history' of the insurgents. The General was certain that the insurrection had not a 'half-chance' of success. He saw it as 'a madness', a 'flagrant crime'.

On 13 August Mikolajczyk sent a telegram to Stalin imploring him, in the name of the future of Russo-Polish relations, to save Warsaw from destruction, by ordering the Red Army to enter the capital of Poland as its 'liberators' rather than as grave-diggers 'to bury the dead in a destroyed city'. Five days later the Polish Premier sent another telegram to Moscow, in which he said that the insurrection seemed premature and that the Soviet High Command could not be held responsible for it. ...[19]

Not only were the highest Polish authorities abroad fully aware, from the beginning of the insurrection, that it had been ill-timed, but in Warsaw itself, a number of high-ranking Home Army officers also regarded the insurrection as premature. Col Bokszczanin wrote in 1965 that he had always considered Bor-Komorowski's decision of 31 July 1944 'as unjustified and premature'. (263)

We can only conclude that the Underground leaders' decision to try to capture Warsaw was dictated more by a desire to forestall occupation of the city by the Russians than by a wish to render unqualified support to the Red Army, as the Soviet appeals requested.

The Warsaw rising was to be the means by which the pro-London Poles were to assume power, initially in the capital and then in the whole of newly-

---

[19] Jan M. Ciechanowski, *The Warsaw Rising of 1944*. London: Cambridge University Press, 1974), p. 262.

> liberated Poland. **The pro-London leaders in-
> tended to forestall, with their rising, the as-
> sumption of power by the Russian-supported
> Polish Communists**.... (266) (Emphasis added, GF)

All these facts are openly discussed in Poland. Snyder's account foregrounds and whitewashes the right-wing nationalist perspective while ignoring all the others.

Snyder has several times condemned the Soviets and communist partisans for being the cause of German reprisals against civilians. This is dishonest of him since, if made at all this criticism should be leveled at all partisan activity, including that of the Home Army and the Western Allies.

All other German reprisals against all civilians for all partisan activities in all German-occupied countries would not the number of Poles the Germans murdered as a reprisal for the Warsaw Uprising. Yet Snyder utters no word of blame!

Did the USSR Prosecute Poles Who Resisted Hitler?

> Later on, when the Soviet Union gained control of
> Poland, resistance to Hitler would be prosecuted as
> a crime, on the logic that armed action not con-
> trolled by the communists undermined the com-
> munists, and that communism was the only legiti-
> mate regime for Poland. (306)

If they did so, it should be easy to find evidence of the fact. But Snyder gives no evidence, not even a citation, in support of his claim that the communists "prosecuted resistance to Hitler as a crime."

> In mid-September, when it could make absolutely
> no difference to the outcome in Warsaw, he [Stalin]
> finally allowed American bombing runs and carried
> out a few of his own. (307)

It is absurd to suggest that any amount of supply drops could *ever* have "made any difference." The reason many Poles considered the Warsaw Uprising a "crime" is precisely because it could not possibly succeed and would obviously result in an unprecedented massacre of Polish civilians and the destruction of the city itself.

The dropping of supplies could never have been decisive. There was no way that the poorly-armed Polish rebels could stand against 20,000 German troops. The Soviets dropped a great many supplies — by some estimates, more than the British did. But both British and Soviet supplies fell mostly into German-occupied areas.

The crime was the Uprising itself. The Warsaw Uprising led to many thousands of rebels being killed. That is a huge number of casualties of brave people. But as many as 200,000 Polish civilians were also killed by the Germans, and most of the city destroyed. The overwhelming majority of these casualties could have been avoided if the Home Army had coordinated their uprising with the Red Army.

But that was precisely what the anticommunist Home Army *refused* to do. The whole purpose of the Warsaw Uprising was to seize power in the city *after the Red Army had forced the Wehrmacht to begin abandoning* it, and then present the Red Army with a "fait accompli" — the Home Army in charge of the city. This would, supposedly, have given the London Polish government leverage with which to demand that the Western Allies support their claim to be the legitimate government in Warsaw and, therefore, in Poland as a whole.

After the Germans, it is the Home Army leadership itself that must bear responsibility for the disaster of the Warsaw Uprising. Many Poles, including Polish commanders in the Home Army, thought the Uprising not only had no chance of success, but was a "crime." Stalin thought so too, and acted accordingly.

Snyder wants it "both ways." He agrees, with the majority of historians, that "the Red Army had been halted, by unexpectedly strong German resistance, just beyond Warsaw." (305) But Snyder cannot resist an attempt to blame the Soviets for the crime of the Uprising. So he says:

> It made perfect Stalinist sense to encourage an uprising, and then not to assist one. Right to the last moment, Soviet propaganda had called for an upris-

> ing in Warsaw, promising Soviet assistance. The up-
> rising came, but the help did not. (305)

This is false and absurd to boot. First, there is no evidence for Snyder's statement. Second, anyone who might heed such a call from the Soviets would certainly coordinate it with the Red Army's advance. Third, the last person on earth that Home Army commanders would have heeded was Stalin!

> While the Red Army hesitated just east of the Vistu-
> la River from early August 1944 through mid-
> January 1945, the Germans were killing the Jews to
> its west. During those five months, the Red Army
> was less than a hundred kilometers from Łódź, by
> this point the largest concentration of Jews left in
> occupied Poland, and less than a hundred kilome-
> ters from Auschwitz, where Polish and European
> Jews were still being gassed. The Red Army's halt at
> the Vistula doomed not only the Polish fighters and
> the civilians of Warsaw but also the Jews of Łódź.
> (310)

But Snyder himself has already stated that the Red Army did not "hesitate" but was "halted by unexpected strong German resistance!" (305) It was not this "halt" that "doomed the Polish fighters" — it was the refusal of the Home Army commanders to coordinate the uprising with the Red Army that doomed them, and 150,000 — 200,000 Polish civilians.

Had the Home Army coordinated its activity with the Red Army it could have put all its efforts into preventing the Germans from blowing up the bridges across the Vistula and greatly facilitated the Red Army's advance from the east bank into Warsaw. The Home Army commanders' refusal to work with the Red Army guaranteed the murder of 200,000 inhabitants of Warsaw, the destruction of most of the city, *and* the deaths of the Jews of Łódź!

It is particularly foul of Snyder to blame the Red Army for the deaths of Jews murdered by the Nazis when the Red Army liberated more Jews, and more concentration and death camps, than all the other Allied forces.

Did the NKVD Shoot Poles Just Like the Germans Had?

When Soviet soldiers finally crossed the Vistula and advanced into the ruins of Warsaw on 17 January 1945, they found very few buildings still standing. The site of Concentration Camp Warsaw, however, was still available. The Soviet NKVD took over its facilities, and used them for familiar purposes. Home Army soldiers were interrogated and shot there by the Soviets in 1945, as they had been by the Germans in 1944.[70] (311; emphasis added GF)

Source:

n. 70 - Kopka, *Warschau*, 51, 116.

It is instructive to follow out the chain of evidence, which Snyder certainly did not bother to do. Snyder's source, Kopka, *Konzentrationslager Warschau* (2007), page 51, simply mentions the fact that the NKVD and UB (*Urząd Bezpieczeństwa*, Polish communist security force) occupied the site of the former KL (= Konzentrationslager) Warsaw. On page 116 Kopka states only this:

Zachowały się fragmentaryczne przekazy o egzekucjach w tym obozie, jak choćby ten: "W Warszawie na ul. Gęsiej odbywają się systematycznie likwidacje członków AK przez NKWD"[2]

Translated:

Fragmentary messages have been preserved about executions in this camp, such as this: "In Warsaw, on Gęsia Street liquidations of AK members by the NKVD regularly take place."

The only evidence cited is a further reference. Note 2 in Kopka reads:

K. Żmuda-Wilczyńska, Prokurator żądał kary śmierci, "Na przedpolu Warszawy" 1995, z. 5, s. 17 (za: S. Kalbarczyk, Sowieckie ... , s. 152-153).

A specific reference to the Kalbarczyk article is given in Kopka's preceding foonote:

> S. Kalbarczyk, Sowieckie represje wobec polskiego podziemia niepodległościowego w Warszawie i okolicach na przełomie 1944 i 1945 roku, "Pamięć i Sprawiedliwość" 2002, nr 2 (2),…"

I have obtained this article. The relevant passage in it (pp. 152-3) reads as follows:

> Inne placówki NKWD w Warszawie opisywane są w materiale źródłowym w sposób wysoce enigmatyczny. Z dostępnych źródeł wynika, że od stycznia 1945 r. przy ul. Gęsiej funkcjonował obóz NKWD ("Gęsiówka"). W straszliwych warunkach przetrzymywano tu żołnierzy Armii Krajowej, a ponadto jeńców niemieckich i innych "przestępców" [93]. Są wzmianki o egzekucjach w tym obozie: "W Warszawic na ul. Gęsiej odbywają się systematycznie likwidacje członków AK przez NKWD."[94]

Translated:

> Other NKVD facilities in Warsaw are described in the source material in a highly enigmatic manner. The available sources indicate that from January 1945, an NKVD camp functioned on Gęsia Street (the "Gęsiówka"). Soldiers of the Armia Krajowa as well as German prisoners of war and other "criminals"were held there in terrible conditions, [93] There is mention of executions in this camp: "In Warszaw on Gęsia Street liquidations take place on a regular basis of members of the AK by the NKVD."

The reference at note 94 is to an archival document, "CAW, O VI SG NW, ll/52. 34, k. 16; ibidem, ll/52. 100, k. 4." But Kalbarczyk gives us no way to evaluate it: no source criticism is given about this document; no information about what it is, why it was produced and by whom, nothing.

To conclude: this is the only evidence that the NKVD was shooting Home Army soldiers in that prison — "mentions" — *wzmianki* — that are "highly enigmatic." No names are given of Home Army victims. Moreover, if Home Army men were shot and could be identified, the question of why they were shot would still remain: what the charges against them were, whether they were given any kind of trial. After all, the underground Home Army was at war with the communist forces, murdering Jews and communists long after the war had ended.

If a charge of "systematic executions" were made against the British, French, or Americans, a close examination of the evidence would certainly take place before any conclusions were drawn. As Kalbarczyk admits, the evidence is "highly enigmatic." This is a red flag, a warning to the reader: "We do not know whether the contents of this document are reliable!"

But Snyder does not bother with scholarly exactness, when the charges are against communists. For Snyder as for the Nazis communists are "unpersons," to be treated unequally; virtually any charge against communists is acceptable for him.

Chapter 13. *Bloodlands* Ch. 10: Accusations of Soviet Crimes Near the War's End

Expulsion of German Colonists — Like Soviet Expulsion of Polish *Osadnicy* ("Settlers")

Snyder says, of the Germans expelled from Poland at the war's end:

> Perhaps 1.5 million of them were German adminis-
> trators and colonists, who would never have come
> to Poland without Hitler's war. They lived in houses
> or apartments that they had taken from Poles ex-
> pelled (or killed) during the war or from Jews who
> had been killed. (314)

But the same had been true of the Polish imperialist "settlers" (Polish "osadnicy") sent by the Polish state after 1921 to "polo-nize" Western Ukraine and Belorussia, the areas seized by Poland from Soviet Russia by military conquest but in which Poles were a minority. Echoing Snyder's words they were indeed "Polish admin-istrators and colonists, who would never have come to Western Belorussia and Western Ukraine without Pilsudski's war."

These lands were east of the Curzon Line. It is impossible to un-derstand the history of this period and region without reference to the Curzon Line. But Snyder never mentions it even once in *Blood-lands.* He writes of these areas as though they were "naturally" part of Poland, and therefore that there was something "unnatu-ral," unjust, etc., that they should be reunited with Eastern Belo-russia and Eastern Ukraine within the USSR. In reality Poland had conquered these lands through an imperialist war and treated their Ukrainian, Belorussian, and Jewish populations like colonial subjects in an imperialist — that is, brutal and racist, manner.

Poles Murdered Polish Jews

There were also many cases of Poles murdering Jews during the war to take their property and of Poles blackmailing Jews not to turn them into the Germans until the Jews ran out of money, and then turning them in. The cruelty and greed of these *szantażysty* or *szmalcowniki* (blackmailers) is commonly portrayed in accounts by Jews who hid in Poland during the war.

This is yet another way in which capitalist Poland resembles Nazi Germany. The Soviet Union was completely different. No one, not even Snyder, has ever accused the Soviet Army or Soviet citizens of acting in this way against Soviet Jews.

After the war was over there were many cases of Poles murdering Jews in order to keep the property they had taken from them while the Jews had been in hiding. The Polish Home Army, now underground "freedom fighters," and other Polish bands and gangs, killed a great many Jews, sometimes for their property, sometimes because, like the Nazis, many Polish nationalists equated Judaism with communism, sometimes because they did not consider Jews to be Poles and wanted Poland *judenrein*, "cleaned of Jews," just as the Nazis did.

Since he cites a number of the works produced by the researchers at the Research Center for the Holocaust ("Centrum Badań nad Zagładą Żydów") Snyder must know about these things. But few of his readers will know about them, and Snyder remains silent about them.

Rapes of German Women by Red Army Soldiers

During the march on Berlin, the Red Army followed a dreadfully simple procedure in the eastern lands of the Reich, the territories meant for Poland: its men raped German women and seized German men (and some women) for labor. The behavior continued as the soldiers reached the German lands that would remain in Germany, and finally Berlin. Red Army soldiers had also raped women in Poland, and in Hungary, and even in Yugoslavia, where a communist revolution would make the country a Soviet

> ally. Yugoslav communists complained to Stalin
> about the behavior of Soviet soldiers, who gave
> them a little lecture about soldiers and "fun."[7] (316)

Source: (n. 7 p. 498): "...Yugoslav quotation: Naimark, *Russians*, 71."

Snyder does not tell his readers the source here, which is Milovan Djilas's book *Conversations with Stalin*. Published in 1961, it appeared long after (a) the events described; (b) the very hostile break between Yugoslavia and the Soviet Union; and (c) Djilas's own rejection of communism.

So Djilas's account, published 17 years after the fact, might be inaccurate because of his bias — Djilas hated Stalin, and by 1961 had come to hate communism — because the passage of time had reshaped his memory of events; or because he had fabricated it. Or, it might be accurate. We can't know. The historical principle of "Testis unus, testis nullus" — means that a single "witness," or piece of evidence to an event, is not enough to establish that the event actually occurred.[1]

This short passage illustrates why good historians insist upon *source criticism* — an examination of the source of the evidence. Any lawyer knows the importance of sources. If a defendant, or a witness, claims that a third party made a certain statement, opposing counsel is sure to ask: "What is your source? How do we know that statement is genuine?" But Snyder doesn't do this. He never does when it might call into question an otherwise perfectly good anti-Stalin or anticommunist statement.

So did Stalin say this? Given the source, we can't be sure. But one thing is certain: Stalin's alleged statement had nothing whatsoever to do with any rapes in Germany. Djilas states that it was made during his trip to Moscow "during the winter of 1944-1945" (p. 93). The war against Hitler was far from over and allegations of rape against German women had not yet been made.

Bottom line: We don't know whether Stalin made this statement — i.e. whether Djilas was reporting the truth or writing anticom-

---

[1] See the explanation at http://dic.academic.ru/dic.nsf/latin_proverbs/2504/Testis

munist propaganda. But we know it was not made with reference to Red Army rapes in Germany. Neither **Naimark** nor Snyder point this fact out.

On pp. 316-318 Snyder expatiates upon the widespread story of mass rapes of German women by Red Army soldiers. There are many Russian responses to this accusation, most of them defensive, some of them quoting accounts of exemplary treatment of German women by Red Army soldiers. There are also accounts of the rape of German women by Red Army soldiers who were then tried and shot or imprisoned. None of them have the kinds of well-founded total numbers that we would like to have.

The whole question has become so ideologically charged that it is hardly possible to get objective information. Nazi propaganda claimed a great many rapes, in order to strengthen resistance to the Red Army. Anticommunist propaganda since the war has made the claim of massive rape a central focus.

So, what was the situation? Were there "more rapes than could be expected" by Red Army men of German women? Most people want simple answers. But there aren't any simple answers here. The "massive rape" story is mainly spread by professional anticommunists who are not objective about anything else, so there's no reason to think they are objective in this matter either.

It has never even been established that there was a higher *rate* of rape by Red Army men — number of confirmed rapes divided by the number of soldiers — than there was in the other Allied armies. Also, the Red Army occupied areas that had sided with the Nazis and participated in the unprecedented slaughter of civilians and murder of Red Army prisoners, whereas much of the areas occupied by the Allies were anti-German. Other factors: German women could get abortions by claiming rape by a Soviet soldier, which must have led to some false claims. Allied soldiers could pay for sex with desperate women with food, cigarettes or other goods. Such arrangements were not considered "rape" though women in desperate need often had no choice.

The question of widespread rape by American soldiers, evidently encouraged by U.S. Army propaganda — moreover, in "friendly" countries such as France, rather than in pro-Nazi countries whose soldiers had participated in enormous atrocities in the USSR like Hungary, Rumania, and Germany — has only recently begun to attract some attention.[2] The issue seems to be that publicity about rape by Red Army soldiers started some years earlier than that about rape by American soldiers and has been vigorously promoted for anticommunist purposes, as Snyder is doing.

Was there a high incidence of rape in the liberated USSR? I have attempted to survey the Russian-language literature on this question. As far as I can tell no one has alleged that this was the case. That tends to make me suspect that anger and resentment towards Germans and their allies were a major factor in whatever rapes occurred. So in one respect this is part of the anticommunist "numbers game" — to fabricate or multiply alleged Soviet atrocities.

On the other hand, given the unprecedented level of atrocities and destruction inflicted on the USSR by the German armies it would be surprising if there were not a higher level of rape of German, Hungarian, Rumanian, etc., women by Red Army men than there were among Allied soldiers. But it is impossible to get any precise figures.

So we really do not know. Historians ought to admit ignorance on the basis of lack of good evidence, which is very often the case. But lack of evidence does not stop ideological anticommunists from drawing the conclusions they desire and then using their own fictions to moralize, in the manner of Josef Goebbels' diaries.

> As so often, Stalin's crimes were enabled by Hitler's policies. (318)

"As so often" what? What "crimes"? *Snyder has yet to establish a single "crime" of Stalin's.* This is Snyder's anticommunism in overdrive again. It seems clear that Snyder will stoop to any propaganda technique in order to dishonestly associate the Soviet Union with Nazi Germany.

---

[2] Jennifer Schluesser, "The Dark Side of Liberation," *New York Times* May 21, 2013 p. C1.

Snyder Barely Refers to the Real Genocide: the "Volhynian Massacres"

The Germans had killed about 1.3 million Jews in the former eastern Poland in 1941 and 1942, with the help of local policemen. Some of these Ukrainian policemen helped to form a Ukrainian partisan army in 1943, which under the leadership of Ukrainian nationalists cleansed the former southwest Poland —which it saw as western Ukraine — of remaining Poles. The OUN-Bandera, the nationalist organization that led the partisan army, had long pledged to rid Ukraine of its national minorities. Its capacity to kill Poles depended upon German training, and its determination to kill Poles had much to do with its desire to clear the terrain of purported enemies before a final confrontation with the Red Army. The UPA, as the partisan army was known, murdered tens of thousands of Poles, and provoked reprisals from Poles upon Ukrainian civilians.[34] (326)

Sources:

n. 34 , p. 500: "Documentation of the UPA's plans for and actions toward Poles can be found in TsDAVO 3833/1/86/6a; 3833/1/131/13-14; 3833/1/86/19-20; and 3933/3/1/60. Of related interest are DAR 30/1/16=USHMM RG-31.017M-1; DAR 301/1/5=USHMM RG-31.017M-1; and DAR 30/1/4=USHMM RG-31.017M-1. These OUN-B and UPA wartime declarations coincide with postwar interrogations (see GARF, R-9478/1/398) and recollections of Polish survivors (on the massacre of 12-13 July 1943, for example, see OKAW, II/737, II/1144, II/2099, II/2650, II/953, and II/775) and Jewish survivors (for example, ŻIH 301/2519; and Adini, Dubno: sefer zikaron, 717-718). The fundamental study is now Motyka, *Ukraińska partyzantka*. See also Il'iushyn, *OUN-UPA*, and Arm-

> strong, *Ukrainian Nationalism*. I sought to explain
> this conflict in "Causes," *Reconstruction*, "Life and
> Death," and Sketches."

This page contains the only reference in *Bloodlands* to the Volhynian Massacres of 50,000 - 100,000 or more Polish civilians by Ukrainian Nationalist forces armed by the Germans but acting on their own initiative. Snyder has researched these important and neglected mass murders and has published on them in the past. Yet he neglects them in *Bloodlands*. Why?

This was true genocide: an attempt to kill so many Poles that survivors would flee and rid the Ukraine of Poles completely.[3] Even if the Soviet NKVD or army had been guilty of killing all the "Katyn" Poles — and we can now be certain that the "official version" of the Katyn massacre is false — that would be less than ½ to less than ¼ of the number of Poles murdered by the Ukrainian Nationalists.[4] Yet the Volhynian massacres are scarcely ever discussed! Snyder himself spends only one-half of one paragraph on it. Why?

Snyder follows contemporary Polish nationalist practice in virtually ignoring the Volhynian massacres in *Bloodlands*. The reason for this neglect seems to be that it is highly embarrassing to today's Ukrainian Nationalists, who heap praise upon the Ukrainian Nationalist forces as anti-Bolshevik "freedom fighters" despite the fact that they fought on the side of the Nazis and murdered, at the very least, hundreds of thousands of Jews and Poles. The state of Ukraine has periodically declared the same forces who were guilty of these horrific and massive atrocities — the OUN-Bandera, the 14th SS Division "Galizien," later renamed the "Ukrainian Insurgent Army" (*Ukraïns'ka Povstans'ka Armiia*) — to be "heroes."

It can hardly be a coincidence that the Volhynian massacres are also neglected in today's right-wing, capitalist Poland. Poland follows what is often called the "Giedroyc doctrine," named for anti-

---

[3] For a brief overview in Polish see Ewa Siemaszko, "Genocyd Polaków na Wołyniu i w Galicji Wschodniej (1942/1943-1946/1947) (December, 2009) at
http://szturman.livejournal.com/260126.html There is a Russian translation: "Геноцид Поляков на Волыни И В Восточной Галиции," at
http://misha18.livejournal.com/35007.html

[4] See the discussion above in Chapter Ten.

communist political theorist Jerzy Giedroyc who proposed that the mass murders by Ukrainian nationalists be "forgotten" in the interests of good relations with post-soviet Ukraine, while the "Katyn massacres" be emphasized as a political tool against Russia. According to Polish historian Bogumił Grott:

> Do dziś pamiętam, jak Jerzy Giedroyć w radiowym wywiadzie, dokładnie dwa tygodnie przed śmiercią, problem mordów UPA na Polakach skwitował krótkim: „należy zapomnieć."

Translated:

> I still remember how Jerzy Giedroyc in a radio interview given just two weeks before his death, briefly summed up the problem of the UPA murders of Poles: "We must forget them."[5]

Since Snyder follows this practice we note that he expresses his gratitude towards Jerzy Giedroyc:

> The late Jerzy Giedroyc, ...helped me to ask some of the right questions. (421)

In the immediate post-Soviet period Polish researchers finally began to publish lengthy, well-documented accounts of the really hair-raising atrocities committed by Ukrainian nationalist soldiers against Polish civilians in order to drive them out of Western Ukraine. This brought attention to these horrific mass murders for the first time and caused a lot of embarrassment between anticommunist Poland and anticommunist Ukraine.

In 2003 the two highly anticommunist states organized a sort of "reconciliation" conference. Since that time the Polish side has relented somewhat. Both sides agreed that "It was a long time ago and everybody who did it is dead" — not true, of course, even today, much less a decade ago. They evidently want to bury the hatchet about all these mass murders, including retributive killings of perhaps 10,000 - 20,000 Ukrainian civilians by Polish forces, so they could get back to their primary business — blaming

---

[5] Bogumił Grott, „Wiktor Poliszczuk - historyk przemilczanych zbrodni, '27 Dywizja Wołyńska AK'" Biuletyn Informacyjny, nr 1(101), styczeń-marzec 2009 Warszawa, s. 27. At http://ien.pl/index.php/archives/1217

Stalin, communism, the Soviet Union, and Russia for all bad things. This attempt at coverup has been under way for the past decade.

The more publicity the Volhynian massacres get, the worse the anticommunist Ukrainian and Polish forces seem. Even the "Katyn massacre" pales in comparison! And this tells us something about the enormous publicity and propaganda given in today's Poland to Katyn. Clearly this is not at all about the victims but about anti-communism, and also about keeping anti-Russian sentiment alive. Polish nationalism is largely based on anti-Russian propaganda. This is a plausible hypothesis to explain why Snyder devotes less than a paragraph to these massacres.

Snyder asserts that the book by his friend Grzegorz Motyka, *Ukraińska partyzantka 1942-1960* is "now the fundamental study." Hardly! Motyka's book is only partly about the Volhynian massacres. Much of the rest of it is about the "heroic" struggle of Ukrainian nationalist — and fascist — partisans against the Soviets.

Motyka has been a member of the "Instytut Pamięti Narodowej," the Polish "Institute of the People's Memory," a fanatically nationalist research-propaganda group funded by the Polish government and innocent of any aim at objectivity. The IPN's President takes an oath "to the Polish people." This is reminiscent of Nazi practice — who is to define what constitutes "loyalty to the people?" And who are "the people" anyway? Moreover, historians are supposed to be loyal to *the truth*, not to their own *Volk*.

Imagine what American historians would think of an organization named "Institute of the American People's Memory." It would be immediately recognized as a far-right nationalist effort and scorned by all respected historians. The IPN is primarily anticommunist and anti-Soviet. No *objective* historian would associate with it, just as no objective historian would associate with the Hoover Institution in Palo Alto, California, a similar anticommunist propaganda mill in the guise of a "research center."

Yet Motyka appears to disagree with Snyder on the question of the Volhynian massacres. Motyka wrote a long essay in *Gazeta Wyborcza* titled "Forget About Giedroyc: Poles, Ukrainians, and the

IPN."[6] He takes the position that the Ukrainian massacres of Poles were "one of the bloodiest Polish episodes of the Second World War and must not be forgotten." Motyka does not shrink from calling these massacres "genocide" (*ludobójstwo*). Motyka also admits that "some actions of the Polish underground could also be called genocide", such as the murders of some dozens of Belorussians in 1946 or murders of 200 Ukrainians in June 1945, both after the war.

According to Motyka there are very few memorials concerning these horrific mass murders in Poland today:

> To wstyd, że do takich miejsc jak masowy grób w wołyńskiej Parośli można dotrzeć tylko leśnym duktem zrytym przez dziki.

Translated:

> It is shameful that places like the mass grave in Parośla, Volhynia, can only be reached only by a forest path cut through wilderness.[7]

Motyka makes the gesture of mentioning Soviet "crimes" and falsely claims that that the Soviets wanted to "annihilate class enemies" — something the Soviets never advocated. These are general remarks apparently obligatory for Polish historians today. If the Soviets, or pro-Soviet partisans, had ever done anything remotely resembling the mass murders carried out not only by Ukrainian nationalist forces but by the Polish Home Army and NSZ underground "in response" to the Ukrainian mass murders, the whole world would have known about it for decades. There would be many large, expensive memorials to the victims, a library of books exposing the "communist atrocities", and no doubt lawsuits for damages before the European Court of Human Rights.

The reality is that there is no evidence that the Soviets and pro-Soviet forces never did anything like this. This is another reminder

---

[6] „Zapomnijcie o Giedroyciu: Polacy, Ukraińcy, IPN." *Gazeta Wyborcza* May 24, 2008.

[7] Parośla is in the Lublin region of Poland almost at the border of Belarus and a little north of the border with Ukraine. The tiny monument can be seen at the Polish Wikipedia page http://pl.wikipedia.org/wiki/Zbrodnia_w_Parośli_I

that it is the Polish and Ukrainian "freedom fighters", rather than the Soviet Union, who most resemble the Nazis.

The point, though, is that Motyka does not advocate downplaying Ukrainian massacres, as in practice Snyder does. The fundamental study of these horrendous events remains that by Władysław and Ewa Siemaszko.[8] A number of books are available in Russian. For a brief English introduction see the Internet page "Genocide Committed by Ukrainian Nationalists in Occupied Poland."[9]

The eagerness of Polish and Ukrainian nationalist elites to "bury the hatchet" over 50,000 to 100,000 or more atrocious murders contrasts with the Polish elite's never-ending complaints about the Katyn massacres which comprised 1/4 or 1/7 the number of victims. Moreover, as we have discussed in a previous chapter the "official" version has now been definitively disproven. In like manner Snyder devotes less than a paragraph to these horrifying massacres while inventing Soviet "atrocities" left and right.

More False Numbers of "Victims"

> Between 1944 and 1946, for example, 182,543 Ukrainians were deported from Soviet Ukraine to the Gulag: not for committing a particular crime, not even for being Ukrainian nationalists, but for being related to or acquainted with Ukrainian nationalists. At about the same time, in 1946 and 1947, the Soviets sentenced 148,079 Red Army veterans to the Gulag for collaboration with the Germans. There were never more Soviet citizens in the Gulag than in the years after the war; indeed, the number of Soviet citizens in the camps and special

---

[8] *Ludobójstwo dokonane przez nacjonalistów ukraińskich na ludności polskiej Wołynia 1939—1945* (Warsaw: Wydawnictwo „von Borowiecky" 2000), in two volumes, 1433 pages in length. Motyka's work has been criticized as apologetic towards the Ukrainian Nationalists. See Zbigniew Małyszczycki, " Motykowanie historii," http://chomikuj.pl/henrypk/Galeria/KRESY/Motykowanie+historii.pdf ; Russian translation, «Мотыкование истории," http://poacher.borda.ru/?1-11-0-00000016-000-0-0

[9] At http://www.electronicmuseum.ca/Poland-WW2/ukrainian_insurgent_atrocities/uia.html The Russian-language Wikipedia page is helpful as an introduction: http://ru.wikipedia.org/wiki/Волынская_резня

settlements increased every year from 1945 until Stalin's death.[36] (328)

Sources: (n. 36 p. 500):

* "On the 182,543 Ukrainians deported from Soviet Ukraine to the Gulag, see Weiner, "Nature," 1137."

* "On the 148,079 Red Army veterans, see Polian, "Violence," 129."

* "See also, generally, Applebaum, *Gulag*, 463."

In an article published since *Bloodlands* Snyder claimed even more:

> At war's end, the Ukrainian nationalists were de-
> feated by the Soviets, who killed tens of thousands
> of Ukrainian civilians and deported hundreds of
> thousands more to concentration camps. (2011-3)

This is all false. Snyder presents no evidence whatsoever that *any* Ukrainian civilians were killed, much less "tens of thousands."

According to the authoritative collection of Soviet documents published by the highly anticommunist "Memorial" society in 2005 the number of all persons deported from the Ukraine between 1944 and 1948 inclusive is 131,935. This number includes 16,996 persons from the following groups: German repatriates, family members of convicted traitors, convicted German citizens of the USSR (e.g. Volga Germans, called "Fol'ksdoich"), and those who had served in German military or police formations. Subtracting these, the total number of Ukrainian nationalists is 114,969 (another possible total number from the same report is 114,936). (*Stalinskie Deportatsii* 630-1) These people were not sent to "camps" but were "exiled" (*ssylka*) to the Eastern USSR.

Snyder cites an article by Amir **Weiner** published in 1999. The citation and its footnote may be found in the Appendix to this chapter.[10] As usual, the "devil is in the details" — the evidence.

Weiner's figure of 110,825 "nationalists killed" (see the first quotation in the Appendix to this chapter) comes from a secondary

---

[10] See Chapter 13 — Appendix at http://tinyurl.com/blood-lies-appendix-ch13

source written by a Ukrainian nationalist, as does the figure of 182,543 deported between 1944 and 1952. The number from Nikolai Fiodrovich Bugai, the leading Russian scholar on deportations, covers the years 1939 to 1945, meaning: all the Polish "settlers" deported from the Western Ukraine in 1939-1940, as well as during the war. Bugai also explicitly includes deportations of Germans and others from this area (Bugai 12, 13). It tells us nothing about the period from 1944 onward.

Weiner claims the Soviets "emphasized almost total annihilation" since they "repeatedly failed to mention prisoners taken alive." This is false. Weiner is in error. Bugai is the acknowledged Russian specialist on deportations and is conventionally anticommunist and anti-Stalin. In the Appendix to this chapter the reader will find primary source evidence printed by Bugai with emphasis added at the passages referring to the *large numbers of prisoners taken*. Bugai cites primary sources — Beria's reports to Stalin — that speak of tens of thousands of prisoners and those who have turned themselves in.

Elsewhere Weiner uses and cites Bugai's work. So how can Weiner — Snyder's source here — state that "the campaign against nationalists" was "a war without prisoners"? How can he talk about "NKVD reports" failing "to mention prisoners taken alive, emphasizing almost total annihilation"? The answer appears to be that Weiner doesn't use Bugai here. Instead he cites Ukrainian nationalist historians. Ukrainian nationalists (like Polish, Baltic, etc. nationalists) have every reason to falsify and exaggerate Soviet "atrocities." This is the only way they have to try to excuse, or at least explain, the important role Ukrainian nationalist forces played in the Holocaust of the Jews and in the Volhynian massacres of 50,000 to 100,000 or more Polish civilians.

The Soviets did indeed "kill tens of thousands" in the Ukraine: not civilians, as Snyder falsely claims, but OUN-UPA fighters. No country would fail to combat armed bands within its own territory. Moreover, these forces had fought on the Nazi side and helped carry out the Holocaust, to say nothing of the mass murders of Polish and Soviet civilians.

As for the number deported, Snyder's claim of "hundreds of thousands" "deported to concentration camps" is fallacious. *Sovetskie deportatsii,* the collection of primary sources cited above, published in 2005, give the figure of 37,145 persons during 1944-1946.

Polian, "Violence," 129, cites same number — 148,079. Here is the passage:

> En 1946-1947, 148 079 "Vlassoviens," furent exilés pour une durée de six ans avec le statut de "colons de travail" dans les regions les plus inhospitalières de l'URSS.[31] (129)

Translated:

> In 1946-1947, 148,079 "Vlassovites" were exiled for a period of six years with the status of "labor colonists" to the most inhospitable regions of the USSR.

Polian's source is a Russian study published in 1992 by Guboglo and Kuznetsov. However, it's just as likely that Polian just copied this from the end of the twelfth chapter of the notorious *Black Book of Communism*, since both the same number and same reference are given.

Snyder, remember, said that these were "Red Army veterans," and then referred to Polian. But his own source Polian calls them "Vlassoviens," men who had been recruited to Nazi armies, such as the Vlasov army. Snyder has lied about this to make it look to the reader as though Red Army soldiers were sent to the Gulag.

Applebaum, Gulag, 463 contains no information of relevance to this paragraph.

Snyder continues:

> In a few days in October 1947, some 76,192 Ukrainians were transported to the Gulag. (329)

Sources: (n. 38 p. 501): Motyka, *Ukraińska partyzantka* , 535.

Motyka, *Ukraińska partyzantka* , 535 does give number 76,192. But Snyder has falsified what occurred. In fact, they were not sent to the Gulag — that is, to camps — but were exiled. The relevant document — by Kruglov, Minister of the MVD (Ministry of Internal

Affairs, successor to the NKVD) may be found in the Appendix to this chapter.

Snyder Cares About "Elites." About Other People? Not So Much…

Snyder:

> Men of elite families were killed at Katyn and other
> sites… (380)

Let's set aside for a moment the fact that Snyder has not even tried to establish what happened at Katyn, nor to inform his readers of the scholarly controversy that exists over this event.[11] Once again, it is revealing that Snyder cares about "elites" so much. It is an example of Snyder's deeply reactionary way of thinking.

Of course it is a historical truism that *all* progressive social and political upheavals and revolutions target "elites." Slave revolts and peasant revolts throughout history; the English Revolution of the mid-17th century; the American Revolution; the French Revolution; the United States' defeat of the Confederacy in the American Civil War; the Russian Revolution, the Yugoslav, Chinese, and Vietnamese revolutions, and many others — all disproportionately targeted "elites" because those "elites" were the exploiters or their agents. History shows that the common working people can do without the wealthy "elites" very well indeed!

> Leading about 120,000 special forces, he [Lavrentii
> Beria] rounded up and expelled 478,479 people in
> just over a week… Because no Chechens or Ingush
> were to be left behind, people who could not be
> moved were shot. Villages were burned to the
> ground everywhere; in some places, barns full of
> people were burned as well. (330; emphasis added,
> GF)

Sources: (n. 41 p. 501):

---

[11] In reality, as we have argued earlier in this book, the "official version" of the Katyn massacre cannot possibly be true — a fact that anticommunists try to hide at any cost. See also Furr, Official Version.

* "See Polian, *Against Their Will*, 134-155, for all of the cited figures."
* "See also Naimark, *Fires*, 96";
* Lieberman, *Terrible Fate*, 206-207";
* Burleigh, *Third Reich*, 749.

Snyder is wrong again. There is *no* evidence that *anyone* "who could not be moved" was "shot"; nor that *any* "villages were burned to the ground," much less "everywhere; nor that "barns full of people were burned as well." The story about *one* barn of people being burned alive — not multiple barns, as Snyder claims — is a forgery, probably American in origin due to the clumsy literal translation into Russian of American "intelligence slang." It is thoroughly discussed and refuted in the two works cited in this footnote.[12] Snyder fails to inform his readers about this research. Does he even know anything about this issue? If not, why write about it — except to make anticommunist propaganda?

Lieberman, *Terrible Fate* 206-7 quotes a Chechen nationalist source that records only that some people did die on the journey. It does not record the number, for which see below.

Nikolai Bugai is the most authoritative Russian expert on deportations, and an anti-Stalinist to boot. Here is what he has written:

> Operation Chechevitsa, which began on 23 February, was completed sometime during the third week of March. NKVD records attest to 180 convoy trains carrying 493,269 Chechen and Ingush nationals and members of other nationalities seized at the same time. **Fifty people were killed in the course of the operation, and 1,272 died on the journey.**
>
> Other reports indicate that during the Cheka military actions and the resettlement 2,016 Chechen and Ingush anti-Soviet elements were arrested, and 20,072 firearms and

---

[12] Pykhalov, Igor'. Mestechkovye strasti v chechenskikh gorakh.. In his book (with A. Diukov), *Velikaia obolgannaia voina, 2*, chapter 2. It may be read online (in Russian) here: http://militera.lib.ru/research/pyhalov_dukov/02.html Nikita Mendkovich. "Khaibakhskoe delo." In the online history journal *Aktual'naia Istoriia* (Current History), at http://actualhistory.ru/poilemics-haibach

479 submachine guns were confiscated.[13] (Emphasis added, GF.)

Naimark, *Fires of Hatred* 96, agrees with Bugai: "the NKVD reported only sporadic cases of resistance."[14]

The "Numbers Game" Again, Falsified Once More

Snyder writes:

> In all of the civil conflict, flight, deportation, and re-
> settlement provoked or caused by the return of the
> Red Army between 1943 and 1947, some 700,000
> Germans died, as did at least 150,000 Poles and
> perhaps 250,000 Ukrainians. At a minimum, anoth-
> er 300,000 Soviet citizens died during or shortly af-
> ter the Soviet deportations from the Caucasus, Cri-
> mea, Moldova, and the Baltic States. If the struggles
> of Lithuanian, Latvian, and Estonian nationalists
> against the reimposition of Soviet power are re-
> garded as resistance to deportations, which in some
> measure they were, another hundred thousand or
> so people would have to be added to the total dead
> associated with ethnic cleansing.[43] (332)

Sources: (n. 43 p. 501):

> * "Weiner ("Nature," 1137) notes that the Soviets reported
> killing 110,825 people as Ukrainian nationalists between
> February 1944 and May 1946.

> * "The NKVD estimated that 144,705 Chechens, Ingush,
> Balkars, and Karachai died as a result of deportation or
> shortly after resettlement (by 1948); see Lieberman, *Terri-
> ble Fate*, 207."

Snyder gives *no source at all* for his figures of the deaths of
700,000 Germans, "at least" 150,000 Poles," and "perhaps 250,000

---

[13] N.F. Bugai and A.M. Gonov. "The Forced Evacuation of the Chechens and the Ingush." *Russian Studies in History*, vol. 41, no. 2, Fall 2002, pp. 43—61, at p. 56.

[14] An associate of the Hoover Institution, Naimark is an ideological anticommunist, so he
writes: "Anyone who resisted was shot." There is no evidence for this assertion. It is likely
that those who offered *armed* resistance were shot, but they were few.

Ukrainians." Nor does he give any evidence for his blaming the Red Army for whatever deaths did occur. Weiner's fraudulent claim of "110,825 people killed" has been refuted above.

Snyder gives no evidence for the deaths of 100,000 Baltic nationalists. Nor does he tell his readers that Nazi collaborators in the Baltics and Baltic participants in the Holocaust described themselves as "nationalists," hoping that the word "nationalist" would "justify" their anti-Soviet terrorism. We should recall that all fascists justified their fascism as "nationalism."

As for this claim of Snyder's:

> The NKVD estimated that 144,705 Chechens, Ingush, Balkars, and Karachai died as a result of deportation or shortly after resettlement (by 1948); see Lieberman, *Terrible Fate*, 207.

This too is a falsification. We have seen that Bugai published the NKVD report that 50 Chechen and Ingush died during deportation. We have no way of knowing how many of the 493,000 who were deported would have died during the same time period had they remained in their villages. Surely some would have, so the 1272 who "died on the journey" cannot all be persons who would not have died as a result of the deportation.

During 1946-47 there was a serious famine in the USSR The famine was caused by catastrophic weather conditions. No doubt it was made even worse by the massive destruction of the war. Nor was the famine was not confined to the USSR According to Stephen Wheatcroft, who has written the latest study of the Soviet famine of 1946-1947:

> The World Food Crisis of 1946—1947 was the most serious global food shortage of modern history, when famine simultaneously threatened Central and Eastern Europe, India, Indo-China and China, and bread rationing was introduced in Britain for the first time ever.[17] The British and American governments had requested food aid from Stalin to ease the World Food Crisis before they became aware of the situation in the USSR. The international context of the Soviet famine of 1946—1947 was strikingly different to 1921, when America

had been able to provide large amounts of relief grain to Russia.[15]

Claiming that deaths of whatever number "by 1948" were "a result of deportation" is plainly dishonest. As Snyder notes, Lieberman makes this claim on page 207 of his book. His source is an early book of Bugai, who cites the number 144,704. Bugai wrote:

> According to the NKVD Department on Special Settlements, among all deported Chechens, Ingush, Balkarians (1944) and Karachai (1943) during 1944-1948, 144,704 persons died (23.7%), i.e. in Kazakhstan, - 101,036 Chechen, Ingush, and Balkarians; in Uzbekistan, - 16,052 (10.6%) persons (during a 6-month stay); in 1948 — 13,883 persons (9.8%).[16]

In this same article Bugai also says that between 1944 and 1946 "1468 deported people died in Kazakhstan." This refutes the accusation that those who died "by 1948" died as a result of deportation. Neither Lieberman nor Snyder mentions this fact. Nor do they calculate the number of deaths above the normal mortality rate for the large population there. Bugai also discusses the extra provisions allotted by the Soviet state to deportees (pp. 117 ff).

Immediately after the paragraph above Bugai adds the sentence:

> The number of sources for this study is very poor.

Neither Lieberman nor Snyder mention that either. In fact, this short book by Bugai, published in English in 1996, is the translation of an article published in 1989 — that is, before the end of the USSR.[17] Better documentation began to appear after the end of the USSR in 1991. In 1998 Bugai and his associate Gomov wrote the account quoted above. It appears that he does not repeat the death

---

[15] Wheatcroft, "The Soviet Famine of 1946—1947, the Weather and Human Agency in Historical Perspective." *Europe-Asia Studies* 64:6 (2012), 1004.

[16] Nikolai F. Bougai. *The Deportation of Peoples in the Soviet Union.* New York: Nova Science Publishers, 1996, page 98

[17] N.F. Bugai. "K voprosu of deportatsii narodov SSSR v 30-40 godakh." *Istoriia SSSR* 6 (1989), 135-144. - Н.Ф. Бугай. "К вопросу о депортации народов СССР в 30-40 годах." *История СССР* 1989 (6), 135-144.

figures he cited in 1989. Lieberman (206-7) repeats *undocumented* stories of many deaths during the deportation. Bugai relates some of them too. But he also reports the official accounts, above.

As others have suggested, it is very likely that the official, and very low, estimates of deaths are accurate. There would certainly have been a head count at the end of the journey. Discrepancies would have raised the suspicion that, for example, NKVD men might have let some persons escape in exchange for bribes. Therefore it is un-likely that many — if indeed any — persons died and were buried along the route, in addition to those reported.

In his 1992 book *Ikh nado deportirovat'* Bugai quotes selections of a "report of the section of special resettlement of the MVD of the USSR concerning work among those resettled" and dated April 10, 1953 where the same number of those who died, 144,705, is also cited.

> (_ ..) **С момента расселения до настоящего времени** на спецпоселении родилось 82 391 чел., в том числе: детей бывших кулаков- 22 209, немцев- 22 210, чеченцев, ингушей, балкарцев, карачаевцев- 26 002, других контингентов- 11 970.
>
> (...) Из общего числа умерших 309 100 чел. умерло после высылки на спецпоселение: чеченцев, карачаевцев, ингушеи, балкарцев- 144 704, немцев- 42 823, спецпоселенцев из Крыма- 44 887, калмыков- 16 594, турок, курдов, хемшинов- 14 895, членов семей оуновцев- 10 384, бывших кулаков- 30 194, других контингентов- 5958 чел.
>
> Наибольший процент смертности имелся среди спецпоселенцев, переселеиных в 1944 г. Так, из общего количества переселенцев в этом году до настоящего времени умерло: чеченцев, ингушей, балкарцев, карачаевцев- 23,7%, крымских татар, болгар, греков, армян-19,6%, калмыков-17,4% турок, курдов, хемшшюв- 14,6%.

- pp. 264-5.

Translated:

> (...) **From the moment of resettlement [February 1944] to the present time** in the special settlements 82,391 people have been born, including: children of former kulaks, 22,209, Germans, 22,210, Chechens, Ingush, Balkars, and Karachai 26,002, others 11,970...

> The greatest per centage of mortality is among those special resettled persons who were resettled in 1944. Of the total number of persons resettled in that year to the present time there have died: Chechens, Ingush, Balkars, Karachai — 23.7%; Crimean Tatars, Bulgarians, Greeks, Armenians — 19.6%, Kalmyks — 17.4%, Turks, Kurds, Khemshshiuv — 14.6%... (Emphasis added.)

It appears as though the relevant figures are for the period between "the moment of resettlement" — i.e., of deportation — "to the present time": that is, between 1944 and 1953.[18] This would contradict Bugai's earlier statement that the period in question was 1944-1948.

Why Did Stalin Reject Marshall Plan Aid?

> In 1947 it [the United States] offered economic aid, in the form of the Marshall Plan, to European countries willing to cooperate with one another on elementary matters of trade and financial policy. Stalin could reject Marshall aid and force his clients to reject it as well,... (335)

The Soviet Union did reject Marshall Plan aid — because it appeared to be an attempt to subvert its influence in Europe. Geoffrey Roberts writes:

---

[18] Because of the excerpted nature of the document Bugai cites it is impossible to be certain what the period of time is.

Although the Americans were thinking mainly in terms of Western Europe, the Soviet Union and Eastern Europe were not excluded from the proposed aid programme. Indeed the British and French governments responded to Marshall's Harvard speech by inviting the Russians to a conference in Paris to discuss a European response to the plan. In Moscow, however, the Soviets were in two minds. On the one hand, they welcomed the possibility of American loans and grants, for themselves and for their East European allies. On the other, they feared that the Marshall Plan was an economic counterpart of the Truman Doctrine — a means of using American financial muscle to build an anti-Soviet alliance in Western Europe.

At the Paris conference in July 1947 Moscow's worst fears were realized. The British and French insisted (in accordance with Marshall's express wishes) that any American aide programme had to be co-coordinated and organized on a pan-Europe basis. This was seen by the Soviets as a western device for interference in the economic and political life of the East European countries. Such interference was completely unacceptable to Stalin. Consequently the USSR withdrew from all negotiations concerning the Marshal Plan and insisted its East European allies did not participate either.[19]

Did Non-collectivized Agriculture "Save" the Ukraine from Famine?

Ukrainians returned to a country where famine was raging again. Perhaps a million people starved to death in the two years after the war. It was western Ukraine, with a private agricultural sector that the Soviets had not yet had time to collectivize, that

---

[19] "Historians and the Cold War," *History Review* December 2000.

saved the rest of Soviet Ukraine from even greater
suffering.[44]"

Source: (n. 44 p. 501): "Survivors of the famine mention this in
their memoirs. See Potichnij, "1946-1947 Famine," 185.

Potichnij's study is published in a right-wing Ukrainian nationalist
book and is not referred to by any expert scholars on the subject.
The latest study of the 1946-7 famine is that by Stephen Wheatcroft. Snyder offers no evidence that uncollectivized Western
Ukraine "saved" the Soviet Union in the famine of 1947 or, indeed,
that collectivization had anything to do at all with the famine. As
the quotation from Wheatcroft's article cited above shows, there
was still a bread shortage in the U.K. although, of course, agriculture was not collectivized there. Wheatcroft says nothing specifically about the harvest in Western Ukraine.

Chapter 14. Snyder's Accusations of Soviet Anti-Semitism in *Bloodlands* Chapter 11

What is the Truth?

> И вдруг на этом обсуждении премий Сталин, обращаясь к членам Политбюро и говорит:
>
> - У нас в ЦК антисемиты завелись. Это безобразие!
>
> - *Так это было. Тихон Хренников о времени и о себе.* М.: «Музыка» 1994, с. 179.

Translated:

> And suddenly during this discussion of the prizes Stalin turned towards the members of the Politburo and said:
>
> - Antisemites have turned up in our Central Committee. It is a disgrace!
>
> - *Thus It Was. Tikhon Khrennikov about His Times and Himself.* Moscow: "Muzyka" 1994, p. 179.

The Lie That Stalin Was Anti-Semitic

Snyder's book is subtitled "Europe Between Hitler and Stalin." He speaks of "twelve years, between 1933 and 1945, while both Hitler and Stalin were in power." (vii) Hitler committed suicide in April 1945.

So why does Snyder have a chapter that deals with events in the USSR from 1948 to 1952, when Hitler was long dead? The reason, presumably, is that Snyder cannot find any anti-Semitism by Stalin, the Soviet government, or pro-Soviet forces like the Polish communist-led People's Army Armia Ludowa, AL). On the contrary: all the anti-Semitism between 1933 and 1945, aside from the Nazis, was by anticommunist forces like the Polish government in exile, its underground Home Army and Ukrainian nationalists. And their anti-Semitism was immense!

Snyder supports, and is supported by, the political forces in present-day Poland and Ukraine that are fiercely anticommunist — Snyder approves of that — but are also anti-Semitic in their unguarded moments. They revere and honor the anticommunist forces of the war and post-war period — but these forces too were violently anti-Semitic. Snyder obviously cannot document any Soviet anti-Semitism before 1945 or he would have done it. So Snyder tries hard to find anti-Semitic acts by Stalin and the Soviet leadership after 1945, even though this violates the parameters Snyder himself has chosen for his book.

The final chapter in Snyder's book is titled "Stalinist Antisemitism." If one is going to sustain a comparison between Hitler and Stalin, as Snyder wishes to do, then it's important to claim, somehow or other, that Stalin was anti-Semitic. This is not easy to do, as the quotation from composer Tikhon Khrennikov's memoirs above shows. There is much evidence that Stalin vigorously opposed anti-Semitism. There is no evidence that Stalin was anti-Semitic and, consequently, no reason to think that he was. But Snyder tries to "square the circle" anyway. We examine his logical contortions and falsifications in the present chapter.

Did Stalin Murder Solomon Mikhoels?

Snyder introduces the chapter as follows:

> In January 1948, Stalin was killing a Jew. Solomon Mikhoels, the chairman of the Jewish Anti-Fascist Committee and the director of the Moscow Yiddish Theater, had been sent to Minsk to judge a play for the Stalin Prize. Once arrived, he was invited to the country house of the head of the Soviet Belarusian state police, Lavrenty Tsanava, who had him murdered, along with an inconvenient witness. Mikhoels's body, crushed by a truck, was left on a quiet street. (339)

This is false. Stalin did not order Mikhoels to be murdered. The documents purporting to "prove" this are crude forgeries. This forgery has been discussed in Russia for over a decade. IUrii Mukhin discussed the evidence of a forgery in *Ubiystvo Stalina i Beria* (2002). Mukhin has written some absurdities in his day, but his discussion of the "Mikhoels murder documents" is very cogent. Zhores Medvedev, a Soviet dissident with strong anti-Stalin and anticommunist credentials, wrote that he does not believe the story to be true either.[1] Snyder shows no familiarity with this issue whatsoever.[2]

Did Stalin"s Daughter Overhear Stalin "Covering Up" Mikhoels" Murder?

> Svetlana Allilueva, Stalin's daughter, overheard her father arranging the cover story for the murder with Tsanava: "car accident." (340)

Here Snyder is misleading his readers by significant omission. In 1966 Svetlana Allilueva, Joseph Stalin's only daughter, emigrated from the USSR to the West. In her first book of memoirs, *Twenty Letters To A Friend*, published in 1967, a year after her arrival in the West, she wrote:

> A new wave of arrests got under way at the end of 1948... Lozovsky was arrested, and Mikhoels was killed. (p. 196)[3]

A footnote to this passage in the English edition (p. 245) states that Mikhoels "died in mysterious circumstances" in 1948.

About a year later Allilueva published a second Alliluyeva's volume of memoirs, *Only One Year* (1969). Here she tells a very different story:

---

[1] *Stalin i Evreiskaia Problema*. Moscow: Izdatel'stvo 'Prava cheloveka', 2003, pp. 10-26.

[2] My Moscow-based colleague Vladimir L. Bobrov and I have an article pending publication that proves conclusively that the documents purporting to prove Stalin's murder of Mikhoels are crude forgeries.

[3] Svetlana's chronology is confused here. There was no such clear connection among the events she cites, for Mikhoels was killed on January 13, 1948, not at the end of the year.

> One day, in father's dacha, during one of my rare
> meetings with him, I entered his room when he was
> speaking to someone on the telephone. Something
> was being reported to him and he was listening.
> Then, as a summary of the conversation, he said,
> "Well, it's an automobile accident." I remember so
> well the way he said it: not a question but an an-
> swer, an assertion. He wasn't asking; he was sug-
> gesting: "an automobile accident." When he got
> through, he greeted me; and a little later he said:
> "Mikhoels was killed in an automobile accident." (p.
> 154)

Had Stalin's daughter somehow "forgotten" to mention this detail in her earlier account? That can hardly be the case. People do not forget details like the involvement of their father in a murder. Nor can people who hear only one side of a phone conversation tell whether a person making a statement is instructing someone else, or repeating a fact just heard from the other party.

One thing is clear: in 1967 Allilueva did not yet "know" that Mikhoels had been murdered at all, much less that it was her father who had murdered him. Most likely she had been "coached" during the year between the two books. Her second volume was written after moving to the US and befriending several virulent anti-communists, some of whom she thanks in the book. No doubt it was they who "convinced" her to put a different interpretation on what she had heard her father say in 1948.

Despite its obvious lack of validity as evidence some writers[4], Snyder among them, still cite Allilueva's statement from *Only One Year* while omitting any mention of her earlier statement in *Twenty Letters To A Friend.* To do so is dishonesty of a high order: prop-aganda, not scholarship.

---

[4] E.g Joshua Rubenstein and Vladimir P. Naumov, *Stalin's Secret Pogrom. The Postwar Inqui-sition of the Jewish Anti-Fascist Committee.* (New Haven CT: Yale University Press, 2001), 39.

Did Stalin Say Russians Had Been the War"s Greatest Victims?

> Given the centrality of the Second World War to the experience of all east Europeans, in the USSR and in the new satellite states, everyone in the new communist Europe would have to understand that the Russian nation had struggled and suffered like no other. Russians would have to be the greatest victors and the greatest victims, now and forever. (347)

Snyder does not even bother to cite any evidence to support this false statement.

Was The Number of Soviet Jews Killed by the Germans a "State Secret"?

> The number of Jews killed by the Germans in the Soviet Union was a state secret. (342)

This statement is also false, and again Snyder does not cite any evidence to support it. (Snyder's footnote to the paragraph that begins with this statement is also false — he vastly understates the number of Soviet citizens killed in the war. We omit this here).

Did the Soviets Try to Hide the Fact of Collaboration with the Germans?

> It was unmentionable that Soviet citizens had staffed Treblinka, Sobibór, and Bełżec. That the Germans needed collaborators, and found them, is not surprising. But collaboration undermined the myth of a united Soviet population defending the honor of the fatherland by resisting the hated fascist invader. (342-3)

Another false statement, and again Snyder cites no evidence. There was no "myth of a united Soviet population..." Trials of collaborators continued throughout the Soviet period, as did prosecutions of, and public attacks upon, Ukrainian and other nationalists who aided the Nazis and who found safe haven in the West.

"Some" Nationalist Partisans Were Antisemitic?

> In the Baltics and Ukraine and Poland, some parti-
> sans were openly anti-Semitic, and continued to use
> the Nazi tactic of associating Soviet power with
> Jewry.
>
> (344; no reference given.)

This is a vast understatement: Baltic and Ukrainian nationalists were *uniformly* anti-Semitic During the German occupation they participated in, and often initiated, mass murders of Jewish civilians, often outdoing the Germans in gruesome sadism. The same was true of most Polish nationalists, including the Home Army.

Polish Anti-Semitism

Prewar Polish society was perhaps the most anti-Semitic society in the world. Polish Jews were not considered "Poles" and were subject to many kinds of discrimination. The Polish Catholic church urged discrimination against Jews, the boycott of Jewish businesses, etc.

During the war Polish civilians carried out many murderous pogroms against Jews. Often the Germans had nothing to do with these attacks. Jewish memoirs repeatedly record that Polish Jews who left the ghettos were more afraid of Poles than they were of Germans. Polish civilians robbed, beat, and murdered Jews, and turned them into the Germans. This last was very important as Germans were not familiar with the clues of Jewish identity and often could not tell Polish Jews from Polish non-Jews. Poles were much more sensitive to these differences and could use their ability to blackmail Jews. *Szmalcownictwo*[5], the blackmailing by Polish civilians of Jews who managed to get outside the ghetto, took place everywhere.

Polish civilians killed Jews to gain favor with the Germans, but also to steal their victims' possessions — homes, lands, belongings, money, clothes — or simply because they were Jews. Sometimes refined forms of torture were used. Jews were burned to death;

---

[5] *Szmalec* means "lard, grease" — that is, money.

Jewish women and girls were often raped before being killed, and so on.

Polish nationalists are fond of pointing out the fact that Israel has named more Poles as "Righteous Among the Nations" — persons who helped Jews during the war — than people of any other nationality. But many Poles who saved Jews during the war were hounded and persecuted by their Polish neighbors and other Poles who learned that they had helped to save Jews. Nationalist historians avoid this issue. Dariusz Libionka, a researcher at the Polish Center for Holocaust Research (Centrum Badań nad Zagładą Żydów) whose work Snyder cites in *Bloodlands,* writes:

> Jak wspomina Michał Borwicz, dyrektor Żydowskiej Komisji Historycznej w Krakowie, po wojnie ukrywający Żydów robili wszystko, aby ich "zbrodnia" nie została ujawniona:
>
> > Zaraz po ukazaniu się pierwszego ŻKH (Dokumenty i zbrodnie męczeństwa) zaczęły się wizyty paradoksalne. Ludzie cytowani po nazwisku (i to właśnie dobroczyńcy!) przychodzili przygnębieni, z wyrzutami: że publikując ich "zbrodnię", [...] wydajemy ich na pastwę zemsty sąsiadów... i nie tylko sąsiadów. Z kolei z podobnymi pretensjami zaczęli się zjawiać niektórzy uratowani Żydzi, wysłani do nas przez swoich dobroczyńców. Inni jeszcze (autorzy zeznań spisanych już, lecz na razie jeszcze nie ogłoszonych) przychodzili prewencyjnie, by zabronić ich ogłaszania w przyszłości [...]. Stanęliśmy, ja i moi współpracownicy, przed kwadraturą koła.

Translated:

> Michael Borwicz, director of the Jewish Historical Commission in Krakow, said that after the war those who had hidden Jews did everything they could to prevent their "crime" from being disclosed:

Immediately after the release of the first ZKH
(Documents and crimes of martyrdom) there
began to occur paradoxical visits. People quoted
by name (and mainly the benefactors [those
who had rescued Jews]!) arrived depressed,
with reproaches: that by publishing their
"crime," [...] we were delivering them to the
mercy of the revenge of their neighbors. ...and
not only of their neighbors. In turn, with similar
claims there began to unexpectedly appear
some rescued Jews, sent to us by their benefactors. Still others (authors of written testimony
but at that time as yet not published) came pre-
ventively, to prohibit their publication in the future [...]. I and my colleagues were faced with
the problem of squaring the circle [i.e. of publishing the names of those who had saved Jews,
and so exposing them to danger from other
Poles, or of not publishing their names, and so
leaving their benevolence unrecognized].[6]

A Polish woman who saved Jews, Marysia Michalska, told one of
those she was hiding, that she had a "guilty conscience" for helping
her Jewish wards:

Byli też i tacy, którzy z powodów religijnych
uważali, że nam, Żydom, wstyd pomagać. Na
przykład Marysia Michalska, osoba dosyć
kulturalna, lecz przesadnie pobożna, zawsze miała
wyrzuty sumienia, że nam udzieliła pomocy ... w
rozmowie ze mną niejednokrotnie zaznaczała, że
modli się, by Bóg jej nie ukarał za to, że nam
pomaga.

Translated:

There were also those who, for religious reasons
thought that it was shameful to help us Jews. For

---

[6] Dariusz Libionka, "Polskie piśmiennictwo na temat zorganizowanej i indywidualnej
pomocy Żydom (1945-2008)", *Zagłada Żydów* 4 (2008), 23.

> example, Mary Michalska, a quite cultured person
> but overly pious, always had a guilty conscience
> that she had provided assistance to us ... in conver-
> sation with me she repeatedly stressed that she was
> praying that God would not punish her for having
> helped us.
> - Leokadia Schmidt, *Cudem przeżyliśmy czas zagłady*
> (Warsaw: Wydawnictwo Literackie, 1983), 160.

Michalska evidently got the idea that helping Jews was sinful from the anti-Semitic Polish Roman Catholic Church, whose influence intensified the ideological anti-Semitism of the Polish elites. After the war many Jews who returned to their homes, shops, and businesses found them occupied by Poles who refused to leave. Many were murdered by their Polish neighbors.

The anticommunist Polish underground that carried out terrorist activity for years after the war also targeted Jews as well as Soviet soldiers and officials, Polish communists, and anyone whom they deemed unpatriotic. Jewish survivors record Home Army units after the war stopping trains, taking the Jewish passengers off and shooting them.

The Center for Holocaust Research (Centrum Badań nad Zagładą Żydów) in Warsaw has published many books and journal articles detailing horrific acts of anti-Semitic violence by Polish civilians and by the Home Army. Polish-American professor Jan Thomasz Gross, a highly anticommunist author, has published a number of books in English detailing Polish anti-Semitism during and after the war that have brought this question to the attention of persons who are not specialists in Polish history.

A recent and very useful account drawn from the works of the Centrum, of Gross, of memoirs of Polish Jews, and other sources, is by Stefan Zgliczyński, *Jak Polacy Niemcom Żydów Mordować Pomagali* - "How Poles Helped Germans Murder Jews." The title is misleading, however, as most of the accounts in the book deal with Poles, both partisans and civilians, murdering Jews on their own initiative without any encouragement or assistance, much less orders, from Germans. Zgliczyński, who is the editor of the Polish edition of the French journal *Le monde diplomatique*, concludes his book with this damning statement:

> Dlatego też logika każe zadać pytanie: z kim przede wszystkim walczyli Polacy podczas ostatniej wojny - z okupantem, czy też ze swoimi żydowskimi sąsiadami i współobywatelami?

Translated:

> Therefore, logic forces us to ask the question: against whom, above all, did Poles fight during the last war — against the occupier or also against their Jewish neighbors and fellow citizens? (265)

Zgliczyński's book serves as an accessible introduction to the large body of research by scholars from the Centrum and of other works such as memoir literature that is available only in Polish. Someone really should translate it.

Most Jews in the former "Kresy," as Western Belorussia and Western Ukraine were called by the Polish imperialists, welcomed the Red Army enthusiastically. There were many Jews in the Red Army, the NKVD (Soviet political police) and the Soviet administrative organs. Likewise, Jewish escapees from the ghettos and Jewish partisans joined the Soviet-backed People's Army (AL), while the Home Army rejected them at best and often murdered them. After the war the communist administration arrested, tried, and punished Poles who participated in pogroms against Jews.

Polish nationalists today do their best to minimize Polish anti-Semitism by ignoring it; by falsely claiming that the Germans "instigated" pogroms by Polish civilians; or by blaming the Jews themselves for being "disloyal" to Poland. Polish nationalists never discuss the official racism against Jews by the prewar Polish government; the role of the Polish schools and Roman Catholic church leadership in actively promoting anti-Semitic ideas; or the admiration of many in the Polish elite for Adolf Hitler's anti-Jewish campaigns. Why *any* Polish Jews should have been loyal to the racist Polish state is the real question, never explained.

Discussion of the official anti-Semitism under the Second Polish Republic, in the Home Army and other Polish formations during and after the war, and of the phenomenal level of anti-Semitism among the Polish population makes the Soviet Union and communist Poles look very good by comparison.

Who Was Harmed By Soviet "Occupation"?

> No Soviet account of the war could note one of its central facts: German and Soviet occupation together was worse than German occupation alone. (344)

This has to be one of the most cynical statements in this highly dishonest book. Snyder makes no argument and cites no evidence to support it. The reality is just the opposite: German and Soviet occupation together was far, far **better** than German occupation alone. Had the Soviets not driven the Germans out, the Germans would have killed not just the millions of Poles and Soviet citizens they did kill, but almost all of them. That was Hitler's expressed aim.

The Soviet retaking of areas formerly occupied by the Germans was certainly far better for Jews, communists, and all those who were fighting or resisting the German occupation. The Red Army saved the majority of Poles, Belorussians, Ukrainians, Russians, and Jews from annihilation or at best slave labor.[7] For example, most of the members of the anticommunist Home Army surrendered in early 1945 when ordered to do so by the London Polish government, and either lived peacefully in postwar Poland or chose to emigrate. Had the Red Army not liberated Poland the Germans would eventually have captured and killed them.

In the article cited previously Grzegorz Motyka, an anticommunist and a researcher whose work Snyder recommends, says that it was the Red Army that stopped the pro-Nazi Ukrainian Nationalists from slaughtering even more Polish civilians and that thou-

---

[7] See the Nazi "Generalplan Ost," now online at http://gplanost.x-berg.de/gplanost.html In Russian translation at http://vk.com/doc-37298103_133818250?dl=a63272a28cd2d43eb8 (accessed February 10, 2014)

sands of Poles joined the pro-Soviet partisan movement as a result.

Of course, the Soviet occupation was indeed "worse" for some people. For Poles who were prosecuted for anti-Semitic and/or anticommunist crimes. For those who had collaborated with the Germans — though it is not clear how many of even these Poles would have survived if Germany had won the war. For those who fought in or supported the underground anticommunist terrorist movements.

In short, the Soviet occupation was worse for fascists, anti-Semites, and those who fought for the restoration of capitalism. The political tendency of *Bloodlands* is aimed to please these very forces, who are honored as "freedom fighters" by today's nationalists in Poland, the Baltics, Ukraine, and to a lesser extent in Belarus.

"The Big Lie" Yet Again: "Soviet Invasion of Poland," "Soviet Alliance with Germany"

> The whole Soviet idea of the Great Patriotic War was premised on the view that the war began in 1941, when Germany invaded the USSR, not in 1939, when Germany and the Soviet Union together invaded Poland. In other words, in the official story, the territories absorbed as a result of Soviet aggression in 1939 had to be considered as somehow always having been Soviet, rather than as the booty of a war that Stalin had helped Hitler to begin. Otherwise the Soviet Union would figure as one of the two powers that started the war, as one of the aggressors, which was obviously unacceptable. (344; no reference given)

And:

> The Soviet citizens who suffered most in the war had been brought by force under Soviet rule right before the Germans came—as a result of a Soviet alliance with Nazi Germany.

> "Also to be forgotten was that the Soviet Union had been
> allied to Nazi Germany when the war began in 1939...
> (345)

This falsehood is crucial to Snyder's thesis. We have thoroughly
discussed it earlier in the present book. We have shown exhaust-
ively in previous chapters that there was no "alliance" with Nazi
Germany and no "Soviet aggression." Apparently Snyder thinks
that his readers will believe this falsehood if he repeats it often
enough. This is the technique of mind-numbing repetition called
"the Big Lie" that Adolf Hitler advocated in *Mein Kampf.*

The following sentence begs for a little more comment:

> ...in the official story, the territories absorbed as a
> result of Soviet aggression in 1939 had to be con-
> sidered as somehow always having been Soviet, ra-
> ther than as the booty of a war that Stalin had
> helped Hitler to begin.

Snyder is referring to Western Ukraine and Western Belorussia,
which had been "the booty of a war" all right — the booty of the
Polish imperialist invasion of Russia in 1919-1921. Poland had
taken these lands by force then, and lost them again in 1939. Evidently Snyder hopes that his readers will be ignorant of this history.

And of course it was not Stalin who had "helped Hitler to begin"
the war. The British, French, and Polish governments did that.
They encouraged Hitler's aggression with the Munich Accord.
Then they torpedoed collective security against Hitler despite the
Soviets' struggle to convince them of its necessity. We have dis-
cussed this, with evidence, in previous chapters.

Was There Official Anti-Semitism in the USSR After World War 2?

> In late 1948 and early 1949, public life in the Soviet
> Union veered toward anti-Semitism. The new line
> was set, indirectly but discernibly, by Pravda on 28
> January 1949. An article on "unpatriotic theater
> critics," who were "bearers of stateless cosmopoli-

tanism," began a campaign of denunciation of Jews
in every sphere of professional life. Pravda purged
itself of Jews in early March. Jewish officers were
cashiered from the Red Army and Jewish activists
removed from leadership positions in the communist party. ...Jewish writers who had taken an interest in Yiddish culture or in the German murder
of Jews found themselves under arrest. As Grossman recalled, "Throughout the whole of the USSR it
seemed that only Jews thieved and took bribes, only
Jews were criminally indifferent towards the suffer-
ings of the sick, and only Jews published vicious or
badly written books."[12] (348)

Sources (n. 12 p. 502):

* "On the *Pravda* article, see Kostyrchenko, *Shadows*, 152."

* "On the decreased number of Jews in high party positions
(thirteen percent to four percent from 1945 to 1952), see
Kostyrchenko, *Gosudarstvennyi antisemitizm*, 352."

* "The Grossman quotation is from Chandler's translation of
Everything Flows.

The *Pravda* editorial discussed by **Kostyrchenko** was written by
Aleksandr A. Fadeev, General Secretary of the Writers Union, and
David I. Zaslavskii, a longtime editor of *Pravda* and of Jewish background himself. The article is available online at a number of places.[8] Many, though not all, of the theatre critics who are criticized in
it do have recognizably Jewish names. But that in itself does not
make the article anti-Semitic, despite the claims of Kostyrchenko
and others. It's impossible to criticize anyone without mentioning
that person's name. It is not anti-Semitic to criticize a Jewish writer. And the criticism in the *Pravda* editorial is not anti-Semitic at
all. Rather, it is directed against criticism that belittled Soviet culture in comparison to Western European culture.

---

[8] At http://www.alexanderyakovlev.org/fond/issues-doc/69512 and
http://www.ihst.ru/projects/sohist/books/cosmopolit/100.htm

By 1952 the per centage of persons "of Jewish origin" in Party organizations had indeed declined to approximately the per centage of Jews in the Soviet population (the correct reference is to the table in **Kostyrchenko**, *Gosudarstvennyi antisemitizm* pp. 353-355). But this is not evidence of anti-Semitism either. Previously the percentage of Jews in high positions in the Party and cultural spheres had been two or more times their proportion in the population. The large-scale *overrepresentation* of Jews in these fields was only possible if other nationalities were seriously *underrepresented*. Reducing the percentage of Jews was inevitable as the percentage of other nationalities was increased.

It was also inevitable that there would be an increase in anti-Semitism in the USSR after the war. Tens of millions of Soviet citizens had lived for several years under German occupation and been subject to an unprecedented barrage of Nazi anti-Semitic propaganda. Nationalists among the Baltic, Belorussian, and Ukrainian population had promoted anti-Semitism too, often more vehemently than the Germans did. This was bound to leave its mark on postwar Soviet society. But Snyder is not discussing *this* anti-Semitism.

Stalin Opposed Anti-Semitism

In the paragraph cited above, Snyder writes:

> A few dozen Jewish poets and novelists who used
> Russian literary pseudonyms found their real or
> prior names published in parentheses. (348)

This is true — and it was Stalin himself who reacted vehemently against it. Stalin opposed the publication of Jewish names after the "pen" names of authors. Noted Soviet author, war correspondent, and editor of literary journals Konstantin Simonov records the following:

> - Почему Мальцев, а в скобках стоит Ровинский?
> В чем дело? До каких пор это будет
> продолжаться? В прошлом году уже говорили
> на эту тему, запретили представлять на
> премию, указывая двойные фамилии. Зачем это
> делается? Зачем пишется двойная фамилия?

Если человек избрал себе литературный
псевдоним - это его право, не будем уже
говорить ни о чем другом, просто об
элементарном приличии. Человек имеет право
писать под тем псевдонимом, который он себе
избрал. Но, видимо, кому-то приятно
подчеркнуть, что у этого человека двойная
фамилия, подчеркнуть, что это еврей. Зачем это
подчеркивать? Зачем это делать? Зачем
насаждать антисемитизм? Кому это надо?
Человека надо писать под той фамилией, под
которой он себя пишет сам. Человек хочет
иметь псевдоним. Он себя ощущает так, как это
для него самого естественно. Зачем же его
тянуть, тащить назад? [9]

Translated:

Why 'Mal'tsev', and then 'Rovinskii' in parentheses?
What's going on here? How long is this going to
continue? ... Why is this being done? We already
spoke about this last year, forbidding double last
names in works presented for the [Stalin] prize.
Why write a double last name? If a person has chosen a literary pseudonym — that's his right. We're
not speaking of anything other than elementary de-
cency. A person has the right to write under a pseudonym he has chosen for himself. But, obviously,
somebody wants to emphasize that this person has
a double name, to emphasize that he is a Jew. Why
emphasize that? Why do that? Why spread anti-
Semitism? Who benefits from that? We must write
down a person with the surname that the person
himself has chosen. A person wishes to have a
pseudonym; he himself feels that this is natural for
him. So why pull him, drag him back?

[9] Konstantin Simonov. *Glazami cheloveka moego pokoleniya.* Moscow: Novosti, 1988, p. 216.
Also online at http://www.hrono.info/libris/lib_s/simonov16.php

Simonov's book and this quotation are well known to students of Soviet history. If Snyder is ignorant of it he is unqualified to write about the subject. If he does know about it but kept it from his readers he is being deliberately dishonest. Stalin made other remarks after the war showing that he personally opposed anti-Semitism.

Snyder cites no evidence that "Jewish officers were dismissed from the Red Army" because they were Jewish or that "Jewish writers... found themselves under arrest." These are serious allegations. If they were made against, say, the American government we would demand evidence. Perhaps Snyder is counting on reflexive, "knee-jerk" anti-Stalinism among his readers to blind them to the absence of any evidence?

The Grossman quotation is from a novel written years after Stalin's death. A quotation from a novel is not documentation of an historical fact. Grossman himself was a tragic case of the consequences of Khrushchev's lies about Stalin and the Stalin years. And the reader should be clear on this point: Khrushchev's "Secret Speech" was deliberately falsified from beginning to end.[10] Grossman believed these slanders and incorporated Khrushchev's false history of the USSR into the book Snyder cites, *Everything Flows (Vsio techiot)*. In it the protagonist accepts Khrushchev's false "revelations" about the Stalin years at face value and decides that all the years of communism have been a cruel hoax, the defendants in the Moscow Trials innocent, and so forth.

Grossman's translator, Robert Chandler, believes this false history himself and has said that Grossman's novels are important "as history."[11] Quite the opposite is the case. Grossman believed Khrushchev's lies and built his novel around them. Many people would

---

[10] See Furr, Khrushchev Lied. The English version of this book was not published until 2011, after *Bloodlands*. But the Russian version was ublished in 2007, long before *Bloodlands*. Гровер Ферр. Антисталинская подлость. М.: Алгортим. 2007. Republished as Тени XX-го съезда, или антисталинская подлость. М.: Эксмо-Алгоритм, 2010. Snyder should have known about it.

[11] See Chandler's remarks in the following interview at BookSerf: "BS... Does it matter what we call different sections of *Everything Flows*, history or fiction? RC: No, I don't think it matters." At http://thebookserf.blogspot.com/2010/01/everything-flows-by-vasily-grossman.html Also, email of Robert Chandler of March 4, 2010.

conclude that this ruins Grossman's novel, for the novel is constructed entirely around Khrushchev's politics. If he had known
Khrushchev's "revelations" were lies Grossman would never have
written this novel in the first place! But many more people than
just Grossman were duped and disillusioned by Khrushchev's lies.

Snyder writes:

> Jews across the Soviet Union were in a state of dis-
> tress. The MGB reported the anxieties of the Jews in
> Soviet Ukraine, who understood that the policy
> must come from the top, and worried that "no one
> can say what form this is going to take." Only five
> years had passed since the end of the German occu-
> pation. For that matter, only eleven years had
> passed since the end of the Great Terror.[13] (348)

Source (n. 13 p. 502): "… For the MGB report, see Kostyrchenko,
Gosudarstvennyi antisemitizm, 327."

The letter in question[12] does indeed show that some Jewish nationalists in the Western Ukrainian city of Chernovtsy reacted negatively to the line on Soviet patriotism of the anti-cosmopolitan
campaign. However, according to the letter, not all the Jewish figures quoted considered it anti-Semitic. Some of them simply
thought it was anti-Marxist. Benjamin Pinkus, Professor of Jewish
History at the Ben-Gurion University in Israel, states that: …."It is
important to emphasise that in these attacks [the anti-
cosmopolitanism campaign] there was no anti-Jewish tone, either
explicitly or implicitly."[13]

The "Berlin Blockade"

Snyder gives the following brief account of the "Berlin Blockade":

---

[12] Online at http://www.alexanderyakovlev.org/fond/issues-doc/68642

[13] *The Jews of the Soviet Union: The History of a National Minority.* Cambridge University
Press, 1989, p 152. Pinkus shows that some Jews "took an active part in the anti-
cosmopolitanism campaign." (157) Pinkus also argues that Jewish writers were attacked
more frequently and perhaps more intensely. So the anti-cosmopolitan campaign may not
have been entirely free of anti-Semitism. But it was not *official* anti-Semitism.

> The western Allies had announced that they would
> introduce a new German currency, the Deutsch-
> mark, in the zones they controlled. The Soviets
> blockaded West Berlin, with the evident goal of
> forcing West Berliners to accept supplies from the
> Soviets, and thus accept Soviet control of their soci-
> ety. The Americans then undertook to supply the
> isolated city by air, which Moscow claimed could
> never work. In May 1949, the Soviets had to give up
> the blockade. The Americans, along with the British,
> proved capable of supplying thousands of tons of
> supplies by air every day. In this one action, good-
> will, prosperity, and power were all on display.
> (349)

This is false. "Soviet control of their society" was not at all the Soviet "goal." Even Snyder does not claim he can demonstrate this,
calling it "the evident goal." Snyder has distorted what the Berlin
crisis was all about. Historian Geoffrey Roberts describes it as follows:

> Although termed a "blockade" by the West, the So-
> viet action consisted of a limited set of restrictions
> on land access to the Western sectors of Berlin from
> West Germany. It did not preclude supplies to West
> Berlin from the Soviet zone of occupation, which
> continued to trickle into the city, nor was air access
> prohibited — hence the famous airlift.
>
> The goal of Stalin's pressure tactics was to force the
> Western allies to rescind their London communiqué
> and return to the CFM [Council of Foreign Minis-
> ters] negotiating forum. Stalin was quite frank
> about his aim in two conversations he held with the
> British, French, and American ambassadors in Au-
> gust 1948. In January 1949 Stalin made this posi-
> tion public when he agreed with a Western inter-
> viewer that the blockade would be lifted if the West
> agreed to convene another CFM session devoted to
> the German question. In May 1949 the blockade

> was lifted when the Western powers agreed to re-
> convene the CFM in Paris.[14]

Smyder does not mention the fact that it was the Soviet Union that offered to reunite Germany — something all Germans wanted — but the Western Allies refused.

Snyder Falsifies — Again — About Litvinov"s Dismissal

> He [Molotov] had been appointed to the job [Soviet
> Foreign Minister] in 1939, in part because he (un-
> like his predecessor Litvinov) was not Jewish, and
> Stalin had then needed someone with whom Hitler
> would negotiate. (351)

We have exposed this falsehood in a previous chapter. There is no evidence to support it. It seems that Molotov was appointed because Stalin wanted desperately to conclude a treaty for mutual defense not with Hitler but with the West, and Molotov was the person closest to him.

> It was very dangerous to be a Jew in postwar Po-
> land—though no more so than to be a Ukrainian or
> a German or a Pole in the anti-communist under-
> ground. (352)

This is a striking admission by Snyder, though he appears to be unaware he has made it. Snyder is comparing the situation of Jewish civilians, who he admits were subject to murderous anti-Semitic pogroms by Poles in Poland, to armed terrorists who were of course being hunted by the police.

Many of these terrorists had collaborated with the Germans — some Home Army men had done this, as had virtually all the Ukrainians and Germans in what Snyder calls "the anti-communist underground." Many of them had participated in the Holocaust and/or themselves taken part in the murder of Polish, Ukrainian, and Russian civilians. It was right that it be "dangerous" for them,

---

[14] Roberts, *Molotov. Stalin's Cold Warrior* (Dulles, VA: Potomac Books, 2012), 118-9.

just as it was wrong that there was so much Polish anti-Semitism that it was dangerous for Jews in Poland.

In this passage and in fact throughout *Bloodlands* Snyder is clearly doing propaganda work for — "rehabilitating" — pro-Nazi, anti-Semitic forces in Eastern Europe who are considered "heroes" by today's right-wing Eastern European nationalists.. Of course these forces were also anti-Soviet, which is the reason Snyder minimizes their crimes.

In 2013 Poland declared a holiday in honor of the "Doomed Soldiers" (in Polish, „Żołnierze wyklęci") of the Polish anticommunist underground, proclaiming them to be "heroes." A Ukrainian newspaper has this to say about them:

> "Прокляті солдати": настав час бачити героїв такими, якими вони були
>
> Парламент Польщі підтримав надання статусу національного свята дню пам'яті т.зв. "проклятих солдатів" - учасників антирадянського збройного підпілля в 1940-1950-ті рр. Серед них є і ті, хто відверто співпрацював з нацистами, і ті, хто по-звірячому вбивав мирних українців.[15]

Translated:

> "Doomed Soldiers" [more accurately, "damned soldiers"] — The Time Has Come to See These Heroes As They Really Were
>
> The Parliament of Poland had supported the proposal for the status of a national holiday to the day of memory of the so-called "Doomed Soldiers" — the participants in the anti-Soviet armed underground of the 1940s and 1950s. Among them are those who openly collaborated with the Nazis and those who viciously killed peaceful Ukrainians.

---

[15] http://www.istpravda.com.ua/digest/2011/03/7/29916/ The reader will recall that anticommunist historian Motyka states that Ukrainian partisans murdered 100,000 or more peaceful Poles in the Volhynian Massacres.

Snyder does not mention the fact that the Soviets and pro-Soviet Poles actively persecuted anti-Semites. For example, the perpetrators of the murderous pogram of Jews in Kielce, Poland in July 1946 were captured, tried, convicted, and executed within a month of their crime.

Did the Polish Communists Claim that Only Communists Led the Warsaw Ghetto Revolt?

> All resistance to fascism was by definition led by communists; if it was not led by communists, then it was not resistance. The history of the Warsaw Ghetto Uprising of 1943 had to be rewritten such that communists could be seen as leading Polish Jews— just as they were supposedly leading the Polish anti-Nazi resistance generally. In the politically acceptable history of the Second World War, the resistance in the ghetto had little to do with the mass murder of Jews, and much to do with the courage of communists. This fundamental shift of emphasis obscured the Jewish experience of the war, as the Holocaust became nothing more than an instance of fascism. It was precisely Jewish communists who had to develop and communicate these misrepresentations, so that they could not be charged with attending to Jewish rather than Polish goals. In order to seem like plausible Polish communist leaders, Jewish communists had to delete from history the single most important example of Jews resisting Nazis from Jewish motivations. The bait in Stalin's political trap was left by Hitler.[22] (322)

Source (n. 22 p. 502): Shore, "Język," 60.

This is contradicted by Snyder's own source. According to Marci Shore Jewish historians did not "delete" the Warsaw Ghetto Uprising from history but continued to celebrate it every year while downplaying the role of the Zionists and exaggerating that of the Communists.

Shore, "Język," 60:

> W ten sposób zakończyła się pewna epoka. Co roku komuniści - z Zachariaszem na czele - obchodzili rocznicę powstania. Nie było już żadnej wzmianki o syjonistach. Generalnie chodziło tu o proces, w którym komuniści żydowscy zdradzali syjonistyczną lewicę, swoich byłych towarzyszy.

Translated:

> Thus ended an era. Every year the communists, with Zacharias in charge, celebrated the anniversary. There was no longer any mention of Zionists. Generally, this meant a process in which Jewish Communists betrayed the Zionist left, their former comrades.

> Po wyjezdie Hermana i innych syjonistów, Ber Mark stał się autorem oficjalnej historii powstania w getcie warszawskim. Według cenzora: "Tow. Markowi udało się przeprowadzić w swej pracy słuszną polityczno-ideologiczną linię ... Tow. Mark przeprowadza w swej pracy tę linię zasadniczą, że jedyną siłę, która rzuciła hasło walki, że jedynym czynnikiem, który zorganizował i kierował ruchem oporu w getcie — była PPR i GL."

Translated:

> After the departure of Herman and other Zionists, Ber Mark was the author of the official history of the Warsaw ghetto uprising. According to the censor: "Comrade. Mark carried out in his work the legitimate political and ideological line ... Comrade. Mark carries out in his work in this line of principle that the only force which threw the signal for the fight that the only factor that organized and directed resistance in the Ghetto, was the PPR and the GL [the Polish Workers Party and the Gardia Ludowa, communist groups]."

But there is reason to doubt the truth of Shore's statement here. Ber Mark's official history, *Powstanie w getcie warszawskim*, published in Polish in 1959, was published in English translation in 1975. Here are two short passages from the early pages of that book, *Uprising in the Warsaw Ghetto*:

> Its [the Anti-Fascist Bloc's] member bodies were the Polish Workers Party (P.P.R.), Hashomer Hatzair, Left and Right Labor Zionists, and Hechalutz. (5)

> Commander-in-chief [of the Jewish Fighting Organization] was [Mordechai] Anielewicz, a twenty-four-year-old Hashomer Hatzair activist. Other members were Hersz Berlinski (Left Labor Zionist), Marek Edelman (Jewish Labor Bund), Itzhak Cukierman (Hechalutz), and Michal Roisenfeld (Polish Workers Party). (6)

Here is one final passage to show that Mark did not neglect the Zionists in the rest of the book:

> In brief, here [at Mila 18] were the mind and heart of the Uprising: the leaderships of the Jewish Fighting Organization, Hashomer Hatzair, and the Communists; plus activists and commanders in D'ror (a Zionist group), the Jewish Labor Bund, and Akiva. (72)

The issue here is not how historically accurate Mark's depiction is. Snyder claims that the postwar communist version of the Warsaw Ghetto uprising portrayed communists as in the lead. Snyder's source Shore claims that Ber Mark wrote that "the only factor that organized and directed resistence in the Ghetto was the PPR and GL." These quotations from Ber Mark 's book prove that this is not true. Mark mentions the communists prominently but often mentions Zionist and other non-communist Jewish forces first. Moreover, Mark does not show communists as the leaders of the Uprising, as Shore claims.

Snyder then again claims, without evidence, that Stalin was anti-Semitic:

> This was Polish-Jewish Stalinist self-defense from Stalin's own anti-Semitism. (356)

Another blatant falsehood by Snyder. As we have seen and will see again, Stalin was not in the least "anti-Semitic" and Snyder has no evidence that he was.

According to Zhores Medvedev,

> Антисемитизм Сталина, о котором можно прочитать почти во всех его биографиях, не был ни религиозным, ни этническим, ни бытовым. Он был политическим и проявлялся в форме антисионизма, а не юдофобии.

Translated:

> Stalin's anti-Semitism, about which one reads in almost all of his biographies, was not based on religion, or race, or culture. It was political and expressed itself in the form of anti-Zionism, and not of racial anti-Semitism [iudofobii].[16]

Here Medvedev takes the position that opposition to Zionism is "anti-Semitic." Of course this is wrong. Many Jews, including Israeli Jews, are strongly anti-Zionist. Medvedev states that there is no evidence that Stalin was anti-Semitic, but anticommunist writers routinely claim that he was. Snyder is one of these.

Again Snyder Claims Stalin "Slandered the Home Army and the Warsaw Uprising"

> The associated slander of the Home Army and the Warsaw Uprising of 1944 was an easy labor. Since it had not been led by communists, it could not have been an uprising. Since the Home Army soldiers were not communists, they were reactionaries, acting against the interests of the toiling masses. The Polish patriots who died seeking to liberate their capital were fascists, little better than Hitler. The Home Army, which had fought the Germans with much greater determination than the Polish com-

---

[16] *Stalin i evreiskaia problema*, p. 92.

munists, was a "bespittled dwarf of reaction."[23]
(356)

n. 23: This was part of the slogan of one of the more striking propaganda posters, executed by Włodzimierz Zakrzewski.[17]

This is false. The communists never called the fighters of the Warsaw Uprising "fascists" and Snyder cannot cite any evidence that they did so. Furthermore, many communists also fought in the Warsaw Uprising.

As we have discussed in an earlier chapter, it was not only Stalin and the communists but General Anders, Jan Ciechanowski, and many other anticommunist Poles thought the Warsaw Uprising of 1944 was a "crime." The criminals were the Home Army leadership, not the ordinary fighters. Many other non-communist Poles came to think the same thing, since the Uprising predictably led only to disaster.

There is no question that the Home Army fought to restore prewar Poland, a violent, imperialist regime, racist against Jews, Ukrainians, and Belorussians, and hostile even to the Polish trade union movement. Snyder cites no evidence at all for his claim that the Home Army fought the Germans "with much greater determination than the Polish communists" of the People's Army. Moreover, here Snyder seems to forget that he has already claimed that the activity of pro-Soviet partisans against the Germans simply brought down German violence upon the local population. To the extent the Home Army fought the Germans their actions would have the same effect.

Snyder omits to inform his readers that the Home Army was conspiring with the German military against the communist forces. Nor does he mention that the Home Army hunted down and killed

---

[17] The Zakrzewski poster, "The giant and the bespittled dwarf of reaction," may be viewed here: http://artyzm.com/obraz.php?id=5569 The "giant" in the poster is either a People's Army (Armia Ludowa) fighter or a Polish Army (Wojsko Polskie) man, and the "bespittled dwarf of reaction" is the AK. The AK attacked and killed pro-Soviet partisans and Jews generally, and had collaborated with the Nazis, so it is neither surprising or unjust that the communists attacked it as "reactionary."

Jews, including Jews who escaped from the Warsaw Ghetto Uprising, and collaborated with the Nazis against the Red Army.

Should Stalin Have Left Terrorists Alone Because A Few Of Them Had Once Tried to Save Jews?

> Berman, a very intelligent man, understood all of this as well as anyone could, and he brought these premises to their logical conclusions. He presided over a security apparatus that arrested members of the Home Army who had accepted the special assignment of saving Jews. (357)

This is a dishonest statement. Snyder apparently wishes to imply that Polish communist security arrested some Home Army men *because* they had been assigned to save Jews. Snyder does not say this in plain language, because it is untrue. Does he then wish to imply that "accepting the special assignment of saving Jews" should have exempted them from arrest no matter what else they did?

Snyder gives no note or citation of evidence for this statement. He does not tell us the names of any of these Home Army men. But one of them — if not the only one — was Witold Pilecki. Pilecki did indeed struggle to save Jews. But he also remained in post-war Poland as a leader of the viiolent underground terrorist Home Army which murdered thousands of Poles, Jews, and Soviet citizens.

This is what he was tried and executed for in 1948. No country, capitalist or communist, permits underground terrorists to roam and murder freely. Zgliczyński's book gives many examples of wartime and, especially, of post-war murders of Jews, communists, Soviet citizens, and others by underground terrorists of the Home Army, the NSZ (Narodowe Siły Zbrojne, "National Armed Forces"). There is at least one book that gives names and details about more than one thousand members and veterans of the pro-communist People's Army (Armia Ludowa, AL) murdered by these underground anticommunist "nationalist" groups *after* the war's end.[18]

---

[18] *Żołnierze Armii Ludowej polegli i zamordowani przez podziemie zbrojne po wyzwoleniu kraju.* Warsaw: Wydawca Rada Krajowa Żołnierzy Armii Krajowej przy ZG Związku

Snyder Lies About Purge of the Polish Communist Party

> Polish communists who were in power in the late
> 1940s usually knew, from personal experience, just
> what had happened to their comrades in the 1930s.
> Back then, Stalin had sent a signal; Polish com-
> munists had duly denounced each other, which led
> to mass murder, and the end of the party itself....[30]
> (359)

Source (n. 30 p. 503): "This explanation of the absence of a communist blood purge in Poland can be found inter alia in Luks,
"Brüche," 47. One Polish communist leader apparently murdered
another during the war; this too might have bred caution."

Evidently Snyder has invented this falsehood. There has never
been any evidence that Stalin gave such a "signal." Luks, "Brüche,"
— the correct page reference to it is p. 43, not p. 47 — says nothing about a "signal" from Stalin, about "Polish communists duly
denouncing each other," "mass murder," or anything of the kind.

The "Doctors" Plot"

Snyder spends more space on this event than on any other in this
chapter. He gets virtually everything wrong, as he has so many
times before. It is hard to believe that Snyder has studied the Doctors' Plot himself. He appears to rely instead on the extremely anticommunist and incompetent secondary accounts by Brent and
Naumov, and by Arno Lustiger. But Snyder, not they, is responsible
for what goes into his book.

> Shcherbakov had died the day after he had insisted,
> against doctors' orders, on taking part in a Victory
> Day parade. (363)

Source (n. 39 p. 503): "On the Victory Day parade, see Brandenberger, "Last Crime," 193."

Kombatantów RP i b. Więźniów Politycznych, 1997. Some excerpts from this book, very
hard to find outside Poland, are online at http://poczmanski-
wieslaw.blog.pl/2013/09/05/w-trosce-o-dobre-imie-prezydenta-iii-rp/ and a few other
sites (accessed March 22 2014).

Brandenberger simply repeats what Brent/Naumov say: that Shcherbakov ignored the doctors' advice to remain in bed — he had suffered a heart attack on December 1944 — and instead went out to view the Victory Day celebrations and died of another heart attack the next day, May 10, 1945. But neither Branderberger nor Brent/Naumov cite any evidence for their contention that Shcherbakov ignored the doctors' advice.

A.N. Ponomarev, author of the only full-length biography of Shcherbakov, had access to evidence from the Moscow Party archive and from the Shcherbakov family. Ponomarev states that Shcherbakov went to the celebration *with his doctors' permission*:

> Вечером (**врачи не возражали**) Александр Сергеевич в сопровождении жены приехал с дачи в столицу, побывал на улицах и площадях, порадовался вместе с москвичами долгожданной победе.[19]

Translated:

> In the evening (**the doctors did not object**) Aleksandr Sergeevich together with his wife drove from his dacha to the capital, spent a while on the streets and in the squares, rejoicing together with the Muscovites over the long-awaited victory.

Ponomarev is honest enough to admit that he is not certain about this, since the testimony came years a few years later during the investigation of the Doctors' Plot. How, then, can Brandenberger, Brent/Naumov, and Snyder claim *without qualification* that Shcherbakov's doctors *did* object?

In the case of Zhdanov things are clearer, and again Snyder gets them wrong:

> Zhdanov, too, had ignored doctors' orders to rest.
> (363)

This can only be a deliberate falsehood either by Snyder or by his source. Snyder cites the Brent/Naumov book so he must know that

---

[19] A.N. Ponomarev. *Aleksandr Shcherbakov. Stranitsy biografii.* M: Izd. Glavarkhiva Moskvy, 2004, p. 275.

even this dishonest book discusses how the doctors in charge of treating Zhdanov allowed him to leave his bed and walk around despite the fact that the consulting cardiologist, Dr. Lidia Timashuk, determined that Zhdanov had suffered a recent heart attack and recommended strict bed rest.

There Really Was a "Doctors" Plot" Against Zhdanov

In fact there was indeed a conspiracy among Zhdanov's doctors to mistreat Zhdanov: to deny that he had suffered not just one heart attack but two recent ones and possibly a third the month before; to ignore the diagnosis of Dr. Timashuk, the cardiologist, and therefore to allow Zhdanov to get out of bed. The direct result of this was Zhdanov's death. Gennady Kostyrchenko quotes from Dr. Vinogradov's note to Beria on March 27, 1953:

> Все же необходимо признать, что у А.А. Жданова имелся инфаркт, и отрицание его мною, профессорами Василенко, Егоровым, докторами Майоровым и Карпай было с нашей стороны ошибкой. При этом злого умысла в постановке диагноза и метода лечения у нас не было."[20]

Translated:

> All the same, it must be admitted that A.A. Zhdanov did have a heart attack and the denial of this fact by myself, professor Vasilenko and Egorov, and doctors Maiorov and Karpai was a mistake on our part. We had no evil intention in making our diagnosis and our treatment.

Brent and Naumov claim to have had access to an even earlier document in which Vinogradov makes the same admission:

> On November 18, 1952, Vinogradov was still able to deny a premeditated plot to kill Zhdanov: "I allowed a mistake in the diagnosis that led to grave consequences and then to [Zhdanov's] death. There was

---

[20] *Tainaia politika Stalina. Vlast' i antisemitizm* (2003), 642.

> no evil plan in my action ... I want only to repeat
> that at the basis of this crime, its original source,
> was medical error that I allowed as a consultant,
> leading the treatment of A.A. Zhdanov.
> (Brent/Naumov, 231)

A semi-official collection of documents cites the following original:

> Я признаю, что по моей вине жизнь А.А.
> Жданова была сокращена. При лечении я
> допустил ошибку в диагностике, приведшую к
> тяжелым последствиям, а затем к его смерти.
> Злого умысла в моих действиях не было.[21]

Translated:

> I admit that it was my fault that A.A. Zhdanov's life
> was shortened. In the course of treating him I made
> a mistake in diagnosis which led to serious conse-
> quences and then to his death. There was no evil in-
> tent in my actions.

Therefore there really was a "doctors' plot" against Zhdanov in 1948! Vinogradov admitted that the consulting doctors ignored the findings and recommendation of the cardiologist, Dr. Ti-mashuk. The only question is whether Vinogradov and the others did this, as Vinogradov claimed, to "hide my mistake in order to protect myself and those who had taken part in Zhdanov's treat-ment,"[22] or whether they had deliberately killed Zhdanov.

Understandably, the Soviet investigators had to investigate the latter possibility. The job of policemen is to be suspicious. If medi-cal doctors in the United States today were to make such an ad-mission they would certainly be stripped of their licenses to prac-tice medicine and face criminal prosecution and civil lawsuits.

Snyder must have known this since both Brent/Naumov and Kostyrchenko relate it. Moreover, many of the primary sources, including this document, have been publicly available for years.

---

[21] At http://www.alexanderyakovlev.org/fond/issues-doc/69180

[22] «...чтобы скрыть свою ошибку, выгородить себя и принимавших участие в лечении А.А. Жданова...» ; see document at previous footnote.

But Snyder failed to tell his readers the facts about this important question.

Did Stalin Order the Doctors To Be Beaten in 1952?

> In autumn 1952 several more Soviet doctors were under investigation. None of them had anything to do with Zhdanov or Shcherbakov, but they had treated other Soviet and foreign communist dignitaries before their deaths. One of them was Stalin's personal doctor, who had advised him to retire in early 1952. At Stalin's express and repeated orders, these people were beaten terribly...[46] (365)

Source (n. 46 p. 503): "Quotation: Brent, *Plot*, 250."

Snyder gives no evidence for the claim that Stalin ordered the doctors to be beaten. Neither do Brent and Naumov, who state that "the doctors were 'beaten to a pulp'" but give no reference.

This opens up an interesting mystery. On August 22, 2011, a purported letter to Beria from Sergei A. Goglidze, Deputy head of the MVD at the time and dated March 26, 1953, was published by "Memorial Society" official and researcher Nikita Petrov in *Novaia Gazeta*.[23] This is an ideologically anticommunist newspaper of which Mikhail Gorbachev is part owner along with a Russian billionaire, while "Memorial" is a highly anticommunist research institution. Neither has any reputation for historical objectivity. In this letter Goglidze supposedly claimed that Stalin himself had told him to beat suspects "with deadly beatings."

Is this document genuine? Petrov claims that he found it "in the 1990s" but does not explain why he waited until 2011 to publish it. It is not mentioned in the "Memorial"-sponsored volume *Lavrentii Beria*, Part I, published in 1991, where Documents 5 and 6

---

[23] Nikita Petrov. "Zavety Stalina: 'Bit', bit', smertnym boem bit'!" - Никита Петров. Заветы Сталина: «Бить, бить, смертным боем бить!»
http://www.novayagazeta.ru/gulag/48143.html For some reason Petrov published only excerpts from this letter. The whole text is available at
http://perpetrator2004.narod.ru/documents/DoctorsPlot/StalinDocsDP.doc

deal with the "Doctors Plot." Nor is it in the 1085-page volume of Beria-related documents published in 2012.[24] Petrov quoted from it in an earlier article in *Novaia Gazeta* of October 16, 2008, but did not publish it at that time. Instead, he published an often-reprinted reproduction the so-called "torture telegram" of January 10, 1939, along with a handwritten facsimile of a letter from Semion Ignat'ev to Stalin of November 15, 1952 that does not mention beatings.

All this raises suspicion about whether this document is genuine. Even if it is, the further question is: was Goglidze telling the truth? The truth is: it is impossible to say. Anti-Stalinists have every reason to fabricate documents to make Stalin look bad, and have done so. Goglidze, if he did write this letter, had every reason to pass the blame for mistreatment of the doctor-prisoners onto the dead Stalin, since doing so might help him avoid punishment (Goglidze was one of six MGB officers shot in December 1953 for their association with Lavrentii Beria).The historian's dictum "Testis unus — testis nullus" applies here too; one "witness" is never enough to establish a fact. Source criticism, an obligation for every responsible historian, is essential here — and once again Snyder fails to give us any.

Snyder also fails to inform his readers of this passage in his daughter's memoir:

> The "case of the Kremlin doctors" was under way that last winter. My father's housekeeper told me not long ago that my father was exceedingly distressed at the turn events took. She heard it discussed at the dinner table. She was waiting on the table, as usual, when my father remarked that he didn't believe the doctors were "dishonest" and that the only evidence against them, after all, was the "reports" of Dr. Timashuk.[25] (Emphasis added)

Snyder quotes Svetlana Allilueva's memoirs elsewhere, so why not here? Obviously because *this* quotation would cast doubt on Sta-

---

[24] *Politbiuro i delo Beria. Sbornik dokumentov.* Moscow: Kuchkovo Pole, 2012.

[25] *Twenty Letters to a Friend*, p. 207.

lin's guilt in the "Doctors' Plot" case. Brent/Naumov also fail to cite this passage, no doubt for the same reason.

We have seen above that Snyder quotes from Svetlana Allilueva's writings — but only when they have an anti-Stalin tendency. When they do not or, as here, when they contradict an anti-communist story, Snyder ignores them. This is not the way a historian is supposed to act. Snyder is writing not history but "anticommunist propaganda with footnotes."

Snyder Falsifies Stalin"s Words

Snyder states:

> Stalin, a sick man of seventy-three, listening to no counsel but his own, pushed forward. In December 1952 he said that "every Jew is a nationalist and an agent of American intelligence," a paranoid formulation even by his standards.[49] (366)

Source (n. 49 p. 503): "For "every Jew…," see Rubenstein, *Pogrom*, 62."

Rubenstein does have this quotation — but it is a lie. Rubenstein refers to the source, the memoirs of Minister Malyshev about a December 1 1952 meeting during which Stalin said:

> Любой еврей-националист, это агент америк[анской] разведки. Евреи-нац[ионалисты] считают, что их нацию спасли США (там можно стать богачом, буржа и т.д.)

Translated:

> Every Jewish nationalist is an agent of American intelligence. Jewish nationalists consider that their nation was saved by the USA (there one can become rich, a bourgeois, etc.)
>
> - *Istochnik* 5 (1997), 140-1.

By "Jewish nationalist" Stalin clearly means "Zionist." Since April 2008 there has even been an Internet page exposing this misquotation, which it attributes to Brent and Naumov. But as recently as

April 2012 Snyder was repeating this false quotation in the standard talk he was giving about *Bloodlands*.[26]

Snyder is either deliberately lying or never bothered to check the source of this quotation. Whatever is the case, it does him no credit as a historian.

Anything To Make Stalin Appear Anti-Semitic? Snyder Falsifies the Draft Letter

Snyder writes:

> In February 1953, the Soviet leadership was drafting and redrafting a collective Jewish self-denunciation, including phrases that might have come straight from Nazi propaganda. It was to be signed by prominent Soviet Jews and published in *Pravda*. Vasily Grossman was among those intimidated into signing the letter....[52] (367)

Sources (n. 52 p. 504):

> * "On the drafting and redrafting, see Kostyrchenko, *Gosudarstvennyi antisemitizm* , 470-478."
> * "On Grossman, see Brandenberger, "Last Crime," 196.
> * "See also Luks, "Brüche," 47."

In an article published in 2009, when *Bloodlands* must have been nearing completion, Snyder wrote:

> In early 1953, the Soviet leadership was circulating a petition among prominent Soviet Jews, who were to apologize to Russians for claiming that Jews had suffered, and thank Russians for saving them."
> (note to Kostyrchenko, *Gosudarstvennyi antisemitizm...* 470-478.) (2009-4)

Snyder's characterization of the unpublished letter is false. The letter in question says nothing whatsoever about any apology, to Russians or to anyone else. It says nothing about "claiming that

---

[26]See http://holocaustcontroversies.blogspot.com/2006/04/correction-corner-1-every-jew-is.html When Snyder repeated this lie during his talk on April 17, 2012 at Kean University I called from the floor: "That's not true!" Snyder's reply was "Yeah, sure!"

Jews had suffered." It says nothing about "thanking Russians" — or anybody — "for saving them." It does not contain any "Jewish self-denunciation," whatever that might mean. It contains no "phrases that might have come straight from Nazi propaganda."

Of course, Snyder's readers will have no idea that he is lying — and here I say "lying" advisedly, because it is not credible that Snyder has simply failed to read the letter himself. But Snyder's readers will not have read the letter. What's more, Snyder has failed to inform them where they might read it. The first draft of the letter in question is translated into English in Brent/Naumov (300-305). Snyder cites this book. But Snyder does not inform his readers that they can read this letter there. Could that be because anyone who does read the letter would see that Snyder is not being truthful about it?

Nor was it "the Soviet leadership" that was circulating this letter. Dmitrii Shepilov, one of the Secretaries of the CPSU, and N.A. Mikhailov, head of the Agitprop section of the Party, sent it to Malenkov, who was in the leadership of the Party, the Politburo. Neither Shepilov nor Mikhailov was in the "Soviet leadership." After criticism by Il'ia Erenburg a second draft was sent to Mikhailov by Shepilov but never circulated farther, much less printed.

Here is what Lazar Kaganovich told Feliks Chuev about this letter:

> Когда Михайлов принес мне бумагу для публикации против этих врачей - я вам рассказываю кое-что личное - по еврейскому вопросу, и там были подписи Рейзена и многих других еврейских деятелей. Михайлов был секретарем ЦК, потом министром культуры. Я ему сказал: «Я не подпишу».
>
> - А что, там осуждали их?
>
> - Да, да. Он говорит: «Как? Мне товарищ Сталин поручил.»- Скажите товарищу Сталину, что я не подпишу. Я ему сам объясню.
>
> Когда я пришел, Сталин меня спрашивает: «Почему вы не подписали?» Я говорю: «Я член Политбюро ЦК КПСС, а не еврейский

общественный деятель, и буду подписывать бумагу как член Политбюро. Давайте такую бумагу я напишу, а как еврейский общественный деятель не буду подписывать. Я не еврейский общественный деятель!»

Сталин внимательно на меня посмотрел: «Ладно, хорошо».

Я говорю: «Если нужно, я напишу, статью, от себя».

«Посмотрим, может, надо будет и статью написать»[27]

Translated:

When Mikhailov brought me the paper for publication against these doctors — I am telling you something personal — concerning the Jewish question, there were the signatures of Reizen and of many other Jewish figures. Mikhailov was a secretary of the Central Committee, and then Minister of Culture. I told him: "I will not sign it."

- What? Are you condemning them?

- Yes, yes. He said: "What? Comrade Stalin gave me this." — Tell comrade Stalin that I will not sign it. I will explain it to him myself.

When I arrived, Stalin asked me. "Why didn't you sign?" I said: "I am a member of the Politburo of the CC of the CPSU, and not a Jewish public figure, and I will sign papers as a member of the Politburo. Give me a paper like this and I will sign it, but I will not sign as a Jewish public figure. I am not a Jewish public figure."

Stalin looked attentively at me. "OK, that's fine."

I said: "If necessary, I will write an article of my own."

---

[27] Feliks Chuev, *Tak govoril Kaganovich*. Moscow: Otechestvo, 1992, p. 174.

"Let's see, maybe we'll need you to write an article."

There is no evidence that Vasili Grossman was "intimidated into signing the letter." His signature simply appears alongside those of many others. **Brandenberger** cites no evidence that Grossman was "coerced." Nor does it seem likely. Judging from his novels, at this time Grossman was making great efforts to be a loyal communist.

> In vicious press attacks, it suddenly emerged that his [Grossman's — GF] recently published novel of the war, *For a Just Cause*, was not patriotic enough. *For a Just Cause* was a vast novel of the Battle of Stalingrad, mostly within Stalinist conventions. (367)

Several of these criticisms are available online. None of them are "vicious," though some are sharp. Their main point is that Grossman's novel is not Marxist enough for a Party member.[28]

Snyder: Rumors Are History — Almost

Snyder writes:

> Judging **by the rumors circulating at the time**, Soviet citizens had no trouble imagining the possible outcomes: doctors would have been show-tried with Soviet leaders who were their supposed allies; remaining Jews would have been purged from the state police and the armed forces; the thirty-five thousand Soviet Jewish doctors (and perhaps scientists as well) might have been deported to camps; and perhaps even the Jewish people as such would have been subject to forced removal or even mass shootings.[54] (368, emphasis added)

It is true that rumors like this circulated at the time in the USSR. Today in the USA rumors are circulating that Israel had advance warning of the 9/11 terrorist attack; that the attack was permitted, maybe even planned, by the Bush Administration itself; that

---

[28] At http://www.hrono.ru/dokum/195_dok/19530324gross.html

the Twin Towers were demolished not by the jetliners' impacts but by explosive charges carefully placed in advance, etc.

In other words, rumor is not history — far from it! There are plenty of rumors in Russia today that reflect very positively on Stalin. Of course, Snyder ignores them. For Snyder, rumor only belongs in an historical work when that rumor conforms to his own prejudices.

Snyder has to know, but does not tell his readers, that Gennady Kostyrchenko, anticommunist, Zionist, and hater of Stalin, has long since disproved the stories about a "planned deportation of Jews." Kostyrchenko's article is titled "Deportatsiia — Mistifikatsiia", and one does not need to know Russian to understand its meaning [29] Snyder also fails to inform his readers that in his book *Stalin i evreiskaia problema* ("Stalin and the Jewish Problem," 2003) Zhores Medvedev writes:

> Можно предположить, что Сталин позвонил в «Правду» либо вечером 27 февраля, либо утром 28 февраля и распорядился прекратить публикацию антиеврейских материалов и всех других статей, связанных с «делом врачей....»

> В Советском Союзе в это время был только один человек, который мог простым телефонным звонком редактору «Правды» или в Агитпроп ЦК КПСС изменить официальную политику. Это мог сделать только Сталин. (216-7)

Translated:

> We can assume that Stalin called Pravda either on the evening of February 27 or in the morning of February 28 and arranged for the cessation of publication of anti-Jewish materials and of all other articles dealing with the "Doctors' Plot."...

---

[29] See his articles "Депортация - мистификация," Лехаим, 9/ 2002, at http://www.lechaim.ru/ARHIV/125/kost.htm ; also in Вопросы Истории 1 (2003), 92-113.

> In the Soviet Union at that time there was only one
> person who was able, with a single telephone call to
> the editor of Pravda or to the Department of Agit-
> prop of the CC CPSU to change official policy. Only
> Stalin could do that...

In their collection of essays *The Unknown Stalin* Zhores and his
brother Roi Medvedev come to a similar conclusion:

> We still have no way of knowing exactly how the
> anti-Semitic campaign was stopped on 1 March or
> who was ultimately responsible. ... It is clear, how-
> ever, that the end of the propaganda campaign was
> associated with a decision to abandon preparations
> for the trial of the doctors. The actual order could
> only have come from Ignatiev. It is also conceivable,
> however, that Stalin had given the instruction him-
> self on 27 or 28 February.[30]

It appears more than unlikely that Ignatiev would have sent such
an order without at least obtaining Stalin's approval. The
Medvedev volumes are very well known but Snyder does not mention these passages. Incompetence? Or deliberate deceit?

Snyder Still Believes Khrushchev"s "Secret Speech"

Snyder:

> He [Nikita Khrushchev] even revealed some of Sta-
> lin's crimes in a speech to a party congress in Feb-
> ruary 1956... (371)

No, he did not. The evidence proving Khrushchev's famous "Secret
Speech" was falsified from beginning to the end was published
Russian in late 2007, long before Snyder's book was completed.[31]
If Snyder did not know about this he is incompetent to write about
the matter.

---

[30] Woodstock and New York: Overlook Press, 2004, p. 32

[31] Г. Ферр, *Антисталинская подлость* (2007). In English since 2011 as *Khrushchev Lied*.

Chapter 15: An Examination of the Falsehoods in *Bloodlands.*

Since *Bloodlands* is not an attempt to give a truthful account of the events it discusses, it is something else: an attempt to convince the reader – including the academic reader – that it is a truthful account. In other words: *Bloodlands* is a work of propaganda disguised as a work of historical research or a summary account of works of historical research. *Bloodlands* is a book that intends to mislead its readers, and it has been very successful.

The main reason for its success is what I have called "the anti-Stalin paradigm." *Bloodlands* tells its readers what they were, broadly speaking, already "knew" – that is, thought they knew: that Stalin and the Soviet leadership were morally evil people who deliberately murdered millions of people and so were, broadly speaking, like the Nazis. *Bloodlands* fills out the paradigm of "Stalin and the Soviets as evil" with examples and scholarly-looking documentation much as hot air fills out a balloon.

In addition to the techniques of scholarly misrepresentation and misdirection, other factors are involved. Chief among them is the power of the anti-Stalin paradigm. This epidemic of self-imposed blindness exists because there is no powerful institution that is devoted to the pursuit of historical truth. The historical profession is supposed to be such an institution. But it is not, at least as regards Soviet history of the Stalin period. In this field falsehood is rewarded as long as it serves anticommunist purposes while the truth is discouraged or penalized when, as is usually the case, it does not serve those purposes.

The techniques of misdirection employed in *Bloodlands* are not original or sophisticated. Once they have been pointed out they appear almost transparent. But they have fooled dozens of reviewers, including academic reviewers. At the time I am writing this

(May, 2014) I have yet to find a single reviewer who has identified even one of the dozens of falsifications in Snyder's book.

If someone were to write a book accusing the American government of atrocities on the scale of those Snyder falsely attributes to Stalin and the Soviet leadership, we can be certain that many scholars would check every statement and examine all the evidence. That up to now no one has done this is, no doubt, due in part to the fact that in *Bloodlands* Snyder is simply telling people that which they have assumed to be true all along.

What we have done in the present book is simply to apply to Snyder's fact-claims, accusations, and allegations against Stalin, the Soviet leadership, and pro-Soviet forces in *Bloodlands* the skeptical attitude that any careful reviewer of a book alleging crimes by the United States government and leadership would adopt. The result is devastating to Snyder's book.

*   *

*

Within the anti-Stalin paradigm, a number of rhetorical techniques of misdirection are employed in *Bloodlands*. In an earlier work I called the different kinds of falsification in Nikita Khrushchev's "Secret Speech" a "typology of prevarication."[1] In that work I was able to show that what Khrushchev stated in this infamous speech was false. Because Russian authorities still keep most primary source documentation of the events of the high politics of the 1930s top secret, in most cases I did not have enough evidence to discover what really happened – only enough to prove that more than 40 "revelations" made by Khrushchev in that speech are deliberate lies and that twenty more are false, probably but not demonstrably deliberate falsehoods.

In *The Murder of Sergei Kirov* I discussed the studies by Matthew Lenoe, Åsmund Egge, and Alla Kirilina. I discovered that these scholars had tortured the available evidence in order to reach the only conclusion congruent with the anti-Stalin paradigm: that Ki-

---

[1] *Khrushchev Lied*, Chapter 10, 137-158.

rov's assassin, Leonid Nikolaev, was a "lone gunman" and that Stalin fabricated the criminal case against everyone else. In the case of Kirov's murder we do have enough evidence to prove that those persons convicted of the murder by the Soviet court in December 1934 were indeed guilty. But I did not give a summary or theoretically-informed account of the errors and methods of misdirection that these prior scholars used.

In the case of *Bloodlands* I think such an account is warranted. The fact-claims against Stalin and the Soviets are so universally false, and the failure of expert reviewers to notice this so complete, that we are forced to admit that the techniques of falsification in *Bloodlands* have been successful. If they have fooled the experts they will also fool the general reader. These techniques of falsification are simple in principle. But they are only disclosed as simple in practice if one studies them closely.

The widespread acceptance of the anti-Stalin paradigm discourages any attempt to verify fact-claims that are convenient to that paradigm, since the process of verification dismantles the paradigm itself. A review of the techniques of misdirection in *Bloodlands* may prove helpful in warning the reader against naive acceptance of the anti-Stalin paradigm. Under its controlling influence every piece of evidence is bent to fit it, while everything that does not fit it is ignored or discarded.

In the ideologically-charged field that is Soviet history of the Stalin period no accusation of wrongdoing against Stalin, the Soviet leadership, or pro-Soviet forces, no matter what its source, should ever be accepted as true unless it has been thoroughly verified. The sooner this fact is generally recognized, and the sooner the practice of verifying everything that "fits" the anti-Stalin paradigm is taken seriously, the better for those who wish to discover the truth.

Methods of Falsification in *Bloodlands*

Avoidance of objectivity takes different specific forms. There are many different ways to make fact claims without evidence.

Technique of Deception	Characteristics	Example[2]
Begging the Question (BQ)	*Petitio principii:* Assuming that which is to be proven.	"The mass starvation of 1933 was the result of Stalin's first Five-Year Plan, implemented between 1928 and 1932." (*Bloodlands* Chapter 3)
Bias of Omission (BO)	Rely on the readers' ignorance	"'Poland never surrendered, but hostilities came to an end on 6 October 1939." (*Bloodlands* Ch. 4); 'Snyder Barely Refers to the Real Genocide: the "Volhynian Massacres."' (Chapter 13)
Fabrication (FA)	Statements that are anticommunist bias only, without any evidence at all	"'Stalin's First Commandment": Another Snyder Fabrication.' (Chapter 3)
The Big Lie (BL)	Repetition of the same falsehood over and over to give the reader the impression that it has previously been established as true.	The USSR and Nazi Germany were "allies"; Molotov-Ribbentrop Pact was an agreement to partition Poland; "joint invasion" of Poland; USSR and Nazi Germany

---

[2] Chapter references are to the chapters in the present book unless *Bloodlands* is specifically mentioned.

		wanted to eliminate "Polish elite." (*passim.*)
Communism – Nazism (CN)	Miss no chance to compare if not to equate them. Communism is to be linked with Nazism whenever possible regardless of logic. Often the attempts to bracket the two together is awkward, even bizarre, and sometimes seemingly irrational. The rationality lies in the BL repetition. The aim to get the reader used to the comparison as though it were a natural one. Nazi actions are blamed on the Soviets whenever possible. Communist motives must be made to appear as similar as possible to Nazi motives.	GULAG prisoners were "slave labor" (*Bloodlands,* Ch. 3); 'Did "Soviet Cruelty" Lead to Support for Nazism?' (Ch. 4); 'Snyder Terms Stalin's Anti-Hitler Move a 'Pro'-Hitler Move.' (Ch. 7); 'Snyder: Noting A Person's Nationality Is "Not So Very Different From" Nazism.' (Ch. 7); 'Snyder Equates Nazi Imperialism with Soviet Anti-Imperialism.' (Ch. 9); 'Did Soviet Partisans Cause Nazi Atrocities?' (Ch. 11)
Antisemitism (AS)	In *Bloodlands* this trope services the CN trope.	'The Lie That Stalin Was Anti-Semitic.' (Ch. 14); 'Did Sta-

		lin's Daughter Overhear Stalin "Covering Up" Solomon Mikhoels' Murder?' (Ch. 14); 'Anything To Make Stalin Appear Anti-Semitic? Snyder Falsifies the Draft Letter.' (Ch. 14)
	The Nazis were anti-Semitic so Stalin and the Soviet leadership must be shown to have been anti-Semitic as well. This is impossible, so fabrications (FA) and Phony Citations (PC; see below) must be employed.	
Numbers Game (NG)	This trope also services the CN trope. For the Communism-Nazism / Stalin-Hitler comparison to work it must be asserted that the Soviets murdered very large numbers of people, since the Nazis did so.	'More False Numbers of "Victims".' (Ch. 13)
Phony Citation (PC)	The work or works cited as evidence in support of a fact-claim do not in reality support it.	'The Lie that Stalin Spoke of an "Alliance" with Hitler.' (Ch. 8); 'Snyder Falsifies Stalin's Words." (Ch. 14)
Anticommunist Scholarship (AC)	Often the PC is taken from secondary sources by other anticommunist scholars.	A great many of Snyder's false fact-claims are taken from AC scholars, such as these: 'Snyder's "Funda-

		mental" Source -- A Hitler Supporter.' (Ch. 4); 'Snyder Falsifies the Nalibocki Massacre.' (Ch. 11)
False or Falsified Quotation (FQ)	This is a hybrid category. Sometimes there is no real source for the quotation at all, which makes it a special kind of FA – a fabricated quotation. Sometimes a genuine quotation is cited incorrectly. The quotation really says, and means, something else.	'Were "Women Routinely Raped, Robbed of Food"?' (Ch. 2); 'Snyder: "Half a Million Youngsters in Watchtowers".' (Ch. 4)
Psychologizing (PS)	Snyder claims that Stalin was "thinking" something.	'"Stalin's New Malice."'(Ch. 3); 'Snyder Reads Stalin's Mood.' (Ch. 7); 'Snyder Claims That Stalin Hated All Poles.' (Ch. 7)
Anticommunist statements that do not prove anything but "sound bad." (SB)		'Stalin's "Personal Politics."' (Ch. 3)
First-Person Accounts (FP)		(See discussion below.)

First-Person Accounts (FP)

A final category that does not lend itself to tabular presentation is that of the first-person account. Snyder uses them a lot in *Bloodlands*. The deception comes when, as in *Bloodlands*, they are used as though they can establish an historical fact.

The problems of first-person accounts are as follows:

> * They are normally collected long after the event. But memory is a creative process. Memories change, often to fit ideological assumptions made later in the person's life. Such memories are useless as historical evidence, even as evidence of the personal experience of the individual whose account it is.

> * The principle *testis unus, testis nullus* applies in all but exceptional cases. One testimony is not sufficient to establish that an event occurred.

> * First-person testimony is often collected in a biased, unrepresentative way. For example, the book by Kovalenko from which Snyder took his story of "Petro Veldii" was compiled by selecting 1000 personal accounts of the famine of 1932-33 from among 6000 collected, but only "negative" accounts were published.

First-person accounts are often used for their emotional appeal. The appeal to emotion has long been recognized as a rhetorical strategy to disarm rational attempts at evaluating evidence: in short, as a technique of propaganda. Snyder uses purported firsthand accounts of the famine. Even without source criticism – some of these accounts come from the works of Nazi collaborators – such accounts are not evidence that any specific event actually occurred. The "Petro Veldii" story in Chapter One of *Bloodlands* that we examine in the Introduction is a good example of this.

Analysis of the Prevarications in *Bloodlands*

The international success of a work as corrupt as *Bloodlands* requires explanation. How can a book that is largely composed of demonstrable, provable falsehoods have been published? Once published, how can it be praised by newspaper and magazine reviewers and by professional historians whose job it is to critically examine historical studies? How can a work utterly lacking in integrity be published in the hundreds of thousands of copies, garner awards in several countries, and be translated into dozens of languages?

Part of the answer lies in the historical role of pseudo-scholarship as propaganda for anticommunist purposes. The demonization of Soviet history dates back to the revolution itself. Already in 1920 Walter Lippmann and Charles Merz showed how the *New York Times*, newspaper "of record" then as today, "reported" the triumph of the Whites and the defeat of the Reds numerous times, always falsely. Lippmann and Merz concluded that the reporters had not deliberately lied. Rather they had reported not what they saw but what they and their bosses *wanted* to see.[3] The *Times's* reporters included Walter Duranty, later to be attacked for being "insufficiently anticommunist" when in the 1930s he insisted on reporting only what he saw or knew for a fact rather than what he had not witnessed.

Bloodlands was published by Basic Books, a commercial rather than an academic publisher. Academic presses require that manuscripts submitted for publication be vetted by academic specialists in the field. This does not guarantee that falsehoods will be caught and that standards of evidence routine in other areas of history will be observed. Nevertheless, I suspect that at least some of the more glaring falsifications in *Bloodlands* might well have been recognized as such by an academic review—unless the reviewers had been selected more for their anticommunist fervor than for excellence of research.

For example, there is a good chance that academic reviewers would not have permitted Snyder's account of the fraudulent "Holodomor" to pass without at least some qualification. And the millions of "deliberate murders" of the Holodomor fraud are essential to Snyder's Stalin-Hitler / Communist-Nazi comparison; without

---

[3] Walter Lippmann and Charles Merz. "A Test of the News." Supplement to *The New Republic* August 4, 1920. It is available online at
https://archive.org/details/LippmannMerzATestoftheNews (Accessed May 5 2014).

them he would have had no book. But academic vetting is not necessary in commercial publishing.

The many awards *Bloodlands* has garnered from newspapers and magazines are understandable. All these publications are dogmatically anticommunist. Indeed some of them, like the WSJ and "Reason Magazine,"stand politically on the far right. But when it comes to hostility to Stalin there is often little or no difference along the continuum from left-liberal to neoconservative. And it is publicity and promotion from these publications that determine commercial success; hence, "non-fiction bestseller," etc. The author and his publisher are making a lot of money! Not a careful search for the truth but profit is the goal of commercial publication, and anticommunist bias is not a barrier but a requirement for mass commercial success.

Bloodlands has not been greeted by scholars with the criticism it deserves. On the contrary, many academic specialists in the field of East European history have praised the book. Although, as the reader of the present study realizes, *Bloodlands* is composed of little except falsehoods concerning the actions of Soviet leaders and Soviet and communist actors, these academic reviewers have managed to miss virtually all of them.

Three "Review Forums" on *Bloodlands*

As illustration of this fact we here consider the first three "review forums" in professional historical journals that Snyder himself listed on his web page as of April 2014.[4] Together they represent considered responses to *Bloodlands* by thirteen prominent academic scholars.

Book reviews and "review forums" are of some value if the participants really are expert in the same field as the subject of the book. But in the present case only two of these thirteen, Hiroaki Kuromiya and Jörg Baberowski, are specialists in Soviet history of the Stalin period. Both of them are on the far right of even the anticommunist scholarly spectrum; both are passionately anticommunist

---

[4] At http://timothysnyder.org/books-2/bloodlands/review-forums/

and make no pretense at objectivity. Baberowski has nothing of interest to say at all. Kuromiya is the only one of the thirteen who questions whether the Soviet famine of 1932-33 was in fact deliberate mass murder. But he does not draw the obvious conclusion: that if the famine was not mass murder the whole framework of Snyder's book collapses. The other twelve all accept without question Snyder's importation of the Ukrainian nationalist myth of the "Holodomor." None of them seems to know that the major Western studies of the famine of 1932-33 by Mark Tauger, Stephen Wheatcroft, and R.W. Davies, even exist. One of them even misspells the clearly unfamiliar term.

Kuromiya is also the only one of the thirteen to point out Snyder's gross error about Japanese military intentions after 1937.[5] Aside from him none of these scholars questions a single one of Snyder's fact-claims. None of them, Kuromiya included, checks even one of Snyder's fact-claims to verify whether it is based on primary source evidence or whether that evidence in fact supports what Snyder claims in his text.

All these scholars (with the exception of the two mild demurrers by Kuromiya) simply accept every one of Snyder's assertions or fact-claims about the actions of Stalin, the Soviet leadership, and communist forces. Yet, as the present study demonstrates, every one of these fact-claims is false. All of these scholars repeat the verbiage about Soviet or Stalinist "mass murders." Yet, as the present study has shown, the evidence is clear that the only mass murder, the terrible *Ezhovshchina,* was not sanctioned by Stalin or the Soviet leadership. Not one of these scholars seems to know anything about this event. Not one of them knows of the long-standing scholarly debate over the Katyn massacre. And so on.

Kuromiya and Baberowski aside, the rest of the reviewers – eleven out of thirteen – are specialists in Nazism, or in the Holocaust of Jews, or in Eastern Europe. They show profound ignorance about the historiography of the Soviet Union during the 1930s. They are not in the least qualified to judge whether Snyder's fact-claims

---

[5] See the discussion in Chapter Five of the present book.

about Soviet history are accurate or not. Of course they themselves knew this. But none of them was forthright enough to admit it.

Whether knowledgeable about the history of the Stalin era or not, all of these scholars could have done what any reviewer should do. They could have selected a few of Snyder's assertions about Soviet history and then checked Snyder's footnotes to see whether those references supported what Snyder claims they support. If unable to read Polish or Ukrainian they could have asked help from colleagues. This is elementary, the kind of thing graduate students are trained to do; what Ph.D. students regularly do in the course of researching for their dissertations.

Moreover, if it is not done then the readership is being deliberately misled. These scholars are giving the impression that they can approve or certify Snyder's research when they know themselves they are in no position to do so. They claim they have have found Snyder's research to be good – most of them say as much – while in reality they are taking Snyder's book "on faith." But they don't admit this.

These scholars cannot escape responsibility for their endorsing Snyder's research when in reality they had no idea whether it is good or not. However, it is not only a question of their individual failures. It is the system of academic review as it exists. They simply acted in accordance with it. It is the system itself that is really at fault. For her review to be of any value to others a reviewer of a scholarly book has to be an expert on the same subject as that of the book itself. Then she has to spend serious time and effort studying the book and its research.

But this seldom happens. Book reviews "count" little in a scholar's career so few scholars spend much time on them. If the book is on a subject the scholar knows very well then her independent judgment can indeed be of value. But when, as in this case, the book is on a subject that the scholar knows little or even nothing about, her judgment is worthless. The scholar should either recuse herself or write only about those aspects of the book she is expert on and openly admit that she does not know enough about the other parts of the book to have any opinion about them. But none of the reviewers in these three "review forums" were forthright enough to do this. Therefore their endorsements of Snyder's book are dishonest. They mislead their readers.

To understand how this can happen we must briefly examine the system of anticommunist pseudo-scholarship on Soviet history of the Stalin period that not only permits but lavishly rewards dishonest works like *Bloodlands*.

Objectivity

In any field of study it is essential that the researcher determine to be objective from the outset of his study. History is no different. The historian must make every effort to survey all the primary sources that bear upon his subject, and all the secondary sources that study this evidence regardless of whether these secondary sources reflect the same biases, preconceived ideas, or values as his own.

Since objectivity is, among other things, an attitude of distrust of the self and of one's own preconceived ideas and biases, the historian must compensate for her own limitations by trying especially hard to give a supportive reading to primary and secondary sources whose tendency is opposed to her own biases and preconceived ideas. At the same time she must determine to be especially suspicious of that evidence and those works of scholarship that tend to confirm or agree with her own biases, to counteract her natural tendency to look with special favor upon statements that reflect her own views.

In her historical practice, the historian must observe the tenets of objective research from the outset, and even before. If the historian does not begin with a determination to find the truth no matter whose ox is gored, ready at every moment to discover a truth that she finds disillusioning, her research is doomed. He will never stumble across the truth by accident along the way. Moreover, if an historian does not begin from a determination to discover the truth we must ask the question: What, then, is her purpose in writing her book? If she is not out to discover the truth and report it to her readers, what *is* she doing?

Snyder ignores every tenet of historical objectivity. Therefore, no one should be surprised that her book is devoid of historical truth. It could not be otherwise.

Anticommunist Scholarship

Snyder's determined flouting of objectivity would be of little consequence if it were an exception. *Bloodlands* and similar works would be rejected during the vetting process and not be published. Those works that for whatever reason managed to evade the vetting process and be published anyway would be quickly critiqued, their errors, carelessness, and deliberate dishonesty identified and exposed. Negative reviews would warn potential readers away. This is how the system of scholarly and semi-popular reviewing is supposed to work.

But in reality it does not work this way. Scholarship on the Stalin period in the Soviet Union is constrained by an informal but strict code of "political correctness." Stalin must be depicted as a moral monster and the Soviet Union during his time as a place of government-sponsored mass murder and repression. No substantive deviation from this formula is tolerated.

Only rarely can one find a refutation of even the most absurd accusations of crimes by Stalin. In his 2010 study that concluded that Stalin did not have a hand in the murder of Sergei Kirov in Leningrad on December 1, 1934 Matthew Lenoe felt compelled to write a two-page profession of his anticommunist and anti-Stalin convictions. Lenoe admits that he did so lest someone suspect him of being "pro-Stalin" for rejecting an interpretation which had been abandoned by Soviet and Russian experts for decades and for which there had never been any evidence in the first place.

Even this is an exception. Claims that Stalin committed some crime, no matter how poorly supported by evidence, are typically passed over in silence if really absurd and otherwise are accepted and even repeated, as Snyder does many times in *Bloodlands*.

In history of the Stalin period a kind of "Gresham's Law" prevails where "bad scholarship drives out the good." When good scholarship is produced it is carefully written so as not to contradict any tenets of anti-Stalinism that the researcher thinks may be an inviolable part of the anti-Stalin paradigm.

Good research is being done in the field of Stalin-era Soviet history. But it is typically confined to the close examination of primary sources, especially when newly-available sources are used. Research that is narrowly focused on specific events, places, and time periods can be very revealing. Even when marred by bias, research that reproduces new primary sources can be valuable because flawed interpretation can be discarded and the texts of the primary sources themselves appropriated for more objective research.

An anticommunist scholarly environment or "industry" has been created where "scholars" churn out anticommunist falsehoods and then cite each other's falsehoods as evidence that the falsehoods are true. Primary sources are distorted by misinterpretation or ignored entirely. The "scholars" or academic practitioners in this "industry" assume in their writings that it is not primary source evidence and its interpretation, but the consensus of anticommunist researchers, that establishes a statement as "true."

Snyder follows this practice with enthusiasm. *Bloodlands* is a product of it. Snyder rarely cites primary sources at all. When he does, he gets them wrong. For the most part Snyder cites secondary sources by "scholars" of the anticommunist "industry" This produces a body of anticommunist pseudo-scholarship based upon bias alone – that is, upon ignorance.

In addition to falsehood this system reproduces ignorance. Anticommunist scholars inevitably become lazy when no one criticizes their research because it has the "correct" anticommunist tendency or "line." Why worry about the truth if what matters is not objectivity in skillful analysis and interpretation of primary source evidence but in striking the right anticommunist tone? Why bother to do the hard, time-consuming work of real research, of discovering the truth, when the path to academic success is to repeat anticommunist assertions without regard to the evidence?

Our study of *Bloodlands* has disclosed that Snyder is not only biased. He is also ignorant about much or most of the history of which he poses as an expert. His readers should not assume that Snyder has worked hard to discover the truth and then gone on to construct deliberate lies in order to disguise this truth. The reverse is much more likely: that Snyder has no idea what the truth is because he has never tried to find it. He has mastered the anticommunist position or "line" on many issues, and this can be got from reading the works of a limited number of recognized anticommunist "scholars" without troubling oneself about primary sources or real research of any kind.

Conclusion:

The Missing "Crimes of Stalinism."

"An Attack on the Enlightenment"

In Chapter 4 of *Bloodlands* Snyder accuses the Soviet Union of "an attack on the very concept of modernity, or indeed the social embodiment of Enlightenment" (153). In Chapter Seven of the present book we proved Snyder's accusation to be fraudulent. But it is true of Snyder's book. In virtually every accusation he makes against Stalin, the Soviet Union, or pro-communist forces such as pro-Soviet partisans and the Red Army, Snyder thrusts falsehoods at his readers and calls them the truth.

Bloodlands is a work completely devoid of integrity. It is a cloth woven of lies and falsifications from beginning to end, an outrage against the canons of historical research and the historian's responsibility. As such it is itself "an attack on the Enlightenment", debauching history to serve political ends.

Failure of the Field of Soviet and East European History

Bloodlands has received many very positive reviews by professional historians in historical journals. A few reviewers have questioned Snyder's historiographical or theoretical paradigm. Still others, experts on the history of the Jewish Holocaust, have criticized him for his tendency to repeat the "nationalist" mythologies of today's right-wing Eastern European regimes.

But at the time of this writing I have yet to read a single review of *Bloodlands* where the reviewer is knowledgeable about the history of the Soviet Union during the 1930s and brings that knowledge to bear in the discussion of Snyder's book. Even reviewers who raise criticisms of other aspects of *Bloodlands* accept Snyder's fact-claims about the actions of Stalin, the Soviet leadership, and pro-Soviet forces. Yet any specialist in Soviet history of this period who has kept abreast of the scholarship and recently published documents could not fail to find a great many false statements in Snyder's presentation.

Here are two examples from major history journals. In his review of *Bloodlands*[1] Thomas Kühne rightly criticizes Snyder for his "move to link Soviet and Nazi crimes":

> As it seems to reduce the responsibility of the Nazis and their collaborators, supporters and claqueurs, it is welcomed in rightist circles of various types: German conservatives in the 1980s, who wanted to 'normalise' the German past, and East European and nationalists today, who downplay Nazi crimes and up-play Communist crimes in order to promote a common European memory that merges Nazism and Stalinism into a 'double-genocide' theory that prioritises East European suffering over Jewish suffering, obfuscates the distinction between perpetrators and victims, and provides relief from the bitter legacy of East Europeans' collaboration in the Nazi genocide.

Kühne is certainly right that Snyder's book plays to the right-wing "nationalists" of Eastern Europe. But Kühne accepts without question Snyder's viewpoint about purported Soviet (often "Stalin's" or "Stalinist") "crimes":

> "Snyder is not the first to think about what Hitler and Stalin had in common and how their murderous politics related to each other."

> "...the Hitler-Stalin Pact as the actual springboard of the two dictators' collaboration in the destruction of Poland..."

> "...the links between Hitler's and Stalin's mass-murder policies."

> "...Stalinist and Nazi terror..."

---

[1] "Great Men and Large Numbers: Undertheorizing a History of Mass Killing." *Contemporary European History*, 21, 2 (2012), pp. 133—143.

> "...Stalin's victims need to be included in these sto-
> ries as well, he points out, that is, victims of Ukrain-
> ian holodomor (death by hunger), of the Great Ter-
> ror in 1937—8, and not least of Stalin's 'ethnic
> cleansings' and antisemitic purges around and after
> 1945."

> "...an account on the mass crimes of the Nazi and
> Soviet regimes which infamously 'turned people in-
> to numbers'..."

None of these accusations against "Stalin" and the Soviet leadership are interrogated in the least. Kühne just accepts them as established, though where they have supposedly been established
and by whom he does not say.

As the reader of this book will now realize, *all* these statements are
false. Stalin had no "murderous politics"; there was no "collaboration in the destruction of Poland"; Stalin had no "mass-murder policies"; there was no "Stalinist terror"; there was no "Holodomor"
but a great famine in which the Soviet government, by all evidence,
did the best it could. There was a "Great Terror", or *Ezhovshchina*,
but it was not that of Stalin or the Soviet state. Stalin had no "ethnic cleansings" or "anti-Semitic purges." The Soviet regime committed no "mass crimes."

In *Kritika*, a journal specializing in Russian and Soviet history, Michael Wildt[2] is rightly critical of *Bloodlands* on many counts. But
Wildt shows no knowledge of scholarship on the Soviet Union and
so he takes the following assertions straight from Snyder's book,
without any question, much less examination:

> "...the two most murderous regimes of the first half
> of the 20th century..."

> "And while the Nazi regime killed about 10,000
> people in concentration camps and prisons before
> the outbreak of World War II in 1939, the Stalinist

---

[2] Wildt review of Bloodlands *in Kritika: Explorations in Russian and Eurasian History* 14, 1
(Winter 2013),197-206.

leadership had already allowed millions to die from hunger and had shot about one million people."

"...Stalin's crimes..."

"The first events Snyder recounts are the deaths from hunger during the early 1930s of millions of people, not only in Ukraine but also in Kazakhstan and other parts of the Soviet Union. These deaths were due to the arbitrary and rash collectivization of agriculture organized by the Stalinist leadership in Moscow."

"After the catastrophic harvest of 1931, which was partly a result of collectivization, the Stalinist leadership exported grain in order to be able to purchase industrial goods abroad. It consciously accepted the mass deaths that resulted from this policy. In December of that year, Stalin decreed that kolkhozes that could not meet their grain delivery quotas should also deliver their seeds to the authorities. Thus in 1932—33 death from hunger became an ineluctable fate for millions of people."

"Stalin was certain that the peasants' falling short of grain delivery quotas was proof of their collaboration with foreign enemies and of their resistance, both of which had to be quashed ruthlessly."

"Between 1934 and 1939, when popular fronts against fascism were forged in Europe, the Soviet repressive organs shot about 750,000 people as alleged enemies of the people and deported an even greater number to the Gulag. The local secret police arrested and murdered according to quotas from above."

"...the Stalinist regime also murdered according to ethnic criteria, as, for instance, in the so-called "Polish operation." "...the assumption that Soviet citizens of Polish nationality were enemies of the Soviet system."

> "...a nonaggression treaty on 23 August 1939, which amounted to nothing less than yet another German—Russian partition of Poland."

> "The Polish elite was shot or deported. The systematic murder of about 15,000 Polish officers, who had fled from the German troops in the east, literally decapitated the Polish army."

> "Snyder is correct in emphasizing the commonalities in the violent practices of the two regimes in Poland. Both Germany and the Soviet Union desired the "decapitation of Polish society" (125) and the ruthless exploitation of the remaining civilian population through forced labor. Both sides waged an ethnic war against the Poles."

> "The millions of dead from famine in the Soviet Union at the beginning of the 1930s were the consequence—no doubt, a foreseeable consequence and one that the Stalinist regime deliberately accepted—of a brutal industrialization policy carried out at the expense of the rural population."

Every one of these claims has been disproven in the present book. Many of them, such as Snyder's account of the famine of 1932-33 which Wildt echoes uncritically here, have been disproven by respectable Western scholars. The "official version" of the "Katyn massacre" has been under sharp criticism by some Russian scholars for fifteen years. Highly anticommunist and anti-Stalin Russian scholars have shown that USSR did not "murder according to ethnic criteria" in the "Polish operation." Wildt appears oblivious to all of this.

Why do Wildt and Kühne repeat Snyder's fact-claims about the Soviet Union uncritically when they are by no means uncritical of other aspects of *Bloodlands*? In part it is because neither knows much about Soviet history. Wildt admits as much:

> ...here I should register the caveat that I am a specialist of Nazism, not Soviet collectivization...

Nobody can be a "specialist" in everything. But most of Snyder's book is about Soviet, not German, actions. Why did Kühne and Wildt agree to review *Bloodlands* when each of them knows he is unqualified to have an independent judgment on Snyder's statements about Soviet actions?

I suggest that the reason is that the anticommunist paradigm, in the form of anti-Stalinism, is simply "taken for granted" in academia in a way that statements about, for example, Hitler and Nazi Germany are not. The scholarship on Hitler is meticulous and detailed. Misstatements about Nazi actions and crimes are caught, parsed, and subjected to criticism. But claims of "Stalin's crimes" are accepted without any interrogation at all.

How Could This Happen?

No scholarly field should function like this. It is a disgrace that a book like Snyder's could be published and widely read for years while his falsifications, phony references, dishonest use of sources, and incorrect statements pass not only unchallenged but accepted, even praised, by professional historians. Any graduate student in this field could check Snyder's evidence and find what I have found: that every allegation of "crimes" against Stalin and the Soviet leadership is false.

Could a collapse of the historian's responsibility of this magnitude happen in any area of American or British history – always excepting the history of the communist movement in those countries? I doubt it. The spectrum of viewpoints in those fields is too broad. There are no "sacred cows" so firmly ensconced as such that all criticism, or all praise, of them is *a priori* ruled out of bounds.

There is no excuse for the ease with which statements about "crimes of Stalinism," unsupported by primary evidence, have been and continue to be accepted as truth. But there is an explanation. From its inception as an academic discipline the primary function of Soviet studies has been to provide a fount of anticommunist propaganda propped up by scholarship or the appearance of it.

For several generations anticommunist Russian exiles were among the most prominent figures in the field. Their anticommunist bias was enhanced by the advent of the Cold War and abetted by an influx of Soviet defectors, some of them former Nazi collaborators. The range of viewpoints acceptable in the field has been stretched to include Trotskyists and socialists of the social democratic type. But pro-communist viewpoints and researchers with an openly pro-communist orientation have always been excluded. This makes sense once one recalls that this field was created as a weapon against Soviet communism from the beginning.

More than two decades after the end of the Soviet Union the field of Soviet history remains first and foremost a weapon of political and ideological warfare. It has never encompassed those who challenge what I have called the "anti-Stalin paradigm" of Soviet history: anyone who insists on drawing conclusions about Soviet history based upon evidence rather than upon ideological grounds.

The Strength of the "Anti-Stalin Paradigm"

Indeed, in important respects the ideological blinders in this field have hardened since the end of the USSR because of the post-Soviet states. Ukraine and Poland and, in a somewhat different way, Russia too have constructed national mythologies along rigidly anticommunist lines and upon historical falsehoods. Today a professional historian in the field of Soviet or Eastern European history cannot get published, get access to archives, be invited to historical conferences, — in short, have a career — if she seriously questions the mendacious historical mythologies propagated by the political and academic elites in these countries such as the "Katyn massacre," the "Holodomor," or the "innocence" of Marshal Tukhachevsky or Nikolai Bukharin.

The history of the Soviet Union is fatally constrained by the anti-Stalin paradigm. It is simply "not done," virtually taboo, to find Stalin *not* guilty of some crime or other he has been charged with. If the evidence does not support the anti-Stalin conclusion, then so much the worse for the evidence! It will be ignored, or phony evidence will be invented, or conclusions based on no evidence at all.

Utter falsehoods are acceptable as long as they conform to the paradigm of "Stalin-as-evil."[3]

The sad fact is that in its broad outlines the field of Soviet history functions more like propaganda than like history. Good research is done on very specific topics, especially when based on archival evidence. But the framework or paradigm of Soviet history during the Stalin period in which such studies situate themselves sets firm limits on what conclusions are acceptable. The academic field of Soviet history of the Stalin period is governed by a form of "political correctness" far more than it is by normal canons of historical research.

This is the context in which Snyder's disgraceful book, one that is nothing but falsehoods, falsifications, rumors, and lies, can receive positive reviews not just from obvious ideologues in the media or avowedly pro-capitalist organizations and publications but from professional academic historians.

What Can We Do?

The most basic conclusion of this book concerns Snyder himself. Nothing he writes about Stalin, the Soviet Union, communism, or Eastern European history can be assumed to be accurate. Every claim he makes must be double-checked. After all, that is what this book presents — a check of every statement of an anticommunist tenor that Snyder makes in *Bloodlands*, with the result that all of them are false, fabrications.

A scientist who is exposed as guilty not just of making an error here and there — that is inevitable — but of nothing but "errors", of making nothing but false statements and therefore of reporting nothing but false results, would be distrusted by fellow scientists forever thereafter. Science functions on the presupposition that the scientists of the past have reported truthful results in their work, results which can be used in the future work of other scientists. We would not trust the "research" of a biochemist hired by

---

[3] The present author has demonstrated this in detail with respect to the December 1 1934 murder of Sergei Kirov, Leningrad Party leader. See Grover Furr, *The Murder of Sergei Kirov. History, Scholarship, and the Anti-Stalin Paradigm* (Kettering, OH: Erythros Press & Media, LLC, 2013).

the Tobacco Institute to provide "evidence" that cigarette smoking was not causally related to lung cancer. We would assume his "research" was, in reality, not research at all but propaganda aimed at a preconceived and false result.

Distrust

Historians work in an analogous way. One historian who does false research and reports untruthful results is a threat to the field as a whole. His work shold never be cited since it cannot be trusted. Like the biochemist hired to produce genuine-looking but phony "research" to support a preconceived conclusion, a historian who writes anticommunist propaganda in the guise of "research" has produced not history but propaganda. He has violated the canons of the historical profession. His work can never be trusted again.

But distrusting Snyder's work in the future is too narrow a response to *Bloodlands*. Snyder has failed to find a single "crime of Stalinism" despite his own best efforts and those of a battalion of Polish and Ukrainian academics. If they had found any such "crimes of Stalinism" we can be sure that they would have reported them. But they did not find any—hence all the falsifications.

This means that, as far as Soviet history of the Stalin period is concerned, *all* allegations of "crimes of Stalinism," "crimes" of communists, should be reflexively distrusted. We should be even more suspicious when such allegations emanate from persons with a preconceived ideological anticommunist commitment.

A Renewed Insistence upon Objectivity

We need to distrust anti-Stalin allegations and anticommunist stories unless and until we can verify them ourselves. But we also need to take steps to ensure, as far as possible, our own objectivity in historical inquiry.

Everyone has preconceived ideas. It is one's own preconceived ideas and biases that are most likely to mislead one. To maintain a determination to be objective a historian must develop the habit of (a) giving an especially generous reading — suspending doubt and suspicion to a considerable extent — to any evidence that appears to go contrary to one's own preconceived ideas; and (b) adopting an especially critical attitude towards any evidence that tends to support one's own preconceived ideas or ideological positions. A further technique is to have colleagues who are aware of your pre-conceived ideas and commitments give a critical pre-publication reading to your research, having been asked in advance to be on the lookout for places where you may have unintentionally al-lowed your own prejudices to override your commitment to objec-tivity.

The Falsehoods of Polish "Nationalist" Mythology

Snyder has chosen to adopt the framework, bias, and falsehoods that characterize the work of Polish anticommunist "nationalist" historians. We have checked the evidence cited by Snyder in sup-port of his fact-claims and found that it is fraudulent. Either it doesn't exist at all or it points to conclusions different from the conclusions Snyder draws, even contrary to what he claims. Since in the main Snyder is rehashing Polish "nationalist" mythology we have in effect, examined the main premises of that mythology and show it to be false.

Specifically, we have examined and refuted the following "myths":

Myth: The "Kresy Wschodnie" (Eastern Borderlands), the Polish term for the Western Ukraine and Western Belorussia, were inal-ienable parts of Poland.

Fact: The "Kresy" became part of Poland in 1921 through military conquest in an imperialist war with Soviet Russia. The Polish gov-ernment held no plebiscites to ask the population whether they wished to be in Poland or not. The "Kresy" never had a majority Polish population. Poland had to have recourse to a large-scale program of "settling" Poles — mainly military men — in these are-as in the hopes of "polonizing" them (making them more "Polish"). These *osadnicy* (settlers) became the imperialist infrastructure of the "Kresy."

Myth: The Second Polish Republic of 1919 to 1939 was a decent society to which its citizens owed loyalty.

Fact: Poland was strongly imperialist. The Polish army seized Vil-nius from Lithuania in 1922 and the Teschen area of Czechoslovakia from that country in October 1938. As late as January 1939 Polish Foreign Minister Josef Beck told German Foreign Minister Joachim von Ribbentrop that Poland had aspirations to the Black Sea — that is, to take over about half of present-day Ukraine. Polish "nationalist" historians never discuss these land-grabs as imperialist.

The long-term aim of the Polish ruling elite was a Poland with the borders of the 18th century, when the Grand Duchy of Poland and Lithuania encompassed Western Ukraine to the Black Sea and most of present-day Belarus.[4] The Polish leadership cared nothing for the desires of the populations of these areas.

The Polish ruling elite was viciously racist. Only Roman Catholics were considered "Poles." All minorities suffered significant discrimination, which increased during the late 1930s.

Myth: The Molotov-Ribbentrop Pact was a plot to destroy Poland and provided for a "joint German-Soviet invasion."

Fact: This is false. The M-R Pact divided Poland into spheres of influence, requiring that the German army would have to withdraw from Eastern Poland. This pact would have preserved an independent Polish state if the Polish government had not abandoned the country and its inhabitants to the Nazis.

Myth: The Soviet Union invaded Poland on September 17, 1939.

Fact: There was no such "invasion." The USSR occupied Western Ukraine and Western Belorussia to prevent the Wehrmacht (German army) from marching up to the Soviet border. The USSR's claim that it remained neutral in the German-Polish was accepted by all the Allies except the Polish Government-In-Exile.

Myth: Hitler's Germany and Stalin's Soviet Union were "allies."

Fact: There was no alliance of any kind. The M-R Pact was a non-aggression pact.

Myth: German and Soviet troops held a "joint victory parade" at Brest-Litovsk.

---

[4] See the map at http://en.wikipedia.org/wiki/File:Poland1764physical.jpg

Fact: The parade was a handing over of power from the German army to the Red Army, since under the M-R Pact Brest was within the Soviet sphere of influence.[5]

Myth: In April and May 1940 the Soviets shot about 22,000 Polish prisoners, including officers, in a series of mass murders known as the Katyn massacre.

Fact: As of 2013 at the latest — some historians would choose a much earlier date — we have clear evidence that the "official version" of the event known to history as the "Katyn massacre" is false.

Since the late 1990s there has been a significant and very interesting scholarly dispute over the supposed "Katyn massacre" and the documents that purport to establish it as a fact. Snyder wrote *Bloodlands* during this period. But he never informs his readers about this dispute. In this he again follows the template of Polish "nationalist" historians and of anticommunist writers generally.

The myth of the "Katyn massacre" is central to right-wing Polish nationalism and important to anticommunist discourse generally. In anticommunist scholarship it is considered "taboo", akin to "Holocaust denial", to question Katyn, regardless of the evidence.

At the very minimum, no one interested in the truth should pay any attention whatever to any account of the "Katyn massacre" that does not include a thorough and objective account of the historical dispute over this subject, including full discussion of the numerous Russian-language studies by Russian scholars who have long rejected and claim to have disproven the "official version" of Katyn.

Myth: After taking them back from Poland in September 1939 the Soviets were guilty of "atrocities" and "terror" in the former "Kresy."

---

[5] A related myth is that the Nazi Gestapo and the Soviet NKVD held three "conferences" at which the killing of the Polish elites was planned. There is no evidence whatever for such conferences. Not all Polish nationalists make this specific claim today. Snyder does not mention it.

Fact: There was no "terror." Anticommunist historians use the word "terror" to describe the arrests and deportation of the Polish imperialist "settlers" (*osadnicy*) in 19439-1941. Claims of "communist", "Soviet", or "Stalinist" "terror" or "atrocities" are a verbal ploy that serves to avoid the issue of Polish imperial conquest and racist oppression in Western Ukraine and Western Belorussia.

Myth: The **myth** of Polish "victimhood": Post-1939 Polish nationalism claims that Poland was "victimized" by two invasions, the German and the Soviet, in September 1939, which destroyed the Polish state.

This is false. In reality the Polish state disappeared because, in an unprecedented act of betrayal, the Polish government abandoned the country, leaving it without a government. We have shown this in our extensive discussion on the Molotov-Ribbentrop Pact and the German-Polish war of September-October 1939.

Myth: The **myth** of Polish "heroism."

Fact: Many Poles did indeed heroically fight against the Germans. But the Home Army, the armed force of the Polish government-in-exile (in Paris until June, 1940, thereafter in London) also fought communist partisans, with whom they were supposedly in alliance. The Home Army routinely murdered Jews who were hiding from the Germans. Some Home Army commanders collaborated with the Germans (see below). Fighting against communist partisans, murdering Jews, and collaborating with the Germans is not "heroic" behavior.

The Polish People's Army (Armia Ludowa, AL) and the pro-Soviet Polish Army (Wojsko Polskie, WP) led by Zygmunt Berling did fight the Germans heroically. They did so without anti-Semitic terror or collaboration with the Germans. These forces were pro-communist and led by communists. Praising Polish communist forces or expressing pride in their accomplishments is "taboo" in mainstream Polish "nationalist" historiography because that historiography promotes not truth but "political correctness" in the form of anticommunist lies.

Myth: Poland faced "two totalitarianisms": Nazi Germany and the USSR.

Fact: This is false, just another verbal ploy, a play on words. For the most part the term "totalitarian" has no fixed meaning. It is simply an epithet meaning "bad." It is sometimes used to refer to a state with only one political party. Nazi Germany and the Soviet Union each had only one legal political party. But Nazi Germany and the USSR were diametrically opposite in every other way. Moreover, the existence of multiple political parties does not constitute real "democracy." Capitalist countries typically have multiple parties while being run by the wealthy either openly or behind the scenes.

Poland was much more similar to Nazi Germany than the Soviet Union was. Like Hitler's regime the Second Polish Republic was authoritarian, imperialist, anticommunist, anti-labor, fiercely racist against ethnic minorities, viciously and officially anti-Semitic, and militarist. Most important, it was capitalist. Not surprisingly, many leading Polish politicians and intellectuals admired Hitler and Nazi Germany.

Myth: The Soviets betrayed the heroic "Warsaw Uprising".

Myth: The murderous postwar Polish underground was a "heroic" war for "freedom" and "liberation."

Why Tells Lies If The Truth Is On Your Side?

Since the end of the Soviet Union in 1991 a flood of primary source documents from former Soviet archives have gradually been made available to researchers. I have been locating, obtaining, and studying these documents — more precisely, those among them dealing with the Stalin period and the historical controversies about it — for more than a decade.

Based on this reading and research I studied Nikita Khrushchev's famed "Secret Speech" to the 20th Congress of the Communist Party of the Soviet Union of February 25, 1956. To my amazement and no little discomfort I made the astounding discovery that every single accusation leveled by Khrushchev in that speech against Stalin and Lavrentii Beria is demonstrably false. [6] To date no one, spe-

---

[6] All but one minor accusation, which I could neither confirm nor disprove. See Furr, *Khrushchev Lied.*

cifically no historian of the Soviet Union, has challenged any of the results of my study. Khrushchev has no defenders.

The implications of the fact that Khrushchev did nothing but lie and falsify in that world-shaking speech prompted me to scrutinize other assertions, "fact-claims" that Stalin or the Soviet government of the 1930s committed some atrocity, crime, or other. I read *Bloodlands* soon after it was published and immediately recognized from my previous research that at least some of the assertions of "crimes" Snyder makes are false.

I proceeded to formulate the hypothesis that many, perhaps even most, of Snyder's accusations of crimes against Stalin and the Soviet Union would turn out to be false. As it turned out, my hypothesis was correct — but it was also incorrect. I did not expect to discover that not many, not most, but virtually *every* accusation involving the claim of a crime of one kind or other, every crime alleged by Snyder against Stalin, the Soviet Union, and pro-Soviet forces, would turn out to be false. Yet that is the case. No ideological bias of mine but the evidence itself demands this conclusion.

Anyone who reads Snyder's book will see that he has tried to include any and all crimes and misdeeds that can be alleged against Stalin and the Soviet Union between the period of collectivization virtually until Stalin's death in 1953. It is worthy of note that Snyder was unable to find even a single genuine crime.

This bears repeating: Not one of the crimes alleged by Snyder against Stalin and the Soviet leadership is genuine. All are fabrications. Snyder was unable to find a single example — not even one — of a "crime" that really was committed by the Stalin and/or the Soviet leadership. The implications of this fact should be considered.

Snyder has not done all his research by himself. He has had the resources of many ideologically-committed anticommunist researchers of Eastern Europe, especially of Poland and Ukraine, whose governments sponsor research facilities specifically devoted to fabricating tales of "communist atrocities." It appears that some of these professional anticommunist researchers may have helped Snyder. In addition Snyder has been able to draw on decades of publication by well-funded Cold War publicists and propa-

gandists. Snyder has also had at his service the magnificent biblio-
graphical and research facilities of the major research libraries
and institutes of the world.

And yet, despite all these resources, human and material, Snyder
has not been able to find even a single crime that Stalin or the Soviet leadership of his day was guilty of. He has not been able to
identify even a single genuine "crime of Stalin" or "crime of Stalinism." He has had to fabricate them all — or, more often, to repeat
fabrications alleged by others before him.

Where Are the "Crimes of Stalinism"?

It is in principle impossible to "prove a negative." You can only
prove a positive. You can't prove that Mr. X was *not* present in, say,
Moscow on a given date and at a given time. All you can do is to
prove that Mr. X *was* somewhere else — say, Leningrad — on that
same date and at that time. This means that in principle no one can
prove that Stalin and the Soviet leadership of his time did not
commit even a single "crime"; that the set of events that historians
conventionally call "crimes of Stalinism" is an empty set.

However, the fact that the combined efforts of all the anticommunist, anti-Stalinist, researchers in the world over a period of
more than 70 years — "all the King's horses and all the King's
men"[7] — and with the facilities of all the world's best libraries and
archives, have not been able to come up with a single, genuine
"crime of Stalin" of the period 1932-1945 — this is a fact that is
worthy of attention. *It is strong evidence in support of the negative
conclusion: that there were no such "crimes of Stalin."* For if there
were any such crimes, surely these highly motivated and well-
provisioned anticommunist researchers, with unprecedented and
privileged access to the archives, would have found them by now.

Of course there are really a number of categories of acts that have
been termed "crimes of Stalinism." One is the category of acts that
are crimes by any definition, such as deliberate killings of innocent
persons. This is the "empty set." The anticommunists of decades
have never yet succeeded in identifying even a single one of them.

---

[7] From the British nursery rhyme "Humpty Dumpty Sat on a Wall."

The second category consists of "crimes" against property and the resistance of the propertied. Collectivization of agriculture deprived many rich, and also many not-so-rich, peasants of their private property in land, just as the Revolution of 1917 deprived capitalists of their private property in the means of production, landlords of their estates, urban landlords of their rentable buildings, and so on. These were "crimes" by a kind of class-conscious definition — the definition of the property-owning class. At the same time they were acts of liberation from the viewpoint of the exploited classes of workers, peasants, and many others. The liberation of Western Ukraine and Western Belorussia by the Red Army is considered a "crime" by the Polish "nationalist"-imperialists.

A third category is the crimes committed by members of the Soviet leadership during Stalin's period. The principle example here is the *Ezhovshchina*, the mass murder of several hundred thousand Soviet citizens under the pretense of fighting organized counter-revolutionary groups. This was certainly a massive crime by any standard. But a truthful account of these horrendous events is not useful to ideological anticommunists because it was carried out unbeknownst to Stalin and the Soviet government who eventually, and far too late, realized what was going on, stopped it, and punished the criminals. We have presented the relevant evidence in chapters 5 and 6 of the present book.

Unquestionably the *Ezhovshchina* represents a massive failure of the Soviet system. Arch Getty termed it "the self-destruction of the Bolsheviks."[8] Some such term certainly applies. But it was not "Stalin's" crime in that he and the Soviet top leadership did not order it or wish it, and when they learned of it they acted to stop it and punish the guilty.

It is crimes of the first kind, and especially alleged atrocities — mass murders — that are the subject of Snyder's book. Without them Snyder's attempt to compare Stalin with Hitler, the USSR with Nazi Germany, and Bolshevism with Nazism, falls apart.

---

[8] J. Arch Getty and Oleg V. Naumov, *The Road to Terror. Stalin and the Self-Destruction of the Bolsheviks, 1932-1939.* New Haven: Yale University Press, 1999.

The Crimes of Western Imperialism

In the absence of such atrocities by the Soviet Union it is the acts of the Western imperialist countries, especially in the colonial world, that most closely resemble the crimes of Nazism. Not "Stalin + Hitler" but "Churchill + Hitler," "Daladier + Hitler," "Roosevelt and Truman + Hitler." To quote again from Professor Domenico Losurdo:

> On a d'ailleurs longtemps comparé le colonialisme anglais et occidental et le colonialisme hitlérien. Gandhi disait : « en Inde nous avons un gouvernement hitlérien, faut-il le camoufler en termes plus légers ? », « Hitler a été le péché de la Grande-Bretagne . »

Translated:

> British and Western colonialism has long been compared to Hitler's colonialism. Gandhi used to say: "In India we have a Hitlerite government. Must we disguise it with softer terms?" "Hitler was Great Britain's sin."

To count the millions of colonial victims of the Western "democratic" powers would be a large task. They certainly amount to the tens of millions. Even as concerns World War II it is hard to be precise in calculating the crimes of the Western Allies against non-combatant civilians such as the victims of the terror-bombings against Japanese and German cities, or of the two atomic bombs which could have been dropped on, for example, the Japanese Kwangtung Army but instead were dropped on defenseless civilians cities virtually devoid of military significance.

There is the "man-made famine" in Bengal, India, which cost the lives of between 1.5 and 5 million persons and for which the British government was completely responsible.[9] Then, shortly after

---

[9] Among many sources for the Bengal famine see Mark Tauger, "The Indian Famine Crises of World War II." *British Scholar* 1, No. 2 (March 2009), 166-196; Scott Horton, "Churchill's Dark Side: Six Questions for Madhusree Mukerjee." *Harper's* November 4, 2010. At http://harpers.org/archive/2010/11/hbc-90007797 ; Gideon Polya, "The Famine of History — Bengal 1943." *International Network on Holocaust and Genocide* 10 (1995) 10-15; "The

the war, the murder of 40,000 Korean peasants on the island of Cheju-do, where with American knowledge and support South Korean leaders, until recently Japanese collaborators, sent in fascist killers against a peasant revolt in an area where peasant revolts had taken place for many years.[10]

There is the horrific mass murder — mass torture campaign by the British against the Kenyan "nationalist" movement. Within the last decade major scholarly works by Western authors have begun to bring to Western attention facts about this world-class atrocity that have been well known in Kenya but suppressed in the "Free World."[11]

The Vietnamese anti-imperialist struggle for independence, first against France, then against Japan, then again against France, then against the United States, cost the lives of between 2 and 4 million Vietnamese. None of them would have been killed if the French imperialists had simply ceded independence. During the course of this thirty-year war both French and American forces committed numerous horrific atrocities against civilians. A recent book about American atrocities in Vietnam is titled *Kill Anything That Moves*.[12]

This is just a short selection. The list of horrors committed by Western anticommunist nations could be greatly lengthened. One can understand, therefore, why it is important that enemies of the communist movement — who are at the same time defenders of Western imperialism and its crimes — find it so important to fabricate "crimes of Stalinism."

Bengal Famine, 1943-45." *Freedom From Famine* . at http://www.duo.uio.no/publ/statsvitenskap/1997/514/3/7/8.html

[10] See John Merrill, "The Cheju-Do Rebellion." *Journal of Korean Studies* 2 (1980), 139-197. This horrific slaughter is thoroughly studied by South Korean scholars but virtually unknown in the West.

[11] Begin with David M. Anderson, "Atoning for the Sins of Empire", *NYT* June 12, 2013. Continue with Anderson's book *Histories of the Hanged: The Dirty War in Kenya and the End of Empire (*2006) and Caroline Elkins, *Imperial Reckoning. The Untold Story of the End of Em;pire in Kenya.* (New York: Henry Holt, 2005).

[12] Nick Turse, *Kill Anything That Moves. The Real American War in Vietnam.* New York: Metropolitan Books — Henry Holt, 2013.

The Crimes of Eastern European "Nationalists"

An equally powerful motive is the ideological requirements of the right-wing "nationalists" of the former Soviet bloc and former Soviet Union. Holocaust researchers centered around the website "Defending History"[13] have increasingly come to realize, and point out to others, the fact that Snyder's *Bloodlands* has become a kind of "Bible" of the anticommunist "nationalists" whose political predecessors sided with the Nazis and helped them murder millions of Jews and others, often outdoing the Nazis themselves.

Snyder's book is also valued by Polish "nationalists" whose have based their claims to legitimacy on the mythology that the prewar Polish regime was heroic and a "victim" of Nazi Germany and the Soviet Union. The truth is almost diametrically the opposite. Prewar Poland was a horrific imperialist regime, ferociously anti-labor, fiercely racist against its non-Polish citizens.

The prewar Polish regime rejected collective security with the Soviet Union, the only policy that could have foiled Hitler's aggression. Once Hitler's forces attacked, the Polish government abandoned first its capital, Warsaw, and then the country itself without forming a government-in-exile. No other government did this. This unique act of cowardice and indifference to the fate of their people guaranteed the destruction of Poland as a state and condemned the Polish population to Nazi occupation and mass murder.

Poland had a shameful history of anti-Semitic attacks against its Jewish citizens — attacks that continued under German occupation and even after the war. Polish anti-Semitism was the fault of the Polish political, religious, cultural, and educational elite. It continues to be very strong on the Polish right today despite the fact that few Jews remain in Poland. The Polish elite also encouraged racist pogroms against Ukrainians. In a previous chapter we have quoted American scholar Jeffrey Burds' brief description of one such anti-Ukrainian pogrom. Research done by the Polish "Center for Holocaust Research" (Centrum Badań nad Zagładą Żydów) and the work of the highly anticommunist scholar Jan T. Gross docu-

---

[13] At http://defendinghistory.com

ment the astounding extent of violent anti-Semitism, as well as anticommunism, in prewar, wartime, and postwar Poland.

During the 1980s the Solidarność "union" made Marshal Pilsudski and the regime of the "colonels" that followed Pilsudski its symbols and its national heroes. The post-1990 capitalist Polish governmental and educational elite have made it their task to "rehabilitate" the prewar Polish elite. This entails denying their crimes. It has also meant fabricating prewar and wartime "crimes" by communists and especially by the Soviet Union.

"Nationalism" Justifies Nothing

The anticommunist Polish and Ukrainian researchers from whose works Snyder draws his allegations in *Bloodlands* have looked hard for "crimes of Stalinism." Snyder has foisted their fabrications upon a Western audience largely unfamiliar with this self-serving, right-wing version of history that predominates in Eastern Europe. In the present book we have proven, citing the evidence, that all of these claims made by Snyder in *Bloodlands* are false.

Snyder's book has won the praise of anticommunists and crypto-fascists. The "Defending History" site quotes enthusiastic praise for *Bloodlands* by a right-wing Lithuanian academic. On first glance one might think this strange, since Snyder says virtually nothing about Lithuania. But the reason is not far to seek. The Lithuanian regime, like most Eastern European regimes, bases its claim to historical legitimacy and nationalism on the prewar regime — an authoritarian, elitist and racist dictatorship, anti-labor, anticommunist, and anti-Semitic — that was closely aligned with Nazi Germany.

Important parts of this elite collaborated in the mass murder of Soviet Jews and fought on Hitler's side in the war. As in the other Baltic countries, Poland, and Ukraine, "nationalist" soldiers went underground after the war and devoted themselves to terrorism — murder and sabotage. This terrorist activity is officially praised as "heroic" in today's Baltic states as in Poland. In some cases like that of the Ukrainian OUN these terrorists received aid from the American CIA just as did Al Qaeda and Osama bin Laden four decades later. Now the soldiers who fought for the Nazis are praised as "freedom fighters" while the Red Army soldiers who liberated these countries from Nazism are called "invaders" and "imperialists."

Most post-socialist countries of Eastern Europe are dominated by anticommunist regimes that justify their reactionary policies in part by their claim to be "true nationalists." All have been engaged in constructing national mythologies — false "nationalist" histories. All these countries, again with very few exceptions, have turned from being allies of the Soviet Union to being allies of NATO and the United States and hostile to post-Soviet Russia.

But "nationalism" justifies nothing. Hitler and his lieutenants were all German "nationalists". The Nazi leaders who went to the gallows after Nuremburg proclaimed with their last words their devotion to Germany. We can assume they were being truthful. Like the Polish, Ukrainian, and other Eastern European "nationalists" the Nazis committed their massive crimes in the name of patriotism, of "the nation."

The Role of NATO and the United States

The United States wasted no time in taking advantage of the collapse of the Soviet Union. It attacked Iraq in 1991, and subsequently organized an embargo that killed a half million Iraqi children.[14] In 2001 the USA led an invasion of Afghanistan and, in 2003, of Iraq, that have cost the lives of at least another 100,000 innocent civilians. None of this would have been possible if the Soviet Union had remained intact. None of it could have been done, or done as thoroughly, without the collaboration of the new "nationalist" regimes of the former Soviet bloc and USSR.

The stability and legitimacy of the countries of the former Soviet bloc and former USSR are of obvious importance to the American elite, which plans to keep military forces in the Middle East indefinitely. This pits the interests of the US elite against those of the

---

[14] Lesley Stahl on U.S. sanctions against Iraq: "We have heard that a half million children have died. I mean, that's more children than died in Hiroshima. And, you know, is the price worth it?" Secretary of State Madeleine Albright: "I think this is a very hard choice, but the price — we think the price is worth it." — "60 Minutes" (American news commentator television program), May 12, 1996.

Russian elite. Snyder's book plays a role in de-legitimizing Russia, as the successor state to the Soviet Union, just as it helps to justify the far-right and even crypto-fascist politics of Eastern Europe.

Apology for Holocaust Perpetrators — But Not Only for Them

Historians of the Holocaust have been the most prominent critics of *Bloodlands*. But neither they nor the few other critics of this book have noted the fact that Snyder has not only falsified World War II and the role of Polish and Ukrainian Nationalists — though he has indeed done that. All of Snyder's claims about Soviet "crimes" are also false. Yet this fact has drawn virtually no attention from Snyder's critics. It seems that they do not realize it, or do not object to it.

This is the task that the present book takes up. The falsehoods in *Bloodlands* are all of apiece: both apology for anticommunist (and anti-Semitic) "nationalists" and falsification of what the Soviet Union did. But the latter has attracted no scholarly attention — until now.

Snyder is a significant figure in American intellectual life. He is a frequent columnist for the most influential intellectual journals. His book is taken as a statement of facts, his lies and falsehoods about the Soviet Union and Stalin are accepted as true. In mainstream Western intellectual circles, and even on most of the Left, it is "taboo" to question any charge against Stalin or the Soviet Union, no matter how absurd.[15] If you try to challenge them — the present author has done so — the response is: "You are a defender of Stalin!"[16]

---

[15] Russia is one of the few countries where some space still remains in intellectual life for honest research into the Stalin period.

[16] An example of an essay that takes Snyder's claims in *Bloodlands* as fact is István Deák's review "Could Stalin Have Been Stopped?" *New York Review of Books*, March 13 2013. As a youth, Deák was in a labor battalion in the fascist Hungarian Army that invaded the Ukraine alongside Hitler's forces and that killed at least hundreds of thousands of Soviet citizens, to say nothing of Red Army soldiers. The present author wrote a response to Deáks' essay, and also sent it to a few email lists.

Therefore, the present book will inevitably be called "an apology for Stalin," even "for Stalin's crimes." But by now the reader knows this is false. This study is simply an attempt to get at the truth. Not to "defend Stalin" or "defend the Soviet Union," but simply to discover and document what really happened, using the best evidence, research methods, and appropriate means of deduction and conclusion.

Any blow in defense of the truth is a blow for the enlightenment, for civilization, and for the future, and against the injustices not just of the past but of the present and against those who lie about the past to justify their exploitative practices today. May this book contribute, however modestly, towards these goals.

Bibliography and Sources; Corrigenda

To reduce the number of pages and, thereby, to keep the cost of this book as low as possible, the bibliography for this book has been put on the Internet at the URL below:

http://msuweb.montclair.edu/~furrg/research/blood_lies_bibliography.html

"Corrigenda" – corrections of errors discovered after this book has been printed – will be listed on the following page as they are discovered:

http://msuweb.montclair.edu/~furrg/research/blood_lies_corrigenda.html

Index.